ESSENTIALS OF PUBLIC RELATIONS

Dennis L. Wilcox
San Jose State University

Phillip H. Ault
South Bend Tribune

Warren K. Agee
University of Georgia

Glen T. Cameron
Missouri School of Journalism

Longman

New York San Francisco Boston
London Toronto Sydney Tokyo Singapore Madrid
Mexico City Munich Paris Cape Town Hong Kong Montreal

Publisher: Priscilla McGeehon
Acquisitions Editor: Michael Greer
Marketing Manager: Megan Galvin-Fak
Supplements Editor: Kristinn Muller
Production Manager: Ellen MacElree
Project Coordination, Text Design, and Electronic Page Makeup: Electronic Publishing
    Services Inc., NYC
Cover Designer/Manager: Nancy Danahy
Cover Photos: © Photo Disc, Inc.; © The Stock Market
Senior Print Buyer: Dennis Para
Printer and Binder: R. R. Donnelly & Sons Company
Cover Printer: Coral Graphics Services

Library of Congress Cataloging-in-Publication Data

Essentials of Public Relations / Dennis L. Wilcox...[et al.].
    p. cm.
  Includes bibliographical references and index.
  ISBN 0-321-08231-1
  1. Public Relations. I. Wilcox, Dennis L.

HM1221 .E87   2001
659.2—dc21   00-044973

Please visit our website at http://www.awl.com

ISBN 0-321-08231-1

 2345678910—DOC—03 02 01

BRIEF CONTENTS

DETAILED CONTENTS

PREFACE

A strong growth in the study and practice of public relations has created a need for a compact textbook. *Essentials of Public Relations* fills that need.

Knowledge of public relations concepts and techniques is important in the careers of students who enter business, social agencies, education, and government. Some colleges that do not offer a major or an extended curriculum in public relations provide a basic course in the fundamentals of the field. Other schools are considering doing so. It is for them that we have created this introductory textbook.

Such a text needs to be authoritative, broad in its survey of the entire field yet concise, and strongly oriented toward practical instructions and examples. That has been our goal.

Essentials of Public Relations is a condensed paperback version of our highly successful sixth edition of *Public Relations:Strategies and Tactics.*

Strategies and Tactics is widely recognized for the breadth and depth of its content, and for its extensive reference material and instruction aids. In *Essentials of Public Relations,* we have eliminated some of the examples and illustrations, and deleted a substantial amount of detail.

A comparison of the contents of the two books shows that the briefer edition contains all the basic textual material of the larger book. The main difference is that Chapters 16, 17, and 18 of the sixth edition—each covering a group of nonprofit organizations—have been consolidated into a new Chapter 16 titled Nonprofit Organizations.

In keeping with the changes in the field, we place emphasis on two issues that are receiving much attention in the practice of public relations: ethical standards and the vigorous growth of global operations. Our hope is that *Essentials of Public Relations* will attract a new audience of students and faculty to the rapidly changing field of public relations.

ORGANIZATION OF THE TEXT

The book is divided into five parts, presenting a logical teaching progression, with a case problem at the close of each chapter.

- **Part One: Role** This defines public relations, traces its development, and discusses the individual's place in the field.

- **Part Two: Process** This section takes students in sequence through the basic steps involved in a public relations program.

- **Part Three: Strategy** This discusses the fundamental concepts of strategy. It explains the formation of public opinion, the identification of target audiences, and methods for reaching them.

- **Part Four: Application** Here we explain the practical ways in which the process and strategies of public relations are applied in major areas of practice.

- **Part Five: Tactics** This final part describes the techniques of day-by-day public relations practice. It explains the use of the Internet as a research tool and as a method for delivering public relations and marketing messages.

UP-TO-DATE COVERAGE

Use of up-to-date examples drawn from recent events to illustrate concepts and methods helps students to understand the realities of public relations practice. Two case studies are examples of this approach:

1. The Clinton impeachment trial. Our study examines the massive public relations battle that took place. It looks at the tactics used by the anti-Clinton forces in the Monica Lewinsky scandal and those employed by the White House to fight back. This study appears at the end of Chapter 1. It gives students an early opportunity to see how public relations operates in a situation of national significance.

2. The tobacco battle, in which state and federal governments have fought to make the tobacco industry pay the cost of treating illnesses caused by smoking and to limit its marketing powers. This study appears in Chapter 14, "Politics and Government."

Here is a sampling of other public relations situations found in this book:

* Salt Lake City Olympic scandal
* High-tech promotion of popular singer Jewel's new book of poetry
* Top celebrity endorser: Bill Cosby
* 100th anniversary of Jell-O
* UConn 2000, a $1 billion fundraiser
* Contrast in Asian and American pop idols
* Northwest Airlines comemoration of 50th anniversary of historic US-Japan flight
* University use of online methods to recruit prospective students

ANCILLARIES
Instructor's Manual/Test Bank

The Instructor's Manual has been completely revised and contains chapter objectives, suggested class projects/discussion questions, case problems, end-of-chapter review questions with answers and page references, PowerPoint duplication masters, and lecture outlines. The Instructor's Manual also contains sample syllabi and course outlines. The Test Bank portion contains hundrerds of challenging multiple choice and true/false questions organized by chapter.

Computerized Testing

The printed Test Bank is also available on a cross-platform CD-ROM through our fully networkable computerized testing system, TestGen-EQ. The program's friendly graphical interface enables instructors to view, edit, and add questions: transfer questions to tests; and print tests in a variety of fonts and forms. Search and sort features help instructors locate questions quickly and arrange them in a preferred order. Six question formats are available, including short-answer, true-false, multiple choice, essay, matching, and bimodal.

Companion Website (www.awl.com/wilcox)

This online course companion provides a wealth of resources for both students and instructors using *Essentials of Public Relations*. Students will find chapter objectives, test questions with page references, annotated web links, a complete guide to conducting research on the Internet, and more! Instructors will have access to the Instructor's Manual and teaching links, and can also put course materials online using Syllabus Manager.

ACKNOWLEDGMENTS

It is a pleasure to express our appreciation to our academic colleagues who reviewed the sixth edition, on which this book is based, and to numerous others in the professional and academic fields who assisted us.

Unfortunately, space does not permit us to list them individually. But to each of them we say a hearty "Thank you!"

Dennis L. Wilcox
Phillip H. Ault
Warren K. Agee
Glen T. Cameron

What Is Public Relations?

Preview

The objective of this introductory chapter is to define public relations, explain its communication and counseling roles, and clarify
the relationship of public relations to journalism, advertising, and
marketing.

Topics covered in the chapter include:
- The challenge of public relations
- Definitions of public relations
- Public relations as a process
- The components of public relations
- How public relations differs from journalism,
  advertising, and marketing
- The integrated approach
- Clinton impeachment trial

THE CHALLENGE OF PUBLIC RELATIONS

It is 9 A.M. and Anne-Marie, an account executive in a San Francisco public relations
firm, is at her computer working on a news release about a client's new software product. She finishes it, gives it a once-over, and e-mails it to the client for approval. She
also attaches a note that an electronic news service can deliver it to newspapers across
the country later in the day.

　　Her next activity is a brainstorming session with other staff members to generate
creative ideas about a campaign to raise funds for the local AIDS foundation. When

she gets back to her office, she finds a number of telephone messages. A reporter for a trade publication needs background information on a story he is writing; a graphic designer has finished a rough draft of a client's brochure; a catering manager has called about making final arrangements for a reception at an art gallery; and a video producer asks if she can attend the taping of a video news release next week.

Lunch is with a client who wants her counsel on how to announce the closing of a plant in another state. After lunch, Anne-Marie heads back to the office. She asks her assistant to check arrangements for a news conference next week in New York. She telephones a key editor to "pitch" a story about a client's new product. Anne-Marie also touches base with other members of her team, who are working on a 12-city media tour by an Olympic champion representing an athletic shoe manufacturer.

At 4 P.M., Anne-Marie checks several computer databases to gather information about the industry of a new client. She also checks online news updates to determine if anything is occurring that involves or affects her firm's clients. At 5 P.M., as she winds down from the day's hectic activities, she reviews news stories from a clipping service about her client, an association of strawberry producers. She is pleased to find that her feature story, which included recipes and color photos, appeared in 150 dailies.

As the previous scenario illustrates, the challenge of public relations is multifaceted. A public relations professional must have skills in written and interpersonal communication, research, negotiation, creativity, logistics, facilitation, and problem-solving.

Indeed, those who want a challenging career with plenty of variety often choose the field of public relations. The U.S. Bureau of Labor Statistics estimates that the management and public relations industry already employs more than a million nationwide, and it is one of the top ten industries with the fastest wage and employment growth through 2008.

GLOBAL SCOPE

It is difficult to estimate worldwide figures, but *Reed's Directory of Public Relations Organizations* lists 155 national and regional public relations associations with an aggregate membership of 137,000 people. Included are such groups as the Public Relations Institute of Southern Africa (PRISA), the Public Relations Association of Mauritius (PRAM), the Association of Public Relations Practitioners in Thailand, and the Public Relations Institute of Australia (PRIA).

Such memberships, however, are usually only a partial indication, because large numbers of public relations practitioners don't belong to professional organizations. The president of the China International Public Relations Association, for example, says that the country has more than 100,000 practitioners and that up to 500,000 are studying aspects of public relations in colleges and training institutes.

In terms of economics, the public relations field is most extensively developed in the United States, where organizations spend an estimated $10 billion annually in such activity. Although statistics are scarce, European companies are estimated to spend $3 billion annually on public relations. This figure continues to increase through implementation of the European Community (EC) and the development of market economies in Eastern Europe and the new nations of the former Soviet Union. Areas with strong growth potential in Europe are public affairs, corporate relations, health care, and marketing communications.

The second area of major growth is Asia. Shandwick, the world's fourth largest firm, sees growth of 20 to 30 percent in such nations as Malaysia, Korea, Thailand, Singapore, Indonesia, and China. Increased privatization of national industries and expansion of free market economies are also fueling major growth in Latin America and Southern Africa. A more detailed discussion of international public relations is found in Chapter 15.

A VARIETY OF DEFINITIONS

People often define public relations by some of its most visible techniques and tactics, such as publicity in a newspaper, a television interview with an organization's spokesperson, or the appearance of a celebrity at a special event.

What people fail to understand is that public relations is a process involving many subtle and far-reaching aspects. It includes research and analysis, policy formation, programming, communication, and feedback from numerous publics. Its practitioners operate on two distinct levels—as advisers to their clients or to an organization's top management, and as technicians who produce and disseminate messages in multiple media channels.

A number of definitions have been formulated over the years. One of the early definitions that gained wide acceptance was formulated by the newsletter *PR News:* "Public relations is the management function which evaluates public attitudes, identifies the policies and procedures of an individual or an organization with the public interest, and plans and executes a program of action to earn public understanding and patience."

Other definitions are provided by theorists and textbook authors. Scott M. Cutlip, Allen H. Center, and Glen M. Broom state in *Effective Public Relations* that "public relations is the management function that identifies, establishes, and maintains mutually beneficial relationships between an organization and the various publics on whom its success or failure depends." The management function is also emphasized in *Managing Public Relations* by James E. Grunig and Todd Hunt. They state that public relations is "the management of communication between an organization and its publics."

The best definition for today's modern practice is offered by Professors Lawrence W. Long and Vincent Hazelton, who describe public relations as "a communication function of management through which organizations adapt to, alter, or maintain their environment for the purpose of achieving organizational goals." Their approach represents the somewhat newer theory that public relations is more than persuasion. It should also foster open, two-way communication and mutual understanding with the idea that an organization also changes its attitudes and behaviors in the process—not just the target audience.

National and international public relations organizations, including the Public Relations Society of America (PRSA), also have formulated definitions. Here is a sampling:

- Public relations is the deliberate, planned, and sustained effort to establish and maintain mutual understanding between an organization and its publics." (British Institute of Public Opinion, whose definition has also been adopted in a number of Commonwealth nations)

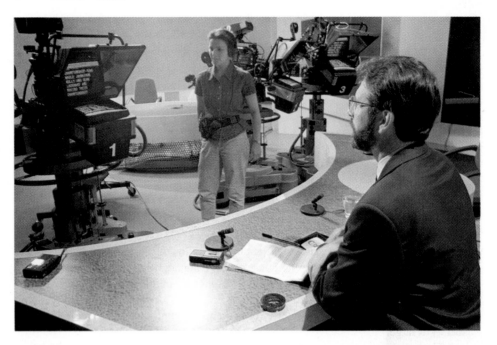

Satellite television makes it possible for audiences to see and hear leaders from other countries, often on controversial issues. Here Gerry Adams, Sinn Fein political leader, broadcasts an election speech from Belfast to Irish voters. The speech is transmitted by satellite to audiences in Canada and the United States. Such transmission is important in global public relations.

- Public relations is the management, through communication, of perceptions and strategic relationships between an organization and its internal and external stakeholders. (Public Relations Institute of Southern Africa)

- Public relations is the sustained and systematic managerial effort through which private and public organizations seek to establish understanding, sympathy, and support in those public circles with which they have or expect to obtain contact." (Dansk Public Relations Klub of Denmark, which also uses the English term)

Careful study of these explanations should enable anyone to formulate a definition of public relations; committing any single one to memory is unnecessary. The key words to remember in defining public relations follow:

Deliberate. Public relations activity is intentional. It is designed to influence, gain understanding, provide information, and obtain *feedback* (reaction from those affected by the activity).

Planned. Public relations activity is organized. Solutions to problems are discovered and logistics are thought out, with the activity taking place over a period of time. It is systematic, requiring research and analysis.

Performance. Effective public relations is based on actual policies and performance. No amount of public relations will generate good will and support if the organization is unresponsive to community concerns. A Pacific Northwest timber company, despite a campaign

PR Insights

Public Relations Society of America Official Statement on Public Relations

Public relations helps our complex, pluralistic society to reach decisions and function more effectively by contributing to mutual understanding among groups and institutions. It serves to bring private and public policies into harmony.

Public relations serves a variety of institutions in society such as businesses, trade unions, government agencies, voluntary associations, foundations, hospitals, and educational and religious institutions. To achieve their goals, these institutions must develop effective relationships with many different audiences or publics such as employees, members, customers, local communities, shareholders, and other institutions, and with society at large.

The managements of institutions need to understand the attitudes and values of their publics in order to achieve institutional goals. The goals themselves are shaped by the external environment. The public relations practitioner acts as a counselor to management, and as a mediator, helping to translate private aims into reasonable, publicly acceptable policy and action.

As a management function, public relations encompasses the following:

- Anticipating, analyzing, and interpreting public opinion, attitudes, and issues which might impact, for good or ill, the operations and plans of the organization.

- Counseling management at all levels in the organization with regard to policy decisions, courses of action and communication, and taking into account their public ramifications and the organization's social or citizenship responsibilities.

- Researching, conducting, and evaluating, on a continuing basis, programs of action and communication to achieve informed public understanding necessary to the success of an organization's aims. These may include marketing, financial, fund-raising, employee, community or government relations, and other programs.

- Planning and implementing the organization's efforts to influence or change public policy.

- Setting objectives, planning, budgeting, recruiting and training staff, and developing facilities—in short, *managing* the resources needed to perform all of the above.

- Examples of the knowledge that may be required in the professional practice of public relations include communication arts, psychology, social psychology, sociology, political science, economics, and the principles of management and ethics. Technical knowledge and skills are required for opinion research, public issues analysis, media relations, direct mail, institutional advertising, publications, film/video productions, special events, speeches, and presentations.

In helping to define and implement policy, the public relations practitioner utilizes a variety of professional communication skills and plays an integrative role both within the organization and between the organization and the external environment.

with the theme "For Us, Every Day Is Earth Day," became known as the villain of Washington State because of its insistence on logging old-growth forests and bulldozing a logging road into a prime elk habitat.

Public Interest. Public relations activity should be mutually beneficial to the organization and the public; it is the alignment of the organization's self-interests with the public's concerns and interests. For example, the Exxon Mobil Corporation sponsors quality programming on public television because it enhances the company's image; by the same token, the public benefits from the availability of such programming.

Two-Way Communication. Public relations is more than one-way dissemination of informational materials. It is equally important to solicit feedback. As Jim Osborne, former vice president of public affairs at Bell Canada, says, "The primary responsibility of the public relations counselor is to provide (management) a thorough grasp of public sentiment."

Management Function. Public relations is most effective when it is an integral part of decision-making by top management. Public relations involves counseling and problem-solving at high levels, not just the dissemination of information after a decision has been made.

To summarize, a person can grasp the essential elements of public relations by remembering the following words: *deliberate . . . planned . . . performance . . . public interest . . . two-way communication . . . management function.*

The elements of public relations just described are part of an interactive process that makes up what is called *public relations activity.* In the following section, public relations as a process is discussed.

PUBLIC RELATIONS AS A PROCESS

Public relations is a *process*—that is, a series of actions, changes, or functions that bring about a result. One popular way to describe the process, and to remember its components, is to use the RACE acronym, first articulated by John Marston in his book *The Nature of Public Relations.* Essentially, RACE means that public relations activity consists of four key elements:

* **R**esearch—What is the problem or situation?

* **A**ction(program planning)—What is going to be done about it?

* **C**ommunication (execution)—How will the public be told?

* **E**valuation—Was the audience reached and what was the effect?

Part Two of this text discusses this key four-step process.

Another approach is to think of the process as a never-ending cycle in which six components are links in a chain. Figure 1.1 shows the process.

The public relations process also may be conceptualized in several steps as follows:

Level 1

a. Public relations personnel obtain insights into the problem from numerous sources.

b. Public relations personnel analyze these inputs and make recommendations to management.

c. Management makes policy and action decisions.

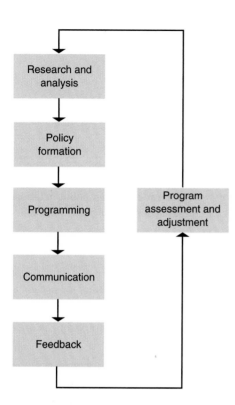

Figure 1.1
In the conceptualization of public relations as a cyclical process, feedback—or audience response—leads to assessment of the program, which becomes an essential element in the development of another public relations project.

Level 2

d. Public relations personnel execute a program of action.

e. Public relations personnel evaluate the effectiveness of the action.

Step A consists of inputs that determine the nature and extent of the public relations problem. These may include feedback from the public, media reporting and editorial comment, analysis of trend data, other forms of research, personal experience, and government pressures and regulations.

In Step B, public relations personnel assess these inputs, establish objectives and an agenda of activity, and convey their recommendations to management. As previously noted, this is the adviser role of public relations.

After management makes its decisions, in Step C, public relations personnel execute the action program in Step D through such means as news releases, publications, speeches, and community relations programs. In Step E, the effect of these efforts is measured by feedback from the same components that made up Step A. The cycle is then repeated to solve related aspects of the problem that may require additional decision making and action.

Note that public relations plays two distinct roles in this process, thus serving as a "middle ground" or "linking agent." On Level 1, public relations interacts directly with external sources of information, including the public, media, and government, and relays these inputs to management along with recommendations. On Level 2, public relations becomes the vehicle through which management reaches the public with assorted messages.

THE COMPONENTS OF PUBLIC RELATIONS

The basic components of public relations, according to a monograph issued by the PRSA Foundation, include the following:

Counseling. Providing advice to management concerning policies, relationships, and communications.

Research. Determining attitudes and behaviors of publics in order to plan public relations strategies. Such research can be used to (1) generate mutual understanding or (2) influence and persuade publics.

Media Relations. Working with mass media in seeking publicity or responding to their interests in the organization.

Publicity. Disseminating planned messages through selected media to further the organization's interests.

Employee/Member Relations. Responding to concerns, informing, and motivating an organization's employees or members.

Community Relations. Planned activity with a community to maintain an environment that benefits both the organization and the community.

Public Affairs. Developing effective involvement in public policy and helping an organization adapt to public expectations. The term is also used by government agencies to describe their public relations activities and by many corporations as an umbrella term to describe multiple public relations activities.

Government Affairs. Relating directly with legislatures and regulatory agencies on behalf of the organization. *Lobbying* can be part of a government affairs program.

Issues Management. Identifying and addressing issues of public concern that affect the organization.

Financial Relations. Creating and maintaining investor confidence and building good relationships with the financial community. Also known as *Investor Relations* or *Shareholder Relations.*

Industry Relations. Relating with other firms in the industry of an organization and with trade associations.

Development/Fund-Raising. Demonstrating the need for and encouraging the public to support an organization, primarily through financial contributions.

Special Events. Stimulating an interest in a person, product, or organization by means of a focused "happening"; also, activities designed to interact with publics and listen to them.

Marketing Communications. Combination of activities designed to sell a product, service, or idea, including advertising, collateral materials, publicity, promotion, direct mail, trade shows, and special events.

These components, and how they function, constitute the substance of this textbook.

OTHER TERMS FOR PUBLIC RELATIONS

Public relations is used as an umbrella term on a worldwide basis. Sixty-four of the 69 national membership associations, from the Arab Public Relations Society to the Zimbabwe Institute of Public Relations, identify themselves with that term.

Individual companies and other groups, however, often use other terms to describe the public relations function. *O'Dwyer's PR Services Report* surveyed *Fortune* magazine's list of the largest 500 corporations and found that the most common name, used by 165 companies, is *corporate communications.* The term *public relations* is a distant second, with 64 companies using it. Other popular names, in descending order, were *public affairs, communication, corporate relations,* and *corporate public affairs.* Some companies link public relations with marketing. Chase Manhattan, for example, has a *corporate marketing and communications* unit.

Public information is the term most widely used by social service agencies, universities, and government agencies. The implication is that only information is being disseminated, in contrast to persuasive communication, generally perceived as the purpose of public relations. Social services agencies often use the term *community relations,* and the military is fond of *public affairs.*

In many cases it is clear that companies and organizations use *public information, public affairs,* or *corporate communications* as euphemisms for *public relations.* This, in part, is a reaction to the misuse of the original term by the public and the media. On occasion, a reporter or government official will use the term *public relations gimmick* or *ploy* to imply that the activities or statements of an organization are without substance or sincerity.

The popularity of *corporate communications* is also based on the idea that the term is broader than *public relations,* which is often incorrectly perceived as only *media relations.* Corporate communications, many contend, encompasses all communications of the

Global PR

High-Flying Public Relations

The continual quest to circle the globe nonstop in a balloon requires extensive ground support, including public relations.

Three veteran balloonists—Richard Branson, Per Lindstrand, and Steve Fosset—made yet another unsuccessful attempt in December 1998 when they traveled 8200 miles from Morocco before bad weather forced them down off the coast of Hawaii. In the process they captured world headlines.

Keeping the media and the public informed along the way was an extensive public relations operation at the London headquarters of the group, ICO Global Challenge. Not only was press given hourly updates on progress, but news releases pro-

claimed each record set. For example, one release maintained that the effort involved the first piloted balloon to cross the full breadth of the Himalayas and the first to traverse the entire Asian land mass.

In addition, the balloonists had their own website so the public could keep track of the adventure. In only a week, the site received millions of visits.

Balloonists Bertrand Piccard and Brian Jones, in March of 1999, also generated worldwide publicity when they successfully circumvented the globe in the Breitlin Orbiter, named after the Swiss watch company that was the corporate sponsor. Anheuser-Busch also got considerable publicity by awarding a million-dollar prize for the feat.

company, including advertising, marketing communications, public affairs, community relations, and employee communications.

Other organizations use a term that better describes the primary activity of the department. It is clear, for example, that a department of investor relations deals primarily with stockholders, institutional investors, and the financial press. A department of marketing communications primarily emphasizes product publicity and promotion. The organization and functions of communications departments are discussed in Chapter 5.

Like departments, individuals specialize in subcategories of public relations. A person who deals exclusively with placement of stories in the media is, to be precise, a *publicist*. A *press agent* is also a specialist, operating within the subcategory of public relations that concentrates on finding unusual news angles and planning events or "happenings" that attract media attention—for example, an attempt to be listed in the *Guinness Book of Records* by baking the world's largest apple pie.

Some Less Flattering Terms   Unfortunately, the public and the press on occasion describe public relations people as "flacks" or "spin doctors."

A *flack* or *flak* is a derisive slang term that journalists often use for a press agent or anyone else working in public relations. Although in recent years most publications, including the *Wall Street Journal* have refrained from using the "F" word in print, trade publications such as *Editor & Publisher* still use it on a regular basis.

The term has an interesting history. According to Wes Pedersen, director of communications for the Public Affairs Council, the term "flack" originated in 1939 in *Variety,* the show business publication. It began using flack as a synonym for press agent, he says, "in tribute to the skills of Gene Flack in publicizing motion pictures." Others say the word "flak" was used during World War I to describe heavy ground fire aimed at aircraft. At times, journalists consider the barrage of daily news releases they receive a form of flak that interferes with their mission of informing the public.

The term *spin doctor* is a more recent entry into the lexicon of public relations. It first appeared in 1984, according to *Safire's Political Dictionary* by William Safire, in a New York *Times* editorial about the activities of President Reagan's reelection campaign. In the beginning, the meaning of "spin" was restricted to what often were considered the unethical and misleading activities and tactics of political campaign consultants. By the mid-1990s, however, the media widely used the term to describe any effort by public relations personnel to put a positive slant on an event or issue.

Robert Dilenschneider, president of his own public relations firm in New York, wrote in a *Wall Street Journal* article: "I think the time has come for public relations professionals to condemn 'spin' and label 'spin doctors' for what they are: purveyors of deception, manipulation, and misinformation. Spin is antithetical to legitimate public relations, which aims to enhance the image of companies and individuals to generate public approval for the programs and policies they advance…Spin is to public relations what pornography is to art.…"

Not all public relations people, however, share Dilenschneider's views. Pat Jackson, publisher of *PR Reporter,* says: "We're all 'spinners'—because it simply means marshaling the data from your viewpoint, attempting to persuade others your viewpoint is legitimate." And Bill Patterson, vice president of reputation management at HMS Partners in Columbus, Ohio, in an article for *Public Relations Tactics* titled "Confessions of a Spin Doctor," wrote: "By 'spin,' I mean that I use all modern methods of communication to tell the most positive story I can about my clients.…"

Indeed, spin seems to have well established itself as a popular slang term for any information with a point of view. It has even become popular as a title in books about public relations, as in *PR: A Social History of Spin,* by Stuart Ewan; *The Father of Spin: Edward L. Bernays & The Birth of Public Relations,* by Larry Tye; *Spin Man: The Topsy-Turvy World of Public Relations,* by Thomas Madden; *Spin Cycle: How the White House and the Media Manipulate the News,* by Howard Kurtz; and *Spin: How to Turn the Power of the Press to Your Advantage,* by Michael Sitrick.

Within the public relations community, feeling also exists that "PR" is a slang term that carries a somewhat denigrating connotation. The late Sam Black, a public relations consultant in the United Kingdom and author of several books on public relations, says, "The use of 'PR' was probably originated as a nickname for 'press relations,'" the primary activity of public relations in its early years (see Chapter 2). Although "PR" is now more than press relations, the nickname is commonly used in daily conversation and is widely recognized around the world.

HOW PUBLIC RELATIONS DIFFERS FROM JOURNALISM

Writing is a common activity of both public relations professionals and journalists. Both also do their jobs in many of the same ways; they interview people, gather and synthesize large amounts of information, write in a journalistic style, and are trained to produce good copy on deadline. In fact, many reporters eventually change careers and become public relations practitioners.

This has led many people, including journalists, to the incorrect conclusion that little difference exists between public relations and journalism. For many, public relations is simply being a "journalist-in-residence" for a nonmedia organization.

However, despite the sharing of many techniques, the two fields are fundamentally different in scope, objectives, audiences, and channels.

Scope. Public relations, as stated earlier, has many components, ranging from counseling to issues management and special events. Journalistic writing and media relations, although important, are only two of these elements. In addition, effective practice of public relations requires strategic thinking, problem-solving capability, and other management skills.

Objectives. Journalists gather and select information for the primary purpose of providing the public with news and information. As Professors David Dozier and William Ehling explain, ". . . communication activities are an end in themselves." Public relations personnel also gather facts and information for the purpose of informing the public, but the objective is different. Communication activity is only a means to the end. In other words, the objective is not only to inform but to change people's attitudes and behaviors, in order to further an organization's goals and objectives.

Audiences. Journalists write primarily for a mass audience—readers, listeners, or viewers of the medium for which they work. By definition, mass audiences are not well defined, and a journalist on a daily newspaper, for example, writes for the general public. A public relations professional, in contrast, carefully segments audiences into various demographic and psychological characteristics. Such research allows messages to be tailored to audience needs, concerns, and interests for maximum effect.

When a corporation and a charitable organization combine in an event, both benefit in public awareness and the charity does so in contributions. GTE Communications Corporation sponsored the GTE Big Ride Across America, a 3,254-mile bicycle tour to benefit the American Lung Association. Each of the 730 riders on the 48-day tour from Seattle to Washington, D.C. pledged at least $6000 to the charity. GTE received much attention for its products en route.

Channels. Most journalists, by nature of their employment, reach audiences through one channel—the medium that publishes or broadcasts their work. Public relations professionals use a variety of channels to reach the audiences previously described. The channels employed may be a combination of mass media outlets—newspapers, magazines, radio, and television. Or they may include direct mail, pamphlets, posters, newsletters, trade journals, special events, and posting messages on the Internet.

HOW PUBLIC RELATIONS DIFFERS FROM ADVERTISING

Just as many people mistakenly equate publicity with public relations, there is also some confusion about the distinction between *publicity* (one area of public relations) and advertising.

Although publicity and advertising both utilize mass media for dissemination of messages, the format and context are different. *Publicity*—information about an event, an individual or group, or a product—appears as a news item or feature story in the mass media. Material is prepared by public relations personnel and submitted to the news department for consideration. Editors, known as *gatekeepers,* determine whether the material will be used or simply thrown away.

Advertising, in contrast, is paid space and broadcast time. Organizations and individuals typically contract with the advertising department of a mass media outlet for a full-page ad or a one-minute commercial, which can cost thousands of dollars. An organization writes the advertisement, decides the type and graphics, and controls where and when the advertisement will be run. In other words, advertising is simply renting space in a mass medium.

Other differences between public relations activities and advertising include:

• Advertising works almost exclusively through mass media outlets; public relations relies on a number of communication tools—brochures, slide presentations, special events, speeches, news releases, feature stories, and so forth.

• Advertising is addressed to external audiences—primarily consumers of goods and services; public relations presents its message to specialized external audiences (stockholders, vendors, community leaders, environmental groups, and so on) and internal publics (employees).

• Advertising is readily identified as a specialized communication function; public relations is broader in scope, dealing with the policies and performance of the entire organization, from the morale of employees to the way telephone operators respond to calls.

• Advertising is often used as a communication tool in public relations, and public relations activity often supports advertising campaigns. Advertising's function is to sell goods and services; the public relations function is to create an environment in which the organization can thrive. The latter calls for dealing with economic, social, and political factors that can affect the organization.

HOW PUBLIC RELATIONS DIFFERS FROM MARKETING

Public relations is distinct from marketing in several ways, although their boundaries often overlap.

The functions overlap, for example, because both deal with an organization's relationships and employ similar communication tools to reach the public. Both have the ultimate purpose of assuring an organization's success and economic survival. Public relations and marketing, however, approach this task from somewhat different perspectives, or worldviews.

This difference is illustrated by the descriptions of each field that a distinguished panel of educators and practitioners in public relations and marketing developed during a colloquium at San Diego State University. After a day of debate, they formed this definition of public relations:

> Public relations is the management process whose goal is to attain and maintain accord and positive behaviors among social groupings on which an organization depends in order to achieve its mission. Its fundamental responsibility is to build and maintain a hospitable environment for an organization.

The group defined marketing's goal in different terms:

> Marketing is the management process whose goal is to attract and satisfy customers (or clients) on a long-term basis in order to achieve an organization's economic objectives. Its fundamental responsibility is to build and maintain markets for an organization's products or services.

In other words, public relations is concerned with building relationships and generating goodwill for the organization; marketing is concerned with customers and selling products and services.

James E. Grunig, editor of *Excellence in Public Relations and Communication Management,* put the differences between public relations and marketing in sharp contrast:

> . . . the marketing function should communicate with the markets for an organization's goods and services. Public relations should be concerned with all the publics of the organization. The major purpose of marketing is to make money for the organization by increasing the slope of the demand curve. The major purpose of public relations is to save money for the organization by building relationships with publics that constrain or enhance the ability of the organization to meet its mission.

In this passage, Grunig points out a fundamental difference between marketing and public relations in terms of how the public is described. Marketing and advertising professionals tend to speak of "target markets," "consumers," and "customers." Public relations professionals tend to talk of "publics," "audiences," and "stakeholders." These groups may be any publics that are affected by or can affect an organization. According to Grunig, "Publics can arise within stakeholder categories—such as employees, communities, stockholders, governments, members, students, suppliers, and donors, as well as consumers."

HOW PUBLIC RELATIONS SUPPORTS MARKETING

Philip Kotler, professor of marketing at Northwestern University and author of a leading marketing textbook, says public relations is the fifth "P" of marketing strategy, which includes four other Ps—Product, Price, Place, and Promotion. As he wrote in the *Harvard Business Review,* "Public relations takes longer to cultivate, but when energized, it can help pull the company into the market."

When public relations is used to support directly an organization's marketing objectives, it is called *marketing communications.* This was identified as a component of public relations earlier in the chapter. Another term, coined by Thomas Harris in his book *The Marketer's Guide to Public Relations,* is *marketing public relations.* He says:

> I make a clear distinction between those public relations functions which support marketing, which I call Marketing Public Relations (MPR) and the other public relations activities that define the corporation's relationships with its non-customer publics, which I label Corporate Public Relations (CPR).

Dennis L. Wilcox in his text *Public Relations Writing and Media Techniques,* list eight ways in which public relations activities contribute to fulfilling marketing objectives:

• Developing new prospects for new markets, such as people who inquire after seeing or hearing a product release in the news media

• Providing third-party endorsements—via newspapers, magazines, radio, and television—through news releases about a company's products or services, community involvement, inventions, and new plans

- Generating sales leads, usually through articles in the trade press about new products and services

- Paving the way for sales calls

- Stretching the organization's advertising and promotional dollars through timely and supportive releases about it and its products

- Providing inexpensive sales literature, because articles about the company and its products can be reprinted as informative pieces for prospective customers

- Establishing the corporation as an authoritative source of information on a given product

- Helping to sell minor products that don't have large advertising budgets

TOWARD AN INTEGRATED PERSPECTIVE

Although well-defined differences exist among the fields of advertising, marketing, and public relations, there is an increasing realization that an organization's goals and objectives can be best accomplished through an integrated approach.

The understanding has given rise, to such terms as *integrated marketing communications, convergent communications,* and *integrated communications.* Don Schulz, Stanley Tannenbaum, and Robert Lauterborn, authors of *Integrated Marketing Communications,* explain the title of their book as follows:

> A concept of marketing communication planning that recognizes the added value of a comprehensive plan that evaluates the strategic roles of a variety of communication disciplines—e.g., General Advertising, Direct Response, Sales Promotion, and Public Relations—and combines these disciplines to provide clarity, consistency, and maximum communication impact.

Several factors have fueled the trend toward integration. One is the downsizing and reengineering of organizations. Many of them have consolidated departments and have also reduced staff dedicated to various communication disciplines. As a result, one department, with fewer employees, is expected to do a greater variety of communication tasks.

Second, there are tighter budgets for organizational marketing and communication. Many organizations, to avoid the high cost of advertising, look for alternative ways to deliver messages. These may include product publicity, direct mail, and sales promotion.

Third, a realization exists that the marketing of products and services can be affected by public and social policy issues. Environmental legislation influences packaging and content of products, a proposed luxury tax on expensive autos affects sales of those cars, and a company's support of Planned Parenthood or health benefits for same-sex partners may spur a product boycott.

Fourth, there is a rise of relationship marketing. As Ken Reich, a marketing communications expert, says, "The fundamental tenets of marketing have indeed shifted to a large degree, from the 1960s' four-Ps (product, price, place, and promotion) to the 1990s' four-Cs (customer needs, cost to meet those needs, convenience to purchase, and

PR Casebook

Integrated Marketing Sells Furby

Every Christmas sees a hot toy that retailers have trouble keeping on the shelves. Furby, a cuddly, furry doll that speaks both Furbish and English, became that toy in 1998, because of an integrated campaign of marketing, promotion, advertising, and public relations activities.

Promotion of Furby began in February when Tiger Electronics, a division of Hasbro, introduced the product to retailers and the media at a toy fair in New York. This led to a 12-page article in *Wired* magazine, a trend-setting publication read by many journalists. *Wired* described Furby as a "Cabbage Patch doll with artificial intelligence." Another early booster was *Playthings,* an influential toy trade magazine. Editors of the publications jointly extolled Furby on network TV shows. *USA Today* did a product feature on the doll. Other journalists did so as well.

In October, Tiger Electronics held major product launches at leading toy stores such as FAO Schwartz that also generated media coverage. A website was set up for Furby, showing live coverage of the toy store launches. Nabisco put Furbies on its cookie packaging, and Hi-C did likewise on its juice boxes. Tiger also saturated children's TV programming with Furby advertising.

The result was impressive. Toy stores nationwide experienced long lines of parents wanting to buy Furby. Sales climbed to two million by Christmas Eve.

communication)—in other words, the building of solid, long-term customer loyalty through service and two-way communication."

The concept of integration, therefore, is the realization that an organization's communications should be consistent. As Michael Lissauer of *Business Wire* says, "It's essential that there be a consistency of message, that the communications effort project a singular voice. Business must deliver the right message in the right medium to elicit the right result."

Figure 1.2
This illustration shows the interplay of messages and feedback in an integrated marketing communication campaign. The targeted database includes customers, media, and sales personnel.

Turf battles between marketing and public relations departments no doubt will continue, but the concept of integrating, or coordinating, communications is here to stay. Paul Alvarez, former chairman of Ketchum Communications, says that if public relations people are going to have credibility with clients and employers, they must acknowledge the roles played by other communication disciplines such as advertising, direct marketing, and sales promotion. By the same token, other disciplines must realize the full potential of public relations.

All disciplines deserve an equal voice at the table when an organization considers its communication objectives and strategies. Integrated marketing communication is also discussed in Chapters 5, 7, and 13.

THE VALUES OF PUBLIC RELATIONS

More than ever, today the world needs not more information but sensitive communicators and facilitators who can explain the goals and methods of individuals, organizations, and governments to others in a socially responsible manner. Equally, these experts in communication and public opinion must provide their employers with knowledge of what others are thinking, to guide them in setting their policies wisely for the common good.

Patrick Jackson, a former president of the Public Relations Society of America (PRSA) and publisher of *PR Reporter,* makes the case for the important role of public relations in today's society. He once wrote:

> As soon as there was Eve with Adam, there were relationships, and in every society, no matter how small or primitive, public communication needs and problems inevitably emerge and must be resolved. Public relations is devoted to the essential function of building and improving human relationships.

PR Casebook

The Clinton Impeachment: An Epic Public Relations Battle

President Clinton became only the second president in U.S. history to be impeached by the U.S. House of Representatives, and he was ultimately acquitted by the U.S. Senate.

Throughout most of 1998, the media world was almost totally saturated by the Clinton/Lewinsky scandal as the President waged a legal and public relations defense while major events unfolded: (1) Independent Counsel Kenneth Starr conducted grand jury proceedings and filed a 445-page report with Congress; (2) the House Judiciary Committee conducted hearings; and (3) the

House of Representatives, in a highly emotional and partisan debate, approved two of four articles of impeachment—charging the President with lying under oath and obstructing justice.

The saga began when President Clinton on January 17 testified under oath in the Paula Jones sexual harassment case that he never had an affair with Monica Lewinsky, a former White House intern. In August, after Lewinsky admitted to Starr's grand jury that she did have an affair, and DNA analysis disclosed Clinton's semen on one of her dresses, the

(continued)

PR Casebook

Clinton Impeachment, continued

President admitted in a nationally televised speech an "improper relationship" and expressed regret about misleading the American public.

Throughout the year, White House legal and public relations advisers were often at odds on how to handle the legal aspects and shape public opinion. Legal advisers cautioned President Clinton to remain silent as much as possible because any admission of guilt could be used by the prosecutor in an impeachment proceeding or could subject the President to further criminal liability after he left office. Clinton's public relations advisers, however, argued that "stonewalling" and failing to admit guilt would just drag out the issue—and that the

President Clinton, describing himself as "profoundly sorry" for his actions, urged reconciliation after the U.S. Senate refused to convict him in the impeachment trial resulting from the White House sex scandal.

American people could more easily forgive his sexual transgressions than his lying about them.

Indeed, many public relations professionals said that Clinton committed a public relations error by not admitting an affair until August. Lynn Morgen, principal of Morgen-Walke, Associates said: "Clinton should have admitted the affair ages ago and gotten to other things." And Betsy Nichols, principal of Nichols & Co., said: "The people wanted to forgive him but his address (in August) about Monica Lewinsky was not forthright."

Aviva Diamond, president of Blue Streak, Inc., a Los Angeles firm specializing in media and speech training, expressed the opinion that Clinton had violated at least four public relations axioms: (1) be honest, (2) don't be defensive, (3) don't destroy public trust, and (4) apologize quickly, sincerely, and fully. In an article in *Public Relations Tactics,* Diamond concluded: "What really sticks in the public's collective craw is the lying, the sense that they are being manipulated, the feeling that they cannot trust their top elected official. It's an object lesson for corporate executives as well as politicians."

But Carole Gorney, a professor at Lehigh University and an expert on litigation public relations, was less convinced. In an article in PRSA's *Strategist,* she observed that Clinton's relative silence may indeed have been the best course of action— from a legal as well as public relations standpoint. She cited the fact that, given the President's high approval ratings throughout the scandal (one poll showed the President's job approval rating skyrocketed to 73 percent immediately after the House impeachment vote), it was good politics to have remained silent about his relationship with Lewinsky as long as he did.

The White House, however, did use a number of public relations strategies throughout the year in an attempt to marshal public support for

(continued)

PR Casebook

Clinton Impeachment, continued

the President. Here are some of the strategies and tactics that were used:

Kenneth Starr as Villain White House spokespersons, as well as the President and Hillary Clinton, criticized Starr as a right-wing zealot whose single mission in life was to get Clinton out of office. Early in the year, Hillary Clinton went on national TV morning talk shows to defend her husband and lambaste Starr for conducting what she described as a highly partisan "witch-hunt." Clinton, in his August speech admitting "an improper relationship," also berated Starr for "prying into personal lives," and spending more than $40 million in a four-year period on an effort to discredit him. The idea was to focus public attention on the flaws of the judicial process, not the President's transgressions.

GOP as Villain As with Starr, Clinton focused on the Republican-dominated Congress as the source of his troubles. The White House positioned the Starr inquiry as simply another partisan battle pitting the Democratic White House against the Republican Congress. Polls showed that Newt Gingrich, the Republican Speaker of the House, was not highly popular with the public and was perceived as an ideologue.

Acting Presidential Clinton continued to act "presidential" and as the military's commander-in-chief. He gave talks about the robust economy and offered new initiatives in health, education, and welfare. He took immediate military action when the U.S. embassies in Kenya and Tanzania were bombed, and even ordered the bombing of Iraq on the eve of his impeachment. Often, his statements were made in settings with the American flag behind him and the presidential seal prominently displayed on the podium—a visual appeal to patriotism.

(continued)

Members of the Capitol police load 36 sealed boxes of evidence from independent counsel Kenneth Starr's grand jury investigation of President Clinton for delivery to the House of Representatives. This evidence led to impeachment charges against Clinton.

Clinton Impeachment, continued

Legal Hairsplitting Clinton continued to argue that he hadn't lied to attorneys for Paula Jones because he had not had "sexual relations" with Lewinsky, defined in most dictionaries as "sexual intercourse."

Grassroots Support White House operatives encouraged citizens to write their congressional representatives opposing impeachment. One California online organization called "Censure and Move On" delivered 300,000 anti-impeachment signatures to Congress that had been collected at the group's website. Another group, liberal People for the American Way, aired radio spots to counter conservative groups and talk-show hosts fueling grassroots support for impeachment.

Lobbying Democratic legislators were lobbied by the White House to stand united against impeachment. In addition, labor union leaders and black leaders were asked to lobby Republican lawmakers in swing districts.

Media Editorial Support Sympathetic columnists and editorial writers were enlisted as third-party support. Lars-Erik Nelson, columnist for the New York *Daily News,* for example, wrote: "Most revolting of all is Starr's prissy piousness, insisting that he had to dump this pornography into our history books because Clinton drove him to it."

Leaked Information about Grand Jury Testimony Washington is famous for leaks, and all sides released details about Clinton's grand jury testimony before it was aired in full on American television. The White House moaned about how degrading the questions were and how terrible it was for the Republicans to release the videotape. By the time the videotape was aired, most Americans were prepared for the worst and, although two of three Americans were convinced

that Clinton had lied under oath, most also concluded that it was "no big deal" because the tapes did not live up to their advance billing.

Quick Response to Starr Report The White House issued a massive rebuttal to the Starr report; it was published in daily newspapers on the same day as the lengthy Starr report. This action helped mute the impact of Starr's allegations.

Election as Referendum President Clinton's fortunes rose considerably, particularly in solidifying the support of the Democratic Party, when the GOP, predicting advances, lost seats in the House, and the Democrats gained. Traditionally, the President's party loses seats in mid-term elections. Although the gains were minor, pundits still saw the election as a major public refutation of the GOP's strategy to proceed with impeachment, and Newt Gingrich even resigned as Speaker of the House. President Clinton also touted the election as a manifestation of the public's opposition to impeachment.

Use of Respected Leaders In a joint letter to the *New York Times,* former Presidents Jimmy Carter and Gerald Ford proposed that Clinton be censured by a bipartisan vote in the U.S. Senate to avoid a lengthy trial that would further divide the country.

In sum, President Clinton's fate was perhaps just as dependent on effective public relations strategies and public opinion as it was on points of law. Media coverage was also a strong factor. As one headline in a major daily newspaper proclaimed: "Clinton saga is benumbing the public, media: To pundits, drama has been bled dry." According to the article, the sheer volume of coverage caused the public to say "no more" and conclude that the whole issue was nothing more than partisan politics as usual.

CASE PROBLEM

The National Company plans to introduce a new line of its battery-powered notebooks and portable computers. The approach is an integrated marketing communications campaign that will incorporate public relations, direct mail, sales promotion, and advertising. The objectives are to:

- Generate awareness of the new product with business audiences.

- Position National as the technology leader in developing and manufacturing notebook/portable computers.

- Increase National's sales and market share.

Do some brainstorming. Can you think of any audience research that could be done before you plan the marketing communications program? What variety of techniques and activities could help accomplish National's objectives?

QUESTIONS FOR REVIEW AND DISCUSSION

1. How many people work in public relations? Is public relations a growing field around the world?

2. There are many definitions of public relations. Of those listed in Chapter 1, select the one you find most satisfying and discuss the reasons for your preference.

3. What ten words characterize the essential elements of public relations?

4. How would you summarize the official statement on public relations issued by the Public Relations Society of America?

5. The RACE acronym is a popular way of describing the public relations process. For what step does each initial stand?

6. Public relations is described as a *loop process*. What component makes it a loop process instead of just a linear process?

7. What are the basic components of public relations practice? Which one sounds the most interesting as a career speciality for you?

8. What other terms are used by organizations to describe the public relations function? Do you have a preference for any of them? Explain your reasons.

9. What is "spin"? To some, it has negative connotations that conjure up manipulation and dishonesty. To others, it's simply a slang term for telling an organization's perspective on an event or issue. What do you think?

10. The case study on White House efforts to influence the American public during the Clinton/Lewinsky scandal raises some complex issues regarding the role of public relations in public affairs. Do you think the White House efforts were appropriate and fair? Why or why not?

11. Do you consider "PR" a slang term that should be avoided? Why or why not?

12. How does public relations differ from journalism? Advertising? Marketing?

13. How can the techniques and activities of public relations support the marketing function?

14. What is marketing communications? What is the concept of integrated marketing communications?

15. What four reasons are given for an organization to establish an integrated approach to its communications strategy?

The Evolution of Public Relations

2

Preview

The objective of this chapter is to make students aware of the significant events and personalities that have helped shape today's public relations practices, to place these in context from ancient times, and to define current trends.

Topics covered in the chapter include:

- The roots of public relations
- The evolving functions—press agentry, publicity, and counseling
- Early leaders—Ivy Ledbetter Lee, Edward L. Bernays, Doris Fleischman, and others
- Trends during World Wars I and II
- Trends since World War II
- Major developments in the 1990s and predictions for the twenty-first century

THE ROOTS OF PUBLIC RELATIONS

Public relations is a twentieth-century phenomenon whose roots extend deep into history; in a sense it is as old as human communication itself. In succeeding civilizations, such as those of Babylonia, Greece, and Rome, people were persuaded to accept the authority of government and religion through techniques that are still used: interpersonal communication, speeches, art, literature, staged events, publicity, and other such devices. None of these endeavors was called public relations, of course, but their purpose and their effect were the same as those of similar activities today.

The following remarks of Peter G. Osgood, president of Carl Byoir & Associates, provide a few examples of the early practice of the art of public relations:

> The art has many roots. For example, the practice of dispatching teams to prepare the way for a traveling dignitary or politician was not invented by Harry Truman or Richard Nixon. Their political ancestors in Babylonia, Greece, and Rome were quite adept at it.
>
> St. John the Baptist himself did superb advance work for Jesus of Nazareth.
>
> Publicity, community relations, speech writing, positioning, government relations, issues analysis, employee relations, even investor relations: when you think about these activities in terms of the skills needed to practice them, it's plain they have deep historical roots.

Other examples abound. In the eleventh century, throughout the far-flung hierarchy of the Roman Catholic Church, Pope Urban II persuaded thousands of followers to serve God and gain forgiveness of their sins by engaging in the Holy Crusades against the Muslims. Six centuries later, the church was among the first to use the word *propaganda,* with the establishment by Pope Gregory XV of the College of Propaganda to supervise foreign missions and train priests to propagate the faith. (See Chapter 10.)

The stories that Spanish explorers publicized of the never-discovered Seven Cities of Gold, and even the fabled Fountain of Youth, induced others to travel to the New World. Some of the explorers probably believed those stories themselves. Two more blatant deceptions—examples of actions unacceptable to public relations people today—occurred when Eric the Red, in 1000 A.D., discovered a land of ice and rock and, to attract settlers, named it Greenland; and when Sir Walter Raleigh in 1584 sent back glowing accounts of what was actually a swamp-filled Roanoke Island, to persuade other settlers to travel to America.

It is clear, then, that the idea of using all forms of human communication—drama and storytelling among them—to influence the behavior of other people is nothing new.

THE EVOLVING FUNCTIONS

An excellent way to understand what public relations is all about today is to examine the evolution of its principal functions—press agentry, publicity, and counseling—along with the methods used to carry out those functions.

Press Agentry

"Hyping"—the promotion of movie and television stars, books, magazines, and so on through shrewd use of the media and other devices—is an increasingly lively phenomenon in today's public relations world. At the center of hyping is the press agent, whom the *Webster's New World Dictionary* defines as "a person whose work is to get publicity for an individual, organization, etc."

Press agentry is simply an extension of the activities of those who, in ancient civilizations, promoted athletic events such as the Olympic Games and built an aura of myth around emperors and heroes. Its modern expression may be found in the press agentry that, during the nineteenth century in America, promoted circuses and exhibitions; glorified Davy Crockett as a frontier hero in order to draw political support from Andrew Jackson; attracted thousands to the touring shows of Buffalo Bill and sharpshooter Annie Oakley; made a legend of frontiersman Daniel Boone; and promoted hundreds of other personalities.

The old-time press agents and the show people they most often represented played on the credulity of the public in its longing to be entertained, whether deceived or not. Advertisements and press releases were exaggerated to the point of being outright lies. Doing advance work for an attraction, the press agent dropped a sheaf of tickets on the desk of a newspaper city editor along with the announcements. Voluminous publicity generally resulted, and reporters, editors, and their families flocked to their free entertainment with scant regard for the ethical constraints that largely prohibit such practices today.

Small wonder then that today's public relations practitioner, exercising the highly sophisticated skills of evaluation, counseling, communication, and influencing management policies, shudders at the suggestion that public relations grew out of press agentry. And yet some aspects of modern public relations have their roots in the practice.

Phineas T. Barnum, the great American showman of the nineteenth century, for example, was the master of the *pseudoevent,* the planned happening that occurs primarily for the purpose of being reported—a part of today's public relations activities.

Barnum, who was born in Connecticut in 1810, was also a hardheaded businessman, devoted to his family, a generous contributor to charities, a nondrinker, an accumulator of property, imaginative and energetic, a man whose primary love in staging his circus performances was to make children smile. Beyond that, however, most of today's public relations people would like to part company—for Barnum, in his advertising and publicity, used extensive flowery language and exaggeration, very much the norm during that period in American life. Even so, a public hungry for entertainment accepted his exaggerations, perhaps because they were audacious. Spectators thrilled to the wonders that he presented:

- Tom Thumb became one of the sensations of the century. Barnum discovered Charles S. Stratton in Connecticut when Stratton was five years old, only an inch over two feet in stature and weighing 15 pounds. Barnum made a public relations event of "General" Tom Thumb's marriage to another midget. After triumphal tours of the United States, where Tom Thumb entertained audiences with singing, dancing, and comedy monologues, Barnum took his attraction to England. A tiny carriage and ponies helped to attract attention to the midget, but Barnum decided that the best way to get public acceptance was first to involve the opinion leaders. Consequently, he invited London society leaders to his townhouse, where they met the quick-witted Tom Thumb. This meeting resulted in an invitation to the palace. Having entertained royalty, Tom Thumb drew full houses every night. Barnum, even in his day, knew the value of third-party endorsement.

- Jenny Lind, the "Swedish Nightingale," was one of Europe's most famous singers but was virtually unknown in the United States. Consequently, Barnum launched an unprecedented press campaign to acquaint the American public with her well-loved voice. He obtained full houses on opening nights in each community by donating part of the proceeds to charity. As a civic activity, the event attracted many of the town's opinion leaders, whereupon the general public flocked to attend succeeding performances—a device still employed today.

- The Barnum & Bailey Circus, with its three rings, two stands, and 800 employees, was proclaimed "The Greatest Show on Earth." Neil Harris, in his book *Humbug: The Art of P. T. Barnum,* describes the circus as the showman's "one enduring monument to fame . . . ."

Publicity

Early Development   Publicity, which consists mainly of the issuing of news releases to the media about the activities of an organization or an individual, is one of the earliest forms of public relations. It has been used for virtually every purpose. Signs such as "Vote for Cicero. He is a good man." have been found by archaeologists in ruins of ancient civilizations. In 59 B.C. Julius Caesar ordered the posting of a news sheet, *Acta Diurna,* outside the Forum to inform citizens of actions of Roman legislators; Caesar's *Commentaries* were published largely to aggrandize the achievements of the emperor.

The Colonial Era   In 1620, broadsides were distributed in Europe by the Virginia Company offering 50 acres of free land to those bringing settlers to America by 1625. In 1641, Harvard College published a fund-raising brochure, and in 1758, Kings College (now Columbia University) issued its first press release, announcing commencement exercises.

Phineas T. Barnum, a master of "hype," created pseudoevents such as the beautiful baby show promoted by this poster. Notice how he appeals to two human instincts: the desires to win money and to look at human oddity, quaterns (called quadruplets in modern usage).

VALENTINE'S MANUAL

BARNUM'S MUSEUM
Every Day and Evening this Week, commencing Monday, June 2nd, 1862

GRAND NATIONAL

Waters & Son

BABY SHOW
100 BEAUTIFUL BABIES
will be on exhibition for prizes, for which upwards of
$2,000 Cash will be Distributed
FOR THE
Finest Babies,
Twins, Triplets,
Quaterns
—AND—
ANOTHER BARNUM'S MUSEUM ATTRACTION, 1862

Mainly through the use of newspapers and pamphlets, a staged event (the Boston Tea Party), and wide publicity accorded the so-called Boston Massacre, fiery Samuel Adams and the Boston Radicals achieved a propaganda triumph in helping persuade the American colonists to revolt against Great Britain. Also highly instrumental in bringing lukewarm citizens into the Revolutionary movement was Tom Paine's *Common Sense;* more than 120,000 copies of the pamphlet were sold in three months. Influencing public opinion both in the colonies and in England were the *Federalist Papers,* comprised of 85 letters written by Alexander Hamilton, James Madison, and John Jay, and a series of articles by John Dickinson titled "Letters from a Farmer in Pennsylvania." The most frequently cited female propagandists of the era included Mercy Otis Warren, Abigail Adams, and Sarah Bache, daughter of Benjamin Franklin.

Nineteenth Century Public affairs were controlled mainly by the aristocratic, propertied class until the revolt of the so-called common man placed rough-hewn Andrew Jackson in the White House in 1828. Amos Kendall, a former Kentucky newspaper editor, became an intimate member of Jackson's "kitchen cabinet" and probably the first presidential press secretary. The appointment demonstrated for the first time that public relations is integral to political policy-making and management.

Jackson's campaign and presidency represented the first attempt in American political life to gain broad-based support for a presidential candidate. Kendall sampled public opinion on issues, advised Jackson, and skillfully interpreted his rough ideas, putting them into presentable form as speeches and news releases.

After the Jacksonian era, American politicians increasingly used press releases, pamphlets, posters, and emblems to win favor. The effort reached a nineteenth-century crescendo during the presidential campaigns of William Jennings Bryan and William McKinley in 1896.

Throughout the century, publicity techniques helped populate Western land. Newly sprung-up villages competed to attract printers, whose newspaper copies and pamphlets describing almost every community as "the garden spot of the West" were sent back East to induce increased settlement.

In addition, the supporters of such causes as antislavery, antivivisectionism, women's rights, and prohibition employed publicity to maximum effect throughout the century. One of the most influential publicity ventures for the abolition of slavery was the publication of Harriet Beecher Stowe's *Uncle Tom's Cabin.* Stowe was among a number of women who, although they were not public relations people, extensively used some of the techniques of public relations to promote their causes. Sarah J. Hale, editor from 1836 to 1877 of *Godey's Ladies Book,* a best-selling magazine with 150,000 circulation, ardently promoted women's rights. After a women's rights convention in Seneca Falls, New York, in 1845, Amelia Bloomer became famous. Now associated with the loose-fitting trousers she wore in protest of the corset, she edited *The Lily,* a women's rights publication. Noted temperance crusader Susan B. Anthony got attention by invading saloons with an axe; in less dramatic fashion she served as business manager of *The Revolution,* which advocated a variety of radical causes. The American Woman Suffrage Association was formed in 1869 with Lucy Stone as editor of its weekly, *The Woman's Journal.* While adoption of the Nineteenth Amendment to the U.S. Constitution in 1920 gave women the right to vote, the movement ended without ensuring women greater property rights.

Professor Carolyn M. Byerly of Ithaca College says that such campaigns for social reform qualify as public relations operations and deserve a place in the history of the field. She cites research by Genevieve Gardner McBride which points out that in Wisconsin the support for a constitutional amendment giving women the right to vote began with a few interested individuals and was carried out through carefully managed informational campaigns that included "publicity, press agentry, publications, petition drives, advertising, merchandising, lobbying, membership recruitment and training, special events, fund-raising . . . and issues management, or 'crisis PR.'"

A wave of industrialization, mechanization, and urbanization swept the nation after the Civil War. Concentrations of wealth developed throughout manufacturing and trade. Amid the questioning of business practices, the Mutual Life Insurance Company in 1888 hired journalist Charles J. Smith to write press releases designed to improve its image. In 1889 Westinghouse Corporation established what is said to be the first in-house publicity department, with a former newspaper reporter, E. H. Heinrichs, as manager. In 1897 the term *public relations* was used by the Association of American Railroads in a company listing.

Twentieth Century   As the use of publicity gained increased acceptance, the first publicity agency, known as the Publicity Bureau, established in Boston in 1900. Harvard College was its most prestigious client. George F. Parker and Ivy Ledbetter Lee opened a publicity office in New York City in 1904. Parker remained in the publicity field, but Lee became an adviser to companies and individuals (as will be discussed in the section that follows).

A second Boston publicity business was opened in 1906 by James D. Ellsworth, who later joined the staff of the American Telephone & Telegraph Company. Theodore N. Vail greatly expanded the press and customer relations operations at AT&T after becoming its president in 1907. In 1909 another pioneer, Pendleton Dudley, established a public relations office in New York.

The Santa Fe Railway, at the beginning of the twentieth century, commissioned dozens of painters and photographers to depict scenes in the then little-known Southwest. The paintings unabashedly prettified the American Indian, and the photographs, colored by hand, showed the Indians weaving, grinding corn, and dancing. This corporate image-making attracted hundreds of tourists and contributed to the romanticizing of the Indian and the West.

The Chicago Edison Company broke new ground in public relations techniques under the skillful leadership of its president, Samuel Insull. Well aware of the special need of a public utility to maintain a sound relationship with its customers, Insull created a variety of techniques—he established an external magazine, *Chicago, The Electric City,* in 1903; used press releases extensively; was the first in business to use films for public relations purposes, in 1909; and started the "bill stuffer" idea in 1912 by inserting company information into customer bills.

Henry Ford was probably the first major industrialist to utilize thoroughly two basic public relations concepts. The first was the notion of *positioning*—the idea that credit and publicity always go to those who do something first—and the second idea was ready accessibility to the press.

In 1900 Ford obtained coverage of the prototype Model T by demonstrating it to a reporter from the Detroit *Tribune.* By 1903 Ford achieved widespread publicity by racing his cars—a practice that is still carried out today by automakers. Ford hired Barney Oldfield, a champion bicycle racer and a popular personality, to drive a Ford car at a record speed of 1 minute and 6 seconds per mile, or a bit less than 60 miles per hour. The publicity from these speed runs gave Ford financial backing and a ready market.

Ford also positioned himself as the champion of the common people and was the first automaker to envision that a car should be affordable for everyone. He produced his first Model T in 1908 for $850 and, by 1915 to 1916, reduced its selling price to $360. Such price reductions made Ford dominant in the auto industry and on newspaper front pages.

Although Ford was the first major industrialist to hire blacks in large numbers, he also wrote a number of anti-Semitic articles. In the 1930s, his earlier image as the champion of the working class was shattered by his resistance to organized labor, which led to several violent confrontations as the United Automobile Workers attempted to organize Ford workers.

In politics, President Theodore Roosevelt proved himself a master in generating publicity. Roosevelt was the first president to make extensive use of news conferences and interviews in drumming up support for his projects. He knew the value of the presidential tour for publicity purposes.

Not-for-profit organizations joined the publicity bandwagon in the century's first decade. The American Red Cross and the National Tuberculosis Association began extensive publicity programs soon after their formation in 1908. The Knights of Columbus and the National Lutheran Council opened press offices in 1918.

Organized fund-raising for American higher education began in 1916 when John Price Jones, a public relations veteran of the Liberty Loan campaign to help finance the U.S. war

American trains were jammed during World War II with soldiers being carried to ports of embarkation for shipping overseas into combat. Many civilians complained that because of military crowding they could not find seats or sleeping berths on the trains. The New Haven Railroad tried to placate the protesters with an emotional appeal to their patriotism and sympathy.

effort, directed a highly successful drive in behalf of Harvard University. The campaign exceeded its $10 million goal by $4 million.

Counseling

Industrialists and Muckrakers

In the latter part of the nineteenth century, the United States was transformed by mighty economic and social forces: industrialization moved forward on a major scale; cities swelled with even more immigrants; production was rapidly being mechanized; and business firms grew through the use of vastly improved transportation and communication facilities, along with new interlocking corporate structures and financing methods.

It was the era of the so-called robber barons, exploiters of natural resources and labor, known in less accusatory terms as founders of great American industries. Heavy concentrations of power were held by men such as John D. Rockefeller, Sr., in oil; Andrew Carnegie in steel; J. Pierpont Morgan and Cornelius Vanderbilt in finance; and other industrial leaders. Labor strife intensified, and the government, upon the urging of populist and progressive forces, began to challenge big business with the enactment of the Interstate Commerce Act and the Sherman Antitrust Act.

Within the dozen years after 1900, several magazines developed a literature of exposure that Theodore Roosevelt called the work of "muckrakers." He was comparing the more sensational writers to the Man with the Muckrake in the seventeenth-century work *Pilgrim's Progress*—a character who did not look up to see the celestial crown but continued to rake the filth. Led by Ida M. Tarbell, these writers posed a serious threat to business. Tarbell wrote a series of articles published by *McClure's* in 1903 titled "History of the Standard Oil Company," an attack on the corruption and unfair practices of the Rockefeller oil monopoly. Other noted muckrakers included Upton Sinclair, who exposed unsanitary and fraudulent practices of the meatpackers in his 1906 book *The Jungle*.

The First Public Relations Counsel

The combination of stubborn management attitudes and improper actions, labor strife, and widespread public criticism produced the first public relations counselor, Ivy Ledbetter Lee. Although, as previously noted, this Princeton graduate and former business reporter for the New York *World* began his private practice as a publicist, he shortly expanded that role to become the first public relations counsel.

The emergence of modern public relations can be dated from 1906, when Lee was hired by the anthracite coal industry, then embroiled in a strike. Lee discovered that, although the miners' leader, John Mitchell, was supplying reporters with all the facts they requested, by contrast the leader of the coal proprietors, George F. Baer, had refused to talk to the press or even to President Theodore Roosevelt, who was seeking to arbitrate the dispute. Lee persuaded Baer and his associates to change their policy. He issued a press notice signed by Baer and the other leading proprietors that began: "The anthracite coal operators, realizing the general public interest in conditions in the mining regions, have arranged to supply the press with all possible information. . . ."

Lee issued a "Declaration of Principles," which signaled the end of the "public be damned" attitude of business and the beginning of the "public be informed" era. Eric Goldman said the declaration "marks the emergence of a second stage of public relations. The public was no longer to be ignored, in the traditional manner of business, nor fooled, in the continuing manner of the press agent."

The continuance of Lee's policy of providing accurate information about corporate and institutional activities has saved American news media millions of dollars in reporter salaries during the intervening four decades. Despite misleading information given out by some public relations people, news releases quickly became extremely valuable—even a necessity—to the media.

Railroads at the time also were seeking to operate secretly in their dealings with the press. Retained by the Pennsylvania Railroad Company to handle press relations after a major rail disaster, Lee persuaded the president of the company to alter his policy. Lee provided press facilities, released all available information, and enabled reporters to view the disaster scene. Although such action appeared to the conservative railway directors to constitute reckless indiscretion, they later acknowledged that the company had received fairer press comment than on any previous such occasion.

In 1914, John D. Rockefeller, Jr., hired Lee in the wake of the vicious strike-breaking activities known as the Ludlow Massacre at the Rockefeller family's Colorado Fuel and Iron Company plant. Lee went to Colorado and talked to both sides. He also persuaded Rockefeller to talk with the miners and their families. Lee made sure that the press was there to record Rockefeller's eating in the workers' dining hall, swinging a pickax in the mine, and having a beer with the workers after hours. The press portrayed Rockefeller as seriously concerned about the plight of the workers. Meanwhile, Lee distributed a factsheet giving management's view of the strike and even convinced the governor of Colorado to write an article supporting the position taken by the company.

Rockefeller's visits with the miners led to policy changes and more worker benefits, but the company also prevented the United Mine Workers from gaining a foothold.

Lee's success in transforming a labor dispute into a positive situation (and public image) for the Rockefeller family was based on the fact, according to Gordon M. Sears, president of T. J. Ross and Associates, that "Lee tried to solve the problem or at least establish the proper course toward solution before turning to communications." Lee's achievement led the Rockefeller family to hire him for a full-scale renovation of the Rockefeller name, badly damaged by the muckrakers who often pictured John D. Rockefeller, Sr., as an exploiter and the king of the greedy capitalists. Lee advised the Rockefellers to announce publicly the millions of dollars that they gave to charitable institutions. When John Senior died in 1937, he was mourned worldwide as a kindly old man and a great humanitarian and philanthropist.

Lee died in 1934. He is remembered for four important contributions to public relations: (1) advancing the concept that business and industry should align themselves with the public interest, and not vice versa; (2) dealing with top executives and carrying out no program unless it had the active support and personal contribution of management; (3) maintaining open communication with the news media; and (4) emphasizing the necessity of humanizing business and bringing its public relations down to the community level of employees, customers, and neighbors.

Wartime Counsel to Government   Both world wars saw a tremendous upsurge in the role of public relations on behalf of the government—especially the Creel Committee during World War I and the Office of War Information during World War II.

PR Insights

Brightening Rockefeller's Public Image

Two New York writers helped John D. Rockefeller, Sr. shed much of his penchant for secrecy and resistance to press coverage, according to historian Ron Chernow, author of a 1997 book, *Titan: The Life of John D. Rockefeller, Sr.*

In 1906, the Standard Oil Company trust hired its first publicist, Joseph I. C. Clarke, an editor at the New York *Herald.* Jovial and outgoing, Clarke "greeted reporters with a quip and a cigar," to warm up the trust's image, Chernow relates. "Before long he was lining up reporters for breezy, lighthearted interviews with Rockefeller, featuring a game of golf with the mogul, who obligingly delivered pithy observations on topical subjects. Articles began to appear with titles like, 'The Human Side of John D. Rockefeller,' as if its existence wasn't taken for granted."

Soon thereafter, Rockefeller and friends sailed for France aboard the *Deutschland.* In an article for the New York *American,* reporter William Hoster speculated that Rockefeller needed to consult a European specialist because of ill health. He, too, boarded the *Deutschland,* spied on Rockefeller, and was surprised "to find . . . a tall, broad-shouldered robust man, with ruddy complexion, clear eyes, alert step and altogether vigorous manner."

At Cherbourg, Hoster confronted his subject. "Mr. Rockefeller, have you ever reflected that perhaps you yourself may be in measure responsible for the way that you have been treated by the newspapers?" For a time, writes Chernow, Rockefeller "gazed stonily at Hoster and dug his walking stick into the gravel path. Then his face relaxed and a faint smile crossed his lips. 'So it is my fault. I suppose there may be something in what you say, though I had never thought of it that way before.'"

Rockefeller invited Hoster to join his party. "After a lifetime spent escaping reporters," Chernow relates. "Rockefeller now converted William Hoster into his bosom companion. They rambled through the forest, golfed, and dined together in local hotels."

After that, perhaps also because of Clarke's influence, Rockefeller seemed to have lost his fear of the press and noticeably loosened up.

The Creel Committee.   "Literally public relations counselors to the United States Government" during World War I is the description given to members of the Committee on Public Information by James O. Mock and Cedric Larson in their book *Words That Won the War.* President Wilson called on George Creel, a former newspaper reporter, to organize a comprehensive public relations effort to advise him and his cabinet, to carry out programs, and to influence United States and world opinion. Wrote Mock and Larson:

> Mr. Creel assembled as brilliant and talented a group of journalists, scholars, press agents, editors, artists, and other manipulators of the symbols of public opinion as America had ever seen united for a single purpose. It was a gargantuan advertising agency, the like of which the country had never known, and the breathtaking scope of its activities was not to be equalled until the rise of the totalitarian dictatorship after the war. George Creel, Carl Byoir, Edgar Sisson, Harvey O'Higgins, Guy Stanton Ford, and their famous associates were literally public relations counselors to the United States Government, carrying first to the citizens of this country and then to those in distant lands, the ideas which gave motive power to the stupendous undertaking of 1917–1918.

John D. Rockefeller, Sr. was often photographed giving dimes to children during the 1920s. His public relations counsel, Ivy Ledbetter Lee, has been credited with suggesting that he do so to improve his image, but Lee says he merely convinced Rockefeller to let news photographers show what he had been doing for years. Rockefeller gave millions to charity. Here he presents a dime to William Gebele, Jr. in Lakewood, N.J. (AP/Wide World Photos)

Among numerous other activities, the committee persuaded newspapers and magazines to contribute volumes of news and advertising space to encourage Americans to save food and to invest heavily in Liberty Bonds, which more than 10 million people purchased. Thousands of businesses set up their own groups of publicity people to expand the effort. Wilson accepted Creel's advice that hatred of the Germans should be played down and loyalty and confidence in the government should be emphasized. The committee publicized the war aims and ideals of Woodrow Wilson—to make the world safe for democracy and to make World War I the war to end all wars. The American Red Cross, operating in cooperation with the committee, enrolled more than 19 million new members and received more than $400 million in contributions during the period.

The massive effort had a profound effect on the development of public relations by demonstrating the success of these full-blown techniques. It also awakened an awareness in Americans of the power of mediated information in changing public attitudes and behavior. This, coupled with postwar analysis of British propaganda devices alleged to have helped get the nation into the war, resulted in a number of scholarly books and college courses on the subject. Among the books was Walter Lippmann's classic *Public Opinion,* in which he pointed out how people are moved to action by "the pictures in our minds."

Another legacy was the training received by the noted practitioners Carl Byoir, associate chairman of the committee, and Edward L. Bernays. Byoir in 1930 founded a company that for more than 50 years was one of the largest public relations firms in the United States.

Global PR

Public Relations Roots in Germany, Great Britain, and Australia

GERMANY

As the Industrial Revolution swept through Europe, few owners, as in the United States, sensed a need to communicate with the public about their operations. In Germany, however, railroad companies and at least one shareholding corporation began publicity efforts as far back as the mid-nineteenth century. Alfred Krupp, founder of the Krupp Company, which became the premier industrial firm in Germany and the base of the Nazi war power, wrote to a financial adviser in 1866:

> We think . . . it is time that authoritative reports concerning factory matters in accordance with the facts should be propagated on a regular basis through newspaper reports which serve the enlightened public. We can supply the material for this purpose, and should qualified experts at times be unavailable, it is our wish to contact responsible newspaper editors ourselves.

As the Krupp public relations efforts expanded internationally, other major industries followed suit.

GREAT BRITAIN

The industrial and communication systems of Great Britain were already developed in 1910, when the Marconi Company established a department to distribute news releases about its achievements in wireless telegraphy.

In 1911 the first government public relations campaign was carried out when, at the instigation of Prime Minister David Lloyd George, the Insurance Commission explained the benefits of the National Insurance Act, an unpopular measure that had attracted much adverse publicity. The Air Ministry appointed the first government press officer in 1919, and a year later the Ministry of Health selected Sir Basil Clarke, a former Reuters correspondent, as director of information.

In 1924, Clarke established a counseling firm, Editorial Services Ltd. in London. For his first client, a dairy group, he promoted the idea of milk pasteurization, an innovation that had met with some resistance from the public.

The first public relations officer so styled in Britain was Sir John Elliott, appointed in 1925 by the Southern Railway Company.

(continued)

In one of the early campaigns that established Byoir's reputation, he mobilized women's groups, along with business and labor groups, and directed a campaign that defeated a proposed New York state anti-chain-store tax. He employed the third-party endorsement technique described in Chapter 10.

Bernays's contributions to public relations will be discussed shortly.

Office of War Information (OWI).   To head the vital war information operation during World War II, President Franklin Roosevelt turned to Elmer Davis, an Indiana-born journalist and a Rhodes Scholar. Davis had spent 15 years as a novelist and freelance writer, 10 years as a New York *Times* reporter, and three years as a radio commentator for the Columbia Broadcasting System.

Public Relations Roots in Germany, Great Britain, and Australia, continued

Beginning in the mid-nineteenth century, the government enjoyed a close working relationship with the Reuters news agency for almost 100 years. Paul Julius Reuter, agency owner, was granted use of cables linking the empire's outposts; in return, agency dispatches did much to further the nation's commercial and political interests, and there is little doubt that the news service was careful to say at crucial points what the British government wished it to say. With such an arrangement, historians have noted, government propaganda was particularly effective in bringing the United States to its side in World War I. Today, Reuters operates with scant if any government influence.

Government public relations was substantially enlarged after World War II. The offices are now organized into three sections: press relations, publicity and inquiry, and intelligence.

Via shortwave, the British Broadcasting Company (BBC), chartered in 1922, carries a British point of view to an estimated 75 million adults around the world each week.

AUSTRALIA

Public relations in Australia largely consisted of publicity efforts until after World War II. When U.S. General Douglas MacArthur arrived in Australia after his escape from Corregidor in 1942, he introduced the term *public relations* and, with a highly skilled staff, demonstrated numerous ways of promoting his image and war policy.

The industry grew steadily, and, in 1960, the Public Relations Institute of Australia (PRIA) was formed. It now includes more than 1500 practitioners. Women, today comprising about one third of the nation's public relations specialists, were among its founders.

Notable practitioners include George Fitzpatrick, credited with being the first Australian to conduct public relations, and Eric White, who, a Hill and Knowlton official said, "virtually created the public relations industry" in Australia. As early as the 1960s White oversaw extensions of his firm in six Pacific Rim countries.

Profiting by knowledge of the techniques so successful in World War I, Davis orchestrated an even larger public relations effort during World War II. His job was exceptionally difficult because his office had to coordinate information from the military and numerous government agencies, wrestle for funds each year with a Congress suspicious that the OWI would become Roosevelt's personal propaganda vehicle, and overcome opposition from a large segment of the press that resented having to do business with an official spokesperson.

As in World War I, the OWI's campaigns were extremely successful in promoting the sale of war bonds and in obtaining press and broadcast support for other wartime necessities.

The Voice of America, established by the Department of State in 1942, carried news of the war to all parts of the world. The film industry provided support through such means as Frank Capra's documentary film for the U.S. Signal Corps, designed to build patriotism; bond-selling tours by film stars; and the production of commercial movies glorifying U.S. fighting forces.

President Franklin D. Roosevelt's radio "fireside chats" from the White House strengthened public morale during the Great Depression of the 1930s and later during World War II.

The OWI was the forerunner of the U.S. Information Agency, established in 1953 under President Eisenhower to "tell America's story abroad." A number of the people who worked with Davis became public relations leaders during ensuing decades.

Further Development of the Counseling Function The role of the public relations practitioner as an adviser to corporate and institutional managements grew in significance as the American economy expanded during the 1920s. The persons most responsible for defining this function and drawing public attention to it were Edward L. Bernays and his wife and partner Doris E. Fleischman. Fleischman was a talented writer, ardent feminist, and former assistant women's page and assistant Sunday editor of the New York *Tribune.* Married in 1922, they were equal partners in the firm of Edward L. Bernays, Counsel on Public Relations, until Fleischman died in 1980.

Fleischman, indeed, was an equal partner in the work of the firm, interviewing clients, writing news releases, editing the company's newsletter, and writing and editing books and magazine articles, among other duties. The gender value system of the time, however, did not allow Fleischman to represent the firm to its clients or even to be included in the firm's title. Other historians have credited to Bernays both his own and their shared public relations achievements, included in the list of early examples of counseling that follows shortly.

The Public Relations Function Explained "In writing this book I have tried to set down the broad principles that govern the new profession of public relations counsel." With this opening sentence of *Crystallizing Public Opinion,* published in 1923, Bernays coined a term to describe a function that was to become the core of public relations. He illuminated the scope and function, methods and techniques, and social responsibilities of public relations. Following by a year Walter Lippmann's insightful treatise on public opinion, the book

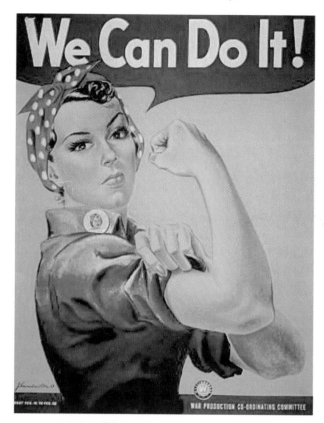

This poster urging women to join the home front workforce during World War II was an extremely effective recruiting tool. It was issued by the War Production Coordinating Committee.

attracted much attention, and Bernays was invited by New York University to offer the first public relations course in the nation.

Even so, the name and definition that Bernays gave to the scope and function of public relations failed for years to gain acceptance by editors and scholars, most of whom equated the new business with press agentry. Following World War I, the newspaper industry conducted a campaign against "spacegrabbers," identified as press agents who demanded free publicity instead of buying advertising space. Later, Stanley Walker, city editor of the New York *Herald Tribune*, leveled his scorn at Bernays:

> Bernays has taken the sideshow barker and given him a philosophy and a new and awesome language. . . . He is no primitive drum-beater. . . . He is devoid of swank and does not visit newspaper offices [as did the circus advance agents]; and yet, the more thoughtful newspaper editors, who have their own moments of worry about the mass mind and commercialism, regard Bernays as a possible menace, and warn their colleagues of his machinations.

This antipathy toward public relations still lingers among many journalists. In 1955 Bernays refined his approach to public relations and, in a book titled *The Engineering of Consent,* he gave the field a new description. To many people, the word *engineering* implied manipulation through propaganda and other devices. Bernays, who himself later

Edward L. Bernays, a legendary figure in
public relations with a career spanning three
quarters of a century, died at the age of 103 in
1995. On his 100th birthday he was honored at
a dinner by the Boston chapter of the Public
Relations Society of America.

railed at use of the word *image* to mean reputation-building, defended his terminology
and concept:

> The term engineering was used advisedly. In our society, with its myriad of group interests,
> interest groups, and media, only an engineering approach to the problems of adjustment,
> information, and persuasion could bring effective results. . . .
>
> Public relations practiced as a profession is an art applied to a science, in which the
> public interest and not pecuniary motivation is the primary consideration. The engineering
> of consent in this sense assumes a constructive social role. Regrettably, public relations, like
> other professions, can be abused and used for anti-social purposes. I have tried to make the
> profession socially responsible as well as economically viable.

Early Examples of Counseling   The following examples illustrate how effectively
Bernays performed his public relations work:

• When, in the 1910s, the actor Richard Bennett wanted to produce *Damaged Goods,* a
  play about sex education, Bernays blunted the anticipated criticism of moralists, and
  possibly avoided a police raid, by organizing the Sociological Fund of the *Medical
  Review of Reviews* journal, with contributors paying $4 each to attend the play as an
  educational event.

• To help Procter & Gamble sell Ivory soap, Bernays attracted the attention of children and
  their parents to cleanliness by developing a nationwide interest in soap sculpture.

• At a time when public opinion and some legislation kept women from smoking in public, Bernays was hired by George Washington Hill, president of the American Tobacco

PR Insights

Edward L. Bernays and the "Big Think"

Journalist Larry Tye, author of *The Father of Spin: Edward L. Bernays & the Birth of Public Relations,* credits Bernays for developing the concept of the "Big Think" in the 1920s and 1930s.

Bernays, in many of his legendary public relations efforts, was a master strategist who often took the indirect approach to solving a client's problem. In the mid–1920s, for example, Beechnut Packing Company hired Bernays to help restore bacon sales as a nation of breakfast eaters got into the habit of having only juice, toast, and coffee. The Bernays solution was to have a famous New York doctor do a national survey of other physicians asking whether they favored a hearty or light breakfast for good health and, of course, "hearty" won big. The media reported that doctors "prescribed" hearty breakfasts to their patients—and sales soared for the two items most identified with big breakfasts—bacon and eggs.

In 1930, book publishers hired Bernays to increase book sales. Bernays came up with the idea of having respected public figures make statements about the importance of books to civilization. He also persuaded architects, contractors, and decorators to build houses with bookshelves. Bernays reasoned, "Where there are bookshelves, there will be books." The sale of books boomed as new home owners wanted to show how "civilized" they were.

Tye writes, "Some analysts have referred to his methods as strategic or lateral thinking—mapping out a solution based on a client's standing in the wider economy and society rather than narrow, vertical considerations like how they were faring against other bacon makers, or book sellers. Bernays preferred the phrase, 'appeals of indirection,' plotting a path to a client's goal that seemed roundabout but ultimately removed underlying as well as immediate impediments. In retrospect, we can pin an even simpler label on what he did: Big Think."

Company, to expand sales of Lucky Strike cigarettes. Bernays consulted a psychoanalyst, who told him that cigarettes might be perceived as "torches of freedom" by women seeking equality with men. Bernays helped break the barrier by inducing ten debutantes to "light up" while strolling in New York's Easter Parade.

Perhaps the most spectacular example of Bernays's skill took place in 1929. To celebrate the fiftieth anniversary of Thomas Edison's invention of the electric light bulb, Bernays arranged the worldwide-attention-getting Light's Golden Jubilee. On October 21, many of the world's utilities shut off their power all at one time, for one minute, in honor of Edison. President Herbert Hoover and many other dignitaries attended a banquet climaxing the celebration. The event achieved such fame that the U.S. Post Office, on its own, issued a commemorative two-cent postage stamp.

Sociologist Leonard W. Doob described the jubilee as "one of the most lavish pieces of propaganda ever engineered in this country during peace time." Bernays, wrote Doob, was working "not for Edison or for Henry Ford, but for very important interests [General Electric had hired Bernays] which saw this historic anniversary as an opportunity to publicize the uses of the electric light."

Light's Golden Jubilee is considered one of Bernays's major accomplishments. It showed, in 1929, the potential of effective public relations. And when television commen-

Doris Fleischman was the partner and wife of Edward L. Bernays in their pioneering public relations counseling firm.

tator Bill Moyers interviewed Bernays in 1984 on a Public Broadcasting Service program about the early beginnings of public relations, Moyers said: "You know, you got Thomas Edison, Henry Ford, Herbert Hoover, and masses of Americans to do what you wanted them to do. You got the whole world to turn off its lights at the same time. You got American women to smoke in public. That's not influence. That's power."

Replied Bernays: "But you see, I never thought of it as power. I never treated it as power. People want to go where they want to be led."

Bernays was widely acknowledged as the founder of modern public relations; one historian has even described him as "the first and doubtless the leading ideologist of public relations." Sigmund Freud, founder of psychoanalysis, must have been proud of his nephew. In 1990 *Life* magazine cited Bernays as one of the 100 most important Americans of the twentieth century.

After Bernays's death in 1995 at the age of 103, journalist Larry Tye searched more than 800 boxes of material that Bernays bequeathed to the Library of Congress and interviewed more than 100 people who knew him. His 1998 book *The Father of Spin: Edward L. Bernays & the Birth of Public Relations* offers a sometimes unflattering portrait of Bernays as an egotistical person who often practiced deception by not revealing the sponsorship of his "Torches of Freedom" parade of female cigarette smokers on New York's Fifth

Avenue. Tye maintains that Ivy Lee and other pre–World War I practitioners could lay greater claim than Bernays to having fathered the craft.

Other Public Relations Pioneers   Benjamin Sonnenberg, Rex Harlow, Leone Baxter, and Henry C. Rogers loom large in the list of other early, influential public relations counselors.

Benjamin Sonnenberg.   It was Sonnenberg who suggested that the Texaco Company sponsor performances of the Metropolitan Opera Company on national radio. Sponsorship of the Saturday afternoon series, which began in 1940, still continues.

Rex Harlow.   Harlow, known as "the father of public relations research," was probably the first full-time public relations educator. As a professor in Stanford University's School of Education, Harlow began teaching a public relations course on a regular basis in 1939. In that same year he founded the American Council on Public Relations (which eventually became the Public Relations Society of America), serving as its president for eight years.

In 1952, Harlow founded the *Social Science Reporter,* one of the first newsletters in the field. In it he actively sought to show practitioners and top management how social science research findings benefit the practice of public relations.

Leone Baxter.   A partner for more than 25 years with Clem Whitaker in the firms of Whitaker & Baxter, Campaigns Incorporated, W&B Advertising, and California Feature Service, Leone Baxter has headed Whitaker & Baxter International since her partner's death in 1961. As president, she counsels clients in the United States and abroad, formulates plans, and directs the staff that carries them out.

The firm is credited with being the first professional political campaign management organization in the United States, setting the pace for many thousands today. The firm orchestrated the advertisements, front groups, and movie shorts that distorted and challenged Upton Sinclair, the muckraking author of *The Jungle* and other exposés of American capitalism's seamy underside, when Sinclair ran for governor of California in 1934. The story of tactics employed in the campaign, which Sinclair lost, is related in Greg Mitchell's 1993 book, *The Campaign of the Century.*

Henry C. Rogers.   In the mid-1930s Rogers, with Warren Cowan, established the public relations firm of Rogers & Cowan, the largest and by most measures the most successful Hollywood image-making operation.

Rogers later became a corporate counsel. Of his image-building years, he said: "Dog food and movie stars are much alike because they are both products in need of exposure."

Among the most widely known advocates of social causes in the twentieth century who effectively used some of the techniques of public relations were Margaret Sanger, founder of the Planned Parenthood Federation of America; singer Kate Smith, who sold thousands of dollars in U.S. bonds during World War II while making Irving Berlin's "God Bless America" almost the national anthem; Dorothy Day, founder of the widely respected *Catholic Worker* magazine in 1933 and its editor until 1980, an active pacifist and worker for the nonviolent achievement of social justice; Gloria Steinem, cofounder with Patricia Carbine of *Ms.* magazine, chronicler of the feminist movement for more than two decades; and Betty Friedan, originator of the National Organization for Women (NOW) in 1966.

Serving on the Management Team   Public relations counseling is at its best when it functions at the very top level of management. American corporate executives have been slow to accept this viewpoint. Its recognition in recent years has resulted mostly from the experiences of companies whose leaders understood much of what public relations is all about.

Arthur W. Page, who served as vice president of public relations for the American Telephone and Telegraph Company from 1927 to 1946, helped shape today's practice by advocating a philosophy that public relations is a management function and that it should have an active voice in management. He also expressed the belief that a company's performance, not press agentry, comprises its basis for public approval.

More than any other individual, Page is credited with laying the foundation for the field of corporate public relations.

Alfred P. Sloan, then president of General Motors Corporation, was among the first executives to place great trust in public relations. In 1931, during the early years of the Great Depression when business was attacked widely for its failures, Sloan hired Paul W. Garrett as his first public relations employee.

Garrett was charged with ascertaining public attitudes and executing a program to bring the company full public approval. For one thing, the board of directors felt that favor might be gained by making the billion-dollar corporation appear small. Garrett considered that approach neither reasonable nor possible. Instead, he informed management that it must interpret itself by words and deeds that had meaning to those outside the company, that it must put the broad interests of the public first, that it must develop sound internal relationships with its employees, and that it must be frank and honest and explain the company's policies clearly through every possible medium.

PUBLIC RELATIONS COMES OF AGE

During the second half of the twentieth century, public relations became firmly established as indispensable to America's economic, political, and social development. And by the turn of the century, it was well integrated into the total communication programs of companies and institutions both nationally and globally.

After World War II

The booming economy after World War II produced rapid growth in all areas of public relations. Companies opened public relations departments or expanded existing ones. Government staffs increased in size, as did those of nonprofit organizations such as educational institutions and health and welfare agencies. Television emerged in the late 1940s as a new challenge for public relations expertise. New firms sprang up nationwide. Many were required not only to sell their own services to potential clients but first to educate many managers on the value of public relations itself.

By 1950 an estimated 17,000 men and 2,000 women were employed as practitioners in public relations and publicity. Typical of the public relations programs of large corporations at midcentury was that of the Aluminum Company of America. Heading the operation was a vice president for public relations-advertising, aided by an assistant public relations director and an advertising manager. Departments included community relations, product

PR Insights

Four Models of Public Relations

To aid in understanding the history of formal public relations as well as its practice today, Professors James E. Grunig of the University of Maryland and Todd Hunt of Rutgers, The State University of New Jersey, have constructed four models of public relations. All four models are practiced today, but the "ideal" one—that in increasing use—is the two-way symmetric model. They explain the models in their 1984 book *Managing Public Relations:*

PRESS AGENTRY/PUBLICITY

Propaganda is the purpose, sought through one-way communication that is often incomplete, distorted, or only partially true. The model is source → receiver. Communication is viewed as telling, not listening, and little if any research is undertaken. P. T. Barnum was the leading historical figure during this model's heyday from 1850 to 1900. Sports, theater, and product promotion are the main fields of practice today.

PUBLIC INFORMATION

Dissemination of information, not necessarily with a persuasive intent, is the purpose. The model is source → receiver. Research, if any, is

likely to be confined to readability tests or readership studies. Ivy Lee is the leading historical figure during this model's early development period from about 1900 into the 1920s. Government, nonprofit associations, and business are primary fields of practice today.

TWO-WAY ASYMMETRIC

Scientific persuasion is the purpose, and communication is two-way, with imbalanced effects. The model is source → receiver, with feedback ← to the source. Research is both formative, helping to plan an activity and to choose objectives, and evaluative, finding if the objective has been met. Edward L. Bernays is the leading historical figure during the model's period beginning in the 1920s. Competitive business and public relations firms are the primary places of practice today.

TWO-WAY SYMMETRIC

Gaining mutual understanding is the purpose, and communication is two-way with balanced effects. The model is group → group with

(continued)

publicity, motion pictures and exhibits, employee publications, news bureau, and industrial economics (speech-writing and educational relations). *Alcoa News* magazine was published for all employees, as well as separate publications for those in 20 plants. The main broadcast effort was sponsorship of Edward R. Murrow's *See It Now* television program.

A British scholar, J.A.R. Pimlott, wrote in 1951: "Public relations is not a peculiarly American phenomenon, but it has nowhere flourished as in the United States. Nowhere else is it so widely practiced, so lucrative, so pretentious, so respectable and disreputable, so widely suspected and so extravagantly extolled."

Census-takers in 1960 counted 23,870 men and 7,271 women engaged in public relations, although some observers put the total figure at approximately 35,000. Since 1960, the number of public relations practitioners has dramatically increased, as stated in Chapter 4. Since 1986, women have comprised more than 50 percent of public relations personnel.

Four Models of Public Relations, *continued*

feedback ←. Formative research is used mainly both to learn how the public perceives the organization and to determine what consequences the organization has for the public, resulting in the counseling of management about policies. Evaluative research is used to measure whether a public relations effort has improved both the understanding publics have of the organization and that which management has of its publics.

Bernays, educators, and professional leaders have been the main historical figures of the two-way symmetric model, followed by some organizations since the 1960s and 1970s.

	Model			
	One-Way		Two-Way	
	Press Agentry/ Publicity	Public Information	Two-Way Asymmetrical	Two-Way Symmetrical
Purpose	Propaganda	Dissemination of information	Scientific persuasion	Mutual understanding
Organizational contribution	Advocacy	Dissemination of information	Advocacy	Mediation
Nature of communication	One-way; complete truth not essential	One-way; truth important	Two-way; imbalanced effects	Two-way; balanced effects
Communication model	Source → Rec.*	Source → Rec.	Source → Rec. feedback	Group → Group
Nature of research	Little; "counting house"	Little; readability, readership	Formative; evaluative of attitudes	Formative; evaluative of understanding

Note. Adapted from Grunig and Hunt, *Managing Public Relations*, 1984, p. 22.

* "Rec." is abbreviation for "Receiver."

Recent surveys show that four out of five large companies and trade organizations now have public relations departments. Additionally, there are more than 6,000 public relations firms.

Journalism and mass communications schools have also felt the impact of public relations majors. In 1999 an estimated 185 colleges and universities offered degrees or sequences in public relations—about 50 percent of the total number of institutions offering journalism and mass communications programs.

The popularity of public relations as a major field of study is reflected in annual statistics gathered by the Association for Education in Journalism and Mass Communication (AEJMC). As early as 1987, Professor Paul Peterson of Ohio State University, who conducted the annual AEJMC survey for many years, declared, "Indications are clear that the areas of advertising and public relations are the leaders in attracting student interests." Reports from Australia, Singapore, England, and Germany also show major increases in public relations enrollments.

The Public Relations Student Society of America, founded in 1968, provides important professional training on campus (see Chapter 4). The International Association of Business Communicators (IABC) also has individual student members and some student chapters, but no national student organization.

Public Relations and Social Growth   Public relations has become essential in modern life because of a multiplicity of reasons, including the following: heavy, continuing population growth, especially in cities where individual citizens have scant direct contact with Big Business, Big Labor, Big Government, Big Institutions, and other powerful organizations influencing their lives; scientific and technological advances, including automation and computerization; the communications revolution; mergers and consolidations, with bottom-line financial considerations often replacing the more personalized decision-making of previous, more genteel times; and the increased interdependence of a complex world society.

The globalization of business and communications has been accompanied by a parallel increase in public relations activity around the world (see Chapter 15). At home, government regulation has brought about the employment of thousands of government public information people and public relations experts helping those regulated to comply with or oppose the regulations.

Many citizens feel alienated, bewildered by such rapid change, cut off from the sense of community that characterized the lives of previous generations. They seek power through innumerable pressure groups, focusing on causes such as environmentalism, human rights, and antinuclear campaigns. Public opinion, registered through continual polling, has become increasingly powerful in opposing or effecting change.

Both physically and psychologically separated from their publics, American business and industry have turned increasingly to public relations specialists for audience analysis, strategic planning, and issues management, among other functions. Corporate social responsibility has become the norm and the expectation. One of the most important tasks of these specialists is that of environmental surveillance—serving, in effect, much like the periscope of a submarine. The continued growth of companies, if not survival itself, depends in large part on the skills of public relations people.

Research has assumed an importance never before known. Back in 1883, Theodore N. Vail had sensed its importance, sending letters to AT&T customers seeking their opinions. In 1912, public-relations-wise Henry Ford had asked 1000 customers why they had purchased his Model T car. These were among the forerunners of the social science research techniques that were developed after World War I. In the 1930s, George Gallup, Elmo Roper, Claude Robinson, and others began to conduct modern public opinion and marketing surveys. With these, public relations specialists and others could evaluate public attitudes quantitatively and obtain objective measurements to supplement personal estimates.

Major Developments in Today's World

Technological and societal changes continued to transform aspects of public relations during the 1990s. As largely foreseen by communications leaders and management executives, the major developments included those pertaining to the global economy, quality of the environment, an increased management role for public relations, and other areas of practice.

A Global Economy   Every national economy and every business is part of an integrated global economy, analysts declare. The internationalization of business means that companies and public relations people must learn foreign cultures, business practices, and languages. The wealth of the world has largely shifted from the West to the Pacific Rim, especially in Japan, Taiwan, Singapore, and Korea, despite major slumps in the Asian economies in late 1998 and early 1999.

Quality of the Environment   Concern for the environment is now a widespread issue; people in many countries believe that protecting it is so important that no requirements and standards can be too high. Environmental issues also translate as a "quality of life" issue: people are concerned about their health and perceive a direct self-interest in such issues as the "greenhouse effect," acid rain, pollution, toxic wastes, and the spread of AIDS. Because such issues are transnational in scope, international dialogue and cooperation are prerequisites for effective solutions.

Corporations must be more sensitive to environmental concerns than in the past and show diverse publics that they are part of the solution, not the problem. At the same time, according to C. J. Silas, chairman of Phillips Petroleum Company, the challenge for industry and government is "to balance the two good, but seemingly paradoxical, objectives of environmental protection and economic growth and development."

Increased Management Role for Business   Impediments to sales success such as environmental concerns have required that public relations play a major role in the strategic planning and policy formulation of companies. John L. Clendenin, chairman of BellSouth Corporation, says, "I can't imagine any institution being able to operate successfully in today's environment without effective and proactive public relations management." (See Fig. 2.1.)

New Emphasis on Issues Management   Many companies are seeking to cope with a flood of public policy issues. Governments as well as corporations are turning to experts skilled in problem analysis and conflict resolution to deal with the tough problems facing society and the planet Earth. (See Chapter 13.)

Proliferation of Publics   The splintering of mass markets into hundreds of smaller markets, begun mainly in the 1980s, has continued. Public relations personnel used microdemographics (closely defining target audiences by age, sex, educational level, and the like) to reach multiple publics with tailored information. In addition to traditional publics such as consumers and stockholders, audiences were increasingly fragmented into special-interest groups.

Decline of Mass Media   The fragmentation of publics has meant the decline of mass media as vehicles with which to reach audiences. Technology is providing many avenues for transmitting messages to specific audiences; the key terms are *niche programming* and *narrowcasting*.

Cynthia Pharr, president of Tracy-Locke-Pharr Public Relations, put it this way: "With mass media rapidly giving way to specialized vehicles of communication, it is essential to tailor messages to narrow, well-defined audiences." This means identifying and understanding particular interest groups, working effectively with the media those groups trust, and developing a variety of messages to reach different audiences. The "one size fits all" news release, she contends, is dead.

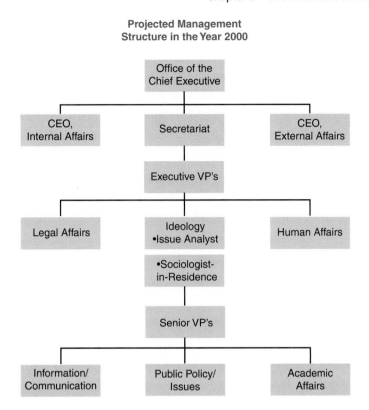

Projected Management
Structure in the Year 2000

Figure 2.1

This idealized
management structure in
the year 2000 was
designed by veteran
counselor John F. Budd, Jr.

(Copyright John F. Budd, Jr. 1998)

Rapid Spread of New Media Technology   During the 1990s, the number of World Wide Web sites increased from four million to more than 20 million. By mid-1999, according to *Nielsen Media Research,* more than 100 million people were using the Internet, with 20 million of them making online purchases.

The Leading Trend in Public Relations   Public relations people are increasingly using the electronic media as their principal method of communication. Reports the *Public Relations Journal*: "Partly what is pushing the electronic public relations frontier is the accessibility of electronic technology and the merging of telephone, cable, and computer companies, as well as the increasing utilization of e-mail and the Internet by journalists, cumulatively creating the information superhighway."

Much More One-to-One Communication   Public relations people are communicating much more on a one-to-one basis rather than seeking a mass audience. Says John Beardsley, past president of the Public Relations Society of America and CEO of Padilla, Speer, Beardsley public relations: "You're dealing with many audiences, many constituencies. The technology makes it possible to subdivide and subdivide—until you get to the point where you're almost talking one-to-one. The people are still there . . . but the way to reach them has absolutely demolished the concept of a mass audience."

International Media Relations   Press conferences and simultaneous briefings by teams of public relations professionals in various countries are being transmitted by satellite. Corporations are maintaining decentralized public relations offices on several continents and publishing newsletters in a variety of languages.

Higher Priority on Employee Communication   The employee ranks of many corporations were severely downsized (reduced) during the 1990s to satisfy the demands of the global marketplace and company stakeholders. At the same time, employees noted huge increases in salaries of chief executive officers of major corporations. Vastly diminished employee loyalty often resulted, causing management to place high priority on using public relations communications to restore or hold employee trust.

The Skilled Practitioner   Public relations personnel of many global corporations increased their training and professional experience in marketing, international business, finance, and government during the 1990s. They were charged with performing like senior-level managers: thinking, visualizing, and implementing strategies.

CASE PROBLEM

The latter part of this chapter lists a number of national and global trends taking place in public relations. One of the most visible trends is the advent of new media technologies and, in particular, the Internet. In fact, more than one public relations professional has declared that the Internet has revolutionized the way public relations is practiced today. Do some research on how the Internet has changed the way journalists and public relations people do their work as compared to how things were done before the "information highway" became part of our lives.

QUESTIONS FOR REVIEW AND DISCUSSION

1. The roots of public relations extend deep into history. What are some of the early antecedents of today's public relations practice?

2. What is meant by "hyping"?

3. Which practices of press agent Phineas T. Barnum should modern practitioners use? Which should they reject?

4. Describe briefly the publicity practices used by Henry Ford and by Theodore Roosevelt.

5. Ivy Lee made four important contributions to public relations. Can you identify them?

6. What effect did the Creel Committee of World War I have on the development of public relations?

7. Who was Doris E. Fleischman? Name at least three other women who used public relations techniques in pursuit of their causes.

8. Identify three of the successful public relations campaigns conducted by Edward L. Bernays.

9. What are some of the aspects of current American social and business life that make public relations essential?

10. What major national and global issues confront public relations practitioners today?

3

Ethics and Professionalism

Preview

The goal of this chapter is to give students an understanding of the ethical standards and professionalism required of public relations practitioners today, and to help them identify their own standards as public relations professionals.

The topics covered in this chapter include:
* What is ethics?
* Codes of ethics
* Professionalism, licensing, and accreditation
* Ethics in individual practice
* Ethical dealings with news media
* "Front groups"

WHAT IS ETHICS?

Ethics refers to the value system by which a person determines what is right or wrong, fair or unfair, just or unjust. It is expressed through moral behavior in specific situations. An individual's conduct is measured not only against his or her conscience but also against some norm of acceptability that has been societally, professionally, or organizationally determined. The difficulty in ascertaining whether an act is ethical lies in the fact that individuals have different standards and perceptions of what is "right" and "wrong." Often the situation is not black or white, but falls into the gray area.

A person's philosophical orientation can also determine how he or she acts in a specific situation. Philosophers say the three basic value orientations are (1) absolutist, (2) existentialist, and (3) situationalist. The absolutist believes every decision is either "right" or "wrong," regardless of the consequences. The existentialist, whose choices are made without a prescribed value system, decides on the basis of immediate rational choice. The situationalist's decisions are based on what would cause the least harm or most good.

Most people, depending on the actual situation, probably choose a course of action somewhere along the continuum of the three types. They make decisions on the building blocks of truth-telling, promise-keeping, loyalty, and commitment.

Public relations professionals have the added dilemma of making decisions that satisfy (1) the public interest, (2) the employer, (3) the professional organization's code of ethics, and (4) their personal values. In the ideal world, the four would not conflict. In reality, however, they often do.

CODES OF ETHICS

Most professional organizations and many businesses have codes of ethics. These documents, also called *codes of professional conduct,* are supposed to set acceptable norms of behavior for working professionals and employees. The Public Relations Society of America (PRSA) and the International Association of Business Communicators (IABC) both have such codes for their members, to be discussed in the following pages. The PRSA code is emphasized because of its age (dating back to 1950) and its enforcement process, unique among communications organizations.

The PRSA Code of Professional Standards

When the Public Relations Society of America was founded in 1948, one of its first concerns, according to the late Rea W. Smith, former executive vice president, was "the development of an ethical code so that (1) its members would have behavioral guidelines, (2) managements would have a clear understanding of standards, and (3) professionals in public relations would be distinguished from shady promoters and ballyhoo advance men who, unfortunately, had been quick to appropriate the words 'public relations' to describe their operations."

Enunciating principles on which the code would be built, members pledged to (1) conduct themselves professionally with truth, accuracy, fairness, and responsibility to the public and (2) improve their individual competence and advance the knowledge and proficiency of the profession through continuing research and education.

The PRSA Code of Professional Standards for the Practice of Public Relations was adopted in 1950 and strengthened by successive revisions. In a unifying step, the 1988 revision was based on the Code of the North American Public Relations Council (NAPRC), an organization of 13 member groups, including PRSA.

PRSA's Code Enforcement

The PRSA has a Board of Ethical and Professional Standards to receive, initiate, and review complaints about members. If a complaint has merit, the case is sent to district-level grievance boards charged with gathering testimony and making a recommendation to the board.

The findings are reviewed and a final decision made by the society's Board of Directors. PRSA may *expel, suspend, censure,* or *reprimand* a member if he or she is found in violation of the code. If a person is expelled from PRSA—the highest sanction—it simply means he or she cannot be a member. PRSA has no legal authority to prohibit an expelled member from continuing to practice public relations.

The threat of condemnation by one's professional peers, however, is a strong incentive for following the code. The bylaws do permit public announcement of actions taken against a member, but this is usually done through insertion of a short item in the society's internal newsletters, and no general news release is made.

The PRSA can discipline only its own members; it has no legal right to condemn non-members for incompetent practice. Since only a comparably small percentage of the public relations people in the United States are members of PRSA, code enforcement provisions possibly are less important than the existence of the code itself.

Types of Complaints

The PRSA Ethics Board currently investigates about 15 to 20 cases annually involving a possible violation of ethics and professional practice, but almost every one comes to a "dead end" with no action taken. The primary reason for this, says Bob Frause, chair of the Ethics Board, is that PRSA is a voluntary organization that doesn't have quasi-legal power to subpoena witnesses, order the presentation of evidence, or even fine individuals for refusing to cooperate fully.

This inability to conduct full-scale inquiries is one reason why, between 1990 and 1998, no member was even reprimanded by the organization for unethical conduct. One case did make it all the way to the PRSA Board of Directors for action, but the board voted to take no action.

Frause says the majority of cases that now come before the Ethics Board deal primarily with Article 7: identifying ". . . publicly the name of the client or employer on whose behalf any public communication is made," and Article 8: members "shall not use any individual or organization professing to serve or represent an announced cause, or professing to be independent or unbiased, but actually serving another or undisclosed interest." Both articles deal mainly with organizing "front groups," to be discussed shortly.

Other situations that come before the Ethics Board with some frequency involve Article 5: intentional communication of false and misleading information; and Article 4: adhering to accuracy and truth and avoiding extravagant claims and unfair comparisons. . . ." These possible violations of the PRSA ethics code are somewhat of a change from previous years, when Article 3: fair dealing with clients, employers, and the public, generated the most complaints.

The biggest headache that the PRSA Ethics Board has, says Frause, is the apparent "disconnect" between employers and supervisors who are PRSA members, and the unethical conduct of non-PRSA staff members whom they are supposed to be supervising. The PRSA code doesn't specifically hold the employer or supervisor responsible for the actions of a junior employee, so management often says, "I wasn't involved in that decision or action."

Other Codes

Practically every national public relations organization has a code of ethics, and such organizations as the Canadian Public Relations Society (CPRS), the Public Relations Institute

PR Insights

PRSA's Code of Professional Standards for the Practice of Public Relations

These articles have been adopted by the Public Relations Society of America to promote and maintain high standards of public service and ethical conduct among its members.

1. A member shall conduct his or her professional life in accord with the *public interest.*

2. A member shall exemplify high standards of *honesty and integrity* while carrying out dual obligations to a client or employer and to the democratic process.

3. A member shall *deal fairly* with the public, with past or present clients or employers, and with fellow practitioners, giving due respect to the ideal of free inquiry and to the opinions of others.

4. A member shall adhere to the highest standards of *accuracy and truth,* avoiding extravagant claims or unfair comparisons and giving credit for ideas and words borrowed from others.

5. A member shall not knowingly disseminate *false or misleading information* and shall act promptly to correct erroneous communications for which he or she is responsible.

6. A member shall not engage in any practice which has the purpose of *corrupting* the integrity of channels of communications or the processes of government.

7. A member shall be prepared to *identify publicly* the name of the client or employer on whose behalf any public communication is made.

8. A member shall not use any individual or organization professing to serve or represent an announced cause, or professing to be independent or unbiased, but actually serving another or *undisclosed interest.*

9. A member shall *not guarantee the achievement* of specified results beyond the member's direct control.

10. A member shall *not represent conflicting* or competing interests without the express consent of those concerned, given after a full disclosure of the facts.

11. A member shall not place himself or herself in a position where the member's *personal interest is or may be in conflict* with an obligation to an employer or client, or others, without full disclosure of such interests to all involved.

12. A member shall *not accept fees, commissions, gifts, or any other consideration* from anyone except clients or employers for whom services are performed without their express consent, given after full disclosure of the facts.

13. A member shall scrupulously safeguard the *confidences and privacy rights* of present, former, and prospective clients or employers.

14. A member shall not intentionally *damage the professional reputation* or practice of another practitioner.

15. If a member has evidence that another member has been guilty of unethical, illegal, or unfair practices, including those in violation of this Code, the member is obligated to present the information promptly to the proper authorities of the Society for action in accordance with the procedure set forth in Article XII of the Bylaws.

16. A member called as a witness in a proceeding for enforcement of this Code is obligated to appear, unless excused for sufficient reason by the judicial panel.

17. A member shall, as soon as possible, sever relations with any organization or individual if such relationship requires conduct contrary to the articles of this Code.

of Southern Africa (PRISA), and the Public Relations Institute of Australia (PRIA) have codes that strongly resemble the PRSA one.

These national organizations also exercise the right to censure or expel members who violate the code, but PRSA, despite flaws in enforcement, is unique in having a highly structured grievance procedure in place. Indeed, during the first 33 years of the code's life, at least 10 members were disciplined by PRSA.

Critics often complain that such codes of ethics "have no teeth," and one cynic, quoted by *Ragan's PR Intelligence Report,* says, "Watching the public relations industry discuss ethics is a little like watching tourists from a foreign country attempting to speak a language they barely understand. They seem enthusiastic and sincere, and many of the right words come out of their mouths, but they just don't quite manage to make sense."

Problems in code enforcement, however, are not unique to public relations groups. Professional organizations in which membership is voluntary are often reluctant to discipline members for several reasons, including lawsuits and the First Amendment guarantee of free speech.

Consequently, most professional membership groups believe that the primary purpose of establishing codes of ethics is not enforcement, but education and information—enunciating standards of conduct that will guide members in their professional lives. The International Association of Business Communicators (IABC) takes this approach.

IABC's Code of Ethics

The International Association of Business Communicators, with members in 52 nations, updated its code of ethics in 1995 to 1996. The new code, which has 12 articles, represents little change in content from the 1985 version, but the major points are more streamlined. It continues to be based on the principles that professional communication not only is legal and ethical but also is in good taste and sensitive to cultural values and beliefs. Members also are encouraged to be truthful, accurate, and fair in all their communications.

According to the *Worldbook of IABC Communicators,* "IABC fosters compliance with its code by engaging in global communication campaigns rather than through negative sanctions." The code is published in several languages, and IABC bylaws require that articles on ethics and professional conduct be published in the organization's monthly publication *IABC: Communication World.* In addition, the organization includes sessions on ethics at its annual meetings, conducts workshops on ethics, and encourages chapters to include ethics discussions in their local programs. In addition, new and renewing members of IABC must sign the following statement as part of their application: "I have reviewed and understand the IABC Code of Ethics for Professional Communicators."

IABC's ethics board, consisting of three accredited members, also answers inquiries about ethics. An IABC spokesperson, however, reports that "very few inquiries" have been received during the past several years, and that the organization has never taken the formal action of suspending or expelling a member. Instead, if a member is conducting his professional activities contrary to the code, the usual procedure is to have an informal conversation with the offender and point out the areas of the code being violated. This is usually enough for the offender to amend his or her ways.

Since 1990, at least two IABC members have voluntarily resigned because they had violated Article 6, which deals with a member who has been found guilty by a government body or judicial body of violating laws governing professional activities. In one case, a member resigned after being charged with embezzling funds from a chapter treasury.

The code of professional conduct of the International Public Relations Association (IPRA), based on the charter of the United Nations, is discussed in Chapter 15.

Video News Release Code of Good Practice

Are video news releases (VNRs) fake news? A survey published in *TV Guide* disclosed that almost half of TV station news directors failed to identify the source of VNRs on their news programs. *TV Guide,* in a cover story, labeled such reports "fake news."

"Don't blame the makers of the VNRs," said Bob Kimmel, senior vice president of the News/Broadcast Network. "We are doing everything we can by putting the source of the material on the VNR. We can't control what happens at the news level, however." Many stations pass off the VNRs as products of their own staffs. (See Chapter 23.)

Six video news producers, members of the Public Relations Service Council in New York, drew up a Code of Good Practice and pointed out that a seal bearing the code's insignia would reassure news directors that the release contained accurate information and was clearly labeled as coming from a corporate sponsor. The code:

> The objective of a VNR is to present information, pictures, and sound that television journalists can use and rely on for quality, accuracy, and perspective.
>
> Information contained in a VNR must be accurate and reliable. Intentionally false and misleading information must be avoided.
>
> A video news release must be clearly identified as such, both on the video's opening slate and on any advisory material and scripts that precede or accompany tape distribution.
>
> The sponsor of the video news release must be clearly identified on a video slate and on the VNR tape. Name and phone number of a responsible party must be provided on the video for journalists to contact for further information.
>
> Persons interviewed in the VNR must be accurately identified by name, title, and affiliation on the video.

PROFESSIONALISM, LICENSING, AND ACCREDITATION

Is public relations a profession? Should its practitioners be licensed? Does the accreditation of practitioners constitute a sufficient guarantee of their talents and integrity? These and other such questions are addressed in the section that follows.

Professionalism

Among public relations practitioners there are considerable differences of opinion about whether public relations is a craft, a skill, or a developing profession. Certainly, at its present level, public relations does not qualify as a profession in the same sense that medicine and law do. Public relations does not have prescribed standards of educational preparation, a mandatory period of apprenticeship, or state laws that govern admission.

PR Insights

Ethical Dilemmas in Public Relations Practice

How would you respond to the following situations? Consider your answers. Then, turn the page to see how your responses correspond with interpretations of the PRSA Code.

1. The company president asks you to write a news release claiming that a new product is four times better than the competition and that it represents a "revolutionary" breakthrough in technology.

2. You're a student intern at a public relations firm. One of your assignments is to call corporations and say you're a student doing a class project. You would like to know what kinds of outside public relations services would be most helpful to the company.

3. An American company wants to increase its visibility and market share in Eastern Europe. As director of public relations, you invite a group of German business editors to visit the firm's headquarters with all expenses paid.

4. Your company, in order to improve the quality and media acceptance of news releases, hires the local daily's business editor on a retainer fee for periodic advice and counsel.

5. Your company, as part of its Christmas tradition, gives journalists who regularly cover it an expensive gift. Last year, it was a weekend at a local resort.

6. You are asked by your employer to establish a "citizens' task force" for the purpose of writing state legislators opposing an environmental bill that negatively affects the company.

7. Your public relations firm is competing for an account with two other firms. As a sales point, you say, "We can get you coverage in the *Wall Street Journal.*"

8. You're looking for a job in public relations, and a tobacco company offers you the highest salary.

9. You work for a public relations firm. A printing company representative contacts you with the following proposal: If you refer clients that result in new business, the representative will pay you a $250 "finder's fee."

Adding to the confusion about professionalism is the difficulty of ascertaining what constitutes public relations practice. John F. Budd, Jr., a veteran counselor, wrote in *Public Relations Quarterly:* "We *act* as publicists, yet we *talk* of counseling. We *perform* as technologists in communication but we *aspire* to be decision-makers dealing in policy."

On the other hand, there is an increasing body of literature about public relations—including this text and many others in the field. PRSA has compiled a Body of Knowledge abstract that contains more than 1000 references, available on computer disk or hard copy. Substantial progress also is being made in developing theories of public relations, conducting research, and publishing scholarly journals.

There is also the idea, advanced by many professionals and PRSA itself, that the most important thing is for the individual to *act like a professional* in the field. This means that a practitioner should have:

1. A sense of independence.

Answers to Ethical Dilemmas in Public Relations Practice

1. Making extravagant claims about a product, which cannot be substantiated, should be avoided. Article 4 says a member shall adhere to the highest standards of truth and accuracy. Article 5 also says that a member shall not knowingly disseminate false and misleading information.

2. Although you're a student, you are acting as an agent of the public relations firm. Consequently, you are not representing yourself with honesty and integrity (Article 2), and you are serving the undisclosed interest (Article 8) of the public relations firm that is seeking the information for marketing and direct mail purposes.

3. Inviting German editors to headquarters, all expenses paid, is permissible under Article 6, which is concerned about corrupting the channels of communication. It can be argued that the visit has legitimate news value, and it furthers press understanding of the company's operations. Article 6 would be violated, however, if the all-expense-paid trip were simply a pleasant holiday.

4. Hiring an editor to be a consultant violates Article 6 about the corruption of communication channels because there is a strong indication that such an arrangement is designed to gain preferential or guaranteed news coverage. Article 6, however, would not necessarily be violated if there were full public disclosure and the editor's employer approved.

5. Article 6 does not forbid gifts of nominal value to the media, especially if the gift is a sample of the company's product. Major gifts, however, raise serious questions about expectations of favorable media coverage in return—and thus could corrupt the channels of communication.

6. The establishment of "citizen task forces" violates Article 8, especially if the intent is to portray the group as independent or unbiased—yet serving the undisclosed interest of the company organizing and funding its activities. This is not in accord with the public interest (Article 1), nor is the practitioner dealing fairly with the public (Article 3).

7. Promising an employer or client that you can get coverage in a specific publication is a violation of Article 9, which says a member shall not guarantee the achievement of specified results beyond the member's direct control. A person can guarantee the quality of work, but not the decisions of editors.

8. The decision to work for a tobacco company is a personal choice. Article 11, however, says that a member should not place himself or herself in a position where the member's personal interest is in conflict with an employer or client. Therefore, if you oppose smoking and believe it is hazardous to health, it would be difficult to fulfill your obligations to your employer.

9. Accepting a "finder's fee" from a printing company representative violates Article 12, which states that such fees should not be accepted unless the employer or client is told and gives consent. Accepting a "finder's fee" places the practitioner in a conflict-of-interest situation (Article 10) because he or she may not act in the best interests of the client or employer.

PR Insights

IABC's Code of Ethics for Professional Communicators

PREFACE

Because hundreds of thousands of business communicators worldwide engage in activities that affect the lives of millions of people, and because this power carries with it significant social responsibilities, the International Association of Business Communicators developed the Code of Ethics for Professional Communicators. The Code is based on three different yet interrelated principles of professional communication that apply throughout the world.

These principles assume that just societies are governed by a profound respect for human rights and the rule of law; that the ethics—the criteria for determining what is right and wrong—can be agreed upon by members of an organization; and, that understanding matters of taste requires sensitivity to cultural norms.

These principles are essential:

• Professional communication is legal.

• Professional communication is ethical.

• Professional communication is in good taste.

Recognizing these principles, members of IABC will:

• engage in communication that is not only legal but also ethical and sensitive to cultural values and beliefs;

• engage in truthful, accurate and fair communication that facilitates respect and mutual understanding; and

• adhere to the following articles of the IABC Code of Ethics for Professional Communicators.

Because conditions in the world are constantly changing, members of IABC will work to improve their individual competence and to increase the body of knowledge in the field with research and education.

ARTICLES

1. Professional communicators uphold the credibility and dignity of their profession by practicing honest, candid and timely communication and by fostering the free flow of essential information in accord with the public interest.

2. Professional communicators disseminate accurate information and promptly correct any erroneous communication for which they may be responsible.

3. Professional communicators understand and support the principles of free speech, freedom of assembly, and access to an open marketplace of ideas; and, act accordingly.

(continued)

2. A sense of responsibility to society and the public interest.

3. Manifest concern for the competence and honor of the profession as a whole.

4. A higher loyalty to the standards of the profession and fellow professionals than to the employer of the moment. The reference point in all public relations activity must be the standards of the profession and not those of the client or the employer.

PR Insights

IABC's Code of Ethics for Professional Communicators,
continued

4. Professional communicators are sensitive to cultural values and beliefs and engage in fair and balanced communication activities that foster and encourage mutual understanding.

5. Professional communicators refrain from taking part in any undertaking which the communicator considers to be unethical.

6. Professional communicators obey laws and public policies governing their professional activities and are sensitive to the spirit of all laws and regulations and, should any law or public policy be violated, for whatever reason, act promptly to correct the situation.

7. Professional communicators give credit for unique expressions borrowed from others and identify the sources and purposes of all information disseminated to the public.

8. Professional communicators protect confidential information and, at the same time, comply with all legal requirements for the disclosure of information affecting the welfare of others.

9. Professional communicators do not use confidential information gained as a result of professional activities for personal benefit and do not represent conflicting or competing interests without written consent of those involved.

10. Professional communicators do not accept undisclosed gifts or payments for professional services from anyone other than a client or employer.

11. Professional communicators do not guarantee results that are beyond the power of the practitioner to deliver.

12. Professional communicators are honest not only with others but also, and most importantly, with themselves as individuals; for a professional communicator seeks the truth and speaks the truth first to the self.

Unfortunately, a major barrier to professionalism is the attitude that many practitioners themselves have toward their work. As James Grunig and Todd Hunt state in their text *Managing Public Relations,* practitioners tend to hold more "careerist" values than professional values. In other words, they place higher importance on job security, prestige in the organization, salary level, and recognition from superiors than on the values listed above.

On another level, many practitioners are limited in their professionalism by what might be termed a "technician mentality." These people narrowly define professionalism as the ability to do a competent job of executing the mechanics of communicating (preparing news releases, brochures, newsletters, and so on) even if the information provided by management or a client is in bad taste, is misleading, lacks documentation, or is just plain wrong.

The *Wall Street Journal* once highlighted the pitfalls of the technician mentality. The story described how Jartran, Inc., used the services of the Daniel J. Edelman, Inc., public relations firm to distribute a press packet to the media. The packet included a letter offering information about wheels falling off trucks owned by U-Haul, its archrival. When the newspaper reporter asked about the ethics of this approach, an Edelman junior account executive was quoted as saying, "It was their idea. We're merely the PR firm that represents them."

In other words, readers may get the impression that the public relations expertise of a firm is available to the highest bidder, regardless of professional values, fair play, and ultimately, the public interest. When public relations firms and departments take no responsibility for what is communicated—only *how* it is communicated in terms of techniques—they reinforce the perception that public relations is more flackery than profession.

Some practitioners defend the technician mentality, however, arguing that public relations people are like lawyers in the court of public opinion. Everyone is entitled to his or her viewpoint and, whether the public relations person agrees or not, the client or employer has a right to be heard. Thus a public relations representative is a paid advocate, just as a lawyer is. The only flaw in this argument is that public relations people are not lawyers, nor are they in a court of law where judicial concepts determine the roles of defendant and plaintiff. In addition, lawyers have been known to turn down clients or resign from a case because they doubted the client's story.

In Chapter 12, which concerns legal aspects of public relations, it is pointed out that courts are increasingly holding public relations firms accountable for information disseminated on behalf of a client. Thus it is no longer acceptable to say, "The client told me to do it."

Licensing

Proposals that public relations practitioners be licensed were discussed before PRSA was founded. One proponent, Edward L. Bernays, who was instrumental in formulating the modern concept of public relations (see Chapter 2), believed that licensing would protect the profession and the public from incompetent, shoddy opportunists who do not have the knowledge, talent, or ethics required.

The problem is stated by PRSA's task force on demonstrating professionalism:

> Pick up any metropolitan newspaper and scan the employment ads. Under the "public relations" classification, you are likely to find opportunities for door-to-door salespersons, receptionists, used-car salesmen, singles bar hostesses and others of less savory reputation. The front pages of the newspapers are full of stories about former government employees peddling influence and calling it public relations.

Thus, under the licensing approach, only those individuals who pass rigid examinations and tests of personal integrity could call themselves "public relations" counselors. Those not licensed would have to call themselves "publicists" or adopt some other designation.

Several arguments for mandatory licensing and registration with legal sanctions exist:

1. It would define the practice of public relations.

2. It would establish uniform educational curricula.

3. It would set uniform ethical and professional standards.

4. It would provide for decertification of violators of ethical standards.

5. It would protect the consumer of public relations services (clients and employers) from impostors and charlatans.

6. It would protect qualified practitioners from unfair competition from the unethical and unqualified.

7. It would raise the credibility of public relations practitioners.

8. Since licensing would not control anyone's right to deal with the media, government, or public, or to speak out in any way, no infringement of First Amendment rights would be involved.

Several arguments against licensing and in favor of continued reliance on a voluntary approach to public relations ethics also exist:

1. Any licensing in the communications field is an infringement on the First Amendment.

2. It is difficult to define public relations.

3. Too much emphasis would be placed on education.

4. Voluntary accreditation is sufficient to establish standards.

5. Civil and criminal laws already exist to deal with malpractice.

6. Legislatures show little or no interest in licensing public relations since the health and welfare of the general public are not at stake.

7. Licensing would be a state function, and public relations people often work on a national and international basis.

8. Licensing assures only minimum competence and professional standards; it doesn't necessarily assure high ethical behavior.

9. The credibility and status of an occupation are not necessarily assured through licensing. Attorneys, for example, don't enjoy particularly high public status and prestige because they are licensed. Nor do licensed practical nurses.

10. The machinery required for government to license and police all public relations practitioners in this country would be elaborate and very costly to the American taxpayer.

A PRSA study group on licensing and registration bluntly reported:

> There is an almost universal disdain for licensing and a sharp dislike for any type of government oversight of public relations practice. It is our judgment . . . that the ethical code and sense of public and professional morality that must be maintained by public relations professionals cannot be delegated to government. The process of morality, while personal, is democratic and cannot be legislated. It can best be sustained through peer-imposed discipline based on a common code of ethics and consistently maintained levels of professional excellence in practice.

In sum, the licensing of public relations professionals is not likely to be initiated. Although many, including Edward L. Bernays, thought it would be a good solution to getting the charlatans out of the field and enforcing ethical practice, the field (unlike medicine or law) is so broad that it's difficult to define. Licensing also raises serious questions about possible violation of First Amendment rights in the United States and even the considerable expense of administering such a system on a state-by-state basis. In addition, neither the public, governmental agencies, nor even the public relations industry, is actively lobbying for any form of licensing.

An alternative to licensing is accreditation, which many national public relations groups actively endorse and promote.

PR Insights

Guidelines for Fair Dealing

Ketchum, a major public relations firm, has established guidelines for its employees on how to deal fairly with clients.

The code deals with (1) truth and accuracy in communications, (2) confidential information, (3) purchasing, (4) gifts and excessive entertainment and other payments, (5) industry groups, (6) union agreements, (7) suppliers to the agency and clients, (8) services for competitors, (9) use of inside information, and (10) misuse of business opportunities.

"We will deal with clients in a fair and businesslike fashion, providing unbiased, professional recommendations to move their business ahead," the code promises.

"We will safeguard their proprietary information and help protect their financial assets."

Many other public relations firms have similar codes.

Accreditation

The major effort to improve standards and professionalism in public relations around the world has been related to establishing accreditation programs. PRSA, for example, began its accreditation program in 1965. Since then, other national groups such as IABC, and the Canadian Public Relations Society (CPRS) have established accreditation programs.

In all cases, public relations practitioners are accredited if they have achieved a high level of experience, competence, and ethical conduct. Accreditation, ideally, is a "seal of approval."

PRSA's approach is somewhat typical. To become an accredited member of the society, with the designation APR, a person must have at least five years' full-time experience in public relations or teaching and pass a written and oral exam. The written exam consists of "textbook knowledge" (key terms, theories, and history), interpretation of the code of ethics, and a case problem that tests the candidate's ability to develop public relations plans to deal with a specific situation. To date, about a fourth of PRSA's 19,000 members have earned the APR designation.

Other national groups have developed written and oral exams, but unlike PRSA, they also require the candidate to submit a portfolio of work samples. IABC, which uses the designation of ABC (Accredited Business Communicator), places a heavy emphasis on a person's professional work samples. The candidate must document the objectives and the overall communication strategy, and provide evaluation of the results. The national public relations groups in Australia, Canada, and South Africa also require candidates to submit a portfolio of work samples and require a written and oral presentation. About 650 of IABC's 12,500 members have ABC designation.

Various national groups also take different approaches to assuring that accredited members are knowledgeable about the history and general concepts of effective public relations practice. PRSA, in a somewhat controversial decision in 1998, decided that all candidates should read one, officially designated, undergraduate textbook. This was a move that Mel Sharpe, chair of the PRSA Educators' Academy, criticized as ". . . a vocational, one-course, one-book entry-level attitude about PR." Other educators also questioned whether accreditation should be based on the concept of reading just one book and having five years' experience. The Canadian Public Relations Society (CPRS) offers a list of readings, while the IABC doesn't recommend any specific articles or books. South Africa's PRISA, on the other hand, assures some knowledge of the field by requiring that each candidate first complete a Certificate in Public Relations Management course before taking the exam.

In the United Kingdom, persons wishing to join the 4000 full members of the Institute of Public Relations must have four years of experience at an executive level and hold a public relations degree from one of seven recognized university programs or from the Communications, Advertising and Marketing Foundation.

Continuing Education PRSA in 1989 adopted a requirement that all accredited members must accumulate 10 points every three years to maintain accreditation. Points could be earned by taking university courses, attending professional workshops, writing articles, or even serving on PRSA committees. The implementation has been somewhat less than successful. By 1996, a large number of APRs had failed to complete the reaccreditation process, so PRSA excused 2782 members who had earned the APR status before 1993 from the requirement.

Other Steps toward Professionalism

PRSA, IABC, and other national groups have various programs designed to advance the profession of public relations. They include (1) working with universities to standardize curricula, (2) establishing research activities, (3) recognizing outstanding senior practitioners, (4) organizing professional development workshops, and (5) establishing international standards for the conduct of business.

Education PRSA, IABC, and other organizations such as the National Communication Association (NCA) have worked with the public relations division of the Association for Education in Journalism and Mass Communication (AEJMC) to improve and standardize the curricula of public relations at the bachelor's and master's degree levels.

One result of this cooperation was the 1999 Commission on Pubic Relations Education, which consisted of leading educators and practitioners representing a number of professional communication groups. This commission examined the role and function of public relations education for the new century and concluded, as did a previous commission report in 1987, that a strong background in liberal arts and social sciences is a necessary foundation for public relations majors. In addition, coursework in a public relations major should comprise 25 to 40 percent of all undergraduate credit hours. Of those, at lease half would be clearly identified as public relations courses in such topics as (1) principles, (2) case studies, (3) research and evaluation, (4) writing and production, (5) planning and management, (6) campaigns, and (7) supervised internships. The commission also recommended a minor or double major in another discipline such as business or the behavioral sciences.

PRSA also has a certification program for colleges and universities that offer public relations majors and degree programs. This was started in 1989, and only six universities have been certified in the voluntary program. One reason for the low number is that the vast majority of journalism units, in which most public relations programs are housed, are accredited by the American Council on Education in Journalism and Mass Communication (ACEJMC). Many public relations educators, as well as unit administrators, feel this is sufficient.

Would You Take This Client?

Here's a hypothetical situation. A well-known professional basketball player is charged with cocaine possession and the rape of a contestant in a local beauty contest. His attorney asks you to advise and assist him in handling the intense media interest in the case. He wants you to try to place favorable stories about the athlete in the media and create a positive pretrial environment for him. If convicted, it would mean the end of his professional basketball career.

You are not asked to do anything unethical, according to the PRSA. The money is quite good and you know the publicity from working on the case will probably help your public relations consulting career, especially if the athlete is found innocent. Would you take the account? The lawyer tells you confidentially that the athlete has admitted that he snorted cocaine and raped the woman, but the plea will be "not guilty." Does this information affect your decision? What are the ethics of the situation as you see them?

Sponsorship of student chapters also is common. PRSA sponsors the Public Relations Student Society of America (PRSSA), which has about 210 chapters and 6000 members nationally. IABC currently has chapters at 45 college and universities.

Research The IABC Foundation and the Institute for Public Relations Research and Education regularly fund research projects that advance the body of knowledge in public relations. Both also sponsor symposiums, fund graduate student research projects, and commission a variety of research studies.

Recognition of Senior Professionals Several national groups, including PRSA and IABC, have established "Fellow" programs that recognize career achievement and contributions to the profession. PRSA, for example, in 1990 established a College of Fellows, which has grown to about 400 members. In addition, annual awards by both PRSA and IABC honor outstanding individuals.

Professional Development The primary purpose of most public relations groups is to advance the profession through education and information. Monthly membership publications, such as PRSA's *Tactics* and *IABC: Communication World*, are one form of education and information. In addition, most national groups usually have a professional practice center that offers everything from one-day seminars and workshops to video-cassettes, topical information packets, certificate programs, audiocassettes, home study programs, and books. PRSA's catalog of resources, for example, is a 34-page booklet. IABC has a similar array of offerings.

ETHICS IN INDIVIDUAL PRACTICE

Despite codes of professional practice and formalized accreditation, ethics in public relations boils down to deeply troubling questions for the individual practitioner: Will I lie for my employer? Will I rig a doorprize drawing so a favorite client can win? Will I deceive in order to gain information about another agency's clients? Will I cover up a hazardous condition? Will I issue a news release presenting only half the truth? Will I seek to bribe a reporter or a legislator? Will I withhold some information in a news conference, and provide it only if a reporter asks a specific question? Will I quit my job rather than cooperate in a questionable activity? In other words, to what extent, if any, will I compromise my personal beliefs?

These and similar questions plague the lives of many public relations people, although a number hold such strong personal beliefs and/or work for such highly principled employers that they seldom need to compromise their personal values. If employers make a suggestion that involves questionable ethics, the public relations person often can talk them out of the idea by citing the possible consequences of such an action—adverse media publicity, for example.

"To thine own self be true," advised New York public relations executive Chester Burger at an IABC conference. A fellow panelist, Canadian politician and radio commentator Stephen Lewis, commented: "There is a tremendous jaundice on the part of the public about the way things are communicated. People have elevated superficiality to an art form. Look at the substance of what you have to convey, and the honesty used in conveying it." With the audience contributing suggestions, the panelists formulated the following list of commendable practices:

- Be honest at all times.

- Convey a sense of business ethics based on your own standards and those of society.

- Respect the integrity and position of your opponents and audiences.

- Develop trust by emphasizing substance over triviality.

- Present all sides of an issue.

- Strive for a balance between loyalty to the organization and duty to the public.

- Don't sacrifice long-term objectives for short-term gains.

Adherence to professional standards of conduct—being truly independent—is the chief measure of a public relations person. Faced with such personal problems as a mortgage and children to educate, practitioners may be strongly tempted to become yes men (or yes women) and decline to express their views forcefully to an employer, or to resign.

Allen H. Center, professor emeritus at San Diego State University and a long-time corporate public relations executive, has written: "Public relations has emerged more as an echo of an employer's standards and interests than that of a professional discipline applied to the employer's problems." Yet many a practitioner has resigned rather than submit to a compromising situation.

In some cases practitioners have been arbitrarily fired for refusing to write news releases that are false and misleading. This happened to an accredited PRSA member in the San Francisco Bay area. The company president wanted him, among other things, to write and send a news release giving a list of company clients when, in fact, none of the companies had signed a contract for services. When the practitioner refused, on the grounds that the PRSA code would be violated, he was fired. In turn, the practitioner sued the company for unlawful dismissal and received almost $100,000 in an out-of-court settlement.

Tommy Ross, pioneer public relations practitioner and partner of Ivy Lee before founding T. J. Ross and Associates, once told a Fortune magazine interviewer: "Unless you are willing to resign an account or a job over a matter of principle, it is no use to call yourself a member of the world's newest profession—for you are already a member of the world's oldest."

ETHICAL DEALINGS WITH NEWS MEDIA

The most practical consideration facing a public relations specialist in his or her dealings with the news media is that anything less than total honesty will destroy credibility and, with it, the practitioner's usefulness to an employer.

Trust is maintained even when practitioners say "no comment" and refuse to answer questions that go beyond information reported in the news releases, according to a study by Professors Michael Ryan and David L. Hartinson, published in *Journalism Quarterly*. Practitioners and journalists tend to agree on how they define lying; both, for example, believe that giving evasive answers to reporters' questions constitutes lying.

Achieving trust is the aim of all practitioners, and it can be achieved only through highly professional and ethical performance. It is for this reason that providing junkets with doubtful news value, extravagant parties, expensive gifts, and personal favors for media representatives should never be done.

CASE STUDY 1: USE OF "FRONT GROUPS" POSES ETHICAL CONCERNS

The proliferation of so-called "front groups" waging purported "grassroots" campaigns to achieve public relations goals has created much debate in the field in recent years.

The establishment of dozens of such groups evoked a strongly worded statement from the board of directors of the Public Relations Society of America:

> PRSA specifically condemns the efforts of those organizations, sometimes known as "front groups," that seek to influence the public policy process by disguising or obscuring the true identity of their members or by implying representation of a much more broadly based group than exists.

Almost every "save the environment" organization has spawned a counter group. For example, the Forest Alliance of British Columbia posed as a grassroots movement opposing the International Coalition to Save British Columbia's Rainforests, composed of 25 "green" groups. It was later revealed that the Canadian timber industry paid Burson-Marsteller $1 million to create the alliance, whose aim was to convince the public that environmental destruction has been exaggerated and to persuade lawmakers to abolish unprofitable environmental regulations.

Names given to many of the organizations are confusing, if not downright deceptive. Northwesterners for More Fish was the name chosen for a "grassroots" coalition of utilities and other companies in the Northwest under attack by environmental groups for depleting the fish population.

In California's Riverside County, a public relations firm organized Friends of Eagle Mountain on behalf of a mining company that wanted to create the world's largest landfill in an abandoned iron ore pit.

A prohunting group that works to convince people that wildlife is already so plentiful there is no reason not to kill some of it is known as the Abundant Wildlife Society of North America.

The involvement of the Hill and Knowlton public relations firm in the work of a front group known as Citizens for a Free Kuwait during the Persian Gulf War is detailed in the accompanying case study.

CASE STUDY 2: HILL AND KNOWLTON'S CAMPAIGN FOR A FREE KUWAIT

The activities of Hill and Knowlton (H&K), one of the largest public relations firms, in promoting U.S. entry into the Persian Gulf War produced a barrage of criticism from print and broadcast sources and in the public relations trade press as well.

The reports charged that Hill and Knowlton, working for the Citizens for a Free Kuwait, misled the American public about atrocities committed by Iraqi soldiers in order to "sell" the war. Precipitating the reports on CBS-TV's *60 Minutes* and ABC-TV's *20/20* was a New York *Times* op-ed piece by John MacArthur, publisher of *Harper's* magazine. MacArthur revealed that the tearful 15-year-old girl who testified about the atrocities before the Congressional Human Rights Caucus, identified only as Nayirah, actually was the daughter of the Kuwait ambassador to the United States, Saud Nasir Al-Sabah. (See Chapter 14.)

Neither of the television programs, nor Amnesty International, could find confirmation of Nayirah's claim that hundreds of babies had been taken from their incubators by Iraqi soldiers and left on the floor to die. Hill and Knowlton was criticized by *60 Minutes* for allegedly showing that "war can be marketed, just like soft drinks and toothpaste."

CBS reported that a video news release of Nayirah's statement was distributed to promote the war. Six senators cited the "babies" story, and the war was approved by a margin of five senators, CBS noted.

Lauri Fitz-Pegado, representing the firm on the programs, said she believed Nayirah was telling the truth. She told CBS she did not know that $11.8 million of the funds for the Citizens for a Free Kuwait account came from the Kuwaiti government and only $17,861 from 78 citizens.

Thomas E. Eidson, president and CEO of Hill and Knowlton, strongly defended the firm's actions. He said Nayirah's identity had been disclosed to the Congressional Human Rights Caucus, which decided, at the request of her father, not to make her identity known in fear of reprisal against those left behind in Kuwait.

Several public relations executives, questioned by *O'Dwyer's PR Services Report,* said H&K had violated the PRSA code article relating to "honesty and integrity" and the article forbidding use of an individual "professing to be independent but actually serving another undisclosed interest." Chicago counselor Philip Lesley said the concealment was a "direct breach" of Article 8 of the code outlawing "fronts." He was quoted as adding that the "overwhelming quest for ever higher profits and volume" has caused firms to "lose sight of ethics."

Case Study Questions

- In view of the sensational nature of Nayirah's testimony, should H&K have investigated its factual basis? Should H&K have foreseen the media repercussions of not frankly stating her connection to the Kuwaiti government?

- Should H&K have disclosed publicly the source of funds supporting Citizens for a Free Kuwait? Is the use of a "front" organization such as Citizens for a Free Kuwait deceptive and a breach of the PRSA code of ethics?

- In the interest of protecting the reputation of public relations practitioners, should other firms refrain from criticizing them?

- Should public relations firms accept controversial clients? Where would you draw the line?

- Did the news media treat H&K fairly in this case?

CASE STUDY 3: HILL AND KNOWLTON'S ANTIABORTION CAMPAIGN

A lively controversy with multiple ethical aspects erupted in 1990 when Hill and Knowlton agreed to conduct an antiabortion campaign for U.S. Roman Catholic bishops. The bishops also hired the Worthlin Group, a leading Republican polling operation that served Ronald Reagan in his campaign for the White House and during his presidency. The aim of the bishops' campaign, costing $3 to $5 million over a three- to five-year period, was to persuade both Catholics and non-Catholics to oppose abortion.

Many Hill and Knowlton employees publicly criticized the decision; two resigned, and the firm lost at least one client. President Robert L. Dilenschneider said any employee could refrain from working on the account with impunity.

"Some organizations have lost sight of fundamental values, such as the sanctity of human life, or they have tried to convince America that the main issue in the abortion debate is the right to choose rather than, as it really is, what is being chosen," said Cardinal John J. O'Connor, archbishop of New York and chairman of the Committee for Pro-Life Activities of the U.S. Catholic Conference.

Critics branded the campaign as a waste of church resources and a violation of the constitutional separation of church and state. Charged Kate Michelman, president of the National Abortion Rights Action League: "They're not just trying to deliver a message, they're trying to interject their religious and moral views into politics."

Jerry Dalton, PRSA president, said in a letter to the New York *Times* that the bishops have a First Amendment right to use public relations counsel to help them shape arguments against abortion.

"However controversial or unpopular a cause, advocates—or opponents—have the right to seek professional PR counsel to help them shape and communicate persuasive arguments," Dalton wrote. "That's what the First Amendment is all about." Other corporate executives, interviewed by the *Public Relations Journal,* echoed Dalton's opinion.

A former priest, Eugene Kennedy, professor of psychology at Loyola University, wrote in the New York *Times* that the bishops had chosen a strategy "that is manipulative at best and numbingly amoral at worst."

A story in the *National Catholic Reporter* titled "What Does H&K Sell?" provided the answer: "Anything the customer is prepared to pay for."

Dilenschneider responded to both attacks: "We do not shy away from controversy but we will not misrepresent a client's position. And if cash were the determinant for representation of a client, we would certainly not have turned away, as we have, representation of Muammar al-Qaddafi, General Noriega, Ferdinand Marcos, South Africa (in its previous posture), Guatemala, and the Colombian drug lords."

Other criticisms of the firm's acceptance of the Catholic account included the following:

1. The firm violated Article 10 of the PRSA code: "A member shall not represent conflicting or competing interests without the express consent of those concerned, given after a full disclosure of the facts." The *Bulldog Reporter* newsletter raised the issue, pointing out that among Hill and Knowlton's hundreds of clients were the Church of Scientology; DNS, a gene-splicing bioengineering firm; Wyeth-Ayerst, makers of contraceptive devices; and Playboy Enterprises, which supports abortion rights. The newsletter said representatives of the Bishops Committee in both New York and Washington said they were unaware of Hill and Knowlton's ties to Playboy.

Asked about a possible conflict of interest, according to the newsletter Dilenschneider replied: "We will not resign any business we currently have."

2. Hill and Knowlton responded slowly in handling the firm's internal communications problem. Staff members complained that they first heard of H&K's agreeing to work for the bishops from newspaper reports. No backup spokesperson was appointed to respond to innumerable press inquiries after the story broke, according to some accounts.

3. The firm should not accept "an assignment whose ultimate goal is to limit our fundamental rights," according to a petition signed by 160 staff members in the company's New York office. Davia Tenin, vice president for marketing at the Wertheim Schroder investment banking firm, said the decision "says to me that it is going to sacrifice women's rights for the pocketbook."

4. Acceptance of the account reinforced with some people the image of public relations professionals as being simply "hired guns" (the accusation of Frances Kissling, president of Catholics for a Free Choice). Other published statements included the stereotypical charge that "PR people don't care whose side they are on so long as the pay is good" and Eugene Kennedy's statement, "You call in public relations operatives when the truth won't do."

Case Study Questions

The Hill and Knowlton controversy raised a number of questions for discussion. Some of the questions involved ethics, while others were operational in nature:

•   Should Hill and Knowlton have accepted the Catholic bishops' account, or should it have adopted Burson-Marsteller's policy of not handling religious or political accounts?

- Do the bishops have a constitutional right to use a public relations firm to develop new strategies?

- Was the principle of separation of church and state violated?

- Did Hill and Knowlton violate an article of the PRSA Code of Professional Standards for the Practice of Public Relations?

- Did the firm follow the precepts of a public relations communications crisis plan?

CASE PROBLEM

Prism Computer Corporation, a manufacturer of personal computers, has developed a new laser printer that is cheaper and more efficient than those produced by competitors. Although prototype models have been built, actual production of the new printer has been stalled up to three months by manufacturing problems.

Despite these difficulties, Prism's top management believes it is important from a marketing stand-point to announce that the new laser printer is now available. Consequently, you are asked as the product information specialist to write and distribute a new product release about the laser printer and its features.

You are told that no mention should be made in the news release that the product won't be available for another three months. What would you do in this situation? Does the situation violate professional ethics in any way? Why or why not?

QUESTIONS FOR REVIEW AND DISCUSSION

1. Sound ethical practice is essential in public relations work. What is meant by *ethics,* and how is it that two individuals can disagree about what constitutes an ethical dilemma?

2. What do you consider the most important points in the PRSA and IABC codes? How do the standards serve the interest of (1) the organizations' members and (2) the public? Can you find any loopholes that might hinder full-fledged enforcement?

3. What are some of the principal problems involved in enforcing the codes?

4. What does the PRSA code say about giving gifts and free trips to representatives of the media? Is it all right to buy drinks or dinner for a news reporter?

5. Under what circumstances should public relations practitioners (1) criticize each other and (2) not criticize each other?

6. To what four standards should a practitioner adhere in acting like a professional?

7. Should TV news directors identify the source of video news releases (VNRs) carried on their programs? Why?

8. Should public relations practitioners be licensed? What are some of the reasons pro and con?

9. Is the primary goal of the PRSA code of ethics enforcement or education?

10. In your opinion, should a PRSA member be held responsible for the ethical misconduct of a non-PRSA member whom he or she is supervising?

11. Is the use of a "front" organization deceptive?

12. What portion of the PRSA code, if any, did Hill and Knowlton violate when it accepted the Catholic bishops' antiabortion account?

The Individual in Public Relations

4

Preview

The objective of this chapter is to give the student a personal perspective on public relations work—how the individual fits into public relations practice and the rewards and challenges for a practitioner.

Topics covered in the chapter include:
- Changing focus in public relations
- The range of public relations work
- Personal qualifications and attitudes
- Professional organizations providing support
- Internships
- Women and ethnic groups in a diversified workforce
- Salaries in public relations

THE PUBLIC RELATIONS ROLE

A person entering public relations may develop a career in numerous areas of this increasingly diverse field. Similarly, the variety of personal traits and skills that bring success is wide. While certain abilities are basic for all, such as writing well, public relations practitioners, as their experience grows, may develop special skills and find personally gratifying niches.

This chapter explains the job opportunities and requirements and discusses the individual attributes most likely to bring success.

A Changing Focus in Public Relations

Traditionally, it was widely held that public relations practitioners should if possible have experience as reporters, to polish their writing skills and to learn firsthand how the media function. In an earlier era, a large percentage of public relations people did have newspaper or broadcast experience. This is no longer true for several reasons, however.

The field of public relations has broadened far beyond working with the mass media. Much writing today in public relations is done for controlled media such as company publications and web sites, direct mail campaigns, and membership newsletters, requiring no media relations savvy or contacts. Writing skill and knowledge of the media are vital, but so is training in management, logistics, and planning. A *PR Reporter* survey showed that there are now just as many practitioners in the field without newspaper experience as there are with such experience.

More universities than in the past are now offering joint public relations/advertising programs, in part because of growing interest in integrated marketing communications.

A study by Billy I. Ross of Louisiana State University and Keith F. Johnson of Texas Tech University, published in 1999, reported public relations enrollment was 15,964 students in undergraduate and graduate programs. In the 1997–1998 academic year, public relations programs graduated 4,841 undergraduates.

Fortunately the number of public relations jobs continues to increase as the field expands. According to the Federal Bureau of Labor Statistics, employment of public relations managers will increase faster than the average for all occupations through the year 2008, placing public relations in the top ten growth industries. Job growth projections are particularly strong in health care and technology sectors, as well as the crisis communications specialty.

The Range of Public Relations Work

Women and men entering public relations may work in company departments, public relations firms that serve clients, or a wide range of organizations that require public relations services. The major areas of public relations work they will find include:

- *Corporations.* Departments seek to protect and enhance a company's reputation. They provide information to the public as well as to special audiences such as stockholders, financial analysts, and employees. Their work also includes community relations and often marketing communications.

- *Nonprofit organizations.* These range from membership organizations, such as trade and environmental associations, to social and cultural groups, hospitals, and other health agencies. Fund-raising is often involved.

- *Entertainment, sports, and travel.* Practitioners in these areas are often concerned with publicity for individuals and promotion of events ranging from football games to motion pictures.

- *Government and the military.* This area includes promotion of political issues, sometimes through lobbying, work with politicians, dissemination of information about government activities to citizens, and distribution of information about the armed forces.

- *Education.* At the college level, public relations people work primarily with alumni, faculty and administration, students, and the public to promote the school's image, recruit students, and raise funds. Secondary schools frequently have specialists to handle community relations.

PR Insights

Job Levels in Public Relations

Entry-Level Technician. Use of technical "craft" skills to disseminate information, persuade, gather data, or solicit feedback.

Supervisor. Supervises projects, including planning, scheduling, budgeting, organizing, leading, controlling, and problem-solving.

Manager. Constituency and issue-trend analysis; departmental management, including organizing, budgeting, leading, controlling, evaluating, and problem-solving.

Director. Constituency and issue-trend analysis; communication and operational planning at departmental level, including planning, organizing, leading, controlling, evaluating, and problem-solving.

Executive. Organizational leadership and management skills, including developing the organizational vision, corporate mission, strategic objectives, annual goals, businesses, broad strategies, policies, and systems.

Source: Adapted from the *Public Relations Professional Career Guide,* Public Relations Society of America, 33 Irving Place, New York, NY 10003.

- *International public relations.* The immense expansion of almost instantaneous global communications has opened an intriguing new area, especially for practitioners with language skills and familiarity with other cultures.

    Detailed discussion of these areas appears in later chapters.

PERSONAL QUALIFICATIONS AND ATTITUDES

Any attempt to define a single public relations type of personality is pointless, because the field is so diverse that it needs people of differing personalities. Some practitioners deal with clients and the public in person on a frequent basis; others work primarily at desks, planning, writing, and researching. Many do both.

Basic Personal Attributes

A few basic personal attributes are evident in all successful practitioners, no matter what their specific assignments. These include:

1. Ability with words, written or spoken

2. Analytical skill, to identify and define problems

3. Creative ability, to develop fresh, effective solutions to problems

4. An instinct for persuasion

5. Ability to make compelling and polished presentations

Veteran public relations executives responsible for hiring staff members emphasize that people with normal personalities possessing the required skills are better suited for most public relations jobs than the brash "glad hand" type.

Public relations professionals use a variety of tools to reach the public. This advertisement by the American Cancer Society urging proper nutrition was published as a public service by 15 magazines with a combined circulation of 10.5 million. Paramount Pictures allowed the society to use the Spock picture without charge.

Source: The American Cancer Society, Inc.

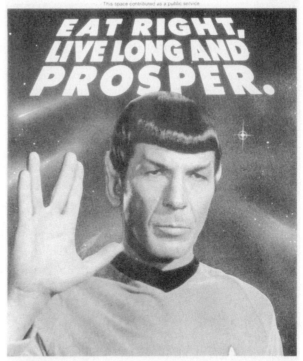

Four Essential Abilities

Those who plan careers in public relations should develop four basic abilities, no matter what area of work they enter. These are writing skill, research ability, planning expertise, and problem-solving ability.

1. *Writing skill.* The ability to put information and ideas onto paper clearly and concisely is essential. Good grammar and good spelling are vital. Misspelled words and sloppy sentence structure look amateurish.

2. *Research ability.* Arguments for causes must have factual support instead of generalities. A person must have the persistence and ability to gather information from a variety of sources, as well as to conduct original research by designing and implementing opinion polls or audits. Too many public relations programs fail because the organization does not assess audience needs and perceptions. Skillful use of the Internet and computer databases is an important element of research work.

3. *Planning expertise.* A public relations program involves a number of communication tools and activities that must be carefully planned and coordinated. A person needs to be a good planner to make certain that materials are distributed in a timely manner, events occur without problems, and budgets are not exceeded.

4. *Problem-solving ability.* Innovative ideas and fresh approaches are needed to solve complex problems or to make a public relations program unique and memorable. Increased salaries and promotions go to people who show top management how to solve problems creatively.

The following three typical help-wanted advertisements illustrate how a public relations career may develop. The first is for an entry-level position of a routine nature, the second for a job with more responsibility, and the third for a high-level director who does strategic planning, directs a staff, and serves as the institution's spokesperson.

Staff Aide

Credit union seeks public relations aide to write and edit monthly newsletter, design and write brochure, and plan a variety of promotions for each quarter. Successful applicant must maintain rapport with members through publications as well as telephone and personal

PR Insights

Public Relations Personality Checklist

This checklist, based on careful evaluation, can measure the effectiveness of your personality in terms of the public relations profession.

Rate each item "yes" or "no." Each "yes" counts for four points. A "no" doesn't count. Anything below 60 is a poor score. A score between 60 and 80 suggests you should analyze your weak areas and take steps to correct them. Scores above 80 indicate an effective public relations personality.

_____ Good sense of humor
_____ Positive and optimistic
_____ Friendly, meet people easily
_____ Can keep a conversation going
_____ with anybody
_____ Take frustration and rejection in stride
_____ Able to persuade others easily
_____ Well-groomed, businesslike appearance
_____ Flair for showmanship
_____ Strong creative urge

_____ Considerate and tactful
_____ Adept in use of words
_____ Able to gain management's confidence
_____ Enjoy being with people
_____ Enjoy listening
_____ Enjoy helping other people
_____ resolve problems
_____ Curious about many things
_____ Enjoy reading in diverse areas
_____ Determined to complete projects
_____ High energy level
_____ Can cope with sudden emergencies
_____ See mistakes as learning experiences
_____ Factual and objective
_____ Respect other people's viewpoints
_____ Perceptive and sensitive
_____ Quickly absorb and retain information

Source: *PRSSA Forum*, Spring 1990.

contact and assist various departments with public relations/promotion activities. Degree in public relations or journalism required. Candidate should be a self-starter with initiative to work independently, be able to work under pressure to meet deadlines, and accept constructive criticism without being offended.

Public Relations Account Coordinator

Public Relations Account Coordinator at fast-growing high-tech public relations agency. Four-year degree preferably in business/public relations. Position involves providing support to account team members and assisting in the implementation of PR programs for our clients. Includes use of strong writing/proofing skills, understanding of AP style, familiarity with Macintosh, strong multitasking capabilities, ability to deal with publications by phone, and ability to be a team player. Familiarity with the Internet, FileMaker Pro, and MS Word a plus.

University Director of Public Affairs

The university seeks an individual to create, direct, and manage a comprehensive and integrated public affairs program in support of the university's mission and goals on a national, regional, and community level. This entails developing communication and public affairs strategies and programs in conjunction with the president and other officers and academic leaders.

Serving as the principal spokesperson for the university, specific responsibilities include directing the dissemination of information within the university itself, to the media and to the many publics involved with the university, promoting special events, enhancing the university's visibility, and identifying areas within the community that could benefit from university resources and facilities.

Systematic research shows that there is a hierarchy of roles in public relations practice. In several studies, Professors Glen Broom and David Dozier of San Diego State University have found four empirically grounded organizational roles. They describe the roles as follows:

Communication Managers. Practitioners playing this role are perceived by others as the organization's public relations experts. They make communication policy decisions and are held accountable by others and themselves for the success or failure of communication programs. They follow a systematic planning process.

Communication Liaisons. Practitioners playing this role represent the organization at public meetings and create opportunities for management to hear the views of priority publics. Predominantly communication facilitators, these practitioners also identify alternative solutions to organizational problems.

Media Relations Specialists. Practitioners playing this role actively seek to place messages about the organization in the mass media. At the same time, they keep others in the organization informed of what is being said about the organization (and about issues important to the organization) in the media.

Communication Technicians. Practitioners playing this role are responsible for producing communication products and implementing decisions made by others. They take photographs, assemble graphics; write brochures, pamphlets and news releases; and handle all aspects of production.

The communication manager usually stands at the top of the hierarchy. Many practitioners, however, to play lower-level organizational roles even after years of professional experience.

Some evidence suggests that women in public relations tend to fulfill the technician role, resulting in lower pay and less power in organizations. In some studies, however, those in technician roles report higher job satisfaction. This may result from the intrinsic rewards of writing and graphic design. The higher satisfaction may also derive from avoiding some of the responsibility and time demands shouldered by managers.

NEEDED: AN UNDERSTANDING OF ECONOMICS

In preparing themselves for public relations careers, students should obtain as solid a grounding in economics as possible. Once they are employed as professionals, they should study the financial aspects of their employers or clients. More and more, public relations involves distribution and interpretation of financial information. To handle this material well, the practitioner first must understand it. Investor relations, which requires detailed financial knowledge, is the highest-paid specialty area in public relations work.

After a few years of work, some public relations people return to the classroom to earn advanced degrees. The Master of Business Administration degree, commonly called the MBA, is probably the most frequently sought, but the list of Master's and Ph.D. degrees held by public relations specialists ranges over many fields. According to professors Katherine Kinnick of Kennesaw State University and Glen T. Cameron of the Missouri School of Journalism, public relations students should be exposed to business-style training in their major coursework. The increasing emphasis on public relations as a management function calls for public relations students to learn the "nuts and bolts" of business. Students who plan to do corporate public relations work should remember the fundamental fact about American business: every company was created to earn a profit for those who risked their money to start it. Businesses can continue to exist only as long as they are profitable. The task of public relations in the business world is to help companies prosper. Unfortunately, many college students believe that American business makes excessive profits. This belief arises from a lack of comprehension of free enterprise economics.

Many progressive companies use a *triangle* concept, representing three basic elements in their business. Customers, shareholders, and employees form the three sides.

PROFESSIONAL SUPPORT SERVICES

Talking with other public relations people about their successes and failures, and exchanging ideas, is an important activity in building a career. Reading professional literature and attending workshops and seminars are also beneficial activities. Public relations organizations provide many opportunities of this nature.

Organizations and Societies

Public relations groups at the local, state, national, and international levels provide an important channel of communication for practitioners in all areas of the profession.

The largest national group is the Public Relations Society of America, with 19,000 members and more than 100 chapters. The society has 14 special interest sections. It is the parent organization of the Public Relations Student Society of America (discussed in the next section).

PR Insights

Qualities for a Successful Career

Art Stevens, president of Lobsenz-Stevens, Inc., in New York City and author of *The Persuasion Explosion,* has formulated what it takes to become successful in public relations. The individual . . .

1. Must be an excellent writer capable of writing client reports, effective article themes to editors, news releases, captions, annual reports, feature stories, and the like. His or her writing must require little editing and supervision.

2. Must be able to do short- and long-range planning, conceive and execute a full public relations plan for each account, and adhere strictly to deadlines.

3. Must be innovative and imaginative, not bound by trite, traditional ideas. Must be willing to keep an open mind to new ideas and to researching better ways.

4. Must be well informed about a client's business and continue to keep abreast of all developments in business and government that have an effect on the client's or company's business. Must function as a counselor as well as a communicator.

5. Must be results-oriented, whether the task is the placement of major stories about a client in important publications or the successful execution of a special event. Must be a doer and a self-starter. Must know what follow-up means and have a solid respect for timetables and deadlines.

6. Must be a thorough "pro," skilled in all the techniques used in the practice of public relations: writing and distribution of news releases, producing press kits, running press conferences, and so on. Must be familiar with feature writers, magazine contributors, and hot current subjects being written about.

7. Must know how to create publicity by conceiving a meaningful idea and carrying it through to its conclusion. Must know how to create sundry ideas where none are evident and must know where to take them.

8. Must know what it takes to establish and maintain acquaintanceship with key media people, since editorial contact is one of the primary functions of the public relations professional. The public relations professional must know how to deal with the media and understand their need for quick and responsive answers.

9. Must be able to learn and grow as new situations and client needs arise. Must draw upon prior experiences in the public relations field to move into new situations effortlessly and effectively.

10. Must be a good manager, capable of organizing and arranging his or her workload for maximum results. Must be capable of carrying many assignments at the same time and be in control of each one.

11. Finally, the public relations professional must not be a yes man/woman. Public relations has outgrown the caricature of second-class professionalism by producing individuals who speak their minds confidently to top management of major corporations and make valuable recommendations to these executives. So long as the public relations professional earns the respect and confidence of the chief executive officer, public relations will grow as a profession and will contribute to the broad communications goal of companies and institutions across the United States.

Source: Newsletter of the PRSA Counselors Academy.

The second largest organization of communication and public relations professionals is the International Association of Business Communicators (IABC), with 13,500 members in 56 countries. Most members live in the United States (72%), with Canada, the United Kingdom, and Hong Kong having significant numbers. Although its membership has diversified somewhat in recent years, a large percentage of IABC members are involved in employee communications. The organization publishes the monthly magazine *Communication World.*

Internships

Internships are extremely popular in the communications industry, and a student whose résumé includes practical work experience along with an academic record has an important advantage. Obtaining an internship offered by a public relations firm, company department, or charitable agency is among the best ways to get this desired experience. The intern, in most cases, earns academic credit and gets firsthand knowledge of work in the professional field.

Although internships offer an advantage in getting a first job, the practice by some companies of using unpaid interns has drawn increasing criticism because it puts downward pressure on wages in fields where internships proliferate. The contention is that when students or recent graduates work for nothing, aspiring professionals will accept low beginning salaries. A trend is growing among colleges and universities, and employers as well, to advocate paid internships.

Another way for students to get experience is through membership in the Public Relations Student Society of America (PRSSA). The society has chapters at about 200 universities and a national membership of 6000. Many students participate in a national case study competition or carry out projects on local campuses as part of a corporate collegiate program. Many chapters also have student-run firms that implement programs for local and campus organizations. A university must offer five courses in public relations before a PRSSA chapter can be established on its campus.

A DIVERSIFIED WORKFORCE

More than half the public relations practitioners in the United States are women, an increasing number of whom hold high-level management positions. Thus the public relations industry provides a healthy diversity of gender perspective as it prepares and delivers its messages.

Public relations falls seriously short, however, in developing a workforce rich in racial diversity. As the industry faces the challenge of addressing the abundance of target audiences in the increasingly multiracial, multicultural American population, its composition remains overwhelmingly white.

Ethnic Groups

More than 25 percent of the U.S. population in the late 1990s consisted of racial minorities—primarily African Americans, Hispanics, Asians and Pacific Islanders, and Native Americans—and the percentage is growing. The number of minority workers in public relations falls far short of equaling that population percentage.

The membership profile for the Public Relations Society of America in 1997 showed that 93 percent of respondents were white, 3 percent black, 2 percent Hispanic, and 1 percent Asian. Because the profile depicts only PRSA members, it does not necessarily represent the total public relations workforce.

Some public relations firms say that they have difficulty hiring minority staff members because they receive so few applications from minority aspirants. Seeking to improve the situation, PRSA has taken several significant steps to stimulate recruitment of minorities. It has a national task force to promote minorities in public relations, a program of seminars and a speakers bureau to identify and encourage candidates, a list of minority candidates available, and a scholarship fund to place minority students in intern programs.

The public relations industry should do more to address various explanations offered for the shortage of minorities in public relations. Among them are inadequate school counseling to steer minority students toward public relations careers, a fear among some young people—usually unfounded—that they will not be accepted by coworkers; a dislike of being paraded as "token" minorities and assigned only to minority clients; and, in some instances, actual discrimination by public relations offices and/or clients.

As public relations practice becomes more and more internationalized, firms entering the world market have an especially strong need for diversified ethnic staffs. With constant communication between their U.S. offices and firms abroad, they need staff members with language skills, personal knowledge of other countries, and sensibility to the customs and attitudes of others. Knowledge of Spanish and the Asian languages is especially valuable.

Women

As more and more young women entered the public relations field during the 1980s, the percentage of female workers rose swiftly. In February 1987, the U.S. Bureau of Labor Statistics for the first time showed women in the majority, at 51.7 percent. Five years later, in 1992, the bureau reported that women's portion of the workforce had risen to 58.5 percent. The percentage of women in other fields has increased similarly.

Today the percentage of women in the public relations field approaches 70 percent. Membership in the International Association of Business Communicators (IABC) consists of 70 percent women. Larry Marshall, a veteran recruiter of individuals for public relations jobs, told a Public Relations Society of America career seminar in 1996 that women constitute 60 to 70 percent of the staffs in public relations firms and about 30 percent in corporate departments.

One reason the proportion of women in public relations is growing rapidly, Marshall pointed out, is that 75 percent of the candidates for junior-level jobs are women. But rapid change is not occurring in the career track taken by women. A 1989 study by DeAnna DeRosa of Menlo College and Dennis L. Wilcox of San Jose State was updated in 1998 by Michael Mitrook of the University of Central Florida, Glen T. Cameron of Missouri, and public relations professional Kimberly V. Wilkes. Both of the studies of majors in public relations suggest that women are very well equipped for business life. They display self-confidence, assertiveness, risk-taking attitudes, and accountability necessary for business success, but are less career-oriented, fully expecting to take family leaves, to limit work hours, and to interrupt their careers for family duties. Kim Wilkes surmised that the public relations major appeals to women because it blends creativity and business. More important, it is a field that lends itself to interrupted careers and freelancing for the sake of child rearing.

Although female undergraduates were strong in aptitudes needed for advancement along the management track, the disinclination to management positions and the stereotyping of women as technicians may pose a problem for the field in general. Martha Lauzen has found that when women are disinclined to handle management duties, preferring to focus on writing and other technical roles, encroachment occurs. Encroachment takes place

This group of high-ranking executives exemplifies the rise of women to senior positions in public relations at large corporations and counseling firms. From left to right, top row: Marcia Appel, senior vice president of corporate advertising and communications, Musicland Corporation; and Margo L. Barnes, senior vice president of corporate communications, Bayer Corporation; Second row: Barie S. Carmichael, vice president of corporate communications, Dow Corning; and Jean L. Farinelli, chief executive officer, Creamer Dickson Basford Public Relations. Third row: Kathleen M. Fitzgerald, senior vice president of public relations, investor relations, and advertising for Lucent Technologies; and Mary C. Linder, senior vice president of global communications, Estee Lauder Companies. Bottom row: Katherine B. Rohrbach, chief communications officer, Charles Schwab & Co.; and Anita K. Russell, director of corporate communications, Coors Brewing Company.

when top management puts people from outside public relations in charge of public relations. As a result, the definition of what is and is not public relations is further muddled or diluted. Lauzen concluded that being a woman in public relations did not lead to encroachment, but being a technician did.

Although women are still concentrated in lower- and middle-level jobs, times are changing, as evidenced by the success of many women in the field. At a banquet celebrating the fiftieth anniversary of Women Executives in Public Relations in 1995, Marilyn Castaldi, its president and senior vice president of the Fleishman-Hillard public relations firm, said, "Women are now ascending en masse into top positions in corporations, major agencies, and firms of their own."

A 70-to-30 percent female-to-male ratio in fields that virtually demand a college education is exceptionally high. For comparison, women on average held less than one third of U.S. radio news positions. The ratio in television, however, is more favorable to women. The Federal Communications Commission reported in 1996 that females constituted 40.7 percent of full-time broadcast employees and 41.9 percent of cable industry employees.

Gender discrimination in public relations is less than in some of the traditional mass media, with discrimination least likely in public relations firms. Firms are driven financially by billable hours charged to clients and by the generation of new business for the firm. In such an analytical reward system, the individual's productivity counts far more than favoritism in earning raises and promotions. Women appear to fare very well on such a level playing field, arguably because they show strength in building personal relationships and offer a fresh perspective toward social problems.

Women Receive Lower Pay.   Despite the numerical superiority of women in public relations, studies show that men earn more than women do. The longtime gap in male versus female salary scales remains substantial at many levels, but is diminishing.

A survey published by the Public Relations Society of America in 1996 reported that on average men's salaries are 45 percent higher than women's—$59,460 against $41,110.

The IABC survey in 1995, in which 4,679 members participated, showed that salaries of U.S. female members amounted to 79 percent of men's salaries. For IABC women members in Canada, the 1995 percentage was 87, compared to 86 in 1989.

The salary advantage for men over women is widespread in most of American business, according to a survey of 28 fields of endeavor conducted in 1996 by *Working Woman* magazine. It found that typically women earned 5 to 15 percent less than men. A fact influencing the salary gap is that corporate/industrial public relations work, traditionally dominated by men, pays the highest salaries, while the public sector and nonprofit organizations, in which women dominate, are among the lowest.

WHAT KINDS OF SALARIES?

Public relations work pays relatively well. This is true from the entry level to the top. The prospect of steady advancement in income as practitioners gain experience and take on more responsibility is attractive.

According to a 1999 national survey commissioned by *PR Week*, the industry average is a person nearly 39 years old making $80,000 annually. By gender, however, it was also found that males averaged $105,000 annually compared to $62,000 for females in the field.

Average salaries vary, of course, depending on type of business and geographical location. *PR Week* found, for example, that the sector of financial services (investor relations) paid the highest average salary—$104,000—while the not-for-profit sector paid the lowest—$56,000. Consumer products paid $87,000, healthcare, $83,000; and hi-tech, $77,000. Salaries are generally higher in the Northeast and the West Coast than the South and the Midwest.

Pay for top-level executives in corporations and public relations firms usually is much higher. A senior vice president, according to the *PR Week* survey, has an average salary of $134,000, and an executive vice president averages $164,000.

Entering the Field

Beginning jobs in public relations, according to a Dow Jones survey, pay an average of $444 per week as compared to daily newspapers at $404 per week, and TV stations at $360 a week. The public relations salary, which comes out to about $23,000 annually, is a nationwide figure. In the Northeast and California, however, average beginning salaries are considerably higher.

Starting salaries in public relations also vary by type of organization. A PRSA survey states that the mean entry-level salary in corporations is $23,550, in government/health care/nonprofit organizations, $23,210, and in public relations firms, $21,110. Although public relations firms offer the lowest entry-level pay of the three categories, staff members of firms, as they gain experience, can expect to earn higher salaries than those in the government/health care/nonprofit organizations category.

According to the 1997 Annual Surveys of Journalism and Mass Communication conducted by Lee B. Becker and Gerald Kosicki, more public relations graduates took full-time work in firms than in departments. The degree provides the most general preparation of all sequences in journalism programs, with public relations majors entering a wide range of communication jobs. The public relations major also enjoyed the highest earnings on graduation from journalism and mass communication programs.

Two factors spur upward mobility once that first job is obtained. Those who are willing to change jobs, called "job jumpers" by executive search specialist Dennis Spring, can expect 12-to-20 percent increases in salary. Changing jobs and locations can be stressful, but does often accelerate salary increases over a career. The sacrifice necessary to earn a graduate degree also reaps rewards. Becker and Kosicki found a $5500 boost in starting salary for those graduating with a Master's degree in any journalism or mass communication major.

CASE PROBLEM

The local Public Relations Society of America (PRSA) chapter is sponsoring an essay contest to select a winner who will receive a $2500 scholarship. The topic is "Why I have what it takes to have a successful career in public relations." Write a 1000-word essay on this topic.

QUESTIONS FOR REVIEW AND DISCUSSION

1. Why do some former newspaper reporters fail in public relations work?

2. Can you name four major areas of public relations work?

3. What are the basic job levels in public relations?

4. Those who plan careers in public relations should develop four basic abilities. What are they?

5. What basic economic fact should students who enter corporate public relations work always keep in mind?

6. Glen Broom and David Dozier say that there is a hierarchy of roles in public relations. What are these roles?

7. What is the largest national organization of public relations professionals? What is another major one?

8. Why is it important for a student to complete an internship while in college?

9. What is the ratio of female-to-male membership in the International Association of Business Communicators?

Public Relations Departments and Firms

Preview

The objective of this chapter is to explain what top management expects from its public relations department and to give students an understanding of how departments and public relations firms operate.

Topics covered in the chapter include:
- The role of public relations departments
- Organization of departments
- Line and staff functions
- Public relations firms
- Advertising and public relations mergers
- Work in a public relations firm
- Fees and charges

PUBLIC RELATIONS DEPARTMENTS

Public relations departments serve various roles and functions within companies and organizations. The following sections discuss the public relations function in organizational structures, names of departments, line and staff functions, sources of friction with other departments, and the pros and cons of working in a department.

Role in Various Organizational Structures

For a century, public relations departments have served companies and organizations. George Westinghouse is reported to have created the first corporate department in

1889 when he hired two men to publicize his pet project, alternating current (AC) electricity. Their work was relatively simple when compared to the mélange of physical, sociological, and psychological elements that contemporary departments employ. Eventually Westinghouse won out over Thomas A. Edison's (DC) direct current system, and his method became the standard in the United States. Westinghouse's public relations department concept has also grown into a basic part of today's electronic world.

Today, public relations is expanding from its traditional functions, enlarged over the years as explained in Chapter 2, to exercise its influence in the highest levels of management.

Importance in Today's World   In a changing environment, and faced with the variety of pressures previously described, executives increasingly see public relations not as publicity and one-way communication, but as a process of negotiation and compromise with a number of key publics. James Grunig, professor of public relations at the University of Maryland, calls the new approach "building good relationships with strategic publics," which will require public relations executives to be "strategic communication managers rather than communication technicians."

Grunig, head of a six-year IABC Foundation research study on *Excellence in Public Relations and Communications Management,* continues:

> When public relations helps that organization build relationships, it saves the organization money by reducing the costs of litigation, regulation, legislation, pressure campaign boycotts, or lost revenue that result from bad relationships with publics—publics that become activist groups when relationships are bad. It also helps the organization make money by cultivating relationships with donors, customers, shareholders and legislators.

The results of the IABC study seem to indicate that chief executive officers (CEOs) consider public relations a good investment. A survey of 200 organizations showed that CEOs gave public relations operations a 184 percent return on investment (ROI), a figure just below that of customer service and sales/marketing.

Importance of Organizational Structure   Research indicates, however, that the role of public relations in an organization often depends on the type of organization, the perceptions of top management, and even the capabilities of the public relations executive.

Research studies by Professor Larissa Grunig at the University of Maryland and Mark McElreath at Towson State University, among others, show that large, complex organizations have a greater tendency than do smaller firms to include public relations in the policy-making process. Companies such as IBM and General Motors, which operate in a highly competitive environment, are more sensitive than many others to policy issues and public attitudes, and to establishing a solid corporate identity. Consequently, they place more emphasis on news conferences, formal contact with the media, writing executive speeches, and counseling management about issues that could potentially affect the corporate bottom line.

In such organizations, classified as mixed organic/mechanical by management theorists, the authority and power of the public relations department are quite high. Public relations is part of what is called the "dominant coalition" and has a great deal of autonomy.

In contrast, a small-scale organization of low complexity, with a standardized product or service, feels few public pressures and little governmental regulatory interest. It has scant public relations activity, and staff members are relegated to such technician roles as producing the company newsletter and issuing routine news releases. Public relations in what is called the traditional organization has little or no input into management decisions and policy formation.

PR Insights

Expertise Required in a Department

The *Excellence in Public Relations and Communication Management* study, funded by IABC, identified 15 areas of specialized expertise that should be present in a public relations department:

STRATEGIC AND OPERATIONAL MANAGEMENT KNOWLEDGE

- Develop strategies for solving problems
- Manage organizational response to issues
- Develop goals and objectives for department
- Prepare budgets
- Manage people

RESEARCH KNOWLEDGE

- Perform environmental scanning
- Determine public reactions to your organization

- Use research to segment publics
- Conduct evaluation research

NEGOTIATION KNOWLEDGE

- Negotiate with activist publics
- Help management understand opinions of publics
- Use conflict resolution theories with publics

PERSUASION KNOWLEDGE

- Persuade a public that your organization is right
- Use attitude theory in a campaign
- Get publics to behave as your organization wants

Source: Dozier, David, with Grunig, James, and Larissa. *The Manager's Guide to Excellence in Public Relations and Communication Management.* Mahwah, NJ: Lawrence Erlbaum Publishers, 1995, p. 64.

Research also indicates that the type of organization involved may be less significant in predicting the role of its public relations department than are the perceptions and expectations of its top management. In many organizations, top-level management perceives public relations as primarily a journalistic and technical function—media relations and publicity. In large-scale mechanical organizations of low complexity, there is also a tendency to think of public relations as only a support function of the marketing department.

Such perceptions by top management severely limit the role of the public relations department as well as its power to take part in management decision making and solve problems. Instead, public relations staff members are relegated to being technicians who simply prepare messages without input on what should be communicated.

A third dimension influencing the role and function of a public relations department is the background and capabilities of its staff. As the IABC Foundation research has pointed out, CEOs want strategic communication managers; yet a large number of public relations managers, many of them journalists by training, self-select technician roles because they lack a knowledge base in research, environmental scanning, problem-solving, and managing total communication strategies.

Instead, they continue to be preoccupied with one-way communication to the mass media even though, as the IABC research points out, the mass media "generally are not the most effective way of communicating with strategic publics—especially at the stage of building relationships rather than responding to issues."

Names of Departments

A public relations department in an organization goes by many names. And most often, it is not "public relations." In the largest corporations (the Fortune 500), the terms *corporate communications* or *communications* outnumber *public relations* by almost four to one.

Among those switching from public relations to corporate communications in recent years are Procter & Gamble and Hershey Candies. In both cases, the companies say that the switch occurred because the department had expanded beyond "public relations" to include such activities as employee communications, shareholder communications, annual reports, consumer relations, and corporate philanthropy.

Such activities, however, are considered subcategories of modern public relations, so consultant Alfred Geduldig has offered another reason. He told *O'Dwyer's PR Services Report* that the term "public relations" had suffered from repeated derogatory usage, causing companies to move away from the term. He also thought that the term "corporate communications" was a sign that public relations people were doing many more things in a company than in the past, reflecting an integration of communications services.

Organization of Departments

The head executive of a public relations or similarly named department usually has one of three titles—manager, director, or vice president. A vice president of corporate communications may have direct responsibility for the additional activities of advertising and marketing communications.

A department usually is divided into specialized sections that have a coordinator or manager. Common sections found in a large corporation are media relations, investor relations, consumer affairs, governmental relations, community relations, marketing communications, and employee communications. A typical organizational chart for a public relations department is shown in Figure 5.1.

Multimillion-dollar corporations often have small departments. A Conference Board survey of 150 major U.S. corporations found that the typical department has nine professionals. The typical department budget, the survey noted, was about $3.5 million.

Public relations personnel may also be dispersed throughout an organization in such a manner that an observer has difficulty in ascertaining the extent of public relations activity. Some may be housed under marketing communications in the marketing department. Others may be assigned to the personnel department as communication specialists producing newsletters and brochures. Decentralization of the public relations function, and the frictions it causes, will be discussed later in this chapter.

Line and Staff Functions

Traditional management theory divides an organization into *line* and *staff* functions. A line manager, such as a vice president of manufacturing, can delegate authority, set production goals, hire employees, and directly influence the work of others. Staff people, in contrast,

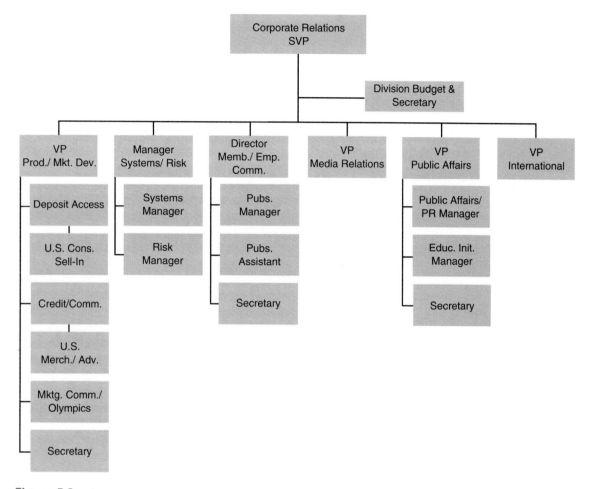

Figure 5.1

This chart explaining the organization of Visa International's corporate relations division shows the diversity of activities carried out under the direction of the executive vice president for corporate relations and communications.

have little or no direct authority. Instead, they indirectly influence the work of others through suggestions, recommendations, and advice.

According to accepted management theory, public relations is a staff function. Public relations people are experts in communication; line managers, including the chief executive officer, rely on them to use their skills in preparing and processing data, making recommendations, and executing communication programs to implement the organization's policies.

Although public relations departments can function only with the approval of top management, there are varying levels of influence that departments may exert.

Levels of Influence   Management experts state that staff functions in an organization operate at various levels of influence and authority. On the lowest level, the staff function may be only *advisory:* line management has no obligation to take recommendations or even request them.

When public relations is purely advisory, it is often not effective. A good example is the Alaska oil-spill crisis (see Chapter 8). Exxon generated a great deal of public, legislative, and media criticism because public relations was relegated to a low level and was, for all practical purposes, nonexistent.

Johnson & Johnson, on the other hand, gives its public relations staff function higher status. The Tylenol crisis, in which seven persons died after taking capsules containing cyanide, clearly showed that the company based much of its reaction and quick recall of the product on the advice of public relations staff. In this case, public relations was in a *compulsory-advisory* position.

Under the compulsory-advisory concept, organization policy requires that line managers (top management) at least listen to the appropriate staff experts before deciding on a strategy. Don Hellriegel and John Slocum, authors of the textbook *Management,* state: "Although such a procedure does not limit the manager's decision-making discretion, it ensures that the manager has made use of the specialized talents of the appropriate staff agency."

Another level of advisory relationship within an organization is called *concurring authority.* For instance, an operating division wishing to publish a brochure cannot do so unless the public relations department approves the copy and layout. If differences arise, the parties must agree before work can proceed. Many firms use this mode to prevent departments and divisions from disseminating materials not in conformity with company standards.

Concurring authority, however, may also limit the freedom of the public relations department. Some companies have a policy that all employee magazine articles and external news releases must be reviewed by the legal staff before publication. The material cannot be disseminated until legal and public relations personnel have agreed upon what will be said. The situation is even more limiting on public relations when the legal department has *command authority* to change a news release with or without the consent of public relations. This is one reason that newspaper editors find some news releases so filled with "legalese" as to be almost unreadable.

Sources of Friction

Ideally, public relations is part of the managerial subsystem. It is, say professors James and Larissa Grunig at the University of Maryland, "the management of communication between an organization and its publics." However, other staff functions also are involved in the communication process with internal and external publics. And, almost invariably, friction occurs. The four areas of possible friction are legal, human resources, advertising, and marketing.

Legal   The legal staff is concerned about the possible effect of any public statement on current or potential litigation. Consequently, lawyers often frustrate public relations personnel by taking the attitude that any public statement can potentially be used against the organization in a lawsuit. Conflicts over what to release and when often have a paralyzing effect on decision-making, causing the organization to seem unresponsive to public concerns. This is particularly true in a crisis, when the public demands information immediately.

Human Resources   The traditional personnel department has now evolved into the expanded role of "human resources," and there are often turf battles over who is responsible for employee communications. Human resources personnel believe they should control the flow of information. Public relations administrators counter that satisfactory external communications cannot be achieved unless effective employee relations are conducted simultaneously. Layoffs, for example, affect not only employees but community and investor relations.

Advertising   Advertising and public relations departments often collide because they compete for funds to communicate with external audiences. Philosophical differences also arise. Advertising's approach to communications is, "Will it increase sales?" Public relations asks, "Will it make friends?" These differing orientations frequently cause breakdowns in coordination of overall strategy.

Marketing   Marketing, like advertising, tends to think only of customers or potential buyers as key publics. Public relations, on the other hand, defines "publics" in a broader way—any group that can have an impact on the operations of the organization. These publics include governmental agencies, environmental groups, neighborhood groups, and a host of other "publics" that marketing would not consider "customers."

The friction between marketing and public relations people reached a new height in the early 1990s when marketing departments began to advocate the concept of "integrated marketing communications."

Some public relations people thought this new trend would mean a loss of autonomy for them and that public relations would lose its counseling role to top management. Others were concerned that marketing-directed public relations would reduce professionals to the role of technicians working to support marketing objectives and functions. Historically, this work has been to handle product publicity.

Another argument was that public relations should do more than get people to buy goods and services. Marketing, by definition, is persuasive in intent. On the other hand, IABC's excellence study concludes that the ideal of public relations is symmetrical communication—the building of mutual understanding and communication between the organization and its various publics.

All this has led James Grunig, editor of the IABC study, to conclude, "We believe, then, that public relations must emerge as a discipline distinct from marketing and that it must be practiced separately from marketing in the organization." Logic dictates, however, that an organization needs a coordinated and integrated approach to communications strategy. The following suggestions may help achieve this goal:

1. Representatives of departments should serve together on key committees to exchange information on how various programs can complement each other to achieve overall organizational objectives.

2. Heads of departments should be equals in job title. In this way, the autonomy of one department is not subverted by another.

3. All department heads should report to the same superior, so that all viewpoints can be considered before an appropriate strategy is formulated.

4. Informal, regular contacts with representatives of other departments help dispel mind-sets and create understanding and respect for each other's viewpoint.

5. Written policies should be established to spell out the responsibilities of each department. Such policies are helpful in settling disputes over which department has authority to communicate with employees or alter a news release.

Some organizational charts for public relations and other departments are shown in Figure 5.2.

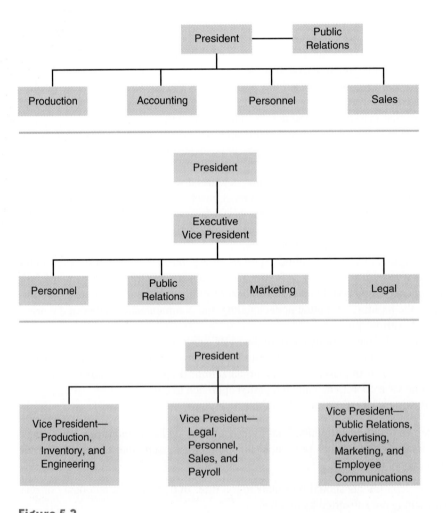

Figure 5.2
This chart depicts three examples of corporate management organization, showing the important position of public relations.

The Trend toward Outsourcing

Although one survey of Fortune 500 companies shows that 47 percent have increased their public relations staffs in the last five years, there is also evidence that organizations are increasingly "outsourcing" their communication activities to public relations firms and independent contractors.

One indication of this is how the budgets of corporate public relations departments are divided. A survey by Thomas Harris & Company and Impulse Research Public Relations, for example, showed that the average large corporation's public relations budget of $3.37 million was split almost evenly between work done internally and work done by public relations firms.

The opportunity to bring resources to the company that are not available internally is the most popular motivation for outsourcing, followed by the need to supplement staff during peak work periods. The most frequently outsourced activity was in the descending order of (1) writing and communications, (2) media relations, (3) publicity, (4) strategy and planning, and (5) event planning.

The trend toward outsourcing, say some experts, follows what has occurred in advertising. Today, about 90 percent of corporate and institutional advertising is handled by advertising agencies instead of in-house departments. As a new century dawns, it appears that the major beneficiary of this trend will be public relations firms, which are discussed next.

PUBLIC RELATIONS FIRMS

Public relations firms are found in almost every nation.

In size, public relations firms range from one- or two-person operations to global giants such as Burson-Marsteller, which employs 2,000 professionals in 35 nations (*www.bm.com*). The scope of services provided to clients varies, but there are common denominators. Big or small, each firm gives counsel and performs technical services required to carry out an agreed-upon program. The firm may operate as an adjunct to an organization's public relations department or, if no department exists, conduct the entire effort.

The United States, because of its large population and economic base, has the world's most public relations firms (about 10,000 according to one count) and generates the most fee income. The J.R. O'Dwyer Company, for example, found that the 50 largest public relations firms in the United States generated revenue of $2.8 billion in 1999, and the top 15 firms generated about three fourths of this total. (See table of the 15 largest U.S. firms). Fueling this growth, as mentioned, was the increased outsourcing of work by corporations.

American public relations firms have proliferated in proportion to the growth of the global economy. Also stimulating the growth of public relations firms were increased urbanization, expansion of government bureaucracy and regulation, more sophisticated mass media systems, the rise of consumerism, international trade, and the demand for more information. Professionals were needed to maintain lines of communication in an increasingly complicated world and to provide much of the material to be distributed. Executives of public relations firms expect double-digit growth for the year 2000 and beyond as more countries adopt free market economies and more international outlets such as CNN are established. In addition, the skyrocketing use of the Internet has fueled the global reach of public relations firms.

Table 5.1 *The 15 Largest Public Relations Firms*

Name*	Fee Income (in Dollars)	Employees
Burson-Marsteller (Young & Rubicam)	$274.6 million	2,000
Hill & Knowlton (WPP Goup)	$243.3 million	1,570
Shandwick International (Interpublic)	$240.4 million	2,054
Porter/Novelli (Omnicom)	$214.9 million	2,483
Fleishman-Hillard (Omnicom)	$213.4 million	1,563
Edelman PR Worldwide	$186.0 million	1,692
Ketchum (Omnicom)	$149.8 million	1,204
BSMG Worldwide (True North)	$144.7 million	858
Ogilvy PR (WPP Group)	$125.0 million	1,100
GCI/APCO Associates (Grey)	$112.7 million	900
Weber PR Worldwide (Inerpublic)	$101.4 million	556
Manning, Selvage & Lee (MacManus)	$95.4 million	520
Brodeur Worldwide (Omnicom)	$70.1 million	700
Golin/Harris Communications (Interpublic)	$59.5 million	427
Ruder Finn	$59.4 million	418

*Advertising agent parent in parentheses

Source: Copyright 2000 by J.R. O'Dwyer Company, Inc.

Services They Provide

Counseling firms today offer services far more extensive than those provided by the nation's first firm, the Publicity Bureau, founded in 1900 in Boston. Today, public relations firms provide a variety of services:

- *Marketing communications.* Promotion of products and services. Such tools as news releases, feature stories, special events, brochures, and media tours are used.

- *Executive speech training.* Top executives are coached on public affairs activities, including personal appearances.

- *Research and evaluation.* Scientific surveys are conducted to measure public attitudes and perceptions.

- *Crisis communication.* Management is counseled on what to say and do in an emergency such as an oil spill or recall of an unsafe product.

- *Media analysis.* Appropriate media are examined for targeting specific messages to key audiences.

Firms Win Golden World Awards

Public relations firms around the world handle a variety of assignments. Here are some that have received a Golden World award from the International Public Relations Association (IPRA):

- **Alpha Beta Ltd. (Denmark)**
  Conducted a program to establish Canal Digital as the leading independent provider of pay TV in the country and to pass a law (enacted) to ban piracy of television programs.

- **Edelman Public Relations Worldwide (Germany)**
  Conducted a public information campaign to make German citizens more aware of Parkinson's disease and the need for early diagnosis and treatment to improve a patient's quality of life.

- **Vulindlela Marketing & Public Relations (South Africa)**
  Conducted a campaign on behalf of the Inner West City Council in Durban to educate black homeowners on the value of paying their util-

ity bills and tax assessments in order to finance public services in their neighborhoods.

- **Green Active PR (Turkey)**
  Conducted a campaign on behalf of Unilever, the market leader in bath and kitchen cleaners, to increase brand awareness in 26 smaller Turkish cities through a program that included the cleaning of local landmarks and monuments.

- **Media In (Slovakia)**
  Helped Slovnaft, the nation's largest petrochemical complex, position itself as ecologically concerned through grants to fund local "green" projects.

- **Japan Counselors, Inc. (Japan)**
  Organized a national information campaign for the Japan Allergy Association to give citizens a better understanding of the actual number of sufferers and to inform doctors on the latest treatments and studies.

- *Community relations.* Management is counseled on ways to achieve official and public support for such projects as building or expanding a factory.

- *Events management.* News conferences, anniversary celebrations, rallies, symposiums, and national conferences are planned and conducted.

- *Public affairs.* Materials and testimony are prepared for government hearings and regulatory bodies, and background briefings are prepared.

- *Branding and corporate reputation.* Advice is given on programs that establish a company brand and its reputation for quality.

- *Financial relations.* Management is counseled on ways to avoid takeover by another firm and effectively communicate with stockholders, security analysts, and institutional investors.

Increasingly, public relations firms emphasize the counseling aspect of their services. This transition to counseling is best expressed by Harold Burson, chairman of Burson-Marsteller, who once told an audience, "In the beginning, top management used to say to us, 'Here's the message, deliver it.' Then it became, 'What should we say?' Now, in smart organizations, it's 'What should we do?'"

Global Reach

Public relations firms, large and small, usually are found in major metropolitan areas. On an international level, the firms and their offices or affiliates are situated in most major world cities. Edelman Public Relations Worldwide, for example, has 35 offices in the United States, Canada, Mexico, Europe, and Asia-Pacific, and more than 50 affiliates worldwide. Other large U.S. firms have firmly planted their flags from Moscow to Bangkok.

The importance of international operations is reflected in the fact that the 15 largest U.S. public relations firms now generate more than 40 percent of their fees outside the United States. Burson-Marsteller and Hill and Knowlton are at the 50 percent level, and The Rowland Company, in the top 20 firms by fee income, now gets about 70 percent of its income from abroad.

International work isn't only for the large firms. Small and medium-sized firms around the world have formed working partnerships with each other. The largest group is WORLD-COM, with 92 firms in 36 nations. And Pinnacle Worldwide is a network of 63 independent firms in 33 nations. Other groups include Public Relations Organization International (PROI) and IPREX.

Essentially, firms in an affiliation cooperate with each other to service clients with international needs. A firm in India may call its affiliate in Los Angeles to handle the details of a news conference for a visiting trade delegation from India. This approach gives small firms with limited resources an opportunity to offer the same kinds of services as the largest firms.

The large international firms, as well as various affiliated groups, have been well established in Western Europe for several years. A new area of expansion is the major cities of Eastern Europe and the former Soviet Union. Another area of new business is Latin America, as free market economies become the rule rather than the exception. Asia, particularly China with its large population, also presents new opportunities.

Public Relations and Advertising Mergers

Until the 1970s, the largest public relations firms were independently owned by their principal officers or, in some cases, by employee stockholders. A significant change began in 1973 when Carl Byoir & Associates, then the third largest U.S. public relations firm, was purchased by the advertising firm of Foote, Cone & Belding.

Today, with the recent purchase of Shandwick (previously the world's largest independent firm) by the Interpublic Group of Companies, 13 of the 15 largest public relations firms are owned by advertising agencies or their holding companies. In addition, several are owned by the same holding company. Omnicom, for example, owns Fleishman-Hillard, Ketchum, Brodeur Worldwide, and Porter Novelli as well as several smaller public relations firms. And the Young & Rubicam advertising conglomerate owns Burson-Marsteller and Cohn-Wolfe. The Interpublic Group also has gone on a buying spree—adding Shandwick, Weber Public Relations Worldwide, and Golin/Harris to its stable that also includes the advertising giant, McCann Erickson Worldwide.

There are several reasons for the acquisition of public relations firms by large advertising conglomerates. One is the natural evolutionary step of integrating various communication disciplines into "total communication networks." Supporters say no single-function agency is equipped with the personnel and resources to handle complex, often global, marketing functions efficiently for a client. In other words, the synergy between advertising and public relations under one corporate banner can more efficiently deliver a consistent message in a multifaceted campaign. In addition, joint public relations and advertising endeavors can increase the pool of potential new clients, generate more referrals, and expand the number of geographical locations.

A second reason is pure business. Advertising firms and their holding companies find public relations firms an attractive investment. According to *PR Week,* revenues from advertising clients have remained somewhat static over the past five years, whereas public relations firms have experienced double-digit growth in the same time frame. Increasingly, public relations firms are becoming the "glittering jewels" in holding company portfolios, according to *PR Week.*

Although earlier efforts to create "total communication networks" often met with limited success, there is now increasing evidence that public relations firms and advertising agencies owned by the same corporate entity are achieving some success in the marketplace. One area is joint pitches for business. Interpublic's McCann-Erickson and Shandwick, for example, got a multimillion-dollar advertising and public relations account from Aon Insurance Company after making a joint pitch. Considerable new business is also generated from units of the same company making referrals to each other.

One development that has fueled more cooperation between advertising agencies and public relations firms is a more sophisticated understanding of public relations by advertising agencies. Traditionally, advertising firms considered public relations as simply a nice add-on to an extensive advertising campaign. Consequently, many advertising firms applied the 90–10 rule: advertising received 90 percent of the budget and public relations got 10 percent. Today, Michael Petruzzello, CEO of Shandwick American says, "Advertising and PR are developing a mutual respect of each other's disciplines."

Focus on Ethics

Should We Represent This Client?

Public relations firms often work for a variety of clients, and the question is often raised whether any client, who is willing to pay, should be entitled to service.

Should a public relations firm, for example, work for a government that tramples human rights? What about a mining company that claims that it has discovered the world's richest gold deposit but can't provide much verifiable evidence except the assurances of the company's president? What about working for the tobacco industry?

Do public relations firms have the obligation to do proper background checks on new clients before signing them onto their rosters? On what basis should a public relations firm accept or turn down a client?

Consequently, a better appreciation now exists of how each specialty—advertising, public relations, direct mail, sales promotion—can complement others in the marketing communications mix. And although there is a strong trend toward "integrated" campaigns, clients who use this method often contract with separate agencies to execute various parts of the plan. When Microsoft introduced Windows 95, it used separate public relations and advertising agencies. Public relations firms, even if owned by an advertising agency, continue to do business under their own names and maintain their own client lists.

Structure of a Counseling Firm

A small public relations firm may consist only of the owner (president) and an assistant (vice president), supported by a secretary. Larger firms have a more extended hierarchy.

The organization of Ketchum Public Relations/San Francisco is fairly typical. The president is based in the New York office of Ketchum Public Relations, so the executive vice president is the on-site director in San Francisco. A senior vice president is associate director of operations. Next in line are several vice presidents who primarily do account supervision or special projects.

An *account supervisor* is in charge of one major account or several smaller ones. An *account executive,* who reports to the supervisor, is in direct contact with the client and handles most of the day-to-day activity. At the bottom of the list is the *assistant account executive,* who does routine maintenance work compiling media lists, gathering information, and writing rough drafts of news releases.

Recent college graduates usually start as assistant account executives. Once they learn the firm's procedures and show ability, promotion to account executive may occur within 6 to 18 months. After two or three years, it is not uncommon for an account executive to become an account supervisor.

Executives at or above the vice-presidential level usually are heavily involved in selling their firm's services. In order to prosper, a firm must continually seek new business and sell additional services to current clients. Consequently, the upper management of the firm calls on prospective clients, prepares proposals, and makes new business presentations. In this very competitive field, a firm not adept at selling itself frequently fails.

Firms frequently organize account teams, especially to serve a client whose program is multifaceted. One member of the team, for example, may set up a nationwide media tour in which an organization representative is booked on television talk shows. Another may supervise all materials going to the print media, including news stories, feature articles, background kits, and artwork. A third may concentrate on the trade press or perhaps arrange special events.

Pros and Cons of Using a Public Relations Firm

Because public relations is a service industry, a firm's major asset is the quality of its people. Potential clients thinking about hiring a public relations firm usually base their decisions on that fact, according to a survey of Fortune 500 corporate vice presidents.

Thomas L. Harris, a consultant who conducted a survey of corporate communication directors, found that clients believe meeting deadlines and keeping promises are the most important criteria for evaluating firms. Other important considerations were, in descending order, (1) client services, (2) honest, accurate billing, (3) creativity, and (4) knowledge of the client's industry.

Advantages   Public relations firms offer the following:

* *Objectivity.* The firm can analyze a client's needs or problems from a new perspective and offer fresh insights.

* *Variety of skills and expertise.* The firm has specialists, whether in speech-writing, trade magazine placement, or helping with proxy battles.

* *Extensive resources.* The firm has abundant media contacts and works regularly with numerous suppliers of products and services. It has research materials, including data information banks, and experience in similar fields.

* *Offices throughout the country.* A national public relations program requires coordination in major cities. Large firms have on-site staffs or affiliate firms in many cities and even around the world.

* *Special problem-solving.* A firm may have extensive experience and a solid reputation in desired areas. For example, Burson-Marsteller is well known for expertise in crisis communications, health and medical issues, and international coordination of special projects. Hill and Knowlton is known for expertise in public affairs, and Ketchum is the expert in consumer marketing.

* *Credibility.* A successful public relations firm has a solid reputation for professional, ethical work. If represented by such a firm, a client will likely get more attention among opinion leaders in mass media, government, and the financial community.

On the Minus Side   Despite many successes, not everything goes smoothly between a firm and its client. There are several drawbacks to using public relations firms:

* *Superficial grasp of a client's unique problems.* While objectivity is gained from an outsider's perspective, there is often a disadvantage in the public relations firm's not thoroughly understanding the client's business or needs.

* *Lack of full-time commitment.* A public relations firm has many clients to service. Therefore, no single client can monopolize its personnel and other resources.

* *Need for prolonged briefing period.* Some companies become frustrated because time and money are needed for a public relations firm to research the organization and make recommendations. Consequently, the actual start of a public relations program may take weeks or months.

* *Resentment by internal staff.* The public relations staff members of a client organization may resent the use of outside counsel because they think it implies that they lack the ability to do the job.

* *Need for strong direction by top management.* High-level executives must take the time to brief outside counsel on specific objectives sought.

- *Need for full information and confidence.* A client must be willing to share its information, including the skeletons in the closet, with outside counsel.

- *Costs.* Outside counsel is expensive. In many situations, routine public relations work can be handled at lower cost by internal staff.

PR Insights

A Job At a Corporation Or a PR Firm?

Recent college graduates often ponder the pros and cons of joining a corporate department or going to work for a PR firm. The following summarizes some of the pluses and minuses:

PR Firm: Breadth of Experience	**Corporate PR: Depth of Experience**
Experience gained quickly; tip—find a mentor you can learn from.	Jobs more difficult to find without experience; duties more narrowly focused.
Variety. Usually work on several clients and projects at same time.	Sometimes little variety at entry level.
Possibility of rapid advancement.	Growth sometimes limited unless you are willing to switch employers.
Fast-paced, exciting.	Can be slower paced.
Seldom see the impact of your work for a client; removed from "action."	Heavy involvement with executive staff, see impact almost instantly. You are an important component in the "big picture."
Abilities get honed and polished. (This is where a mentor really helps.)	Strength in all areas expected. Not a lot of time for coaching by peers.
Networking with other professionals leads to better job opportunities.	Sometimes so involved in your work, you don't have time for networking.
Learn other skills, such as how to do presentations and budgets, and establish deadlines.	Same "client" all the time. Advantage: get to know organization really well. Disadvantage: can become boring.
Intense daily pressure on billable hours, productivity. Some firms are real "sweatshops."	Less intense daily pressure; more emphasis on accomplishing longer-term results.
Somewhat high employment turnover.	Less turnover.
Budgets and resources can be limited.	More resources usually available.
Salary traditionally low at entry level.	Salaries tend to be higher.
Insurance, medical benefits can be minimal.	Benefits usually good, sometimes excellent.
Little opportunity for profit-sharing, stock options.	More opportunities available.
High emphasis on tactical skills, production of materials.	Can be more managerial and involved in strategic planning.

Fees and Charges

A public relations firm charges for its services in several ways. The three most common methods, also used by law firms and management consultants, are:

1. *Basic hourly fee, plus out-of-pocket expenses.* The number of hours spent on a client's account is tabulated each month and billed to the client. Work by personnel in the counseling firm is billed at various hourly rates. Out-of-pocket expenses, such as cab fares, car rentals, airline tickets, and meals, are also billed to the client. In a typical $100,000 campaign, about 70 percent of the budget is spent on staff salaries.

2. *Retainer fee.* A basic monthly charge billed to the client covers ordinary administrative and overhead expenses for maintaining the account and being "on call." Many retainer fees also specify the number of hours the counseling firm will spend on the account each month. Additional work is billed at normal hourly rates. Out-of-pocket expenses are normally billed separately.

3. *Fixed project fee.* The public relations firm agrees to do a specific project, such as an annual report, a newsletter, or a special event, for a fixed fee. For example, a counseling firm may write and produce a quarterly newsletter for $30,000 annually. The fixed fee is the least popular of the three methods because it is difficult to estimate accurately all work and expenses in advance.

The primary basis for all three methods is to estimate the number of hours that a particular project will take to plan, execute, and evaluate. The first method—the basic hourly fee—is the most flexible and most widely used among large firms. It is preferred by public relations people because they are paid for the exact number of hours spent on a project and because it is the only sound way that a fee can be determined intelligently. The retainer fee and the fixed project fee are based on an estimate of how many hours it will take to counsel a client.

How Estimates Are Made   A number of variables are considered when a public relations firm estimates the cost of a program. These may include the size and duration, geographical locations involved, the number of personnel assigned to the project, and the type of client. A major variable, of course, is billing the use of the firm's personnel to a client at the proper hourly rate.

An account supervisor, for example, may earn $60,000 annually and receive benefits (health insurance, pension plan, and so on) that cost the firm an additional $13,000. Thus the annual cost of the employee to the firm totals $73,000. Using 1600 billable hours in a year (after deducting vacation time and holidays), the account executive makes $45.63 per hour.

The standard industry practice, however, is to bill clients at least three times a person's salary. This multiple allows the firm to pay for office space, equipment, insurance, supplies, and try to operate at a profit level of about 10 to 20 percent before taxes. Thus the billing rate of the account supervisor (3 × $45.63) rounds off at $137 per hour. The principals of a counseling firm, because of their much higher salaries, often command $175 to $500 per hour depending on the size and capabilities of the firm.

The primary income of a public relations firm comes from the selling of staff time, but some additional income results from markups on photocopying, telephone, fax, and artwork the firm supervises. The standard markup in the trade is between 15 and 20 percent.

CASE PROBLEM

You will graduate from college in several months and plan a career in public relations. After several interviews, you receive two job offers.

One is with a high-technology company that makes inkjet printers and scanners for the consumer market. The corporate communications department has about 20 professionals, and it is customary for beginners to start in employee publications or product publicity. Later, with more experience, you might be assigned to do marketing communications for a product group or work in a specialized area such as investor relations, governmental affairs, or even community relations.

The second job offer is from a local office of a large, national public relations firm. You would begin as an assistant account executive and work on several accounts, including a chain of fast-food restaurants and an insurance company. The jobs pay about the same, but the corporation offers better insurance and medical plans. Taking into consideration the pros and cons of working for public relations firms versus corporations, what job would best fit your abilities and preferences? Explain your reasons.

QUESTIONS FOR REVIEW AND DISCUSSION

1. How have the role and function of public relations departments changed in recent years?

2. In what ways do the structure and culture of an organization affect the role and influence of the public relations department?

3. What kinds of knowledge does a manager of a public relations department need today?

4. Many departments are now called "corporate communications" instead of "public relations." Do you think the first term is more appropriate? Why or why not?

5. What is the difference between a line and staff function? To which function does public relations belong, and why?

6. Why is a compulsory-advisory role within an organization a good one for a public relations department to have?

7. What four areas of the organization cause the most potential for friction with public relations? Explain.

8. In your opinion, should public relations or human resources be responsible for employee communications?

9. Public relations people express a fear that they will lose influence and be relegated to purely technical functions if they are controlled by the marketing department. Do you think their fears are justified? Why or why not?

10. Name at least seven services that a public relations firm offers clients.

11. What are the three largest public relations firms in the world?

12. How important is international business to American public relations firms?

13. Why do large advertising agencies and holding companies find the acquisition of public relations firms so attractive?

14. What are the pros and cons of using a public relations firm?

15. What are the standard methods used by a public relations firm to charge for its services?

6

Research

Preview

The objective of this chapter is to demonstrate the necessity for research as a basic element in public relations programs, and to give students an understanding of techniques and applications in informal and formal research.

Topics covered in the chapter include:
- The importance and use of research
- Informal research methods
- Use of online databases and the Internet
- Formal research: random sampling
- Questionnaire design
- Ways of reaching respondents

THE IMPORTANCE OF RESEARCH

Effective public relations is a process, and the essential first step is research. Today, research is widely accepted by public relations professionals as an integral part of the planning, program development, and evaluation process.

In basic terms, research is a form of listening. Professors Glen Broom and David Dozier of San Diego State University, in their book, *Using Research in Public Relations,* say simply, "Research is the controlled, objective, and systematic gathering of information for the purpose of describing and understanding."

Before any public relations program can be undertaken, information must be gathered, data collected, and interpretation done. Only by performing this first step can an organization begin to make policy decisions and map out strategies for effective communication programs.

Various kinds of research can be used to accomplish an organization's objectives and meet its need for information. The choice really depends on the subject and situation. Time and budget are important considerations, as is the perceived importance of the situation. Consequently, many questions should be asked before formulating a research design, such as:

1. What is the problem?

2. What kind of information is needed?

3. How will the results of the research be used?

4. What specific public (or publics) should be researched?

5. Should the organization do the research or hire an outside consultant?

6. How will the research data be analyzed, reported, or applied?

7. How soon are the results needed?

8. How much will the research cost?

These questions will help the public relations person determine the extent and nature of the research needed. Only informal research, for example, may be required, because of its lower cost and the need for immediate information. Or a random scientific survey may be selected, despite its cost and time, because a political candidate wants to know exactly how he or she stands in the polls. The pros and cons of each method will be discussed later in the chapter.

Using Research

Research is a multipronged tool that is involved in virtually every phase of a communications program. In general, studies show that public relations departments spend about 3 to 5 percent of their budget on research. Some experts contend that it should be 10 percent. These are ways that public relations professionals use research.

Achieve Credibility with Management   Executives want facts, not guesses and hunches. The inclusion of public relations personnel in an organization's policy- and decision-making, according to the findings of IABC's exhaustive research on excellence in communication management, is strongly correlated with their ability to do research and relate their findings to the organization's objectives.

Define Audiences and Segment Publics   Detailed information about the demographics, lifestyles, characteristics, and consumption patterns of audiences helps to assure that messages reach the proper audiences. A successful children's immunization information campaign in California was based on State Health Department statistics that showed: (1) past immunization programs had not reached rural children, and (2) Hispanic and Vietnamese children were not being immunized in the same proportion as other ethnic groups.

PR Insights

Rules for Publicizing Surveys and Polls

The Council of American Survey Research Organizations (CASRO), a nonprofit national trade organization for more than 150 survey research companies, says survey findings released to the public should contain the following information:

- Sponsorship of the study

- Name of the research company conducting the study

- Description of the study's objectives

- Description of the sample, including the size and the population to which the results are intended to generalize

- Dates of data collection

- Exact wording of the questions asked

- Any information the researcher believes is relevant to help the public make a fair assessment of the results

In addition, CASRO recommends that other information should be readily available if anyone asks. This includes (1) the type of survey conducted, (2) methods for selecting the survey sample, (3) how respondents were screened, and (4) the procedure for data coding and analysis.

Formulate Strategy   Much money can be spent pursuing the wrong strategies. Officials of the New Hampshire paper industry, given the bad press about logging and waterway pollution, thought a campaign was needed to tell the public what it was doing to reduce pollution. An opinion survey of 800 state residents by a public relations firm, however, indicated that the public was already generally satisfied with the industry's efforts. Consequently, the new strategy focused on reinforcing positive themes such as worker safety, employment, and environmental responsibility.

Test Messages   Research is often used to determine what particular message is most salient with the target audience. A campaign to encourage car pooling, according to one focus group study, found that the message most significant with commuters was saving time and money, not air quality or environmental concern. Consequently, the campaign emphasized how many minutes could be cut from an average commute by using car pool lanes, and the annual savings in gasoline, insurance, and car maintenance.

Help Management Keep in Touch   In a mass society, top management is increasingly isolated from the concerns of employees, customers, and other important publics. Research helps bridge the gap by periodically surveying key publics about problems and concerns. This feedback is a "reality check" for top executives and often leads to better policies and communication strategies.

Prevent Crises.   An estimated 90 percent of organizational crises are caused by internal operational problems rather than unexpected natural disasters. Research can often uncover trouble spots and public concerns before they become page-one news. (See section on issues management in the next chapter.) Analyzing complaints on a toll-free number or monitoring "chat rooms" on the Internet can often tip off an organization that it should act before the problem attracts media attention.

Monitor the Competition   Savvy organizations keep track of what the competition is doing. This is done through surveys asking consumers to comment on competing products, content analysis of the competition's media coverage, monitoring the competition's websites, checking Internet chat groups, and reviewing industry reports in trade journals. Such research often helps an organization shape its marketing and communications strategy to counter a competitor's strengths and capitalize on any weaknesses.

Sway Public Opinion   Facts and figures, compiled from a variety of primary and secondary sources, can change public opinion. Shortly before an election in Ohio, 90 percent of the voters supported a state ballot measure that would require cancer warnings on thousands of products from plywood to peanut butter. A coalition called Ohioans for Responsible Health Information, opposing the bill, commissioned universities and other credible outside sources to research the economic impact of such legislation on consumers and major industries. The research, used as the basis of the grassroots campaign, caused the defeat of the ballot measure.

Generate Publicity   Polls and surveys can generate publicity for an organization. Indeed, many surveys seem to be designed primarily with publicity in mind. Simmons Mattress once polled people to find out if they slept in the nude. And Reynolds Metals did a study about the latest trends in the kitchen and the preparation of the family dinner. Results of the study got placement on the food pages of major dailies and even on nationally syndicated radio programs.

Measure Success   The bottom line of any public relations program is whether the time and money spent accomplished the stated objective. As one of its many programs to boost brand awareness, Miller Genuine Draft sponsored a "reunion ride" on Harley Davidson Corporation's 90th anniversary. Ketchum Public Relations, Chicago, generated extensive media publicity about the "ride" and Miller's sponsorship that was 98-percent positive. Perhaps more importantly, sales increased in all but two of the cities included in the event. Evaluation, the last step of the public relations process, is discussed in Chapter 9. The next sections will discuss ways of doing research.

RESEARCH TECHNIQUES

When the word "research" is used, people tend to think only of scientific surveys and complex statistical tabulations. In public relations, however, research techniques are also used to gather data and information.

In fact, a survey of practitioners by Walter K. Lindenmann, senior vice president and director of research for Ketchum Public Relations, found that three fourths of the respondents described their research techniques as casual and informal, rather than scientific and precise. The technique cited most often was literature searches and database information retrieval.

This technique is called *secondary research* because existing information in books, magazine articles, and electronic databases is used. This contrasts with *primary research,* in which "new" and "original" information is generated through a research design that is specific and directed to answer a specific need. Some examples are in-depth interviews, focus groups, surveys, and polls.

Another way of categorizing types of research is by using the terms *qualitative* and *quantitative*. Lindenmann contrasts the basic differences between the two in Table 6.1.

The following sections briefly describe the most common research techniques.

Organizational Materials

Robert Kendall, in his book *Public Relations Campaign Strategies,* calls organizational materials *archival* research. The material may include the organization's policy statements, speeches by key executives, past issues of employee newsletters and magazines, reports on past public relations and marketing efforts, and news clippings. Marketing statistics, in particular, often provide the baseline data for public relations firms that are hired to launch a new product or boost awareness and sales for an existing product or service.

Library Methods

Reference books, academic journals, newspapers, and trade publications are found in every library. In many cases, these materials are found on CD-ROMs. One source is *Hoover's Company and Industry Database,* which provides information analyzing industries and companies.

Table 6.1 *Differences Between Qualitative and Quantitative Research*

Qualitative	Quantitative
"Soft" data	"Hard" data
Usually open-ended free response, unstructured	Usually closed-ended, forced choice, highly structured
"Exploratory," probing, fishing expedition type of research	"Descriptive" or "explanatory" type of research
Usually "valid," but not reliable	Usually "valid" and reliable
Rarely "projectable" to larger audiences	Usually very "projectable" to larger audiences
Generally uses nonrandom samples	Generally uses random samples
Examples	*Examples*
Focus groups	Telephone polls
One-on-one, depth interviews	Mall surveys
Observation, participation, role-playing studies	Mail intercept studies
Convenience polling	Face-to-face interview studies Shared cost or omnibus studies Panel studies

Some common reference sources for public relations professionals are the *Statistical Abstract of the United States,* which summarizes census information; the *Gallup Poll* and the *Gallup Index,* which give an index of public opinion on a variety of issues; *American Demographics,* which reports on population shifts and lifestyle trends; and *Simmons' Media and Markets,* an extensive annual survey of households in terms of product usage by brand and exposure to various media.

Online Resources

Although the library offers numerous sources of information, the information revolution has made it possible for working professionals to do much of this research in their offices through online databases.

Literature searches, the most often used form of informal research in public relations, can be done by using a computer and a modem to extract information from an estimated 1500 electronic databases that store an enormous amount of current and historical information.

Public relations departments and firms use online databases in a number of ways:

- Researching facts and figures to support a proposed project or campaign that requires top management approval.

- Keeping up to date with news about clients and their competitors.

- Tracking the media campaigns of an organization and the press announcements of its competitors.

- Finding a special quotation or impressive statistic for a speech or report.

- Tracking the press and business reaction to an organization's latest actions.

- Finding an expert for advice on an issue or a possible strategy.

- Keeping top management apprised of current business trends and issues.

- Learning the demographics and attitudes of target publics.

Online databases are available on a subscription basis and usually charge by the minute in the same way that a telephone company charges for long-distance calls.

Here are some of the online databases commonly used in public relations:

ABI/Inform. Offers indexing and full-text access to basic business magazines and scholarly journals in business and economics.

Disclosure. Fastest way to locate in-depth information about 11,1000 publicly traded companies and rulings by the Securities Exchange Commission (SEC).

Dow Jones News Retrieval System. Offers full-text newspaper, newswire, and business magazine articles. The Publications Library contains more than 5500 full-text trade, professional, and scholarly articles.

Dun & Bradstreet Million Dollar Directory. Comprehensive directory of U.S. companies, including sales, number of employees, and executive profiles.

Expanded Academic Index. An index to over 3.5 million articles in periodicals, magazines and journals.

LEXIS/NEXIS.   A very current online system that accesses the full text of newspapers, newswires, magazines, and television news scripts.

STATUSA.   Offers information gathered from 50 federal agencies, with more than 300,000 reports and statistical charts.

Online Networks

The use of online networks has skyrocketed in recent years. They not only have many of the same services that commercial online databases provide, but they enable users to send e-mail, participate in chat groups on specific subjects, post notes on computer bulletin boards, and fully access millions of documents on the Internet, including the World Wide Web containing thousands of home pages for various individuals and organizations. Largest of the online networks is America Online, with about 20 million subscribers and about 40 percent of the market. Another service is the Microsoft Network (MSN).

The Internet and World Wide Web

The Internet provides a powerful research tool for the public relations practitioner. Any number of corporations, nonprofits, trade groups, special interest groups, foundations, universities, think tanks, and government agencies post reams of data on the Internet, usually in the form of "home pages" on the World Wide Web.

Online search engines are the essential key to finding information about virtually any subject on the Internet and the World Wide Web. With literally millions of possible websites, search engines make it possible for the researcher simply to type in a keyword or two, click "Go," and receive in a few seconds all the links that the search engine has found relating to the topic.

Relevant Knowledge (*www.relevantknowledge.com*) surveys the web's top domains. One of the more popular search engines is Yahoo (*www.yahoo.com*), which in one month alone had 30.6 million visitors. Other popular engines are Excite (*www.excite.com*), Infoseek (*www.infoseek.com*), Lycos (*www.lycos.com*), AltaVista (*www.altavista.digital.com*), and Hot Bot (*www.hotbot.com*).

An extensive discussion of the Internet's development and operation appears in Chapter 18.

Content Analysis

This research method can be relatively informal or quite scientific in terms of random sampling and establishing specific subject categories. It is often applied to news stories by (1) tabulating the number of times that a key message is mentioned, or (2) analyzing whether the coverage was positive, negative, or neutral. This is further discussed in Chapter 9 in terms of evaluating a program.

A good example of content analysis is the way a company evaluated press coverage of its publicity campaign to celebrate its 100th anniversary. According to Lindenmann: "A low-budget content analysis was carried out on 427 newspaper, magazine, radio, and television placements referring both to the client and its product. The research found that the client's principal themes and copy points were referred to in most of the media coverage the company had received."

PR Insights

Surfing the Internet

Public relations requires research and fact-finding. Here's a sample of sites on the Internet helpful to public relations professionals:

- Population Profile of the United States

  www.census.gov/prod/3/98pubs/p23-194.pdf

- Domestic and International English-language media online

  www.newsdirectory.com

- *PR Week*

  www.prweek.com

- International Public Relations Association (IPRA)

  ipranet.org

- PRCentral (array of case studies listed by subject)

  www.prcentral.com

- *O'Dwyer's PR Services Report*

  www.odwyerpr.com

- *PR Tactics* (Public Relations Society of America)

  www.prsa.org/tactics.html

- *Communication World* (International Association of Business Communicators)

  www.iabc.com/cw/index.html

- PR Web

  www.prweb.com

- Electronic Newstand

  enews.com

- National Investors Relations Institute (NIRI)

  www.niri.org

Another use of content analysis is to determine if a need exists for additional public relations efforts. Faneuil Hall Marketplace in Boston stepped up its public relations activities after it was found that the number of travel articles about it had decreased. An anniversary celebration of the marketplace helped generate increased coverage.

Content analysis can be applied also to letters and phone calls. They provide good feedback about problems with the organization's policies and services. A pattern of letters and phone calls pointing out a problem is evidence that something should be done.

Interviewing

As in content analysis, there are several levels of interviewing. Almost everyone, on a daily basis, talks to colleagues and calls other organizations to gather information. Public relations personnel, faced with solving a particular problem, often "interview" other public relations professionals for ideas and suggestions.

If research is needed on public opinion and attitudes, many public relations firms conduct short interviews with people in a shopping mall or at a meeting. This kind of research is called *intercept interviewing,* because people are literally intercepted in public places and asked their opinion.

The intercept interview is not scientific in terms of sampling method, but it does give an organization a sense of current thinking or exposure to certain key messages. A health group wanted to find out if the public was actually receiving its message and retaining crucial aspects of the message. To gather such information, shopping center or "mall" intercept interviews were conducted with 300 adults at six malls. Both unaided and aided recall questions were asked to assess overall publicity impact.

Intercept interviews last only two to five minutes. At other times, the best approach is to do in-depth interviews to get more comprehensive information. Major fund-raising projects by charitable groups, for example, often require in-depth interviewing of community and business opinion leaders. The success of any major fund drive is the support of key leaders and wealthy individuals. This approach is called *purposive interviewing* because the interviewees are carefully selected for their expertise, influence, or leadership.

Focus Groups

A good alternative to individual interviewing is the focus group. The technique is widely used in advertising, marketing, and public relations to help identify attitudes and motivations of important publics. Another purpose of focus groups is to formulate or pretest message themes and communications strategies before launching a full campaign.

The Paging Services Council used six focus groups in three cities to plan a campaign that would help consumers understand that "beepers" were more than little, black boxes worn only by doctors and drug dealers. The groups helped the council and its public relations firm (1) define target audiences, (2) test program messages, (3) explore consumer attitudes about paging, and (4) evaluate product positioning statements.

Focus groups usually consist of 6 to 12 people representing the characteristics of the target audience, such as employees, consumers, or community residents. The Paging Services Council used baby boomers and users of pagers.

A trained facilitator uses nondirective interviewing techniques that encourage group members to talk freely about a topic or give candid reactions to suggested message themes. The setting is usually a conference room, and the discussion is informal. A focus group may last one or two hours, depending on interaction and subject matter.

A focus group, by definition, is an informal research procedure that develops qualitative information instead of hard data. Results cannot be summarized by percentages or even projected onto an entire population. Nevertheless, focus groups are useful in identifying the range of attitudes and opinions in the participants. Such insights can help an organization structure its messages or, on another level, formulate hypotheses and questions for a quantitative research survey.

Copy-Testing

All too often, organizations fail to communicate effectively because they produce and distribute materials that the target audience can't understand. In many cases, the material is written above the educational level of the audience.

Consequently, representatives of the target audience should be asked to read or view the material in draft form before it is mass-produced and distributed. This can be done on a one-to-one basis or in a small group setting.

Was This News Release Misleading?

Organizations often publicize the favorable findings of survey research, and the International Franchise Association (IFA) is no exception. It sent out a news release quoting a Gallup survey, with the headline, "Gallup Survey: 92 percent Franchise Owners Successful." The text continued, "Whether you're serving burgers or bagels, tending to taxes or helping the bereaved select a casket, franchise owners consider themselves successful. . . ."

The news release didn't include the fact that the survey involved only those still operating and not those who failed. It also didn't specify how the sample was derived and whether bagel or even casket franchise owners were sampled. The IFA also grouped two categories of the survey results together—those who said "very successful"—and those who said "somewhat successful" to come up with the 92 percent.

If you were the public relations director for IFA, would you have allowed this news release to be distributed? Why or why not?

A brochure about employee medical benefits or pension plans, for example, should be pretested with rank-and-file employees for readability and comprehension. Executives and lawyers who must approve the copy may understand the material, but a worker with a high school education might find it difficult to follow.

Another approach is to determine the degree of difficulty by applying a readability formula to the draft copy. Fog, Flesch, and similar techniques have formulas that relate the number of words and syllables per sentence or passage to reading level. Highly complex sentences and multisyllable words require an audience with a college education.

Scientific Sampling

The research techniques discussed so far can provide good insights to public relations staff and help them formulate effective programs. On occasion, however, there is a need to conduct polls and surveys using highly precise scientific sampling methods. Such sampling is based on two important factors—randomness and large numbers of respondents.

Random-Sampling Procedures. For best results, a random sample is taken. In statistics, this means that everyone in the targeted audience (as defined by the researcher) has an equal chance of being selected for the survey. This is also called a *probability* sample.

In contrast, a *nonprobability* survey is not random at all. Mall intercept interviews, for example, are usually restricted to shoppers in the mall at the time interviewers are working. A number of factors affects exactly who is interviewed, including the time of day and the location of the intercept interviews. Researchers doing interviews in the morning may have a disproportionate number of homemakers, while interviews after 5 P.M. may include more high school students and office workers. Also, if the researcher stands outside a record store or athletic shoe outlet, the age of those interviewed may be much younger than that of the general population.

The most precise random sampling is usually done from lists that give the name of everyone in the targeted audience. This is relatively simple when doing a random survey of an organization's employees or members because the researcher can randomly select, for example, every 25th name on a list.

Another common method to ensure representation is to draw a random sample that matches the characteristics of the audience. This is called *quota sampling*. Human resource departments usually have breakdowns of employees by job classification, and it is relatively easy to proportion a sample accordingly. If 42 percent of the employees work on the assembly line, for instance, then 42 percent of the sample should be assembly-line workers. A quota sample can be drawn on any number of demographic factors—age, sex, religion, race, in come—depending on the purpose of the survey.

Random sampling becomes more difficult when there are no comprehensive lists. In that case, researchers surveying the general population often use telephone directories or customer lists to select respondents at random.

The Size of the Sample.   In any probability study, there is always the question of sample size. National polling firms usually sample 1000 to 1500 persons and get a highly accurate idea of what the U.S. adult population is thinking. The average national poll samples 1500 people, and the margin of error is within three percentage points 95 percent of the time. In other words, 19 out of 20 times that the same questionnaire is administered, the results should be within the same three percentage points and reflect the whole population accurately.

In public relations, the primary purpose of poll data is to get indications of attitudes and opinions. Therefore it is not usually necessary or practical to do a scientific sampling of 1500 people. A sample of 250 to 500 will give relatively accurate data—with a 5- or 6-percent variance—that will help determine general public attitudes and opinions. A sample of about 100 people, accurately drawn according to probability guidelines, will include about a 10-percent margin of error.

This percentage of error would be acceptable if a public relations person, for example, asked employees what they want to read in the company magazine. Sixty percent may indicate that they would like to see more news about opportunities for promotion. If only 100 employees were properly surveyed, it really doesn't matter if the actual percentage is 50 or 70 percent. The large percentage, in either case, would be sufficient to justify an increase in news stories about advancement opportunities.

QUESTIONNAIRE DESIGN

Although correct sampling is important in gaining accurate results, pollsters generally acknowledge that sampling error may be far less important than the errors that result from the wording and order of questions and even the timing of the survey.

The Problem of Semantics

The wording of questions on a questionnaire is a time-consuming process, and it is not unusual for a questionnaire to go through multiple drafts in order to achieve maximum clarity. There is a difference between one question, "Is it a good idea to limit handguns?" and another, "Do you think registration of handguns will curtail crime?" On first glance, they seem to be asking the same thing. On closer examination, however, one can realize that a respondent could easily answer "yes" to the first question and "no" to the second.

The first question asks if the limiting of handguns is a good idea. The second asks if people think it will curtail crime. A third question that might elicit a different response would be, "Do you think laws curtailing the use of handguns would work?" Thus, the questions emphasize three different aspects of the problem. The first stresses the value of an idea, the second explores a possible effect, and the third examines the practicality of a proposed solution. Research shows that people often think something is a good idea, but do not think it would work. Another related problem is how respondents might interpret the words *limit* and *curtail.* To some, they may refer to a total ban on handguns, while others may think the words suggest that all guns should be kept away from people with criminal records.

Avoid Biased Wording

Questionnaires should avoid questions that use highly charged words to elicit a particular response. Such a question was used by Republican Party pollsters who asked respondents whether they agreed or disagreed that "We should stop *excessive* legal claims, *frivolous* lawsuits, and *overzealous* lawyers." Not surprisingly, an overwhelming majority of the respondents agreed.

Such statements and questions, in a survey, are indications that "advocacy research" is being conducted. That is, the questionnaire is intentionally skewed to promote a cause or product. Such studies tarnish the reputation of legitimate research and make the public increasingly skeptical of any survey results.

Timing and Context

Responses to survey questions are influenced by events, and this should be taken into consideration when reviewing the results of a survey. The public's esteem for an airline, for example, will get lower marks if a survey is conducted just after a plane crash. Intel's corporate reputation took a dip in company surveys just after major news coverage about a flaw in its Pentium microchip.

On the positive side, surveys by Coca-Cola about its reputation and corporate citizenship showed very favorable public attitudes just after its massive investment in the Atlanta Olympic Games.

Large organizations such as Exxon Mobil, General Electric, and AT&T counterbalance the effects of one-time events by conducting quarterly surveys. Called *benchmarking,* this is discussed in Chapter 9.

Political Correctness

Another problem with questionnaire design involves questions that tend to elicit the "correct" response. This is also called a *courtesy bias.* Respondents choose answers that won't offend the interviewer and reflect mainstream thinking. Surveys, for example, show that 80 percent of Americans consider themselves "environmentalists." As skeptics point out, however, would anyone admit that he or she was not concerned about the environment?

Those conducting employee surveys also fall into the "courtesy" trap by posing such questions as "How much of each newsletter do you read?" or "How well do you like the column by the president?" Employees may never read the newsletter and think the column is ridiculous, but they know the "correct" answer should be that they read the "entire issue" and the column is "excellent."

Researchers try to avoid the "politically correct" answers by making questionnaires confidential and promising anonymity to people who are interviewed. Because employees often perceive the public relations department to be part of management, it is often best to employ an outside research firm to conduct employee surveys.

The Answer Categories

Answer categories can skew a questionnaire. It is important that answer choices are provided to cover a range of opinions. A national polling organization several years ago asked the question "How much confidence do you have in business corporations?" but provided only the following answer categories: (*a*) a great deal, (*b*) only some, and (*c*) none at all. A large gap exists between "a great deal" and the next category, "only some." Such categories invariably skew the results to show very little confidence in business. A better list of answers might have been (*a*) a great deal, (*b*) quite a lot, (*c*) some, (*d*) very little, and (*e*) none. Perhaps an even better approach would be to provide the answer categories (*a*) above average, (*b*) average, and (*c*) below average. The psychological distance between the three choices is equal, and there is less room for respondent interpretation of what "quite a lot" means.

In general, "yes or no" questions are not very good for examining respondents' perceptions and attitudes. A "yes" or "no" answer provides little feedback on the strength or weakness of a respondent's opinion. A question such as "Do you agree with the company's policy of requiring drug testing for all new employees?" can be answered by "yes" or "no," but more useful information would be obtained by setting up a Likert-type scale: (*a*) Strongly agree, (*b*) Agree, (*c*) Undecided, (*d*) Disagree, and (*e*) Strongly disagree. These types of answers enable the surveyor to probe the depth of feeling among respondents, and may serve as guidelines for management in making major changes or just fine-tuning the existing policy.

Another way of designing a numerical scale in order to pinpoint a respondent's beliefs or attitudes is to use, for example, a 5-point scale. Such a scale might look like this.

> **Question:** How would you evaluate the company's efforts to keep you informed about job benefits? Please circle one of the following numbers ("1" being a low rating and "5" being a high rating).

The advantage of numerical scales is that medians and means can be easily calculated. In the previous example, the average from all respondents might be 4.25, which indicates that employees think the company does keep them informed about job benefits but that there is still room for communication improvement.

Questionnaire Guidelines

Here are some general guidelines for the construction of questionnaires:

1. Decide what kinds of information are needed and in what detail.

2. State the objectives of the survey in writing.

3. Decide which group will receive the questionnaire.

4. Decide on the size of the sample.

5. State the purpose of the survey and guarantee anonymity.

6. Use close-ended (multiple-choice) answers as much as possible. Respondents find it easier and less time-consuming to check answers than compose them in an open-ended (essay) questionnaire.

7. Design the questionnaire in such a way that answers can be easily coded for statistical analysis.

8. Strive to make the questionnaire no more than 25 questions. Long questionnaires "put people off" and reduce the number of responses.

9. Use categories when asking questions about education, age, and income. People are more willing to answer when a category or range is used. For example, what category best describes your age? (*a*) Under 25, (*b*) 26 to 40, etc.

10. Use simple, familiar words. Readability should be appropriate for the group being sampled. At the same time, don't "talk down" to respondents.

11. Avoid ambiguous words and phrases that may confuse the respondent.

12. Edit out leading questions that suggest a specific response or bias an answer.

13. Remember context and placement of questions. One question close to another can influence response to the later question.

14. Provide space at the end of the questionnaire for respondents' comments and observations. This allows them to provide additional information or elaboration that may not have been covered in the main body of the questionnaire.

15. Pretest the questions for understanding and possible bias. Representatives of the proposed sampling group should read the questionnaire and make comments for possible improvement.

WAYS OF REACHING RESPONDENTS

A questionnaire is only as good as the delivery system that gets it to respondents. The following sections discuss the pros and cons of (1) mail questionnaires, (2) telephone surveys, (3) personal interviews, and (4) piggyback or omnibus surveys.

Mail Questionnaires

Questionnaires may be used in a variety of settings. They may be handed out at a manufacturing plant, at a county fair, or even in a bank lobby. Most survey questionnaires, however, are mailed to respondents. There are several reasons for this:

1. Because the researchers have better control as to who receives the questionnaire, they can make sure the survey is representative.

2. Large geographical areas can be covered economically.

3. It is less expensive to administer them than to hire an interviewer to conduct personal interviews.

4. Large numbers of people can be included at minimal cost.

Mail questionnaires have some disadvantages. The biggest is a low response rate. A mail questionnaire by a commercial firm to the general public usually produces a response rate of 1 to 2 percent. If the survey concerns issues affecting the general public, the response rate might be 5 to 20 percent. A much better response rate would be generated, however, if the questionnaire were mailed by an organization to its members. In this case, the response rate may be 30 to 80 percent. The more closely people identify with the organization and the questions, the better the response.

The response rate to a mail questionnaire can be increased, say the experts, if all the guidelines of questionnaire construction are followed. In addition, a researcher should keep the following suggestions in mind:

1. Include a stamped, self-addressed return envelope and a personally signed letter.

2. Provide an incentive. Commercial firms often encourage people to fill out questionnaires by including a token amount of money or a discount coupon.

3. Mail questionnaires by first-class mail. Some research shows that placing special issue stamps on the envelope attracts greater interest than simply using a postage meter.

4. Mail a reminder postcard three or four days later.

5. Do a second mailing (either to nonrespondents or to the entire sample) two or three weeks after the first mailing.

Telephone Surveys

Surveys by telephone, particularly if the survey is locally based, are extensively used by research firms. The telephone survey has several advantages:

1. There is an immediate response or nonresponse.

2. A telephone call is personal. It is effective communication, and it is much cheaper than a personal interview.

3. A phone call is less intrusive than going door to door and interviewing people. Surveys show that many people are willing to talk on the phone for up to 45 minutes but will not stand at a door for more than 5 or 10 minutes.

4. The response rate, if the survey is properly composed and phone interviewers trained, can reach 80 to 90 percent.

The major disadvantage of phone interviews is the difficulty in getting access to everyone's phone number. In many urban areas, a third to half of the numbers are unlisted. Although researchers can let a computer program pick numbers through random-digit dialing, this method is not as effective as actually knowing who is being called. Another barrier is convincing respondents that a legitimate poll or survey is being taken. Far too many salespeople have attempted to sell goods by posing as researchers.

Personal Interviews

The personal interview is the most expensive form of research because it requires trained staff and travel. If travel within a city is involved, a trained interviewer can often interview only eight or ten people a day—and salaries and transportation costs make it expensive. There is also the need for considerable advance work in arranging interviews and appointments and, as previously pointed out, researchers encounter reluctance by residents to admit strangers to their homes.

Personal interviews, on the other hand, can be cost-effective and can generate a wealth of information if the setting is controlled. Many research firms conduct personal interviews at national conventions or trade shows, where there is a concentration of people with similar interests.

The Piggyback Survey

An alternative method of reaching respondents is the *piggyback survey,* also known as the *omnibus survey.* In basic terms, an organization "buys" a question in a national survey conducted by a survey organization such as Gallup or Harris.

For example, General Mills may place one or two questions in a national poll asking respondents what professional athlete they most admire, as a way to find new endorsers for its breakfast foods. In the same survey, the American Cancer Society may place a question asking how the public feels about sporting events sponsored by tobacco companies.

The method is attractive to public relations people for two reasons. One is cost. An organization pays much less to participate in a piggyback poll than to conduct its own survey. A second reason is expertise. Firms such as Gallup or Harris have the skill and organization to do a survey properly and efficiently; few public relations departments or firms do.

Piggyback surveys, however, have limitations. An organization can get only a small snapshot of public opinion with one or two questions, and the subject matter must be relevant to the general public.

Web and e-mail Surveys

The newest way to reach respondents is through electronic communication. One way is to post the questionnaire on the organization's website and ask visitors to answer it online. The advantage is instant reply, with a running tabulation of the results instantly available.

Researchers use several methods to attract respondents to the website, including (1) banner ads announcing the survey on other websites or online networks, (2) e-mailing invitations to a target audience, (3) telephoning individuals with an invitation to participate, and (4) sending a postal card. The major disadvantage of a Web survey is how to control the exact characteristics of the respondents, since a website is accessible to virtually anyone with a computer and a modem.

If reaching the exact target audience is important, another approach is the e-mailed survey, sent to a list of known respondents. Organizations can compile e-mail lists of clients or customers, but it's also now possible to purchase e-mail address lists from a variety of sources.

CASE PROBLEM

Universal Manufacturing Corporation is located in a midwestern city of 500,000 people. Its 6000 employees make it one of the largest employers in the country, and the company has been in its present location for the past 50 years. Despite this record, management believes that the company doesn't have a strong identity and visibility in the community.

The director of public relations is asked to prepare a new public relations plan for the coming fiscal year. She recommends that the company first do research to determine exactly what its image is in the community.

If you were the public relations director, what informal methods of research would you use? What more formal research methods could be used? What kinds of information about the company's image should be researched?

QUESTIONS FOR REVIEW AND DISCUSSION

1. Why is research important in public relations work?

2. What kinds of questions should a person ask before formulating a research design?

3. Name at least five ways to use research in public relations.

4. How can survey research be used as a publicity tool?

5. Name at least five informal research methods.

6. What are online databases and how are they used?

7. How can the Internet and World Wide Web be used as research tools?

8. What is the procedure for organizing and conducting a focus group? What are the pros and cons of using focus groups?

9. What is an intercept interview?

10. What is the difference between probability (random) and nonprobability samples?

11. What guidelines should be followed when releasing the results of a survey to the media and the public?

12. What percentage margin of error is associated with various sample sizes? What size samples are usually adequate for public relations work?

13. Name at least five guidelines that should be followed when preparing a survey questionnaire.

14. What are the pros and cons of mail questionnaires, telephone surveys, personal interviews, piggyback survey, and Web/e-mail surveys.

7

Program Planning

Preview

This chapter describes how to organize a well-planned public relations campaign, step-by-step, and how planning applies to issues management.

Topics covered in the chapter include:
* The value of planning
* Systematic approaches to planning
* Elements of a program plan
    Situation
    Objectives
    Audience
    Strategy
    Tactics
    Calendar/Timetable
    Budget
    Evaluation
* Issues management planning

THE VALUE OF PLANNING

The second step in the public relations process, after research, is program planning. Before any public relations activity can be implemented, it is essential that considerable thought be given to what should be done and in what sequence to accomplish an organization's objectives.

A good public relations program should be an effective tool to support an organization's business, marketing, and communications objectives. As Larry Werner, executive vice president of Ketchum public relations, points out, "No longer are we simply in the business of putting press releases out; we're in the business of solving business problems through communications."

In other words, public relations planning should be strategic. As Glen Broom and David Dozier say in their text, *Using Public Relations Research,* "Strategic planning is deciding where you want to be in the future (the goal) and how to get there (the strategies). It sets the organization's direction proactively, avoiding 'drift' and routine repetition of activities." A practitioner must think about a situation, analyze what can be done about it, creatively conceptualize the appropriate strategies and tactics, and determine how the results will be measured. Planning also involves the coordination of multiple methods—news releases, special events, press kits, news conferences, media interviews, brochures, newsletters, speeches, and so on—to achieve specific results.

Paying attention to systematic planning prevents haphazard, ineffective communication. Having a blueprint of what is to be done and how it will be executed makes programs more effective and public relations more valuable to the organization.

APPROACHES TO PLANNING

Planning is like putting together a jigsaw puzzle. Research, discussed in Chapter 6, provides the various pieces. Next it is necessary to arrange the pieces so that a coherent design, or picture, emerges. The best planning is systematic, the process of gathering information, analyzing it, and creatively applying it for the specific purpose of attaining an objective.

Management by Objective (MBO)

One popular approach is a process called *management by objective (MBO).* In other words, the idea is to formulate a strategy that will accomplish an organization's specific objective. MBO provides focus and direction for this type of thinking. According to Robert E. Simmons, author of *Communication Campaign Management,* the use of MBO in planning ensures the ". . . production of relevant messages and establishes criteria against which campaign results can be measured."

Norman R. Nager and T. Harrell Allen, in their book *Public Relations Management by Objectives,* discuss nine basic MBO steps that can help a practitioner conceptualize everything from a simple news release to a multifaceted communications program. The steps, adapted from their book, are as follows:

1. *Client/Employer Objectives.* What is the purpose of the communication and how does it promote or achieve the objectives of the organization? Specific objectives such as "to make consumers aware of the product's high quality" are more meaningful than "to make people aware of the product."

2. *Audience/Publics.* Who exactly should be reached with the message, and how can that audience help achieve the organization's objectives? What are the characteristics of the

audience, and how can demographic information be used to structure the message? The primary audience for a campaign to encourage carpooling consists of people who regularly drive to work, not the general public.

3. *Audience Objectives.* What is it that the audience wants to know, and how can the message be tailored to audience self-interest? Consumers are more interested in how a new computer will increase their productivity than in how it works.

4. *Media Channels.* What is the appropriate channel for reaching the audience, and how can multiple channels (news media, brochures, special events, and direct mail) reinforce the message among key publics? An ad may be best for making consumers aware of a new product, but a news release may be better for conveying consumer information about the product.

5. *Media Channel Objectives.* What is the media gatekeeper looking for in a news angle, and why would a particular publication be interested in the information? A community newspaper is primarily interested in a story with a local angle.

6. *Sources and Questions.* What primary and secondary sources of information are required to provide a factual base for the message? What experts should be interviewed? What database researches should be conducted? A quote from a project engineer about a new technology is better than a quote from the marketing vice president.

7. *Communication Strategies.* What environmental factors will affect the dissemination and acceptance of the message? Are the target publics hostile or favorably disposed to the message? What other events or pieces of information negate or reinforce the message? A campaign to conserve water is more salient if there has been a recent drought.

8. *Essence of the Message.* What is the planned communication impact on the audience? Is the message designed merely to inform or is it designed to change attitudes and behavior? Telling people about the value of physical fitness is different from telling them how to achieve it.

9. *Nonverbal Support.* How can photographs, graphs, films, and artwork clarify and visually enhance the written message? Bar graphs or pie charts are easier to understand than columns of numbers.

ELEMENTS OF A PROGRAM PLAN

Writing a plan for a public relations program is nothing more than preparing a document identifying what is to be done and how to accomplish it. By preparing such a plan, either as a brief outline or an extensive document, the practitioner can make certain that all the elements have been properly considered and that everyone involved understands the "big picture."

It is common practice for public relations firms to prepare a program plan for client approval and possible modification before implementing it. At that time, both the public relations firm and the client reach a mutual understanding of the objectives and how to accomplish them. Public relations departments of organizations also map out a particular campaign or show the department's plans for the coming year.

Observance of the 100th anniversary of the automobile was an event created by the automobile industry and the Detroit Convention & Visitors Bureau to promote American-made automobiles and attract visitors to Detroit, "the Motor City." Display of early automobiles, such as this Packard, attracted crowds. Note the hand crank, small tires, and steering wheel on the right-hand side.

Although there can be some variation, public relations plans include eight basic elements. They are:

- Situation

- Objectives

- Audience

- Strategy

- Tactics

- Calendar/Timetable

- Budget

- Evaluation

The following sections will elaborate on these elements and give examples from campaigns that received PRSA Silver Anvil awards for excellence.

PR Casebook

The 100th Anniversary of Jell-O

A public relations plan contains eight basic elements. The following is an outline of a plan that Kraft Foods and its public relations firm, Hunter & Associates, developed for Jell-O's 100th anniversary celebration.

SITUATION

- Sales of this famous dessert were flat. Brand research shows Jell-O, on the eve of its 100th anniversary celebration, was not top-of-mind with consumers, who were moving to "newer" desserts. Research in company archives provided extensive historical information and graphics about the use and promotion of Jell-O through the years.

OBJECTIVES

- Increase brand awareness in order to increase sales.
- Generate widespread awareness of Jell-O's 100th anniversary in high-profile media.

TARGET AUDIENCE

- Current and lapsed Jell-O consumers; women, aged 25–44, with families.

STRATEGIES

- Use the nostalgic appeal of this brand to capture major media interest.
- Develop many story angles around three key messages for a broad range of media.
- Introduce a new Jell-O product to convey the idea that the brand is still in sync with the times.
- Involve LeRoy, NY, where Jell-O was invented, in the anniversary celebration.

- Involve Kraft Food employees with anniversary celebrations at each plant and corporate location.
- Generate stories emphasizing three key messages: (1) Jell-O is fun, (2) Jell-O is contemporary, and (3) Jell-O is an American and Canadian icon.

TACTICS

- Host gala event with Bill Cosby, Jell-O spokesperson, as master of ceremonies.
- Introduce new flavor—Champagne.
- Publish new cookbook.
- Open new museum and tour exhibits around the country.
- Use Jell-O's hometown, LeRoy (NY), to host a Jell-O Jubilee.
- Establish a new website.
- Provide print and broadcast media with press kits that include historical backgrounders and artwork.

CALENDAR

- 18 months for entire campaign.
- Three months for research, planning.
- Four months for preparing press kits, media lists, etc.
- Eleven months of scheduled events and news releases at quarterly intervals.

(continued)

Situation

Valid objectives cannot be set without a clear understanding of the situation that led to the conclusion that a public relations program was needed.

PR Casebook

The 100th Anniversary of Jell-O, *continued*

First Quarter—Jell-O celebrates its 100th anniversary.
Second Quarter—Champagne flavor introduced, cookbook promoted.
Third Quarter—Jell-O museum opens and begins touring the nation.
Fourth Quarter—Jell-O builds new float for Macy's Thanksgiving Parade.

BUDGET

• $450,000 for 18 months.

EVALUATION

• Brand awareness was established through extensive media coverage. Research showed 6617 positive stories, 7893 minutes of TV time, 101 minutes of radio time. This included extensive stories in the New York *Times,* inclusion of Jell-O in a Jay Leno monologue, and Jell-O featured on Oprah Winfrey's Mother's Day Special.

• Survey research showed 48 percent of respondents heard about the anniversary from television, while another 37 percent found out about it from newspapers or magazines.

• Sales of Jell-O increased more than 5 percent from the previous year.

Three kinds of situations often dictate the conduct of a public relations program. They are (1) the organization must conduct a remedial program to overcome a problem or situation that negatively affects the organization, (2) the organization needs to conduct a specific one-time project, and (3) the organization wants to reinforce an ongoing effort to preserve reputation and public support.

Loss of market share and declining sales often require a remedial program. Mack Trucks, for example, initiated an extensive public relations campaign after seeing its share of market decline from 21 percent to less than 9 percent in a 10-year period. Other organizations launch such campaigns to change public perceptions. The Turkish government conducted an extensive tourism campaign designed to combat negative public perceptions that the country was "uncivilized" and an "underdeveloped, Third-World Middle Eastern country."

One-time, specific events often lead to public relations programs. One such campaign was for the grand opening of San Antonio's new public library. It was important to plan a celebration that showcased the facility as an educational, cultural, and entertainment resource for everyone. The introduction of Microsoft's Windows 95 computer program was also a one-time event; it required a program plan that covered 20 months of prelaunch activities.

In the third situation, program plans are initiated to preserve and develop customer or public support. Department 56, a leading designer and manufacturer of miniature lighted village collectibles, already had a successful business but wanted new customers. Its public relations program to accomplish this included distribution of brochures on home decoration for the Christmas holidays and participation by its dealers in local efforts to decorate Ronald McDonald houses.

In a program plan, relevant research often is included as part of the situation. In the case of Department 56, consumer market analysis revealed a strong link between consumers interested in home decorating and those involved in collecting. Microsoft found in focus groups that consumers would respond favorably to messages about a "faster and easier" computing experience. In the Turkish campaign, research showed little public awareness of Turkey as a European travel destination, and a content analysis of press clippings disclosed a large percentage of negative stereotypes. Other research portrayed the typical American traveler to Turkey as sophisticated, 40-plus years old, with an income of at least $50,000.

Such research provides the foundation for setting program objectives and shaping other elements of the program plan.

Objectives

Once the situation or problem is understood, the next step is to establish objectives for the program. A stated objective should be evaluated by asking (1) does it really address the situation? (2) is it realistic and achievable? and (3) can success be measured in meaningful terms?

An objective is usually stated in terms of program outcomes instead of inputs. Or, put another way, objectives should not be the "means" but the "end." A poor objective, for example, is "generate publicity for a new product." Publicity is not an "end" in itself. The actual objective is to "create consumer awareness about a new product." This is accomplished by such tactics as news releases, special events, and brochures.

It is particularly important that public relations objectives complement and reinforce the organization's objectives. Professor David Dozier of San Diego State University expressed the point well in a *Public Relations Review* article: "The prudent and strategic selection of public relations goals and objectives linked to organizational survival and growth serves to justify the public relations program as a viable management activity."

Basically there are two kinds of objectives: informational and motivational.

Informational Objectives. A large percentage of public relations plans is designed primarily to expose audiences to information and to increase awareness of an issue, an event, or a product. The five objectives of public relations activity will be discussed in Chapter 8. The first two of these—message exposure and accurate dissemination of messages—are the most common. Many communication and marketing professionals believe the major criteria for public relations effectiveness are (1) increase in public awareness, and (2) delivery of key messages.

Some examples of informational objectives are:

Mack Trucks: "Increase awareness and understanding of Mack highway vehicles and engine technology."

Microsoft: "Create broad-based awareness among all audiences of Windows 95 as a 'must upgrade.'"

National Association of Manufacturers (NAM): "Educate target audiences on the fundamental importance of manufacturing to our nation's current competitiveness and future prosperity."

One difficulty with an informational objective is in measuring how well the objective has been achieved. Public awareness and the extent of education that takes place are somewhat abstract and difficult to quantify. Survey research is often required, as will be explained in Chapter 9; many organizations, however, infer "awareness" by counting the number of media placements. In reality, message exposure doesn't necessarily mean increased public awareness.

Motivational Objectives   Although changing attitudes and influencing behavior are more difficult to accomplish in a public relations campaign, motivational objectives are easier to measure. That's because they are "bottom-line"-oriented and are based on clearly measurable results that can be quantified. This is true whether the goal is an increase in product sales, a sellout crowd for a theatrical performance, or expanded donations to a charitable agency.

Some examples of motivational objectives are:

Mack Trucks: "Increase Mack's market share and support Mack's drive to become a dominant player in the highway truck market."

San Antonio Library: "Increase the number of people visiting the Central Library by 25 percent and the number of materials circulated by at least 50 percent."

M&M's Chocolate Candies: "Build consumer sales and market category share."

Turkish Government Tourism Campaign: "Increase the number of U.S. visitors to Turkey."

A public relations program will often have both informational and motivational objectives. A good example is the Fighting Hunger in Wisconsin campaign. Its objectives were to (1) increase public awareness of hunger in Wisconsin, (2) enlist additional volunteers, and (3) raise more money than in the previous year to support hunger-relief programs around the state.

Objectives, and how to measure the accomplishment of them, will be discussed in Chapter 9 on evaluation.

Audience

Public relations programs should be directed toward specific and defined audiences or publics. Although some campaigns are directed to a "general public," such instances are the exception. Even the M&M's Chocolate Candies national "election" campaign to select a new color (blue) for its famous mix was designed to reach consumers 24 years of age or under.

In other words, public relations practitioners target specific publics within a "general public." This is done through market research that can identify key publics by such demographics as age, income, social strata, education, existing ownership or consumption of specific products, and where people live. Market research, for example, told M&M's Candies that young people were the primary consumers of its product. On a more basic level, a water conservation campaign defines its target audience by geography—people living in a particular city or area.

In many cases, common sense is all that is needed to define adequately a specific public. Take, for example, the Ohio vaccination program for children under the age of 2. The primary audience for the message is parents with young children. Other audiences are pregnant women and medical professionals who treat young children.

The following are examples of how organizations already mentioned defined target audiences:

Mack Trucks: "Licensed Class 6, 7, and 8 truck drivers, truck fleet owners, and 600 Mack dealers."

San Antonio Library: "Citizens of San Antonio."

Turkish Government Tourism Campaign: "Seasoned travelers (40-plus years old, with an income of at least $50,000), consumer travel magazines, tour agents, and travel agents in the primary markets of New York, Chicago, and Los Angeles."

Microsoft Windows 95: "(1) industry-computer manufacturers, software vendors, trade/business press, analysts, (2) consumers who own computers, and (3) corporate customers."

As previously noted, some organizations identify the media as a "public." On occasion, in programs that seek media endorsements or try to change how the media report on an organization or an issue, editors and reporters can become a legitimate "public." In general, however, mass media outlets fall in the category of a "means" to an "end." They are channels to reach defined audiences that need to be informed, persuaded, and motivated.

A thorough understanding of the primary and secondary publics is essential if a program's objectives are to be accomplished. Such knowledge also provides guidance on the selection of appropriate strategies and tactics that would reach these defined audiences.

The manufacturer of the CD-ROM on home improvement, for example, might completely bypass the general press and concentrate on specialized publications in the home improvement and CD-ROM fields. Cost is a driving factor; spending large sums to reach members of the general public on matters in which they have no stake or interest is nonproductive and a waste of money.

Strategy

A strategy statement describes how, in concept, an objective is to be achieved, providing guidelines and themes for the overall program. One general strategy may be outlined, or a program may have several strategies, depending on the objectives and the designated audiences.

The public relations programs for Mack Trucks and Microsoft Windows 95 illustrate the basic concept of formulating and writing a strategy. Note that the strategies listed below are broad statements; specific activities are part of tactics, to be covered in the next section.

Mack Trucks summarized its strategies as follows: "1) build a dominant share-of-voice in the trucking trade media; 2) use proprietary media to reach current and prospective Mack customers and dealers; 3) stimulate product trial through the Bulldog National Test Drive Tour; and 4) further the Mack brand identity through cause-related marketing."

Microsoft's strategies were "1) build momentum and a sense of excitement through press activities designed to explode at launch; 2) communicate the technical superiority and leadership of Windows 95 and its benefits; 3) demonstrate industry momentum and breadth of support; and 4) preempt negative news by refocusing media on positive attributes of Windows 95 throughout the volatile prelaunch period."

Key Messages/Themes   The strategy element of a program plan should state key themes and messages to be reiterated throughout the campaign on all publicity materials. The Ohio immunization program, for example, was based on the concept that parents love their children and want them to be healthy. Thus a key message was to tell parents how important vaccinations were to keep their children out of danger. Carrying out this message was the theme of the campaign, "Project L.O.V.E" with the subhead "Love Our Kids Vaccination Project."

In the Turkish tourism campaign, the strategy of combating "negative stereotypes and lack of knowledge about Turkey . . ." included key messages designed to reinforce historical/cultural sites, natural beauty, upscale accommodations, great shopping, excellent cuisine, ideal weather, and friendly people. In an effort to position Turkey as part of Europe instead of the Middle East, the themes of "Center of World History" and "Where Europe Becomes Exotic" were used.

Tactics

This is the "nuts and bolts" part of the plan that describes, in sequence, the specific activities that put the strategies into operation and help to achieve the stated objectives. Tactics involves using the tools of communication to reach primary and secondary audiences with key messages. Chapters 18 to 21 discuss communication tools in greater detail.

Planning a public relations program requires conferences like this one, at which participants weigh information on such diverse topics as objectives, graphics, media selection, demographics, and timing.

The Tactics of Mack Trucks In many cases, each strategy is supported by specific tactics. In the Mack Truck campaign, the first strategy to build a dominant share-of-voice in the trucking trade media was supported by the following tactics:

• A toll-free number facilitated product literature requests generated through publicity efforts.

• New models of Mack trucks were driven to key trucking publications in various cities for demonstrations and background briefings.

• A press conference for trucking trade editors was held at a major trade show to introduce a new Mack engine.

• A press kit featuring news and features about the company's 95-year history was sent to the trade press.

• News releases were sent regularly to the trade press that promoted new products, major customer orders, and awards earned by the company for product quality.

The second strategy—use proprietary media—was supported by these tactics:

• A 24-page quarterly magazine, *The Bulldog,* was sent to more than 15,000 Mack customers and dealers.

• More than 100 customer testimonials were collected and installed on software for use by Mack sales representatives.

The third strategy—stimulate product trial through the Bulldog National Test Drive Tour—was accomplished by having two fully loaded Mack trucks criss-cross the continent visiting truck stops, Mack dealerships, and key prospective customers.

The fourth strategy—enhance the Mack brand through cause-related marketing—arranged with the U.S. Forest Service to haul America's Christmas tree from California to Washington, D.C. Along the way, the truck stopped at dealerships and distributed toy Bulldogs (the company's trademark) to local Toys for Tots programs. This tactic generated considerable local print and broadcast coverage.

The Tactics of Windows 95 Microsoft also used a number of tactics to support the objectives and strategies in the program to launch Windows 95. Industry support and momentum were generated by establishing almost daily contact with the top 50 trade editors and analysts. In addition, three workshops were organized, each with 200 trade editors and analysts in attendance. The effort helped communicate technical superiority, preempted negative news, and generated a flow of positive publicity.

Microsoft's strategy was also to build a sense of excitement and anticipation among consumers. Some of the major tactics used were:

• Sought extensive media placement of publicity materials, with a concentrated effort to obtain cover articles in consumer and trade publications.

• Used 50,000 consumers in 23 cities to pretest early versions of Windows 95 and coordinated media coverage of their "testimonials."

• Organized a workshop for consumer media at Lincoln Center in New York that focused on the many practical applications of Windows 95.

- Publicized the licensing agreement with the Rolling Stones to use their song, "Start Me Up," as the Windows 95 theme song in a television advertising campaign. The agreement generated extensive media coverage because it was the first time that the Rolling Stones had allowed one of their songs to be used for commercial purposes.

- Arranged for the *Times* of London to be distributed free throughout London on August 24, the day of the Windows 95 launch. The newspaper contained a supplement promoting the wonders of Windows 95.

- Arranged to have the Empire State Building in New York lighted in the colors of Windows 95 on the eve of the product's launch.

- Released Windows 95 at midnight August 24 in various world markets. Retail stores stayed open until midnight, long lines formed, and media around the world covered the "midnight madness."

- Staged a daylong celebration at Microsoft's headquarters with Bill Gates and Jay Leno as hosts. More than 500 media representatives attended.

Calendar/Timetable

The three aspects of timing in a program plan are: (1) deciding when a campaign should be conducted, (2) determining the proper sequence of activities, and (3) compiling a list of steps that must be completed to produce a finished product. All three aspects are important to achieve maximum effectiveness.

The Timing of a Campaign   Program planning should take into account the environmental context of a situation and the time when key messages are most meaningful to the intended audience. A campaign to encourage carpooling, for example, might be more successful if it follows a major price rise in gasoline or a government report that traffic congestion has reached gridlock proportions.

Some subjects are seasonal. Department 56, the designer and manufacturer of miniature lighted village collectibles and other holiday giftware, timed the major bulk of its campaign in November to take advantage of the Christmas holidays, when there was major interest in its product lines. Charitable agencies, such as the Wisconsin Project on Hunger, also gear their campaigns around Christmas, when there is increased interest in helping the unfortunate.

By the same token, strawberry producers increase public relations efforts in May and June, when a crop comes to market and the stores have large supplies of the fruit. Similarly, a software program on income tax preparation attracts the most audience interest in February and March, just before the April 15 filing deadline. In another situation, a vendor of a software program designed to handle personal finances launched a public relations/marketing program in January. The timing was based on research indicating that people put "getting control of personal finances" high on their list of New Year's resolutions.

Other kinds of campaigns depend less on environmental or seasonal context. The Mack Truck and Microsoft campaigns, for example, could be conducted at almost anytime.

Focus on Ethics

Should Public Relations Writers Join In?

Microsoft, under attack from the U.S. Department of Justice and its major competitors for monopolistic business practices, asked a public relations firm for a plan to tell its side of the story and influence public opinion. One suggestion from the firm was for Microsoft to ask influential supporters to write op-ed pieces and letters to the editor in states whose regulators were also considering possible antitrust violations.

A copy of this memo was leaked to the Los Angeles *Times* and an article appeared accusing Microsoft of secretly trying to place articles or editorials. A Washington *Post* columnist also called it, "a phony grass-roots campaign" in the same leagues as the tactics used by "Big Tobacco." Other critics accused Microsoft of unethical behavior. On the other side, others wondered what the big fuss is about. They say it's standard practice for PR firms to solicit articles from opinion leaders and even assist in the writing of them.

What do you think? Should such an idea be a legitimate part of a public relations plan? Why or why not?

Scheduling of Tactics   The second aspect of timing is the scheduling and sequencing of various tactics or activities. A typical pattern is to concentrate effort at the beginning of a campaign, when a number of tactics are implemented. This launch phase of a campaign, much like that of a rocket, takes a burst of activity just to break the awareness barrier. After the campaign has achieved orbit, however, less energy and fewer activities are required to maintain momentum.

To further the rocket analogy, public relations campaigns are often the first stage of an integrated marketing communications program. Once public relations has created awareness and customer anticipation of a new product, the second stage may be an advertising and direct-mail campaign. Microsoft used this approach for Windows 95.

Compiling a Calendar   An integral part of timing is advance planning. A video news release, a press kit, or a brochure often takes weeks and months of work to prepare. Arrangements for a special event also take considerable time. Practitioners must take into account the deadlines of publications. Monthly periodicals, for example, frequently need information at least six to eight weeks before publication. A popular talk show may book guests three or four months in advance.

In other words, the public relations professional must think ahead to make things happen in the right sequence at the right time. One way to achieve this goal is to compile timelines and charts that list the necessary steps and their required completion dates.

Shown in Figure 7.1 is an excerpt from a timeline the Charles Schwab Company used when it planned a "town hall" meeting for its employees.

Gantt Charts are also used for planning purposes. Essentially, the format is a column matrix that has two sides. The left side has a vertical list of activities that must be accomplished, and the top has a horizontal line of days, weeks, or months. Figure 7.2 is a simplified example.

Materials Project Plan

Week of October 11-15

Date	Item/Issue	Contact	Notes
Mon. 10/11	Broch copy due	H. Cameron	Deliver to B.Ross
	Save the Date design due	B. Reuter	Needs approval by IPS
Tues. 10/12	Brochure design due	B. Reuter	
Wed. 10/13	Initial poster design due	B. Reuter	
	Save the Date copy final	D. Cohn	
Thurs. 10/14	Revisions to brochure/ Poster	B. Reuter	Review with Dave
	Save the Date disk due	B. Reuter	Deliver to T. Jones for producti
Fri. 10/15	Revised brochure/poster due	B. Reuter	Incorporate DSP revisions

Figure 7.1
This chart shows part of the schedule required to produce a public relations project. Adherence to such schedules is essential.

Budget

No program plan is complete without a budget. Both clients and employers ask, "How much will this program cost?" In many cases, the reverse approach is taken. Organizations establish an amount they can afford, then ask the public relations staff or firm to write a program plan that reflects the amount allocated.

Some budgets of campaigns already discussed were as follows:

Mack Trucks: $204,000 annually, plus expenses.

M&M Chocolate Candies: $555,000.

Department 56: $160,000 for 500,000 brochures, $85,000 for a video seminar, and $24,250 for a satellite tour. Fees for event planning and media relations activities by public relations firm, $100,000.

Turkish Government Tourism: $650,000 for 15-month program: $450,000 in public relations firm fees and $200,000 in expenses.

A budget can be divided into two categories: staff time and out-of-pocket (OOP) expenses. Staff and administrative time usually takes the lion's share of any public relations budget. In a $100,000 campaign done by a public relations firm, for example, it is not unusual for 70 percent to be salaries and administrative fees. Information about how public relations firms charge fees is in Chapter 5.

IIT PR Timeline

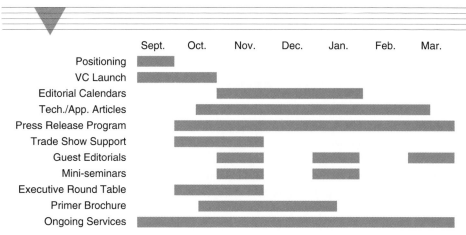

Figure 7.2
A typical Gantt chart.

One method of budgeting is to use two columns. The left column will list the staff cost for writing a pamphlet or compiling a press kit. The right column will list the actual OOP for having the pamphlet or press kit designed, printed, and delivered. Internal public relations staffs, whose members are on the payroll, often complete only the OOP expenses. It is good practice to allocate about 10 percent of the budget for contingencies, or unexpected costs.

Budgets, in a program plan, are usually estimated on the basis of experience and requests from vendors for estimates. After the program is completed, part of the evaluation (see Chapter 9) is to compile a form that shows estimated expenses versus actual expenses.

Evaluation

The evaluation element of a plan relates directly back to the stated objectives for the program. As discussed earlier, objectives must be measurable in some way to show clients and employers that the program accomplished its purpose.

Consequently, evaluation criteria should be realistic, credible, specific, and in line with client or employer expectations. The evaluation section of a program plan should restate the objectives, then name the evaluation methods to be used.

Evaluation of an informational objective often entails a compilation of news clips and an analysis of how often key message points were mentioned. Other methods might be to determine how many brochures were distributed, or the estimated number of viewers who saw a video news release. Motivational objectives are often measured and evaluated by increases in sales or market share, the number of people who called an 800 number for more information, or by benchmark surveys that measure people's perceptions before and after a campaign.

Chapter 9 discusses evaluation techniques and refers to many of the campaigns mentioned here.

PLANNING IN ISSUES MANAGEMENT

We have been discussing the step-by-step progression of planning for all types of public relations programs. Now we will see how planning can be applied in an area of practice called *issues management.*

The interaction of organizations with various elements of society has led to the emergence of issues management as an important part of effective public relations and strategic planning. Essentially, issues management is a proactive and systematic approach to (1) predict problems, (2) anticipate threats, (3) minimize surprises, (4) resolve issues, and (5) prevent crises. Martha Lauzen, a professor at San Diego State University, says effective issue management requires two-way communications, formal environmental scanning, and active sense-making strategies.

Another definition of issues management has been formulated by Coates, Coates, Jarratt, and Heinz in their book *Issues Management: How You Can Plan, Organize, and Manage for the Future.* They say, "Issues management is the organized activity of identifying emerging trends, concerns, or issues likely to affect an organization in the next few years and developing a wider and more positive range of organizational responses toward the future."

The basic concept of issues management is proactive planning. Philip Gaunt and Jeff Ollenburger, writing in *Public Relations Review,* say, "Issues management is proactive in that it tries to identify issues and influence decisions regarding them before they have a detrimental effect on a corporation."

Gaunt and Ollenburger contrast this approach with crisis management (see Chapter 8) that is essentially reactive in nature. They note, "Crisis management tends to be more reactive dealing with an issue after it becomes public knowledge and affects the company." In other words, active planning and prevention through issues management can often mean the difference between a noncrisis and a crisis. Or, as one practitioner put it, the difference between little or no news coverage and a page one headline. This point is particularly relevant since studies show (see Chapter 8) that the majority of organizational crises are self-inflicted because management ignored early warning signs.

The issue about the exploitation of women and children in Third-World sweatshops to make clothes for American companies, for example, simmered for several years before it finally broke into headlines after a worker activist group finally accused television celebrity Kathie Lee Gifford of using "sweatshop" labor to make her clothing line for Wal-Mart Stores. (See Chapter 17.)

Such revelations put the entire U.S. garment industry on the defensive. David Birenbaum, a consultant to the garment industry, wrote in the *Wall Street Journal* that the issue of using cheap Third-World labor was not really new, but the public reaction to such practices was different. He wrote in an op-ed article, "What's changed is that for the first time human rights concerns could become a major marketing issue. . . . More and more importers are now considering safety and other conditions in Asian factories. Few can afford not to, because all it takes is one disaster to damage a label's reputation."

All the publicity and public outrage, however, might have been avoided if the various clothing and athletic shoe manufacturers had paid attention to the concepts of issues management.

Public relations counselors W. Howard Chase and Barrie L. Jones were among the first practitioners to specialize in issues management. They defined the process as five basic steps: (1) issue identification, (2) issue analysis, (3) strategy options, (4) action plan, and (5) evaluation of results. The following is an illustration of how these steps could have been used by the garment industry.

Issue Identification   Organizations should track the alternative press, mainstream media, online chat groups, and the newsletters of activist groups to learn what issues and concerns are being discussed. Of particular importance is establishing a trendline of coverage. Concern about the working conditions of women and children in the garment industry began showing up as an emerging issue several years before the Kathie Lee Gifford exposé.

Issue Analysis   Once an emerging issue is identified, the next step is assessment of its potential impact on the organization. Another consideration is whether the organization is vulnerable on the issue. Are its policies exploitative? Is the company being ethical and socially responsible by turning a blind eye to violations of human rights in the interest of high-profit margins? Can revelations about sweatshop conditions affect sales or damage the label's reputation?

Strategy Options   If the company decides that the emerging issue is potentially damaging, the next step is to consider what to do about it. One option might be to set higher standards for foreign contractors seeking the company's business. Another option: work with human rights groups to monitor possible violations in foreign factories that produce the company's products. A third option might be to establish a new policy that would assure Third-World workers decent pay and health benefits. The pros and cons of each option are weighed against what is most practical and economical for the company.

Action Plan   Once a policy is decided, the fourth step is to communicate it to all interested publics. These may include consumers, the U.S. Department of Labor, labor unions and worker activist groups, company employees, and the financial community. The action may be an opportunity to use the new policy as a marketing tool among consumers who make buying decisions based on a company's level of social responsibility.

Evaluation   With the new policy in place and communicated, the final step is to evaluate the results. Has news coverage been positive and favorable? Have activist groups called off boycotts of your product? Have the working conditions for women and children in the factories improved? Is the company being positioned as an industry leader? Have public perceptions of the company and the industry improved? If the company has acted soon enough, perhaps the greatest measurement of success is avoiding the media coverage that occurs when the problem eventually becomes a crisis.

How issues and situations become crises is discussed further in Chapter 8.

CASE PROBLEM

Sunshine Cafe, a chain of coffee houses, did some market research and found that college students would be an excellent audience to reach. To this end, Sunshine Cafe contacts your public relations firm and asks that you develop a comprehensive plan to (1) create brand awareness among college students, and (2) increase walk-in business at their local stores in college towns.

Using the eight-point planning outline described in this chapter, write a public relations program for Sunshine Cafe. You should consider a variety of communication tools, including events on a campus. However, no money is allocated for advertising.

QUESTIONS FOR REVIEW AND DISCUSSION

1. Why is planning so important in the public relations process?

2. What is MBO and how can it be applied to public relations planning?

3. Name the eight elements of a program plan.

4. Name the three situations that often require a public relations campaign.

5. Explain the difference between an "informational" objective and a "motivational" objective.

6. Should a practitioner define an audience as "general public"? Why or why not?

7. What is the difference between a "strategy" and an "objective"?

8. Review Microsoft's strategies and tactics for the introduction of Windows 95. Do you think it was a well-conceived campaign?

9. Why are timing and scheduling so important in a public relations campaign?

10. What is the largest expense in a campaign conducted by a public relations firm?

11. What are the five steps in the issues management process?

12. How can effective issues management prevent organizational crises?

Communication

8

Preview

In this chapter, the objective is to explain the basic process of communication, the theories that underlie it, and its techniques, in order to help students formulate and disseminate effective messages.

Topics covered in this chapter include:
* A public relations perspective
* Paying attention to the message
* Understanding the message
* Believing the message
* Remembering the message
* Acting on the message
* Crisis communication, with case studies
* Risk communication

THE GOALS OF COMMUNICATION

The third step in the public relations process, after research and planning, is communication. This step, also called *execution,* is the most visible part of public relations work.

In a public relations program, as pointed out in Chapter 7, *communication is the implementation of a decision,* the process and the means by which *objectives* are achieved. A program's *strategies and tactics* may take the form of news releases, news conferences, special events, brochures, speeches, bumper stickers, newsletters, rallies, posters, and the like.

The goals of the communication process are to inform, persuade, motivate, or achieve mutual understanding. To be an effective communicator, a person must have basic knowledge of (1) what constitutes communication and how people receive messages, (2) how people process information and change their perceptions, and (3) what kinds of media and communication tools are most appropriate for a particular message.

Concerning the last point, Kirk Hallahan of Colorado State University makes the point that today's communication revolution has given public relations professionals a full range of communication tools and media, and the traditional approach of simply obtaining publicity in the mass media—newspapers, magazines, radio, and television—is no longer sufficient, if it ever was. He writes, "PR program planners need to reexamine their traditional approaches to the practice and think about media *broadly* and *strategically*. PR media planners must now address some of the same questions that confront advisers. What media best meet a program's objectives? How can media be combined to enhance program effectiveness? What media are most efficient to reach key audience?"

Hallahan's concept of an integrated public relations media model, which outlines five categories of media, is shown in Figure 8.3. Many of these media are discussed in Part 5, Tactics, at the end of this book.

A Public Relations Perspective

A number of variables must be considered when planning a message on behalf of an employer or client.

One is the content of the proposed message. Patrick Jackson, editor of *PR Reporter* and a senior counselor, says the communicator should ask whether the proposed message is (1) appropriate, (2) meaningful, (3) memorable, (4) understandable, and (5) believable to the prospective recipient. "Many a wrongly directed or unnecessary communication has been corrected or dropped by using a screen like this," Jackson says.

In addition to examining the proposed content, a communicator should determine exactly what objective is sought through the communication. James Grunig, professor of public relations at the University of Maryland, lists five possible objectives for a communicator:

1. *Message exposure.* Public relations personnel provide materials to the mass media and disseminate other messages through controlled media such as newsletters and brochures. Intended audiences are exposed to the message in various forms.

2. *Accurate dissemination of the message.* The basic information, often filtered by media gatekeepers, remains intact as it is transmitted through various media.

3. *Acceptance of the message.* Based on its view of reality, the audience not only retains the message but accepts it as valid.

4. *Attitude change.* The audience not only believes the message but makes a verbal or mental commitment to change behavior as a result of the message.

5. *Change in overt behavior.* Members of the audience actually change their current behavior or purchase the product and use it.

Grunig says that most public relations experts usually aim at the first two objectives, exposure to the message and accurate dissemination. The last three objectives depend in large part on a mix of variables—predisposition to the message, peer reinforcement, feasibility of the suggested action, and environmental context, to name a few. The first two objectives are easier to ascertain than attitude change (see Chapter 10).

Although the communicator cannot always control the outcome of a message, researchers recognize that effective dissemination is the beginning of the process that leads to opinion change and adoption of products or services. Therefore it is important to review all components of the communication process.

David Therkelsen, director of marketing for the American Red Cross in St. Paul, Minnesota, succinctly outlines the process:

> To be successful, a message must be *received* by the intended individual or audience. It must get the audience's *attention*. It must be *understood*. It must be *believed*. It must be *remembered*. And ultimately, in some fashion, it must be *acted upon*. Failure to accomplish *any* of these tasks means the entire message fails.

Therkelsen appropriately places the emphasis on the audience and what it does with the message. The following sections elaborate on the six elements he enumerates.

RECEIVING THE MESSAGE

Several communication models explain how a message moves from the sender to the recipient. Some are quite complex, attempting to incorporate an almost infinite number of events, ideas, objects, and people that interact on the message, channel, and receiver.

Most communication models, however, incorporate four basic elements. David K. Berlo's model is an example. It has *sender/source (encoder), message, channel,* and *receiver (decoder)*. A fifth element, *feedback* from the receiver to the sender, is now incorporated in modern models of communication.

Mass media researcher Wilbur Schramm's early models (see Figure 8.1) started with a simple communication model (top), but he later expanded the process to include the concept of "shared experience" (middle diagram). The importance of "shared experience" becomes apparent when a highly technical news release about a new computer system causes a local business editor to shake his or her head in bewilderment.

Schramm's third model (bottom) incorporates the idea of continuous feedback. Both the sender and the receiver continually encode, interpret, decode, transmit, and receive information. The loop process also is integral to all models showing the public relations process of research, planning, communication, and evaluation. This concept was illustrated in Chapter 1, which showed public relations as a cyclical process.

The Importance of Two-Way Communication

Another way to think of feedback is two-way communication. One-way communication, from sender to receiver, only disseminates information. Such a monologue is less effective than two-way communication, which establishes a dialogue between sender and receiver.

Grunig goes even further to postulate that the ideal public relations model is two-way symmetrical communication. That is, communication is balanced between the sender and

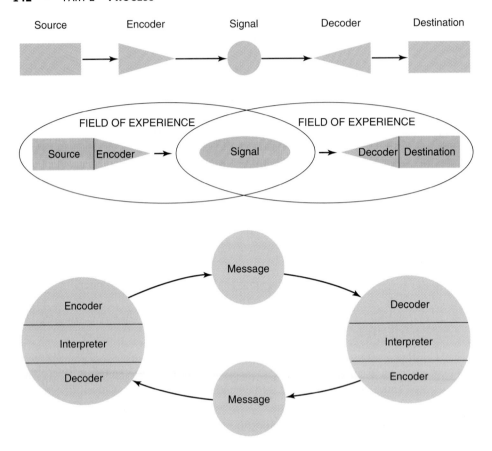

Figure 8.1
These three models (A, B, C) formulated by Wilbur Schramm show the evolution of portraying communication as an interactive process between sender and receiver. Effective communication takes place within a sphere of "shared experience."

the receiver. He says: "In the symmetric model, understanding is the principal objective of public relations, rather than persuasion."

In reality, research shows most organizations have mixed motives when they engage in two-way communication with targeted audiences. Although they may employ dialogue to obtain a better sense of how they can adjust to the needs of an audience, their motive is often asymmetrical—to convince the audience of their point of view through dialogue.

The most effective two-way communication, of course, is two people talking to each other. Small-group discussion is also effective. In both forms the message is fortified by gestures, facial expressions, intimacy, tone of voice, and the opportunity for instant feedback. If the listener asks a question or appears puzzled, the speaker has an instant cue and can rephrase the information or amplify a point.

Barriers to communication tend to mount as one advances to large-group meetings and, ultimately, to the mass media. Organizational materials can reach thousands and, through

PR Insights

A Behavioral Communication Model

The above behavioral communication model, suggests *PR Reporter,* is better than traditional communication models because it forces practitioners to think in terms of what behaviors they are trying to motivate in target publics, rather than what information is being communicated. The process is described as follows:

1. **Awareness.** Salience or relevance is the key to reaching awareness. The purpose of communication here is to create awareness, which is the start of any behavioral process.

2. **Latent readiness.** Either positive or negative readiness to behave in a certain way starts to form, often subconsciously (latently). People get ready to act by accumulating and developing experience, information, word-of-mouth, beliefs, opinions, and emotions.

3. **Triggering event.** The triggering event step gives people a chance to act on their latent readiness. Triggering events may be an election day, a store sale, distribution of a company's annual report, or even a major event announcing a new product or service. Public relations people should build triggering events into their planning: this moves the emphasis from communication to behavior motivation.

4. **Behavior.** Although the ultimate goal is to motivate people to buy something or act in a certain way, they may adopt intermediate behaviors such as requesting more literature, visiting a showroom, or trying the product or idea experimentally.

the mass media, even millions of people at the same time, but the psychological and physical distance between sender and receiver is considerably lengthened. Communication is less effective because the audience no longer is involved with the source. No immediate feedback is possible, and the message may undergo distortion as it passes through mass-media gatekeepers.

Models of communication emphasize the importance of feedback as an integral component of the process. As they implement communication strategies, public relations personnel need to give it careful attention.

PAYING ATTENTION TO THE MESSAGE

Sociologist Harold Lasswell has defined the act of communication as "Who, says what, in which channel, to whom, with what effect?"

Although in public relations much emphasis is given to the formation and dissemination of messages, this effort is wasted if the audience pays no attention. It is therefore important to remember the axiom of Walt Seifert, professor emeritus of public relations at Ohio

State University. He says: "Dissemination does not equal publication, and publication does not equal absorption and action." In other words, "All who receive it won't publish it, and all who read or hear won't understand or act upon it."

Seifert and social psychologists recognize that the majority of an audience at any given time is not particularly interested in a message or in adopting an idea. This doesn't mean, however, that audiences are merely passive receivers of information. Werner Severin and James Tankard, in their text *Communication Theories,* quote one researcher as saying:

> The communicator's audience is not a passive recipient—it cannot be regarded as a lump of clay to be molded by the master propagandist. Rather, the audience is made up of individuals who demand something from the communication to which they are exposed, and who select those that are likely to be useful to them.

This is called the *media uses and gratification theory* of communication. Its basic premise is that the communication process is interactive. The communicator wants to inform and even persuade; the recipient wants to be entertained, informed, or alerted to opportunities that can fulfill individual needs.

In other words, audiences come to messages for very different reasons. People use mass media for such purposes as (1) surveillance of the environment to find out what is happening, locally or even globally, that has some impact on them, (2) entertainment and diversion, (3) reinforcement of their opinions and predispositions, and (4) decision-making about buying a product or service.

Uses and gratification theory assumes that people make highly intelligent choices about which messages require their attention and fulfill their needs. If this is true, as research indicates it is, the public relations communicator must tailor messages that focus on fulfilling audience needs.

One approach is to understand the mental state of the intended audience. Grunig and Hunt, in *Managing Public Relations,* suggest that communication strategies be designed to attract the attention of two kinds of audiences, those who actively seek information and those who passively process information.

Passive audiences may initially pay attention to a message only because it is entertaining and offers a diversion. They can be made aware of the message through brief encounters—with a billboard glimpsed on the way to work, a radio announcement heard in the car, a television advertisement broadcast before a show begins, and information available in a doctor's waiting room. In other words, they use communication channels that can be utilized while they are doing little else.

For this reason, passive audiences need messages that have style and creativity. The person must be lured by photos, illustrations, and catchy slogans into processing information. Press agentry, the dramatic picture, the use of celebrities, radio and television announcements, and events featuring entertainment can make passive audiences aware of a message. The objectives of a communication, therefore, are simply exposure to and accurate dissemination of a message. In most public relations campaigns, communications are designed to reach primarily passive audiences.

A communicator's approach to audiences that actively seek information is different. These people are already at the *interest* stage of the adoption process (discussed later) and seek more sophisticated supplemental information. The tools may include brochures, in-depth newspaper and magazine articles, slide presentations, videotape presentations, symposiums and conferences, major speeches before key groups, and demonstrations at trade shows.

At any given time, of course, the intended audience has passive and active information-seekers in it. It is important, therefore, that multiple messages and a variety of communication tools be used in a full-fledged information campaign.

Public relations personnel have two ways by which to determine strategies. First, research into audience attitudes can give insight into the extent of group interest in, or apathy toward, a new product or idea. Second, more efficient communication can be achieved if the intended audience is segmented as much as possible. After dividing an audience into segments, a practitioner can select the appropriate communication tools.

Other Attention-Getting Concepts

Communicators should think in terms of the five senses—sight, hearing, smell, touch, and taste. Television and film or videotape are effective methods of communication because they engage an audience's senses of sight and hearing. In addition are their attractions of color and movement. Radio, on the other hand, relies on only the sense of hearing. Print media, although capable of communicating a large amount of information in great detail, rely only on sight.

Individuals learn through all five senses, but psychologists estimate that 83 percent of learning is accomplished through sight. Hearing accounts for 11 percent. Fifty percent of what individuals retain consists of what they see and hear. For this reason speakers often use visual aids.

These figures have obvious implications for the public relations practitioner. Any communication strategy should, if possible, include vehicles of communication designed to tap the senses of sight or hearing, or a combination of the two. In other words, a variety of communication tools is needed, including news releases, publicity photos, slide presentations, videotapes, billboards, newsletters, radio announcements, video news releases, media interviews, and news conferences. This multiple approach not only assists learning and retention, discussed later, but provides repetition of a message in a variety of forms that accommodate audience needs.

Other research suggests that audience attention can be generated if the communicator raises a "need" level first. The idea is to "hook" an audience's attention by beginning the message with something that will make its members' lives easier or benefit them in some way. An example is a message from the Internal Revenue Service. It could begin with a reminder about the necessity of filing tax returns on time, but it would get far more audience attention if it opened by urging people to take all the exemptions for which they were eligible. The prospect of paying less tax would be alluring to most people.

UNDERSTANDING THE MESSAGE

Communication is the act of transmitting information, ideas, and attitudes from one person to another. Communication can take place, however, only if the sender and receiver have a common understanding of the symbols being used.

Words are the most common symbols. The degree to which two people understand each other is heavily dependent on their common knowledge of word symbols. Anyone who has traveled abroad can readily attest that very little communication occurs between two people who speak different languages. Even signs translated into English for tourists often lead to some confusing and amusing messages. A brochure for a Japanese hotel, for example, said, "In our hotel, you will be well fed and agreeably drunk. In every room there is a large window offering delightful prospects."

Even if the sender and receiver speak the same language and live in the same country, the effectiveness of their communication depends on such factors as education, social class, regional differences, nationality, and cultural background.

Employee communication specialists are particularly aware of such differences as a multicultural workforce becomes the norm for most organizations. One major factor is the impact of a global economy in which organizations have operations and employees in many countries. A second factor is the increasing multicultural composition of the American work-force. One study says that 85 percent of new entries into the workforce in the year 2000 will be white women, immigrants, African Americans, Hispanics, and Asians. For many of these workers, English will be a second language.

These statistics will require communicators to be better informed about cultural dif-ferences and conflicting values in order to find common ground and build bridges between various groups. At the same time, a major task will be to communicate in clear and simple terms. A national survey by the Educational Testing Service found that 42 million Ameri-can adults fall within the lowest category of literacy. Other studies show that one in eight employees reads at no better than fourth-grade level.

Writing for Clarity

The nature of the audience and its literacy level are important considerations for any com-municator. The key is to produce messages that match, in content and structure, the char-acteristics of the audience.

The Illinois Public Health Department had the right idea when it commissioned a song in rap-music style as one way to inform low-income, poorly educated groups about the dan-

Global PR

Different Worlds of Value Systems

Many theories that explain the communication process are applicable around the world. The application of communication theory, however, is closely tied to the values of a particular culture. A.H. Tobaccowala of Voltas Limited in India makes this observation:

> While galloping modernization and the impact of global value systems will acceler-ate, as of now the idols and heroes of most

people in Asia are not the highly successful wealthy industrialists or the stars of the enter-tainment world or the record breakers in sports. Those who are most honored, admired, and almost worshipped are the Gandhis, the Mandelas, the Mother Theresas, the monks, and the ascetics. This is a world of very different value systems that the West-ern PR person must deal with.

gers of AIDS. The words and music of the "Condom Rag," however, were offensive to elected officials, who cancelled the song.

This example poses the classic dilemma for the expert communicator. Should the message be produced for supervisors, who may be totally different in background and education from the intended audience, or should it be produced with the audience in mind? The obvious answer is the latter, but it is often difficult to convince management of this. One solution is to copy-test all public relations materials on a target audience. This helps convince management—and communicators—that what they like isn't necessarily what the audience wants, needs, or understands.

Another approach is to apply readability and comprehension formulas to materials before they are produced and disseminated. Learning theory makes the case: the simpler the piece of writing, the easier it will be for audiences to understand.

The most widely known readability formula is by Rudolph Flesch. Another is by Barr, Jenkins, and Peterson. Both are based on average sentence length and the number of one-syllable words per 100 words. If a randomly selected sample of 100 words contains 4.2 sentences and 142 syllables, it is ranked at about ninth-grade level. This is the level for which most news releases and daily newspapers strive. In other words, long, complex sentences (more than 19 words) and multisyllable words ("compensation" instead of "pay") reduce comprehension for the average reader.

Audience understanding and comprehension can also be increased by following some of the following concepts.

Use Symbols, Acronyms, and Slogans Clarity and simplicity of message are enhanced by these devices. Each is a form of shorthand that quickly conceptualizes ideas and travels through extended lines of communication.

The world is full of symbols, such as the Christian cross, the Star of David, and the crusading sword of the American Cancer Society. Corporate symbols such as the Mercedes Benz star, the Nike Swoosh, and the multicolored apple of Apple Computer are known throughout the world. The concept is called branding, and corporations invest considerable time and money to make their names and logos become a symbol for quality and service.

A symbol should be unique, memorable, widely recognized, and appropriate. Organizations spend considerable time and energy searching for unique symbols that convey the essence of what they are or hope to be. Considerable amounts of money are then spent on publicizing the symbols and creating meanings for them.

Acronyms also are shorthand for conveying information. An acronym is a word formed from the initial letters of other words. The Group Against Smokers' Pollution goes by the acronym GASP; Juvenile Opportunities in Business becomes JOB. The National Organization for Women has the acronym NOW, which says a great deal about its political priorities.

In many cases, the acronym—because it is short and simple—becomes the common name. The mass media continually use the term AIDS instead of "acquired immune deficiency syndrome." And "UNESCO" is easier to write and say than United Nations Educational, Scientific, and Cultural Organization.

Slogans help condense a concept. Massive advertising and promotion have made "Don't Leave Home Without It" readily identified with American Express. "The Ultimate Driving Machine" is strongly identified with BMW, an acronym for Bavarian Motor Works.

Avoid Jargon   One source of blocked communication is technical and bureaucratic jargon. When delivered to a general audience, it is called *semantic noise* by social scientists. Jargon interferes with the message and impedes the receiver's ability to understand it. An example of a useless news release is the following, which was actually sent to business editors of daily newspapers. This is how it began:

> Versatec, a Xerox Company, has introduced the Graphics Network Processor-SNA (Model 451). The processor, operating as a 377x RJE station, sends and receives EBCDIC or binary data in IMB System Network Architecture (SNA) networks using Synchronous Data Link Control (SDLC) protocol. . . .

This news release may be perfectly appropriate for an engineering publication serving a particular industry, but the information needs to be written in simple terms for the readers of a daily newspaper. A failure to understand the audience means a failure in communication.

Avoid Clichés and Hype Words   Highly charged words with connotative meanings can pose problems, and overuse of clichés and hype words can seriously undermine the credibility of the message.

The *Wall Street Journal,* for example, mocked the business of high-technology public relations with a story titled "High-Tech Hype Reaches New Heights." A reporter analyzed 201 news releases and compiled a "Hype Hit Parade" which included the 11 most overused and ineffective words. They were *leading, enhanced, unique, significant, solution, integrated, powerful, innovative, advanced, high performance,* and *sophisticated.*

Similar surveys have uncovered overused words in business and public relations. A New York firm, John Rost Associates, compiled a list of words and phrases used excessively in business letters and reports. The list includes: *agenda, proactive, interface, networking, finalize, done deals, impact, bottom-line, vis-à-vis, world class, state-of-the-art, user-friendly, competitive edge, know-how, win-win, breakthrough, fast track, hands-on, input, dialogue,* and *no-brainer.*

Avoid Euphemisms   A euphemism, according to Frank Grazian, founding editor of *Communication Briefings,* is "an inoffensive word or phrase that is less direct and less distasteful than the one that represents reality."

Public relations personnel should use positive, favorable words to convey a message, but they have an ethical responsibility not to use words that hide information or mislead. Probably little danger exists in substituting positive words such as saying a person has a "disability" rather than using the word "handicapped." Some euphemisms can even cause amusement when car mechanics become "automotive internists" and luxury cars are called "pre-owned" on the used car lot.

More dangerous are euphemisms that actually alter the meaning or impact of a word or concept. Writers call this doublespeak—words that pretend to communicate but really don't. Governments are famous for doublespeak. In the Persian Gulf War, U.S. military briefing officers described civilian casualties and destruction as "collateral damage." And Serbian authorities use the term "ethnic cleansing" to sanitize the murder of thousands in Kosovo. A government economist once called a recession "a meaningful downturn in aggregate output."

Corporations also use euphemisms and doublespeak to hide unfavorable news. Reducing the number of employees, for example, is often called "right-sizing," "skill mix adjustment," or "career assignment and relocation." An airline once called the crash of a plane "the involuntary conversion of a 727."

Use of euphemisms to hide or mislead obviously is contrary to professional public relations standards and the public interest. As William Lutz writes in *Public Relations Quarterly,* "Such language breeds suspicion, cynicism, distrust, and, ultimately, hostility."

Avoid Discriminatory Language   In today's world, effective communication also means *nondiscriminatory* communication. Public relations personnel should double-check every message to eliminate undesirable gender, racial, and ethnic connotations.

In regard to gender, it is unnecessary to write about something as being *man-made* when a word like *synthetic* or *artificial* is just as good. Companies no longer have *manpower* but *employees, personnel,* and *workers.* Most civic organizations have *chairpersons* now, and cities have *firefighters* instead of *firemen,* and *police officers* instead of *policemen.* Airlines, of course, have *flight attendants* instead of *stewardesses.*

Writers also should be careful about descriptive phrases for women. *Bulldog Reporter,* a West Coast public relations newsletter, once criticized a Chicago public relations firm for describing a female company president as "a tall, attractive blonde who could easily turn heads on Main Street [but] is instead turning heads on Wall Street."

Nor is it appropriate in professional settings to say that a woman is the wife of someone also well known. A female vice president of a public relations firm cried foul when a local newsletter described her as the wife of a prominent journalist. The newsletter editor apologized in the next issue.

Messages should not identify any individual by ethnic designation, but it may be necessary in some situations to designate a particular ethnic or racial group. Although fashions and preferences change, today's writers use *Asian-American* instead of the now pejorative *Oriental.* And the term *Hispanic* is now more acceptable than the politically charged *Spanish-speaking.* The term *Latino,* however, raises some controversy; some women say that it is sexist because the "o" in Spanish is male.

The term *black* seems to be making a comeback, according to the U.S. Department of Labor. Forty-four percent of the *blacks* in a survey preferred this designation, while another 28 percent preferred *African-American* and 12 percent chose *Afro-American.* As a matter of policy, many newspapers use *African-American* on first reference and *black* on second reference. Headlines almost always use *black* because it is short.

BELIEVING THE MESSAGE

One key variable in the communication process, discussed further in Chapter 10, is *source credibility.* Do members of the audience perceive the source as knowledgeable and expert on the subject? Do they perceive the source as honest and objective or just representing a special interest? Audiences, for example, ascribe lower credibility to statements in an advertisement than to the same information contained in a news article because news articles are selected by media gatekeepers.

Source credibility is a problem for any organizational spokesperson because the public already has a bias. In one study conducted for the GCI Group, Opinion Research Corp.

found that more than half of the Americans surveyed are likely to believe a large company is probably guilty of some wrongdoing if it is being investigated by a government agency or if a major lawsuit is filed against the company. At the same time, only one third would trust the statements of a large company.

A second variable in believability is the *context* of the message. Action (performance) speaks louder than a stack of news releases. A bank may spend thousands of dollars on a promotion campaign with the slogan, "Your Friendly Bank—Where Service Counts," but the effort is wasted if employees are not trained to be friendly and courteous.

Incompatible rhetoric and actions can be somewhat amusing at times. At a press briefing about the importance of "buying American," the U.S. Chamber of Commerce passed out commemorative coffee mugs marked in small print on the bottom, "Made in China."

Another barrier to the believability of messages is the audience's predispositions. This problem brings to mind the old saying, "Don't confuse me with the facts, my mind is already made up."

In this case, Leon Festinger's theory of *cognitive dissonance* should be understood. In essence, it says that people will not believe a message contrary to their predispositions unless the communicator can introduce information that causes them to question their beliefs.

Creating dissonance can be done in at least three ways. First, make the target audience aware that circumstances have changed. "In other words," says Patrick Jackson of *PR Reporter,* "they needn't rationalize any longer; it's safe and OK to change because the situation has changed." Second, give information about new developments or discoveries. This is an unthreatening way to break through a person's opinions. Third, use an unexpected spokesperson. Chevron, for example, sought to overcome opposition to some of its oil exploration policies by getting endorsements from several respected leaders in the conservation movement.

REMEMBERING THE MESSAGE

Many messages prepared by public relations personnel are repeated extensively, for several reasons:

- Repetition is necessary because members of a target audience don't all see or hear the message at the same time. Not everyone reads the newspaper on a particular day or watches the same television news program.

- Repetition reminds the audience, so there is less chance of a failure to remember the message. If a source has high credibility, repetition prevents erosion of opinion change.

- Repetition helps the audience remember the message itself. Studies have shown that advertising is quickly forgotten if not repeated constantly.

- Repetition can lead to improved learning and increase the chance of penetrating audience indifference or resistance.

Researchers say that repetition, or redundancy, is also necessary to offset the "noise" surrounding a message. People often hear or see messages in an environment filled with distractions—a baby crying, the conversations of family members or office staff, a barking dog, or even the receiver daydreaming or thinking of other things.

Consequently, communicators often build repetition into a message. Key points may be mentioned at the beginning and then summarized at the end. If the source is asking the receiver to call for more information or write for a brochure, the telephone number or address is repeated several times. Such precautions also fight *entropy,* which means that messages continually lose information as media channels and people process the information and pass it on to others. In one study about employee communications, for example, it was found that rank-and-file workers got only 20 percent of a message that had passed through four levels of managers.

A good example of using multiple communication tools is a campaign to get a bond issue passed for Macomb Community College in Michigan. The message was quite simple: Vote "Yes." A nonprofit citizens group used 13 communication tools to put the message across: *news releases, media interviews, news conferences, rallies, debates, campaign buttons, speaker's bureau, posters, direct mail, flyers, newsletters, phone calls to registered voters,* and *an essay contest.* The bond issue passed.

ACTING ON THE MESSAGE

The ultimate purpose of any message is to have an effect on the recipient. Public relations personnel communicate messages on behalf of organizations to change perceptions, attitudes, opinions, or behavior in some way. Marketing communications, in particular, has the objective of convincing people to buy goods and services.

The Five-Stage Adoption Process

Getting people to act on a message is not a simple process. In fact, research shows that it can be a somewhat lengthy and complex procedure that depends on a number of intervening influences. One key to understanding how people accept new ideas or products is to analyze the adoption process. The five stages are summarized as follows:

1. *Awareness.* A person becomes aware of an idea or a new product, often by means of an advertisement or a news story.

2. *Interest.* The individual seeks more information about the idea or the product, perhaps by ordering a brochure, picking up a pamphlet, or reading an in-depth article in a newspaper or magazine.

3. *Evaluation.* The person evaluates the idea or the product on the basis of how it meets specific needs and wants. Feedback from friends and family is part of this process.

4. *Trial.* Next, the person tries the product or the idea on an experimental basis, by using a sample, witnessing a demonstration, or making qualifying statements such as, "I read. . . ."

5. *Adoption.* The individual begins to use the product on a regular basis or integrates the idea into his or her belief system. The "I read . . ." becomes "I think . . ." if peers provide support and reinforcement of the idea.

It is important to realize that a person does not necessarily go through all five stages with any given idea or product. The process may be terminated after any step. In fact, the process is like a large funnel. Although many are made aware of an idea or a product, only a few will ultimately adopt it.

This is because a number of factors affect the adoption process. Everett Rogers, author of *Diffusion of Innovation,* lists at least five:

- *Relative advantage.* The degree to which an innovation is perceived as better than the idea it replaces.

- *Compatibility.* The degree to which an innovation is perceived as being consistent with the existing values, experiences, and needs of potential adopters.

- *Complexity.* The degree to which an innovation is perceived as difficult to understand and use.

- *Trialability.* The degree to which an innovation may be experienced on a limited basis.

- *Observability.* The degree to which the results of an innovation are visible to others.

The communicator should be aware of these factors and attempt to implement communication strategies that will overcome as many of them as possible. Repeating a message in various ways, reducing its complexity, taking into account competing messages, and structuring the message to meet the needs of the audience are ways to do this.

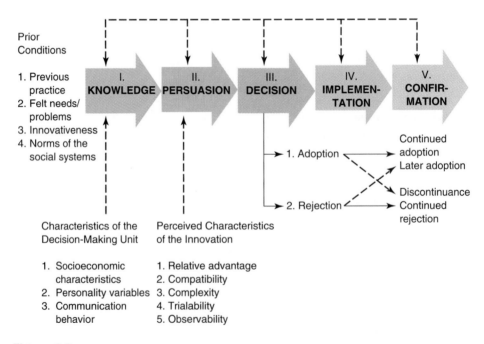

Figure 8.2
This graph shows the steps through which an individual or other decision-making unit goes in the innovation-decision process from first knowledge of an innovation to decision to adopt it, followed by implementation of the new idea and confirmation of the decision.

The Time Factor

Another aspect that confuses people is the amount of time needed to adopt a new idea or product. Depending on the individual and situation, the entire adoption process can take place almost instantly if the result is of minor consequence or requires low-level commitment. Buying a new brand of soft drink or a bar of soap is relatively inexpensive and often done on impulse. On the other hand, deciding to buy a new car or vote for a particular candidate may involve an adoption process that takes several weeks or months.

Rogers's research shows that people approach innovation in different ways, depending on their personality traits and the risk involved. "Innovators" are venturesome and eager to try new ideas, while "Laggards" are traditional and the last to adopt anything. Between the two extremes are "Early Adopters," who are opinion leaders; "Early Majority," who take the deliberate approach; and "Late Majority," who are often skeptical but bow to peer pressure.

How Decisions Are Influenced

Of particular interest to public relations people is the primary source of information at each step in the adoption process. Mass media vehicles such as advertising, short news articles, feature stories, and radio and television news announcements are most influential at the *awareness* stage of the adoption process. A news article or a television announcement makes people aware of an idea, event, or new product. They also are made aware through such vehicles as direct mail, office memos, and simple brochures.

Individuals at the *interest* stage also rely on mass-media vehicles, but they are actively seeking information and pay attention to longer, in-depth articles. They rely more on detailed brochures, specialized publications, small-group seminars, websites, and meetings to provide details. At the *evaluation, trial,* and *adoption* stages, group norms and opinions are the most influential. Feedback, negative or positive, from friends and peers may determine adoption. If a person's friends generally disapprove of the candidate, the movie, or the automobile brand, it is unlikely that the individual will complete the adoption process even if he or she is highly sold on the idea. If a person does make a commitment, mass-media vehicles become reinforcing mechanisms. Studies show, for example, that owners of a new car are the most avid readers of that car's advertising. The complexities of the adoption process show that public relations communicators need to think about the entire communication process—from the formulation of the message to the ways in which receivers ultimately process the information and make decisions. By doing so, communicators can form more effective message strategies and develop realistic objectives for what can actually be accomplished.

A special kind of communication problem comes up when an organization faces a crisis. The following section gives some tips and case studies on how to communicate in such a situation.

CRISIS COMMUNICATION

The communication process, difficult in the best of times, is severely tested in crisis situations when a high degree of uncertainty exists. At such times verifiable information about what is happening or has happened may be lacking.

This causes people to become more active seekers of information and, as research suggests, more dependent on the media for information to satisfy the human desire for closure.

A crisis situation, in other words, puts a great deal of pressure on organizations to respond with accurate, complete information as quickly as possible. How an organization responds in the first 24 hours, experts say, often determines whether the situation remains an "incident" or becomes a full-blown crisis.

What Is a Crisis?

Academics cite many dimensions of what constitutes a crisis for an organization. Ole R. Holsti, author of several articles on crisis theory, defines crises as "situations characterized by surprise, high threat to important values, and a short decision time." Thierry C. Pauchant and Ian J. Mitroff, authors of *Transforming the Crisis-Prone Organization,* use this definition: "A disruption that physically affects a system as a whole and threatens its basic assumptions, its subjective sense of self, its existential core." Steven Fink, author of *Crisis Management: Planning for the Inevitable,* states, "Crises are forewarning situations that run the risk of escalating in intensity, falling under close media or government scrutiny, interfering with normal operations, jeopardizing organizational image and damaging a company's bottom line."

Perhaps the best definition, however, is provided by Pacific Telesis, the parent company of Pacific Bell. Its manual on crisis communication says a crisis is "An extraordinary event or series of events that adversely affects the integrity of the product, the reputation or financial stability of the organization; or the health or well-being of employees, the community, or the public at large."

Nor are crises always unexpected. One study by the Institute for Crisis Management, Indiana, found that only 14 percent of business crises are unexpected. The remaining 86 percent are what the Institute called "smoldering" crises in which an organization is aware of potential business disruption long before the public finds out about it. The study also found that management—or in some cases, mismanagement—caused 78 percent of the crises. "Most organiztions have a crisis plan to deal with sudden crises, like accidents," says Robert B. Irvine, president of the Institute. "However, our data indicates many businesses are denying or ducking serious problems that eventually will ignite and cost them millions of dollars and lost management time."

A Lack of Crisis Planning

Echoing Irvine's thought, another study by Steven Fink found that 89 percent of the chief executive officers of Fortune 500 companies reported that a business crisis was almost inevitable; however, 50 percent admitted that they did not have a crisis management plan.

This situation has caused Kenneth Myers, a crisis consultant, to write, "If economics is the dismal science, then contingency planning is the abysmal science." As academics Donald Chisholm and Martin Landry have noted, "When people believe that because nothing has gone wrong, nothing will go wrong, they court disaster. There is noise in every system and every design. If this fact is ignored, nature soon reminds us of our folly."

Here is a sampling of major crises that have hit various organizations:

• Odwalla, the natural juice maker, had to recall about 70 percent of its product line after several cases of E. coli poisoning—including one death—were linked to its unpasturized apple juice. The company pleaded guilty to criminal charges and agreed to pay a $1.5 million fine.

Characteristic	Public Media	Interactive Media	Controlled Media	Events/ Groups	One-on-One
Key use	Build awareness	Respond to queries; Exchange information	Promotion; provide Detailed information	Motivate attendees; Reinforce attitudes	Obtain commitments; Resolve problems
Examples	Newspapers, magazines, radio, television	Computer-based World Wide Web, databases, e-mail, listservs, newsgroups, chat rooms, bulletin boards	Brochures, newsletters, sponsored magazines, annual reports, books, direct mail, point of purchase displays, videobrochures	Speeches, trade shows, exhibits, meetings/ conferences, demonstrations, rallies, sponsorships, anniversaries	Personal visits, lobbying, personal letters, telephone calls, telemarketing
Nature of communication	Nonpersonal	Nonpersonal	Nonpersonal	Quasi-personal	Personal
Direction of communication	One-way	Quasi-two-way	One-way	Quasi-two-way	Two-way
Technological sophistication	High	High	Moderate	Moderate	Low
Channel ownership	Media organizations	Common carrier or institution	Sponsor	Sponsor or other organization	None
Messages chosen by	Third-parties and producers	Receiver	Sponsor	Sponsor or joint organization	Producer and audience
Audience involvement	Low	High	Moderate	Moderate	High
Reach	High	Moderate-low	Moderate-low	Low	Low
Cost per impression	Extremely low	Low	Moderate	Moderate	High
Key challenges to effectiveness	Competition; media clutter	Availability, accessibility	Design, distribution	Attendence, atmosphere	Empowerment, personal dynamics

Figure 8.3

An Integrated Public Relations Media Model. The variety and scope of media and communication tools available to public relations professionals runs the spectrum from mass media (public media) to one–on–one communication (interpersonal communication). Here, in chart form, is a concept developed by Professor Kirk Hallahan at Colorado State University.

- McDonald's got negative publicity when an 81-year-old woman won a multimillion-dollar lawsuit against the company because she suffered third-degree burns from a scalding cup of coffee.

- Intel, the leading manufacturer of computer chips, faced a major problem in corporate reputation and credibility when it tried to downplay flaws found in its Pentium chip.

Each of these examples, as Irvine suggests, started as a "smoldering" crisis that management could have prevented if it had used more environmental scanning and issues management. Instead, it left the issue to fester and ultimately ignite in national headlines. In the McDonald's case, the company had received at least 700 complaints of coffee burns during the last decade and had settled claims from scalding injuries for more than $500,000.

Intel worsened its problem by treating the Pentium flaw as a trivial matter and failing to offer customers an explanation or a replacement. Indeed, the Intel crisis finally got national attention when IBM announced its decision to halt the sale of Pentium-based personal computers. This decision was made six weeks after Intel knew there was a problem but failed to take corrective action. Alfonso Gonzalez-Herrero and Cornelius B. Pratt, writing about the Intel situation, said, "Intel possibly forgot two key principles of modern corporate communications: (a) image is perceptual reality, and (b) passiveness is a transitory state that can change when publics feel outraged."

PR Casebook

West Point Averts a Crisis

Charges of sexual harassment can seriously damage an organization's reputation and diminish public support.

Officials at West Point knew they had a potential crisis on their hands when a group of women cadets on a "spirit run" were groped as they ran through a cordon of football players at a practice session.

After the women complained, the academy triggered its crisis communication plan. Four points were covered: (1) the academy's investigation would be conducted swiftly, fairly, and openly; (2) the incident was an exception; (3) the complaint should not be equated with the infamous Tailhook scandal; and (4) West Point has a zero tolerance of sexual harassment.

The academy's superintendent, as the spokesperson, reported the incident at a scheduled meeting with the New York *Times*. The academy also communicated with the cadets, faculty, employees, alumni, parents, admission officers, the Pentagon, and members of Congress. The public relations staff coordinated media interviews with cadets and officials at the academy.

Two weeks after the incident, the academy issued a news release announcing final results of the investigation and the punishment awarded to the guilty cadets. Media reports were uniformly positive about how West Point handled the problem.

By being open, forthright, and candid, and by effectively communicating its policy that sexual harassment would not be tolerated, West Point got its key messages across and emerged from the incident with an enhanced reputation. In fact, acceptance of admission offers from women increased 50 percent from the previous year.

How to Communicate during a Crisis

There are many lists giving advice on what to do during a crisis. Here's a compilation of good suggestions:

* *Put the public first.*

* *Take responsibility.* An organization should take responsibility for solving the problem.

* *Be honest.* Don't obscure facts and try to mislead the public.

* *Never say "No comment."* A Porter/Novelli survey found that nearly two thirds of the public feel that "no comment" almost always means that the organization is guilty of wrongdoing.

* *Designate a single spokesperson.*

* *Set up a central information center.*

* *Provide a constant flow of information.* When information is withheld, the cover-up becomes the story.

* *Be familiar with media needs and deadlines.*

* *Be accessible.*

* *Monitor news coverage and telephone inquiries.*

* *Communicate with key publics.*

How Various Organizations Respond to Crises

The above list offers sound, practical advice, but recent research has shown that organizations don't all respond to a crisis in the same way. Indeed, W. Timothy Coombs of Illinois State University postulates that an organization's response may vary on a continuum from *defensive* to *accommodative.* Here is his list of crisis communication strategies that an organization may use:

* *Attack the accuser.* The party that claims a crisis exists is confronted and its logic and facts are faulted. Sometimes a lawsuit is threatened.

* *Denial.* The organization explains that there is no crisis.

* *Excuse.* The organization minimizes its responsibility for the crisis. Any intention to do harm is denied, and the organization says it had no control over the events that led to the crisis. This strategy is often used when there is a natural disaster or product tampering.

* *Justification.* Crisis is minimized with a statement that there was no serious damage or injuries. Sometimes, the blame is shifted to the victims. This is often done when a consumer misuses a product or there is an industrial accident.

* *Ingratiation.* Actions are taken to appease the publics involved. Consumers who complain are given coupons or the organization makes a donation to a charitable organization.

Burlington Industries, for example, gave a large donation to the humane society after the discovery that it had imported coats from China with fur collars containing dog fur instead of "coyote" fur.

• *Corrective action.* Steps are taken to repair the damage from the crisis and to prevent a repetition.

• *Full apology.* Organization takes full responsibility and asks forgiveness. Some compensation of money or aid is often included.

The Coombs typology gives a list of choices for a crisis communication manager depending on the situation. However, he notes that organizations do have to consider more *accommodative* strategies (*ingratiation, corrective action, full apology*) if *defensive* strategies (*attack accuser, denial, excuse*) are not effective in repairing the organization's reputation or restoring previous sales levels. He says, "Accommodative strategies emphasize image repair, which is what is needed as image damage worsens. Defensive strategies, such as denial or minimizing, logically becomes less effective as organizations are viewed as more responsible for the crisis."

Often, however, an organization doesn't adopt an appropriate strategy because of corporate culture and other constraints. Glen T. Cameron at the University of Missouri has developed a contingency theory of conflict management in public relations that seeks to explain why agencies don't always engage in two-way communication and accommodative strategies when confronted with a crisis or a conflict with some publics.

Some variables proscribing the organization, according to Cameron, might be (1) management's moral conviction that the public is wrong, (2) moral neutrality when two contending publics want the organization to take sides on a policy issue, (3) legal constraints, (4) regulatory constraints such as FTC, SEC, (5) prohibition by senior management against an accommodative stance, and (6) possible conflict between departments of the organization on what strategies to adopt.

In some cases, Cameron contends that Grunig's ideal goal of symmetrical communication to achieve mutual understanding and accommodation doesn't occur because both sides have staked out highly rigid positions and are not willing to compromise their strong moral positions. For example, it is unlikely that the "prolife" and "prochoice" forces will ever achieve mutual understanding and accommodation.

How Some Organizations Handled a Crisis

The crisis communication strategies outlined by Coombs are useful when evaluating how various organizations *handled* a crisis. Intel, for example, first denied there was a problem with its Pentium chip. As the crisis deepened and was covered in the mainstream press, Intel then tried the strategy of *justification* by saying the problem wasn't serious enough to warrant replacing the chips. It minimized the concerns of end users such as engineers and computer programmers. Only after considerable damage had been done to Intel's reputation, and IBM had suspended orders for the chip, did Intel take *corrective action* to replace the chips and Andy Grove, Intel's president, issued a *full apology.*

Exxon, still highly identified in the public mind with a major oil spill in Prince William Sound, Alaska, also chose a *defensive strategy* when one of its ships, the *Exxon*

Valdez, hit a reef in 1989 and spilled nearly 240,000 barrels of oil into a pristine environment. The disaster, one of history's worst environmental accidents, was badly mismanaged from the beginning.

Exxon management started its crisis communication strategy by making *excuses.* Management claimed that Exxon, as a corporation, wasn't at fault because (1) the weather wasn't ideal, (2) the charts provided by the U.S. Coast Guard were out of date, and (3) the captain of the ship was derelict in his duties by drinking while on duty. As cleanup efforts began, Exxon also tried to shift the blame by maintaining that government bureaucracy and prohibitions against the use of certain chemicals hampered the company's efforts.

Exxon also used the strategy of *justification* to minimize the damage, saying that environmentalists and the government were exaggerating the ill effects on bird and animal life. Meanwhile, negative press coverage was intense and public outrage continued to rise. William J. Small of Fordham University, who researched the press coverage, wrote, "Probably no other company ever got a more damaging portrayal in the mass media." More than 18,000 customers tore up their Exxon credit cards, late night talk-show hosts ridiculed the company, and congressional committees started hearings. Exxon dropped from eighth to 110th on *Fortune*'s list of most-admired companies.

Exxon's response to all these developments was somewhat ineffective. It did try the strategy of *ingratiation* by running full-page advertisements stating that the company was "sorry" for the oil spill—but didn't take responsibility for it. Instead of calming the storm, that approach only further enraged the public.

Exxon also took *corrective action* and cleaned up the oil spill, spending about $3 billion in its efforts. The company received little credit for this action, however, because most of the public believed it was done only under government pressure. And by the time the cleanup was finished, public attitudes about Exxon had already been formed.

In the case of Intel and Exxon, Cameron's ideas also come into play. Neither company first initiated an accommodative strategy, perhaps because (1) management morally thought that the public was wrong, or (2) the companies were concerned about possible liability lawsuits.

Odwella and Pepsi provide examples of more successful crisis communication strategies.

Odwella didn't bother with a *defensive* strategy when it got a phone call from Washington State health officials that the company's apple juice was implicated in several cases of E. coli poisoning. Only 20 minutes later, Odwella at a press conference announced its recall of all products containing unpasturized apple juice.

Within 72 hours, the company set up a crisis-related website with the aid of its public relations firm, Daniel Edelman Worldwide. The company's website, widely publicized, contained links to the Food and Drug Administration (FDA) and the Centers for Disease Control and Prevention so consumers could get additional information about E. coli contamination.

Company management, from the very beginning, initiated an *accommodative* strategy. The press conference and the website were an *ingratiation* strategy to retain consumer confidence, *corrective action* was taken immediately by recalling the product and taking steps to change the production process. The company president, early on, also issued a *full apology* and garnered much public support by announcing that the company would pay any medical bills of the approximately 70 people poisoned. The company also offered to replace any bottles of apple juice on consumer shelves. The result was widespread public approval, and in one survey almost 90 percent of consumers said they would continue to buy the product.

Focus on Ethics

How Do You Write This News Release?

You work in public relations for a large medical center, and one of your duties is publicizing major research studies by the staff.

One study that comes across your desk shows that postmenopausal women taking estrogen experience a 30-percent increase in the risk of breast cancer. You talk with the head of the research study, and she says that this percentage—when you consider other factors—actually means that a woman who doesn't take estrogen increases her odds of avoiding cancer by only about 1 percent—to 96 percent from 95 percent.

You know the media won't be very much interested in the latter figure because there is no psychological effect of an impressive number. So what do you do? Would you just go ahead and use the 30-percent figure, which is technically correct, or would you write a news release emphasizing the minimal difference?

It is important to note, however that not all successful crisis communication strategies need to be *accommodative.* Pepsi-Cola was able to mount an effective *defensive* crisis communication strategy and avoid a recall when a hoax of nationwide proportions created an intense but short-lived crisis for the soft-drink company.

The crisis began when the media reported that a man in Tacoma, Washington, claimed that he had found a syringe inside a can of Diet Pepsi. As the news spread, men and women across the country made similar claims of finding a broken sewing needle, a screw, a bullet, and even a narcotics vial in their Pepsi cans. As a consequence, demands for a recall of all Pepsi products arose, an action that would have major economic consequences for the company.

Company officials were confident that insertion of foreign objects into cans on the high-speed, closely controlled bottling lines was virtually impossible, so they chose to defend their product. The urgent problem, then, was to convince the public that the product was safe, and any foreign objects found had been inserted after the cans were opened.

The company officials and their public relations staff set about doing this with several strategies. One approach was to *attack the accuser.* Pepsi officials said the foreign objects probably got into the cans after they were opened, and even explained that many people make such claims just to collect compensation from the company. The company also announced that it would pursue legal action against anyone making false claims about the integrity of the company's products.

Pepsi also took the strategy of *denial,* saying that no crisis actually existed. Pepsi president Craig E. Weathrup immediately made appearances on national television programs and gave newspaper interviews to state the company's case that its bottling lines were secure. Helping convince the public was U.S. Food and Drug Administration Commissioner David Kessler, who said that a recall was not necessary.

In addition, Pepsi prepared video news releases (VNRs) to provide visual evidence. These showed pictures of a bottling line moving at nearly 200 cans a minute, so fast that tampering with a can before it was sealed appeared impossible. The first of these VNRs, at the peak of the panic, was seen by a record 183 million viewers, according to a Nielsen survey.

These quick actions deflated the public's concern and polls showed considerable acceptance of Pepsi's contention that the problem was a hoax. A week after the scare began, Pepsi ran full-page advertisements with the headline, "Pepsi is pleased to announce . . . Nothing." It stated, "As America now knows, those stories about Diet Pepsi were a hoax. . . ."

In sum, no one crisis communication strategy is appropriate for all situations, as the above examples indicate. Therefore, as Coombs indicates, "It is only by understanding the crisis situation that the crisis manager can select the appropriate response for the crisis." Corporate culture and management mindsets also influence how an organization responds to a developing crisis.

Pepsi is pleased to announce...

...nothing.

After proof emerged that claims of finding syringes and other foreign objects in Pepsi soft drink cans were false, Pepsi-Cola management published a full-page newspaper advertisement with an eye-catching headline.

As America now knows, those stories about Diet Pepsi were a hoax. Plain and simple, not true. Hundreds of investigators have found no evidence to support a single claim.

As for the many, many thousands of people who work at Pepsi-Cola, we feel great that it's over. And we're ready to get on with making and bringing you what we believe is the best-tasting diet cola in America.

There's not much more we can say. Except that most importantly, we won't let this hoax change our exciting plans for this summer.

We've set up special offers so you can enjoy our great quality products at prices that will save you money all summer long. It all starts on July 4th weekend and we hope you'll stock up with a little extra, just to make up for what you might have missed last week.

That's it. Just one last word of thanks to the millions of you who have stood with us.

Drink All The Diet Pepsi You Want.
Uh Huh.

This message is brought to you by the Pepsi-Cola Company 4242 E. Raymond, Phoenix, Arizona

DIET PEPSI and UH HUH are registered trademarks of PepsiCo.

CASE PROBLEM

Extensive information campaigns are being mounted throughout the world to inform people about the dangers of acquired immune deficiency syndrome (AIDS). Information specialists must utilize a variety of communication strategies and tactics to create public awareness and cause changes in individual behavior patterns.

At the same time, the communication process is very complex because a number of variables must be considered. Using this chapter as a guide, how would you apply the various communication concepts and theories to the task of informing people about AIDS?

QUESTIONS FOR REVIEW AND DISCUSSION

1. Kirk Hallahan lists five categories of media and communication tools. What are they, and what are some of the pros and cons of each?

2. James Grunig says there are at least five possible objectives for a communicator. What are they? What two objectives do most public relations campaigns try to achieve?

3. What are the five basic elements of a communication model?

4. Why is two-way communication (feedback) an important aspect of effective communication?

5. What are the advantages and disadvantages, from a communication standpoint, of reaching the audience through mass media channels?

6. Explain the behavioral communication model. What is the importance of the "triggering event"?

7. What is the premise of the media uses and gratification theory?

8. What kinds of messages and communication channels would you use for a passive audience? An active information-seeking audience?

9. Why is it necessary to use a variety of messages and communication channels in a public relations program?

10. Why is it important to write with clarity and simplicity? How can symbols, acronyms, and slogans help?

11. Explain the concept behind readability formulas.

12. Why is it important to build repetition into a message?

13. Explain the five steps in the adoption process. What are some of the factors that affect the adoption of an idea or product?

14. Both Exxon and Pepsi used *defensive* crisis communication strategies. However, one succeeded and the other failed. What factors do you think made the difference?

Evaluation

Preview

In this chapter the objectives are to explain the critical role of evaluation in public relations, to describe the advantages and disadvantages of various evaluation methods, and to help students select the ones most suitable for specific programs.

Topics covered in the chapter include:
* The purpose of evaluation
* Objectives: A prerequisite for evaluation
* Current status of measurement and evaluation
* Measurement of production
* Message exposure
* Audience comprehension
* Audience change and action
* Supplemental activities

THE PURPOSE OF EVALUATION

The fourth step of the public relations process is evaluation. It is the measurement of results against established objectives set during the planning process discussed in Chapter 7.

Evaluation is well described by Professor James Bissland of Bowling Green State University. He defines it as "the systematic assessment of a program and its results. It is a means for practitioners to offer accountability to clients—and to themselves."

Results and accountability also are themes of Professors Glen Broom and David Dozier of San Diego State University. In their text *Using Research in Public Relations,* they state, "Your program is intended to cause observable impact—to change or maintain something about a situation. So, after the program, you use research to measure and document program effects."

A desire to do a better job next time is a major reason for evaluating public relations efforts, but another equally important reason is the widespread adoption of the management-by-objectives system by clients and employers of public relations personnel. They want to know if the money, time, and effort expended on public relations are well spent and contribute to the realization of an organizational objective, such as attendance at an open house, product sales, or increased awareness of ways to prevent the spread of AIDS.

OBJECTIVES: A PREREQUISITE FOR EVALUATION

Before any public relations program can be properly evaluated, it is important to have a clearly established set of measurable objectives. These should be part of the program plan, discussed in chapter 7, but some points need reviewing.

First, public relations personnel and management should agree on the criteria that will be used to evaluate success in attaining objectives. A Ketchum public relations monograph simply states, "Write the most precise, most results-oriented objectives you can that are realistic, credible, measurable, and compatible with the client's demands on public relations."

Second, don't wait until the end of the public relations program to determine how it will be evaluated. Albert L. Schweitzer at Fleishman-Hillard public relations in St. Louis, makes the point: "Evaluating impact/results starts in the planning stage. You break down the problem into measurable goals and objectives, then after implementing the program, you measure the results against goals."

If an objective is informational, measurement techniques must show how successfully information was communicated to target audiences. Such techniques fall under the rubric of "message dissemination" and "audience exposure," but they do not measure the effect on attitudes or overt behavior and action.

Motivational objectives are more difficult to accomplish. If the objective is to increase sales or market share, it is important to show that public relations efforts caused the increase rather than advertising or other marketing strategies. Or if the objective is to change attitudes or opinions, research should be done before and after the public relations activity to measure the percentage of change.

Although objectives may vary, the following checklist contains the basic evaluation questions that any practitioner should ask:

1. Was the activity or program adequately planned?

2. Did recipients of the message understand it?

3. How could the program strategy have been more effective?

4. Were all primary and secondary audiences reached?

5. Was the desired organizational objective achieved?

6. What unforeseen circumstances affected the success of the program or activity?

7. Did the program or activity fall within the budget set for it?

8. What steps can be taken to improve the success of similar future activities?

CURRENT STATUS OF MEASUREMENT AND EVALUATION

During the past decade, public relations professionals have made considerable progress in evaluation research and the ability to tell clients and employers exactly what has been accomplished. More sophisticated techniques than previously are being used, including computerized news-clip analysis, survey sampling, and attempts to correlate efforts directly with sales.

Today, the trend toward more systematic evaluation is well established. Katherine Delahaye Paine, founder of her own public relations measurement firm, says that the percentage of a public relations budget devoted to measurement and evaluation was about 1 percent a decade ago, but is now more like 5 percent. In the coming decade of the new century, it is projected that the amount will increase to 10 percent. One reason: there is increasing pressure on all parts of the organization—including public relations—to prove their value to the "bottom line."

There are, however, still those who say public relations is not an exact science and is extremely difficult to measure. Walter K. Lindenmann, senior vice president and director of research of Ketchum public relations, takes a more optimistic view. He wrote in *Public Relations Quarterly:* "Let's get something straight right off the bat. First, it is possible to measure public relations effectiveness. . . . Second, measuring public relations effectiveness does not have to be either unbelievably expensive or laboriously time-consuming."

Lindenmann suggests that public relations personnel use a mix of evaluation techniques, many borrowed from advertising and marketing, to provide more complete evaluation. In addition, he notes that there are at least three levels of measurement and evaluation (see Figure 9.1).

On the most basic level are compilations of message distribution and media placements. The second level, which requires more sophisticated techniques, deals with the measurement of audience awareness, comprehension, and retention of the message. The most advanced level is the measurement of changes in attitudes, opinions, and behavior.

The following sections outline the most widely used methods for evaluating public relations efforts. These include: measurement of production, message exposure, audience awareness, audience attitudes, and audience action. Supplemental activities also are discussed. In most cases, a skilled practitioner will use a combination of methods to evaluate the effectiveness of a program.

MEASUREMENT OF PRODUCTION

One elementary form of evaluation is simply to count how many news releases, feature stories, photos, letters, and the like are produced in a given period of time.

This kind of evaluation is supposed to give management an idea of a staff's productivity and output. Public relations professionals, however, do not believe that this evaluation is very meaningful because it emphasizes quantity instead of quality. It may be more cost-effective to write fewer news releases and spend more time on the few that really are newsworthy. It may, for example, be more important for a staff person to spend five weeks working on an article for the *Wall Street Journal* or *Fortune* than to write 29 routine personnel releases.

Another side of the production approach is to specify what the public relations person should accomplish in obtaining media coverage. One state trade association once evaluated its director of media relations on the expectation that (1) four feature stories would be run in any of the 11 largest newspapers in the state and (2) news releases would be used by at least 20 newspapers, including five or more among the 50 largest.

Such evaluation criteria are not only unrealistic but almost impossible to guarantee, because media gatekeepers—not the public relations person—make such decisions. Management may argue, however, that such placement goals provide incentive to the public relations staff and are tangible criteria in employee performance evaluation.

Closely allied to the production of publicity materials is their distribution. Thus a public relations department might report, for instance, that a total of 756 news releases were sent to 819 daily newspapers, 250 weeklies, and 137 trade magazines within one year, or that 110,000 copies of the annual report were distributed to stockholders, security analysts, and business editors.

MEASUREMENT OF MESSAGE EXPOSURE

The most widely practiced form of evaluating public relations programs is the compilation of press clippings and radio and television mentions. Public relations firms and company departments working primarily on a local basis often have a secretary or intern clip the area newspapers. Large companies with regional, national, or even international outreach usually hire clipping services to scan large numbers of publications. It also is possible to have "electronic" clipping services monitor and tape major radio and television programs on a contractual basis. Burrelle's, for example, monitors nearly 400 local TV stations in 150 cities.

The firm of Waggener Edstrom used news clips as one measure of its campaign to publicize the introduction of Microsoft's Windows 95. According to its report, which was the basis for the firm's receipt of a Silver Anvil award from PRSA:

> News coverage consistently communicated key product and corporate messages in more than 240 cover stories in major trade and national news publications during the 20-month launch cycle; 13,000 consumer news stories in publications including the New York *Times,* Washington *Post,* and *Money* magazine; 2,000 TV segments, including all three network morning shows during the 11 days surrounding launch; and 100 syndicated radio spots during the 48-hour launch period. This explosion of media interest was unprecedented for a new product introduction, outpacing even the media coverage of the O. J. Simpson trial, which occurred simultaneously.

Such a compilation measures media acceptance of the story and shows that Microsoft received massive coverage. Clearly, the publicity effort accomplished the first stage of the adoption process by making people aware of Windows 95.

Media Impressions

In addition to the number of media placements, public relations departments and firms report how many people may have been exposed to the message. These numbers are described as *media impressions,* the potential audience reached by a periodical or a broadcast program.

If, for example, a story about an organization appears in the local daily with a circulation of 130,000, the media impressions are 130,000. If another story is published the next day, this counts for 130,000 more impressions. Estimated audiences for radio and television programs, certified by auditing organizations, are also used to compile media impressions.

A regional or national news story can generate millions of impressions by simple multiplication of each placement times the circulation or audience of each medium. Two examples:

• The American College of Obstetricians and Gynecologists organized a public relations campaign to celebrate the 35th anniversary of the birth control pill. According to its report, total media impressions were almost 61 million from print, radio, and television stories.

• M&M Chocolate Candies conducted a national contest to name a new color for M&M candies. Public relations activities generated 1.06 billion impressions from 10,000 TV, radio, and print placements; these included 36,000 print column inches, 12 hours of television news coverage, and 74 hours of radio broadcast time.

Media impressions are commonly used in advertising to illustrate the penetration of a particular message. Such figures give a rough estimate of how many people are exposed to a message. They don't, however, disclose how many people actually read or heard the stories and, more important, how many absorbed or acted on the information. Other techniques needed for this kind of evaluation are discussed later in this chapter.

"Hits" on the Internet

A cyberspace version of media impressions is the number of people reached via an organization's World Wide Web site or home page. Each time a person accesses a site, it is called a "hit" or a "visit."

BayBank of Boston, for example, established a website as part of its sponsorship of the Charles River Regatta. In evaluating its public relations program, the bank also noted that 10,000 visits were recorded at its website in the two weeks prior to the event. Another 33,000 visits were recorded in the month after the regatta, to review results and see cyberspace recreations of the races.

Another example is MCI, which included a website to make consumers aware of its Internet services. The website provided information and also included a test that visitors could take to measure their Internet skills. According to the company and its public relations firm, Ruberry Communications, "More than 2.3 million hits were recorded for the web test site. More than 16,500 people actually completed the test and recorded a score. The test was taken by people from 12 countries."

Advertising Equivalency

Another approach is to calculate the value of message exposure. This is done by converting stories in the regular news columns or on the air into equivalent advertising costs. In other words, a 5-inch article in a trade magazine that charges $100 per column inch for advertising would be worth $500 in publicity value.

Mack Trucks, for example, evaluated its public relations campaign to improve its image in the trucking industry by using advertising equivalency. It reported, "The program generated more than 9,000 inches of editorial coverage with an advertising equivalency of more than $1.2 million—more than five times the company's investment in the program."

Some practitioners even take the approach of calculating the cost of advertising for the same amount of space and then multiplying that total three or six times to reflect a number of research studies that show a news story has higher credibility than an advertisement. Consequently, if Mack Trucks multiplied the equivalent advertising space by three, it could say that the editorial space was worth $3.6 million in publicity.

Although such dollar amounts apparently impress some top managements, the technique of calculating advertising equivalency is really comparing apples and oranges. In fact, Ron Levy, president of North American Precis Syndicate, told *O'Dwyer's Public Relations Newsletter* that he thought the technique was "blatantly ridiculous."

One reason is the fundamental difference between advertising and publicity. Advertising copy is directly controlled by the organization and can be oriented to specific objectives. The organization also controls the size and placement of the message. News mentions, on the other hand, are determined by media gatekeepers and can be negative, neutral, or positive. In addition, a news release can be edited to the point that key corporate messages are deleted. In other words, the organization can't control size, placement, or content.

It becomes a question of what is being measured. Should an article be counted as equivalent advertising space if it is negative? It also is questionable whether a 15-inch article that mentions the organization only once among six other organizations is comparable to 15 column-inches of advertising space. And the numbers game doesn't take into account that a 4-inch article in the *Wall Street Journal* may be more valuable in reaching key publics than a 20-inch article in the Denver *Post*.

In summary, the dollar-value approach to measuring publicity effectiveness is somewhat suspect, and there has been a rapid decline of such statistics in PRSA award entries. The equating of publicity with advertising rates for comparable space also does not engender good media relations. The technique reinforces the opinion of many media gatekeepers that all news releases are just attempts to get "free advertising."

Systematic Tracking

As noted earlier, message exposure has traditionally been measured by sheer bulk. New advances in computer software and databases, however, now make it possible to track media placements in a more sophisticated way.

Computer databases can be used to analyze the content of media placements by such variables as market penetration, type of publication, tone of coverage, sources quoted, and mention of key copy points. Ketchum public relations, for example, can build up to 40 variables into its computer program, including the tracking of reporter bylines to determine if a journalist is predisposed negatively or positively to the client's key messages. Other firms, such as Carma International and The Delahaye Group, do extensive analysis for clients using databases such as NEXIS/LEXIS.

Table 9.1, prepared by The Delahaye Group for a client, illustrates the type of analysis that can be done.

The value of systematic tracking is manifested in several ways. One is continuing, regular feedback during a campaign to determine if an organization's publicity efforts are paying off in terms of placements and mention of key messages. Tracking coverage and comparing it over a period of time is called *benchmarking.*

An example is the campaign that Capitoline/MS&L public relations conducted on behalf of the Turkish government to make Americans more aware of Turkey as a travel destination. By comparing the number of stories before and after the campaign was launched, Carma International found that articles with Turkey as the primary destination increased 400 percent. Favorable articles on Turkey increased 90 percent from a previous year.

At other times, an organization may wish to do a systematic analysis comparing its media coverage with the competition's. Is a major competitor getting more favorable publicity? Is the company being portrayed as an innovative leader, or is its size the only major message being mentioned? Such evaluation allows an organization to fine-tune its public relations efforts and concentrate on problem areas.

Another form of analysis is comparing the number of news releases sent with the number actually published and in what kinds of periodicals. Such analysis often helps a public relations department determine what kinds of publicity are most effective and earn the most return on investment (ROI).

Requests and 800 Numbers

Another measure of media exposure is to compile the number of requests for more information. A story in a newspaper or an appearance of a company spokesperson on a broadcast often provides information as to where people can get more information about a subject.

Table 9.1 *Total Coverage*

	Total
Total impressions	89,641,378
Percent of positive impressions	26.98%
Percent of negative impressions	19.85%
Total articles	1,049
Percent of positive articles	35.65%
Percent of negative articles	16.02%
Percent of articles containing one or more positive messages	52.43%
Percent of articles containing one or more negative messages	18.78%

In many cases, a toll-free 800 number is provided. Dayton Hudson Corporation, owner of several department store chains, used a toll-free hotline number as part of its "Child Care Aware" program to help educate parents about quality child care and how to get it. In a six-month period, 19,000 calls were received seeking advice and copies of a brochure. Dole Food Company, through its toll-free 800 number, got requests for more than 100,000 copies of its brochure titled, "Fun with Fruits and Vegetables: Kid's Cookbook."

Requests for materials also can show the effectiveness of a public relations program. An information program by the U.S. Centers for Disease Control on AIDS prevention, for example, received nearly 2000 phone calls on its information hotline after its "Safe Sex" program on the Public Broadcasting Service (PBS). In addition, the program and resulting publicity generated 260 requests for videotapes and 400 requests for "Smart Sex" organization kits.

Cost-per-Person

Another way to evaluate exposure to the message is to determine the cost of reaching each member of the audience.

The technique is commonly used in advertising in order to place costs in perspective. Although a 30-second commercial during the 2000 Super Bowl telecast cost about $1.5 million ($50,000 per second), advertisers believed it was well worth the price because an audience of more than 125 million was reached for less than a half-cent each. This was a relatively good bargain, even if several million viewers probably visited the refrigerator while the commercial played.

Cost-effectiveness, as this technique is known, also is used in public relations. *Cost-per-thousand* (CPM) is calculated by taking the total of media impressions (discussed earlier) and dividing it by the cost of the publicity program. SkyTel, for example, spent $400,000 to publicize its new two-way paging and messaging system and obtained 52 million impressions, about seven tenths of a cent per impression. According to counselor Ford Kanzler, "CPMs for print publicity programs usually fall well below media space advertising and about 100 percent above direct mail promotions."

In another example, a campaign by the Virginia Department of Tourism to attract Canadian visitors cost $5,500 but generated 90,000 consumer inquiries. This made the cost per inquiry only six cents. The same approach can be done with events, brochures, and newsletters. Nike produced a sports video for $50,000 but reached 150,000 high school students—for a per-person cost of 33 cents.

Audience Attendance

Counting attendance at events is a relatively simple way of evaluating the effectiveness of preevent publicity.

The New York Public Library centennial day celebration, for example, attracted a crowd of 10,000 for a sound-and-laser show and speeches. In addition, 20,000 visitors came to the library on the designated centennial day, and more than 200,000 people from around the world visited the library's exhibitions during the year.

Poor attendance at a meeting or event can indicate inadequate publicity and promotion. Another major cause is lack of public interest, even when people are aware that a meeting or event is taking place. Low attendance usually results in considerable finger-pointing; thus an objective evaluation of exactly what happened—or didn't happen—is a good policy.

MEASUREMENT OF AUDIENCE AWARENESS

So far, techniques of measuring audience exposure and accurate dissemination have been discussed. A higher level of evaluation is to determine whether the audience actually became aware of the message and understood it.

Walter Lindenmann calls this the second level of public relations evalutaion. He notes:

At this level, public relations practitioners measure whether target audience groups actually *received* the messages directed at them: whether they paid *attention* to those messages, whether they *understood* the messages, and whether they have *retained* those messages in any shape or form.

The tools of survey research are needed to answer such questions. Members of the target audience must be asked about the message and what they remember about it. Such research, for example, found that Microsoft achieved a phenomenal 99 percent public awareness that Windows 95 was coming and available for purchase.

Public awareness of what organization sponsors an event also is important. BayBank found that only 59 percent of the spectators recognized the bank as sponsor of the Charles Regatta. Through various innovations, increased publicity efforts, and more signage at the next year's regatta, BayBank raised public awareness to 90 percent.

Another way of measuring audience awareness and comprehension is the day-after recall. Under this method, participants are asked to view a specific television program or read a particular news story; then they are interviewed to learn which messages they remembered.

Ketchum public relations, on behalf of the California Prune Board, used this technique to determine if a 15-city media tour was conveying the key message that prunes are a high-fiber food source. Forty women in Detroit considered likely to watch daytime television shows were asked to view a program on which a Prune Board spokesperson would appear. The day after the program, Ketchum asked the women questions about the show, including their knowledge of the fiber content of prunes. Ninety-three percent remembered the Prune Board spokesperson and 65 percent, on an unaided basis, named prunes as a source of high fiber.

MEASUREMENT OF AUDIENCE ATTITUDES

Closely related to audience awareness and understanding of a message are changes in an audience's perceptions and attitudes.

A major technique to determine such changes is the *baseline study.* Basically, it is a measurement of audience attitudes and opinions before, during, and after a public relations campaign. Baseline studies, also called *benchmark studies,* graphically show the percentage difference in attitudes and opinions as a result of increased information and publicity. A number of intervening variables may account for changes in attitude, of course, but statistical analysis of variance can help pinpoint how much the change is attributable to public relations efforts.

Measuring Use of a Client's Name

You've been hired as an intern at a public relations firm for the summer. One of your duties is to go through recent issues of trade magazines and clip any article in which the name of a client appears. You are then asked to look up advertising rates for these publications and calculate what the comparable space in advertising would cost. The idea, says the account supervisor, is to count entire articles even if the client's name is only mentioned once. "The client is impressed with big numbers," she says, "so count anything you can find." Does this approach raise any ethical concerns on your part? Why or why not?

The Prudential, the insurance company, regularly conducts baseline studies. One survey found that the company scored high in respondent familiarity, but achieved only a 29 percent favorable rating in fulfilling its corporate social responsibilities.

As a result, the company launched "The Prudential Helping Hearts Program." This provided $2 million in matching grants to volunteer emergency medical squads (EMS) to help purchase portable cardiac arrest equipment used to treat heart-attack victims before they reach the hospital. After a year of publicizing the program and making grants, The Prudential found that its overall corporate image rose 29 percent.

The American Iron and Steel Institute also did a baseline study to determine the effectiveness of its campaign to inform the public about the industry's recycling efforts. Before the program, only 52 percent of the respondents in Columbus, Ohio, were aware that steel cans are recyclable. After the campaign, the percentage had risen to 64 percent.

The value of the baseline survey is underscored by Frank R. Stansberry, manager of guest affairs for Coca-Cola. He told the *Public Relations Journal:* "The only way to determine if communications are making an impact is by pre- and posttest research. The first survey measures the status quo. The second one will demonstrate any change and the direction of that change."

MEASUREMENT OF AUDIENCE ACTION

The ultimate objective of any public relations effort, as has been pointed out, is to accomplish organizational objectives. As David Dozier of San Diego State University aptly points out, "The outcome of a successful public relations program is not a hefty stack of news stories. . . . Communication is important only in the effects it achieves among publics."

The objective of the amateur theater group is not to get media publicity; the objective is to sell tickets. The objective of an environmental organization such as Greenpeace is not to get editorials written in favor of whales, but to motivate the public to (1) write elected officials, (2) send donations for its preservation efforts, and (3) get protective legislation passed. The objective of a company is to sell its products and services, not get 200 million media impressions. In all cases, the tools and activities of public relations are a means, not an end.

Figure 9.1

Evaluation goals for public programs can be grouped at three levels of measurement, as shown in this chart.

Source: Ketchum Public Relations, New York, published in Public Relations Quarterly.

Thus it can be seen that public relations efforts are ultimately evaluated on how they help an organization achieve its objectives. Here are some bottom-line examples:

- The M&M's Chocolate Candies color contest campaign caused a 6.5-percent increase in sales.

- The Mack Truck image and customer service campaign increased the company's market share from 9.2 to 12 percent, lifting Mack Trucks from sixth to third place in the large truck market.

- The campaign to promote Turkish tourism caused a 10-percent increase in the number of U.S. travelers to Turkey.

- BayBank saw a 10-percent increase in the number of student bank accounts during the Charles Regatta it sponsored.

- During its centennial year celebration, the National Association of Manufacturers (NAM) had a growth of 800 members; membership retention set a new record.

- A public information campaign on behalf of Fighting Hunger in Wisconsin raised $170,000—$70,000 more than the previous year.

MEASUREMENT OF SUPPLEMENTAL ACTIVITIES

Other forms of measurement can be used in public relations activities. The following sections discuss (1) communication audits, (2) pilot tests and split messages, (3) meeting and event attendance, and (4) newsletter readership.

Communication Audits

The entire communication activity of an organization should be evaluated at least once a year to make sure that every primary and secondary public is receiving appropriate messages.

A communication audit, as an assessment of an organization's entire communication program, could include the following:

1. Analysis of all communication activities—newsletters, memos, policy statements, brochures, annual reports, position papers, mailing lists, media contacts, personnel forms, graphics, logos, advertising, receptionist contacts, waiting lounges for visitors, and so on

2. Informal interviews with rank-and-file employees and middle management and top executives

3. Informal interviews with community leaders, media gatekeepers, consumers, distributors, and other influential persons in the industry

A number of research techniques, as outlined in Chapter 6, can be utilized during a communication audit—including mail and telephone surveys, focus groups, and so forth. The important point is that the communications of an organization should be analyzed from every possible angle, with the input of as many publics as possible.

Pilot Tests and Split Messages

Evaluation is important even before a public relations effort is launched. If exposure to a message is to be maximized, it is wise to pretest it with a sample group from the targeted audience. Do its members easily understand the message? Do they accept the message? Does the message motivate them to adopt a new idea or product?

A variation of pretesting is the *pilot test*. Before going national with a public relations message, companies often test the message and key copy points in selected cities to learn how the media accept the message and how the public reacts. This approach is quite common in product marketing because it limits the costs and enables the company to revamp or fine-tune the message for maximum exposure.

The *split-message approach* is common in direct mail campaigns. Two or three different appeals may be prepared by a charitable organization and sent to different audiences. The response rate is then monitored (perhaps the amount of donations is totaled) to learn what message and graphics seemed to be the most effective.

Meeting and Event Attendance

It has already been pointed out that meetings can be evaluated to some degree by the level of attendance. Such data provide information about the number of people exposed to a message, but still don't answer the more crucial question of what they thought about the meeting.

Public relations people often get an informal sense of an audience's attitudes by its behavior. A standing ovation, spontaneous applause, complimentary remarks as people leave, and even the expressions on people's faces provide clues as to how a meeting was received.

Public relations practitioners also employ more systematic methods. The most common technique is an evaluation sheet that participants fill out at the end of the meeting.

A simple form asking people to rate such items as location, costs, facilities, and program on a 1-to-5 scale (5 being the best) can be used. Other forms may ask people to rate aspects of a conference or meeting as excellent, good, average, and could be better.

Evaluation forms also can ask how people heard about the program and what suggestions they would make for future meetings.

Newsletter Readership

Editors of newsletters should evaluate readership annually. Such an evaluation can help ascertain (1) reader perceptions, (2) the degree to which stories are balanced, (3) kinds of stories that have high reader interest, (4) additional topics that should be covered, (5) credibility of the publication, and (6) the extent to which it is meeting organizational objectives.

Systematic evaluation, it should be emphasized, is not based on whether all the copies are distributed or picked up. This information doesn't tell the editor what the audience actually read, retained, or acted upon. A newsletter, newspaper, or even a brochure can be evaluated in the following ways:

Content Analysis   From a representative sample of past issues, stories may be categorized under general headings such as (1) management announcements, (2) new product developments, (3) new personnel and retirements, (4) features about employees, (5) corporate finances, (6) news of departments and divisions, and (7) job-related information.

Such a systematic analysis will show what percentage of the publication is devoted to each category. It may be found that one division is rarely covered in the employee newsletter or that management pronouncements tend to dominate the entire publication. Given these findings, editors may wish to shift the content somewhat.

Readership Interest Surveys   The purpose of these surveys is to get feedback about the types of stories employees are most interested in reading.

The most common method is simply to provide a long list of generic story topics and have employees rate each as (1) important, (2) somewhat important, or (3) not important. The International Association of Business Communicators (IABC) conducted such a survey on behalf of several dozen companies and found that readers were not very interested in "personals" about other employees (birthdays, anniversaries, and the like).

Article Recall   The best kind of readership survey occurs when trained interviewers ask a sampling of employees what they have read in the latest issue of the publication.

Employees are shown the publication page by page and asked to indicate which articles they have read. As a check on the tendency of employees to report that they have read everything, interviewers also ask them (1) how much of each article they have read and (2) what the articles were about. The results are then content-analyzed to determine which kinds of articles have the most readership.

CASE PROBLEM

The Ohio Department of Transportation, with 17 rideshare groups, is planning a Rideshare Week. The objective is to increase participation in carpooling and use of mass transit during this special week. A long-term objective, of course, is to increase the number of people who use carpools or mass transit on a regular basis.

Your public relations firm is retained to promote Ohio Rideshare Week. Your campaign will include a news conference with the governor encouraging participation, press kits, news releases, interviews on broadcast talk shows, special events, and distribution of Rideshare information booklets at major businesses.

What methods would you use to evaluate the effectiveness of your public relations efforts on behalf of Ohio Rideshare Week?

QUESTIONS FOR REVIEW AND DISCUSSION

1. What is the role of stated objectives in evaluating public relations programs?

2. What primary method of evaluation do public relations people use? Is there any evidence that other methods are increasingly being used?

3. What are some general types of evaluation questions that a person should ask about a program?

4. Name four ways by which publicity activity is evaluated. What, if any, are the drawbacks to each one?

5. Do you think news stories about a product or service should be evaluated in terms of comparable advertising costs? Why or why not?

6. What are the advantages of systematic tracking and content analysis of news clippings?

7. How are pilot tests and split messages used to determine the suitability of a message?

8. How does measurement of message exposure differ from measurement of audience comprehension of the message?

9. How are benchmark studies used in evaluation of public relations programs?

10. What is a communication audit?

11. What methods of evaluation can be done for a company newsletter or magazine?

10

Public Opinion and Persuasion

Preview

The objectives of this chapter are to explain what constitutes public opinion and how it is formed, and to guide students in selecting the appropriate techniques for public relations situations.

Topics covered in the chapter include:

* What is public opinion?
* Opinion leaders as catalysts
* The media's role
* Persuasion: pervasive in our lives
* Factors in persuasive communication
* Propaganda
* Persuasion and manipulation
* The ethics of persuasion

WHAT IS PUBLIC OPINION?

Americans talk about public opinion as if it were a monolithic entity overshadowing the entire landscape. Editorial cartoonists, in contrast, humanize it in the form of John Q. or Jane Public, characters who symbolize what people think about any given issue. The reality is that public opinion is somewhat elusive and extremely difficult to measure at any given moment.

In fact, to continue the metaphor, public opinion is a number of monoliths and John and Jane Q. Publics all existing at the same time. Few issues create unanimity of thought among the population, and public opinion on any issue is split in several directions. It may also come as a surprise to note that only a small number of people at any given time take part in public opinion formation on a specific issue.

There are two reasons for this. First, psychologists have found that the public tends to be passive. Few issues generate an opinion or feeling on the part of an entire citizenry. It is often assumed that a small, vocal group represents the attitude of the public when, in reality, it is more accurate to say that the majority of the people—are apathetic because the issue doesn't interest or affect them. Thus "public" opposition to such issues as nuclear power, gay rights, abortion, and gun control may really be the view of a small but significant number of concerned people.

Second, one issue may engage the attention of one part of the population, while another arouses the interest of another segment. Parents, for example, may form public opinion on the need for improved secondary education, while senior citizens constitute the bulk of public opinion on the need for increased Social Security benefits.

These two examples illustrate the most common definition of public opinion: "Public opinion is the sum of individual opinions on an issue *affecting* those individuals." Another popular definition states: "Public opinion is a collection of views held by persons *interested* in the subject." Thus a person unaffected by or uninterested in (and perhaps unaware of) an issue does not contribute to public opinion on the subject.

Inherent in these definitions is the concept of *self-interest*. The following statements appear in public opinion research:

1. Public opinion is the collective expression of opinion of many individuals bound into a group by common aims, aspirations, needs, and ideals.

2. People who are interested or who have a vested or *self-interest* in an issue—or who can be affected by the outcome of the issue—form public opinion on that particular item.

3. Psychologically, opinion basically is determined by *self-interest*. Events, words, or any other stimuli affect opinion only insofar as their relationship to *self-interest* or a general concern is apparent.

4. Opinion does not remain aroused for any long period of time unless people feel their *self-interest* is acutely involved or unless opinion—aroused by words—is sustained by events.

5. Once *self-interest* is involved, opinion is not easily changed.

How practitioners utilize the concept of self-interest in focusing their message to fit the audience is discussed under "Appeal to Self-Interest," later in this chapter.

Research studies also emphasize the importance of *events* in the formation of public opinion. Social scientists, for example, have made the following generalizations:

1. Opinion is highly sensitive to *events* that have an impact on the public at large or a particular segment of the public.

2. By and large, public opinion does not anticipate *events*. It only reacts to them.

3. *Events* trigger formation of public opinion. Unless people are aware of an issue, they are not likely to be concerned or have an opinion. Awareness and discussion lead to crystallizing of opinions and often a consensus among the public.

4. *Events* of unusual magnitude are likely to swing public opinion temporarily from one extreme to another. Opinion does not stabilize until the implication of the event is seen with some perspective.

People also have more opinions and are able to form them more easily with respect to goals than with the methods necessary to reach those goals. Fairly strong public opinion, according to polls, favors improving the quality of the nation's schools. There is little agreement, however, on how to do this. One group advocates higher salaries for "master" teachers, another endorses substantial tax increases for school operations. A third group urges more rigorous standards. All three groups, plus assorted other ones with still other solutions, make up public opinion on the subject.

OPINION LEADERS AS CATALYSTS

Public opinion on an issue may have its roots in self-interest or in events, but the primary catalyst is public discussion. Only in this way does opinion begin to crystallize, and pollsters can measure it.

Serving as catalysts for the formation of public opinion are people who are knowledgeable and articulate about specific issues. They are called *opinion leaders.* Sociologists describe them as (1) highly interested in the subject or issue, (2) better informed on the issue than the average person, (3) avid consumers of mass media, (4) early adopters of new ideas, and (5) good organizers who can get other people to take action.

Types of Leaders

Sociologists traditionally have defined two types of leaders. First are the *formal opinion leaders,* so called because of their positions as elected officials, presidents of companies, or heads of membership groups. Often news reporters ask them for statements when a specific issue relates to their areas of responsibility or concern. People in formal leadership positions are also called *power leaders.*

Second are the *informal opinion leaders,* who have clout with peers because of some special characteristic. They may be *role models* who are admired and emulated, or opinion leaders because they can exert peer pressure on others to go along with something. In general, informal opinion leaders exert considerable influence on their peer groups by being highly informed, articulate, and credible on particular issues.

A survey of 20,000 Americans by the Roper Organization found that only 10 to 12 percent of the general public are opinion leaders. These "influentials," those whom other people seek out for advice, fit the profile of (1) being active in the community, (2) having a college degree, (3) earning relatively high incomes, (4) regularly reading newspapers and magazines, (5) actively participating in recreational activities, and (6) showing environmental concern by recycling.

Regis McKenna, a marketing communications expert responsible for the original launch of the Apple Macintosh, likes to think of opinion leaders as *luminaries* because, "There are about 20 to 30 key people in every industry who have major influence on trends, standards, and an organization's reputation." He also knows that journalists seek quotes from key opinion leaders in an industry whenever a new product is introduced.

The Role of Mass Media

One traditional way that public relations personnel reach opinion leaders and other key publics is via the mass media—radio, television, newspapers, and magazines. Mass media, as the term infers, means that information from a public relations source can be efficiently and rapidly disseminated to literally millions of people.

PR Insights

The Life Cycle of Public Opinion

Public opinion and persuasion are important catalysts in the formation of a public issue and its ultimate resolution. The natural evolution of an issue involves five stages:

DEFINITION OF THE ISSUE

Activist and special interest groups raise an issue, perhaps a protest against scenic areas being threatened by logging or strip mining. These groups have no formal power but serve as "agenda stimuli" for the media that cover controversy and conflict. Visual opportunities for television coverage occur when activists hold rallies and demonstrations.

INVOLVEMENT OF OPINION LEADERS

Through media coverage, the issue is put on the public agenda and people become aware of it. Opinion leaders begin to discuss the issue and perhaps see it as symbolic of broader environmental issues.

PUBLIC AWARENESS

As public awareness grows, the issue becomes a matter of public discussion and debate, with

extensive media coverage. The issue is simplified by the media into "them versus us." Suggested solutions tend to be at either end of the spectrum.

GOVERNMENT/REGULATORY INVOLVEMENT

Public consensus begins to build for a resolution as government/regulatory involvement occurs. Large groups identify with some side of the issue. Demand grows for government to act.

RESOLUTION

The resolution stage begins as people with authority (elected officials) draft legislation or interpret existing rules and regulations to make a statement. A decision is made to protect the scenic areas, or to reach a compromise with advocates of development. If some groups remain unhappy, however, the cycle may repeat itself.

In order to better understand how public relations people strive to inform the public and shape public opinion via the mass media, it is necessary to review briefly several theories about mass media effects.

Agenda Setting Theory One of the early theories, developed by Paul Lazarsfeld and Elihu Katz, contends that media content sets the agenda for public discussion. People tend to talk about what they see or hear on the 6 o'clock news or read on the front page of the newspaper. Media, by the selection of stories and headlines, tell the public what to think about, but not necessarily what to think. The Clinton/Lewinsky sex scandal, for example, was high on the media agenda for many months, but public opinion polls indicated a variety of viewpoints on the subject.

Social scientist Joseph Klapper calls this the "limited effects" model of mass media. He postulates, "Mass media ordinarily does not serve as a necessary and sufficient cause for audience effects, but rather functions among and through a nexus of mediating factors and influence." Such factors may include the way that opinion leaders analyze and interpret the information provided by the mass media.

From a public relations standpoint, even getting a subject on the media agenda is an accomplishment that advances organizational goals. Sales of Apple's new product, the iMac, rose as the media reported its success and the public became aware of this "hot" item.

Media Dependency Theory Although the agenda-setting function of the media is generally valid, other research indicates that mass media can have a "moderate" or even "powerful" effect on the formation of opinions and attitudes. When people have no prior information or attitude disposition regarding a subject, the mass media play a role in telling people what to think.

Mass media effects are also increased when people cannot verify information through personal experience and knowledge. They are highly dependent on the media for information. Therefore, if much of this information comes from official spokespersons of organizations, it's an opportunity for public relations to shape the tone and content of a story—or, as was noted in Chapter 1, put a particular "spin" on the story. At the University of North Dakota, researchers Debbie Steele and Kirk Hallahan researched a crisis situation for a blood bank and found, "Official sources enjoy an advantage in the early phases of a crisis or issue, particularly when media and others are still in the discovery phase of coverage and the primary emphasis is merely to identify the extent of the problem."

Framing Theory The term "framing" has a long history in mass media research. Traditionally, framing was related to journalists and how they selected certain facts, themes, treatments, and even words to "frame" a story. According to researchers Julie L. Andsager at Washington State University and Angela Powers at Northern Illinois University, "Mass media scholars have long argued that it is important to understand the ways in which journalistic framing of issues occurs because such framing impacts public understanding and, consequently, policy formation." For example, how media frame the debate over health care and the role of HMOs often plays a major role in public perceptions of the problem.

Increasingly, however, scholars are also applying framing theory to public relations efforts. One research paper, by James Tankard and Bill Israel of the University of Texas, was titled, "PR Goes to War: The Effects of Public Relations Campaigns on Media Framing of the Kuwait and Bosnian Crises." Their basic contention was that the governments involved used public relations professionals to help "frame" the issues involved, which were then picked up by the press.

In the case of Kuwait, Hill and Knowlton (see Chapter 3) used the theme of Iraqi atrocities to frame the issue in support of Kuwait. In Bosnia, Ruder-Finn framed the issue as Serb genocide against Bosnian Muslims. Almost overnight, the media were also equating the Serbs with the Nazis in the public mind by using highly emotional words such as "ethnic cleansing" and "concentration camps."

Tankard and Israel point out that the media dependency of most Americans—who have little direct knowledge of these places and the complex issues involved—means that they accept the media's version of reality—which originally came from what the two researchers describe as "special interest groups or other groups with particular causes."

Most public relations personnel rarely find themselves framing the issues of an international conflict, but they do exercise "framing" or "positioning" strategies on any number of products and services. When Edelman Worldwide, for example, was considering strategy for the launch of Apple's iMac computer, one of the strong themes (or frames) was that Apple was on the way back to prosperity after several years of massive losses and erosion of customer support. Indeed, one headline in a daily newspaper proclaimed, "Apple Regains Its Stride." Such "framing" obviously bolsters investor and consumer confidence in the company.

Cultivation Theory   Communication researchers like to call the news content of mass media "mediated reality" since events are repackaged to be more succinct, logical, and interesting to a reader or viewer. This mediated reality, however, can influence beliefs and even conduct if repeated often enough. George Gerbner, of the University of Pennsylvania, conducted the first research on the topic of violence on television and how it affects people. He and his associates found that constant violence portrayed in TV shows eventually "cultivated" viewers to the idea that crime was rampant, and their fears about violence in their own neighborhoods became highly exaggerated.

Again, from a public relations perspective, does that mean that public relations professionals are able, via the media, to "cultivate" viewers into the "mediated reality" to perceive that a company is a solid citizen or that the brand name does mean quality? Or does a corporate advertising campaign, repeated often enough, really "cultivate" consumers to accept the image of the organization portrayed? The vote is still out.

PERSUASION: PERVASIVE IN OUR LIVES

Persuasion has been around since the dawn of human history. It was formalized as a concept more than 2000 years ago by the Greeks, who made *rhetoric,* the art of using language effectively and persuasively, part of their educational system. Aristotle was the first to set down the ideas of *ethos, logos,* and *pathos,* which roughly translate as "source credibility," "logical argument," and "emotional appeal."

More recent scholars, such as Richard Perloff, author of *The Dynamics of Persuasion* (Lawrence Erlbaum, 1993), say "Persuasion is an activity or process in which a communicator attempts to induce a change in the belief, attitude, or behavior of another person or group of persons through the transmission of a message in a context in which the persuadee has some degree of free choice."

Such a definition is consistent with the role of public relations professionals in today's society. Indeed, Professor Richard Heath says:

> . . . public relations professionals are influential rhetors. They design, place, and repeat messages on behalf of sponsors on an array of topics that shape views of government, charitable organizations, institutions of public education, products and consumerism, capitalism, labor, health, and leisure. These professionals speak, write, and use visual images to discuss topics and take stances on public policies at the local, state, and federal levels.

The dominant public view of public relations, in fact, is one of persuasive communication actions performed on behalf of clients, according to Professors Dean Kruckeberg at the University of Northern Iowa and Ken Starck at the University of Iowa. Gandy adds that ". . . the primary role of public relations is one of purposeful, self-interested communications." And Edward Bernays even called public relations the "engineering" of consent to create "a favorable and positive climate of opinion toward the individual, product, institution or idea which is represented." See Chapter 2 for definitions by Edward L. Bernays.

To accomplish this goal, public relations personnel use a variety of techniques to reach and influence their audiences. At the same time, persuasion or rhetoric should be considered more than a one-way flow of information, argument, and influence. In the best sense, Toth and Heath in their book *Rhetorical and Critical Approaches to Public Relations,* say persuasion should be a dialogue between points of view in the marketplace of public opinion, where any number of persuaders are hawking their wares.

PR Insights

A Sampler on Persuasion

A number of research studies have contributed to a basic understanding of persuasion concepts. Here are some basic ideas from the text *Public Communication Campaigns,* edited by Ronald E. Rice and William J. Paisley:

- Positive appeals are generally more effective than negative appeals for retention of the message and actual compliance.

- Radio and television messages tend to be more persuasive than print but, if the message is complex, better comprehension is achieved through print media.

- Strong emotional appeals and fear arousal are most effective when the audience has minimal concern about or interest in the topic.

- High fear appeals are effective only when a readily available action can be taken to eliminate the threat.

- Logical appeals, using facts and figures, are better for highly educated, sophisticated audiences than strong emotional appeals.

- Altruistic need, like self-interest, can be a strong motivator. Men are willing to get a physical checkup more to protect their families than to protect themselves.

- A celebrity or an attractive model is most effective when the audience has low involvement, the theme is simple, and broadcast channels are used. An exciting spokesperson attracts attention to a message that would otherwise be ignored.

Indeed, persuasion is an integral part of democratic society. It is the freedom of speech used by every individual and organization to influence opinion, understanding, judgment, and action.

Uses of Persuasion

Persuasion is used to (1) change or neutralize hostile opinions, (2) crystallize latent opinions and positive attitudes, and (3) conserve favorable opinions.

The most difficult persuasive task is to turn hostile opinions into favorable ones. There is much truth to the adage "Don't confuse me with the facts; my mind is made up." Once people have decided, for instance, that HMOs are making excessive profits or that a nonprofit agency is wasting public donations, they tend to ignore or disbelieve any contradictory information. Everyone, as Walter Lippmann has described, has pictures in his or her head based on an individual perception of reality. People generalize from personal experience and what peers tell them. For example, if a person has an encounter with a rude clerk, the inclination is to generalize that the entire department store chain is not very good.

Persuasion is much easier if the message is compatible with a person's general disposition toward a subject. If a person tends to identify Toyota as a company with a good reputation, he or she may express this feeling by purchasing one of its cars. Nonprofit agencies usually crystallize the public's latent inclination to aid the less fortunate by asking for a donation. Both examples illustrate the reason that organizations strive to have a good reputation—it is translated into sales and donations. The concept of message channeling will be discussed in more detail later in the chapter.

The easiest form of persuasion is communication that reinforces favorable opinions. Public relations people, by providing a steady stream of reinforcing messages, keep the reservoir of goodwill in sound condition. More than one organization has survived a major problem because public esteem for it tended to minimize current difficulties. Continual efforts to maintain the reservoir of goodwill is called *preventive public relations*—the most effective of all.

FACTORS IN PERSUASIVE COMMUNICATION

A number of factors are involved in persuasive communication, and the public relations practitioner should be knowledgeable about each one. The following is a brief discussion of (1) audience analysis, (2) source credibility, (3) appeal to self-interest, (4) clarity of message, (5) timing and context, (6) audience participation, (7) suggestions for action, (8) content and structure of messages, and (9) persuasive speaking.

Audience Analysis

Knowledge of audience characteristics such as beliefs, attitudes, concerns, and lifestyles is an essential part of persuasion. It helps the communicator tailor messages that are salient, answer a felt need, and provide a logical course of action.

Basic demographic information, readily available through census data, can help determine an audience's gender, income level, education, ethnic background, and age groupings. Other data, often prepared for marketing departments, give information on a group's buying habits, disposable income, and ways of spending leisure time.

Polling and surveys, discussed in Chapter 6, tap a target audience's attitudes, opinions, and concerns. Such research tells about the public's resistance to some ideas, as well as its predisposition to support other ideas. Recycling programs, for example, made a slow start in the early 1990s because the public resisted changing its habit of throwing everything into the same garbage container. Yet surveys showed that although the public was concerned about the environment, "convenience" was king. The only way to change habits was to make it easy for homeowners to recycle by providing sorting bins that, in turn, were regularly picked up. Many cities also opened neighborhood recycling centers that paid people for bottles and cans. Today, recycling is the norm.

Such audience analysis, coupled with suitably tailored messages in the appropriate media outlets, is the technique of *channeling.* Persuasive messages are more effective when they take into account the audience's lifestyles, beliefs, and concerns.

Source Credibility

A message is more believable to the intended audience if the source has *credibility.* This was Aristotle's concept of *ethos,* mentioned earlier, and it explains why organizations use a variety of spokespeople, depending upon the message and the audience.

The California Strawberry Advisory Board, for example, arranges for a home economist to appear on television talk shows to discuss nutrition and to demonstrate easy-to-follow strawberry recipes. The viewers, primarily homemakers, identified with the representative and found her highly credible. By the same token, a manufacturer of sunscreen lotion uses a professor of pharmacology and a past president of the State Pharmacy Board to discuss the scientific merits of sunscreen versus suntan lotions.

The Three Factors   Source credibility is based on three factors. One is *expertise.* Does the audience perceive the person as an expert on the subject? Companies, for example, use engineers and scientists to answer news conference questions about how an engineering process works or whether an ingredient in the manufacturing process of a product presents a potential hazard.

The second component is *sincerity.* Does the person come across as believing what he or she is saying? Robin Williams may not be an expert on all the products he endorses, but he does get high ratings for sincerity.

The third component, even more elusive, is *charisma.* Is the individual attractive, self-assured, and articulate, projecting an image of competence and leadership?

Ideally, a source will exhibit all three attributes. Steve Jobs, president of Apple, is a good example. He is highly credible as an expert on Apple products because he is one of the company's founders and also a "geek" in his own right. In countless media interviews and trade show presentations, he comes across as a candid, open individual who really believes in the company's products. Jobs also has charisma; he is self-assured, confident, and articulate. His standard uniform—the open-neck shirt, the vest, and the designer jeans—gives him additional aura as a legendary figure in the computer industry.

Not every organization, however, has a Steve Jobs for its president. Depending on the message and the audience, various spokespersons can be used and quoted for source credibility. A news release for a new product, for example, might quote the director of research and development (R&D) for the company. If the information is about an organization's financial picture, the most credible person would be the chief executive officer (CEO) or the vice president of finance, primarily because of perceived expertise.

Expertise is less important than sincerity and charisma if celebrities are used as spokespersons. Their primary purpose is to call attention to the product or service. Another purpose is to associate the celebrity's popularity with the product. This technique is called *transfer,* mentioned later in this chapter as a propaganda device.

Bill Cosby, for example, is a perennial favorite as a product endorser in terms of effectiveness, credibility, and popularity. In a survey by American Research Company, Cosby scored No. 1 as the best product endorser in 1998, which was exactly where he ranked in 1988. Other surveys, such as one conducted by Video Storyboard, highly rank Candice Bergen, Cosby, Kathie Lee Gifford, and Michael Jordan as good product endorsers.

Using celebrities has its problems, however. One is the increasing number of endorsements to the point that the public sometimes can't remember who endorses what. Candice Bergen endorses Sprint, but a third of the Video Storyboard respondents thought she endorsed AT&T or MCI. A second problem can be overexposure of a celebrity such as Michael Jordan, who gets about $40 million annually for endorsing more than a dozen products.

The third problem occurs when an endorser's actions undercut the product or service. Actress Cybil Shepherd, who once starred in commercials for beef, caused considerable anguish in the cattle industry when she was quoted in a magazine as saying that she rarely ate beef. Florida orange juice producers immediately cancelled Burt Reynolds as a spokesperson because of his bitter breakup with Loni Anderson. The producers thought his marital problem was at odds with the image of orange juice as a healthful, happy, family product.

In summary, the use of various sources for credibility depends, in large part, on the type of audience being reached. That is why audience analysis is the first step in formulating persuasive messages.

Appeal to Self-Interest

Self-interest was described during an earlier discussion about the formation of public opinion. Publics become involved in issues or pay attention to messages that appeal to their psychic or economic needs.

Publicity for a personal computer can serve as an example. A news release to the trade press serving the computer industry might focus on the technical proficiency of the equipment. The audience, of course, consists of engineers and computer programmers. A brochure prepared for the public, however, may emphasize how the computer can (1) help people keep track of personal finances, (2) assist youngsters in becoming better students, (3) fit into a small space, and (4) offer good value. Consumers are interested in how the personal computer can make life easier for them.

Charitable organizations don't sell products, but they do need volunteers and donations. This is accomplished by careful structuring of messages that appeal to self-interest. This is not to say that altruism is dead. Thousands of people give freely of their time and money to charitable organizations, but they do receive something in return, or they would not do it. The "something in return" may be (1) self-esteem, (2) the opportunity to make a contribution to society, (3) recognition from peers and the community, (4) a sense of belonging, (5) ego gratification, or even (6) a tax deduction. Public relations people understand psychic needs and rewards, and that is why there is constant recognition of volunteers in newsletters and at award banquets. (Further discussion of volunteerism appears in Chapter 16).

Sociologist Harold Lasswell says people are motivated by eight basic appeals. They are power, respect, well-being, affection, wealth, skill, enlightenment, and physical and mental vitality. Psychologist Abraham Maslow, in turn, says any appeal to self-interest must be based on a *hierarchy of needs*. The first and lowest level involves basic needs such as food, water, shelter, and even transportation to and from work. The second level consists of security needs. People need to feel secure in their jobs, safe in their homes, and confident about their retirement. At the third level are "belonging" needs—people seek association with others. This is why individuals join organizations.

"Love" needs comprise the fourth level in the hierarchy. Humans have a need to be wanted and loved—fulfilling the desire for self-esteem. At the fifth and highest level in Maslow's hierarchy are self-actualization needs. Once the first four needs are met, Maslow says, people are free to achieve maximum personal potential; for example, through traveling extensively or perhaps becoming experts on orchids.

The challenge for public relations personnel, as creators of persuasive messages, is to tailor information to fill or reduce a need. Social scientists have said that success in persuasion largely depends on accurate assessment of audience needs and self-interests.

Clarity of Message

Many messages fail because the audience finds the message unnecessarily complex in content or language. The most persuasive messages are direct, are simply expressed, and contain only one primary idea. Peter Drucker, a management expert, once said, "An innovation, to be effective, has to be simple and it has to be focused. It should do only one thing, otherwise it confuses." The same can be said for the content of any message.

Timing and Context

A message is more persuasive if environmental factors support the message or if the message is received within the context of other messages and situations with which the individual is familiar. These factors are called timing and context.

Information from a utility on how to conserve energy is more salient if the consumer has just received the January heating bill. A pamphlet on a new stock offering is more effective if it accompanies an investor's dividend check. A citizens' group lobbying for a stoplight gets more attention if a major accident has just occurred at the intersection.

Political candidates are aware of public concerns and avidly read polls to learn what issues are most salient with voters. If the polls indicate that crime and unemployment are key issues, the candidate begins to use these issues—and to offer his or her proposals—in the campaign.

Timing and context also play an important role in achieving publicity in the mass media. Public relations personnel, as pointed out earlier, should read newspapers and watch television news programs to find out what media gatekeepers consider newsworthy. A manufacturer of a locking device for computer files got extensive media coverage about its product simply because its release followed a rash of news stories about thieves' gaining access to bank accounts through computers. Media gatekeepers found the product newsworthy within the context of actual news events.

Audience Participation

A change in attitude or reinforcement of beliefs is enhanced by *audience involvement and participation.*

An organization, for example, may have employees discuss productivity in a quality-control circle. Management may already have figured out what is needed, but if workers are involved in the problem-solving, they often come up with the same solution or even a better one. And, from a persuasion standpoint, the employees are more committed to making the solution work because it came from them—not as a policy or order handed down by higher management.

Participation can also take the form of samples. Many companies distribute product samples so the consumer can conveniently try them without expense. A consumer who samples the product and makes a judgment about its quality is more likely to purchase it.

Activist groups use participation as a way of helping people actualize their beliefs. Not only do rallies and demonstrations give people a sense of belonging, but the act of participation reinforces their beliefs. Asking people to do something—conserve energy, collect donations, or picket—activates a form of self-persuasion and commitment.

Suggestions for Action

A principle of persuasion is that people endorse ideas only if they are accompanied by a proposed action from the sponsor.

Recommendations for action must be clear. Public relations practitioners must not only ask people to conserve energy, for instance, but also furnish detailed data and ideas on how to do it.

A campaign conducted by Pacific Gas & Electric Company provides an example. The utility inaugurated a Zero Interest Program (ZIP) to offer customers a way to implement energy-saving ideas. The program involved several components:

1. *Energy kit.* A telephone hotline was established and widely publicized so interested customers could order an energy kit detailing what the average homeowner could do to reduce energy use.

2. *Service bureau.* The company, at no charge, sent representatives to homes to check the efficiency of water heaters and furnaces, measure the amount of insulation, and check doors and windows for drafts.

3. *ZIP.* The cost of making a home more energy-efficient was funded by zero-interest loans to any qualified customer.

Content and Structure of Messages

A number of techniques can make a message more persuasive. Writers throughout history have emphasized some information while downplaying or omitting other pieces of information. Thus they addressed both the *content and structure of messages.*

Expert communicators continue to use a number of devices, including (1) drama, (2) statistics, (3) surveys and polls, (4) examples, (5) testimonials, (6) mass media endorsements, and (7) emotional appeals.

Drama   Because everyone likes a good story, the first task of a communicator is to get audience attention. This is often accomplished by graphically illustrating an event or situation. Newspapers often dramatize a story to get reader interest in an issue. Thus we read about the family evicted from its home in a story on the increase in bankruptcies; the old man who is starving because of welfare red tape; or the worker disabled because of toxic waste. In newsrooms, this is called *humanizing an issue.*

Dramatizing is also used in public relations. Relief organizations, in particular, attempt to galvanize public concern and donations through drama, as shown in the photographs below. The UNICEF fund-raising letter's description of a child dying of malnutrition, like the stark black-and-white photographs used by other relief organizations, creates powerful imagery, emotion, and drama.

A more mundane use of dramatizing is the so-called *application story,* sent to the trade press. This is sometimes called the *case study technique,* in which a manufacturer prepares an article on how an individual or a company is using the product. IBM, for example, provides a number of application stories about the unique ways in which its products are being used.

Faith, Hope and Love.
But the greatest of these is
Love.

Emotional appeals emphasizing children are used frequently by charitable organizations to stimulate fund-raising. This solicitation by Save the Children appeals to readers' instinct for seeking love, personalizing the message with winsome photographs of children.

your sponsored child. You'll learn firsthand that the most valuable thing you can give this young girl or boy is your love.

Please call 1-800-736-1818 or mail the coupon below today. Thank you.

Yes. I'll help needy children through sponsorship.

I prefer to sponsor a __boy __girl __either in the area I've checked below.

Please send my child's photo and personal history.

☐ Where the need is greatest ☐ Caribbean/Latin America
☐ Middle East ☐ Africa ☐ Asia

Name _____
Phone (____) _____
Address _____ Apt. _____
City _____ State _____ Zip _____

Established in 1932. The original child sponsorship agency. YOUR SPONSORSHIP CONTRIBUTIONS ARE U.S. INCOME TAX DEDUCTIBLE. We are indeed proud of our use of funds. Our annual report and audit statement are available upon request.
©1995 Save the Children Federation, Inc.

Please charge my monthly sponsorship contribution of $20 to my credit card automatically each month: ☐ Mastercard ☐ Visa ☐ Discover ☐ Amex
Account # _____
Exp. Date _____
Signature _____

☐ I prefer to pay by check each month. My first monthly sponsorship contribution of $20 is enclosed.

☐ Instead of becoming a sponsor at this time, I am enclosing a contribution of $_____.

☐ Please send me more information.

Save the Children.
50 Wilton Road, Westport, CT 06880

Statistics   People are impressed by statistics. Use of numbers can convey objectivity, size, and importance in a credible way that can influence public opinion. Caterpillar, for example, got considerable media publicity for its new 797 mining dump truck by combining statistics and some humor. In the news release for the largest truck in the world, it announced that the bed of the truck was so large that it could haul the following payloads: four blue whales, 217 taxicabs, 1,200 grand pianos, and 23,490 Furbies.

Surveys and Polls   Airlines and auto manufacturers, in particular, use the results of *surveys and polls* to show that they are first in "customer satisfaction," "service," and even "leg room" or "cargo space." The most credible surveys are those conducted by independent research organizations, but readers still should read the fine print to see what is being compared and rated. Is an American-made auto, for example, being compared only with other U.S. cars or with foreign cars as well?

Examples   A statement of opinion can be more persuasive if some *examples* are given. A school board can often get support for a bond issue by citing examples of how the present facilities are inadequate for student needs. Environmental groups tell how other communities have successfully established greenbelts when requesting a city council to do the same. Automakers promote the durability of their vehicles by citing their performance on a test track or in a road race.

Testimonials   A form of source credibility, *testimonials* can be either explicit or implied. A campaign to curtail alcohol and drug abuse may feature a pop singer as a spokesperson, or have a young woman talk about being paralyzed and disfigured as the victim of a drunk driver. Implied testimonials also can be effective. Proclamations by mayors and governors establishing Red Cross Day or Library Week are implied testimonials. The testimonial as a propaganda device is discussed later in the chapter.

Endorsements   In addition to those by paid celebrities, products and services benefit from favorable statements by experts in what is called a *third-party endorsement.* A well-known medical specialist may publicly state that a particular brand of exercise equipment is best for general conditioning. Organizations such as the American Dental Association and the National Safety Council also endorse products and services.

Media endorsements, usually unpaid, can come through editorials, reviews, surveys, and news stories. A daily newspaper may endorse a political candidate, review restaurants and entertainment events, and even compile a survey ranking the best coffeehouses. The media also produce news stories about new products and services which, because of their perceived objectivity, are considered a form of *third-party endorsement.* The idea is that media coverage bestows legitimacy and newsworthiness on a product or service.

Emotional Appeals   Fund-raising letters from nonprofit groups, in particular, use this persuasive device. Amnesty International, an organization dedicated to human rights and fighting state terrorism, began one direct-mail letter with the following message in large red type:

> "We Are God in Here . . ."
>   . . . That's what the guards taunted the prisoner with as they applied electrical shocks to her body while she lay handcuffed to the springs of a metal bed. Her cries were echoed by the screams of other victims and the laughter of their torturers.

Such emotional appeals can do much to galvanize the public into action, but they also can backfire. Such appeals raise ego defenses, and people don't like to be told that in some way they are responsible. A description of suffering makes many people uncomfortable, and, rather than take action, they may tune out the message. A relief organization runs full-page advertisements in magazines with the headline "You Can Help Maria Get Enough to Eat . . . Or You Can Turn the Page." Researchers say that most people, their ego defenses raised, turn the page and mentally refuse to acknowledge that they even saw the ad. In sum, emotional appeals that attempt to lay a guilt trip on the audience are not very successful.

Strong fear arousals also can cause people to tune out, especially if they feel that they can't do anything about the problem anyway. Research indicates, however, that a moderate fear arousal, accompanied by a relatively easy solution, is effective. A moderate fear arousal is: "What would happen if your child were thrown through the windshield in an accident?" The message concludes with the suggestion that a baby, for protection and safety, should be placed in a secured infant seat.

Psychologists say the most effective emotional appeal is one coupled with facts and figures. The emotional appeal attracts audience interest, but logical arguments are also needed.

PROPAGANDA

No discussion of persuasion would be complete without mentioning propaganda and the techniques associated with it.

Garth S. Jowett and Victoria O'Donnell in their book, *Propaganda and Persuasion* (Sage), say "Propaganda is the deliberate and systematic attempt to shape perceptions, manipulate cognitions, and direct behavior to achieve a response that furthers the desired intent of the propagandist." Its roots go back to the seventeenth century, when the Roman Catholic Church set up the *congregatio de propaganda* (congregation for propagating the faith). The word took on extremely negative connotations in the twentieth century.

In World Wars I and II, propaganda was associated with the information activities of the enemy. Germany and Japan were sending out "propaganda" while the United States and its allies were disseminating "truth." Today, propaganda connotes falsehood, lies, deceit, disinformation, and duplicity—practices that opposing groups and governments accuse each other of employing.

Some have even argued that propaganda, in the broadest sense of the word, also includes the advertising and public relations activity of such diverse entities as Exxon and the Sierra Club. Social scientists, however, say that the word *propaganda* should be used only to denote activity that sells a belief system or constitutes political or ideological dogma.

Advertising and public relations messages for commercial purposes, however, do use several techniques commonly associated with propaganda. The most common are the following:

1. *Plain folks.* An approach often used by individuals to show humble beginnings and empathy with the average citizen. Political candidates, in particular, are quite fond of telling about their "humble" beginnings.

2. *Testimonial.* A frequently used device to achieve credibility, as discussed earlier. A well-known expert, popular celebrity, or average citizen gives testimony about the value of a product or the wisdom of a decision.

Is "Framing" an Issue OK?

The chapter includes information about the efforts of public relations firms to "frame" issues that would, in turn, be reflected by media coverage. Others might call this kind of effort "positioning" or even putting a "spin" on a particular event. The objective, of course, is to define the issues involved for the media and subsequently for the public. Hill and Knowlton, for example, helped frame the invasion of Kuwait by Iraq, using the theme of atrocity stories to generate anti-Iraq sentiment in the American people. Is "framing" a legitimate and ethical aspect if today's public relations practice? Why or why not?

3. *Bandwagon.* The implication or direct statement that everyone wants the product or that the idea has overwhelming support. "Millions of Americans support a ban on abortion" or "Every leading expert believes. . . ."

4. *Card-stacking.* The selection of facts and data to build an overwhelming case on one side of the issue, while concealing the other side. The advertising industry says a ban on beer advertising would lead to enormous reductions in network sports programming, and a ban on cigarette advertising would kill many magazines.

5. *Transfer.* The technique of associating the person, product, or organization with something that has high status, visibility, or credibility. Many corporations, for example, paid millions to be official sponsors of the 2000 Olympic Games, hoping that the public would associate their products with excellence.

6. *Glittering generalities.* The technique of associating a cause, product, or idea with favorable abstractions such as freedom, justice, democracy, and the American way. Las Vegas bills itself as "The American Way to Play," and American oil companies argue for offshore drilling to keep "America energy-independent."

A student of public relations should be aware of these techniques, if only to make certain that he or she doesn't intentionally use them to deceive and mislead the public. Ethical responsibilities exist in every form of persuasive communication; guidelines are discussed at the end of the chapter.

PERSUASION AND MANIPULATION

The discussion on previous pages examined ways in which an individual can formulate persuasive messages. The ability to use these often leads to charges that public relations practitioners have great power to influence and manipulate people.

In reality, the effectiveness of persuasive techniques is greatly exaggerated. Persuasion is not an exact science, and no surefire way exists to predict that people or media gatekeepers will be persuaded to believe a message or act on it. If persuasive techniques were as refined as the critics say, all people might be driving the same make of automobile, using the same soap, and voting for the same political candidate.

This doesn't happen because several variables intervene in the flow of persuasive messages. Katz says the two major intervening variables are selectivity and interpersonal relations; these are consistent with the "limited effects" model of mass communications.

For purposes of discussion, the limitations on effective persuasive messages can be listed as (1) lack of message penetration, (2) competing messages, (3) self-selection, and (4) self-perception.

Lack of Message Penetration

The diffusion of messages, despite modern communication technologies, is not pervasive. Not everyone, of course, watches the same television program or reads the same newspapers and magazines. Not everyone receives the same mail or attends the same meetings. Not everyone the communicator wants to reach will be in the audience eventually reached, despite advances in audience segmentation techniques. There is also the problem of messages being distorted as they pass through media gatekeepers. Key message points often are left out, or the context of the message is changed.

Competing Messages

In the 1930s, before much was known about the complex process of communication, it was believed that people received information directly without any intervening variable. This was called the *bullet theory* or the *hypodermic needle theory* of communication.

Today communication experts realize that no message is received in a vacuum. Messages are filtered through a receiver's entire social structure and belief system. Nationality, race, religion, gender, cultural patterns, family, and friends are among the variables that filter and dilute persuasive messages. In addition, people receive countless competing and conflicting messages daily. Social scientists say a person usually conforms to the standards of his or her family and friends. Consequently, most people do not believe or act on messages that are contrary to group norms.

Self-Selection

The people most wanted in an audience are often the least likely to be there. As any minister attests, sinners don't go to church on a regular basis. Vehement supporters or loyalists frequently ignore information from the other side. They do so by being selective in the messages that they want to hear. They read books, newspaper editorials, and magazine articles and view television programs that support their predispositions. This is why social scientists say that the media are more effective in reinforcing existing attitudes than in changing them.

Self-Perception

Self-perception is the channel through which messages are interpreted. People will perceive the same information differently, depending on predispositions and already formulated opinions. *Inside PR* newsletter describes how people react to news stories: "If they believe something to be true and see a story affirming that belief, their belief is strengthened. If they believe something to be true and see a story challenging that belief, they assume the story is biased or just plain wrong."

Thus, depending on a person's views, an action by an organization may be considered a "great contribution to the community" or a "self-serving gimmick."

THE ETHICS OF PERSUASION

Public relations people, by definition, are advocates of clients and employers. The emphasis is on persuasive communication to influence a particular public in some way. At the same time, as Chapter 3 pointed out, public relations practitioners must conduct their activities in an ethical manner.

The use of persuasive techniques, therefore, calls for some additional guidelines. Professor Richard L. Johannesen of Northern Illinois University, writing in *Persuasion, Reception and Responsibility,* a text by Charles Larson, lists the following ethical criteria for using persuasive devices that should be kept in mind by every public relations professional:

1. Do not use false, fabricated, misrepresented, distorted, or irrelevant evidence to support arguments or claims.

2. Do not intentionally use specious, unsupported, or illogical reasoning.

3. Do not represent yourself as informed or as an "expert" on a subject when you are not.

4. Do not use irrelevant appeals to divert attention or scrutiny from the issue at hand. Among the appeals that commonly serve such a purpose are "smear" attacks on an opponent's character, appeals to hatred and bigotry, innuendo, and "God" or "devil" terms that cause intense but unreflective positive or negative reactions.

5. Do not ask your audience to link your idea or proposal to emotion-laden values, motives, or goals to which it actually is not related.

6. Do not deceive your audience by concealing your real purpose, your self-interest, the group you represent, or your position as an advocate of a viewpoint.

7. Do not distort, hide, or misrepresent the number, scope, intensity, or undesirable features of consequences.

8. Do not use emotional appeals that lack a supporting basis of evidence or reasoning or that would not be accepted if the audience had time and opportunity to examine the subject itself.

9. Do not oversimplify complex situations into simplistic, two-valued, either/or, polar views or choices.

10. Do not pretend certainty when tentativeness and degrees of probability would be more accurate.

11. Do not advocate something in which you do not believe yourself.

It is clear from the preceding list that a public relations professional should be more than a technician or a "hired gun." This raises the issue that public relations personnel often lack the technical and legal expertise to know whether information provided to them by the client or employer is accurate.

Richard Heath makes it clear that this doesn't excuse public relations professionals from ethical responsibility. He writes:

> The problem of reporting information that they cannot personally verify does not excuse them from being responsible communicators. Their responsibility is to demand that the most accurate information be provided and the evaluation be the best available.

Persuasive messages require truth, honesty, and candor for two practical reasons. First, Heath says that a message is already suspect because it is advanced on behalf of a client or organization. Second, half-truths and misleading information do not serve the best interests of the public or the organization.

CASE PROBLEM

The school system of a major city wants to draw attention to the need for more volunteer adult tutors in the city's 200 public schools. Budget cutbacks in teaching staff and other resources have made it a vital necessity to recruit volunteers who would work with students on an individual basis to improve reading and math skills.

Your public relations firm has volunteered to organize a public information campaign. Explain what you would do in each of the following categories that relate to the structure and content of persuasive messages: drama, statistics, examples, testimonials, endorsements, and emotional appeals.

QUESTIONS FOR REVIEW AND DISCUSSION

1. Public opinion is highly influenced by self-interest and events. What are these concepts?

2. What is the importance of opinion leaders in the formation of public opinion?

3. What theories about mass media effects have relevance for public relations?

4. What are the stages of public opinion in the life cycle of an issue?

5. Name the three objectives of persuasion in public relations work. What objective is the most difficult to accomplish?

6. Can you name and describe the nine factors involved in persuasive communication?

7. What are three factors involved in source credibility?

8. What are the pros and cons of using celebrities for product endorsements?

9. What are the levels of Maslow's hierarchy of needs? Why is it important for public relations people to understand the basic needs of people?

10. Why is audience involvement and participation important in persuasion?

11. What kinds of techniques can a person use to write persuasive messages?

12. Name several propaganda techniques. Should they be used by public relations people?

13. What are some ethical responsibilities of a person who uses persuasion techniques to influence others?

The Audience and How to Reach It

Preview

The objective of this chapter is to explain the characteristics of the audiences public relations people seek to address and how the various media can be used to reach them.

Topics covered in the chapter include:
- Nature of the public relations audience
- Two special audiences: seniors and ethnic groups
- Matching audience and media
- Newspapers
- Created events: making news happen
- Magazines and books
- Radio
- Television and films
- Online media

THE NATURE OF THE PUBLIC RELATIONS AUDIENCE

If the audience on which public relations practitioners focus their messages were a monolithic whole, their work would be far easier—and far less stimulating. The audience, in fact, is just the opposite: a complex intermingling of groups with diverse cultural, ethnic, religious, and economic attributes whose interests coincide at times and conflict at others.

For the public relations professional, knowledge of these shifting audience dynamics is essential. A successful campaign must be aimed at those segments of the mass audience that are most desirable for its particular purpose and must employ those media most effective in reaching them. Some of these segments are easily identifiable and reachable, a category that Zoe McCathrin of Kent State University calls "prepackaged publics." These are well-organized groups whose members have banded together in a common interest; they constitute ready-made targets for practitioners who have projects of concern to them. Examples of such prepackaged publics are businesspeople in Rotary Clubs and animal lovers in the Humane Society.

Diversity is the most significant aspect of the mass audience in the United States. Differences in geography, history, and economy among regions of the sprawling country are marked; ranchers in Montana have different attitudes from residents in the heavily populated Eastern seaboard cities. Yet people in the two areas have national interests in common. Ethnic cultures also shape the audience segments public relations practitioners address.

Identification of target audiences can be accomplished through computer technology to conduct both secondary and primary research. The rich lode of geographical and social statistics found in Census Bureau reports provides a foundation. Many of these are broken down by census tract and ZIP code.

Other data sources, such as automobile registration, voter registration, sales figures, mailing lists, and church and organization memberships, can be merged into the computer database. For example, one marketing research organization, Claritas Inc., has divided the Chicago metropolitan district into 62 lifestyle clusters. It assigned a name to each cluster, such as "Boomers & Babies," whose buying habits, it says, include "rent more than five videos a month, buy children frozen dinners, read parenting magazines."

Increasingly, public relations professionals employ the computer for primary research to identify target audiences and to develop effective strategies for each. Publics PR Research Software™ was developed specifically to identify target publics using the situational theory created by University of Maryland professor James E. Grunig. The theory posits that groups define themselves as active publics when they identify an issue as a problem (problem recognition component) that affects them personally (involvement component) and that they feel empowered to address in some way (constraint recognition component).

Active publics merit attention by organizations dealing with an issue because their members seek information about the issue and will likely play a role in the outcome of the issue (by informing and influencing others.) (Chapter 6 provides details about the research process.)

SENIOR AND ETHNIC MARKETS

As the demographic makeup changes dramatically in the United States, two major target audiences have emerged that deserve special attention. One is the *seniors*. This group frequently is defined as men and women 65 years or older, although some sociologists and marketing experts include everyone over age 50. The other group consists of *ethnic minorities*.

Similar audiences are developing to various degrees in other countries.

Seniors

Medical advances have improved life expectancy so much that today almost 35 million Americans are 65 or older, according to the U.S. Bureau of the Census. A heavy upsurge in the senior population will occur after 2010, when the post-World-War-II "baby boomers" begin to reach the age of 65. These older citizens form an important opinion group and a consumer market with special interests.

When appealing to seniors, public relations people should try to ignore the stereotypes of "old folks" so often depicted in the movies and television. Some 80-year-old women sit in rocking chairs, knitting or snoozing, but others cheer and boo ardently while watching professional basketball on TV. Nor are all grandfathers crotchety complainers with quavering voices or kindly patriarchs who fly kites with their grandsons. As many differences in personality, interest, financial status, and living styles exist in the older audience as among their young adult grandchildren.

Public relations practitioners should remember these characteristics of seniors:

- With the perspective of long experience, they are often less easily convinced than young adults, demand value in the things they buy, and pay little attention to fads.

- They vote in greater numbers than their juniors and are more intense readers of newspapers.

- They form an excellent source of volunteers for social, health, and cultural organizations because they have time and often are looking for something to do.

- They are extremely health-conscious, out of self-interest, and want to know about medical developments.

Financially, the elderly are better off than the stereotypes suggest. The Census Bureau found that people aged 65 to 74 have more discretionary income than any other group.

Ethnic Groups

Historically, the United States has welcomed millions of immigrants and assimilated them into the cultural mainstream. They bring a bubbling mixture of personal values, habits, and perceptions that are absorbed slowly, sometimes reluctantly. The questions of assimilation—how much, how little?—also exist with two longtime indigenous minorities, African Americans and Native Americans. This diversity is a great strength of the United States but also a source of friction and misunderstandings. Communication campaigns have been employed in Malaysia and the Mideast to build understanding and interaction among diverse ethnic groups. Called nation-building, this important public relations work will become invaluable in building a relevant new definition of nationhood in the United States as it embraces growing diversity.

Recently the easily identifiable ethnic groups—primarily Hispanics, African Americans, Asian Americans, and Native Americans—as a whole have been growing five times faster than the general population. The U.S. Census Bureau predicted that by the year 2010 Hispanics and African Americans will each make up 13 percent of the U.S. population, a total of 26 percent, while Anglos will be 58 percent. Asian Americans and Native Americans will provide the remaining percentage. Even greater changes will occur by 2050, the Census Bureau predicted. Notably, Hispanics will form nearly one fourth of the U.S. population. (See Figure 11.1.)

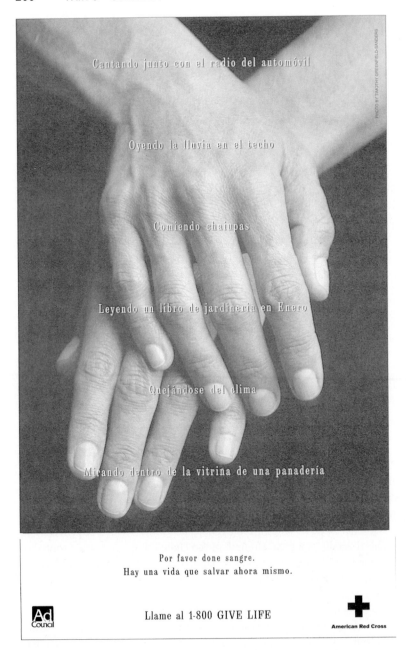

The Red Cross appeals for blood donations in Spanish as well as English to reach the large and growing Hispanic population in the United States. This message was prepared by the Advertising Council.

A basic point to remember is that the minority population forms *many* target audiences, not a massive monolithic group whose interests are identical.

Expanding populations have been accompanied by an increase in the number and strength of the minority media through which messages can be delivered. The 1999 *Gale Directory of Publications and Broadcast Media* lists 158 Hispanic publications and 235 black publications; Spanish and African-American radio stations have increased correspondingly. Two Spanish-language TV networks, Univision and Telemundo, serve millions of viewers. The Black Entertainment Television Network has a large national audience. Thus a substantial number of outlets exist for public relations messages, provided news releases and story pitches are translated and culturally appropriate.

The swift expansion of the Hispanic population is a challenge for public relations practitioners. Merely translating their messages into Spanish is not enough. They must shape communications to the Hispanic culture, in particular the group's family ties. According to the U.S. Census Bureau, 12 million Hispanic children lived in the United States in 1996, up

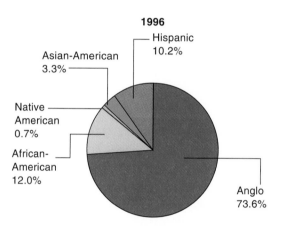

1996

Hispanic 10.2%
Asian-American 3.3%
Native American 0.7%
African-American 12.0%
Anglo 73.6%

Figure 11.1
Predicted changes in U.S. population groups.

(Source: U.S. Census Bureau 1996)

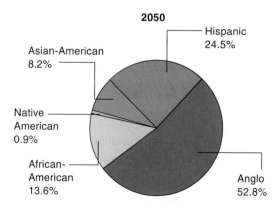

2050

Hispanic 24.5%
Asian-American 8.2%
Native American 0.9%
African-American 13.6%
Anglo 52.8%

from 9.8 million six years earlier. This compares to 50.8 million Anglo children and 11.4 million non-Hispanic blacks.

Radio is an especially important way to reach this ethnic group. Surveys show that the average Hispanic person listens to radio 26 to 30 hours a week, about 13 percent more than the general population.

Television also has a large, rapidly expanding Hispanic audience. The Nielsen rating service in 1997 estimated the number of Hispanic households in the United States with television sets at 7,500,000.

Hispanic-owned businesses are multiplying in the United States. These offer new client possibilities, not only for Hispanic-owned firms but for general public relations firms that adapt their services to Hispanic needs. A Census Bureau report in 1996 showed a 76-percent increase in the number of Hispanic companies in the United States during the five-year period from 1987 to 1992.

Public relations people should give particular attention to the sensitivities of minority audiences. For example, the familiar figure of Aunt Jemima on packages of Quaker Oats food products was widely regarded in the black community as a patronizing stereotype. To change this perception, Quaker Oats cooperated with the National Council of Negro Women to honor outstanding African-American women in local communities, who then competed for a national award. At the local award breakfasts, all food served was Aunt Jemima brands, and Quaker Oats officials participated in the programs. The project generated an atmosphere of mutual understanding.

CHARACTERISTICS OF THE AUDIENCE

Human drives have changed little over the centuries. As we move into the twenty-first century, we continue to love, hate, worship, work for food and shelter, protect our families, and respond to our neighbors' needs much as our forefathers did 300 years ago. Knowing how to appeal to these basic emotions is essential.

Even with these drives constant, specific aspects and attitudes of the audience change. In numerous respects, audience trends of the 1990s differed from those of the 1930s, for example, in ways significant to the public relations practitioner:

1. *The public is increasingly visually oriented.* The enormous impact of television on daily life is largely responsible for an increased visual orientation. Many people obtain virtually all their news from the TV screen. Several recent studies indicate local television is the most credible and frequently used news source, supplanting the local newspaper. Television also serves as a potent communicator of manners and mores.

    Never has a country had as much information available to its citizens as the United States has today—yet the rate of illiteracy is disgracefully high.

2. *Fervent support is generated for single issues.* Many individuals become so zealously involved in promoting or opposing a single favorite issue that they lose the social and political balance so needed in a country. Such vehement behavior may create severe public relations problems for the objects of their attacks.

3. *Heavy emphasis is placed on personality and "celebrity."* Sports stars, television and movie actors, and rock music performers are virtually worshipped by some fans. When stars embrace causes, many people blindly follow them. More and more, we see them being used as spokespersons and fund-raisers.

4. *Strong distrust of authority and suspicion of conspiracy exist.* People have been so inundated with exaggerated political promises, seen so much financial chicanery, and been exposed to so many misleading television advertisements that many of them distrust what they read and hear. They suspect evil motives and tend to believe rumors. The need for public relations programs to develop an atmosphere of justifiable, rational trust is obvious.

5. *The international audience for public relations is expanding swiftly.* Growth of global corporations and expanded foreign marketing by smaller firms open new public relations situations, as does increased foreign ownership of U.S. companies.

MATCHING AUDIENCE AND MEDIA

With an array of printed, spoken, visual, and computer communication methods available, practitioners must make choices in order to use their time and budgets efficiently. Some general guidelines exist for matching audience and media:

- Print media are the most effective for delivering a message that requires absorption of details and contemplation by the receiver. Newspapers are the fastest with the most widespread impact.

- Television has the strongest emotional impact of all media. Its visual power makes situations seem close to the viewer. The personality of the TV communicator creates an influence that print media cannot match.

- Radio's greatest advantages are flexibility and the ability to reach specific target audiences. Messages can be prepared for and broadcast on radio more rapidly than on television, at much lower cost.

- The online media are usually used as a supplemental method of reaching a generally well-educated, relatively affluent audience interested in new ideas and fresh approaches. However, usage patterns are changing almost weekly, and major breaking news stories now reach a large audience online.

In some campaigns the most cost-effective results come from use of a single medium. Other campaigns work best when several types of media are used. Wise selection of media, based on the audience sought and the money available, is an important skill for public relations practitioners to develop.

MEDIA RELATIONS

Editors and reporters on the one hand, and public relations people on the other, need each other. The media must have material and ideas from public relations sources, and practitioners must have the media as a place to display their stories.

Public relations people should remember several things about editors and reporters:

1. They are busy. When you approach them with a story idea, either verbally or on paper, make your sales pitch succinctly and objectively.

2. Editors pride themselves on making their own decisions about what stories to run and how to run them. That is their job. Excessive hype of a story often turns them against it. An urgent demand that editors *must* run a story may lead to rejection.

3. Able editors and competent public relations people respect each other and work well together. If editors discover, however, that they have been misled or fed false information, they will never again fully trust the offending practitioner.

Practitioners also need to remember several things about themselves when dealing with the media:

1. Your job is important in keeping the public informed. You are performing a service, not asking a favor, when you submit a story idea or a news release.

2. You should assume that your story will be judged on its merits as seen by the editor, and should not demean yourself by begging an editor to use it.

3. Your role continues after the story or idea has been accepted. You cannot control the tone of the story that appears, but you can influence it by providing favorable story angles and additional information.

THE PRINT MEDIA

Printed words can be kept indefinitely and can be reread. Messages delivered in that form through newspapers, magazines, and books are a fundamental element in public relations work.

Newspapers

Every edition of a newspaper contains hundreds of news stories and pieces of information, in much greater number than the largest news staff can gather by itself. More than most readers realize, and many editors care to admit, newspapers depend upon information brought to them voluntarily.

The *Columbia Journalism Review* noted, for example, that in one edition the *Wall Street Journal* had obtained 45 percent of its 188 news items from news releases. Because of its specialized nature, the *Journal*'s use of news releases may be higher than that of general-interest daily newspapers.

Approximately 1500 daily newspapers and 7200 weekly newspapers are published in the United States. While some metropolitan newspapers have circulations of more than a million copies a day, approximately two thirds of the daily newspapers have circulations of 20,000 or less.

Newspapers published for distribution in the late afternoon, called evening or P.M. papers, outnumber morning (A.M.) papers approximately three to one. Especially in larger cities, however, a substantial trend toward morning publication is in progress. Knowledge of a newspaper's hours of publication and the deadlines it enforces for submission of copy is essential for everyone who supplies material to the paper.

A Commercial Institution   In dealing with a newspaper, public relations people should remember that it is a commercial institution, created to earn a profit as a purveyor of news and advertising. Publishers and editors as a whole seek to serve the public interest, and often succeed admirably in doing so. Management decisions about what appears in a newspaper must be made with the balance sheet in mind.

Newspapers receive nearly 80 percent of their income from advertising and about 20 percent from selling papers to readers. They cannot afford to publish press releases that are nothing more than commercial advertising; to do so would cut into their largest source of income. To be published, a release submitted to a newspaper must contain information that an editor regards as news of interest to a substantial number of readers.

Since newspapers are protected by the First Amendment to the Constitution, they cannot be forced to publish any material, including news releases, nor need they receive permission from the government or anyone else to publish whatever they desire.

Nevertheless, editors do not enjoy the unfettered privilege of publishing whatever they desire. Two severe limitations hang over their decisions:

1. *The laws of libel and invasion of privacy.* Publication of material that, if challenged in court, is ruled to be libelous or an unreasonable invasion of privacy can cost a newspaper extremely heavy judgments and legal expenses. The newspaper management is legally responsible for everything a newspaper publishes, including material submitted by outsiders, even letters to the editor.

2. *The interests and desires of their readers.* If a newspaper fails to publish news and features that readers find to be valuable or entertaining, its circulation will dwindle and it will perish. Alert editors, therefore, are receptive to fresh ideas. Their doors are open to public relations representatives who can supply useful information.

Organization of a Newspaper   The editor has overall responsibility for the news and editorial content of the newspaper. The managing editor heads the news operations. The city editor, who is responsible for local news coverage, and the editors of other departments such

PR Insights

Three Cardinal Rules for News Releases to Newspapers

A news release submitted to a newspaper should:

1. Contain information that is newsworthy in that newspaper's circulation area.

2. Be addressed to the city editor if it is of general interest, or to the appropriate section editor if it contains special-interest material such as sports news.

3. Be delivered to the newspaper well in advance of the desired publication date to provide time for processing.

as sports and financial, report to him. The associate editor directs the editorial pages. Weekly newspapers have a different focus from that of daily newspapers, and much smaller staffs. The weekly concentrates exclusively on its own community.

Public Relations Opportunities in Newspapers

Material for a newspaper should be submitted either as a news release ready for publication or as a factsheet from which a reporter can develop a feature story or interview. When an invitation to a news conference is sent to a newspaper, it should include a factsheet containing basic information. Frequently, the reporter to whom an editor assigns a news release for processing rewrites and expands it, developing additional story angles and background. When a public relations representative presents an important story idea in factsheet form rather than as a news release for publication, a personal conversation with the appropriate editor, if it can be arranged, helps to sell the concept and expand its potential. *Such personal calls on editors should last no longer than is necessary to explain the idea adequately.* Although some practitioners make a follow-up phone call shortly after the factsheet has arrived, this practice irritates many editors.

A public relations representative wishing to discuss a large-scale project such as a communitywide fund drive should do so by appointment with the managing editor or city editor after the deadline hour has passed. A cooperative plan of publicity can be developed at such a session. A newspaper is more likely to give a major project sympathetic treatment if its editors receive background information before the first stories break. This allows them time to plan coverage.

At times, an organization's representative or other individual needs to discuss a policy issue with the newspaper management—a complaint against perceived mistreatment by the newspaper, for example, or an attempt to obtain editorial support. Usually this is done by appointment with the editor or associate editor or, in the case of a news story, with the managing editor. Often problems arise from misunderstanding rather than from intent.

Public relations representatives should never assume that editors and reporters are all-knowing about projects being planned in a community. A basic rule: when you have news to announce, tell the media; don't wait for them to come to you.

Created Events: Making News Happen

Some news stories *happen.* Other stories must be *created.* Successful public relations practitioners must do more than produce competent, accurate news releases about routine occurrences in the affairs of their clients or employers. They must use ingenuity and organizing ability to create events that attract coverage in the news media. Historian Daniel Boorstin calls these projects "pseudoevents." This extra dimension of creativity is the difference between acting to make news and merely reacting to news that happens. We are not speaking here of feeding phony stories to the media or doing anything else unethical. We are talking about causing something to occur.

Such created events vary in scope from the huge antiabortion and prochoice marches in Washington, staged by ardent advocates of opposite positions, to small, clever publicity promotions that draw media coverage because they are unusual, involve prominent people, or are just plain fun.

The 100th anniversary of the invention of Jell-O gelatin dessert posed a challenge to Kraft Foods' public relations firm, Hunter and Associates: celebrate the traditions of Jell-O in American life without contributing to a consumer perception in the 1990s that Jell-O was old-fashioned (see Chapter 7).

Every one of the events in a list later in this chapter represents a legitimate news story that the local newspaper and other media might cover. But these stories exist only because a public relations adviser convinced the company to sponsor or conduct them. Once this decision is made, the practitioner must produce a flow of news releases with fresh angles, as well as use other techniques to build public interest.

Openings of stores and shopping centers, as well as groundbreakings, happen so frequently that the ingenuity of public relations representatives is challenged. Editors dislike pictures of the traditional, rigidly posed group of men in dark business suits and incongruous hard-hats lined up behind one man with a shovel.

Magazines

Magazine editors in most instances aim carefully at special-interest audiences. They fire rifle bullets at limited, well-defined readership groups.

The more than 12,000 periodicals published in the United States may be classified in several ways. For purposes of this discussion, periodicals are grouped into two broad categories, those for the public at large and those for specific audiences. Each is in turn broken down into several subdivisions.

Focus on Ethics

Information Pollution in Trade Publications?

It is not uncommon in the trade press for an editor to make a subtle demand on a public relations person who wants to place a story in the magazine or newsletter. There is a "linkage" between getting the story published and buying advertising space in the trade publication. If a company wants a good editorial spread, it must help "pay the freight" through an advertising buy. Some trade press publishers defend this "linkage," saying that the publication cannot survive without advertising—so it is only fair for the companies that want coverage to contribute to the financial stability of the publication. From another perspective, editors simply give preference to advertisers when selecting stories to cover. Either view violates the Public Relations Society of America code of ethics, which says that the exchange of advertising for "good" copy is one form of "corrupting the media."

Imagine that you pitch a story by telephone to the editor of a trade publication. The editor knows that you really want coverage for your client and she implies that you need to buy ad space to assure your story will be run. What would you do?

Do you think that advertiser influence on stories diminishes the value of public relations?

In your mind, is there a qualitative difference between trade publications that require advertising and more independent publications such as newspapers? Which has more value for the practice of public relations?

Periodicals for the Public at Large   Among the types in this category are the following:

General Interest. Only a few national magazines with across-the-board appeal exist today. Prominent among them are *Reader's Digest,* enormously successful worldwide; *People,* which capitalizes on the contemporary interest in personalities; and *National Geographic.*

News Magazines. High-circulation weekly newsmagazines report and interpret the news, adding background that daily newspapers lack time to develop. The biggest periodicals of this type are *Time, Newsweek,* and *U.S. News & World Report.*

Women's Interest. Magazines designed for women have a very large audience. Prominent in this group are *Ladies' Home Journal, Cosmopolitan, Working Woman, Better Homes and Gardens, Good Housekeeping,* and *Family Circle.*

Men's Interest. Growing participation of women in athletics has increased female readership of traditionally male sports magazines. *Sports Illustrated* and *Field and Stream* are perhaps the best known of these magazines.

The categories of magazines just listed offer tremendous public relations opportunities. They are difficult markets to hit, however, except by highly experienced specialists well acquainted with the magazines' operating methods. Far more abundant opportunities for placing public relations material exist with the other periodicals, those aimed at more specific audiences.

Periodicals for Specific Audiences   The specific-interest group includes a wide array of publications, including the following:

Special-Audience Magazines. Hundreds of these prosper because they are carefully edited on single themes. Each attracts an audience with strong interest in its particular topic; this audience in turn draws advertisers whose products are especially relevant to these readers. A glance at the magazine rack in a supermarket gives an indication of the diversity of special-interest magazines—only an indication, however, because such periodicals are distributed primarily by subscription.

A few examples include *Dog World, Backpacker, Stereo Review, Car Craft, Skin Diver, Surfing, Ski, International Photographer,* and *World Oil.*

Trade Journals. Trade journals are designed for persons who read them for business and professional reasons, not recreational ones. While virtually unknown to the public, these periodicals are vital channels of communication within various industries and professions. In their pages, readers learn about the activities of their competitors, new products and trends in their field of work, and the movement of individuals from one job to another. Often trade journals have the same intimacy in their respective fields as weekly newspapers do in their communities.

The following small sampling of trade journals indicates the extremely specialized nature of their contents: *American Christmas Tree Journal, Mini-Micro Systems, Fleet Owner, The Indian Trader, Insulation Outlook, Progressive Grocer,* and *Wire Journal International.*

Placement of material in trade journals is an essential assignment for many public relations representatives. A story about a new product published in an appropriate trade journal may be more valuable to the manufacturer of that product than a story about it in a large newspaper, because the information reaches a target audience containing potential purchasers.

Company and Organizational Magazines. There are two types of company and organizational magazines:

1. *Internal,* designed for and distributed primarily to employees, retirees, influential outsiders who may have some interest in the organization, and often stockholders of the firm.

2. *External,* distributed to selected portions of the public. Published by companies and organizations to promote public appreciation of the sponsor and to form a psychological tie between sponsor and recipient. The magazines that airline travelers find in the seat pockets in front of them, such as *American Way* (American Airlines), are prime examples of this group.

Public Relations Opportunities in Magazines

A study of the annual *Writer's Market* and the monthly periodicals *Writer's Digest* and *The Writer* will provide abundant information about individual magazines.

Operating with much smaller staffs than newspapers have, magazines are heavily dependent on material submitted from outside their offices. Some, are almost entirely staff-written. The staffs create ideas and cover some stories; they also process public relations material submitted to them. The more carefully the submitted material is tailored to the particular periodical's audience and written in a style preferred by the editor, the more likely it is to be published, with or without rewriting by the staff.

A public relations practitioner has four principal approaches for getting material into a periodical:

1. Submit a story idea that would promote the practitioner's cause either directly or subtly, and urge the editor to have a writer, freelance or staff, develop the story on assignment.

2. Send a written query to the editor outlining an article idea and offering to submit the article in publishable form if the editor approves the idea.

3. Submit a completed article, written either by the practitioner or by an independent writer under contract, and hope that the editor will accept it for publication. In this and the two previously mentioned instances, however, the editor should be made fully aware of the source of the suggestion or article. As pointed out in Chapter 3, allowing a freelance writer to place what presumably is an "independent" article is a violation of Article 9 of the PRSA Code of Professional Standards, which forbids using third parties who are purported to be independent but serve the special interests of the employer or client.

4. For trade journals and other periodicals that use such material, submit news releases in ready-to-publish form.

Books

Because their writing and publication is a time-consuming process, often involving years from the conception of an idea until appearance of the volume, books are not popularly recognized as public relations tools. Yet they can be. A book, especially a hardcover one, has stature in the minds of readers. They read it with respect and give attention to the message it carries.

Books are promulgators of ideas. As channels of communication, they reach thoughtful audiences, including opinion leaders. Often publication of a book starts a trend or focuses national discussion on an issue.

The standard method of book publishing is for an author and publisher to sign a contract describing the material the author will deliver to the publisher and the conditions under which the publisher will issue and sell the book. The publisher pays the cost of production and marketing. The author receives a royalty fee on each copy sold, perhaps 10 to 15 percent of the retail price. Publishers often make advance payments to authors against the royalties their books are expected to earn.

A book published in hardcover often requires a year from acceptance of the manuscript to publication. Thus, a public relations effort made through publication of a hardcover book must be long range in nature and aimed at the broad-stroke influencing of public opinion.

The tremendous growth of paperback publishing has opened new avenues for use of books as public relations vehicles. Hundreds of titles, ranging from classical literature to how-to-do-it books on gardening, plumbing, and sex, are on sale. An examination of nonfiction titles on the paperback shelves will show the range of opportunity that exists to promote products, ideological movements, personalities, and fads.

The traditional royalty system of hardcover books also is used for paperback books, but various forms of fee payments to authors are employed as well.

Although the fact is seldom mentioned publicly, companies and nonprofit organizations sometimes pay subsidies to both hardcover and paperback publishers to help defray production costs of a book they wish to see published. The subsidy may take the form of a guarantee to purchase a specific number of copies.

The idea for a beautifully illustrated book on New England, to cite an example, might come from a state travel agency, which approaches the publisher either directly or through an author. The state agency pays part of the publisher's cost, knowing that the book will draw visitors to the area.

Public Relations Opportunities in Books

As indicated previously, books as public relations tools, both hardcover and paperback, usually are best suited to promote ideas and create a favorable state of mind. Political movements often are publicized through books by proponents. On a more mundane level, every book published about gardening indirectly helps the sale of garden tools. Although a specific brand of tools may not be mentioned in such a book, it benefits from the book's existence. The manufacturer's public relations representative can help the company's cause by assisting the author in assembling material.

THE SPOKEN AND VISUAL MEDIA

Radio, television, motion pictures, and video have strong impact on virtually everyone. The messages they contain usually are delivered by individuals whose personality, expressed through voice and/or visual manner, adds emphasis to the words.

PR Insights

32 Ways to Create News for Your Organization

1. Tie in with news events of the day.
2. Work with another publicity person.
3. Tie in with a newspaper or other medium on a mutual project.
4. Conduct a poll or survey.
5. Issue a report.
6. Arrange an interview with a celebrity.
7. Take part in a controversy.
8. Arrange for a testimonial.
9. Arrange for a speech.
10. Make an analysis or prediction.
11. Form and announce names for committees.
12. Hold an election.
13. Announce an appointment.
14. Celebrate an anniversary.
15. Issue a summary of facts.
16. Tie in with a holiday.
17. Make a trip.
18. Make an award.
19. Hold a contest.
20. Pass a resolution.
21. Appear before public bodies.
22. Stage a special event.
23. Write a letter.
24. Release a letter you have received.
25. Adapt national reports and surveys for local use.
26. Stage a debate.
27. Tie into a well-known week or day.
28. Honor an institution.
29. Organize a tour.
30. Inspect a project.
31. Issue a commendation.
32. Issue a protest.

Radio

Speed and mobility are the special attributes that make radio unique among the major media of communication. If urgency justifies such action, messages can be placed on the air by radio almost instantly upon their receipt at a radio station. They need not be delayed by the time-consuming production processes of print. Since radio programming is more loosely structured than television programming, interruption of a program for an urgent announcement can be done with less internal decision-making. Although most public relations material does not involve such urgency, moments of crisis do occur when quick on-the-air action helps a company or other organization get information to the public swiftly.

Radio benefits, too, from its ability to go almost anywhere. Reporters working from mobile trucks can be broadcasting from the scene of a large fire within minutes after it has been discovered. They can hurry from a press conference to a luncheon speech, carrying only a small amount of equipment.

So is flexibility among listeners. Radios in automobiles reach captive audiences, enhancing the popularity of drive-time disc jockeys. The tiny transistor or mini earphone-type radio brings programs to mail carriers on their routes, carpenters on construction sites, and homeowners pulling weeds in their gardens.

More than 12,000 radio stations reach over 150 million Americans each day, with stations ranging from low-powered outlets operated by a handful of staff members to large metropolitan stations audible for hundreds of miles. Slightly less than half of these stations are of the amplitude modulation (AM) type; the others use frequency modulation (FM), which has shorter range but generally clearer reception. A public relations practitioner should study each station's format and submit material suitable to it. Don't send information about senior citizen recreational programs to the news director of a hard-rock station with an audience primarily of teenagers.

Public Relations Opportunities in Radio

Commercial radio is highly promotional in nature and provides innumerable opportunities for public relations specialists to further their causes. Radio programs may be divided into two general categories: news-talk and entertainment. A station's news director is responsible for the former, the program director for the latter. At least eight possible targets exist in radio:

1. *Newscasts.* Many stations have frequent newscasts, of which the five-minute variety is the most common. If the station has a network affiliation, some newscasts it carries are national in content. Of much more interest to the public relations practitioner are the local newscasts. Brevity is fundamental on radio. A story that runs 400 words in a newspaper may be told in 50 words or fewer on radio. Lengthy news releases for radio stations are unnecessary, indeed unwise.

2. *Community calendars.* Stations broadcast a daily program called the "Community Bulletin Board," or a similar title. This listing of coming events is an excellent place to circulate information about a program the practitioner is handling.

3. *Actualities.* Radio news directors brighten their newscasts by including *actualities.* These are brief reports from scenes of action, either live or on tape. Public relations representatives may supply stations with actualities to be used on newscasts. If a high executive of a practitioner's client speaks at a luncheon, a brief taped highlight from that speech, if sent to a radio station, may find a place on a local newscast.

4. *Talk shows.* Another goal is the radio talk show, on which a moderator and guests discuss issues. Placement of a client on a talk show provides exposure for the individual and for the cause being espoused.

    Call-in talk shows on current events are an important factor in forming public opinion, although the verbal excesses of certain hosts and their callers weaken their influence with some people.

5. *Editorials.* Powerful radio stations often broadcast editorials, comparable to newspaper editorials, usually delivered by the station manager. Public relations specialists may be able to persuade a station to carry an editorial of endorsement for their cause. They

should stay alert, too, for editorials that condemn a cause they espouse. The representative should request equal time on the air for a rebuttal. Hundreds of smaller stations, however, do not carry editorials.

6. *Disc jockey shows.* On the entertainment side, disc jockeys in their programs of music and chitchat frequently air material provided by public relations sources. The DJs conduct on-the-air contests and promotions, give away tickets to shows, discuss coming local events, offer trivia quizzes—whatever they can think of to make their programs distinctive and lively.

7. *Community events.* At times, radio stations sponsor community events such as outdoor concerts or long-distance runs. Repeated mention of such an event on the air for days or weeks usually turns out large crowds. Here, too, is an opportunity for the public relations person to convince a station either to sponsor such an event or to develop tie-ins with it.

8. *Public service announcements (PSAs).* These commercials promoting public causes such as health care and civic programs are run free of charge by stations, usually in unsold time slots during scheduled commercial breaks. PSA scripts should be written to run 20, 30, or 60 seconds. Use of celebrity voices is common.

Television

Our lives feel the impact of television more than that of any other communications medium. More than 1500 television stations are in operation, projecting over-the-air visual programming. According to estimates provided by the A. C. Nielsen Company, the major rating firm for national programming, more than 95 million American households own television sets. According to Nielsen statistics, the average American family watches television about seven hours a day.

The fundamental factor that differentiates television from the other media and gives it such pervasive impact is the visual element. Producers of entertainment shows, newscasts, and commercials regard movement on the screen as essential. Something must happen to hold the viewer's attention. Persons talking on the screen for more than a brief time without movement, or at least a change of camera angle, are belittled as "talking heads."

Because of this visual impact, television emphasizes personality. Entertainment programs are built around stars. Only on television do news reporters achieve "star quality." When public relations people plan material for television, they should remember the importance of visual impact and personality.

Television shows live and die by their ratings. A scorecard mentality dominates the selection of programs and program content, especially on the networks. The viewing habits of a few thousand Americans, recorded by the Nielsen, Arbitron, and other rating services, determine what programs all TV watchers can see. The explanation is money. Networks and local stations determine the prices they charge to show commercials by the estimated size of the audience watching a program when the commercial is shown.

A tremendous battle for admission to the home viewer's screen has developed among cable TV, video, and the traditional over-the-air stations and networks. In the mid–1970s, the three basic commercial networks were viewed by 92 percent of the audience during

Governor Jesse Ventura of Minnesota, a former professional wrestler, talks to David Letterman about his new political role during taping of "The Late Show with David Letterman" on CBS. Appearances on the television networks' late-night interview programs are much sought-after promotional opportunities.

prime-time evening hours. This figure had fallen to 42 percent in 1998 as the total television audience was fragmented.

Although most television stations are on the air for 18 hours or more a day, only a few hours of programming originate in their studios—mostly newscasts, local talk shows, and mid-morning homemaker programs—all good public relations targets.

Cable Television   Because television networks and individual stations, especially those in major cities, gear their programming to large audiences, public relations practitioners have difficulty in obtaining airtime for projects lacking mass appeal. Cable television, however, often presents valuable opportunities.

More than 62 million U.S. households were wired for cable TV by 1997. However, the number of viewers for a cable channel is usually relatively small because the total TV audience is fragmented among the numerous competing channels. On the plus side, the public relations specialist faces fewer editing and management barriers in getting a program or short segment broadcast.

Municipal authorities have the right to demand that cable systems to which they grant operating franchises include an *access channel* for public, educational, or government programming, without advertising. Public relations directors for cultural, social, and other nonprofit agencies—and even for commercial interests—can use these so-called PEG channels effectively to promote public-service causes by creating interesting programs.

Some cable systems also produce *local origination* (LO) programming. LO programs may carry advertising. They offer an outlet for public relations material that provides substantial information without being obviously commercial in tone.

Public Relations Opportunities in Television

The possibilities for the public relations specialist to use television are so numerous that they are worth examining on two levels: network and local.

Mick Jagger and the Rolling Stones exemplify the power generated by rock musicians to deliver emotional messages to youthful audiences. When Jagger explodes on stage—striding, shouting, and gesticulating—his performance stirs boisterous reactions from the crowd.

The Network Level   There are six principal methods commonly used:

1. *Guest appearances on news and talk shows.* Placement of clients on such programs as the *Tonight* and *Today* shows allows them to give plugs to new products, books, films, and plays, and to advocate their causes. Guests on network interview shows must be articulate and poised, so they won't freeze up before the camera. Consequently they are carefully screened by show production staffs before being granted an appearance.

   Public relations people wishing to place guests on these programs should apply to the producers of the shows.

2. *News releases and story proposals to network news departments.* This process is identical to that followed with radio stations.

3. *Video news releases,* commonly called VNRs. These are ready-to-broadcast tapes or background footage for use in news programs. News programs will use VNRs in some form if they are well done and avoid delivering an obvious commercial message. (VNRs are discussed in Chapter 23.)

4. *Program ideas.* The representative of an important cause may propose to a network that it build an episode in a dramatic or situation comedy series around this cause. The public relations person can assist the program producer by supplying technical information.

   Characters in situation comedies or dramas quite frequently take strong advocacy positions in the plotline, thus delivering a message to viewers.

5. *Silent publicity.* There are almost subliminal impacts in entertainment programs that quietly publicize a representative's cause. In a private detective show, for example, the

star may be shown chasing the villain through an airport terminal past a TWA sign. Or the automobiles used by the lead characters may be Ford products exclusively.

6. *Public service announcements.* These are run occasionally by stations nationwide as public relations gestures. The Advertising Council prepares material for national non-profit organizations as a public service.

The Local Station Level   The methods listed for network public relations apply just as effectively on the local level—indeed, even more so in some instances, because competition for time on local stations often is less intense. The more intimate nature of local programming increases public relations opportunities. Even a diaper-changing contest at a shopping mall can gain airtime.

There are four most frequently used techniques:

1. *Guest appearances on local talk shows.* Visiting experts in such fields as homemaking crafts, sponsored by companies and trade associations, demonstrate their skills for moderator and audience. National public relations firms send such clients around well-established circuits of local television and radio shows in each city they visit. The North American Precis Syndicate, Inc. (NAPS) claims great results for a service that edits and reuses an organizations's VNR material in pitches to local talk shows.

2. *Protest demonstrations.* Filmed demonstrations are such a staple on some television stations in large cities as to be a visual cliché. A group supporting or opposing a cause notifies a station that it will march at a certain time and place. Carrying placards, the marchers parade before the camera and a representative is shown explaining their cause. Although, for fairness, stations should put on an advocate for the other side in the same sequence, some stations neglect this responsibility, and so the marching group's point of view dominates.

3. *Videotapes for news shows.* Smaller TV stations, in particular, lack enough staff to cover all potentially newsworthy events in their areas. Practitioners can fill the gaps by delivering videotapes of events they handle, for inclusion in newscasts.

4. *General-interest films.* Local cable channels sometimes will show films of 15- or 20-minute duration produced by corporations in which the direct commercial message is nonexistent or muted. The purpose of such films is to strengthen a company's image as a good community citizen. Films explaining large civic programs by nonprofit organizations also may be used.

Motion Pictures

Mention of motion pictures brings to mind, first and inevitably, the commercial entertainment film turned out by that nebulous place called Hollywood. From a public relations point of view, possibilities for influencing the content of commercial motion pictures for client purposes are relatively limited. Practitioners who know their way through the labyrinth of Hollywood financing and production can make deals for silent publicity through use of brand-name merchandise, negotiating how the product will be used and whether there will be a fee.

PR Insights

How to Place a Client on a TV Talk Show

Television stations are looking for interesting, articulate guests for their talk shows. The larger the station, the more stringent are its requirements for accepting a guest. This summary of needs and procedures for *AM/San Francisco,* the morning show on KGO-TV, the ABC network outlet in San Francisco, is typical of those for metropolitan stations. The information is from an article published in *Bulldog,* a West Coast public relations newsletter.

The station wants guests "who will provide information that will help our viewers to save money and save time, helpful hints around the house, consumer-type things." The station also uses guests from the business community who can comment on money, taxes, the stock market, and similar topics.

KGO-TV defines the audience for this show as primarily nonworking women, 18 to 49, married, with at least one child. The show also attracts working viewers before they leave for their jobs.

Segments on the one-hour show run from six to 10 minutes. The usual pattern is to open with a celebrity-entertainer, then offer two segments on consumer topics. Segments 4, 5, and 6 cover "more serious subjects."

The production staff will normally consider for appearance only those who have appeared on television previously. Usually it asks to see a video clip of a prior TV appearance; an effective clip is an important way to gain acceptance.

"TV is a visual medium and a lot of our audience isn't just sitting there watching. They're folding clothes or ironing, so we need a voice that will grab their attention."

The public relations practitioner should submit a brief written query to the show's producer—"a 1-page letter getting straight to the basics: whom you're offering, what their experience is, exactly what their topic would be, what shows they've been on previously, a bio (biographical statement) and all other information available on the person, as well as clippings, copies of articles on the person or topic."

Staff members try to answer queries in about a week, perhaps sooner. The show is booked at least a week in advance but sometimes has last-minute openings.

In terms of specific public relations results similar to those obtainable from the other mass media, however, commercial films are a minor channel.

Sponsored Films

In other forms, the motion picture is an important public relations tool.

Corporations and nonprofit organizations use motion pictures and videotapes for internal purposes as part of audiovisual programs to train and inform their employees, or for external purposes to inform and influence the public and the financial community.

When, for example, Levi Strauss & Co. needed to explain to its employees a new personnel management program called Teamwork, it prepared a video for them. This was built around an a cappella singing group, which demonstrated the importance of individuals working together. Virtually all employees who saw it called the unusual approach beneficial.

A significant use of the motion picture or video in public relations is directly promotional. Although avoiding frontal-attack sales messages such as those in television commercials, these films seek to whet the interest of audience members who are potential purchasers of the sponsor's product or contributors to the sponsor's cause. For example, a travel agency shows members of an invited audience a film about a Caribbean cruise. Colorful photography with voice-over narration depicts the scenery cruise passengers will see. Shipboard activities, including a few humorous touches, are shown. So are the luxurious accommodations and the enormous buffet tables from which travelers select their meals (no passenger ever is seasick in such films, of course).

Similarly, a university president at a dinner meeting of alumni shows a film of the campus as it is today. The film is a carefully contrived balance of nostalgia and progress, with scenes of football games and students at work in the new science building. Having rekindled alumni interest in the old school, the film closes with a recital of the university's plans and aspirations.

ONLINE MEDIA

Communication by computer is a significant, swiftly expanding tool for public relations practitioners. Its ability to deliver information about client projects, establish contacts with reporters, and exchange ideas through the commercial online services and the global Internet is fascinating and not yet fully realized.

The World Wide Web portion of the Internet, which provides on-screen graphics, photographs, audio, and video clips along with text, is an especially effective form of cyberspace public relations.

Companies, public relations firms, nonprofit organizations, newspapers, and broadcasters, even individuals, maintain *home pages* about themselves on the Web. By calling up a desired home page on their computer screens, viewers can obtain information from the sponsor. As one example from thousands on the Web, the San Francisco Giants baseball team's home page carries game schedules, ticket information, photographs of players, and Giant merchandise.

PUBLIC RELATIONS OPPORTUNITIES
IN ONLINE MEDIA

Home pages on the World Wide Web offer an unusual opportunity to reach an audience with a message in the exact form a public relations practitioner conceives it, because the Web is not subject to editing by any media gatekeeper. Tens of thousands of companies, nonprofit organizations, and individuals maintain sites on the World Wide Web, on which they explain and promote their services. Specific examples of how the Web is used in public relations appear in Chapter 18. By participating in online discussion groups and similar online interchanges, public relations people often reach opinion leaders in specific fields with facts and opinions favorable to their cause. Among these key online contacts are reporters and editors of Web-based publications that increasingly offer breaking news more immediately than print or broadcast outlets. The pace of media relations has increased as public relations professionals monitor online news, striving for what Professor Stephen Thomsen of Brigham Young University calls real-time response. The public relations person hopes to catch errors or offer balancing comments for stories as they break online and before they pick up momentum through print and broadcast dispersion.

CASE PROBLEM

Cygna Labs, a medium-sized pharmaceutical firm located in Salt Lake City, has developed a sunscreen lotion. The product, Sun-Cure, joins a number of similar products on store shelves. Independent laboratory testing shows that Sun-Cure is particularly effective in blocking UVB rays, which cause burning and even premature aging of the skin. It is a good product and gets high ratings from dermatologists.

Unfortunately, the public still shows confusion about the differences between sunscreens and suntan lotions, as well as the merits of competing brands. Your public relations firm is retained to develop a product publicity program for Sun-Cure that would reach daily newspapers, selected magazines, radio, and television. What communication strategies would you develop for getting coverage in each medium?

QUESTIONS FOR REVIEW AND DISCUSSION

1. Why is the senior audience so important in the United States, and what are some of its characteristics?

2. On what basis do newspaper editors select the news releases they publish?

3. A good public relations person knows how to create news events. Why is this important?

4. What significant differences between magazines and newspapers must a public relations practitioner keep in mind when submitting material to them?

5. Why are special-audience magazines and trade journals such important targets for many public relations people?

6. What are the three factors in Professor James Grunig's situational theory that help identify active publics for an issue?

7. What two special attributes make radio distinctive among the major media of mass communication?

8. Do local radio newscasts have a good potential as an outlet for news releases? If so, why?

9. Ratings determine which television programs survive and which die. Why do ratings have such power?

10. How should public relations representatives go about trying to place their clients on television interview shows?

11. Can you describe three ways in which public relations practitioners use online media?

12

Public Relations and the Law

Preview

In this chapter the objective is to provide a general understanding of legal considerations involved in public relations and to show students specifically how laws on defamation, copyright, and trademarks, as well as government agency regulations, affect the distribution of messages.

Topics covered in this chapter include:
* A sampling of legal problems
* Libel and defamation
* Invasion of privacy
* Copyright law and trademark law
* Regulations of government agencies, including the Federal Trade Commission and Securities and Exchange Commission
* Corporate/employee free speech
* Liability for sponsored events
* Working with lawyers

A SAMPLING OF LEGAL PROBLEMS

The law and its many ramifications are somewhat abstract to the average person. Many people may have difficulty imagining exactly how public relations personnel can run afoul of the law, or generate a suit, simply by communicating information.

To bring things down to earth, and to make this chapter more meaningful, we provide here a sampling of recent government regulatory agency cases and lawsuits that involved public relations materials and the work of practitioners.

* The Princeton Dental Resource Center paid a $25,000 settlement after the New York attorney general's office charged the organization with making false and misleading claims in its newsletter.

* Labtest International, a New Jersey firm, was ordered by a U.S. District Court to pay $111,000 to Washington Business Information, Inc., for copyright infringement. It had illegally photocopied the company's weekly *Product Safety Letter.*

* The Securities and Exchange Commission (SEC) stopped the mailing of 45,000 prospectuses from Krupp Securities of Boston because the company had attached a sales brochure to the prospectus, a violation of SEC guidelines.

* The estate of the late children's author, Dr. Seuss, won a $1.5 million judgment against a Los Angeles T-shirt maker for infringement of copyright. The manufacturer portrayed a parody of Dr. Seuss's Cat in the Hat character smoking marijuana and giving the peace sign.

* The owner of a Detroit public relations firm, asked to write a news release about an impending corporate merger, ran afoul of SEC regulations when he used the confidential information to purchase stock before the merger became public.

* The Federal Trade Commission filed false advertising charges against three national diet firms after they failed to provide factual evidence that clients actually achieved weight-loss goals or maintained the loss.

These examples provide some idea of the legal pitfalls that a public relations person may encounter. Many of the charges were eventually dismissed or settled out of court, but the organizations paid dearly for the adverse publicity and the expense of defending themselves.

Public relations personnel must be aware that they can be held legally liable if they provide advice or tacitly support an illegal activity of a client or employer. This area of liability is called *conspiracy*. A public relations person can be named as a coconspirator with other organizational officials if he or she:

* participates in an illegal action such as bribing a government official or covering up information of vital interest to the public health and safety

* counsels and guides the policy behind an illegal action

* takes a major personal part in the illegal action

* helps establish a "front group" whereby the connection to the public relations firm or its clients is kept hidden

* cooperates in any other way to further an illegal action

These five concepts, it is emphasized, also apply to public relations firms that create, produce, and distribute materials on behalf of clients. The courts have ruled on more than one occasion that public relations firms cannot hide behind the defense of "the client told me to do it." Public relations firms have a legal responsibility to practice "due diligence" in the type of information and documentation supplied by a client. Regulatory agencies such as the Federal Trade Commission (discussed shortly) have the power under the Lanham Act to file charges against public relations firms that distribute false and misleading information.

LIBEL AND DEFAMATION

Public relations professionals should be thoroughly familiar with the concepts of libel and slander. Such knowledge is crucial if an organization's internal and external communications are to meet legal and regulatory standards with a minimum of legal complications.

Traditionally, *libel* was a printed falsehood and *slander* was an oral statement that was false. Today, as a practical matter, there is little difference in the two, and the courts often use *defamation* as a collective term.

Essentially, defamation is any false statement about a person (or organization) that creates public hatred, contempt, ridicule, or inflicts injury on reputation. A person filing a libel suit usually must prove that: (1) the false statement was communicated to others through print, broadcast, or electronic means, (2) the person was identified or is identifiable, (3) there is actual injury in the form of money losses, loss of reputation, or mental suffering, and (4) the person making the statement was malicious or negligent.

In general, private citizens have more success winning defamation suits than public figures or corporations. With public figures–government officials, entertainers, political candidates, and other newsworthy personalities–there is the extra test of whether the libelous statements were made with actual malice (*New York Times v. Sullivan*).

Corporations, to some degree, are also considered "public figures" by the courts for several reasons: (1) they engage in advertising and promotion offering products and services to the public, (2) they are often involved in matters of public controversy and public policy, and (3) they have some degree of access to the media–through regular advertising and news releases–that enables them to respond and rebut defamatory charges made against them.

This is not to say that corporations don't win lawsuits regarding defamation. A good example is General Motors, which filed a multimillion-dollar defamation suit against NBC after the network's *Dateline* news program carried a story about gas tanks on GM pickup trucks exploding in side-impact collisions.

GM's general counsel, in a news conference, meticulously provided evidence that NBC had inserted toy rocket "igniters" in the gas tanks, understated the vehicle speed at the moment of impact, and wrongly claimed that the fuel tanks could be easily ruptured. Within 24 hours after the suit was filed, NBC caved in. It agreed to air a nine-minute apology on the news program and pay GM $2 million to cover the cost of its investigation.

Increasingly, corporations are using fraud and contract law to sue news organizations, instead of pursuing harder-to-prove libel claims. In *Food Lion v. Capital Cities/ABC* (1995), for example, the grocery chain was awarded $315,000 after it sued ABC News for fraud and trespassing; two TV producers had lied on job applications and hidden cameras in their wigs to report an expose on alleged health violations at several stores.

Avoiding Libel Suits

There is little investigative reporting in public relations, but libel suits can be filed against organizational officials who make libelous accusations during a media interview, send out news releases that make false statements, or injure someone's reputation.

Some executives have been sorry that they lost control during a news conference and called the leaders of a labor union "a bunch of crooks and compulsive liars" Suits have been filed for calling a news reporter "a pimp for all environmental groups" Such language, while highly quotable and colorful, can provoke legal retaliation, merited or not.

Accurate information, and a delicate choice of words, must be used in news releases. For example, a former employee of J. Walter Thompson advertising agency claimed she was libeled in an agency news release that stated she had been dismissed because of financial irregularities in the department she headed. Eventually, the $20 million lawsuit was dismissed because she couldn't prove that the agency acted in a "grossly irresponsible manner."

In situations involving personnel, organizations often try to avoid lawsuits by saying that an employee left "for personal reasons" or to "pursue other interests," even if the real reason was incompetence or a record of sexual harassment. News releases and product publicity should also be written in accordance with FTC and SEC regulations, to be discussed shortly.

Another potentially dangerous practice is making unflattering comments about the competition's products. Although comparative advertising is the norm in the United States, a company must walk a narrow line between comparison and "trade libel," or "product disparagement" Statements should be truthful, with factual evidence and scientific demonstration available to substantiate them. Companies often charge competitors with overstepping the boundary between "puffery" and "factual representation."

An organization can offer the opinion that a particular product or service is the "best" or "a revolutionary development" if the context clearly shows that the communication is a statement of opinion attributed to someone. Then it is classified as "puffery" and doesn't require factual evidence.

Don Sneed, Tim Wulfemeyer, and Harry Stonecipher, in a *Public Relations Review* article, say that a news release should be written to indicate clearly statements of opinion and statements of fact. They suggest that (1) opinion statements be accompanied by the facts upon which the opinions are based, (2) statements of opinion be clearly labeled as such, and (3) the context of the language surrounding the expression of opinion be reviewed for possible legal implications.

The Fair Comment Defense

Organizations can do much to assure that their communications avoid materials that could lead to potential lawsuits. By the same token, organizations are somewhat limited in their ability to use legal measures to defend themselves against criticism.

Executives are often incensed when an environmental group includes their corporation on its annual "dirty dozen" polluters or similar lists. Executives are also unhappy when a broadcast consumer affairs reporter flatly calls the product a "rip-off."

A corporate reputation may be damaged and product sales may go down, but a defamation case is difficult to win because, as previously mentioned, the accuser must prove actual malice. Also operating is the concept of fair comment and criticism.

This defense is used by theater and music critics when they lambaste a play or concert. Fair comment also means that when companies and individuals voluntarily display their wares to the public for sale or consumption, they have no real recourse against criticism done with honest purpose and lack of malicious intent.

INVASION OF PRIVACY

An area of law that particularly applies to employees of an organization is *invasion of privacy.* Public relations staff must be particularly sensitive to the issue of privacy in at least four areas: (1) employee newsletters, (2) photo releases, (3) product publicity and advertising, and (4) media inquiries about employees.

Employee Newsletters

It is no longer true, if it ever was, that an organization has an unlimited right to publicize the activities of its employees. In fact, Morton J. Simon, a Philadelphia lawyer and author of *Public Relations Law,* wrote, "It should not be assumed that a person's status as an employee waives his right to privacy." Simon correctly points out that a company newsletter or magazine does not enjoy the same First Amendment protection that the news media enjoy when they claim "newsworthiness" and "public interest." A number of court cases, he says, show that company newsletters are considered commercial tools of trade.

In sum, one should avoid anything that might embarrass or subject an employee to ridicule by fellow employees. Here are some guidelines to remember when writing about employee activities:

* Keep the focus on organization-related activities.

* Have employees submit "personals" in writing.

* Double-check all information for accuracy.

* Ask: "Will this embarrass anyone or cause someone to be the butt of jokes?"

* Don't rely on secondhand information; confirm the facts with the person involved.

* Don't include racial or ethnic designations of employees in any articles.

Photo Releases

Ordinarily, a public relations practitioner doesn't need a signed release if a person gives "implied consent" by posing for a picture and is told how it will be used. This is particularly true for "news" photographs published in internal newsletters.

Public relations departments, however, should take the precaution of (1) filing all photographs, (2) dating them, and (3) giving the context of the situation. This precludes the use of old photos that could embarrass employees or subject them to ridicule. In other cases, it precludes using photographs of persons who are no longer employed or have died. This method also helps to make certain that a photo taken for the employee newsletter isn't used in an advertisement.

If a photo of an employee or customer is used in product publicity, sales brochures, or advertisements, the standard practice is to obtain a signed release. Here is a simplified release used by Hewlett-Packard Company:

> I grant to Hewlett-Packard Company ("HP"), its representatives and employees the right to take photographs of me and my property in connection with the above identified subject and I authorize HP, its assigns and transferees to copyright, use, and publish the same in print and/or electronically.
>
> I agree that HP may use such photographs of me with or without my name and for any lawful purpose, including for example, such purposes as publicity, illustration, and advertising.

PR Insights

Litigation PR: The New Game in Town

One of the newer specialties in public relations practice is *litigation public relations* (LPR). According to Mary Gottschall, a legal affairs correspondent for the New York *Times,* "This has emerged as an increasing trend, especially where major litigation is involved. The idea is that the case might be tried in the court of public opinion as well as before the jury."

Dirk Gibson, a professor at the University of New Mexico, says four types of legal proceedings are likely to elicit significant publicity: tabloid-type titillating cases; shocking, heinous crimes; cases with celebrity victims; and cases with celebrity defendants. The O.J. Simpson murder trial, for example, involved considerable LPR as lawyers on both sides continually held news conferences and leaked information to the media. In the JonBenet Ramsey murder case, the parents of the murdered child hired not only lawyers but also a public relations counselor to defend themselves against leaks by the district attorney's office that they were under suspicion.

More recently, the year-long sparring between Independent Counsel Kenneth Starr and President Clinton (see Chapter 1) involved considerable public relations activity as each side tried to bolster its case in the court of public opinion. William Ginsburg, a trial attorney who first represented Monica Lewinsky, gave so many press interviews that he suffered from overexposure and was eventually replaced.

Corporations have also realized the value of LPR when litigation attracts extensive media coverage. Microsoft and its chairman, Bill Gates not only hired a platoon of lawyers to do battle with the U.S. Justice Department about monopoly and antitrust, but also hired several public relations firms to present the company's case to the public. Good public relations is needed, experts say, because surveys show that nearly one third of the public believes an organization is automatically guilty after being accused of wrongdoing.

Hill and Knowlton, responding to the trend toward more publicized and potentially damaging lawsuits, has even created an LPR specialty group to help clients sway public opinion. Jim Cox, head of the new group, told *PR Tactics:* "Litigation communications is something whose time has come. More people are willing to sue and when they do they are more likely to sue big corporations. Big Business needs to defend itself and not naively believe they will have their day in court."

Product Publicity and Advertising

As already noted, an organization must have a signed release on file if it wants to use the photographs or comments of employees and other individuals in product publicity, sales brochures, and advertising. An added precaution is to give some financial compensation to make a more binding contract.

Chemical Bank of New York unfortunately learned this lesson the hard way. The bank used pictures of 39 employees in various advertisements designed to "humanize" the bank's image, but the employees maintained that no one had requested permission to use their photos in advertisements. Another problem was that the pictures had been taken up to five years before they began appearing in the series of advertisements.

An attorney for the employees, who sued for $600,000 in damages, said, "The bank took the individuality of these employees and used that individuality to make a profit." The judge agreed and ruled that the bank had violated New York's privacy law. The action is called *misappropriation of personality,* which is discussed later in this chapter. Jerry Della Femina, an advertising executive, succinctly makes the point: get permission. "If I used my mother in an ad," he said, "I'd get her permission—and I almost trust her 100 percent."

Written permission also should be obtained if the employee's photograph is to appear in sales brochures or even in the corporate annual report. This rule also applies to other situations. A graduate of Lafayette College sued the college for using a photo of his mother and him at graduation ceremonies, without their permission, in a financial aids brochure.

Media Inquiries about Employees

Because press inquiries have the potential of invading an employee's right of privacy, public relations personnel should follow basic guidelines as to what information will be provided in the employee's behalf.

In general, employers should give a news reporter only basic information. This may include (1) confirmation that the person is an employee, (2) the person's title and job description, and (3) date of beginning employment, or, if applicable, date of termination.

Unless it is specified by law or permission is given by the employee, a public relations person should avoid providing information about an employee's (1) salary, (2) home address, (3) marital status, (4) number of children, (5) organizational memberships, and (6) job performance.

If a reporter does seek any of this information, because of the nature of the story, several methods may be followed.

First, a public relations person can volunteer to contact the employee and have the person speak directly with the reporter. What the employee chooses to tell the reporter is not then a company's responsibility. Second, many organizations do provide additional information to a reporter if it is included on an optional biographical sheet that the employee has filled out. In most cases, the form clearly states that the organization may use any of the information in answering press inquiries or writing its own news releases.

COPYRIGHT LAW

Should a news release be copyrighted? How about a corporate annual report? Can a *New Yorker* cartoon be used in the company magazine without permission? What about reprinting an article from *Fortune* magazine and distributing it to the company's sales staff? Are government reports copyrighted? What constitutes copyright infringement?

These are some of the bothersome questions that a public relations professional should be able to answer. Knowledge of copyright law is important from two perspectives: (1) what organizational materials should be copyrighted, and (2) how correctly to utilize the copyrighted materials of others.

Before going into these areas, however, it is important to know what copyright means. In very simple terms, *copyright* means protection of a creative work from unauthorized use. A section of the U.S. copyright law of 1978 states: "Copyright protection subsists . . . in the original works of authorship fixed in any tangible medium of expression now known or later developed." The word *authorship* is defined in seven categories: (1) literary works, (2) musical works, (3) dramatic works, (4) pantomimes and choreographic works, (5) pictorial, graphic, or sculptural works, (6) motion pictures, and (7) sound recordings. The word *fixed* means that the work is sufficiently permanent or stable to permit it to be perceived, reproduced, or otherwise communicated.

The shield of copyright protection was reduced somewhat in 1991 when the Supreme Court ruled unanimously that directories, computer databases, and other compilations of facts may be copied and republished unless they display "some minimum degree of creativity." The court stated, "Raw facts may be copied at will."

Thus a copyright does not protect ideas, but only the specific ways in which those ideas are expressed. An idea for promoting a product, for example, cannot be copyrighted—but brochures, drawings, news features, animated cartoons, display booths, photographs, recordings, videotapes, corporate symbols, slogans, and the like that express a particular idea can be copyrighted.

Because much money, effort, time, and creative talent are spent on organizational materials, copyright protection is important. By copyrighting materials, a company can prevent competitors from capitalizing on its creative work or producing a facsimile brochure that tends to mislead the public.

The 1978 law presumes that material produced in some tangible form is copyrighted from the moment it is created. This is particularly true if the material bears a copyright notice. One of the following methods may be employed:

1. Using the letter "c" in a circle (©), followed by the word *copyright.*

2. Citing the year of copyright and the name of the owner.

This presumption of copyright is often sufficient to discourage unauthorized use, and the writer or creator of the material has some legal protection if he or she can prove that the material was created before another person claims it.

A more formal step, providing full legal protection, is official registration of the copyrighted work within three months after creation. This is done by depositing two copies of the manuscript (it is not necessary that it has been published), recording, or artwork with the Copyright Office, Library of Congress, Washington, DC 20559. Copyright registration forms are available from U.S. post offices. Registration is not a condition of copyright protection, but it is a prerequisite to an infringement action against unauthorized use by others.

Copyright protection of a work lasts for the life of the author plus 50 years, and no longer. Material copyrighted by a business or organization is protected for 75 years from the time the material is published. In 1998, Congress passed and the President signed the Copyright Term Extension Act, which extends the period of copyright protection on existing copyrightable material by another 20 years. The Disney organization, in particular, lobbied hard for the extension since it kept Mickey Mouse and all his friends out of the public domain.

Fair Use versus Infringement

Public relations people are in the business of gathering information from a variety of sources, so it is important to know where *fair use* ends and *infringement* begins.

Fair use means that part of a copyrighted article may be quoted directly, but the quoted material must be brief in relation to the length of the original work. It may be, for example, only one paragraph in a 750-word article and up to 300 words in a long article or book chapter. Complete attribution of the source must be given regardless of the length of the quotation. If the passage is quoted verbatim, quote marks must be used.

It is important to note, however, that the concept of fair use has distinct limitations if part of the copyrighted material is to be used in advertisements and promotional brochures. In this case, permission is required. It also is important for the original source to approve the context in which the quote is used. A quote out of context often runs into legal trouble if it implies endorsement of a product or service.

The copyright law does allow limited copying of a work for fair use such as criticism, comment, or research. However, in recent years, the courts have considerably narrowed the concept of "fair use" when multiple copies of a copyrighted work are involved.

A landmark case was a successful lawsuit in 1991 by book publishers against Kinko's, a national chain of photocopying stores. The chain was charged with copyright infringement because it reproduced excerpts from books without permission and sold them in anthologies to college students. Although Kinko's argued "fair use" for educational purposes, the court rejected this defense.

Even the unauthorized photocopying of newsletters and published articles can cost the organization large sums of money. Texaco, for example, lost a lawsuit filed by publishers of scientific journals, who claimed that the company violated the copyright law by permitting employees to photocopy articles for their files. Such lawsuits can be avoided if an organization orders quantity reprints from the publisher or pays a licensing fee permitting it to make paper or electronic copies.

The same concept applies to videotaping television shows or news programs. The Supreme Court has ruled that it is "fair use" to make a videotape of a television show for later personal viewing, but a public relations staff must get permission from the television producer if widespread use of the videotape is planned.

Government documents (city, county, state, and federal) are in the public domain and cannot be copyrighted. Public relations personnel, under the fair use doctrine, can freely use quotations and statistics from a government document, but care must be exercised to ensure that the material is in context and not misleading. The most common problem occurs when an organization uses a government report as a form of endorsement for its services or products.

Photography and Artwork

The copyright law makes it clear that freelance and commercial photographers retain ownership of their work. In other words, a customer who buys a copyrighted photo owns the item itself, but not the right to make additional copies. That right remains with the photographer unless transferred in writing.

In a further extension of this right, the duplication of copyrighted photos is also illegal. This was established in a 1990 U.S. Federal District Court case in which the Professional Photographers of America (PP of A) sued a nationwide photofinishing firm for ignoring copyright notices on pictures sent for additional copies.

Freelance photographers generally charge for a picture on the basis of its use. If it is used only once, perhaps for an employee newsletter, the fee is low. If, however, the company wants to use the picture in the corporate annual report or on the company calendar, the fee may be considerably higher. Consequently it is important for a public relations person to tell the photographer exactly how the picture will be used. Arrangements and fees then can be determined for (1) one-time use, (2) unlimited use, or (3) the payment of royalties every time the picture is used.

Computer manipulation of original artwork can also violate copyright. One photographer's picture of a racing yacht was used on a poster after the art director electronically changed the numbers on the sail and made the water a deeper blue. In another case, a photo distribution agency successfully sued *Newsday* for unauthorized use of a color image after the newspaper reconstructed the agency's picture using a computer scanner, then failed to credit the photographer. In sum, slightly changing a copyrighted photo or a piece of artwork can be considered a violation of copyright if the intent is to capitalize on widespread recognition of the original art.

The Rights of Freelance Writers

Although the rights of freelance photographers have been established for some years, it was only recently that freelance writers gained more control over the ownership of their work.

In the now famous Reid Case (*Community for Creative Nonviolence v. Reid*), the U.S. Supreme Court in 1989 ruled that writers retained ownership of their work and that purchasers of it simply gained a "license" to reproduce the copyrighted work.

Prior to this ruling, the common practice was to assume that commissioned articles were "work for hire" and the purchaser owned the copyright. In other words, a magazine could reproduce the article in any number of ways and even sell it to another publication without the writer's permission.

Under the new interpretation, ownership of a writer's work is subject to negotiation and contractual agreement. Writers may agree to assign all copyright rights to the work they have been hired to do, or they may give permission only for a specific one-time use.

In a related matter, freelance writers are pressing for additional compensation if an organization puts their work on CD-ROM, online databases, or the Internet's World Wide Web. Traditionally, newspapers and magazines have resisted pressure to compensate writers, but *Harper's* magazine in 1996 became the first publication to share its profits from electronic publishing with writers.

Public relations firms and corporate public relations departments are responsible for ensuring compliance with the copyright law. This means that all agreements with a freelance writer must be in writing, and the use of the material must be clearly stated. Ideally, public relations personnel should negotiate multiple rights and even complete ownership of the copyright.

Copyright Issues on the Internet

The emergence of the information superhighway, particularly the Internet and World Wide Web, has raised new issues about the protection of intellectual property. Three issues regarding copyright are: (1) the downloading of copyrighted material, (2) the unauthorized uploading of such material, and (3) the responsibilities of online carriers to police copyright violations.

The Downloading of Material In general, the same rules apply to cyberspace as to more earthbound methods of expressing and disseminating ideas. Original materials in digital form are still protected by copyright. The fair-use limits for materials found on the Internet are essentially the same as the fair use of materials disseminated by any other means.

The Uploading of Material In many cases, owners of copyrighted material have uploaded various kinds of information with the intention of making it freely available. Some examples are software, games, and even the entire text of *The Hitchhikers Guide to the Galaxy*. The problem comes, however, when third parties upload copyrighted material without permission. Consequently, copyright holders are increasingly patrolling the Internet and World Wide Web to stop the unauthorized use of material. Some examples:

- Dutton Children's Books threatened a lawsuit against a New Mexico State University student for using Winnie the Pooh illustrations on his home page.

- Paramount Pictures sent warning notes to *Star Trek* fans against using the Internet to disseminate photos from the TV series.

- Elvis Presley Enterprises ordered the removal of sound clips of "Blue Suede Shoes" and "Hound Dog" from a home page that also displayed images from Graceland postcards.

The unauthorized use of copyrighted material on the Internet has led to calls for Congress to update the existing law to cover online information. One measure considered by the Senate would make it illegal to evade copyright protections built into electronically distributed material.

Copyright Guidelines

A number of points have been discussed about copyright. A public relations person should keep the following in mind:

1. Ideas cannot be copyrighted, but the expression of those ideas can be.

2. Major public relations materials (brochures, annual reports, videotapes, motion pictures, position papers, and the like) should be copyrighted, if only to prevent unauthorized use by competitors.

3. Although there is a concept of *fair use,* any copyrighted material intended directly to advance the sales and profits of an organization should not be used unless permission is given.

4. Copyrighted material should not be taken out of context, particularly if it implies endorsement of the organization's services or products.

5. Quantity reprints of an article should be ordered from the publisher.

6. Permission is required to use segments of television programs or motion pictures.

7. Permission must be obtained to use segments of popular songs (written verses or sound recordings) from a recording company.

8. Photographers and freelance writers retain the rights to their works. Permission and fees must be negotiated to use works for other purposes than originally agreed upon.

9. Photographs of current celebrities or those who are now deceased cannot be used for promotion and publicity purposes without permission.

10. Permission is required to reprint cartoon characters, such as Snoopy or Garfield. In addition, cartoons and other artwork or illustrations in a publication are copyrighted.

11. Government documents are not copyrighted, but caution is necessary if the material is used in a way that implies endorsement of products or services.

12. Private letters, or excerpts from them, cannot be published or used in sales and publicity materials without the permission of the letter writer.

13. Original material posted on the Internet and the World Wide Web has copyright protection.

14. The copyrighted material of others should not be posted on the Internet unless specific permission is granted.

TRADEMARK LAW

What do the names Coca-Cola, Marlboro, IBM, the Olympic rings, and the logo of the Dallas Cowboys have in common? They are all registered trademarks protected by law.

A trademark is a word, symbol, or slogan, used singly or in combination, that identifies a product's origin. According to Susan L. Cohen, writing in *Editor & Publisher*'s annual trademark supplement, "It also serves as an indicator of quality, a kind of shorthand for consumers to use in recognizing goods in a complex marketplace." Research indicates, for example, that 53 percent of Americans say brand quality takes precedence over price considerations.

The concept of a trademark is nothing new. The ancient Egyptians carved marks into the stones of the pyramids, and the craftsmen of the Middle Ages used guild marks to identify the source and quality of products.

The Protection of Trademarks

Trademarks are always capitalized and never used as nouns. They are always used as adjectives modifying nouns. For example, the proper terms are kleenex tissues, xerox copies, and Rollerblade skates. A person who uses a kleenex, makes a xerox, or goes "rollerblading" is violating trademark law.

In addition, organizations take the step of designating brand names and slogans with various marks. The registered trademark symbol is a superscript, small capital "R" in a circle—®. "Registered in U.S. Patent and Trademark Office" and "Reg. U.S. Pat. Off" may

PR Casebook

Use the Logo, Pay the Fee

Sports logos are registered trademarks, and a licensing fee must be paid before anyone can use logos for commercial products and promotions.

Teams in the National Football League and the National Basketball Association earn more than $3 billion annually just selling licensed merchandise, and the sale of college and university trademarked goods is rapidly approaching that mark. Schools such as Notre Dame, Michigan, and Ohio State rake in more than $3 million a year in royalties from licensing their logos to be placed on everything from beer mugs to T-shirts.

The penalty for not paying a licensing fee is steep. The NFL, during Super Bowl week, typically confiscates about $1 million in bogus goods and files criminal charges against the offending vendors.

---

also be used. A "TM" in small capital letters indicates a trademark that isn't registered. It represents a company's common-law claim to a right of trademark, or a trademark for which registration is pending.

A service mark is like a trademark, but it designates a service rather than a product, or is a logo. An "SM" in small capitals in a circle—(SM)—is the symbol for a registered service mark. If registration is pending, the "SM" should be used without the circle.

These symbols are used in advertising, product labeling, news releases, company brochures, and so on to let the public and competitors know that a name, slogan, or symbol is protected by law. See the advertisement on page 233 for an example of how organizations publicize their trademarks and service marks.

Public relations practitioners play an important role in protecting the trademarks of their employers. They safeguard trademarks and respect nonorganizational trademarks in the following ways:

1. Ensure that company trademarks are capitalized and used properly in all organizational literature and graphics. Lax supervision can cause loss of trademark protection.

2. Distribute trademark brochures to editors and reporters and place advertisements in trade publications, designating names to be capitalized.

3. Educate employees as to what the organization's trademarks are and how to use them correctly.

4. Monitor the mass media to make certain that trademarks are used correctly. If they are not, send a gentle reminder.

5. Check publications to ensure that other organizations are not infringing on a registered trademark. If they are, the company legal department should protest with letters and threats of possible lawsuits.

6. Make sure the trademark is actually being used. A 1988 revision of the Trademark Act no longer permits an organization to hold a name in reserve.

7. Assure that the trademarks of other organizations are correctly used and properly noted.

FedEx® Is Not Synonymous With Overnight Shipping.

That's why you can't FedEx or Federal Express your package. Neither FedEx® nor Federal Express® are nouns, verbs, adverbs or even participles. They are adjectives and identify our unique brand of shipping services. So if you want to send a package overnight, ask for FedEx® delivery services.

When you do, we think you'll know why we say "Why Fool Around With Anyone Else?"® After all, FedEx is "Absolutely, Positively the Best in the Business."® Help us protect our marks. Ask us before you use them, use them correctly, and, most of all, only ask for FedEx® delivery services.

Be absolutely sure.

www.fedex.com

© 1998 Federal Express Corporation

Protection of trademarks requires corporate diligence. Some companies deliver warning messages through advertisements in trade magazines, as in this FedEx example.

8. Avoid the use of trademarked symbols or cartoon figures in promotional materials without the explicit permission of the owner. In some cases, to be discussed, a licensing fee is required.

Organizations adamantly insist on the proper use of trademarks in order to avoid the problem of having a name or slogan become generic. Or, to put it another way, a brand name becomes a common noun through general public use. Some trade names that have become generic include *aspirin, thermos, cornflakes, nylon, cellophane,* and *yo-yo.* This means that any company can use these names to describe a product.

The Problem of Trademark Infringement

Today, when there are thousands of businesses and organizations, finding a trademark not already in use is extremely difficult. The task is even more frustrating if a company wants to use a trademark on an international level.

A good example is what happened to Nike at the 1992 Olympic Games in Barcelona. The athletic shoe manufacturer paid millions to be an official sponsor of the games, and it planned to introduce a new line of clothes at the event. There was a snag, however. A Spanish high court ruled that the Beaverton, Oregon, firm's trademark infringed on the trademark of a Barcelona sock company that had registered "Nike" more than 60 years ago. The court barred Nike from selling or advertising its sports apparel in Spain, an action that cost the company about $20 million in marketing potential.

The complexity of finding a new name, coupled with the attempts of many to capitalize on an already known trade name, has spawned a number of lawsuits claiming trademark infringement. Here are some examples:

- Axiom, Inc. was ordered to change its name after a court found that it infringed on the registered trademark of a competing company, Acxiom Corp.

- Phi Beta Kappa, the academic honor society, filed a $5 million trademark infringement suit against Compaq Computer Corp. after the company launched a "Phi Beta Compaq" promotion to college students.

- Anheuser-Busch filed a trademark infringement suit against a University of North Carolina student after he designed and sold T-shirts saying "Nag Head, N.C.—King of Beaches." The back of the shirt said, "This beach is for you."

In all these cases organizations claimed that their registered trademarks were being improperly exploited for commercial or organizational purposes. Some guidelines used by courts to determine if there has been trademark infringement are as follows:

1. Has the defendant used a name as a way of capitalizing on the reputation of another organization's trademark—and does the defendant benefit from the original organization's investment in popularizing its trademark?

2. Is there an intent (real or otherwise) to create confusion in the public mind? Is there an intent to imply a connection between the defendant's product and the item identified by trademark?

3. How similar are the two organizations? Are they providing the same kinds of products or services?

4. Has the original organization actively protected the trademark by publicizing it and by actually continuing to use it in connection with its products or services?

5. Is the trademark unique? A company with a trademark that merely describes a common product might be in trouble.

Misappropriation of Personality

A form of trademark infringement also can result from the unauthorized use of well-known entertainers, professional athletes, and other public figures in an organization's publicity and advertising materials. A photo of Tom Cruise may make a company's advertising campaign more interesting, but the courts call it "misappropriation of personality" if permission and licensing fees have not been negotiated.

Airbus Industrie got into trouble, for example, by featuring a photo of Sir Roger Bannister, famous for the four-minute mile, in one of its advertisements without seeking prior permission. As part of the settlement, the company had to run a full-page apology in *Fortune* and other magazines that had used the advertisement, as well as make a substantial donation to a charity approved by Sir Roger.

Deceased celebrities are also protected. In order to use a likeness of a personality such as Elvis Presley, Marilyn Monroe, or even Albert Einstein, the user must pay a licensing fee to an agent representing the family, studio, or estate of the deceased. The estate of Princess Diana also has exclusive rights to approve and license the use of her image for any commercial purpose.

Legal protection also extends to the use of "sound-alikes" or "look-alikes." Bette Midler won a $400,000 judgment against Young & Rubicam (later affirmed by the Supreme Court on appeal) after the advertising agency used another singer to do a "sound-alike" of her singing style in a rendition of the song, "Do You Wanna Dance?" for a Ford commercial.

REGULATIONS BY GOVERNMENT AGENCIES

The promotion of products and services, whether through advertising, product publicity, or other techniques, is not protected by the First Amendment. Instead, the courts have traditionally ruled that such activities fall under the doctrine of *commercial speech*. This means that messages can be regulated by the state in the interest of public health, safety, and consumer protection.

Consequently, the states and the federal government have passed legislation that regulates commercial speech and even restricts it if standards of disclosure, truth, and accuracy are violated. One consequence was the banning of cigarette advertising on television in the 1960s. A more difficult legal question is whether government can completely ban the advertising or promotion of a legally sold product such as cigarettes or alcohol.

Public relations personnel involved in product publicity and the distribution of financial information should be aware of guidelines established by such government agencies as the Federal Trade Commission and the Securities and Exchange Commission.

Federal Trade Commission

The Federal Trade Commission (FTC) has jurisdiction to determine that advertisements are not deceptive or misleading. Public relations personnel should also know that the commission has jurisdiction over product news releases and other forms of product publicity such as videos and brochures.

In the eyes of the FTC, both advertisements and product publicity materials are vehicles of commercial trade—and therefore subject to regulation. In fact, Section 43(a) of the Lanham Act makes it clear that anyone, including public relations personnel, is subject to liability if that person participates in the making or dissemination of a false and misleading representation in any advertising or promotional material. This includes advertising and public relations firms, which also can be held liable for writing, producing, and distributing product publicity materials on behalf of clients.

An example of an FTC complaint is one filed against Campbell Soup Company for claiming that its soups were low in fat and cholesterol and thus helpful in fighting heart disease. The commission charged that the claim was deceptive because publicity and advertisements didn't disclose that the soups also were high in sodium, a condition that increases the risk of heart disease.

The Campbell Soup case raises an important aspect of FTC guidelines. Although a publicized fact may be accurate in itself, FTC staff also considers the context or "net impression received by the consumers." In Campbell's case, advertising copywriters and publicists ignored the information about high sodium, which placed an entirely new perspective on the health benefits of the soup.

FTC investigators are usually on the lookout for unsubstantiated claims and various forms of misleading or deceptive information. Some of the words in promotional materials that trigger FTC interest are: *authentic, certified, cure, custom-made, germ-free, natural, unbreakable, perfect, first class, exclusive,* and *reliable.*

In recent years, the FTC has also established guidelines for "green" marketing because of extensive consumer confusion about the environmental claims of various products. Words such as *recycled content, recyclable, ozone-safe*, and *biodegradable* can now be used only if the product meets specific FTC definitions of these terms.

The following guidelines, adapted from FTC regulations, should be taken into account when writing product publicity materials:

- Make sure the information is accurate and can be substantiated.

- Stick to the facts. Don't "hype" the product or service by using flowery, nonspecific adjectives and ambiguous claims.

- Make sure celebrities or others who endorse the product actually use it. They should not say anything about the product's properties that cannot be substantiated.

- Watch the language. Don't say "independent research study" when the research was done by the organization's staff.

- Provide proper context for statements and statistics attributed to government agencies. They don't endorse products.

- Describe tests and surveys in sufficient detail so the consumer understands what was tested under what conditions.

- Remember that a product is not "new" if only the packaging has been changed or the product is more than six months old.

- When comparing products or services with a competitor's, make certain you can substantiate your claims.

- Avoid misleading and deceptive product demonstrations.

Securities and Exchange Commission

The megamergers and the IPOs (initial public offerings) of many new companies have made the Securities and Exchange Commission (SEC) a household term in the business world. This federal agency closely monitors the financial affairs of publicly traded companies and protects the interests of stockholders.

SEC guidelines on public disclosure and insider trading are particularly relevant to corporate public relations staff members who must meet the requirements. The distribution of misleading information or failure to make a timely disclosure of material information may be the basis of liability under the SEC code. A company may even be liable if, while it satisfies regulations by getting information out, it conveys crucial information in a vague way or "buries" it deep in the news release.

The SEC has volumes of regulations, but the three concepts most pertinent to public relations personnel are as follows:

1. *Full information must be given on anything that might materially affect the company's stock.* This includes such things as (1) dividends or their deletion, (2) annual and quarterly earnings, (3) stock splits, (4) mergers or takeovers, (5) major management changes, (6) major product developments, (7) expansion plans, (8) change of business purpose, (9) defaults, (10) proxy materials, (11) disposition of major assets, (12) purchase of own stock, and (13) announcements of major contracts or orders.

2. *Timely disclosure is essential.* A company must act promptly (within minutes or a few hours) to dispel or confirm rumors that result in unusual market activity or market variations. The most common ways of dispensing such financial information are through use of electronic news release services, contact with the major international news services (Dow Jones Wire), and bulk faxing.

3. *Insider trading is illegal.* Company officials, including public relations staffs and outside counsel, cannot use inside information to buy and sell company stock. The landmark case on insider trading occurred in 1965, when Texas Gulf Sulphur executives used inside information about an ore strike in Canada to buy stock while at the same time issuing a news release downplaying rumors that a rich find had been made.

The courts are increasingly applying the "mosaic doctrine" to financial information. Maureen Rubin, an attorney writing in *Public Relations Journal,* explains that a court may examine *all* information released by a company, including news releases, to determine whether, taken as a whole, they create an "overall misleading" impression. One such case was *Cytryn v. Cook* (1990), in which a U.S. District Court ruled that the proper test of a company's adequate financial disclosure was not the literal truth of each positive statement, but the overall misleading impression that it combined to create in the eyes of potential investors.

As a result of such cases, investor relations personnel must also avoid such practices as:

- Unrealistic sales and earnings reports

- Glowing descriptions of products in the experimental stage

- Announcements of possible mergers or takeovers that are only in the speculation stage

- Free trips for business reporters and offers of stock to financial analysts and editors of financial newsletters

- Omission of unfavorable news and developments

- Leaks of information to selected outsiders and financial columnists

- Dissemination of false rumors about a competitor's financial health

The SEC, in 1998, passed new regulations supporting the use of "plain English" in prospectuses and other financial documents. The new rules are supposed to make information understandable to the average investor by removing sentences littered with lawyerisms such as *aforementioned, hereby, therewith, whereas,* and *hereinafter.* According to SEC Chairman Arthur Levitt, the cover page, summary, and risk factor sections of prospectuses must be clear, concise, and understandable.

Focus on Ethics

To Buy or Not to Buy?

One of your clients at a public relations firm is a medium-sized company that has been somewhat successful in the marketplace. One day, while talking to a corporate vice president on another matter, she tells you off-hand that there's a pretty good chance that the company will be acquired by a large, multinational corporation in the next four to six weeks. If that happens, that means the company's stock will be worth more than the current selling price. Given this tip, would it be a good idea to call your broker immediately and buy some stock?

The SEC's booklet on "plain English" gives helpful writing hints such as (1) make sentences short, (2) use *we* and *our, you* and *your,* and (3) say it with an active verb. More information about SEC guidelines can be accessed at its website: *www.sec.gov/consumer/plaine.htm.*

Other Regulatory Agencies

Although the FTC and the SEC are the major federal agencies concerned with the content of advertising and publicity materials, the Food and Drug Administration (FDA) and the Bureau of Alcohol, Tobacco and Firearms (ATF) have also established guidelines.

The FDA oversees the advertising and promotion of prescription drugs, over-the-counter medicines, and cosmetics. Under the federal Food, Drug, and Cosmetic Act, any "person" (which includes advertising and public relations firms) who "causes the misbranding" of products through the dissemination of false and misleading information may be liable.

The FDA, for example, has strict guidelines on the production and distribution of video news releases (VNRs) on health care topics. Agency staff reviews the scripts to assure that the information is accurate, doesn't exaggerate the benefits of a particular product, and doesn't mislead the public that a "cure" has been found.

Prescription drugs, in particular, have major FDA curbs on advertising and promotion, so the drug companies try to sidestep the regulations by publicizing diseases. Eli Lilly & Co., the maker of Prozac, provides a good example. The company sponsors ads and distributes publicity about depression. And the Glaxo Institute for Digestive Health conducts information campaigns about the fact that stomach pains can be an indication of major problems. Of course, Glaxo also makes the ulcer drug Zantac.

A recent development in state legislation is "food slander" laws. A dozen states have put "agricultural product disparagement" laws on their books, making it a crime to criticize or denigrate food with information that is not based on scientific fact.

The legislation, which resulted from the U.S. apple industry's losing almost $100 million because of the Alar scare, is designed to curtail activist groups that often use scare tactics and faulty information to disparage a particular food product. Millions of Americans learned about such laws when popular television celebrity Oprah Winfrey was sued by several Texas cattlemen for allegedly disparaging beef on her talk show. The trial, held in San Antonio, was a publicity bonanza for Oprah–and the jury acquitted her.

CORPORATE/EMPLOYEE FREE SPEECH

Although there are a number of restrictions on "commercial speech" by regulatory agencies, the Supreme Court has also upheld the right of corporations to express their views of public policy and interest.

A series of court cases has supported the concept of corporate free speech. These are some of the landmark cases:

- *First National Bank of Boston (1978).* The Supreme Court struck down a Massachusetts law that prohibited corporations from publicizing their views on issues subject to the ballot box. The ruling essentially gave corporations the same status as an individual under the First Amendment.

- *Consolidated Edison (1980).* The Supreme Court ruled that a New York Public Utilities Commission regulation prohibiting utilities from making statements on matters of public policy and controversy was unconstitutional.

- *Pacific Gas & Electric (1986).* The Supreme Court ruled that the California Public Utilities Commission could not require PG&E to include messages from activist consumer groups in its mailings to customers. The utility argued that inclusion of such messages impaired the company's right to communicate its own messages.

Although corporations can speak out on public issues in the context of First Amendment rights, a 1990 decision by the Supreme Court seems to indicate that this "free speech" right doesn't extend to endorsement of political candidates.

In a six to three decision in *Austin v. Michigan Chamber of Commerce,* the Court said a Michigan law that prohibits corporations from buying newspaper advertisements on behalf of a political candidate did not violate the chamber's right to free speech. The Michigan legislation, which applies to all incorporated bodies (even the Sierra Club and the American Civil Liberties Union) is part of a campaign finance law.

Employee Free Speech

A modern, progressive organization encourages employee comments and even criticisms. Many employee newspapers carry letters to the editor because they breed a healthy atmosphere of two-way communication and make company publications more credible.

Yet, at the same time, recent developments have indicated that not all is well for employee freedom of expression. A *Time* magazine essay by Barbara Ehrenreich, for example, gives startling examples of organizations denying free speech to employees. A grocery worker in Dallas was fired for wearing a Green Bay Packers T-shirt to work when the Dallas Cowboys were scheduled to play Green Bay in the conference playoffs. A worker at Caterpiller, Inc. was suspended for wearing a T-shirt titled "Defending the American Dream," a slogan of the union that had bitterly fought the company in a strike.

Employee freedom of expression and the issue of privacy have also been raised by court decisions that give employers the right to read employees' e-mail. Pillsbury, for example, fired a worker who posted an e-mail message to a colleague calling management "back-stabbing bastards." The employee sued, but the court sided with the company. In another case, Intel got a court injunction against a former employee who complained about the company in e-mails sent to thousands of employees. The Electronic Frontier Foundation, a group devoted to civil liberties in cyberspace, worried about violation of First Amendment rights. The company, however, contended that it wasn't a matter of free speech, but trespassing on company property.

Companies say internal e-mail systems are company property and can be used only for official company business. Kmart Corporation even has a policy stating, "Misuse of the e-mail system could result in denial of access to the Kmart computing environment, or dismissal."

WORKING WITH LAWYERS

This chapter has outlined a number of areas in which the release of information (or the lack of release) raises legal issues for an organization. Public relations personnel must be aware of legal pitfalls, but they are not lawyers. By the same token, lawyers aren't experts in public relations and often have a poor understanding of how important the court of public opinion is in determining the reputation and credibility of an organization.

In today's business environment, with its high potential for litigation, it is essential for public relations professionals and lawyers to have cooperative relationships. Although much is written about the tug-of-war between public relations people and lawyers concerning the release of information, a survey by Kathy R. Fitzpatrick, a public relations professor now at Virginia Tech University, found that almost 85 percent of the public relations respondents said their relationship with legal counsel was either "excellent" or "good."

A number of steps can be taken by an organization to ensure that the public relations and legal staffs have a cordial, mutually supportive relationship:

- The public relations and legal staffs should report to the same top executive, who can listen to both sides and decide on a course of action.

- Public relations personnel should know basic legal concepts and regulatory guidelines in order to build trust and credibility with the legal department.

- Both functions should be represented on key committees.

- The organization should have a clearly defined statement of responsibilities for each staff and its relationship to the other. Neither should dominate.

- Periodic consultations should be held during which materials and programs are reviewed.

- The legal staff, as part of its duties, should brief public relations personnel on impending developments in litigation, so press inquiries can be answered in an appropriate manner.

CASE PROBLEM

Expresso Unlimited, a chain of coffee shops, hires you as director of public relations and marketing. Some of your ideas include (1) a series of advertisements showing pictures and quotes from satisfied customers; (2) hiring a freelance photographer to build up a photo file for use in possible magazine articles, brochures, newsletters, and advertising; (3) reprinting and distributing various magazine articles that have been written about the company; (4) starting an employee newsletter with emphasis on employee features and "personals"; (5) including in the newsletter and advertisements cartoons about coffee drinking from various publications, including the *New Yorker;* (6) citing a government study that rates the quality of coffee beans from around the world, and pointing out that Expresso Unlimited uses only the highest-quality beans; (7) writing a news release that quotes a survey showing that eight out of 10 serious coffee drinkers prefer Expresso Unlimited; and (8) creating a home page on the Internet that would include pictures of famous people drinking a cup of coffee.

Prepare a memo outlining the legal and regulatory factors that should be considered in implementing the above activities.

QUESTIONS FOR REVIEW AND DISCUSSION

1. Why do public relations staff and firms need to know the legal aspects of creating and distributing messages?

2. How can a public relations person take precautions to avoid libel suits?

3. What is the concept of fair comment and criticism? Are there any limitations?

4. What precautions should a public relations person take to avoid invasion of privacy suits?

5. If an organization wants to use the photo or comments of an employee or a customer in an advertisement, what precautions should be taken?

6. When the media call about an employee, what kinds of information should the public relations person provide? What other approaches can be used?

7. What basic guidelines of copyright law should public relations professionals know about?

8. What rights do photographers and freelance writers have regarding ownership of their works?

9. How do public relations people help an organization protect its trademarks?

10. What is "misappropriation of personality"?

11. What should public relations people know about the regulations of the Federal Trade Commission?

12. What should public relations personnel know about the regulations of the Securities and Exchange Commission?

13. Many companies contend that they have the right to read the e-mail of employees. What do you think? Is this a violation of privacy and employee free speech?

14. What should be the relationship between public relations staff and legal counsel in an organization?

13

Corporations

Preview

The objective of this chapter is to give students a better understanding of public relations in corporations, whose dealings with customers, communities, governments, stockholders, employees, and the financial world heavily influence their reputations with the public.

Topics covered in this chapter include:
- The corporate role
- The human factor and downsizing
- Consumerism
- Community relations
- Corporations and the environment
- Financial information
- Sensitivity to ethnic groups
- Marketing communications
- Employee communications

THE CORPORATE ROLE

This is an era of giantism in American and, indeed, world business. International conglomerates control subsidiary companies that often produce a grab bag of seemingly unrelated products and services under the same corporate banner. These conglomerates must deal with government at many levels. Their operations affect the environment, control the employment of thousands, and have an impact on the financial and social well-being of millions. Truly, they have a compelling influence on contemporary life.

Bigness brings remoteness. The popular phrase "the faceless corporation" may be a cliché, but it represents a genuine distrust in the public mind—a distrust often based on lack of knowledge about a corporation rather than on actual unfavorable experiences. When U.S. gasoline prices soared in early 2000, for example, suspicion spread that the oil companies had conspired to gouge the public, a distrust that the oil companies never fully allayed.

Since a corporation's impact on society is felt at so many levels, those who plan and conduct its public relations face a complex task. Even relatively small corporations need public relations programs that show them conducting their affairs, both external and internal, in a socially responsible manner.

Figure 13.1 presents in schematic form the way one company—General Electric—categorizes the various concerns it must take into consideration at every step of executive decision-making.

THE HUMAN FACTOR

The fundamental, irreplaceable element in every business is people. A successful company must treat its customers honestly and in a friendly manner. Equally, it must conduct relations with its employees with a responsible, compassionate, evenhanded policy. And it must heed the desires and attitudes of people in the communities where it operates.

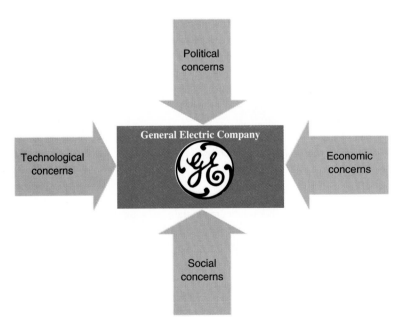

Figure 13.1
General Electric Company sees four factors that must be taken into consideration whenever a management decision is made: (1) Political—How do government regulations and other pressures affect the decision? (2) Technological—do we have engineering knowledge to complete the goal? (3) Social—What is our responsibility to society? (4) Economic—Will it make a profit?

The Public Perception

What corporations *do* is not enough. The public's perception of their conduct also matters. A corporation may operate in a completely legal, technically sound, and financially efficient manner yet find itself viewed by segments of the public as cold, greedy, and heedless of cherished social values. The public relations practitioner's job is to see that this does not happen. The practitioner must work within the company to foster constructive, socially aware behavior and outside the company to convince the public that the firm is a worthy, caring, corporate citizen.

Downsizing Stirs Resentment

The public relations task is especially difficult when a corporation announces large-scale dismissals, as many companies did during the 1990s.

When corporations engage in *downsizing*—dismissing thousands of employees to increase profits—they magnify the public's distrust.

Most citizens feel vaguely uneasy about the concentration of vast economic power in a few hands when one corporation buys another for more than $10 billion, although they don't understand the financial maneuvers involved.

The public relations challenge in downsizing is twofold:

- To convince top management, before the cuts are announced, that it should think of the employees as individuals, not as statistics—recognize the company loyalty most of them have shown, provide as much financial cushion and insurance protection as possible, and offer retraining and job-placement assistance.

- To make the public understand why the layoffs are justified. The electronic age has caused enormous changes in production and marketing procedures; jobs essential 20 years ago

PR Casebook

Starbucks' Response to Tragedy Makes a Profound Statement

The Starbucks Coffee Company reopened seven months after the brutal after-hours killing of three young employees at the Washington, D.C. area store. Residents welcomed the reopening, stating that business must go on and that criminals cannot "win." But the opening was made special through several extraordinary efforts by the large coffee chain. The company made the store a living memorial, installing a floor-to-ceiling maplewood mural that features three boxes with the initials of the slain employees. Family members placed photos and other mementos in the boxes. Starbucks also immediately offered a $100,000 reward for apprehension of the murderers and paid for funerals of the victims as well as counseling of family members. And since the store reopened, all net profits have gone to a foundation that promotes nonviolence. The company's efforts have been well received in the community and by many of the 23,000 Starbucks employees, who are described as company partners.

no longer are needed. Changes in the company's line of products, needed to stay competitive, have altered workforce needs. A company that remains static in a fiercely competitive world will not survive. Mergers of corporations and spin-offs of company divisions have created many job duplications.

If a corporation's layoff announcement has shown genuine regard for the employees affected, the public may acknowledge some validity in the dismissals. If the announcement sounds cold and heartless, the justifications will be largely brushed aside.

What Can Happen When Businesses Overlook the Human Factor

Businesses sometimes fail to recognize the human factor. They become so engrossed in computer technology, cash-flow charts, and management techniques that they overlook personal sensitivities. In a public relations blunder, the U.S. Bank of Washington in Spokane did exactly that, to its regret. A man in shabby clothes parked his pickup truck in the bank's parking lot, cashed a check, then asked the teller to validate his 60-cent parking ticket. She refused, claiming that cashing a check wasn't a transaction, as required for parking validation. When the man protested, she called a supervisor, who looked distastefully at the ragged character and also refused.

"Fine," the man replied. "You don't need me and I don't need you." Whereupon he closed his account and took the $1 million he had on deposit to a competing bank down the street.

Taco Bell made a costly blunder, too. It fired one of its restaurant managers in Portland, Oregon, because she ran out from her restaurant to aid a teenager wounded in a street fight. In doing so, she broke a company rule requiring employees to remain in the restaurant and call police if trouble occurs.

Public indignation at this harsh treatment for a humanitarian act was so intense that Taco Bell apologized in a full-page newspaper advertisement. It offered the manager her job back, but she refused, taking another job elsewhere.

"Sometimes corporations make mistakes," Taco Bell said. "In this case we did, and we've learned from it."

The lesson is clear: before a company takes an action affecting the public, its management should attempt to view the move through the eyes of others. Providing management with these outside perceptions is the job of the public relations specialists. Their antennae must be sensitive to changes in public attitudes.

Similarly, corporate managements should pay heed to how their actions are perceived by their employees. If employees believe that management is treating them unfairly, their work suffers and internal tensions develop. Absenteeism rises.

A disturbing difference in how a company's top management and how its employees perceive the workplace atmosphere sometimes develops, with potentially dangerous consequences. The problem can exist, as well, in large nonprofit organizations.

A survey by *Industry Week* and the Wyatt Company points up this conflict in attitudes. It reported that while 69 percent of senior managers responding believed their organizations' management style encouraged treating employees with respect, only 24 percent of their line managers believed this was true. Moreover, 64 percent of the top management respondents believed their firms encouraged freedom of expression, while only 29 percent of the line supervisors thought so. Since line supervisors are in personal contact with most employees, their opinions should be closer to that of the workforce than are those of top management's.

These findings define the challenge for company public relations departments, since they, in conjunction with the human relations department, have the responsibility for communication between management and employees.

Computers versus Humans

As computer wizardry multiplies, and increasingly ingenious automated voice equipment comes into service, companies are tempted to substitute this technology for human contact with customers. This should be done with extreme caution. Unwise use of electronic response may alienate the very people the company needs to please. A dissatisfied customer who telephones to protest a billing error or shipping mistake resents being answered by a recording. Far too many consumers have had bad experiences such as this actual example: a newcomer to an area needed information about a telephone installation he had ordered, so he called the customer service number of the phone company. He was answered by a recorded voice, which gave him a choice of numbers to press on his touchtone phone. That produced another recorded answer, which gave him a further set of extension numbers from which to choose. That brought a third recorded answer, stating that all customer service representatives were busy but one would answer him shortly. He was put on hold for nearly 30 minutes. Each minute a recorded voice told him that his call was important to the company and asked him to keep holding. Then he was abruptly disconnected. He had to start again from the beginning. About 40 minutes elapsed before he reached a live voice. The result: an infuriated customer. This from a telephone company that was running TV commercials praising its splendid service!

This is an extreme instance, but it illustrates how a company can alienate the public. Here is an area in which corporate public relations practitioners should exercise influence with management to maintain the human touch.

CONSUMERISM

The day when business could operate successfully on the Latin precept of *caveat emptor*— "Let the buyer beware"—is long gone. In today's society, sellers are expected to deliver goods and services of safe, acceptable quality on honest terms, without misleading claims and deceptive financing practices. Consumers have rights protected by the federal government and enjoy the assistance of government and private agencies in enforcing those rights. Consumerism is a significant and growing force in the conduct of business. The manner in which public relations practitioners help to guide a company in handling the pressures of consumerism strongly affects the public's attitude toward that company.

Development of the Consumer Movement

The consumer movement developed during the past three decades because far too often business firms were caught either cheating their customers or carelessly giving them inferior products, then making it difficult for them to obtain adjustments. Public trust in business diminished. When the firm of Yankelovich, Skelly and White took a poll in 1967 to measure public trust, the result showed confidence in business at about 70 percent. In a similar poll 14 years later, public confidence had plummeted to 19 percent. Opinion Research Corporation concluded from its 1998 survey findings that companies are *guilty until proven innocent,* suggesting that mistrust of business will persist in the new century.

The high priest of the consumer movement during its growth stages was Ralph Nader, a youthful attorney in Washington, D.C. His book *Unsafe at Any Speed,* published in 1965, was a searing indictment of automobile safety standards. Nader organized study groups that published generally critical reports on other industries and dwelt heavily upon corporate responsibility to consumers.

Rising consumer protests coincided with a period of rapid expansion in the "watchdog" role of government. The power of federal regulatory agencies over business expanded in numerous directions.

Consumerism Today

Today, Americans as a whole, in their roles as consumers, appear to want enforcement of rules protecting them from fraud, dangerous food products and medicines, highway perils, toxic wastes, and other threats to their personal well-being.

In a study by Louis Harris and Associates, strong sentiment was expressed favoring continued government regulation of safety, health, and truth in advertising.

Use of Boycotts

The *boycott*—refusal to buy the products or services of an offending company—is a widely used tool of the consumer movement, aimed at firms for many different reasons.

Typical boycotts in recent years were those against Kraft Foods and Nabisco for allegedly selling cigarettes to minors, Levi Strauss for moving plants abroad, and Burger King for allegedly promoting sex and violence on TV with its commercials.

The Southern Baptist Convention, representing 16 million church members, drew national attention in 1996 with a threat to boycott the Walt Disney Company's animated films, toys, and theme parks because it believed that Disney was promoting homosexuality over family values. The convention was especially disturbed about Disney's decision to extend health benefits to same sex partners of homosexual employees.

Although the convention's resolution did not set a deadline for enforcing the boycott, many individual members said that they would start obeying it immediately.

In the private sector, the nationwide network of Better Business Bureaus provides machinery through which wronged consumers may seek satisfaction. Nader's operations in Washington continue to publicize defective products and services. Other consumer organizations do similar work. *Consumer Reports* is widely read.

Corporate willingness to accept blame when justified softens consumer anger. The PECO Energy Company received favorable reaction when it did so. An explosion caused by a reported but unrepaired gas leak in a company line killed two people. The utility's chief executive quickly apologized publicly, stating, "PECO Energy takes full responsibility."

PRODUCT RECALLS

Recalls of defective products from the purchasers are the most visible and frequently very expensive aspect of corporate relations with consumers. Hundreds of recalls, from major to relatively insignificant, are issued every year. In a typical year they ranged from 920,000 pickup trucks by General Motors (GM) for seat and safety-belt problems to 78,000 cases of animal crackers by Consolidated Biscuit Company for improper labeling.

Millions of automobiles have been called back for correction of defects that might endanger the safety of riders. Some recalls have been made voluntarily by manufacturers, others under government pressure.

Ten automobile companies recalled 8.8 million vehicles to replace seat belts, the largest recall ever. Ford called back 8.5 million vehicles to replace faulty ignition switches.

When the U.S. Food and Drug Administration found E. coli bacteria in a sample of unpasteurized Odwalla apple juice, the maker of the drink responded quickly with a frank, vigorous series of actions. It withdrew all its apple-based products and formed a research council of scientists, industry officials, and health specialists to examine its production process. The company's founder apologized for the outbreak during a news conference in Seattle and offered to pay the medical bills of any person stricken with E. coli infection from Odwalla juice.

In a full-page newspaper advertisement, Odwalla corporate heads said that the outbreak "has shaken all of us at Odwalla." They announced creation of a website and an 800 telephone number to provide information and answer inquiries. "We want to hear from you," their open letter said.

BUSINESS PUBLIC AFFAIRS

"Corporate citizenship" is a basic tenet of business and industry for several reasons.

First, many business executives have realized that to reduce government regulation they must take the initiative and voluntarily exercise a sense of social responsibility. Historically, business has been regulated in direct proportion to its social abuses.

The so-called robber barons of the late nineteenth century exploited labor and resources, generating considerable regulation of railway, utility, oil, and other companies (see Chapter 2). More recently, industry's failure to solve many of the environmental problems caused by manufacturing has increased demands for government regulation. One result was the creation of the Environmental Protection Agency (EPA).

Second, business and industrial leaders realize that they can survive and prosper only in a stable society that provides safety, security, and economic well-being for its citizens. Business needs to help find solutions to a number of societal problems. Such assistance not only improves the quality of life but creates a reservoir of public support for business.

Third, corporate citizenship enhances a company's reputation and its ability to market goods and services. A survey conducted by Opinion Research Corporation for *Fortune* magazine, for example, showed that 89 percent of adults said a company's reputation often determined what products they bought. *California Business,* commenting on the survey, added, "Companies involved in social issues are considered more sensitive to their customers."

With this thought in mind, companies in recent years have undertaken a variety of projects under the rubric of public affairs and community relations. Some examples:

* Dayton-Hudson Corporation, a Minneapolis-based retailer, conducted a "Child Care Aware" program to help educate parents about quality child care and how to find it. The

Focus on Ethics

Ethical Guidelines for Business Public Affairs Professionals

a. The public affairs professional maintains professional relationships based on honesty and reliable information, and therefore:

1. Represents accurately his or her organization's policies on economic and political matters to government, employees, shareholders, community interests, and others.

2. Serves always as a source of reliable information, discussing the varied aspects of complex public issues within the context and constraints of the advocacy role.

3. Recognizes diverse viewpoints within the public policy process, knowing that disagreement on issues is both inevitable and healthy.

b. The Public Affairs Professional seeks to protect the integrity of the public policy process and the political system, and therefore:

1. Publicly acknowledges his or her role as a legitimate participant in the public policy process and discloses whatever work-related information the law requires.

2. Knows, respects, and abides by federal and state laws that apply to lobbying and related public affairs activities.

3. Knows and respects the laws governing campaign finance and other political activities, and abides by the letter and intent of those laws.

c. The Public Affairs Professional understands the interrelation of business interests with the larger public interests, and therefore:

1. Endeavors to ensure that responsible and diverse external interests and views concerning the needs of society are considered within the corporate decision-making process.

2. Bears the responsibility for management review of public policies which may bring corporate interests into conflict with other interests.

3. Acknowledges dual obligations—to advocate the interests of his or her employer, and to preserve the openness and integrity of the democratic process.

4. Presents to his or her employer an accurate assessment of the political and social realities that may affect corporate operations.

Source: Public Affairs Council, a Washington-based organization of public affairs executives for major corporations.

program included in-store information booths, distribution of 1.7 million brochures, and a toll-free national hotline.

• Liz Claiborne, the apparel manufacturer, commissioned leading American women artists to create works of public art to address issues of concern to women. In San Francisco, for example, six artists developed a public service campaign on the issue of domestic violence. The company also funded a domestic violence hotline.

- Arby's restaurant chain set up a "Neighbors in Need" program with local social service groups to give families down on their luck two meals a day for one month. Through its various franchises, the chain provided more than 670,000 meals.

- Lenscrafters, in association with Lions Clubs International, sponsored a program in England to recycle eyeglasses for distribution by its clubs to underprivileged families in developing nations. More than 50,000 pairs of glasses were collected.

COMMUNITY RELATIONS

A business slogan says, "Think globally, act locally." Community relations, particularly in those towns and cities where the company maintains an office, retail outlets, or a manufacturing facility, carries out that advice.

Because a corporation relies on local governments for construction permits, changes in zoning laws, even tax concessions, a good working relationship with city hall and community groups is important. A vigorous program also helps in the recruitment of employees and gives the company influence in community affairs.

Public affairs specialists often serve as representatives of their companies on community boards, task forces, and commissions. The purpose is to develop a dialogue between the company and the community. Public affairs personnel presenting the company's viewpoint listen and monitor emerging issues. Thus they can inform management about any public or governmental concerns that directly or indirectly affect the company.

CORPORATE AID TO EDUCATION

In recent years, many corporations have become involved in supporting schools, in part because their human relations directors are disturbed by the poor education shown by some of their job applicants. Some companies "adopt" schools, supplying needed equipment and company employees to assist teachers. Contributions of computer equipment are one form of assistance. Two examples of corporate aid:

- Westinghouse sponsors an annual Science Talent Search that draws entrants from nearly two thousand high schools. The top prize is a $40,000 scholarship.

- Dow Chemical Company and Ketchum Public Relations, seeking to spark students' interest in chemistry, created ChemTV, a multimedia show patterned in the MTV music style, which toured high schools in 16 large cities. Later Dow released a 45-minute video version for other interested schools.

A word of caution: any company entering the educational field should be certain that its efforts are primarily intended to improve education, not to sell products to students. Otherwise, it can be criticized for crass commercialism. The National Education Association warns teachers not to use ready-made contributed lesson plans if they advance "merely PR purposes." (See Chapter 16.)

CORPORATE PHILANTHROPY

Company financial contributions to community and national social programs and institutions are closely related to community relations. The campaign to balance the federal budget, with resulting cutbacks in government contributions to many programs, has put pressure on corporations to increase their philanthropy. The Independent Sector, a coalition of nonprofit foundations and charities, estimates that charitable organizations nationwide depend on the government for about 29 percent of their income.

Many corporations follow a policy of "enlightened self-interest" in their giving. That is, they select the charitable institutions they will support, and the forms of support to offer that will assist company goals and objectives. (See "Focus on Ethics" on page 304.)

Hewlett-Packard, for example, is a manufacturer of computers, medical equipment, and test equipment. Product gifts account for most of its philanthropy. The company's philosophy is simply stated: "HP giving to college and universities meets university needs for products while attracting highly skilled workers to the industries we support."

On the other hand, Philip Morris uses philanthropy for constituency-building and generating favorable perceptions among opinion leaders. The giant beer, tobacco, and food conglomerate donated more than $17 million in one recent year to schools, hospitals, cultural organizations, and charity groups. Many of these funds, activist critics say, were targeted to minority organizations that might help defeat tax and antismoking bills. In other words, corporate giving is based on where there might be political benefit.

American corporations in 1998 contributed $9 billion to philanthropic organizations, according to the American Association of Fund-Raising Counsel (AAFRC). This represents 5.1 percent of the total $175 billion in contributions reported by the AAFRC. (See Chapter 16.)

Company giving takes many forms—cash, as in the case of Philip Morris; company products, as done by Hewlett-Packard; food and clothing to the needy; loans of company employees to assist fund drives by charitable organizations; and other methods.

A widely used technique is matching funds: a company matches every dollar an employee contributes to a charitable organization. Corporations also encourage employees to do volunteer work, either on company time or after work hours.

An example of creative corporate philanthropy:

• Eight companies in Santa Rosa and San Mateo Counties of California competed to see which one could contribute the most food to the Second Harvest Food Bank at Christmas. Winner of the Corporate Food Bowl Challenge was Cisco Systems. Company management vigorously encouraged its approximately five thousand employees to participate. They contributed 914,525 pounds of food to the needy. For convenience, many donated cash, which was used to purchase food.

Corporate philanthropy does have its limitations. Contributions generate a reserve of public support but cannot offset company performance that the public considers unsatisfactory.

Philanthropy also may come under attack from special-interest groups. This is particularly true regarding extremely emotional issues. Prolife groups, for example, often target companies that give grants to Planned Parenthood and ask supporters to boycott the company's products.

Pioneer Hi-Bred International, a seed corn company headquartered in Iowa, canceled its $25,000 annual gift to Planned Parenthood of Greater Iowa after a prolife group called Rescue the Perishing started distributing leaflets to farmers asking them to boycott the company's products. The company president flatly told the *Wall Street Journal,* "We were blackmailed" but added, "You can't put the corn business at risk."

Prolife groups had originally forced Dayton-Hudson Corporation, a department store chain, to cancel its contribution to Planned Parenthood, but the company reversed its decision after hundreds of irate customers sent in cut-up credit cards.

CORPORATIONS AND THE ENVIRONMENT

Public demand for protection of the environment, born of a growing realization that the earth's resources are limited, places a heavy burden on corporations. Much of the world's pollution, but far from all, has been created by their manufacturing processes and use of their products. The public wants those products but protests against the pollution they have created. In earlier decades, smoking factory smokestacks were applauded as a sign of prosperity. Today they are a badge of corporate dishonor, because medical science has established that air pollution damages health.

Social responsibility requires that companies eliminate, to the best of their ability, the sources of environmental damage they have created. At the same time, corporate

Focus on Ethics

Corporate Philanthropy Is Really Strategic Communication

Corporate giving is best described as strategic philanthropy, according to *PR Reporter* (November 16, 1998). The newsletter offers a definition of strategic philanthropy by Paul Davis Jones and Cary Raymond of IDPR Group: ". . . the long-term socially responsible contribution of dollars, volunteers, products and expertise to a cause *aligned with the strategic business goals of an organization.*" Such giving can reap an array of benefits for the corporation.

1. Strengthened reputation and brand recognition
2. Increased media opportunities
3. Improved community and government relations
4. Facilitation of employee recruitment and retention
5. Enhanced marketing
6. Access to research and development
7. Increased corporate profitability

Questions worth asking:

• Do you think that when strategic philanthropy is at work, more giving is made to more worthy organizations than would be true if the corporation ignored the seven benefits of strategic philanthropy?

• Should corporate giving be based in part or entirely on strategic considerations?

• Can the most needy causes be "shortchanged" because they do not serve strategic interests of corporate givers?

• Why shouldn't a corporation strive "to do good and to do well" at the same time?

managements must protect the interests of their stockholders. Corporations face what writer William H. Miller called the green wall: "the towering, though invisible, barrier that separates firms' environmental good intentions from the realities of the bottom line." Activist groups representing many different environmental causes focus the public mood by conducting campaigns against individual companies, sometimes in a highly emotional manner.

Even the best-intentioned corporations sometimes have difficulty in eliminating their offenses because the cost can be extremely high. Nevertheless, companies are increasingly aware that the cost savings of waste reduction, recycling, and elimination of future cleanup efforts can be considerable. The combination of genuine actions to achieve sustainable, low-impact production and effective communication programs can earn goodwill from many of the corporation's stakeholders, including employees, regulators and shareholders.

Alice Rivlin, director of the Office of Management and Budget in the Clinton administration and an environmental activist, summarized the problem many industries face:

> It's sometimes difficult for companies to be as environmentally responsible as they'd like to be, because it's costly in the short run. That's part of the general problem of short-term focus in American companies. But I think if they take a long-range view, especially with the rising concern about the environment in the general public, it's clear that long-term profitability will be aided by environmental responsibility.

The Public Relations Role

Public relations people representing corporations concentrate on three areas concerning the environment:

1. Present to the public the company's environmental accomplishments, its plans for long-term cleanup, and explanations of the company's problems in achieving its goals.

2. Inform top management of the public's perceptions and concerns about the company's environmental record. If management is reluctant to address the problems, public relations experts should persuade senior officials that they should act to protect the company's reputation.

3. Conduct environmental cleanup campaigns within the company, urging employees to follow good environmental practices such as recycling on and off the job.

Specialists recommend that as a first step a company should take an environmental audit. This involves a detailed investigation of every aspect of the business for its impact on the environment. An audit by a qualified outsider may be more objective than a self-examination. Next, management should create a long-range cleanup program. Some environmental faults may be overcome quickly and cheaply, others only at high cost and with retooling.

A company may need to raise prices of its products to remain profitable. Willingness to spend money and take risks is what Alice Rivlin was talking about. Jobs may be in jeopardy because of these decisions, a painful personnel problem.

Bad news always attracts more attention than good news. Public disclosure that a company is committing an environmental sin automatically gets more headlines than the success of a three-year program to reduce wastepaper by 25 percent. Two ways in which a public relations practitioner can respond to this psychological fact are:

- Search out all the environmentally positive actions the company has taken and publicize them in a creative manner, such as through videotaped presentations to community groups. This projects a "good citizen" image.

- Have a crisis plan ready in case a company environmental blunder comes to light. Be ready to explain how it came about; why it is difficult to correct, if that is true; and the company's plans to correct it. All defensive words fail, of course, if the company does not act vigorously to solve the problem.

Corporate products and methods viewed as dangerous today often were quite acceptable to society when they were created. Pesticides were hailed as a boon to agricultural production; further research has revealed their danger to humans. Asbestos was regarded as valuable fire insulation material; today it is known to cause cancer, yet removing it from buildings is costly and difficult. Lead was used widely in manufactured products; now medical evidence shows the peril of lead poisoning, especially to children. In explaining why a corporation is violating one of today's taboos, the practitioner can make a valid point by emphasizing the historical perspective. Realistic people recognize that complex solutions take time, but they must be convinced that the company is taking action, not just talking.

One Company's Program

The 3M Company, operating in 20 countries worldwide, has won numerous awards for its "Pollution Prevention Pays" program. The manufacturing company calculates that the program has saved it $500 million since its inception in 1975.

Company management decided to concentrate on reducing the air pollution created by its production processes. This involved identifying pollution sources, modifying operations, installing control equipment, changing products, recycling, and encouraging suggestions from employees. More than 2500 projects have been put in operation around the world. These have reduced 3M's air pollutants by 120,000 tons. In the early 1990s, 3M decided to invest another $150 million in air pollution control equipment and renamed the project "3P Plus."

Vital to the program is the public relations department, which is responsible for all environmental communications—internal, to stimulate employee understanding and appreciation, and external, to inform the public about what is happening. For employees, the department conducts motivational meetings, shows videotapes, and issues special publications. For external use, it distributes news releases and other material, holds media briefings, and conducts plant tours for community leaders.

THE BUSINESS-MEDIA RELATIONSHIP

Reporting by the media is a basic source of public information about the performance and objectives of business. Too frequently it generates misunderstanding and irritation between these two essential segments of society, a situation for which both sides are partially responsible. The trouble arises most frequently when a corporation becomes involved in a communication crisis.

Many business executives regard media stories about their companies as inaccurate, incomplete, and biased, an opinion at odds with the view of many business editors and writers. The pattern emerges in most polls taken on the relationship. A poll by Louis Harris and Associates asked, "Would you rate business journalism positively on being fair, balanced and accurate?" Results showed a striking discrepancy in the percentage of "Yes" responses among the four groups polled:

Business executives	27 percent
Writers and editors	84 percent
Business academics	64 percent
Journalism academics	72 percent

A majority of all four categories agreed, however, that the quality of business reporting had improved substantially during the past 25 years or so.

Corporate managers' principal complaints against media coverage are inaccuracy, incomplete coverage, inadequate research and preparation for interviews, and antibusiness bias. Business editors and reporters state in response that often they cannot publish or broadcast thorough, evenhanded stories about business because many company executives, uncooperative and wary, erect barriers against them. Writers complain about failing to obtain direct access to decision-making executives and being restricted to using public relations statements that don't contain information they need. Journalists assert, too, that some business leaders don't understand the concept of objectivity and assume that any story involving unfavorable news about their company is intentionally biased.

Public relations practitioners serving business stand in the middle. They must interpret their companies to the media while showing their chief executive officers and other high officials how open, friendly press relations can serve their interest.

FINANCIAL INFORMATION

At a time when corporate mergers, takeovers, and financial scandals make headlines almost daily, the role of investor relations is essential in corporate operations. This falls within the general scope of public relations.

The men and women who handle investor relations work are specialists. In large corporations they may function as a separate unit, in smaller companies as part of the public relations department. No matter how the organization chart is designed, cooperation between the general public relations function and this special field should be close.

The two primary targets for a company's financial information are (1) its stockholders, and (2) the financial analysts whose advice to brokers and bankers about a company's financial situation affects the price of its stock. Since large blocks of stock often are held by a single investor, such as a pension fund, special attention must be paid to those investors, as well as to the growing number of foreign stockholders.

Annual meetings of corporations commonly are routine and dull, with everything going precisely as management has arranged it. Proxy votes obtained in advance assure management solid control of the voting. Management often presents slide and videotaped shows to illustrate achievements, serves light refreshments, and in general tries to create an atmosphere of competence and geniality. Behind the scenes, many hours of public relations department work have been spent in planning the meetings.

At times abrasive moments of controversy may arise if stockholders challenge management policies. Although antimanagement resolutions rarely pass, they obtain publicity and at times gather enough votes to influence management thinking.

SENSITIVITY TO ETHNIC GROUPS

Swift expansion of the minority population in the United States, bringing with it intensified problems of language and cultural differences, demands heightened sensitivity by corporate management. Traditionally, senior executives have been white males, although female and minority faces are increasingly evident in executive suites. Feedback on attitudes of minority customers and employees collected by public relations departments helps broaden management perspectives.

The racial mixture of workforces sometimes becomes an issue if a large minority group in a community believes that a company fails to hire enough of its members. Communications within a company also can be a problem if some employees speak little or no English. These difficulties can be overcome if management handles them in a sensitive manner. When it fails to do so, the cost in money and public respect can be great.

Texaco Inc. provides a notorious example. After lingering in federal court more than two years, a suit against the oil company by 1377 employees charging racial discrimination was blown wide open by disclosure of a tape recorded secretly at a meeting of high company executives. They were heard using racial slurs against employees and discussing the destruction of documents the employees might use in their suit.

Eleven days later Texaco agreed to pay $176 million to settle the case, the largest settlement ever in a racial discrimination suit. It agreed to begin intensive sensitivity training, and the corporate chairman apologized publicly. One former executive was charged by the federal government with shredding documents.

Repercussions against Texaco were intense. Black leaders called a boycott but cancelled it after Texaco announced plans to diversify its workforce. Some organizations sold their Texaco stock in protest.

MARKETING COMMUNICATIONS

Many companies use the tools and tactics of public relations extensively to support the marketing and sales objectives of their businesses. This is called *marketing communications* or *marketing public relations.* Personnel who work in this specialty area usually serve in, or work closely with, the marketing, advertising, and promotion departments of the company.

Thomas L. Harris, author of *A Marketer's Guide to Public Relations,* defines marketing public relations (MPR) as: "The process of planning, executing, and evaluating programs that encourage purchase and consumer satisfaction through credible communication of information and impressions that identify companies and their products with the needs, wants, concerns, and interests of consumers."

PR Casebook

Eddie Bauer's Blunder

The Eddie Bauer Inc. clothing chain, caught in a racial discrimination crisis, responded so slowly and clumsily that it compounded its problem.

Two black teenage youths were shopping at an Eddie Bauer store in Maryland. As they left, police officers moonlighting as security guards accused one youth of shoplifting the shirt he was wearing. He told them he had purchased the shirt on a previous visit to the store and didn't have with him the sales receipt they demanded. The officers ordered him to take off the shirt and leave it until he brought in the receipt. He returned with the receipt the next day and was given the shirt. A company spokesperson later called the incident "minor" and implied that the company had done the young man a favor by returning it.

Angered at her son's treatment, the youth's mother phoned the Eddie Bauer corporate headquarters to complain. She said she was told someone would call her back. When weeks passed without a return call, she told the story to the Washington *Post*, which published it.

In response to public criticism and a threatened lawsuit, Eddie Bauer hired Hill and Knowl-

ton, the public relations firm, to help. With Hill and Knowlton's guidance, the company president issued a belated apology and went to Washington, where he conferred with officials of the National Association for the Advancement of Colored People (NAACP). He promised a sensitivity training program for employees. The company donated truckloads of clothing to homeless shelters.

These gestures were insufficient to placate critics. Other black customers told stories of discrimination. The young man's mother pointed out that while the company president was in Washington he spoke with NAACP officials but didn't apologize to the two young men or see them or their families.

Even Bauer's act of hiring Hill and Knowlton drew criticism. Washington *Post* columnist Jonathan Yardley wrote, "Taking on a high-octane public relations firm is prima facie evidence of guilt."

The company's delay in response and perceived failure to recognize the personal feelings of the individuals involved made a bad situation even worse.

In many cases, marketing public relations also is coordinated with a company's messages in advertising, marketing, direct mail, and promotion. This has led to the concept of *integrated marketing communications* (IMC) in which companies manage all sources of information about a product or service in order to assure maximum message penetration.

In an integrated program, for example, public relations activities are often geared to obtaining early awareness and credibility for a product.

The Volkswagen Beetle was introduced in just such a way. Volkswagen won early support of key auto trade and business media by inviting them to participate in background sessions on the car during the preproduction stage. The car was introduced using video news releases and interactive satellite feeds that resulted in 800 individual TV segments, including appearances on *The Today Show* and *Good Morning America*. After this initial introduction using the tools of publicity, advertising was used to keep the auto in the public eye.

The objectives of marketing public relations, often called *marcom* in industry jargon, are accomplished in several ways.

Companies that request comments from customers about the service they received accomplish a double purpose: they show their concern for customer satisfaction and obtain information for future marketing efforts. This questionnaire on a business reply card distributed by Firestone Tire and Service Centers is typical.

As your Firestone store manager, my job is customer satisfaction.

If you have any comments about our service, please contact me directly. We care about more than your car.

(Optional)

NO POSTAGE
NECESSARY
IF MAILED
IN THE
UNITED STATES

BUSINESS REPLY MAIL

FIRST CLASS MAIL   PERMIT NO. 2215   ARLINGTON HEIGHTS, IL

POSTAGE WILL BE PAID BY ADDRESSEE

FIRESTONE TIRE AND SERVICE CENTERS
MANAGER-CUSTOMER RETENTION
P O BOX 8700
ROLLING MEADOWS, IL 60008-9878

Product Publicity   The cost and clutter of advertising and sales promotion have mounted dramatically, and companies have found that product publicity is a cost-effective way of reaching potential consumers. Products, if presented properly, can be newsworthy and catch the eyes of reporters and editors. Clorox, for example, generated many news articles and broadcast mentions for its Combat cockroach killer by sponsoring a contest to find America's five worst cockroach-infested homes.

Other forms of product publicity are found on the food, auto, real estate, business, travel, and sports pages of newspapers and magazines as news and feature stories. Radio and television talk shows and consumer programs contain large amounts of publicity.

Information Bureaus   Several companies operate information bureaus that help position their products in the marketplace. Quaker's Gatorade has its Sports Science Institute, Reebok has an Aerobic Information Bureau, and Nutri/System operates a Health and Fitness Information Bureau. One primary function of these "information bureaus" is the distribution of news releases and press kits that report research results.

Cause-Related Marketing   Companies in highly competitive fields often strive to stand out by supporting causes that appeal to various market segments. Dannon yogurt brand, for example, donates 1.5 percent of its sales to the National Wildlife Federation.

Corporate Sponsorships   Companies spend about nine billion annually sponsoring activities ranging from the Olympic Games, the Indianapolis 500-mile race, and the Kentucky Derby, to the Three Tenors Opera Tour. Experts say that corporate sponsorship is a growth industry averaging a 30- to 40-percent increase annually.

Product publicity: Cucumbers received national publicity from this photograph of a man spreading them in an eleven-foot-deep wooden tank at Hausback Pickle Company in Saginaw, Michigan. Publicists can draw attention even to unexciting products by creating unusual photographs like this one.

The popularity of sponsored events is due to several reasons. These events (1) enhance the reputation and image of the sponsoring company through association, (2) give product brands high visibility among key purchasing publics, (3) provide a focal point for marketing efforts and sales campaigns, and (4) generate publicity and media coverage.

Sponsorships can be more cost-effective than advertising. Visa International, for example, spends about $200,000 a year sponsoring the USA-Visa Decathlon Team—about the price of a 30-second prime-time TV commercial.

The array of sponsorship activity and opportunities is so great that the International Events Group publishes the eight-page *IEG Sponsorship Report* every two weeks. Sports is an especially popular area. Local stadiums almost everywhere now have corporate names.

The demographic characteristics of potential customers determine for the most part what events a company will sponsor. Manufacturers of expensive products sponsor events that draw the interest of affluent consumers. That's why Lexus, a luxury car, sponsors polo championships. General Motors GMC division, however, is interested in selling pickup trucks, so it sponsors a 15-city country western music tour.

EMPLOYEE COMMUNICATIONS

The employees of a company form a crucial audience for its public relations department. The department, often working with or within the human resources department, must concentrate on communicating with employees just as vigorously as it does on delivering the corporate story to the outside world. A workforce that respects its management, has pride in its products, and believes that it is being treated fairly is a key factor in corporate success.

In these days of corporate turmoil, unrest and uncertainty among employees create a greater need than ever for effective employee communications. Surveys indicate a drop-off in employees' loyalty to their companies, based in part on their belief that remote corporate managements feel no loyalty to them.

Job security and financial protection against illness are two principal concerns among employees. As much as the facts justify, they need to be reassured. Company magazines, brochures, newsletters, and policy manuals written for employees are a fundamental form of internal communication. These are discussed in detail in Chapter 19.

Much employee communication work is relatively standard—distribution of information about working conditions, retirement benefits, new company products, changes in management and supervisory personnel, and corporate plans for expansion or alterations in operating procedures. *The better informed employees are, the less likely they are to spread erroneous and possibly damaging misinformation.* Gossip flourishes in an information vacuum. Accurate information from management can make the always-present company grapevine a positive rather than a negative force.

Health and Social Issues

The skyrocketing cost of health insurance for employees has become a heavy and still-growing burden on employers. Yet with personal medical and hospital bills so high, employees regard medical insurance for themselves and their families as extremely important. Company attempts to trim benefits have encountered fervent resistance.

Circle K, which operates convenience stores nationwide, found that out when, with little preparation, it denied new employees coverage for illnesses and accidents related to "personal lifestyle decisions."

This meant no coverage for new employees if they became ill with acquired immune deficiency syndrome (AIDS) or had drug or alcohol problems. Circle K was accused, among other things, of making a thinly veiled attack on homosexuality. The dispute was covered on national television and the front pages. Reaction was so severe that Circle K suspended implementation of the plan.

Other social issues in the workplace:

Sexual Harassment   This worries both employees and management, the latter for legal as well as ethical reasons. The U.S. Supreme Court ruled in *Monitor Savings Bank v. Vinson* (1986) that a company may be held liable in sexual harassment suits even if management is unaware of the problem and has a general policy against discrimination.

One major corporation, the DuPont Company, meets the problem of sexual harassment thus, as reported in *Public Relations Journal:* a travel safety seminar for female employees, a personal safety program that includes a rape-prevention workshop, a managers' workshop to define their role in helping employees who have been assaulted, legal assistance, liabil-

An open letter to customers and other interested parties, presented in an advertisement, is an effective way to explain a corporation's actions and strengthen its image. Here Aetna and U.S. Health Care answer questions about their planned merger.

ity coverage, and public relations assistance in handling publicity that might result from a rape trial. The company promotes the program in internal publications, on the company news hotline, and in monthly safety meetings.

Policies concerning smoking by employees on company property and testing of employees for drug use are other issues of concern.

CASE PROBLEM

Women's sports, both amateur and professional, have attracted an increasing number of participants in recent years. Nike, recognizing this trend, has developed a new shoe designed for women basketball players. Develop a marketing public relations program for this product that also would be coordinated with an advertising and promotion program.

Provide the unique perspective and value of your public relations expertise. Include a response plan for critics of Nike's use of cheaper overseas labor to make shoes. This plan could range from steps to remedy injustices to a defense of open labor markets, depending upon your view.

QUESTIONS FOR REVIEW AND DISCUSSION

1. Why is the public perception of a corporation so important to its success?

2. What caused the growth of the consumer movement between 1960 and 1980 in the United States? Who was its best-known leader?

3. Have you ever participated in a boycott? If so, do you believe the boycott achieved its goal? If it failed, why did it?

4. As a corporate public relations director, what actions might you recommend to top management in order to establish your company's image as a socially responsible organization?

5. What are some of the methods government relations specialists use to obtain favorable treatment for their companies?

6. Why are investor relations specialists so important to the financial well-being of a corporation?

7. What is marketing public relations? What primary audience is involved? What kind of activities does it include?

8. Why are corporate sponsorships so popular?

9. What two primary concerns of employees need to be addressed by public relations and human relations departments of companies?

Politics and Government

14

Preview

In this chapter, the objective is to provide an understanding of the work performed by governmental relations specialists, lobbyists, and political fund-raisers.

Topics covered in the chapter include:
- Corporate government relations
- Lobbying
- The problem of "influence peddling"
- Grassroots lobbying efforts
- Political action committees (PACs)
- Fund-raising by candidates
- Political campaigns
- Public affairs in government
- Attacks on government information services

GOVERNMENT RELATIONS

A major component of corporate public affairs is government relations. This activity is so important that many companies, particularly in highly regulated industries, have separate departments of government relations. The reason is simple. The actions of governmental bodies at the local, state, and federal level have a major impact on how a business operates.

Government relations specialists have a number of functions: they gather information, disseminate management's views, cooperate with government on projects of mutual benefit, and motivate employees to participate in the political process.

As the eyes and ears of a business or industry, practitioners spend much time gathering and processing information. They monitor the activities of many legislative bodies and regulatory agencies to keep track of issues coming up for debate and possible vote. Such intelligence gathering enables a corporation or an industry to plan ahead and, if necessary, adjust policies or provide information that may influence the nature of government decision-making.

Government relations specialists also spend much time disseminating information about the company's position to a variety of key publics. Spoken tactics may include an informal office visit to a government official or testimony at a public hearing. In addition, public affairs people are often called upon to give a speech or write one for a senior executive.

Written tactics may include writing letters and op-ed articles, preparing position papers, producing newsletters, and placing advocacy advertising. Although legislators are a primary audience, the Foundation for Public Affairs reports that nine of 10 companies also communicate with employees on public policy issues, while another 40 percent communicate with retirees, customers, and other publics such as taxpayers and government employees.

The importance of effective governmental relations to the economic well-being of a company is best summarized by a New York *Times* writer thus:

> Public relations executives can rightly point out that, with the cacophony of interests clamoring for attention in Washington, there is a role for professional advice on how to insure that one's message is heard. With the expanding role of Congress and the increasing complexity of government, this probably is true now more than ever. There are undoubtedly times that public relations firms can help journalists, politicians and clients.

LOBBYING

Lobbying is closely aligned with governmental relations, and the distinction between the two areas often blurs. In general, government relations is a broader term that denotes a number of activities related to the monitoring of government and the dissemination of information to various publics, including elected officials.

Lobbying, on the other hand, is a more specific activity. *Webster's New World Dictionary* defines a *lobbyist* as "a person acting for a special-interest group, who tries to influence the voting on legislation or the decisions of government administrators." In other words, a lobbyist directs his or her energies to the defeat, passage, or amendment of proposed legislation and regulatory agency policies.

Lobbyists can be found at the local, state, and federal levels of government. California, for example, has about 900 registered lobbyists who represent more than 1600 special-interest groups.

The number and variety of special interests multiply at the federal level. One directory of Washington lobbyists lists 20,000 individuals and organizations. The interests represented include virtually the entire spectrum of U.S. business, educational, religious, local, national, and international pursuits.

The diversity of those groups can be illustrated with the debate about new regulations for managed health care. Opposing the regulations were (1) insurance companies, (2) HMO trade groups, (3) the Blue Cross-Blue Shield Association, (4) the National Federation of Independent Business, and (5) the U.S. Chamber of Commerce.

Collectively, they spent $60 million on lobbying in the first half of 1998—an average of $112,000 per lawmaker—in an effort to make sure no damaging legislation was passed by Congress. In addition, another $11 million was spent on advertising. The groups opposed new regulations because they believed the restrictions would push the cost of health plans so high that small businesses no longer could afford to insure workers.

On the other side, the American Medical Association, the AFL-CIO, the Association of Trial Lawyers, and various consumer groups spent about $14 million trying to get new regulations such as a Patient's Bill of Rights passed. From their perspective, legislation was needed to guarantee quality health care.

The Nature of Lobbying

Although the public perceives that only big business lobbies, a variety of special interests do it. *Fortune* magazine, for example, ranked the top 25 lobbying groups in Washington in terms of influence, and the American Association of Retired Persons (AARP) was first on the list. The next four rankings, in descending order, were (1) the American Israel Public Affairs Committee, (2) the National Federation of Independent Business, (3) the National Rifle Association, and (4) the AFL-CIO.

Collectively, interest groups spent $1.42 billion on lobbying in 1998, according to the nonprofit Center for Responsive Politics (CPR). For perspective, the center noted that this amount was enough to cover the entire budget of the Food and Drug Administration (FDA). Businesses involved in real estate, insurance, and finance spent the most money—$203 million. Tobacco companies spent $67.4 million on lobbying, almost double what they spent in 1997. Leading the pack was Philip Morris Companies, spending the most—$3.62 million.

Competing lobbying efforts often cancel each other out. All this leaves legislators and regulatory personnel the responsibility to weigh the pros and cons of an issue before voting. Indeed, *Time* magazine notes that lobbyists representing all sides of an issue "do serve a useful purpose by showing busy legislators the virtues and pitfalls of complex legislation." A classic conflict is the debate between saving jobs and improving the environment. A coalition of environmental groups constantly lobbies Congress for tougher legislation to clean up industrial pollution or protect endangered species. Simultaneously, local communities and unions often argue that the proposed legislation would mean the loss of jobs and economic chaos.

The Problem of "Influence Peddling"

Although a case can be made for lobbying as a legitimate activity, deep public suspicion exists about former legislators and officials who capitalize on their connections and charge large fees for doing what is commonly described as *influence peddling*.

Indeed, the roster of registered lobbyists in Washington includes a virtual "who's who" of former legislators and government officials from both Democratic and Republican parties. A good example is Powell Tate, a major public affairs firm in Washington, D.C. The president is Sheila Tate, who served as Nancy Reagan's press secretary and President Bush's transition press secretary when he was elected in 1988. Tate's partner is Jody

Beer Lobbyists Keep the Suds Flowing

The outcry over tobacco as a public-health menace has raised the inevitable question. Is booze next?

Beer producers and wholesalers are taking no chances. The National Beer Wholesalers Association (NBWA), for example, has increased its PAC donations to political candidates from $430,000 to $1.5 million per two-year cycle, an amount more than the powerful AFL-CIO gives through its various PAC groups. The group also makes major contributions to political candidates at the local and state level.

The industry is concerned that its product will make it the next "tobacco wars" because much public concern exists about such issues as (1) underage drinking, (2) binge drinking on college campuses, (3) drunken driving, and (4) how beer is marketed and advertised.

George Hacker, a nationally recognized alcohol-control activist, says, "Like tobacco, alcohol imposes enormous costs on society because this is an addictive substance. And because it can be purchased 24 hours a day and is sold in colorfully packaged containers that appeal to kids."

Powell, the former press secretary of President Carter. Together, they know on a first-name basis key Republican and Democratic lawmakers as well as the major journalists covering the Capitol.

"Influence peddling," always an issue in Washington, came into sharp public focus when Michael Deaver quit his job as White House deputy chief of staff for President Reagan and promptly became a public affairs consultant. In short order, he had a list of corporations and foreign governments as clients, including a $1-million contract with South Korean interests. Although he claimed to be doing "strategic planning," Deaver was found guilty of perjury and violation of the Ethics in Government Act.

The Ethics in Government Act forbids government officials from actively lobbying their former agencies for one year after leaving office. Critics say it has little or no impact. Marlin Fitzwater, press secretary to President Bush, and Mike McCurry, former press secretary to President Clinton, also became lobbyists shortly after leaving office. Although the law prevented them from lobbying the White House for a year, it placed no such restriction on lobbying members of Congress.

Members of Congress can also become lobbyists immediately upon leaving office. Congress has passed no legislation restricting the lobbying efforts of former legislators and their chief aides. A good example is former Senator Bob Packard, who resigned in the face of ethics charges of sexual and official misconduct. Within three months, he opened a Capitol Hill consulting firm to give clients ". . . advice on legislation and how they ought to lobby Congress."

A New Lobbying Reform Bill

Politicians of both parties have regularly decried the influence of lobbyists, but reform has taken a half-century. At least ten times since the first loophole-riddled lobbying regulations were passed in 1946, efforts to update the law failed to get past the legislative obstacles.

In 1995, however, Congress finally passed a measure designed to reform lobbying, and President Clinton signed it. Part of the impetus, no doubt, was the impact of polls indicating that the public believed lobbyists had runaway influence in Washington.

One key provision was an expanded definition of what is considered to be a "lobbyist." The new law defines a lobbyist as "someone hired to influence lawmakers, government officials or their aides, and who spends at least 20 percent of his or her time representing any client in a six-month period."

Another key provision requires lobbyists to register with Congress and disclose their clients, the issue areas in which lobbying is being done, and roughly how much is being paid for it. Violators face civil fines of up to $50,000.

The tougher restrictions on lobbyists also apply to eating and drinking. Under the new law, lobbyist-paid lavish lunches and drawn-out dinners are forbidden. Receptions at which finger food is served are allowed. Lobbyists call this the *toothpick rule.* The law also prohibits a lobbyist from buying a meal for a lawmaker unless at least 25 people from an organization attend. That is considered a "widely attended event" at which a lobbyist could not monopolize a lawmaker's time.

New rules also exist for gifts and travel. Senators, their aides, and other Senate officers are barred from accepting gifts worth more than $50 and from accepting privately paid travel to "recreational events." Similar rules about gift-giving govern the executive branch of government.

One area exempted from the lobby reform bill was financial disclosures for so-called "grassroots" lobbying. In many respects, it is the fastest growing area in the political persuasion business.

Grassroots Lobbying

Grassroots lobbying is now an $800 million industry, according to *Campaigns and Elections,* a bimonthly magazine for "political professionals." What makes it so attractive to various groups is that there are virtually no rules or regulations.

The tools of such lobbying are advocacy advertising, toll-free phone lines, bulk faxing, websites, and computerized direct mail aimed at generating phone calls and letters from the public to Congress, the White House, and governmental regulatory agencies.

One major firm, Bonner & Associates, has a highly sophisticated communications system that includes banks of telephones and computers that can call or send letters to thousands of citizens within hours. For example, the American Bankers Association hired Bonner to kill a Congressional bill that would lower credit card interest rates. The firm orchestrated 10,000 phone calls from citizens and community leaders to ten members of the House Banking Committee. The bill died in committee.

Grassroots lobbying also involves coalition-building. The basic idea is to get individuals and groups with no financial interest in an issue to speak on the sponsor's behalf. The premise is that letters and phone calls from private citizens are more influential than arguments from vested interests.

A good example comes from another Bonner campaign. In this case, Congress was considering an auto pollution bill opposed by car manufacturers. The auto companies sought opposition to the bill from beyond the auto industry. Key legislators soon began hearing from disabled and elderly people who were convinced the bill would force the

PR Insights

Guidelines for Grassroots Lobbying

Legitimate coalitions of companies, associations, and citizens are effective grassroots tools, but "misleading front groups and sneak attacks are recipes for trouble," says Jay Lawrence, senior vice president of Fleishman-Hillard public relations.

Lawrence gives these tips for effective grassroots lobbying:

- *Target the effort.* Few campaigns need to reach every congressman or state legislator.

- *Go after "persuadables."* Narrow the audience by concentrating on fence-sitters.

- *Build coalitions on economic self-interest.* Go after individuals and organizations who would be financially affected.

- *Think politically.* Find people who know legislative decision-makers or have some connection with them.

- *Letters are best.* Personal letters are the most effective—far better than postcards, mailgrams, and petitions. The best letters are short and simple.

- *Make it easy.* Provide sample drafts of letters, as well as pens, paper, and even stamps.

- *Arrange meetings.* The best single communication is a meeting in the official's home district with a group of interested constituents.

- *Avoid stealth tactics.* If you can't say up front whose interest you are promoting and why, it is a good idea to take another look at the effort.

Source: *O'Dwyer's PR Services Report,* June 1996, p. 12.

industry to build cars too small to hold walkers and wheelchairs, and from Little League parents worried that fuel-efficient station wagons would not accommodate a whole team. The bill was defeated.

Although public involvement in legislative issues is admirable, critics say "grassroots" lobbying, with its orchestration of public feedback, often slips into the category of unethical behavior.

Another problem involves doing grassroots lobbying under the cover of front groups (see Chapter 3). This is called *stealth lobbying,* because the public isn't told what vested interests are behind a particular campaign.

In one example, APCO Associates, a unit of GCI public relations, organized the Mississippians for a Fair Legal System (M-Fair) to solicit public support for tort reform. What the public didn't know was that the sponsoring organization, the American Tort Reform Association, included large tobacco and chemical companies, which wanted legislation limiting liability for dangerous or defective products.

Such "grassroots" campaigns make public interest groups wonder if they really shouldn't be called "Astroturf" campaigns, since the "grass" is artificial. Michael Pertschuk, codirector of the Advocacy Institute in Washington, D.C., told *O'Dwyer's PR Services Report,* "Astroturf groups are usually founded with corporate seed money that is funneled through PR firms."

POLITICAL ACTION COMMITTEES

A specialized area of lobbying, unaffected by the reform bill, is the organization and administration of political action committees, commonly known as PACs. They were created as a labor union mechanism during the 1930s, but campaign finance reforms in the 1970s, which prohibited corporate contributions to candidates for federal elections, made PACs an effective alternative.

Today, there are more than 4000 PACs organized by labor unions, business, trade groups, professional societies, and single-issue groups. Under the law, a PAC can give a maximum of $5,000 to a federal candidate in a primary election and another $5,000 for the general election, a maximum of $10,000 total.

This doesn't sound like much, but a corporation with multiple plant sites and operations may have a score of individual PACs. In addition, each local of a national labor union may have its own PAC. As a result, the tobacco industry as a whole gave $6.1 million in donations to political candidates in 1998.

PAC funds come from employees or members of organizations. Corporations encourage employees (particularly managers) to contribute through payroll deduction or by writing an annual check. Union members usually contribute through their local unions as part of their membership, and professionals in medicine and law use PACs organized by their membership societies.

PACs are a major way of funding political campaigns, particularly at the federal level. In 1995, Republican members of Congress received almost $84 million in campaign contributions, including $25.3 million from PACs. Democratic incumbents received $46 million, including $18 million from PACs.

The most PAC money flows to the majority party in the Congress. After years of favoring Democrats 60 to 40 percent or better, corporate PACs flip-flopped when the Republicans took control of the Congress in 1995. When it appeared that Republican House members were in some reelection trouble and the Democrats might retain the White House in 1996, there was some shift back to funding incumbent Democrats.

Another common practice is that chairmen and members of key committees get the most PAC money, primarily because they can exert the most influence on legislation. Commerce committee chairman Larry Pressler a Republican from South Dakota, for example, led the Senate in fund-raising during 1995 with $1.7 million while his committee was considering the Telecommunications Reform Act of 1996. A large percentage of the contributions came from corporate PACs in the telecommunications, broadcast, and entertainment industries.

PAC monies, however, are only one method used in funding incumbents and election campaigns. Corporations and other special interest groups can also give unlimited "soft" money directly to local, state, and national political committees for various races or for "voter registration" drives and issue advertising. In addition, the host cities for the national conventions set up nonprofit organizations to collect money from companies that sponsor receptions and dinner parties for the media and the delegates.

In 1998, both parties used soft money to buy issue advertising in the congressional elections. According to preelection reports filed with the Federal Election Commission, soft money contributions to Republican Party committees grew 144 percent over the last mid-term elections, while Democratic soft money totals increased 84 percent. Together, the two parties received $173 million in soft money.

FUND-RAISING BY CANDIDATES

American-style campaigning is the most expensive in the world. The Center for Responsive Politics estimates that total spending on the 1996 primaries and presidential election was $800 million, more than 2.5 times the 1992 expenditure of $311 million.

In the 1998 mid-term congressional elections, the two parties spent a record $283 million—the Republicans spent $177.5 million, the Democrats $105.5 million. Experts predict even higher spending in the 2000 presidential elections.

At least 94 House candidates in 76 districts broke the $1 million spending barrier, according to the Federal Election Commission. In some cases, candidates considerably exceeded the amount.

On a higher level, presidential aspirants were also raising millions before the first primary was held. Experts believe that a serious candidate for the presidency would need a minimum of $22 million before the selection of delegates. George W. Bush, for example, had raised more than $70 million before the first state primary was even held.

Incumbent lawmakers utilize professionals to organize fund-raising activities. A popular activity in Washington, D.C., is the luncheon, reception, or dinner on behalf of a legislator's reelection campaign. *The Wall Street Journal,* for example, reported that on a single day in one October, 14 such events were held, raising $650,000.

Attending such events are individual donors and lobbyists. Although a chicken dinner is not exactly worth $5000 per plate, the contact with legislators is. No business is actually discussed, but the occasion gives lobbyists an opportunity to say, "Don't forget us in the markup"—the drafting of a bill.

Some consultants specialize in direct mail and telemarketing. They are helped by firms that specialize in computer databases and mailing lists. Aristole Publishers, for example, claims to have records on 128 million people. A political candidate can get a tailored list of prospects using any number of demographic variables, including party affiliation, voting record, contribution record, age, geographic location, and opinions on various issues.

Other firms in the Washington, D.C., area handle mass mailings on behalf of the candidates. Kiplinger Computer and Mailing Services is capable of running envelopes at 10,000 per hour and printing personalized letters at 120 pages per minute.

PUBLIC RELATIONS AND CAMPAIGNING

The tools of today's political campaign are many and varied. Constant focus groups and polls continually test messages and determine the "hot" buttons of the voter. Extensive use of modern communications technology such as satellite media tours and video news releases, bulk faxing of background material, and the use of the Internet have greatly expanded message delivery.

Helping the candidates use these tools is another force of consultants and technicians who work to advance the election of their clients—writers of position papers, speech writers, graphic artists, computer experts, photographers, and media strategists. Advance peo-

Presidential spokesman Joe Lockhart responds to a question from reporters concerning the Kosovo War in 1999 during a White House News briefing.

ple spend many hours trying to organize events and generate crowds in an age when most people would rather stay home and watch television.

Indeed, even in this age of the Internet and interactive media, television remains the major tool for reaching the American voter. But prime-time television is increasingly expensive and is cited as one of the major reasons that campaigns costs so much. California GOP consultant Sal Russo told *PR Week:* "A good buy in California in the closing weeks of a campaign used to be $1 million a week. Now, it's $2.5 million."

An attractive alternative is the establishment of websites where citizens can get information. Public relations professionals are enthusiastic about the potential. Phil Noble of Politics Online told *PR Week:* "We are seeing the birth of digital politics." One survey shows that 40 percent of regular voters are not online, but other experts claim that only 25 percent of the electorate is currently on the Internet—and a candidate can't win an election with those numbers.

In the 1998 elections, however, many candidates did supplement traditional media such as television with websites and the sending of messages to thousands of e-mail addresses. According to one survey, around 80 to 90 percent of the gubernatorial candidates and 50 percent of the Congressional candidates established campaign websites.

ETHICAL GUIDELINES FOR POLITICAL PUBLIC RELATIONS

Here are several ethical guidelines for people working in political public relations formulated by the Public Relations Society of America:

1. It is the responsibility of professionals practicing political public relations to be conversant with the various local, state, and federal statutes governing such activities and to adhere to them strictly.

2. Members shall represent clients or employers in good faith, and while partisan advocacy on behalf of a candidate or public issue is expected, members shall act in accord with the public interest and adhere to truth and accuracy and to generally accepted standards of good taste.

3. Members shall not issue descriptive material or any advertising or publicity information or participate in the preparation or use thereof which is not signed by responsible

persons or is false, misleading, or unlabeled as to its source, and are obligated to use care to avoid dissemination of any such material.

4. In avoiding practices which might tend to corrupt the processes of government, members shall not make undisclosed gifts of cash or other valuables which are designed to influence specific decisions of voters, legislators, or public officials.

5. Members shall not, through the use of information known to be false or misleading, conveyed directly or through a third party, intentionally injure the public reputation of an opposing candidate.

Such principles, however, get trampled on in every presidential election. As campaign consultant Mark Goodin once said, "Getting people elected, whether we like it or not, isn't pretty. It, unfortunately, has a lot to do with dividing, setting up bases of support and fracturing off those that—you know, it's like busting a big rock."

PUBLIC AFFAIRS IN GOVERNMENT

Since the time of the ancient Egyptians 5000 years ago, governments have always engaged in what is known in the twentieth century as public information, public relations, and public affairs.

The Rosetta Stone, discovered by Napoleon's troops and used by scholars as the key to understanding Egyptian hieroglyphics, turned out to be a publicity release for the reign of Ptolemy V. Julius Caesar was known in his day as a master of staged events in which his army's entrances into Rome after successful battles were highly orchestrated.

There has always been a need for government communications, if for no other reason than to inform citizens of the services available and the manner in which they may be used. In a democracy, public information is crucial if citizens are to make intelligent judgments about the policies and activities of their elected representatives. Through information it is hoped that citizens will have the necessary background to participate fully in the formation of government policies.

The objectives of government information efforts have been summarized by William Ragan, former director of public affairs for the United States Civil Service Commission:

1. Inform the public about the public's business. In other words, communicate the work of government agencies.

2. Improve the effectiveness of agency operations through appropriate public information techniques. In other words, explain agency programs so that citizens understand and can take actions necessary to benefit from them.

3. Provide feedback to government administrators so that programs and policies can be modified, amended, or continued.

4. Advise management on how best to communicate a decision or a program to the widest number of citizens.

5. Serve as an ombudsman. Represent the public and listen to its representatives. Make sure that individual problems of the taxpayer are satisfactorily solved.

6. Educate administrators and bureaucrats about the role of the mass media and how to work with media representatives.

"Public Information" versus "Public Relations"

Although many of the objectives described by Ragan would be considered appropriate goals in almost any field of public relations, in government such activities are never referred to as "public relations." Instead, various euphemisms are used. The most common titles are (1) public information officer, (2) director of public affairs, (3) press secretary, (4) administrative aide, and (5) government program analyst.

In addition, government agencies do not have departments of public relations. Instead, the FBI has an External Affairs Division; the Interstate Commerce Commission has an Office of Communications and Consumer Affairs; and the Environmental Protection Agency has an Office of Public Awareness. The military services usually have Offices of Public Affairs.

Such euphemisms serve to reconcile two essentially contradictory facts: (1) the government needs to inform its citizens, and (2) it is against the law to use appropriated money for the employment of "publicity experts."

Congress as early as 1913 saw a potential danger in executive branch agencies' spending taxpayer dollars to sway the American public to support programs of various administrations. Consequently, the Gillett Amendment (Section 3107 of Title V of the United States Code) was passed: it stated: "Appropriated funds may not be used to pay a publicity expert unless specifically appropriated for that purpose." The law was reinforced in 1919 with prohibition of the use of any appropriations for services, messages, or publications designed to influence a member of Congress. Another law that year required executive agencies to utilize the U.S. Government Printing Office so that publications could be more closely monitored than in the past. Restrictions also prohibit executive departments from mailing any material to the public without a specific request.

Although most citizens would agree that government should not use tax money to persuade the public of the merits or demerits of a particular bill or program, there is a thin line between merely providing information and using information as a lobbying tool.

If a public affairs officer for the Pentagon testifies about the number of surface-to-air missiles deployed by Iraq or Libya, does this constitute information or an attempt to influence congressional appropriations? Or, to use another example, is a speech by the Surgeon General about the dangers of passive smoking only information or support of legislation that would ban cigarette smoking from all federal buildings?

Scope of Federal Government Information

The U.S. government is said to be the world's premier collector of information. It also is maintained, without much disagreement, that the government is one of the world's greatest disseminators of information.

Ascertaining the exact size of the government's "public relations" effort, however, is like trying to guess the number of jelly beans in a large jar. One of the major difficulties is forming a standard definition of what constitutes "public affairs" activity.

The General Accounting Office (GAO) once estimated that probably $2.3 billion was spent each year by federal agencies and the White House on "public relations" activity. Others, often critics of government public relations, have estimated that between 10,000 and 12,000 federal employees are involved in what might be called "public relations" work. It is said, for example, that the Department of Defense has about 1,000 people working in public affairs/information jobs.

Such figures, however, give a false impression of government agencies in general. At the Commerce Department, for example, there are 25 public affairs people out of 36,000 employees. The Immigration and Naturalization Service has eight public affairs officers in a staff of 24,000. The Customs Department has 15 public affairs officers in a staff of 18,000. *O'Dwyer's PR Services Report* says, "That translates to 1/10 of one percent of its workforce. . . ."

Government Agencies Public information specialists and public affairs officers engage in tasks common to the public relations department of a nongovernmental organization. They typically answer press and public inquiries, write news releases, work on newsletters, prepare speeches for top officials, and oversee the production of brochures. Senior-level public affairs specialists also counsel top management about communication strategies.

One of the longest-running public relations efforts has been the preparation and distribution of "hometown" releases by the military. The Fleet Home Town News Center, established during World War II, sends approximately a million news releases annually about the promotions and transfers of U.S. Navy personnel (including the Marine Corps and Coast Guard) to their hometown media.

Another long-term effort has been the FBI's legendary list of the ten most-wanted fugitives. Initiated in 1950, the list immediately captured the attention of the public and the media. Over the years, the list has led to the apprehension of more than 500 fugitives.

Other federal agencies also conduct public relations programs to inform citizens. Some examples include these: (1) the Department of Health and Human Services produced public

Global PR

Danish Post Office Races to a New Image

After 350 years as the Royal Danish Mail, the national postal service had been privatized and had become Post Denmark. The public, however, still perceived it as out of touch and bureaucratic.

Post Denmark wanted to position itself in the public mind as a modern, dynamic organization with a new logo, so it sponsored a Round Denmark bicycle race under the auspices of the Danish Cycle Union.

The race covered 860 kilometers through 30 cities. Sixteen teams from 14 countries competed,

and the race was watched on the roadside by more than 1.2 million spectators. Besides press briefings and regular news releases, TV spots extolled the post office during the five-day event.

About 77 percent of the population saw or read about the race and all the Post's 1254 offices conducted special promotions. Awareness of Post Denmark as a new, dynamic entity increased dramatically and the logo became widely recognized.

Time to Register

13 14 15 16 17 18

Selective Service & You

The federal government publishes a wide range of brochures and other material to provide Americans with information that concerns them. This brochure telling young men how to register for the military draft, and urging them to do so as required, is typical.

service announcements about Medicare fraud, (2) the U.S. Soil Conservation Service urged urban dwellers to help protect the environment, (3) the Environmental Protection Agency (EPA) communicated new regulatory information to companies responsible for underground storage of chemicals, and (4) the U.S. Center for Disease Control conducted a comprehensive campaign about the prevention of AIDS through "smart sex." Every year, at income tax time, the Internal Revenue Service (IRS) distributes news releases loaded with graphics to help people fill out their tax forms. Two other government agencies, the Voice of America (VOA) and the United States Information Service (USIS), are discussed in Chapter 15.

Congressional Efforts   The House of Representatives and the Senate are great disseminators of information. Members regularly produce a barrage of news releases, newsletters, recordings, brochures, taped radio interviews, and videotapes—all designed to inform voters back home about Congress.

Critics complain that most materials are self-promotional and have little value. The franking privilege (free postage) is singled out for the most criticism. The late Senator John Heinz, a Republican from Pennsylvania, once distributed 15 million pieces of mail, financed by taxpayers, during one election year. Obviously, the franking privilege is a real advantage for an incumbent.

All members of Congress also employ a press secretary. According to Edward Downes of Boston University, "Capitol Hill's press secretaries play a significant role in the shaping of America's messages and consequent public policies. In their role as proxy for individual members, the press secretaries act as gatekeepers, determining what information to share with, and hold from, the media; thus, they have command over news shared with the citizenry."

White House Efforts   At the apex of government public relations efforts is the White House. The president receives more media attention than all the federal agencies and Congress combined. It is duly reported when the president goes jogging, tours a housing development, meets a head of state, or gives a speech. All presidents have taken advantage of the intense media interest to implement public relations strategies that would improve their popularity, generate support for programs, and explain embarrassing policy decisions.

The top public relations person in the White House is the Director of Communications. The most visible person, on a daily basis, is the president's press secretary, who has the high-pressure duty of briefing reporters.

Mike McCurry, former press secretary to President Clinton, had the unenviable job of facing the media daily during most of 1998 when his boss was under the microscope during the Kenneth Starr inquiry into President Clinton's activities. To retain his credibility, McCurry had to be honest with the press, but was often hard-pressed to choose his words in walking the fine line between loyalty and the media's incessant need for more revelations.

One approach that McCurry tried to placate the press, with somewhat limited success, was to have the president's legal advisors answer questions regarding President Clinton's relationship with Monica Lewinsky. Despite the pressure-cooker enviroment, former Bush and Reagan press secretary Marlin Fizwater says, "It's the greatest job in the world and worth taking no matter how much trouble you President is in. Now, you may die in the job, it may ruin your life and reputation. But it still will have been the greatest experience of your life."

State Information Services

Every state provides public information services. In California, for example, there are about 175 public information officers (PIOs) in about 70 state agencies. On a daily basis, PIOs provide routine information to the public, and the press on the policies and activities of the agencies. On occasion, state agencies also conduct massive public information campaigns. Some examples include:

Focus on Ethics

What Shall A Spokesperson Say?

Being a press spokesperson for a member of Congress or even the CEO of a corporation has its occupational hazards. You are supposed to be loyal to your employer and accurately reflect his or her points of view to the press. Often you know more "inside" information than you can tell the press.

Suppose you are a press secretary to a legislator, and several former female employees claim that he made unwelcome sexual advances. You know that your boss is somewhat of a "lecher," but he tells you to deny strongly the women's charges when the media pick up the story. What would you do?

- Maryland's Department of Health conducted a public relations and advertising campaign about teenage pregnancy. One commercial shows a teenage couple embracing. In the next scene, the boy has vanished and the girl is holding a squalling baby. A voice-over says, "If you're going to have sex, be ready to go it alone."

- California's Department of Food and Agriculture ran a campaign aimed at educating the Hispanic population about the dangers of importing vegetables, and fruits to California that might contain the Mediterranean fruit fly. Any infestation could cause major problems for the state's $63-billion-dollar agricultural industry.

- Michigan's Department of Agriculture held a campaign to educate the public that aerosol cans should be recycled. Part of the campaign was directed at expanding the number of recycling firms handling steel containers.

- The New York State Canal System used a promotion campaign to make citizens more aware of the system's recreational opportunities.

City Information Services

Cities employ information specialists to disseminate news and information from numerous municipal departments. Such agencies may include the airport, transit district, redevelopment office, parks and recreation, convention and visitors bureau, police and fire, city council, and the mayor's office.

The information flow occurs in many ways, but all have the objective of informing citizens and helping them take full advantage of opportunities. The city council holds neighborhood meetings; an airport commission sets up an exhibit showing the growth needs of the airport; the recreation department promotes summer swimming lessons; and the city's human rights commission sponsors a festival promoting multiculturalism.

Cities also promote themselves in an effort to increase tourism, which is further discussed in Chapter 17. An example of city information efforts is Virginia Beach, Virginia.

Virginia Beach drew thousands of visitors and reaped international publicity by commemorating the 50th anniversary of the "D-Day" invasion of Normandy in World War II.

The key event was a reenactment of the famous landing that included 1200 men in authentic uniforms, vintage tanks, artillery, aircraft, and landing craft. In addition, the city scheduled a weekend of activities that included World War II exhibits, a parade, a 1940s-era canteen, and a "victory" dance.

While anniversaries are a good "hook" for creating international visibility and tourism for a city, extensive information efforts are also needed when a natural disaster strikes. When Des Moines, Iowa, was flooded several years ago and the city's water supply became contaminated, the city conducted an aggressive information campaign to keep the public informed of flood developments and hold anxiety to a minimum.

Attacks on Government Information Services

Although the need for government to inform citizens and publicize programs is accepted in principle, many critics still express skepticism about the activity, as mentioned earlier.

To some, such as book authors James Bennett and Thomas DiLorenzo (*Official Lies: How Washington Misleads Us*), the federal government operates a huge self-serving propaganda machine with tens of thousands of employees paid by taxpayers.

Indeed, taxpayer groups often oppose the employment of information officers as costly and unnecessary. Others, including journalists, criticize public information activities in general because legislators send reams of useless news releases that often merely promote the senders. Such abuse, coupled with snide news stories about the cost of maintaining government "public relations" experts, rankles dedicated public information officials (PIOs) who work very hard to keep the public informed and the press supplied with a daily diet of news stories.

One PIO for a California agency said, "I'd like to see the press find out what's going on in state government without us." Her comment is echoed by another PIO in the Department of Water Resources. He is now called a "government analyst" but says the news media and the public still want and demand information about the state's water supply.

Indeed, a major source of press hostility seems to stem from the fact that reporters are heavily dependent on handouts. In one study Professors Lynne Masel Walters (Texas A&M) and Timothy Walters (Stephen F. Austin State University) found that 86 percent of a state government's news releases were used by daily and weekly newspapers.

One text, *Media: An Introductory Analysis of American Mass Communications* by Peter M. Sandman, David M. Rubin, and David B. Sachsman, puts it bluntly: "If a newspaper were to quit relying on press releases, but continued covering the news it now covers, it would need at least two or three times as many reporters."

News releases, however, are only one aspect of helping the media do their job. The city of Homestead, Florida, spent $70,000 on facilities and staff just to handle the deluge of reporters who descended on the city in the aftermath of Hurricane Andrew. Congress also subsidizes the media by spending millions of dollars annually on press facilities and services for working reporters.

And although there is much congressional and media criticism of the government's extensive publications, these are defended on the basis of cost efficiency. A deputy director of the Department of Agriculture publications branch, for example, reported that his office alone receives about 350,000 inquiries a year. Two thirds of the requests, he says, can be answered with pamphlets that cost between half a cent and 12 cents each, whereas individual responses could cost up to $20 each when personnel costs are included. In other words, the sheer volume of public requests requires a large array of printed materials.

Preventative public relations can bring savings. The taxpayers of California spend about $7 billion annually to deal with the associated costs of teenage pregnancy, so $5.7 million spent on a successful education campaign could save the state considerably more in reduced welfare costs. Michigan's $100,000 expenditure to educate citizens about recycling steel aerosol cans does much to reduce the costs of opening more landfills.

PR Casebook

The Tobacco Bill: A Monumental Lobbying Battle

Few legislative battles have matched the intensity of lobbying that occurred when a bill was introduced in the U.S. Congress to force the tobacco industry to pay billions toward the cost of treating sick smokers.

The industry conducted an intensive public relations, advertising, and lobbying campaign that led to the defeat of the legislation after antismoking groups had successfully lobbied Congress to increase the amount of compensation from $368.5 billion to $516 billion. Industry leaders said the high amount would virtually bankrupt the companies involved, so they must oppose the legislation.

LOBBYING EFFORTS

Consequently, the industry poured at least $43 million into lobbying during the first six months of 1998. This included the employment of almost 200 lobbyists, one for every three members of Congress. The lobbyists included two former Senate majority leaders, an ex-governor, and a former chairman of the Republican Party.

Legislators—particularly the 51 members of the House Commerce Committee responsible for drafting tobacco legislation—also received major campaign donations. Since 1991, committee members had received more than $1 million for their campaigns. In addition, 20 members of the Senate commerce panel received $400,000 during the same period. Trent Lott, a Republican from Mississippi and the majority leader of the U.S.

Senate, had received about $165,000 in campaign and PAC money from tobacco interests over the years. In all, tobacco companies and their employees gave $26.8 million to national party committees and candidates between 1991 and 1998, according to the Federal Election Commission.

Antitobacco groups criticized the industry's donations, but a Philip Morris spokesperson countered: "The American political system relies on a free and open exercise of First Amendment freedoms. Philip Morris is an active citizen participating in the political process by expressing our views on issues that affect our business."

ADVERTISING AND PUBLIC RELATIONS

The tobacco industry also conducted print and television advertising campaigns that cost between $40 and $50 million. The campaign capitalized on the public's traditional concerns about big government and taxes. Key messages claimed that the bill would (1) generate "lots of money for a new government bureaucracy," (2) generate "a half trillion dollars in new taxes," and (3) tax the average citizen "to pay millionaire trial lawyers." Even the U.S. Chamber of Commerce produced an ad opposing the bill on the grounds that such legislation would open the door for all kinds of other industries to be regulated by big government, portrayed as a "tax and spend monster."

(continued)

The Tobacco Bill: A Monumental Lobbying Battle, *continued*

Public relations activities included (1) organizing grassroots opposition among America's estimated 45 million smokers, who would pay hefty tax increases on tobacco products, (2) maintaining that thousands of farm workers in tobacco-growing states would be harmed economically, and (3) marshaling support from outside the industry. Representatives of police organizations, for example, issued public statements saying the proposed legislation would raise cigarette prices to the level that it would create a "thriving black market in cigarettes, posing huge problems for law enforcement at every level."

FROM THE ASHES, A NEW DEAL

After the defeat of the legislation by a Republican-dominated Senate, the industry negotiated a settlement with a coalition of state attorneys-general in which it would pay only $206 billion over a period of 25 years. It also agreed to pay another $1.45 billion to fund antismoking advertising campaigns by state health agencies.

The industry also agreed to voluntary marketing conditions that would end tobacco billboards as well as ads in stadiums, and would ban tobacco logos on caps, T-shirts, and bags. Tobacco product placement in films and on TV shows would also end, and sponsorship of major sporting events would be restricted to only one per year.

Antitobacco critics pointed out that the agreement still allows tobacco companies to (1) advertise and promote their products at the sponsored event, (2) run ads in newspapers and magazines, (3) do direct marketing, and (4) use their corporate names to sponsor cultural events. But some legal experts said that a total ban on tobacco advertising would raise significant First Amendment problems.

PROSPECTS FOR ADDITIONAL REGULATION

The political influence of the tobacco industry, although somewhat diminished by finally agreeing to take legal responsibility for the effects of its products, is still a powerful lobbying force with the ability to challenge any further attempts to regulate the industry.

And no doubt there will be further battles. President Clinton, toward the end of 1998, urged Congress to bolster the Food and Drug Administration's regulatory power to take other steps to counter underage smoking. And antitobacco groups are already lobbying for the FDA to take a more active role in regulating the entire industry. If new legislation is drafted, the tobacco industry could easily reach into its deep pockets to mount another multi-million dollar lobbying campaign.

An Associated Press reporter acknowledged in a story that government information does have value. He wrote:

While some of the money and manpower goes for self-promotion, by far the greater amount is committed to an indispensable function of a democratic government—informing the people.

What good would it serve for the Consumer Product Safety Commission to recall a faulty kerosene heater and not go to the expense of alerting the public to its action? An informed citizenry needs the government to distribute its economic statistics, announce its antitrust suits, tell about the health of the president, give crop forecasts.

In a tense confrontation Senator John McCain (R.-Arizona) argues with representatives of the tobacco industry, whose multimillion dollar advertising campaign helped to defeat Senator McCain's tobacco control bill in the Senate.

CASE PROBLEM

The city council of Lakewood (population 150,000), in cooperation with a citizens' commission, has decided that there is a need to improve citizen participation in the city's curbside recycling program. Such a program is environmentally sound, and there are other reasons to increase participation. The city's only landfill is rapidly filling up, and there are new state mandates for recycling.

Recycling is still a relatively new concept for the majority of Lakewood households—only 45 percent of them are separating their trash for recycling. The percentage is even lower among residents in the middle- to lower-income brackets. The objective is to get 80 percent of the households to use the curbside recycling program.

What kind of public information would you recommend to accomplish this objective? Develop a list of program strategies and communication tactics.

QUESTIONS FOR REVIEW AND DISCUSSION

1. What is the difference between someone working in governmental relations and a lobbyist?

2. The public, in general, has low esteem for lobbyists. Do you think the perception is justified? Why or why not?

3. Many lobbyists are former legislators and government officials. Do you think they exercise undue influence in the shaping of legislation? Why or why not?

4. What are the major points of the new lobbying reform act? Do you think the law will curtail excessive "influence peddling"? Why or why not?

5. The issue is raised about the use of "front groups" in grassroots lobbying efforts. Do you think such approaches are unethical? Should there be laws prohibiting the use of such groups?

6. Name at least five guidelines for effective grassroots lobbying.

7. Explain how a political action committee (PAC) works. What are the pros and cons?

8. How do political candidates raise money? Would you like to be a political fund-raiser? Why or why not?

9. Do you think other nations should adopt American methods of political campaigning? Why or why not?

10. In what ways are reporters dependent on government information efforts?

11. Explain the various laws that regulate government "public relations" efforts.

12. How is "public information" used by states and cities?

13. Do you think attacks on governmental informational efforts are justified? Why or why not?

15

International Public Relations

Preview

The objective of this chapter is to provide students with an understanding of international public relations and the complications and
benefits of working in this cross-cultural area.

Topics covered in the chapter include:
- Global marketing
- Language, culture, and other problems
- Representing foreign corporations in the United
  States
- Representing U.S. corporations in other countries
- International government public relations
- Public relations by international groups
- Foreign public relations organizations
- Opportunities in international work

WHAT IS INTERNATIONAL PUBLIC RELATIONS?

International public relations may be defined as the planned and organized effort of
a company, institution, or government to establish mutually beneficial relations with
the publics of other nations. These publics, in turn, may be defined as the various
groups of people who are affected by, or who can affect, the operations of a particular firm, institution, or government.

International public relations may also be viewed from the standpoint of its practice in individual countries. Although public relations is commonly regarded as a concept developed in the United States at the beginning of the twentieth century, some of its elements, such as countering unfavorable public attitudes by means of disclosure of operations through publicity and annual reports, were practiced by railroad companies and at least one shareholding corporation in Germany as far back as the mid-nineteenth century, to mention only one such country. (See Chapter 2.)

Even so, it is largely American techniques that have been adapted to national and regional public relations practices throughout the world, including many totalitarian nations. Today, although in some languages there is no term comparable to *public relations,* the practice has spread to most countries, especially those with industrial bases and large urban populations. This is primarily the result of worldwide technological, social, economic, and political changes and the growing understanding that public relations is an essential component of advertising, marketing, and diplomacy.

INTERNATIONAL CORPORATE PUBLIC RELATIONS

In this section we explore the new age of global marketing and point out that differences in language, laws, and cultural mores must be overcome when companies conduct business in foreign countries. We also discuss how U.S. public relations firms represent foreign interests in this country as well as U.S. corporations in other parts of the world. Aspects of public relations practice in some other countries are delineated.

The New Age of Global Marketing

For decades, hundreds of corporations based in the United States have been engaged in international business operations including marketing, advertising, and public relations. These activities swelled to unprecedented proportions during the 1990s, largely because of new communications technologies, development of 24-hour financial markets almost worldwide, the lowering of trade barriers, growth of sophisticated foreign competition in traditionally "American" markets, and shrinking cultural differences bringing the "global village" ever closer to reality.

Today almost one third of all U.S. corporate profits are generated through international business. In the case of Coca-Cola, probably the best-known brand name in the world, international sales account for 80 percent of the company's operating profit.

At the same time, overseas investors are moving into American industry. It is not uncommon for 15 to 20 percent of a U.S. company's stock to be held abroad. The United Kingdom, for example, has a direct foreign investment in the United States exceeding $122 billion, followed by Japan and the Netherlands with nearly half that sum each, according to the U.S. Department of Commerce.

Public relations is an essential ingredient in the global megamarketing mix being created. The 15 largest public relations organizations now generate more than 40 percent of their fees outside the United States. Giant companies such as Burson-Marsteller, Hill and Knowlton, and Shandwick earn about half of their fees abroad. Because of fax machines, e-mail, online services, and the Internet, boutique firms are challenging the big agencies for international business. (See Chapter 5.)

Fueling the new age of global marketing are satellite television, computer networks, electronic mail, fax, fiber optics, cellular telephone systems, and emerging technologies such as integrated services digital networks (ISDN) allowing users to send voice, data, graphics, and video over existing copper cables. For example, Hill and Knowlton has its own satellite transmission facilities, and the General Electric Company has formed an international telecommunications network enabling employees to communicate worldwide, using voice, video, and computer data, simply by dialing seven digits on a telephone. Using three satellite systems, Cable News Network (CNN) is viewed by more than 200 million people in more than 140 countries. A number of newspapers and magazines are reaching millions with international editions. *Reader's Digest,* to cite one instance, distributes about 11.5 million copies abroad—44 national editions in more than a dozen languages.

Differences in language, laws, and cultural mores among countries (to be discussed shortly) pose serious problems. There also is a need for both managers and employees to learn to think and act in global terms as quickly as possible. Already, Burson-Marsteller, with offices in many countries, has been spending more than $1 million a year on training tapes and traveling teams of trainers and seminars to foster a uniform approach to client projects.

Much of the new business jousting took place on West European terrain, where a nearly unified European Community (EC) attracted enormous attention. Although hampered by recession in the early 1990s, public relations expenditures increased significantly. The growth was precipitated in part by expansion of commercial television resulting from widespread privatization, the desire of viewers for more varied programming, satellite technology, and slowly developing EC business patterns. Satellite TV reached well over 30 million

Focus on Ethics

Bribery to Get a Story Published?

Paying a print journalist or a television news director to run a favorable story about a business or social enterprise has long been a common practice in many parts of the world, especially in emerging nations where reporters' salaries are low.

Journalists in Russia, China, Southeast Asia, and Latin America have often asked for some form of payment. One common expectation is that the organization seeking coverage will pay "transportation money" to reporters covering news conferences; an envelope containing cash is part of the press kit. Another approach is to give cash to a news director, which is then split among crew members covering the story.

These practices, considered a normal part of doing business in many of these nations, raise questions for American companies and their public relations staffs. Article 6 of the Public Relations Society of America ethics code expressly forbids practitioners from "...corrupting the integrity of the channels of communications," but the code of the International Public Relations Association (IPRA) makes no mention about the payment of "bribes" to reporters.

If you were doing public relations for an American or European firm in China, should you go along with local customs in media relations, or would you refuse to offer payments to media reporters?

people, mostly through cable systems; direct transmission of programming to homes by high-powered satellites bypassed conventional networks, local stations, and cable systems. On the print side, the business press was growing about 20 percent every year, and there were about 15,000 trade publications in Western Europe.

Although the EC promoted the phrase "a single Europe," corporations and public relations firms still faced the complex task of communicating effectively to 320 million people in 12 countries speaking nine languages.

Language, Cultural Differences, and Other Problems

Fundamentally, companies operating in foreign countries are confronted with essentially the same public relations challenges as those in the United States. These include (1) the formation and maintenance of favorable climates for their operations, involving relationships with local and national government officials, consumer groups, the financial community, and employees, (2) the monitoring and assessment of potentially adverse situations and the establishment of ways to counteract them, and (3) the containment of crises before serious damage is done.

These problems, however, may be aggravated by conditions such as the following:

- Differences in languages and the multiplicity of languages in some countries

- Longer chains of command, stretching back to the home country

- Evident and subtle differences in customs

- The varying levels of development of the media and public relations

- Antipathy expressed toward "multinationals," a pejorative word in many countries

- A dislike grounded in such factors as national pride, past relationships, envy, and apprehension, especially in regard to the United States, concerning foreign cultural, economic, political, and military influence

Introduction of the Euro in 1999 as the common currency of 11 countries of the European Union created an uncertain factor in international trade. An extensive public relations campaign helped citizens of the participating countries to change from their traditional national currencies to the new form. Pictured here is a unit of the Euro currency.

The following are some examples of the types of language problems encountered:

* The style of communication is important to the French, who tend to be dramatic and even emotional. Germans, on the other hand, rely heavily on facts and the written word.

* In Asian and African countries, communication often is vague; nonnatives must learn to "read between the lines."

* In communicating, Arabs emphasize form over function, effect over accuracy, and image over meaning. Seeking mainly to convey information, Americans emphasize function and, by extension, substance, meaning, and accuracy.

* Words translate differently in different countries. Chevrolet executives could not figure out why the Chevy Nova was not selling well in Latin America. Then they learned that, although *Nova* means "new" in Spanish, *No va* means "It doesn't go."

Cultural differences provide additional pitfalls, as shown by the following examples:

* In the United States white signifies purity; in most Asian countries, white is the color of death. An Asian bride in one of these countries would never wear a white dress; she would wear red, the color of luck and happiness in China. In Latin America, though, red is the color of passion and love.

* In China, tables at a banquet are never numbered. The Chinese think such tables appear to rank guests, so it is better to direct a guest to the "primrose" or "hollyhock" table.

* German and Swiss executives think a person is uncouth if he or she uses first names, particularly at public events.

* The proper etiquette for drinking in Korea is to fill your neighbor's glass as well as your own.

* News releases in Malaysia should be distributed in four languages to avoid alienating any segment of the press.

* Americans, perhaps because of their strong freedom-of-expression tradition, tend to be perceived throughout the world as extremely vocal and opinionated.

* When Japanese executives suck in air through their teeth and exclaim, "*Sa!* That will be *very* difficult," they really mean just plain "no." The Japanese consider an absolute "no" offensive and try to respond euphemistically.

All of these illustrations indicate that Americans not only must learn the customs of the country to which they are assigned but should rely on native professionals to guide their paths. And, although they should study the language both before and after their arrival, they must realize that only by residing in the country for many years will they be free—if ever— of language problems.

Representing Foreign Corporations in the United States

Industries in other countries frequently employ American public relations firms to advance their needs in this country. Carl Levin, vice president and senior consultant, Burson-Marsteller, Washington, D.C., tells why:

* To hold off protectionist moves threatening their company or industry

---

International Public Relations Manager

Triton Energy Corporation, an international oil and gas company, has an immediate opening for an International Public Relations Manager. Responsibilities include identifying international public relations opportunities and implementing specific programs to take advantage of these opportunities. This individual would also act as Triton's advance team on international public relations/media visits by the CEO, work closely with journalists, direct media relations including such activities as preparation of news releases and feature articles, and arrange for interviews between company executives and the media.

Position requires 50 percent international travel with durations of approximately one week. Spanish speaking ability (as well as other languages) considered a strong positive in this position. Three to five years of international public relations experience required.

Please send resume to:

Triton Energy Corporation
Attention: Personal Services
6688 N. Central Expressway, Suite 1400
Dallas, Texas 75206
(214) 619-5200
(214) 691-0432 Fax
E-mail: gunsberg@tritonenergy.com

Figure 15.1
This advertisement in *WorldView*, published by the Public Relations Society of America, shows one firm's requirements for employment of an international public relations manager.

- To defeat legislation affecting the sale of a client's product

- To support expansion of the client's markets in the United States

- To provide ongoing information on political, sociological, and commercial developments in the United States that could bear on the client's business interests, not only here but worldwide. In the well-organized foreign company, this information is factored into day-to-day policy decisions as well as periodic strategic plans.

Representing U.S. Corporations in Other Countries

On a global basis, public relations as an occupation has achieved highest development in the industrialized nations of the world—United States, Canada, Western Europe, and parts of Asia. It emerges more readily in nations that have multiple-party systems, considerable private ownership of business and industry, large-scale urbanization, and relatively high per-capita income levels—which also relate to literacy and educational opportunities. By the same token, public relations as a specialized activity is less developed in Third-World nations in which the vast majority of the citizens are still rural villagers.

U.S. and other Western public relations firms began exporting their expertise to the People's Republic of China during the mid–1980s. Hill and Knowlton, then active in Asia for about 30 years, began its Beijing operation with three U.S. expatriates and a locally hired employee

Technology Is Bad, But Visit Our Website

Increasingly, national governments are establishing websites on the Internet to explain their culture and national policies to the rest of the world. Even the Taliban, a group of hard-liners ruling Afghanistan, has a website (*www.taliban.com*) despite the fact that they are arguably the world's most vociferous enemies of modern technology.

Among Taliban Online features are news commentaries from the pages of the weekly newspaper, *Dharb-i-Mumin,* which chronicles efforts to enforce *sharia,* or Islamic law, in Afghanistan. Online visitors can also click on various topics such as "Why Women Should Stay in Their Homes."

There are also Q&A sections. One question is why the Taliban have banned women from getting an education or even holding jobs. The answer, in part, is a criticism of Western nations for the way they treat women. According to the Taliban, "Men in the West have made women an object of their lusts and desires. Women are made to work in offices, restaurants, shops, and factories for the gratification of male desires. Even in matters of dress, she is exploited. Men wear trousers which cover their ankles, while women are forced to wear skirts with their legs bare in every kind of weather."

dispatching news releases and organizing receptions and conferences from headquarters in a hotel. Today more than 1,200 public relations firms have been established, employing between 30,000 and 40,000 people, including more than 5,000 professionals. After the first Chinese nongovernmental public relations organization, the Guangdong Public Relations Club, was formed in 1986, more than 400 others have been established, including the Public Relations Society of China. More than 20 universities and 300 institutes and colleges offer public relations courses.

In the Republic of China on Taiwan, public relations experienced rapid growth in recent years, paralleling the economic growth of the country.

Australia and New Zealand have public relations industries that are among the most active and developed in the Western world, according to David Potts, a senior public relations counselor in Sydney, Australia. Global public relations firms, as well as many small and medium-sized companies, operate in the two countries. "Some overseas corporations, however, make the mistake of assuming that public relations styles and campaigns which have worked overseas, especially in the U.S.A., will work in [these countries]," said Potts. "They don't always."

Potts has additional observations about public relations in other Pacific Rim countries:

• Hong Kong, because of its international financial, trading, and tourist links and the fact that Western management techniques are widely used, exhibits a widespread understanding of public relations. There are more advertising and public relations practitioners in Hong Kong than in any other Asian country. Their expertise, however, underwent its greatest test after Britain relinquished the country to China in 1997.

• Singapore and Malaysia enjoy well-developed public relations practices, both local and global. Singapore operations are heavily oriented to visual public relations, and many firms have strong graphics capabilities.

- In Indonesia, public relations consultancies and advertising agencies must be domestically owned.

- Thailand has a great deal of foreign investment and international tourism. The public relations industry is handicapped by a lack of skilled practitioners.

- Unlike most major Asian countries, no global public relations firm operates in the Philippines; instead, outside companies work through local firms on a referral basis. P. A. Chanco III, of the Orientations firm in Manila, advises public relations representatives of foreign corporations to "know the Filipino culture and how it works before anything else."

- In Japan public relations practice is centered on reaching the media through one or more of the 400-plus reporters' "clubs," with about 12,000 members representing 160 newsgathering organizations.

INTERNATIONAL GOVERNMENT PUBLIC RELATIONS

In this section we explore how and why the governments of most nations seek to influence the opinions and actions of governments and people in other countries. Many employ U.S. public relations firms for this purpose.

Influencing Other Countries

The governments of virtually every country have one or more departments involved in communicating with other nations. Much effort and millions of dollars are spent on the tourism industry, attracting visitors whose expenditures aid their hosts' economies. Even larger sums are devoted to lobbying efforts to obtain favorable legislation for a country's products; for example, Costa Rica urged the U.S. Congress to let its sugar into the nation at favorable rates, and the Department of State threatened to enact trade sanctions against countries such as Korea and Taiwan that persisted in "pirating" U.S. products such as computers and books without payment.

Many countries send shortwave broadcasts worldwide to foster their national interests and prestige, keep in touch with nationals abroad, disseminate news, and influence the internal affairs of other nations.

Information Efforts by the Western World In the United States, companies such as General Electric, NBC, and CBS operated shortwave transmitters, relaying mostly domestic programs but also transmitting some in foreign languages. Pearl Harbor convinced the U.S. government that it could not rely solely on commercial broadcasting for an international service, so the Voice of America (VOA) was created in 1942 as a part of the Department of State.

During the latter years of the Cold War era, Radio Moscow was on the air more than 2000 hours a week. The United States countered with more than 16 hours daily of Russian-language VOA broadcasts into the former Soviet Union, and the U.S.-backed Radio Free Europe broadcast into Eastern Europe and Radio Liberty into various parts of Russia.

For decades, people throughout the People's Republic of China have listened to Western radio broadcasts, particularly those of the U.S.-based Voice of America and the British Broadcasting Corporation (BBC). During and after the prodemocracy uprisings in China in 1989, the VOA's 24-hour service in English and particularly its nearly 13 hours of Mandarin and Cantonese broadcasts each day helped get the facts out to the Chinese population even as the state- and Communist-Party-controlled media tried to hide them. The BBC supplemented its regular English-language broadcasts with two and a half hours of programming in Chinese each day.

For more than 40 years the broadcasts of the VOA, BBC, other European stations, and America's Radio Liberty, which transmitted programs in 14 languages from Munich, Germany, conveyed Western-style news and values to the former Soviet Union and Eastern-bloc nations. Despite the jamming that persisted into the late 1980s, millions of Soviet citizens listened. The effect of these broadcasts and of TV programming from (then) West Germany in helping to provide the climate for acceptance of Mikhail Gorbachev's reform campaigns in the midst of economic deprivations is uncertain.

For four decades Radio Free Europe in Munich transmitted programs in native languages to Eastern-bloc nations. In Romania, where demonstrations in December, 1989, ended with the capture and execution of President Nicolae Ceauşescu and his codictator wife Elena, student leaders told reporters they would not have taken to the streets had they not been listening for months to British and American shortwave reports. Said a national student magazine editor: "There was something like a wind of liberty coming from the radio stations from other countries."

With the Cold War over, the Voice of America focused its efforts on information-deprived countries. One step was the creation in 1994 of Radio Free Asia, beaming programs from the United States into the Chinese mainland, Burma, Cambodia, Laos, North Korea, Tibet, and Vietnam.

The VOA also increased its programming to countries such as Iran, Iraq, and Cuba, whose governments portrayed the United States as a demonic country.

The main fare of the service is regional and local news, features, music, and English lessons. News reports and features are produced independently of the State Department, which offers editorial comment only. The VOA operated under a severely reduced budget during the 1990s.

Radio Free Europe and Radio Liberty moved their operations from Munich to less expensive headquarters in Prague and trimmed their staffs from 1100 to 300.

In 1990 the United States also reaffirmed its 1985 decision to withdraw from membership in the United Nations Educational, Scientific, and Cultural Organization (UNESCO) on grounds of mismanagement, politicization, and "endemic hostility" toward a free press, free markets, and individual human rights. A State Department announcement stated that the United States would continue to support educational, scientific, cultural, and communications activities through other global agencies.

Since the mid-1970s, Department of State officials have been aided materially by American news media organizations, operating mainly through the World Press Freedom Committee, to respond to complaints of Third-World countries. These nations have sought, among other goals, independence and equity in access to global communication resources in order that their own views, values, and developmental efforts might be reported more fully.

Global PR

Historic Flight to Japan Commemorated

What would you do if asked to develop a public relations program to celebrate, on two continents, the 50th anniversary of the first commercial flight along the Great Circle Route from the United States to Asia?

Northwest Airlines and Shandwick public relations people faced that mammoth task in 1997. Northwest had become the dominant U.S. carrier in Asia after the flight from Minneapolis-St. Paul to Tokyo, followed by nonstop flights to Beijing and other U.S.-Asia markets. Here's what they did:

Research

Northwest marketing staff helped identify 19 markets strategically important to the past and future of the airline's Pacific business. Researchers unearthed details about the original flight and collected memorabilia. Northwest and Shandwick employees in the 19 cities were consulted and charged with handling the anniversary activities.

Planning

Planning for the year-long celebration, Bridging the Pacific, was handled by Asian and American communications, marketing, and advertising staffs and agencies, and was designed to involve whole communities. A Northwest Boeing 747–400, dubbed WorldPlane, became the portable, visually appealing focal point for the entire trans-Pacific marketplace. Target audiences were current and potential Northwest Airlines employees ands customers in those markets. A children's art contest was planned. The total budget of $750,000 included nearly $125,000 in cash and in-kind WorldPlane charity donations.

Execution

The celebration began with a WorldPlane launch event honoring the child artists. During the month of the original 1947 flight, Northwest produced a week-long celebration. Included were a commemorative exhibit created jointly by the airline and the Minnesota Historical Society, a salute to the original crew members, and a dramatic tarmac event at the airport. Similar events took place in Tokyo and Osaka.

The children's art contest was conducted in 10 Asian and nine North-American communities, with school and media assistance. Winners and two adults from each city were flown to Minneapolis-St. Paul for a weekend party. Fourteen news conferences exposed many members of the target audiences to the artists, as each presented a $5000 check to his or her designated charity.

Almost $100,000 was donated to nonprofit organizations in target communities as a part of the WorldPlane community support program. All Northwest international travelers viewed commemorative videos and/or images of the children's art on seat placards and menus. Major newspapers commemorated the historic flight, along with Northwest's employee newspaper and on-board magazines.

Evaluation

Objective No. 1—raising awareness of the airline's 50-year trans-Pacific history—was achieved. An estimated several million people were exposed to knowledge of the activities. For Asia and North America combined, there were 54 confirmed broadcasts and 260 print articles in large target markets. Also achieved was objective No. 2, raising awareness among trans-Pacific communities and the people Northwest serves.

The Public Relations Society of America gave the initiative its coveted Silver Anvil award.

Information Efforts in Other Nations   *Russian Federation.*   After decades during which the "vulgarity" of Western capitalism and advertising was condemned, Russian television in 1988 carried commercials by Visa, Pepsi, and Sony. In 1989 the government newspaper *Izvestia* began running advertisements weekly in its foreign and Moscow editions.

Public relations practice began gradually under government monitoring as firms entered into partnership arrangements with foreign companies. Nongovernment public relations became increasingly more sophisticated. For most state institutions, such as government parliament, courts, and ministries, however, freedom of the press "made [bureaucrats'] lives so difficult that relations between them and the mass media tended to be adversarial," according to Alexandre G. Nikulaev and Alexander G. Goregin, Russian public relations professionals, writing in *IABC: Communication World.*

"The main problem was not because there were no media relations departments in the state institutions in Russia," they wrote. The people working there were the problem, most of them bureaucrats who had lost other jobs and accepted assignments working with the press without knowing how to do so, the writers contended.

Consequently, in 1994 the Professional Communications Guild of Russia was established in Moscow to compensate for the lack of theoretical knowledge through the exchange of practical experience in workshops and seminars for members; to obtain official recognition of public relations as a profession; and to create standards.

China.   The People's Republic of China has the world's fastest-growing economy, but its lack of public relations skills continues to tarnish its international image, according to global business and political consultants.

Crisis management skills were badly needed when China threatened Hong Kong prior to China's taking control from Great Britain in 1997; when it tried to affect elections in the Republic of China on Taiwan with military exercises; when it tested nuclear weapons in defiance of international pressure; and when it jailed dissidents in violation of its own laws, among other such actions.

"The weakness of China is its policy: never explain, never apologize," said Raymond K. F. Chi'en, a Hong Kong industrialist. Critics point out that in China's powerful communist-led system, to concede error or solicit outside views is tantamount to admitting the system's fallibility.

Nevertheless, China took a tentative step toward seeking public relations help when, in late 1995, its Washington embassy invited the communications firm of Robinson Lerer Sawyer Miller to present an ambitious three-year public relations strategy for Beijing. No immediate action followed, and the Chinese government continued to exercise tight control of print, broadcast, and cable communications while in 1998 stepping up regulation of Internet activities, including the leaking of state secrets, pornography, and political subversion. Periodically, Chinese residents and visitors found it difficult or impossible to access BBC and CNN cable outlets.

In contrast, Taiwan has pursued a vigorous public relations campaign for the last two decades, paying $4.5 million over three years to the Washington lobbying firm Cassidy & Associates. Thousands of American political, industrial, education, and civic leaders have toured Taiwan as guests of the government.

South Africa. With the unfolding of democratic processes in South Africa after decades of apartheid, hundreds of business firms and organizations returned to the nation that produces 40 percent of sub-Saharan Africa's gross domestic product and is known by many as "the gateway to Africa."

Public relations firms and advertising agencies are helping to address the needs of a population of approximately 40 million residents, largely through the 22 internal radio services and three television channels of the South African Broadcasting Corporation and more than 5000 newspapers, periodicals, and journals.

Market surveys reveal different levels of sophistication in both black and white markets, so audiences must be addressed across all racial boundaries. English is the most-used language.

On the continent of Africa, South Africa is the only nation that has a sufficient industrial base to support an extensive number of public relations professionals.

U.S. Firms Working for Foreign Governments

For fees ranging upward of $1 million per year, more than 150 American public relations firms work in this country for other nations. In recent years, for example, Hill and Knowlton has represented Indonesia and Morocco; Burson-Marsteller has represented Argentina, Costa Rica, Hungary, and the USSR (the latter mainly in trade fairs); and Ruder, Finn & Rotman has represented El Salvador, Israel, and Japan. Especially active in representing foreign countries is Doremus & Company, whose clients have included Egypt, Iran, Jordan, the Philippines, Saudi Arabia, and Tunisia.

In many cases, the objective is to influence U.S. foreign policy, generate tourism, create favorable public opinion about the country, or encourage trade. Table 15.1 shows a sampling of accounts reported by *O'Dwyers Newsletter:*

The Countries' Goals What do these countries seek to accomplish? Burson-Marsteller's Carl Levin says that, among other things, the countries pursue several goals:

* To advance political objectives

Table 15.1 *International Accounts Handled by U.S. Firms*

Client	Public Relations Firm	Contract
Mexico	Burson-Marsteller	$853,000
Turkey	Abernathy MacGregor Group	$540,000
Democratic Republic of the Congo	EAW Group	$500,000
Yugoslavia	American International Development Group	$450,000
Saudi Arabia	Powell Tate	$320,000
India	Washington Group	$300,000

- To be counseled on the United States' probable reaction to the client government's projected action

- To advance the country's commercial interests—for example, sales in the United States, increased U.S. private investment, and tourism

- To assist in communications in English

- To counsel and help win understanding and support on a specific issue undermining the client's standing in the United States and the world community

- To help modify laws and regulations inhibiting the client's activities in the United States

Under the Foreign Agents Registration Act of 1938, all legal, political, fund-raising, public relations, and lobbying consultants hired by foreign governments to work in the United States must register with the Department of Justice. They are required to file reports with the Attorney General listing all activities on behalf of a foreign principal, compensation received, and expenses incurred.

Action Programs   Normally hired by an embassy after open bidding for the account, the firm first gathers detailed information about the client country, including past media coverage. Attitudes toward the country are ascertained both informally and through surveys.

The action program decided on will likely include the establishment of a national information bureau to provide facts and published statements of favorable opinion about the country. Appointments are made with key media people and other influential citizens, including educators, business leaders, and government officials. These people are often invited to visit the client country on expense-paid trips, although some news media people decline on ethical grounds. (Ethical questions will be discussed in more detail shortly.)

Gradually, through expert and persistent methods of persuasion and the expenditure of what may run into millions of dollars, critical public attitudes may be changed or reinforced. Success is difficult to judge.

Public relations firms have played a major role in the worldwide sales of state-owned enterprises (a process known as privatization) during the last decade. More than 2700 such enterprises were transferred into private hands in more than 95 countries from 1988 to 1993, according to the International Finance Corporation. Tens of thousands of companies were privatized in Eastern Europe. For example, Burson-Marsteller designed and implemented public education campaigns in Russia, Kazakstan, and Ukraine in support of market reform and privatization.

Problems and Rewards   The toughest problems confronting the firm are often as follows:

- Deciding to represent a country, such as China, whose human rights violations may reflect adversely on the agency itself

- Persuading the heads of such a nation to alter some of its practices so that the favorable public image sought may reflect reality

- Convincing officials of a client country, which may totally control the flow of news internally, that the American press is independent from government control and that they should never expect coverage that is 100-percent favorable

• Deciding to represent an autocratic head of state, such as Mobutu Sese Seko of Zaire, whose lavish living and large Swiss bank accounts have stood in stark contrast to an average family income among the lowest in the world

Amnesty International, the Nobel-Prize-winning human rights monitor, picketed Burson-Marsteller's offices because of its Argentine account. The Council on Hemispheric Affairs criticized Ruder, Finn & Rotman for working for the government of El Salvador. Norman Wolfson, chairman of Norman, Lawrence, Patterson & Farrell, fled Nicaragua with would-be assassins close on his heels after serving during most of 1978 as the public relations counselor for the late dictator General Anastasio Somoza. A Doremus & Company executive working for the economic development of the Philippines, whose government, headed by Ferdinand Marcos, had placed the country under military law, was also threatened with death.

Why, then, do these firms work for unpopular governments? Wolfson put it this way: "I felt that I was performing a better service for my country by trying to help Americans understand Somoza than I did even by serving my country in the Navy during the Second World War." Said Burson-Marsteller's Carl Levin: "I do not think it is overreaching to state that in helping friendly foreign clients we also advance our national interests. And we help in ways that our government cannot." Black, Manafort, Stone & Kelly felt the same way, but dropped its $950,000 contract with an agency close to the Philippines president when President Reagan called on Marcos to resign. And, of course, retainers are large: Wolfson earned $20,000 to $30,000 per month, including expenses, for example.

Intervention Tactics   Placing full-page advertisements in major papers such as the Washington *Post* and New York *Times* is almost invariably the first action taken by agents of foreign governments in seeking to influence American public opinion during a crisis. Surveys have shown that a high percentage of the nation's lawmakers and administrators read the *Post* before or soon after arriving in their offices. The *Times,* in particular, is read by opinion leaders throughout the country, and the advertisements gain important visibility, influencing editorial writers and others. Members of Congress often use these political statements in addresses to their colleagues and obtain permission to insert their remarks in the *Congres-*

Focus on Ethics

"Sweatshop" Labor Practices under Fire

The University of North Carolina has signed a new contract under which Nike, the athletic shoe maker, will pay $7.1 million to outfit the institution's sports team, the Tar Heels, with Nike apparel. The university signed its original contract with Nike for $4.5 million.

Student protesters at a rally argued that the university should not do business with a company accused of allowing "sweatshop" labor practices at its Southeast Asia factories. According to the Associated Press, Chancellor Michael K. Hooker responded that it would be hard to find "a consumer good in the United States right now that it not made in a low-wage factory somewhere."

In your opinion, should the university (1) seek to cancel its contract or (2) keep it in effect but urge that Nike improve its labor practices?

sional Record. The advertisements are generally followed by personal visits and telephone calls by foreign government agency people and their key supporters. Arrangements are made to place representatives on broadcast network and cable programs. Press conferences are arranged, and newsletters are hastily dispatched to media, government, and other leaders.

Some examples of such campaigns include:

• The American-Albanian Community urged President Clinton to lead United Nations action in stopping the killing by Serbian forces, led by Slobodan Milosevic, of thousands of Albanian citizens living in Kosovo. "No More Broken Promises: Stop the Genocide in Kosovo," the headline implored, long before NATO intervened militarily in 1999 to stop the eviction and killing of Albanians living in Kosovo.

• "The Time Has Come to End the Embargo Against Cuba." So proclaimed the headline of an appeal that Americans urge Congress and the President to pass H.R. 2229, the Free Trade with Cuba Act. The appeal was made by the Faculty Committee for Human Rights in the Americas (FACHRAS), whose names and addresses filled the page.

• An advertisement by Japan's Save the Ozone Network took that country to task for failing to take steps to keep tons of ozone-destroying chlorofluorocarbons (CFCs) from escaping into the atmosphere. Readers were asked to petition Japan's Prime Minister and its Minister of International Trade & Industry.

Global PR

Prince Charles Gets New Image

A public relations makeover for Prince Charles?

The *Economist* magazine says "the most audacious rebranding attempt yet attempted" is under way to transform the image of the heir to the British throne.

"The prince had employed public relations professionals before the death of Diana," the magazine confided in its November 1998 issue. "But, in the aftermath of her death, they came to the fore," led by Mark Bolland, an assistant private secretary to the prince, "who is said to be close to Peter Mandelson, the man who rebranded the Labour Party." Another assistant private secretary, Elizabeth Buchanan, was recruited from the Bell Pottinger public relations agency.

The goals: (1) "to take a leaf out of Diana's book, and to emphasize Charles's role as a parent and as a man with a populist streak"; (2) "to play down those of the prince's interests that might get

him labeled as a fuddy-duddy, or a weirdo. He is talking a lot less about architecture and spiritualism these days"; (3) "to cultivate informal contacts with the press" [as Diana did]; and (4) "to get out the good news about their man, in particular the great success of the Prince's Trust, which works with young people in difficult circumstances to set up small businesses, and which is now running part of the government's 'New Deal' programme" All that, and more.

A major public relations problem remains— the future of the prince's relationship with Mrs. Camilla Parker Bowles. A MORI poll taken in October 1998 showed that only 53 percent of the public thought that the prince should be allowed to become king if he married Camilla; and only 19 percent were prepared to accept the idea of Camilla as queen.

Stand by. . . .

People at a shopping center in Shanghai walk past a giant billboard showing actress Gong Li advertising French cosmetics with a message in Chinese—a vivid example of how world trade crosses national boundaries.

The successful fight for ratification of the North American Free Trade Agreement (NAFTA) by the U.S. Congress was one of the most expensive lobbying campaigns ever seen in Washington. Mexico assembled a high-powered team of public relations specialists, lobbyists, lawyers, and consultants to promote passage of the agreement at an annual cost of about $15 million, according to Justice Department records.

U.S. public relations firms helped line up speaking engagements for Mexican officials; former U.S. high government officials mapped strategy; and congressional lobbyists worked Capitol Hill. Many members of Congress and their staffs took trips to Mexico provided by the campaign. Lobbying expenditures by Mexico and U.S. corporations in one year alone were estimated at $100 million.

Burston-Marsteller public relations was paid $4.5 million to develop brochures, organize a speakers bureau, monitor media coverage, produce speeches, and supervise the work of several lobbying firms. In a separate contract, the Office of the President of Mexico paid the firm $1.5 million in fees and expenses to develop a series of television and newspaper ads that promoted Mexico's efforts to combat drug trafficking.

PUBLIC RELATIONS BY INTERNATIONAL GROUPS

Hundreds of noncorporate groups depend on international support for their undertakings. Such organizations as the International Red Cross, World Council of Churches, International Council of B'nai B'rith, and International Chamber of Commerce, along with numerous foundations, educational enterprises, labor unions, and government-support agencies, maintain vigorous public relations programs. For effective operation, their images must be kept as spotless as possible; like corporations, they must constantly monitor their environments, maintain proper relationships with the governments and publics of the countries in which they operate, and be prepared to handle crises.

The International Red Cross is often plagued with reports that relief goods and services are diverted into private hands or that aid has not been forthcoming as quickly as it might have been in major disasters around the world. Rumors that Red Cross representatives sold rather than gave cigarettes to troops in past wars still provide people who heard those reports years ago with an excuse for not giving.

Criticized after World War II for its failure to speak out about the Holocaust, the International Red Cross in 1998 admitted a "moral failure" for its silence, while handing over 60,000 documents to an Israeli archive in Jerusalem. The Roman Catholic Church also apologized for its silence over French collaboration with the Holocaust.

UNICEF, a United Nations agency that provides food, medical supplies, and other aid for millions of children on three continents, must constantly respond to charges, leveled mainly by those who dislike the United Nations, that too many of the dollars raised through card and gift sales and Halloween door-to-door solicitations are used improperly, in part to pay heavy administrative expenses.

NATIONAL PUBLIC RELATIONS ORGANIZATIONS

In virtually every country where public relations has become an economic and social force, practitioners have organized to exchange information, maintain and improve standards of professional performance, and aid in the development of international public relations. Codes of conduct are commonplace, and many organizations seek to enhance the standing of their members through certification and accreditation programs. Journals or newsletters are published, awards recognize outstanding performance, and scholarships and other assistance are provided to educational centers.

Public relations associations have been formed in about 70 countries. Many are comparable to the Public Relations Society of America; a smaller number relate exclusively to the business world, such as the International Association of Business Communicators.

OPPORTUNITIES IN INTERNATIONAL WORK

The 1990s, according to many experts, have represented a new golden age of global marketing and public relations. The opening of the European Market, coupled with economic and social reforms in East European countries and the former Soviet Union, hastened the reality of a global economy.

All of these developments led Jerry Dalton, past president of the Public Relations Society of America, to say: "I think more and more American firms are going to become part of those overseas markets, and I expect a lot of Americans in public relations will be living overseas." Indeed, Dalton believes that the fastest-growing career field for practitioners is international public relations. He adds: "Students who can communicate well and are fluent in a

Assistance with the local language and customs is of critical value to public relations practitioners handling programs in foreign countries. This advertisement offers help to those working in Hungary.

foreign language may be able to write their own ticket." But the coming of the "global village," as Marshall McLuhan once described it, still means that there will be a multiplicity of languages, customs, and values that public relations professionals will have to understand.

Many transnational corporations, putting an increased emphasis on international customer relations, are hiring "corporate protocol" officers to be responsible for doing everything from booking hotels, planning banquets, and hiring limousines, to scheduling plant tours, arranging security, and selecting gifts for foreign officials and major customers. They even brief company executives on current events, advise on the correct protocol for greeting royalty, and "hand out sheet music for sing-alongs at Korean banquets," according to a New York *Times* article.

Its author, Paul Finney, says: "Corporations tend to fill their protocol jobs with people who have backgrounds in public relations, marketing, [and] meeting planning and who have a knowledge of the industry." Although knowledge of foreign languages is a plus, it is not a prerequisite. One protocol officer is quoted as saying, "At AT&T, we're dealing with over 100 countries. You can rent language skills—interpreters, translators—if you need them."

Gavin Anderson, chairman of Gavin Anderson & Company, which has several offices abroad, is an expert in international public relations. He writes:

Practitioners of either global or international public relations are cultural interpreters. They must understand the business and general culture of both their clients (or employers) and

A rooftop advertisement for Philips, the international electronic firm, stands out above a billboard for a downtown Moscow bank, indicative of the extensive entry of foreign companies into Russia.

the country or countries in which they hope to do business. Whether as an outside or in-house consultant, the first task is to tell a U.S. company going abroad (or a foreign party coming to the United States) how to get things done. How does the market work? What are the business habits? What is the infrastructure? The consultant also needs to understand how things work in the host country, to recognize what will need translation and adaptation . . .

The field needs practitioners with an interest in and knowledge of foreign cultures on top of top-notch public relations skills. They need a good sense of working environments, and while they may not have answers for every country, they should know what questions to ask and where to get the information needed. They need to know where the potential dangers are, so as to not replenish the business bloopers book.

The decision to seek an international career should be made during the early academic years, so that a student can take multiple courses in international relations, global marketing techniques, the basics of strategic public relations planning, foreign languages, social and economic geography, and cross-cultural communication. Graduate study is an asset. Many students serve internships with international corporations as a desirable starting point.

PR Insights

Code of Ethics—International Public Relations Association (IPRA)

The following code of professional conduct, based on the charter of the United Nations, has been published in 20 languages:

IPRA MEMBERS SHALL ENDEAVOR:

1. To contribute to the achievement of the moral and cultural conditions enabling human beings to reach their full stature and enjoy the indefeasible rights to which they are entitled under the "Universal Declaration of Human Rights."

2. To establish communication patterns and channels which, by fostering the free flow of essential information, will make each member of the group feel that he/she is being kept informed, and also gives him/her an awareness of his/her own personal involvement and responsibility, and of his/her solidarity with other members.

3. To conduct himself/herself always and in all circumstances in such a manner as to deserve and secure the confidence of those with whom he/she comes in contact.

4. To bear in mind that, because of the relationship between his/her profession and the public, his/her conduct—even in private—will have an impact on the way in which the profession as a whole is appraised.

IPRA MEMBERS SHALL UNDERTAKE:

5. To observe, in the course of his/her professional duties, the moral principles and rules of the "Universal Declaration of Human Rights."

6. To pay due regard to, and uphold, human dignity, and recognize the right of each individual to judge for himself/herself.

7. To establish the moral, psychological, and intellectual conditions for dialogue in its true sense, and to recognize the right of the parties involved to state their case and express their views.

8. To act, in all circumstances, in such a manner as to take account of the respective interests of the parties involved: both the interests of the organization which he/she serves and the interests of the publics involved.

9. To carry out his/her undertakings and commitments, which shall always be so worded as to avoid any misunderstanding, and to show loyalty and integrity in all circumstances so as to keep the confidence of his/her employers, past or present, and of all the publics that are affected by his/her actions.

IPRA MEMBERS SHALL REFRAIN FROM:

10. Subordinating the truth to other requirements.

11. Circulating information which is not based on established and ascertainable facts.

12. Taking part in any venture or undertaking which is unethical or dishonest or capable of impairing human dignity or integrity.

13. Using any manipulative methods or techniques designed to create subconscious motivation which the individual cannot control of his/her own free will and so cannot be held accountable for the action taken on them.

Taking the U.S. Foreign Service Officers' examination is the first requirement for international government careers. Foreign service work with the innumerable federal agencies often requires a substantial period of government, mass media, or public relations service in this country before foreign assignments are made.

CASE PROBLEM

As part of the liberalization of Eastern Europe, the former Czechoslovakia is now two republics with freely elected governments. In the Czech Republic, to improve the country's economy, the national tourist agency wants to promote Prague as the premier tourist destination in Eastern Europe for foreign tourists.

The Czech Republic has many features to recommend it. Much of the country was spared extensive bombing during World War II, and it has ancient castles, buildings, and medieval churches that are among the finest in Europe. Prague, the capital, is a particularly beautiful city with Old-World charm. Food and lodging are relatively inexpensive, in comparison to costs in other European capitals.

Your public relations firm is retained by the Czech Tourist Agency to attract American tourists. What are your recommendations regarding (1) specific audiences to be reached, (2) key themes that should be emphasized, and (3) the publicity and promotional techniques that would be used?

QUESTIONS FOR REVIEW AND DISCUSSION

1. What is meant by international public relations? What are some of the reasons for its growth in recent decades?

2. How does public relations fit into the new mix of global marketing operations?

3. What are some of the difficulties that a corporation is likely to encounter when it conducts business in another country? Enumerate some of the pitfalls that may await its public relations, advertising, and marketing personnel in such enterprises. How may these be partially or fully overcome?

4. What objectives do foreign countries seek to accomplish by hiring U.S. public relations firms to represent them in America?

5. Describe some of the United States' public relations activities internationally.

6. How did shortwave radio transmissions help end the Cold War?

7. Name three reasons why the United States and many other countries engage in shortwave broadcasting.

8. What problems have the Russian Federation encountered in operating a government public relations program?

9. What prevents the People's Republic of China from pursuing sound public relations goals?

10. Describe some of the goals of members of the International Public Relations Association.

16

Nonprofit Organizations

Preview

The purpose of this chapter is to explain how public relations serves nonprofit organizations, as compared to work for business and government, and to identify the types of organizations recognized as nonprofit.

Topics covered in the chapter include:
- Membership organizations
- Social, cultural, and health agencies
- Importance of volunteer workers
- Fund-raising
- College and university public relations
- Contemporary issues in secondary schools

THE ROLE OF PUBLIC RELATIONS

A major broad area of public relations work includes nonprofit institutions. The goal of these institutions is not to make a commercial profit but to improve the human condition in many ways.

The range of nonprofit institutions is astounding, from small city museums to gigantic international foundations. Membership organizations such as trade associations form one category. Social, cultural, religious and health organizations form another segment. Educational institutions fall into a third group.

Much as they differ in purpose, nonprofit organizations have common problems and needs. They are tax-exempt, yet such organizations as a whole face an unending task of raising money to pay their expenses and finance their projects.

The role of public relations in promoting the work of these organizations and aiding them financially is essential.

MEMBERSHIP ORGANIZATIONS

A membership organization consists of people with a common interest, in either business or social life. Their purpose is mutual help and self-improvement. They often use the srength of their common bond to improve community welfare, endorse legislation, and support socially valuable causes.

Trade Associations

At last count, there were about 6000 trade and professional associations in the United States. Because federal laws and regulations often can affect the fortunes of an entire industry, about one third of these groups are based in the Washington, D.C., area. There, association staffs can monitor congressional activity, lobby for or against legislation, communicate late-breaking developments to the membership, and see government officials on a regular basis.

The membership of a trade association usually consists of manufacturers, wholesalers, retailers, or distributors in the same field. Memberships are held by corporate entities, not individuals. For example:

* Electronic Industries Association

* National Soft Drink Association

* National Association of Home Builders

Although individual members may be direct rivals in the marketplace, they work together to promote the entire industry, generate public support and share information of general interest to the entire membership.

By representing its entire industry, an association often is more effective as a news source than is an individual company. When a news situation develops involving a particular field, reporters often turn to the spokesperson of its association for comment.

Labor Unions

Since the mid-1970s, labor unions in the United States have suffered serious losses in membership and consequently in political clout. A perception of unions as money-hungry, inflexible, lacking in concern for the public interest, and at times arrogant created a severe image problem. Media coverage often showed union members in negative, adversarial positions that sometimes inconvenienced the public.

Today total union membership amounts to less than 15 percent of all American workers, with the figure dropping to about 10 percent in the private sector.

A college fraternity, Pi Kappa Phi, created this poster featuring the classic *Rape of the Sabine Women* as a contribution to the campaign against a campus social problem.

Nevertheless, labor unions still are very much a part of the American scene, from players in the National Basketball Association to employees of UPS scurrying with deliveries in each of our communities. Each and every union movement relies on public relations tools in an attempt to regain strength and influence. The unions must seek to build new memberships, protect the job security of members, and improve their public images.

In every national political campaign, the unions spend millions of dollars in support of candidates they regard as friendly. Some of this money goes directly to candidates, while significant amounts are devoted to "issue ads" that do not explicitly endorse an individual. This questionable practice enables support of candidates beyond individual campaign spending limits; probusiness organizations counter with their own issue ads. Significant sums of union money are also spent on lobbying efforts.

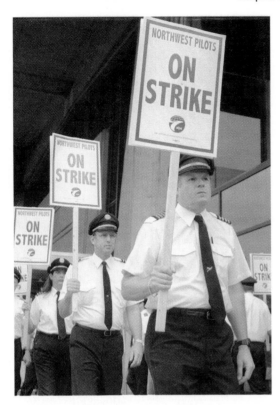

Public demonstration: Northwest Airlines pilots march in a picket line at Detroit Metropolitan Airport during their 1998 strike that tied up the airline's service. Such protests, as well as mass demonstrations in support of causes, are a frequently used method of public relations.

Like corporations, union managements need to employ public relations extensively with their internal audiences. They must keep their memberships informed about what they receive in return for their dues, including social and recreational programs and the representation to company management the union leadership supplies.

Professional Associations

Members of a profession or skilled craft organize for mutual benefit. In many ways, their goals resemble those of labor unions in that they seek improved earning power, better working conditions, and public acceptance of their role in society. Unlike their labor union counterparts, however, members of professional organizations place emphasis on setting standards for professional performance, establishing codes of ethics, determining requirements for admission to the field, and encouraging members to upgrade skills through continuing education. In some cases, professional organizations have quasi-legal power to license and censure members. In most cases, however, professional groups use the techniques of peer pressure and persuasion to police their membership.

In general, professional associations are national in scope, with district, state, or local chapters. Many scientific and scholarly associations, however, are international, with chapters

Religious denominations and ecumenical organizations use public relations to attract membership, spread their beliefs, and promote their social welfare programs. This advertisement publicizes the Religious Communication Congress, commonly called RCC 2000, in Chicago.

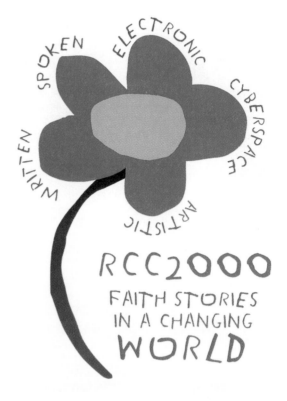

SPOKEN ELECTRONIC CYBERSPACE ARTISTIC WRITTEN

RCC2000
FAITH STORIES IN A CHANGING *WORLD*

RELIGIOUS COMMUNICATION CONGRESS 2000

March 29—April 1, 2000 • Chicago Marriott Downtown
RCC 2000 • 475 Riverside Drive, Room 1948A • New York, NY 10115
212-870-2985 • Fax: 212-870-3578 • http://www.RCC2000.org

in many nations. Organizations such as the Public Relations Society of America (PRSA) and the International Association of Business Communicators (IABC) are classified as professional associations.

The lobbying power exercised in Washington by major professional associations was especially evident during one of the most noteworthy political battles of the 1990s, the Clinton administration's unsuccessful promotion of its health care reform plan. The American Medical Association, with 220,000 physician members, applied both public and backstage pressures in an effort to shape the plan to its advantage. So did other health organizations. A barrage of full-page advocacy advertisements by health organizations appeared in Washington newspapers and magazines, and in national magazines with strong congressional readership. They contained such lines as "Price controls on health care would be a costly mistake" (AMA) and "What we're doing to hold down the high cost of cancer" (pharmaceutical companies).

Public relations activity on behalf of individual professionals is a relatively new development but has increased sharply since the Supreme Court said that regulation by professional organizations infringed on free speech. And the Federal Trade Commission ruled in 1980 that the American Medical Association couldn't tell its members not to advertise.

Chambers Of Commerce

A *chamber of commerce* is an association of business persons, often joined by professionals, who work to improve their city's commercial climate and to publicize its attractions. State chambers of commerce and, nationally, the Chamber of Commerce of the United States provide guidance to local chambers and speak for business interests before state legislatures and the federal government. In the first half of 1998, for example, the U.S. Chamber of Commerce spent more on lobbying in the health care debate—$8 million—than any other group. The primary focus of most members, however, is local.

Often, the chamber of commerce is the public relations arm of city government. Attracting conventions and new businesses to the city also is an important part of chamber work.

ENVIRONMENTAL AND SOCIAL ISSUE ACTIVIST GROUPS

Environmental cleanup holds a high place on the public agenda, primarily because of vigorous campaigns by environmental organizations. By promoting recycling, elimination of toxic waste sites, purification of air and water, and preservation of natural resources, they strongly influence our collective conscience. Organizations that fight for social causes also achieve significant impact, both positive and negative.

Some of these organizations work relatively quietly through lobbying, litigation, and public education. Others are stridently confrontational.

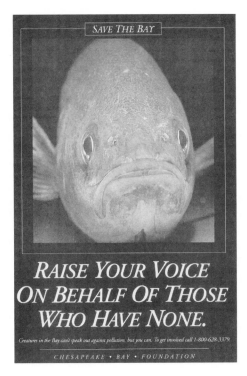

SAVE THE BAY

RAISE YOUR VOICE
ON BEHALF OF THOSE
WHO HAVE NONE.

Creatures in the Bay can't speak out against pollution, but you can. To get involved call 1-800-628-3379

CHESAPEAKE • BAY • FOUNDATION

An intriguing photograph and challenging headline, with a minimum of text, promote the Chesapeake Bay Foundation's drive to enlist volunteers in the fight against bay pollution.

Environmental Groups

Greenpeace, an organization that operates in 30 countries including the United States, with five million members, is perhaps the best known of the confrontational groups. Television viewers are familiar with the daredevil efforts of some members in small boats to stop nuclear warships and whaling fleets. Recently contributions to Greenpeace have declined; so has its political influence. In total membership, Greenpeace is second to the much less flamboyant National Wildlife Foundation, followed by the Sierra Club, and the Nature Conservancy.

The principle ways in which environmental organizations work to achieve their goals are lobbying, litigation, mass demonstrations, boycotts, and reconciliation.

Other Activist Groups

The work of major organizations that receives frequent national attention is illustrative of intense efforts by other prominent associations as well. The National Rifle Association, for example, influences Congress and state legislatures by lobbying and campaign contributions. The American Tobacco Institute fights hard to defeat laws limiting smoking (see Chapter 14).

Focus on Ethics

Sensitivity or Defiance? The NRA Makes a Choice

Few membership groups generate as much public debate and emotion as the National Rifle Association. Its traditional strong defense of the "right to bear arms" was severely tested in the wake of the Columbine High School massacre in Littleton, Colorado, a suburb of Denver.

Charlton Heston, the president of the NRA, continued to defend the NRA's opposition to gun control by telling the press on the day of the shootings that armed guards on the campus might have saved lives. And at the national convention, held the next week in Denver, one keynoter made a rousing defense of the constitutional right to bear arms. She said, "Guns are not the issue. Hate, what pulled the trigger of violence, is the issue."

To many critics, the NRA seemed to be more concerned with enunciating its traditional opposition to gun control than expressing sympathy and concern for the victims of the tragedy. *PR Week* editorialized, "Although the association scaled down its conference and issued a statement of sympathy, there was little evidence of real concern."

The NRA response, or the lack of it, raises the question of ethical actions and responsibility. Given the situation, with public opinion running high for increased gun control in the wake of Columbine, what would have been an ethical stance for the NRA to take? Should the group use the opportunity to press its agenda? Should it simply keep a low profile until the memory of the massacre fades from public view? Should it initiate a new strategy to lead a public campaign about responsible gun use?

LAST CALL.

When closing time comes around, don't get behind the wheel.
Get in front of a phone. Call a friend, or call a cab.

MADD
Mothers Against Drunk Driving

Mothers Against Drunk Driving (MADD) urges people who have been drinking to call a friend or a cab to take them home. This poster with its succinct headline delivers the message graphically.

SOCIAL, CULTURAL, AND HEALTH AGENCIES

Traditionally, nonprofit social agencies have been seen as the "good guys" of society—high-minded, compassionate organizations whose members work to help people achieve a better life. Recently, that perception has changed in some cases.

Numerous agencies have been caught by the recent American urge to scrutinize all aspects of the governmental and social establishment. Famous organizations usually regarded as sacrosanct have found themselves in trouble. The Girl Scouts of America were accused of having such heavy overhead expense for their annual national cookie sale that the girls themselves received little direct benefit. The Boy Scouts of America ran into difficulty for barring homosexuals from membership. The United Way of America, which collects charitable contributions to aid many agencies, suffered scandal and public indignation when news stories revealed that its president received an annual salary of $463,000 and used United Way funds to support a lavish lifestyle. Other investigative reporting disclosed that most top executives of major nonprofit institutions receive salaries above $100,000 and some above $300,000.

These controversies and disclosures were coupled with deep cuts in federal spending on social programs by the 1995 Republican Congress, pursuing its Contract with America. Scandal and economic changes put additional fund-raising pressure on private charities, emphasizing the need for public relations representatives to tell the charity's story more effectively. Like their colleagues in the corporate world, agency communicators feel the need to put crisis management plans in place.

For many nonprofit groups, obtaining operating funds is a necessity that dominates much of their effort. Without generous contributions from companies and individuals whose money is earned in the marketplace, nonprofit organizations could not exist. As an indication of the scope of philanthropy in the United States and of the money needed to keep voluntary service agencies operating, American contributions to charity were $175 billion in 1998, according to the American Association of Fund-Raising Counsel (see Figure 16.1). Additional funds are donated to specialized nonprofit organizations that do not fall under the "charity" mantle, and still more are contributed by federal, state, and local governments. Competition among nonprofit agencies for their share of donations is intense.

In general terms, nonprofit organizations are of two types—*service,* typified nationally by the Visiting Nurse Association and the Boys Clubs of America, and *cause,* whose advocacy role is exemplified by the National Safety Council and the National Association for the Advancement of Colored People (NAACP). Frequently organizations have dual roles, both service and advocacy.

Categories of Social Agencies

For purposes of identification, nonprofit organizations and their functions may be grouped into seven categories:

1. *Social service agencies.* Serving the social needs of individuals and families in many forms are social service agencies. Among prominent national organizations of this type are Goodwill Industries and the American Red Cross. Local chapters carry out national programs. Service clubs such as Rotary Club also raise significant amounts of money for charitable projects.

2. *Health agencies.* Many health agencies combat a specific illness through education, research, and treatment, while others deliver generalized health services in communities. Typical national organizations include the American Heart Association, the American Cancer Society, and the National Multiple Sclerosis Society.

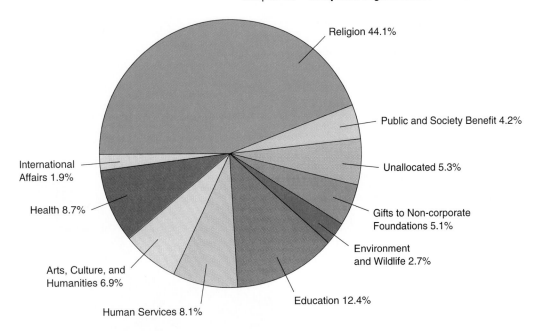

Figure 16.1

This chart shows how the more than $140 billion in charitable giving in the United States each year is divided. The percentages vary slightly from year to year. Contributions from individuals far outnumber those from corporations and foundations, providing about 76 percent of the annual total.

3. *Hospitals.* Public relations work for hospitals is a large and expanding field. The role of a hospital has taken on new dimensions. In addition to caring for ill and injured patients, hospitals conduct preventive health programs and provide other health-related social services that go well beyond the traditional institutional concept. Hospitals may be tax-supported institutions, nonprofit organizations, or profit-making corporations.

4. *Religious organizations.* The mission of organized religion, as perceived by many faiths today, includes much more than holding weekly worship services. Churches distribute charity, conduct personal guidance programs, provide leadership on moral and ethical issues in their communities, and operate social centers where diverse groups gather. Some denominations operate retirement homes and nursing facilities for the elderly. At times, religious organizations assume political roles to further their goals. The nondenominational Salvation Army provides the needy with shelter, food, and clothing. It has a vigorous public relations program to generate support.

A recent study by the Brookings Institution, *Fiscal Capacity of the Voluntary Sector,* stated in this regard: "Because religion occupies a stable, central role in American life, religious institutions will be looked to as a backup finance and delivery mechanism by other subsectors . . . particularly . . . in the human service field."

Twenty thousand participants in the AIDS Walk through downtown Phoenix contributed $1 million to AIDS agencies in the fight against the illness. Organized walks and runs of this type are a popular fund-raising method.

5. *Welfare agencies.* Most continuing welfare payments to persons in need are made by government agencies, using tax-generated funds. Public information officers of these agencies have an important function—to make certain that those entitled to the services know about them and to improve public understanding of how the services function.

6. *Cultural organizations.* Development of interest and participation in the cultural aspects of life falls heavily into the hands of nonprofit organizations. So, in many instances, does operation of libraries, musical organizations and museums. Such institutions frequently receive at least part of their income from government sources; many are operated by governments. Even government-operated cultural institutions depend upon private-support organizations such as Friends of the Museum to raise supplementary funds.

7. *Foundations.* The hundreds of tax-free foundations in the United States constitute about nine percent of total charitable giving. Money to establish a foundation is provided by a wealthy individual or family, a group of contributors, an organization, or a corporation. The foundation's capital is invested, and earnings from the investments are distributed as grants to qualified applicants.

The public knows about such mammoth national organizations as the Ford Foundation, the Rockefeller Foundation, and the National Science Foundation. It is probably not aware, however, of many smaller foundations, some of them extremely important in their specialized fields, that distribute funds for research, education, public performances, displays, and similar purposes.

Giving away money constructively is more difficult than most people realize. Again, public relations representation has a significant role. The requirements of a foundation must be made known to potential applicants for grants. Inquiries must be handled and announcements of grants made.

From this summary, the student can see what diverse, personally satisfying opportunities are available to public relations practitioners in the social agency fields.

Public Relations Goals

Every voluntary agency should establish a set of public relations goals. In doing so, its management should heed the advice of its public relations staff members, for they are trained to sense public moods and are responsible for achieving the goals. In general, nonprofit organizations should design their public relations to achieve these objectives:

1. Develop public awareness of the organization's purpose and activities

2. Induce individuals to use the services the organization provides

3. Create educational materials—especially important for health-oriented agencies

4. Recruit and train volunteer workers

5. Obtain funds to operate the organization

The sections that follow discuss ways in which each of these goals can be pursued.

Public Awareness   The news media provide well-organized channels for stimulating public interest in nonprofit organizations and are receptive to newsworthy material from them. Newspapers usually publish advance stories about meetings, training sessions, and similar routine activities. Beyond that, much depends upon the ingenuity of the public relations practitioner in proposing feature articles and photographs. Television and radio stations will broadcast important news items about organizations and are receptive to feature stories and guest appearances by organization representatives. *Stories about activities are best told in terms of individuals, rather than in high-flown abstractions.* Practitioners should look for unusual or appealing personal stories, such as a retired teacher helping Asian refugee children to learn English.

Creation of events that make news and attract crowds is another way to increase public awareness. Such activities might include an open house in a new hospital wing, or a concert by members of the local symphony orchestra for an audience of blind children.

Novelty stunts sometimes draw attention to a cause greater than their intrinsic value seems to justify. For example, a bed race around the parking lot of a shopping center by teams of students at the local university who are conducting a campus fund drive for the March of Dimes could be fun. It would draw almost certain local television coverage and raise money, too.

Very serious, dramatic messages can also be widely dispersed by staging an event made for television coverage. A North Carolina sheriff was saddened and frustrated by the number of unwanted animals put to death in his county animal shelter. He arranged for telecast of the euthanasia death of a 35-pound collie mix during his local public affairs show, *Sheriff's Beat.* Response was tremendous in the area, with adoptions up 300 percent and markedly increased spaying or neutering by local veterinarians.

Publication and distribution of brochures explaining an organization's objectives, operation of a speaker's bureau, showings of films provided by general headquarters of national nonprofit organizations, and periodic news bulletins distributed to opinion leaders are quiet but effective ways of telling an organization's story.

Use of Services   Closely tied to creation of public awareness is the problem of inducing individuals and families to use an organization's services. Free medical examinations, free clothing and food to the urgently needy, family counseling, nursing service for shut-ins, cultural programs at museums and libraries, offers of scholarships—all these and many other services provided by nonprofit organizations cannot achieve their full value unless potential users know about them.

Because of shyness or embarrassment, those who would benefit from available services sometimes hesitate to use them. Written and spoken material designed to attract these people should emphasize the ease of participation and the privacy of the consultations. The American Cancer Society's widely publicized warning list of cancer danger signals is an example of private self-examination.

Creation of Educational Materials   Public relations representatives of nonprofit organizations spend a substantial portion of their time preparing written and audiovisual materials. These are basic to almost any organization's program.

The quickest way to inform a person about an organization is to hand out a brochure. Brochures provide a first impression. They should be visually appealing and contain basic information, simply written. The writer should answer a reader's obvious questions: What does the organization do? What are its facilities? What services does it offer me? How do I go about participating in its activities and services? The brochure should contain a concise history of the organization and attractive illustrations.

Organizations may design logos, or symbols, that help them keep their activities in the public eye. Another basic piece of printed material is a news bulletin, usually monthly or quarterly, mailed to members, the news media, and perhaps to a carefully composed list of other interested parties. This bulletin may range from a single duplicated sheet to an elaborately printed magazine.

A source of public relations support for national philanthropic organizations is the Advertising Council. This is a not-for-profit association of advertising professionals who volunteer their creative and technical skills for organizations. The council handles more than 30 public service campaigns a year for nonsectarian, nonpartisan organizations, chosen from 300 to 500 annual requests. Newspapers and radio and television stations publish or broadcast free of charge the advertisements the council sends them.

One of the best ways to tell an organization's story succinctly and impressively is with an audiovisual package. This may be a slide show or a video, usually lasting about 20 minutes, to be shown to community audiences and/or on a continuing basis in the organization's building.

Volunteer Workers

A corps of volunteer workers is essential to the success of almost every philanthropic enterprise. Far more work needs to be done than a necessarily small professional staff can accomplish. Recruiting and training volunteers, and maintaining their enthusiasm so they will be dependable long-term workers, are important public relations functions. Organizations usually have a chairperson of volunteers, who works with the public relations (often called community relations) director.

The statistics are impressive. One in five American adults volunteers time for charitable causes, according to a Bureau of Labor Statistics survey. The median weekly time volunteers contribute is slightly more than four hours. Yet the demand for more volunteers is intense.

The concept of voluntary, private charity activity, so strongly developed in the United States, is spreading to other parts of the world. It has taken root recently in Eastern Europe and in those Asian countries that are prospering with new wealth. Volunteerism long has been a factor in Western Europe. More than 400 U.S. voluntary agencies also do work overseas. Rotary International, for example, has raised millions of dollars in a drive to eliminate polio from the world by the year 2000.

What motivates men and women to volunteer? The sense of making a personal contribution to society is a primary factor. Volunteer work can fill a void in the life of an individual who no longer has business or family responsibilities. It also provides social contacts. Why does a former business leader living in a retirement community join a squad of ex-corporate executives who patrol its streets and public places each Monday, picking up wastepaper? The answer is twofold: pride in making a contribution to local well-being and satisfaction in having a structured activity that partially replaces a former business routine. These motives are basic to such volunteerism.

Social prestige plays a role, too. Appearing as a model in a fashion show that raises funds for scholarships carries a social cachet. So does selling tickets for a debutante ball, the profits from which go to the American Cancer Society. Serving as a docent, or guide, at a historical museum also attracts individuals who enjoy being seen in a prestigious setting. Yet persons who do well at these valuable jobs might be unwilling to stuff envelopes for a charity solicitation or spend hours in a back room sorting and mending used clothing for resale in a community thrift shop—jobs that are equally important. Such tasks can be assigned to those volunteers who enjoy working inconspicuously and dread meeting the public. Religious commitment is another powerful motivating force for volunteers.

Retirees Make Excellent Volunteers   Retired men and women, who are increasing in number, form an excellent source of volunteers. The Retired Senior Volunteers Program (RSVP) operates 750 projects nationwide, staffing them from its membership of 365,000. The largest organization of seniors, American Association of Retired Persons (AARP), directs its members into volunteer work through its AARP Volunteer Talent Bank.

How to Recruit Volunteers   Recruiters of volunteers should make clear to potential workers what the proposed jobs entail and, if possible, offer a selection of tasks suitable to differing tastes. A volunteer who has been fast-talked into undertaking an assignment he or she dislikes will probably quit after a short time.

Jon Ramer, RSVP Volunteer
Orlando Science Center

Senior volunteers have the experience to work wonders.

For 40 years, Jon Ramer engineered ways to get aerospace projects off the ground. Today, he is an RSVP volunteer at a science center. And the exhibits he invents launch kids' imaginations into the wonders of science.

Jon is one of nearly half a million RSVP volunteers across the country. **RSVP** stands for **Retired and Senior Volunteer Program**. It's part of the Senior Corps, the national network for senior service. RSVP volunteers are men and women, age 55 and over from all walks of life, who put their life experience to work for their communities.

Jon was an aerospace engineer. Now he makes imaginations fly.

Through RSVP, volunteers match their talent, creativity and wisdom to community needs. Volunteers like Jon choose how and where they want to serve. They ease over-stressed education systems. They help with health concerns. And RSVP volunteers tackle public safety and environmental issues. The needs and the opportunities are vast. So are the rewards.

Join us. To learn more about volunteer opportunities with **RSVP** and the **Senior Corps** call 800-424-8867, TDD: 800-833-3722.

Senior Corps. The Experience of a Lifetime.

 200

Older citizens make excellent volunteers for many organizations. They have available time, are often looking for an activity, and can draw on long experience in many fields.

The public relations practitioner can help in recruiting by providing information resources to explain the organization's purpose, and to show the essential role its volunteers play. Testimony from successful, satisfied volunteers is an excellent recruiting tool.

Like all persons, volunteers enjoy recognition, and they should receive it. Certificates of commendation and luncheons at which their work is praised are just two ways of expressing appreciation. Hospital auxiliaries, in particular, keep charts showing how many hours of service each volunteer has contributed. Service pins or similar tokens are awarded for certain high totals of hours worked. Every organization that uses volunteers should be sure to say, "Thank you!"

FUND-RAISING

At board meetings of voluntary agencies, large and small, from coast to coast, the most frequently asked question is: "Where will we get the money?" Discussion of ways to maintain present programs and to add new ones revolves around that inevitable query.

Finding ways to pay the bills is a critical problem for virtually all nonprofit organizations, even those that receive government grants that finance part of their work. Fund-raising has been elevated to a highly developed art.

Although the largest, most publicized donations are made by corporations and foundations, the total of individual contributions far exceeds combined corporate and foundation giving, amounting to about 76 percent of the more than $175 billion annual U.S. philanthropic donations. Depending on their needs, voluntary organizations may try to catch minnows—hundreds of small contributions—or angle for the huge marlin—large gifts from big-money sources. Some national organizations raise massive sums. The Salvation Army, Catholic Charities USA, and the United Jewish Appeal are among the largest recipients.

Public relations representatives may participate directly in fund-raising by organizing and conducting solicitation programs, or they may serve as consultants to specialized development departments of their organizations. Organizations often employ professional firms to conduct their campaigns on a fee basis. In that case, the organization's public relations representatives usually have a liaison function.

Fund-raising on a major scale requires high-level planning and organization. An organizational chart for a typical fund-raising campaign is shown in Figure 16.2.

The Risks of Fund-Raising

Fund-raising involves risks as well as benefits. Adherence to high ethical standards of solicitation and close control of money-raising costs, so that expenses constitute only a reasonable percentage of the funds collected, are essential if an organization is to maintain public credibility. Numerous groups have suffered severe damage to their reputations from disclosures that only a small portion of the money they raised was applied to the cause they advocated. The rest was consumed in solicitation expenses and administrative overhead.

These fund-raising and administrative costs fluctuate widely among organizations, depending on circumstances, and it is difficult to establish absolute percentage standards for acceptable costs. New organizations, for example, have special start-up expenses. In general, an organization is in trouble if its fund-raising costs are more than 25 percent of what it takes in, or if fund-raising and "administrative overhead" exceed 40 to 50 percent.

The American Cancer Society, for example, applies 78.2 cents of every dollar it raises to its anticancer work; solicitation costs are 12.1 cents and administrative overhead 9.7 cents. The National Charities Information Bureau sets a standard that 70 percent of funds raised by a charity should go into programs.

The United Way scandal, in which the national president was forced from office after disclosures of his excessive expenditures of the charity's funds, and later convicted of embezzlement, caused a severe drop in contributions to that organization. It needed years to recover.

Organizational Chart for Communitywide Fund Drive

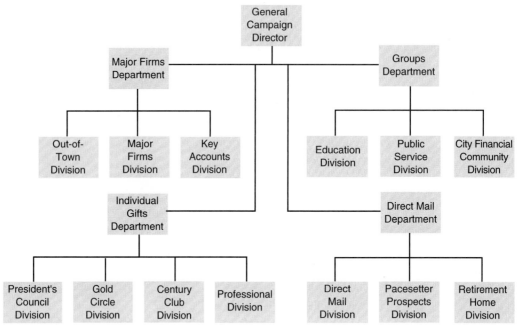

Figure 16.2

This chart shows the basic structure of a fund drive. Specialized groups should be added in each division as necessary to meet local organizational and geographical needs.

Motivations for Giving

An understanding of what motivates individuals and companies to give money is important to anyone involved in fund-raising. An *intrinsic desire to share* a portion of one's resources, however small, with the needy and others served by philanthropic agencies is a primary factor—the inherent generosity possessed in some degree by almost everyone. Another urge, also very human if less laudable, is *ego satisfaction.* Those who are motivated by it range from donors to large institutions who insist that the buildings they give be named for them, down to the individuals who are influenced to help a cause by the knowledge that their names will be published in a list of contributors. *Peer pressure* is a third factor; saying "no" to a request from a friend is difficult. The cliché about "keeping up with the Joneses" applies here, openly or subtly.

While many companies truly desire to contribute a share of their profits to the community well-being, they also are aware that news of their generosity improves their images as good corporate citizens. Individuals and corporations alike may receive income-tax deductions from their donations, a fact that is less of a motivating factor in many instances than the cynical believe.

Fund-raisers know that while many contributors desire nothing more than the personal satisfaction of giving, others like to receive something tangible—a plastic poppy from a vet-

University of California, Berkeley
Museum of Paleontology

"Own a Piece of the Rex"

"Own a piece of the **rex**", and YOU can help
the Museum of Paleontology exhibit this fearsome Cretaceous carnosaur
for everyone to see in the new Valley Life Sciences Building.

Donate towards any bone in the skeleton, including the skull, femur, scapula, tail vertebrae, or
one of the many razor-sharp teeth. Donate a bone in someone else's name - it's a gift for
dinosaur enthusiasts that will last for generations to come!

In a unique fund-raising drive, the University of California, Berkeley, Museum of Paleontology requested donations toward any bone in the dinosaur's skeleton—from the skull for $5,000, to toes and claws for $50. Contributions helped the museum to display the skeleton in its new Valley Life Sciences Building.

erans' organization, for example. This fact influences the sale of items for philanthropic purposes. When a neighbor high school girl rings the doorbell, selling candy to raise a fund for a stricken classmate, multiple forces are at work—instinctive generosity, peer pressure (not to be known in the neighborhood as a tightwad), and the desire to receive something for the money given. Even when householders are on a strict diet, they almost always will accept the candy in return for their contribution rather than merely give the money.

The Competitive Factor

The soliciting organization also should analyze the competition it faces from other fund-raising efforts. The competitive factor is important. The public becomes resentful and uncooperative if approached too frequently for contributions. That is why the United Way of America exists—to consolidate solicitations of numerous important local service agencies into a single unified annual campaign.

The voluntary United Way management in a community, with professional guidance, announces a campaign goal. The money collected in the drive is distributed among participating agencies according to a percentage formula determined by the United Way budget committee.

Types of Fund-Raising

Philanthropic organizations raise funds in several ways:

- Corporate and foundation donations
- Structured capital campaigns
- Direct mail
- Sponsorship of events
- Telephone solicitations
- Use of telephone numbers with "800" and "900" area codes for contributors
- Commercial enterprises

Corporate and Foundation Donations   Organizations seeking donations from major corporations normally should do so through the local corporate offices or sales outlets. Some corporations give local offices a free hand to make donations up to a certain amount. Requests to foundations generally should be made to the main office, which will send application forms.

Corporations make donations estimated at more than $9 billion a year to all causes, of which roughly 40 percent goes to education. Much of this is distributed in large sums for major projects, but an increasing amount is going to smaller local programs. A directory, *Guide to Corporate Giving,* published by the American Council for the Arts in New York, describes the contribution programs of 711 leading corporations. Corporations often fix the amount they will contribute each year as a certain percentage of pretax profits. This ranges from less than 1 percent to more than 2.5 percent.

Increasingly, corporations make donations on a matching basis with gifts by their employees. The matching most commonly is done on a dollar-for-dollar basis; if an employee gives $1 to a philanthropic cause, the employer does the same. Some corporations match at a two-to-one rate or higher.

Corporations make contributions to charities in less direct ways, too, some of them quite self-serving. (The practice of cause-related marketing is explained in Chapter 13.) When applying for a charitable donation, an applicant should submit a "case for support" letter that covers these elements: background of the organization, current status of organization's services, need for organization's services, sources of current funding, administration of the organization, community support, current needs of organization, benefits to the community of the donation, and request for specific amount of funds.

Structured Capital Campaigns   The effort to raise major amounts of money for a new wing of a hospital, for an engineering building on a campus, or even for the reconstruction and renovation of San Francisco's famed cable car system is often called a capital campaign.

In a capital campaign, emphasis is placed on substantial gifts from corporations and individuals. One key concept of a capital campaign, in fact, is that 90 percent of the total amount raised will come from only 10 percent of the contributors. In a $10 million-campaign to add a wing to an art museum, for example, it is not unusual that the lead gift will be $1 or $2 million.

Steps in Running a Capital Campaign

Robert B. Sharp, California professional consultant, recommends these steps in running a capital campaign:

CONDUCT A FEASIBILITY STUDY

Commission an objective review of the cause behind the proposed campaign. This should . . . provide a monetary goal for the campaign, as well as a "gift model"—a chart breaking down the goal into individual gift amounts and indicating how many of each are needed. The review should also lead to the development of a clear "case statement."

GET THE BOARD'S APPROVAL AND SUPPORT OF THE FEASIBILITY STUDY

The board should take steps to carry out the recommendations. (This often results in delays.)

ENLIST VOLUNTEER LEADERSHIP

Choose a campaign chairman and a volunteer chairman. These volunteers will carry the campaign through the private phase to achieve a major portion of the goal before soliciting the general public.

BEGIN SOLICITING GIFTS

Using the feasibility study's gift model and suggested campaign phases, begin solicitation of prospects, moving from attempts to get larger gifts to efforts to obtain lesser ones.

STOP FOR A MIDPOINT EVALUATION

This evaluation, taking place well into the campaign, should make needed adjustments in the drive's timeline, financial goal, or strategy. It is here that the campaign is usually announced to the public through the media. Announcement of the campaign should be made only when the goal is assured.

DETERMINE CLOSING STRATEGIES

Decide what changes need to be made to meet or exceed the original goal. Also, determine when and how to begin general public solicitation.

HONOR VOLUNTEER LEADERSHIP

Plan special events and permanent recognition.

PERFORM "ADMINISTRATIVE WRAP-UP"

Because many large gifts may be divided into pledge payments, set up a procedure to process these and to encourage timely payments. Review what the campaign has achieved and then consider the campaign's implications for future fund-raising efforts.

Source: Condensed from *Chronicle of Philanthropy.* February 2, 1990.

Capital campaigns require considerable expertise and, for this reason, many organizations retain professional fund-raising counsel. There are a number of firms in the country that offer these services, but the most reputable are those belonging to the American Association of Fund-Raising Counsel.

Traditionally, professional fund-raisers were paid by organizations for their work either in salary or by a negotiated fee. In a controversial decision, however, the National Society of Fund-Raising Executives changed its code of ethics in 1989 to permit its members to accept commissions based on the amount of money their drives raise.

The preparation for a capital campaign, whether managed by a professional counseling firm or by the institution's own development staff, is almost as important as the campaign itself. The accompanying box on the previous page describes the steps to be taken in organizing and conducting a capital campaign.

A fund campaign usually is organized along quasi-military lines, with division leaders and team captains.

Donors often are recognized by the size of their gifts—and terms such as *patron* or *founder* are used. Major donors may be given the opportunity to have rooms or public places in the building named after them. Hospitals, for example, prepare "memorial" brochures that show floor plans and the cost of endowing certain facilities.

Direct Mail   Direct mail can be an expensive form of solicitation because of the costs of developing or renting mailing lists, preparation of the printed matter, and postage. An organization can reduce costs by conducting an effective local, limited, direct-mail campaign on its own if it develops an up-to-date mailing list of "good" names—known to be potential donors—and can provide enough volunteers to stuff and address the solicitation envelopes. Regional and national organizations, and some large local ones, either employ direct-mail specialists or rent carefully chosen mailing lists from list brokers.

The old days when direct-mailing pieces came addressed to "Occupant" are largely gone, thanks to the wonders of computerized mailing lists. Now the letters arrive individually addressed. Inside, the appeal letter may bear a personalized salutation and include personal allusions within the text.

The abundance and diversity of mailing lists for rent are astounding. One company offers more than 8000 different mailing lists. A common rental price is $40 per thousand names. Other lists cost more, depending on their special value. The best lists contain donors to similar causes. Direct Media List Management Group, for example, offered a list of almost 1.5 million "aware" women who have contributed to at least one of 27 causes.

Recently, however, the *Chronicle of Philanthropy* has reported a sharp decline in direct-mail contributions received by several large national organizations, such as the Disabled American Veterans and National Easter Seals. The publication asserts, "Americans have become increasingly fed up with direct-mail appeals from charities."

Direct e-mail campaigns can also be arranged at reasonable costs with companies that compile e-mail addresses similar to the print mail lists. A response of 1 percent on a mailing usually is regarded as satisfactory; two percent is excellent.

Take the following steps to make a profitable return of direct mail investments:

1. Make use of an attention-getting headline.

2. Follow with an inspirational lead-in on why and how a donation will benefit clients of the charitable agency.

3. Give a clear definition of the charitable agency's purpose and objectives.

4. Humanize the cause by giving an example of a child or family who benefited.

5. Include testimonials and endorsements from credible individuals.

6. Ask for specific action and provide an easy method for the recipient to respond. Self-addressed stamped envelopes and pledge cards often are included.

7. Close with a postscript that gives the strongest reason for reader response.

One marketing research firm enhanced direct-mail precision by identifying 34 human factors such as age, gender, education, and levels of economic well-being. It fed these factors into computers along with a list of 36,000 ZIP code markets and produced 40 neighborhood types. An organization interested in reaching one of these types—the supereducated top income level, for example—could use suitable mailing lists broken down to postal area routes.

The classic direct-mail format consists of a mailing envelope, letter, brochure, and response device, often with a postage-paid return envelope.

Direct Mail List Rates and Data, updated bimonthly by Standard Rate & Data Service, Inc., is a basic reference book for direct mail lists.

Sponsorship of Events   The range of events a philanthropic organization can sponsor to raise funds is limited only by the imagination of its members.

Participation contests are a popular method. Walkathons and jogathons appeal to the current American emphasis on using the legs for exercise. Nationally, the March of Dimes holds an annual 32-kilometer WalkAmerica in 1100 cities on the same day. Local organizations do the same in their own communities. Bikeathons are popular, too. The money-raising device is the same in all such events: each entrant signs up sponsors who promise to pay a specified amount to the fund for each mile or kilometer the entrant walks, jogs, runs, or cycles.

Staging of parties, charity balls, concerts, and similar events in which tickets are sold is another widely used approach. Often, however, big parties create more publicity than profit, with 25 to 50 percent of the money raised going to expenses. Other methods include sponsorship of a motion picture opening, a theater night, or a sporting event. Barbecues flourish as money-raisers in Western cities. Seeking to attract donors from the under-30 age-group, some organizations use the "fun" approach by raffling off such items as Madonna's sequined brassiere (for $2,500) and a T-shirt by artist Felix Gonzalez-Torres with the message "Nobody Owns Me" (for $50).

Sale of a product, in which the organization keeps a portion of the selling price, ranges from the church baked-goods stand, which yields almost 100-percent profit because members contribute homemade products, to the massive national Girl Scout cookie sale, which grosses about $375 million annually. *A key to success in all charity-fund sales is abundant publicity in the local news media.*

Direct solicitation of funds over television by *telethons* is used primarily in large cities. A television station sets aside a block of airtime for a telethon sponsored by a philanthropic organization. Best known of the national telethons is the one conducted annually by comedian Jerry Lewis for muscular dystrophy.

Telephone Solicitations   Solicitation of donations by telephone is a relatively inexpensive way to seek funds, but of uncertain effectiveness. Many groups hold down their cost of solicitation by using a WATS (Wide Area Telephone Service) line that provides unlimited calls for a flat fee, without individual toll charges. Some people resent receiving telephone solicitations. If the recipient of the call is unfamiliar with the cause, it must be explained clearly and concisely—not always easy for a volunteer solicitor to do. The problem of converting verbal promises by telephone into confirmed written pledges also arises. The normal method is for the sponsoring organization to send a filled-in pledge form to the donor for signature.

Use of "800" or "900" Telephone Numbers   Toll-free telephone numbers with area codes of 800, permitting callers to phone an organization long-distance without cost to themselves, have been in use for years. A 900 code has been added by the telephone companies that requires users to pay a fee for each call placed. The phone company takes a service charge from this fee, and the remainder goes to the party being called.

Charitable organizations increasingly are using "900" numbers in fund-raising. Although the callers must pay for their calls, they have the convenience of making a pledge without having to read solicitation material and write a response. Public television station WNET in New York used a 900 number in an annual pledge drive and received $235,000 in contributions through it.

Commercial Enterprises   Rather than depending entirely on contributions, some nonprofit organizations go into business on their own or make tie-ins with commercial firms from which they earn a profit. Use of this approach is growing, but it contains risks.

The risks for an organization are obvious. Entrepreneurship requires good business management, not always available in charitable organizations. Businesses can lose money as well as make it. Ill-advised lending of an organization's name to a shoddy product or a high-pressure telemarketing scheme can damage a charity's reputation.

Any nonprofit organization contemplating operation of a business should check the tax laws, which require that the enterprise be "substantially related" to the purpose of the nonprofit group.

Case Study: A Lesson in Fund-Raising   The Old Globe Theater in San Diego's Balboa Park is an integral part of the city's cultural life. It attracts about 300,000 playgoers a year to its 325 evening performances and has a splendid professional reputation.

The theater's board of directors knew that it needed rehearsal space, refurbishing, and a concession area. They also wanted to pay off debt incurred from rebuilding part of the theater damaged by fire and to acquire a $2 million endowment and reserve fund.

The board decided to conduct a $10 million capital fund campaign. An article in *The Chronicle Of Philanthropy* tells how they did so successfully, despite severe obstacles.

First, the directors conducted a feasibility study. This showed that San Diego's community leaders did not regard the theater's financial needs as compelling; it also showed that the theater's volunteer leadership lacked members who could make large personal contributions and solicit major campaign gifts.

After a delay caused in part by the death of the theater's campaign consultant, Robert B. Sharp took the job and the campaign was revitalized. New volunteer leaders were recruited. Several events then occurred:

- A four-color brochure was published to be given to donor prospects.

- A few donors made large gifts as a nucleus of the drive.

- At cocktail parties, board members and major donors heard presentations about the campaign. They were asked to pick names of people they knew from a list of 20,000 season ticket holders. This provided a list for solicitation.

- A precise goal was set for each prospect—2 to 5 percent of the donor's estimated "adjusted gross worth." The campaign hired a researcher to examine various credit and public records to determine what these goals should be.

With this list, the campaign reached full speed. The cochair made a challenge gift of $500,000 that required the theater to raise $1.5 million within seven months.

Prospective donors were invited to dinner and a play, taken backstage, and given a slide presentation before seeing the play. The campaign used slides rather than a videotape because they enabled the speaker to pause during the presentation for questions.

Solicitors went after the largest gifts first, then moved step by step to the smaller prospects. They had a gift model showing the various sizes of gifts sought, from a high of $1 million down to $1000, and the number of prospects for each size (three for $1 million, 1500 for $1000). Actual donors in each category proved to be about one third of the category's prospects.

So far, everything had been done on a personal basis without major publicity. A total of $8.5 million was raised from individuals, corporations, and foundations.

Then the campaign went public with a media blitz to solicit gifts under $10,000 from the general public. The final phase involved sending direct-mail pieces to theater constituents who had not contributed.

Large donors were recognized by having their family coats of arms incorporated in the design of the new facilities and they received framed versions of the coats of arms. An importing company donated research to find coats of arms for families lacking them.

A crucial part of this successful campaign was the identification of potential large donors and the analysis of how much each might donate, so that solicitors could make their calls with specific money targets in mind.

HEALTH CARE PUBLIC RELATIONS

The $400-billion-a-year health care industry has an impact on all Americans who are concerned about their personal health and the often-burdensome cost of medical service. Since most medical services—primarily treatments by physicians, hospital stays, sale of medicines, and health insurance—function in a competitive environment, public relations and marketing programs are essential in their operations.

One multifaceted campaign dealt with a serious health scare. The communication program addressing tainted food employed two firms in the implementation of nearly a dozen distinct strategies over more than a year. The issue was bacterial contamination of precut vegetables. Television news producers were particularly avid to produce "buyer beware" segments about precut salad ingredients, citing lists of common, harmless bacteria while suggesting that their presence could mean dangerous bacteria might also appear. The Londre Group and Fineman Associates undertook communication efforts for the salad suppliers. Tactics included publicity of university food scientists debunking stories about the innocuous bacteria, video news releases to set forth the scientific facts, trade media briefings, face-to-face meetings with food editors, national opinion surveys, and an array of additional actions. Also indicative of the growing sophistication of health care public relations is the targeting of women as health care consumers because they comprise 60 percent of doctor visits and 59 percent of prescription drug purchases, according to Kym White, Managing Director of Ogilvy PR Worldwide's Health & Medical Practice.

Audience targeting was also the thrust of a study entitled "Femstat 3 Report: American Women and Self Care." It analyzed where women obtain their health care information and found that about 50 percent get information mainly from their primary care doctors; 24 per-

Tough Calls on Health Care Issues

Doctors and nurses joined forces in the Ad Hoc Committee to Defend Health Care, an activist group opposed to purportedly excessive profits of hospitals. Their Boston Tea Party reenactment, covered in *O'Dwyer's PR Services Report,* won publicity for their claim that $125 billion in corporate health care revenues could be better spent on research and improved patient care. Decrying rushed hospital stays, denial of services, and wasteful bureaucracy, the activists tossed annual reports of for-profit hospitals and HMOs into Boston Harbor.

The other side in the dispute responded that so-called "jungle capitalism" bankrolls research to develop lifesaving techniques and provides a stable health care system best able to serve patients. One could add that competition and profit are what drive innovation and excellence throughout the American system.

Which side in this fight would you most want to help with your developing public relations knowledge and skills?

Would you turn down a good job offer from the opposing side for this issue?

Do you think that you could change the organization's stance with your public relations counsel? In other words, could you take a job with the opposition to shape it up enough "to live with yourself every payday"?

cent cited magazines and newspapers as their main source, 7 percent, television and radio, and 5 percent, self-help books. Much of the information in these categories is provided by public relations sources.

Concern about the high number of Americans, around 40 million, who have no medical insurance has created proposals to change the American system, with little result. President Clinton's ambitious program in 1993 met political defeat. Federally financed Medicaid assists low-income patients; it has been under recurring political attack. Older Americans are eligible for Medicare, a form of government-operated insurance they help pay for from their Social Security benefits. Health maintenance organizations (HMOs), in which individuals and families can buy memberships, seek to hold down medical costs by limiting their members' choice of doctors and reserving the right to refuse payment for certain procedures. Although used by millions of Americans, the HMOs face frequent complaints from patients about allegedly insufficient treatment and premature discharge from hospitals. Many American hospitals are operated as commercial enterprises.

Public Relations for Hospitals

The public relations staff of a hospital has two specific roles: (1) to strengthen and maintain the public's perception of the institution as a place where medical skill, compassion, and efficiency are paramount; and (2) to help market the hospital's proliferating array of services. Many hospitals have sought to redefine themselves as community health centers. Basically, hospitals, like hotels, must have high room-occupancy rates to succeed financially. They supplement this fundamental source of income by creating and marketing supplementary services, an area that offers a challenge to public relations people.

Typical of these supplementary services are alcoholism rehabilitation, childbirth and parenting education.

Hospital Audiences

Hospital public relations programs have four basic *audiences:* patients, medical and administrative staffs, news media, and the community as a whole. The four audiences overlap, but each needs a special focus. Careful scrutiny can identify significant subaudiences within these four—for example, the elderly; women who have babies or soon will give birth; victims of heart disease, cancer, and stroke who need support groups after hospitalization; potential donors of money to the hospital; and community opinion leaders.

A Sample of Public Relations Efforts

Here are a few examples of methods hospitals use to project a positive image:

- Sponsorship of community health fairs, offering free screenings to detect symptoms of certain diseases and low-cost comprehensive blood tests

- A "direct line" telephone system within the hospital on which patients and visitors can register complaints and suggestions 24 hours a day

- Bingo games on a closed-circuit television system, for which patients pay a small fee and win cash prizes. This brightens the patients' day

Global PR

The Web Pushes European Limits on Medical Self-Care

Americans have long enjoyed moderate regulation of medical information, enabling U.S. citizens to make judgments about their own medical care. Now public relations firms are setting their sights on European markets for health care products and prescription pharmaceuticals. Firms in the United States are developing communication programs that offer medical information needed for people to take more initiative in their own well-being. One particularly promising new audience for self-care information will be European nations as they liberalize rules about availability of medical information to all citizens.

What the health communication industry calls direct-to-consumer campaigns have empowered American consumers to make many of their own medical decisions. Although advertising plays a role by announcing availability, it is really the public relations materials that enable education about medical matters. These materials are increasingly available on the World Wide Web, where Europeans may read them, in spite of traditional restrictions by continental governments that are just now changing.

This globalization of medical information probably will accelerate the direct-to-consumer movement in Europe, with consequent increases in medical knowledge and self-care, as well as increased commerce for health-related products.

Source: *O'Dwyer's PR Services Report,* October 1998.

Colleges and Universities

Public relations and development offices fulfill important functions for colleges and universities.

Development and Public Relations Offices   The president (or chancellor) is the chief public relations officer of a college or university; he or she sets policy and is responsible for all operations, under the guidance of the institution's governing board.

In large universities, the vice president for development and university relations (that person may have some other title) supervises the office of development, which includes a division for alumni relations, and also the office of public relations; these functions are combined in smaller institutions. Development and alumni personnel seek to enhance the prestige and financial support of the institution. Their primary responsibilities are to build alumni loyalty and to generate funding from private sources.

The public relations director, generally aided by one or more chief assistants, supervises the information news service, publications, and special events. Depending on the size of the institution, perhaps a dozen or more employees will carry out these functions, including writing, photography, graphic design, broadcasting, and computer networking.

Figure 16.3 shows the organization of the public relations staff at a typical-sized university.

Public Information Bureau   The most visible aspect of a university public relations program is its public information bureau. Among other activities, an active bureau produces hundreds of news releases, photographs, and special columns and articles for the print media. It prepares programs of news and features about faculty activities and personalities for stations. It provides assistance and information for reporters, editors, and broadcasters affiliated with the state, regional, and national media. The staff responds to hundreds of telephone calls from members of the news media and the public seeking information.

Serving the Publics   In order to carry out their complex functions, top development and public relations specialists must be a part of the management team of the college or university. At some institutions this is not so, and the public relations program suffers. Ideally, these leaders should attend all top-level meetings involving the president and other administrators.

Faculty and Staff.   College administrators communicate with their faculty and staff members through e-mail and in-house newsletters and newspapers; journals describing research, service, and other accomplishments (which also are sent to outside constituencies); and periodic meetings.

Students.   Because of their large numbers and the many families that they represent, students make up the largest public relations arm—for good or bad—that a university has. The quality of the teaching they receive is the greatest determinant of their allegiance to the institution. However, a sound administrative attitude toward students, involving them as much as possible in decisions that affect their campus lives, is extremely important. So are other forms of communication, achieved through support of student publications and broadcast stations and in numerous other ways. When, upon graduation, they are inducted en masse into the university's alumni society, chances are good that, if they are pleased with their collegiate experience, many will support the university in its future undertakings. Public relations effort directed at students is thus essential.

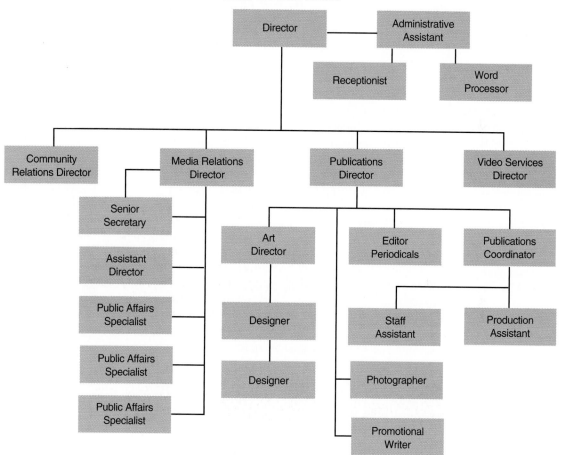

Figure 16.3

Organizational chart of the University of Miami's public affairs office, showing the division of responsibility for the various areas of operation.

Alumni and Other Donors. Fund-raising activities have increased dramatically at most colleges and universities in recent years. As a result, private financial support for these institutions rose almost 9 percent over the preceding fiscal year to $16 billion in gifts during fiscal year 1997, according to the Council for Aid in Education.

The demand for experienced fund-raisers has created a shortage among those qualified, and salaries in some instances have skyrocketed well beyond $100,000 annualy. Women are increasingly holding top positions in the field.

PR Casebook

Universities Open Electronic Doors

Universities are increasingly opening electronic doors to prospective students, inviting them to tour their World Wide Web campus sites no matter how far away they live. In addition, they are using the Internet to teach courses, provide employment bazaars for those about to graduate, and arrange chat rooms and other specialized services for alumni.

"Students can apply from any part of the globe and take a walking tour of the university by computer," said Joel Stitzel, a computer specialist at the University of Minnesota. On many campuses, the websites are replacing viewbooks sent to prospective students in previous years.

Many students gain college admission via the computer. Penn State University aims to process at least 80 percent of its applications electronically by 2000. The 22-campus system receives about 50,000 applications a year.

On many campuses, computer job banks allow employers to post openings and students to see the listings almost immediately and to learn more about the companies.

Videoconference hookups permit companies to interview students without going on campus. For example, in 1996 Procter & Gamble held 28 interviews at Case Western Reserve University in Cleveland using Viewnet, a commercial system that shows a résumé on the left of the screen, the student's image on the bottom right, and the corporate interviewer's image at the top right.

Because many in a new generation of college graduates appear to prefer online communication to what they call "snail-mail," a growing number of alumni associations are creating online sites. On these sites alumni talk about their families, read the school newspaper and alumni newsletter, share jokes, and discuss innumerable issues.

Many universities are using their World Wide Web sites to appeal for financial support. An increasing number of the sites have been secured to decrease loss to hackers. Mississippi State University, one of the first institutions to use a secure system, has received fairly large gifts online, including two for $5000. Cornell University receives about one gift per week online, ranging from $5 to $300. On secured sites, alumni and others may make gifts by credit card numbers without fear that their card numbers will be compromised.

The Alumni Center for Education on the World Wide Web includes an area with both public and private sections featuring chat rooms, bulletin boards, electronic mail, and a searchable member directory. A security feature allows subscribers to make a pledge or gift by credit card online.

University Online Inc. leases about 200 ready-made high school and college courses for extension and corporate training credit purposes. George Washington University and George Mason University were among its first clients.

Colleges and universities use the money they raise mainly to attract and pay new faculty, to buy equipment and provide support for faculty research, and to attract and offer financial aid for students.

The placement of universities' endowment funds often poses a public relations problem. Organizations such as the Tobacco Investment Project persuaded Harvard University and the City University of New York to sell their highly profitable stock holdings in the tobacco companies.

The movement's spread brought a similar dilemma to other universities: how and if they could withdraw their holdings in tobacco companies without sacrificing the firms' large annual grants.

Universities increasingly conduct long-range capital fund campaigns for very large sums, such as the $1.5-billion goal at Yale University and the $1.15-billion goal at Cornell University.

Many institutions employ students to participate in fund-raising phonothons. At the University of Michigan, students called 970,000 alumni and raised $8.3 million during a nine-month period. Computerized dialing systems are often used.

At most institutions, letters are mailed to specific graduating classes over the names of members who have agreed to be class agents for that purpose. Not only year-by-year contributions are sought, but bequests and annuities as well. In return, the colleges publish honor rolls listing donors, invite contributors to join honorary clubs (the President's Club, for example), and name rooms and buildings for the largest givers.

Influential alumni and other important friends of colleges and universities are also encouraged, through personal contact and correspondence, to provide political clout with legislative bodies and boards of regents in support of the institutions' financial and other objectives. Such support is also important in the recruitment of students with outstanding academic, athletic, or other achievement.

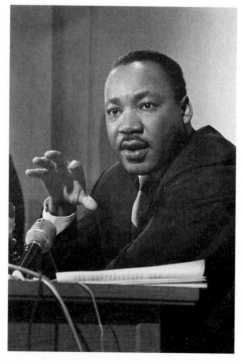

Martin Luther King, Jr.'s leadership was a prime factor in the civil rights battle. The United Negro College Fund has used him as a role model in its fund-raising based on the slogan, "A mind is a terrible thing to waste." He is shown at a news conference in Atlanta.

PR Casebook

University Campaign Seeks $1 Billion

The University of Connecticut mounted a campaign in the mid–1990s to win support for UConn 2000, a 10-year, $1 billion program to rebuild the university's infrastructure and to renew and equip academic and research facilities.

As an opening shot, Institutional Advancement leaders persuaded the Hartford *Courant* to examine editorially the condition of the university's aging infrastructure. The resulting six-part editorial series set the groundwork for the drive.

Working with the public relations firm of Mintz & Hoke, leaders sought to establish the message that Uconn—while maintaining the quality of its academic programs and its faculty and staff—had serious problems with its infrastructure. The message had to be conveyed to as large an audience as possible yet target key groups such as alumni and other friends as well as key legislators and their constituents. The message had to be conveyed during the most critical time for the recruitment of freshmen for the fall semester of the 23,000-student institution.

PLANNING/EXECUTION

UConn advancement leaders and public relations firm representatives met to establish messages, through means such as focus groups, and to design the communications plan. Other action:

- University officials met with more than a dozen newspaper editorial boards and the board of a Hartford-based television station that editorialized on the air.

- A direct-mail brochure was sent to 25,000 parents, alumni, and other friends of the university in targeted legislative districts. Included was a postage-paid postal card expressing support for the project. The objective was to establish the level of support and to add names and addresses to a databank of supporters. Additional postal cards were distributed at university sports events and at the Hartford Civic Center.

  Of 40,000 cards distributed, about 10,000 came back, giving a return of 25 percent. In addition, nearly 2,000 phone calls of support were made to a special 800-number hotline.

- University President Harry J. Hartley sent letters to faculty, staff, and students as well as to alumni, parents, and other friends of the institution. The objective was to give each constituency an overview of the proposal and urge support.

(continued)

Government.   State and federal governments often hold the vital key to whether universities receive sufficient monies to maintain facilities, faculty, and programs. Most large institutions have someone who regularly monitors the state legislature on appropriations and issues ranging from laboratory experiments on animals to standardized tests and taxes. Said Robert Dickens, coordinator of government relations for the University of Nevada at Reno: "When I say I'm a lobbyist, some people look at me as if I need a shower. It's a new business with the universities, and some people think it's a dirty business. But nothing's dirtier than not having resources."

Government relations experts represent universities in Washington, D.C. Their work complements that of the American Council on Education, the National Association of Land-Grant Universities, and the Association of American Universities.

University Campaign Seeks $1 Billion, continued

• A 30-second video spot was aired on local and network broadcasts of men's and women's basketball games. A five-minute video—a minidocumentary—was distributed to key alumni and all legislators. The video was also sent to cable access outlets.

• A news conference at the state capitol building was attended by a bipartisan group of legislators who announced their support. Large display charts, graphs, and photo blowups portrayed the story.

• Letters to the editor and letters to individual legislators were solicited during the spring as the project, in bill form, made its way through the legislative process. A second direct-mail piece was then sent to targeted UConn friends who were constituents in "swing" legislative districts.

• Upon passage of the bill, President Hartley sent thank-you letters to legislative leaders, Connecticut newspaper editors, and others. Community leaders were among those invited to a closing victory celebration on the steps of the university library.

BUDGET

The budget was $82,550. Funding was provided primarily by the University of Connecticut Foundation, with additional support from the UConn chapter of the American Association of University Professors, UConn Professional Employees Association, and UConn Alumni Association.

RESULTS

Not only was the legislation approved, but the first bond issue for the reconstruction project was successfully completed. The direct mailings, producing responses of more than 10,000 postal cards and nearly 2,000 telephone calls, enlarged the scope of the Institutional Advancement Office's future activities.

The University Relations Office of the University of Connecticut won a silver medal in the annual competition sponsored by the Council for the Advancement and Support of Education.

The Community.   As in the case of industry, a college or university must maintain a good relationship with the members of the community in which it is situated. The greatest supporters that an institution may have are the people within its immediate sphere of influence.

In order to bridge the town-gown gap that is often evident, faculty and staff members are encouraged to achieve community visibility through work with civic and other organizations. Business groups often take the lead. The Chamber of Commerce in Lawrence, Kansas, for example, for many years sponsored an annual barbecue, including various other activities, to give faculty and townspeople an opportunity to get to know each other better.

Prospective Students.   Many colleges have turned to highly competitive recruiting methods. Some, in the "hard-sell" classification, use extensive advertising in print and broadcast media and on billboards. Other colleges and universities have replaced their catalogues and brochures with four-color, slick materials that use bright graphics and catchy headlines to lure students. Many use the World Wide Web.

Various other recruiting devices are used. Vanderbilt University sent personalized video-tapes to about 40 highly coveted high school seniors. The College of the Atlantic took prospective students on a 90-foot sailing yacht party. Stanford University was host to 750 high school students who stayed overnight in dormitory rooms, visited classes, attended a musical program, and participated in a campus scavenger hunt. Brown University sponsors a party each spring for up to 250 prospects on an Amtrak train traveling between Washington

Faced by a financial crisis that was forcing faculty members into early retirement, the University of California, Berkeley, made an unusual public appeal for contributions to help it retain tenured professors. The provocative headline, with its play on words, stimulated much interest.

INNOCENT PROFESSOR GOES TO THE CHAIR.

You'd better sit down for this.

Faced with our worst financial crisis since the Great Depression, we've been forced to start asking professors to retire early. Talk about drastic measures.

Last year alone, one-tenth of our tenured professors left. And with hundreds more eligible this year, Cal will continue to lose many of its most distinguished minds. Frankly, we'd much rather have our faculty members win Nobel Prizes than plant rhododendrons in the backyard. This is where you come in.

Your donations have supported endowed chairs before, and are now helping us to improve facilities and attract a slew of top-ranked faculty recruits. Seeing how it's your alma mater's reputation on the line, we need you this time more than ever. Please, give whatever you can afford.

And help us keep some professors on their feet.

UC BERKELEY
It's not the same without you.

UC Berkeley Foundation, 2440 Bancroft Way, Room 301, Berkeley, CA 94720
To help, call the Development Office at (510) 642-7374.

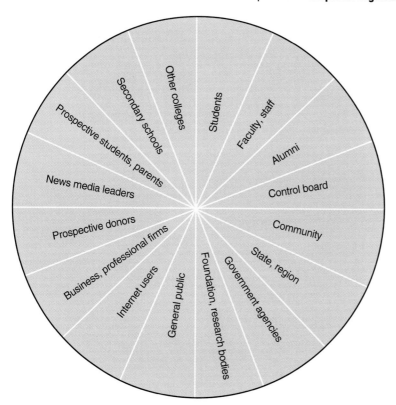

and Providence, Rhode Island. As competition for students has increased, so have the costs of recruiting them.

The purchase of mailing lists is a common tool of student recruitment. Each of approximately 900 colleges annually buys from 10,000 to 15,000 names and addresses of high school students who have taken College Board Examinations. The most sought-after prospects are National Merit Scholarship winners, and it is not uncommon for competing universities to shower a prospect with such lures as free tuition for four years, a private dorm room, guarantees of priority registration, and so on.

Other Publics. Representing more than 2400 institutional members, CASE serves nationally as a principal public affairs arm for education, monitoring federal rights legislation and regulations and working with the American Council on Education and other associations on education-related issues. The organization provides district conferences and institutes, evaluation and critique services, a certification program, awards, reference materials, and placement opportunities. Thousands each summer attend its four-day assembly, replete with workshops.

The University of Calgary's campaign to enroll more students makes a double appeal in this poster. It emphasizes the school's achievements in engineering and space research, and at the same time it makes the point that going to college can be fun.

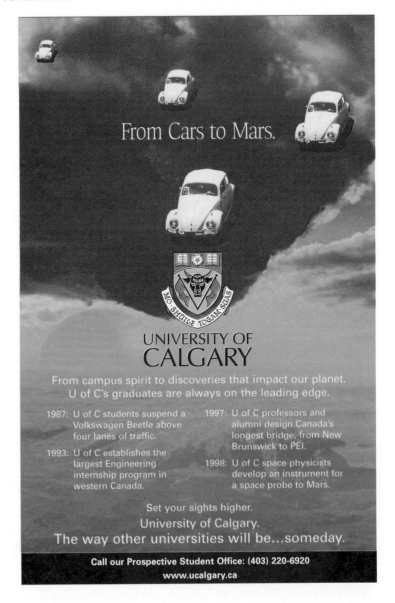

Elementary and Secondary Schools

The strategic planning and skillful execution of public relations programs have materially strengthened many of the nation's elementary and secondary school systems during recent decades.

Response to Contemporary Issues   Should public tax money be used so that parents disaffected with the public schools can send their children to private, religion-supported schools?

Should affirmative action guidelines be followed in admitting students to colleges and universities?

Many questions such as these confronted the nation and its educational systems as the new century dawned. They followed almost two decades of widespread debate since the National Commission on Excellence in Education, citing "a nation at risk," called for massive educational reform. Integration, busing, accountability, book censorship, sex education, discipline, crime, and drugs—all these issues and more commanded public concern.

The 18-member commission proposed increasing requirements in five major areas: content, standards and expectations, time, teaching, and leadership and financial support—all deemed inadequate.

Governors and business leaders then began a decade of annual National Education Summits to plan school advancement. Corporations formed alliances with schools. In many classrooms, however, corporate logos and learning went hand in hand. Among the deals was a 10-year contract that the Colorado Springs schools signed with the Coca-Cola Company for $9 million. Pepsi paid $2.1 million to the Jefferson County school district in Colorado. Many found such exclusive contracts troubling because they limit student choice and can require educational institutions to toe the line. One boy was even suspended for a day for wearing a Pepsi shirt on Coke day.

Reaching the Publics   The primary publics of a school system are teachers, children, parents, staff, and the community. As in all public relations, research, planning, action,

PR Casebook

High School Forms Hall of Fame

A high school Hall of Fame honoring prominent graduates from two Chicago suburbs provides a close tie between the school's administration and the community.

Lyons Township High School, principally serving the towns of La Grange and Western Springs, has an enrollment of nearly 3000 students on two campuses. In more than 100 years of operation, it counts nearly 50,000 graduates and former students.

Each year a citizens' committee, administered by the school's community relations coordinator, elects graduates to the Hall of Fame. These men and women are invited to speak to classes for two days, then are honored at a large community banquet. Plaques of the honorees are placed on a school wall. The honorees receive individual plaques.

Among the 33 inductees during the hall's first three years of operation were two admirals, a university president, corporate presidents, a journalist, a major league baseball player, a cancer surgeon, a children's author, and a television star.

"These individuals provide splendid role models for our students," an administrator said, "and show the community the quality of education LTHS provides."

and evaluation comprise the essential steps with which to reach these publics. On the desks of information directors, communication coordinators, and school-community relations specialists (or whatever the title may be, and it varies widely) are booklets prepared by national and state offices detailing hundreds of ways in which they may carry out their mission. Perhaps the best way to describe school public relations in its major aspects is to examine some of the outstanding programs accorded the Gold Medallion award of the National School Public Relations Association.

Building Community Support When almost one third of the elementary schools in the Fort Worth Independent School District tested low in pupils' reading skills, the superintendent asked the public for help. Business leaders, librarians, and teachers, coordinated by the schools' community relations division, developed a year-long awareness campaign with the theme, "Reading Takes You Places."

Communication plans included news releases, bilingual fliers to parents and community leaders, TV and cable messages, with personal contacts before each activity. Newspapers, the city transportation authority, and advertising companies provided free advertising.

Business firms supported such activities as book donations to libraries and a Reading Rodeo attended by more than 700 children in 69 schools. Community groups such as the Dallas Mavericks, and museums also participated. A Reading Summit involving sponsorship by the Governor's Business Council drew broad media coverage.

By year's end, only three schools failed to meet state expectations and a 91-percent improvement rate was recorded in the number of low-performing schools.

Marketing of Public School Education A pioneer in public opinion surveying in education, William J. Banach, administrative director at the Macomb Intermediate School District in Mount Clemens, Michigan, developed a two-year plan designed to discover what the public wants from its schools. The plan also sought ways to respond to those desires and to educate citizens about actions the school could and could not take. Banach based the campaign on what he termed "the 90–7–3 concept of school communication":

> Ninety percent of the school's image is who we are and what we do 24 hours a day. How school people think, act, and appear and what they say are key factors in marketing. This is why staff training is an integral part of a marketing program—to help people understand their communication roles and how important they are.
>
> Seven percent of the marketing effort is listening—tuning in to find out what people like, don't like, want, don't want. Anything we do to know more about our "customers" is worth doing.
>
> Three percent of marketing is outbound communication—publications, posters, news releases, and other visible and tangible items.

In successive phases, the marketing plan was targeted at (1) elementary parents, with a focus on reading, writing, and arithmetic; (2) secondary students and their parents, emphasizing "the basics and beyond" and beginning with specific objectives based on survey results and meetings with student leaders; and (3) citizens without children in school.

Arrangements were made for teachers to apply "No. 1 apple" stickers to outstanding student papers, and all classroom papers were sent home each Friday. Posters welcoming visitors were placed at each school. The slogan "Your public schools . . . There's no better place to learn" was displayed on billboards, calendars, bookmarks, bumper stickers, T-shirt transfers, and thank-you cards.

A survey made a year after the campaign began revealed enhanced public confidence in the schools. The Macomb Plan, as it is called, has attracted national attention.

CASE PROBLEM

The Vision Council of America is a trade group representing the optical industry. Its three core membership groups are ophthalmologists, opticians, and optometrists.

The group decides to launch a consumer education program after research reveals a reluctance to take children for eye exams because parents rely on free in-school screenings. Additional research shows that 80 percent of learning before the age of 12 is accomplished through vision, yet traditional in-school vision screenings miss between 70 and 80 percent of children's vision problems.

Your public relations firm is retained to conduct a national consumer education program emphasizing the importance of annual eye exams for children. What would you suggest? Program elements that you should consider include key publics, message themes, time of year, strategies, and types of communication tools.

CASE PROBLEM

The facts: for 20 years a Western city of 150,000 population has operated a volunteer Meals on Wheels program, taking food to shut-ins. Financial contributions to help support the project have dwindled, however, as has the force of volunteers to deliver the meals, endangering continuation of this humanitarian service. Your public relations firm has been hired by a local church to revitalize the program.

Following the four-step process explained in Part Two of this book, develop a program to achieve this objective. Define the audiences you should address. Explain specifically what you would seek to learn during your research, describe the plan of action you would use, tell how you would communicate your message, and draw up a plan of evaluation.

CASE PROBLEM

Southwestern University has a public relations problem. The campus administration, taking the route of many other universities, has signed a contract with Carl Jr. to open a fast-food franchise on campus. The decision was based on competitive bidding, and campus administrators made the decision that Carl Jr. was the best choice to answer the needs of hungry students. Remodeling of a space in the Student Union has already begun to accommodate the new franchise when, much to everyone's surprise, the student/faculty gay and lesbian association of the university publicly denounces the contract.

Representatives of the organization say the university should not let Carl Jr. operate on campus because the founder of the company, Carl Karcher, is antigay. About 20 years ago, they say, he gave a political donation to a state senator who introduced a bill in the state legislature that would have banned homosexual teachers from the classroom. The bill, however, was never passed. Although Karcher is no longer actively involved in the management of the restaurant chain, the gay and lesbian association says the university should honor its commitment to diversity and equality by denying the franchise. The university president is caught in a bind, since he has been most vocal about campus climate and expressing zero tolerance about any form of "hate" speech.

If you were the vice president of public relations for the university, what would you recommend? Should the university cancel the contract to satisfy the gay/lesbian association? What about the numerous university students who are looking forward to having the fast-food franchise on campus? What steps would you recommend to resolve the issue?

QUESTIONS FOR REVIEW AND DISCUSSION

1. Trade associations, like other membership organizations, often have headquarters in Washington, D.C., or a state capital. Why?

2. What challenges do labor unions face today?

3. What are the differences and similarities among trade groups, labor unions, and professional associations?

4. What has caused the recent intensified scrutiny of nonprofit organizations?

5. Name the seven categories of social agencies.

6. What motivates men and women to serve as volunteer workers?

7. Describe four commonly used types of fund-raising.

8. What two principal roles does a hospital public relations staff fulfill?

9. Who is the chief public relations officer on a college or university campus? Why?

10. A college news bureau is involved in a vast array of day-to-day public relations operations. Name five or six of these functions.

11. With what primary public does a sound university public relations program begin? Why? List eight other constituencies that must be addressed in such a program.

12. In what ways may powerful alumni and other friends provide support for an institution of higher learning? What is the role of the development office in gaining this support?

13. The National Commission on Excellence in Education called for massive educational reform. How did school officials respond?

14. Do you agree with the marketing concept used by public relations people in the Macomb Intermediate School District in Mount Clemens, Michigan? Describe the key points of this plan in explaining your answer.

17

Entertainment, Sports, and Travel

Preview

In this chapter, the objective is to show students how public relations promotes these three vigorous, growing forms of recreation and helps develop the careers of entertainers, public figures, and athletes.

Topics covered in the chapter include:

- Fascination with celebrity and the mystique of personality
- The practitioner's responsibility and ethical problems in handling individual clients
- Operation of a personality campaign
- Promotion of an entertainment
- Sports publicity
- Goals of travel promotion
- Reaching target travel audiences

FASCINATION WITH CELEBRITY

A dominant factor in today's mass media is the publicizing and glorification of celebrities. Sports heroes and television personalities in particular—along with radio talk-show hosts, members of the British royal family, movie stars, high-profile criminals, and some politicians—are written about, photographed, and discussed almost incessantly.

Such celebrity results in some cases from natural public curiosity about an individual's achievements or position in life. Frequently, however, it is carefully nurtured by publicists for the client's ego satisfaction or commercial gain.

The publicity buildup of individuals is outside the mainstream of public relations work, and some professional practitioners are embarrassed by the exaggerations and tactics used by promoters of so-called "beautiful people." Nevertheless, all students of public relations should learn how the personal publicity trade operates. At some point in their careers they may find a knowledge of its techniques useful.

A CASE STUDY: PRINCESS DIANA

Princess Diana, for example, was a celebrity worldwide as the divorced wife of Prince Charles, heir to the British throne. Her svelte, gracious manner, and high-fashion clothing, plus public interest in the collapse of her once-romantic marriage, created huge media attention to her. She appeared on the cover of *People Magazine* 41 times in a 16-year period and became known to headline writers as Princess Di.

Princess Diana's death in a dramatic, high-speed race to elude press photographers captured world attention.

In death, this ideal though distant relationship is severed, and the youthful image is frozen in time. The tragedy and the timeless glamor galvanize us into a mass audience. Princess Diana's funeral was viewed by an estimated 2.5 billion people around the world. An estimated 152,000 visitors to her burial shrine on the family estate paid $24 each to see her childhood home and family movies in a remodeled stable and to gaze at her island mausoleum. Even in death, both adulation and revenue can follow from celebrity.

THE MYSTIQUE OF PERSONALITY

Why is the public so eager to read about and watch personalities it regards as celebrities? What drives individuals to seek such attention?

The abundance of mass-media outlets today and their intense competition for audiences has vastly stimulated the natural instinct of humans to know about each other's lives. Appearances on talk shows, often-fawning TV interviews, magazine articles whose tone is influenced by publicists, question-and-answer periods on online computer services and the Internet, and ghost-written books contribute to the buildup.

Christine Kelly of *Sassy* magazine writes bluntly, "No-talents become celebrities all the time," a fact that she attributes largely to television. "Once TV started, the whole celeb-creation and worship careened out of control. . . . TV gives the false impression that celebrities are talking right to you, and you feel like they're your friends."

Here are some of the motivating factors in the cult of personality:

Fame   Public attention is drawn to some individuals by their accomplishments or positions. The President of the United States is automatically a celebrity; so is the Pope.

Notoriety   Even people who commit major crimes or are involved unfavorably in spectacular trials are treated as celebrities.

Barbara Goldsmith commented on this fact in the New York *Times:*

> The line between fame and notoriety has been erased. Today we are faced with a vast confusing jumble of celebrities: the talented and the untalented, heroes and villains, people of accomplishment and those who have accomplished nothing at all, the criteria of their celebrity being that their images encapsulate some form of the American dream, that they give enough of an appearance of leadership, heroism, wealth, success, danger, glamour and excitement to feed our fantasies. We no longer demand reality, only that which is real-seeming.

Self-Glorification   Donald Trump, a New York real-estate high-roller with an insatiable desire for publicity, is a striking example of this urge. He put his name on the buildings and casinos he bought and had a personal press agent in addition to the Trump Organization's aggressive public relations department. He telephoned reporters with stories about himself.

Trump's announcement that he planned to divorce his wife, Ivana, leaving her with a mere $25 million of his reputed $1 billion wealth, received major nationwide coverage.

He stayed in the public eye, first by announcing that he was the father of a boy born to actress Marla Maples and then by marrying her before an audience of 1500 people described by a publicist as "close friends." The cynical tone of media coverage is indicated by the opening sentence of the Philadelphia *Inquirer* story: "Donald Trump finally married Marla Maples on Monday—till death, tabloid scandal or prenuptial agreement do they part." Eventually, the marriage did break up.

Repair of a Bad Image   Public relations counselors who specialize in handling individuals sometimes work to create a positive image for a prominent person who has been cast in an unfavorable light by news stories.

Kathie Lee Gifford, a perky TV host, suffered a severe blow to her reputation when it was revealed that some of her "Kathie Lee" line of clothing sold by Wal-Mart was made by Honduran child labor and in New York sweatshops.

Gifford hired Howard Rubenstein, a counselor, to help her. She proclaimed her dismay and lack of knowledge that her name was being used in such practices, then sent her husband with a large amount of cash to pay some of the mistreated workers. Under Rubenstein's guidance, she sought to reverse her role from apparent offender to righteous crusader against such mistreatment of workers.

The climax of Kathie Lee's campaign came when she stood beside President Clinton in the White House Rose Garden as he signed an agreement with ten manufacturers who promised to put labels on their products stating that they had not been made in sweatshops.

Desire for Money   Sarah Ferguson, Duchess of York and former sister-in-law of Princess Diana, found herself in serious difficulty after her divorce from Prince Andrew. At 36, she was heavily in debt, had two daughters but no job, and was known for her extravagance and flamboyant behavior.

Ferguson also hired Rubenstein. His assignment was a classic job of celebrity public relations: keep "Fergie's" name mentioned favorably in magazines and newspapers, obtain television coverage, emphasize her sponsorship of charities, and help her win lucrative endorsements and public appearances. He said he planned to emphasize her "intelligence, devotion to her kids," and respect for the royal family.

When Fergie published a book, she was interviewed on major TV programs, pictured on two *People* covers, and held autographing parties at large bookstores. The book appeared on the New York *Times* best-seller list.

Personal publicity can build on itself. A publicist may arrange for an obscure film actress to attend a party as the guest of a well-known performer and issue a news release about the couple. Another party and another news release follow. Soon the news releases refer to the actress as a celebrity. Presto, she is one. No one officially proclaims that status, any more than some mysterious remote Solomon sends down word that a sports "star" has officially become a "superstar."

Indicative of the commercialization of personality is the success of Celebrity Service International, which keeps a 400,000-card databank on well-known persons and publishes daily bulletins in five cities on their comings and goings. It also publishes an annual enter-tainment-industry contact book that gives the names of managers, lawyers, and publicists who represent celebrities. The daily bulletin, priced at $1250 annually, tips off the media as to what prominent people might be available for a television talk show or a feature inter-view. The contact book helps business, industry, and charities locate celebrities who might serve as a spokesperson or a charity chairperson, or add glamor to a hotel opening.

Psychological Explanations

Psychologists offer varied explanations of why the public becomes impressed—often *fas-cinated* is the more accurate word—by highly publicized individuals. In pretelevision days, the publicity departments of the motion picture studios promoted their male and female stars as glamour figures who lived in a special world of privilege and wealth. Dreaming of

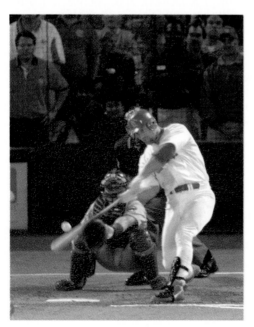

Celebrity endorsements: After Mark McGwire hit his 62nd home run in the 1998 major league baseball season, breaking a longtime record, he was deluged with lucrative offers from marketers to endorse products from soft drinks to automobiles. Top celebrities, especially sports stars, earn millions of dollars from such endorsements. Some expand their income by making personal appearances.

achieving such glory for themselves, young people with and without talent came to Hollywood to crash the magical gates, almost always in vain. Thousands more back home spun fantasies about being Rita Hayworth or Cary Grant. They cherished machine-autographed pictures of their favorites and read with relish inflated stories about the stars in fan magazines, visualizing themselves in the glamour figures' places.

In the earlier days of personality buildup, *wish fulfillment* was a compelling force. It still is. Exposure on television in the intimacy of the family living room, however, makes personalities seem much closer to admiring viewers today than the remote gods and goddesses were in the glory days of the major motion picture studios.

Many ordinary people leading routine lives yearn for heroes. Professional and big-time college sports provide personalities for *hero-worship*. Publicists emphasize the performances of certain players, and television game announcers often build up the stars' roles out of proportion to their achievements; this emphasis creates hero figures for youthful sports enthusiasts to emulate. Similar exaggerated treatment is applied to entertainers and politicians. Syndicated gossip columnist Liz Smith once tried to explain the American cult of personality by saying: "Maybe it's because we all want someone to look up to or spit on, and we don't have royalty."

In addition to admiration for individual performers, members of the public develop a *vicarious sense of belonging* that creates support for athletic teams. Sports publicists exploit this feeling in numerous ways. A winning baseball team becomes "our" team in conversations among patrons of a bar. To signify their loyalty, children and adults alike wear baseball caps bearing the insignia of their favorite major league teams.

Still another factor is the *desire for entertainment* most people feel. Reading fan magazines, or watching their favorite stars being interviewed, or lining up in front of a box office hours before it opens to be sure of getting a ticket—these are ways to bring variety and a little excitement into the daily routine of life.

A public relations practitioner assigned to build up the public image of an individual should analyze the ways in which these psychological factors can be applied. Since the client's cooperation is vital in promotional work, a wise publicist explains this background and tells the client why various actions are planned.

THE PRACTITIONER'S RESPONSIBILITY

A practitioner handling publicity for an individual carries special responsibilities. Often the client turns to the publicist for personal advice, especially for guidance when trouble arises.

Damage Control

A practitioner handling an individual client is responsible for protecting the client from bad publicity as well as generating positive news. When the client appears in a bad light because of misbehavior or an irresponsible public statement, the publicist must try to minimize the harm done to the client's public image. To use a naval term, the objective is *damage control*.

Often politicians who say something controversial in public, then wish later that they hadn't, try to squirm out of the predicament by claiming they were misquoted. This is a foolish defense unless the politician can prove conclusively that he or she was indeed quoted incorrectly. Reporters resent accusations of inaccuracy and may hold a grudge against the accuser. If the accused reporter has the politician's statement on tape, the politician appears even worse. A better defense is for the politician to explain what he or she intended and to express regret for the slip of the tongue.

A similar approach is recommended for Hollywood celebrities who are caught in scandalous acts or unfounded rumor mills. Experts suggest immediate response so that the momentum of subsequent stories is minimized. A brief, honest statement of regret for bad behavior or denial of rumors works well. Television's mass audience enjoys celebrity news. TV lends itself to a short statement that makes a perfect, 20-second sound bite to fit in a brief story. Then the celebrity needs to disappear from sight and take care of personal matters.

Ethical Problems for Publicists

Personal misconduct by a client, or the appearance of misconduct, strains a practitioner's ingenuity and at times his or her ethical principles. Some practitioners will lie outright to protect a client, a dishonest practice that looks even worse if the media show the statement to be a lie.

Issuing a prepared statement to explain the client's conduct, while leaving reporters and their editors dissatisfied, is regarded as safer than having the client call a news conference, unless the client is a victim of circumstances and is best served by talking fully and openly. The decision about holding a news conference also is influenced by how articulate and self-controlled the client is. Under questioning, a person may say something that compounds the problem. (Defensive news conferences are discussed further in Chapter 20.)

CONDUCTING A PERSONALITY CAMPAIGN

A campaign to generate public awareness of an individual should be planned just as meticulously as any other public relations project. This is the fundamental process, step by step, for the practitioner to follow.

Interview the Client

The client should answer a detailed personal questionnaire. The practitioner should be a dogged, probing interviewer, digging for interesting and possibly newsworthy facts about the person's life, activities, and beliefs.

Perhaps, for example, the client is a little-known actress who has won a role as a Midwestern farmer's young wife in a motion picture. During her get-acquainted talks with the publicist, she happens to mention in passing that while growing up in a small town she belonged to the 4-H Club. The feature angle can be the realism she brings to the movie role: when she was a member of the youth organization, she actually did the farm jobs she will perform in the film.

Not only must practitioners draw out such details from their clients, they must also have the ingenuity to develop these facts as story angles. When the actress is placed as a guest on a television talk show, the publicist should prompt her in advance to recall incidents from her 4-H experience. Two or three humorous anecdotes about mishaps with pigs and chickens, tossed into the TV interview, give it verve.

Prepare a Biography of the Client

The basic biography should be limited to four typed pages, perhaps less. News and feature angles should be placed high in the "bio," as it is termed, so an editor or producer can find them quickly. The biography, a portrait and other photographs of the client, and, if possible, additional personal background items should be assembled in a press kit for extensive distribution. Usually the kit is a cardboard folder with inside pockets.

Plan a Marketing Strategy

The practitioner should determine precisely what is to be sold and which types of audience are the most important to reach. For instance, an interview with a romantic operatic tenor on a rock 'n' roll radio station would be inadvisable. But an appearance by the singer on a public television station's talk show would be right on target. A politician trying to project herself as a representative of minority groups should be scheduled to speak before audiences in minority neighborhoods and placed on radio stations whose demographic reports show that they attract minority listeners.

Conduct the Campaign

The best course normally is to project the client on multiple media simultaneously. Radio and television appearances create public awareness and often make newspaper feature stories easier to obtain. The process works in reverse as well. Using telephone calls and "pitch" letters to editors and program directors, the publicist should propose print and on-air interviews with the client. Every such approach should include a news or feature angle for the interviewer to develop. Since magazine articles take longer to reach print, the publicist should begin efforts to obtain them as early as feasible.

An interview in an important magazine—a rising female movie star in *Cosmopolitan* or *People* magazine, for example—has major impact among women readers. Backstage maneuvering often takes place before such an interview appears. Agents for entertainers on their way up eagerly seek to obtain such an interview. When a personality is "hot" or at the top of the ladder, however, magazine editors compete for the privilege of publishing the interview. The star's agent plays them off against each other, perhaps offering exclusivity but demanding such rewards as a cover picture of the star, the right to choose the interviewer (friendly, of course), and even approval of the article. Editors of some magazines yield to publicists' demands. Other publications refuse to do so.

News Releases   News releases are an important avenue of publicity, but the practitioner should avoid too much puffery.

Photographs   Photographs of the client should be submitted to the print media as often as justifiable. Basic in the press kit is the standard head-and-shoulders portrait, often called a "mug shot." Photographs of the client doing something interesting or appearing in a newsworthy group may be published merely with a caption, without accompanying story. If the client seeks national attention, such pictures should be submitted to the news services so that, if newsworthy, they will be distributed to hundreds of newspapers. (Requirements for photographs are discussed in Chapter 21.)

The practitioner and the photographer should be inventive, putting the client into unusual situations. The justification for a successful submission can be thin if the picture is colorful and/or timely.

Sharply increased awareness among editors of women's concern about sexual exploitation has largely eliminated from newspaper pages "cheesecake" pictures—photographs of nubile young women in which the news angle often is as skimpy as their attire. At one time such pictures were published frequently as editors tried to spice up their pages. Occasionally such a picture shows up in print today, blatantly contrived and perhaps in bad taste, such as the one of a smiling man pointing to the replica of a check painted on the bare stomach of a belly dancer. The caption read: "Julian Caruso, an entertainment manager, arrived in court in Stafford, England, yesterday to pay a parking fine. He didn't want to pay the fine, the equivalent of $17, because, he said, Stafford lacks adequate parking. To emphasize his displeasure, he presented the court a check written on the stomach of a belly dancer, Sandrina. Court officials took a look at her real name, Sandra Audley—and decided they couldn't handle the check in that form."

Stunts like this are a throwback to old-time gimmick press agentry, yet sometimes they succeed. The picture was distributed by the Associated Press and published large-size in at least one metropolitan newspaper.

Cheesecake photographs still are printed in the trade press, even though they are seldom seen in daily newspapers. Certain British and Australian newspapers, however, continue to publish large photos of skimpily clad young women, often topless.

Public Appearances   Another way to intensify awareness of individual clients is to arrange for them to appear frequently in public places. Commercial organizations at times invite celebrities of various types or pay them fees to dress up dinner meetings, conventions, and even store openings. A major savings and loan association employed a group of early-day television performers to appear at openings of branch offices. Each day for a week, for two hours, an entertainer stood in a guest booth signing autographs and chatting with visitors, who received a paperback book of pictures recalling television's pioneer period. Refreshments were served. A company photographer took pictures of the celebrity talking to guests. Visitors who appeared in the pictures received them as a souvenir. These appearances benefited the sponsor by attracting crowds and helped the entertainers stay in the public eye.

Awards   A much-used device, but still successful, is to have a client receive an award. The practitioner should be alert for news of awards to be given and nominate the client for appropriate ones. Follow-up communications with persuasive material from the practitioner may convince the sponsor to make the award to the client. In some instances, the idea of an award is proposed to an organization by a practitioner, whose client is then conveniently declared the first recipient. The entertainment business generates immense amounts of publicity for individuals and shows with its Oscar and Emmy awards. Winning an Academy Award greatly strengthens a performer's career. Psychologists believe that televised awards ceremonies give viewers a sense of structure in life.

Nicknames and Labels   Creating catchy nicknames for clients, especially sports and entertainment figures, helps the practitioner get their names into print. Celebrity worshippers like to call their heroes and heroines by nicknames, as though the practice denoted a personal relationship. Thus we see and hear such familiarities for professional basketball players as "Air Jordan" and "Sir Charles" Barkley, and "Old Blue Eyes" and "The Boss" for entertainers.

Record the Results   Those who employ practitioners want tangible results in return for their fees. The practitioner also needs to compile and analyze the results of a personality campaign in order to determine the effectiveness of the various methods used. Tearsheets, photographs, copies of news releases, and, when possible, videotape clips of the client's public appearances should be given to the client. Clipping services help the practitioner assemble this material. At the end of the campaign, or at intervals in a long-term program, summaries of what has been accomplished should be submitted.

PROMOTING AN ENTERTAINMENT

Attracting attendance at an event—anything from a theatrical performance to a fund-raising fashion show or a street carnival—requires a well-planned publicity campaign.

Publicity to Stimulate Ticket Sales

The primary goal of any campaign for an entertainment is to sell tickets. An advance publicity buildup informs listeners, readers, and viewers that an event will occur and stimulates their desire to attend it. Rarely, except for community events publicized in smaller cities, do newspaper stories and broadcasts about an entertainment include detailed information on ticket prices and availability. Those facts usually are deemed too commercial by editors and should be announced in paid advertising. However, some newspapers may include prices, times, and so on in tabular listings of scheduled entertainments. Performance dates usually are included in publicity stories.

Stories about a forthcoming theatrical event, motion picture, rock concert, or similar commercial performance should concentrate on the personalities, style, and history of the show. Every time the show is mentioned, public awareness grows. Thus astute practitioners search for fresh news angles to produce as many stories as possible.

An Example: Publicizing a Play

Let us look at the way a new play can be publicized. The methods are the same whether the work will be performed on Broadway by professionals or in the local municipal auditorium by a little theater group.

Stories include an announcement that the play will be presented, followed by releases reporting the casting of lead characters, start of rehearsals, and opening date. Feature stories, or "readers," discuss the play's theme and background, with quotations from the playwright and director inserted to emphasize an important point. In interviews the play's star can tell why he or she finds the role significant or amusing.

Photographs of show scenes taken in costume during rehearsal should be distributed to the media. In some instances, publicity also can be generated through use of e-mail and World Wide Web pages.

The "Drip-Drip-Drip" Technique of Publicity

Motion picture studios, television production firms, and networks apply the principle of "drip-drip-drip" publicity when a show is being shot. In other words, there is a steady output of information about the production. A public relations specialist, called a unit man or woman, assigned to a film during production, turns out a flow of stories for the general and trade press and plays host to media visitors to the set. The television networks mail out daily news bulletins about their shows to media television editors. They assemble the editors annually to preview new programs and interview their stars. The heaviest barrage of publicity is released shortly before the show openings.

As an example of the uncertainty and high stakes surrounding television programming, the national television networks—ABC, CBS, NBC, Fox, UPN, and WB—offered 26 pilot programs in May 1998, many of which lacked staying power. Other such pilots may survive near-death experiences the way *Seinfeld* did in 1989, when its ratings were dismal. A year later, the comedy series reappeared to begin a rise in popularity that culminated in the hype surrounding the final episode. An audience estimated as being as high as 80 million generated advertising revenues at $1.6 million for a 30-second spot.

A much-publicized device is to have a star unveil his or her star in the cement of the Hollywood Walk of Fame just before the star's new film appears. Videotaped recordings of the event turn up on TV stations across the country.

One danger of excessive promotion of an event, however, is that audience expectation may become too high, so that the performance proves to be a disappointment. A skilled practitioner will stay away from "hype" that can lead to a sense of anticlimax.

A Look at the Motion Picture Industry

Through market research and interpretation of demographics and psychographics, motion picture public relations departments define target audiences they seek to reach. Most motion picture publicity is aimed at 18-to 24-year-olds, where the largest audience lies. Seventy-five percent of the film audience is under the age of 39, although increased attendance by older moviegoers has become evident recently.

Professional entertainment publicity work is concentrated in New York and Los Angeles, the former as the nation's theatrical center and the latter as the motion picture center. (American television production is divided primarily between the two cities, with the larger portion in Los Angeles.)

A typical Los Angeles-area public relations firm specializing in personalities and entertainment has two staffs: one staff of "planters," who deliver to media offices publicity stories about individual clients and the projects in which they are engaged, and another staff of "bookers," whose job is to place clients on talk shows and in other public appearances. Some publicity stories are for general release; others are prepared especially for a single media outlet such as a syndicated Hollywood columnist or a major newspaper. The latter type is marked "exclusive," permitting the publication or station that uses it to claim credit for "breaking" the story.

Another device is to provide supplies of tickets for a new movie or show to radio stations, whose disc jockeys award them to listeners as prizes in on-the-air contests. In the process, these announcers mention the name of the show dozens of times.

Chris Berman does a National Football League television commentary on ESPN. Sports broadcasting occupies a large, expanding portion of TV time. When the all-sports network began, it had a potential audience of 1.4 million homes. Today its potential audience is about 90 million homes worldwide.

For such services to individual or corporate entertainment clients, major Hollywood publicists charge at least $3000 a month, with a three-month minimum. The major studios and networks have their own public relations staffs.

Entertainment firms may also specialize in arranging product placement in movies and television programs. Usually the movie or television producers trade visible placement of a product in the show in exchange for free use of the item in the film. For example, Ford Motor Company provided the Explorer sport utility vehicle that was destroyed by a dinosaur in the movie, *Jurassic Park*. The vehicle was then marketed with Mattel Toys as the Jurassic Park Explorer.

The fast food industry also provides excellent opportunities for market-based public relations involving giveaways of film characters with meals. Movies such as *The Lion King* receive huge boosts in visibility and ticket sales. Characters from the film can provide a key incentive to young customers in the highly competitive takeout business, providing a large but transitory advantage in the so-called burger wars.

SPORTS PUBLICITY

The sports mania flourishing in the United States and in various forms around the world is stimulated by intense public relations efforts. Programs at both the big-time college and professional levels seek to arouse public interest in teams and players, sell tickets to games, and publicize the corporate sponsors who subsidize many events. Increasingly, too, sports publicists work with marketing specialists to promote the sale of booster souvenirs and clothing, a lucrative sideline for teams.

Sports publicists use the normal tools of public relations—press kits, statistics, interviews, television appearances, and the like—to distribute information. But dealing with facts is only part of their role; they also try to stir emotions. For college publicists, this means creating enthusiasm among alumni and making the school glamorous and exciting in order to recruit high school students. Publicists for professional teams work to make them appear to be hometown representatives of civic pride, not merely athletes playing for high salaries.

Sometimes this effort succeeds spectacularly—if the team is a winner. When a team is an inept loser, however, the sports publicist's life turns grim. He or she must find ways to soothe public displeasure and, through methods such as having players conduct clinics at playgrounds and make sympathetic visits to hospitals, create a mood of patient hopefulness: "Wait 'til next year!"

Emerging sports increasingly compete for prominence and fan loyalty against other, more established sports. Soccer is widely popular among youth in America, leading to hopes among its promoters that the professional game will make inroads where traditional U.S. sports dominate. The Professional Golf Association (PGA) bought an 11-page advertising supplement in *Business Week* magazine to promote the professional golfer as a great athlete, philanthropic leader, and consummate professional in the face of rigorous travel and performance pressures.

Focus on Ethics

A Difficult Sports Secret

You are a sports information officer for a university whose high-scoring basketball team hopes to win the national championship. One late evening in the locker room you overhear two top players talking about how they shaved points in two recent games by intentionally missing free throws. Your team won the games, but by a smaller margin than the Las Vegas "oddsmakers" had predicted. Gamblers rewarded them with gifts of expensive sports cars, kept hidden at an off-campus location. You hear that the players are planning to shave points again in the early rounds of the tournament for hefty cash payments.

If you keep the cheating secret, the university might win the national title and obtain generous contributions from enthusiastic alumni. If you report your information to an academic or police authority, and a public gambling scandal occurs, the school will suffer disqualification, shame, and financial loss. You will be vilified by many in the university community for "blowing the whistle" when the outcome of games was never put in jeopardy by these players. You consider a constructive approach since your team did win the previous games. You could tell the players that you know about their scheme and demand that they play competitively from now on or you will report them to the NCAA.

If you don't report the circumstantial evidence you have, will you be guilty of unethical behavior?

What about criminal charges against you for aiding and abetting a criminal act?

If you do report the previous incident, what sort of crisis management approach would you develop?

Since the public yearns for heroes, publicists focus on building up the images of star players, sometimes to excess. They know that stars sell tickets. The 1998 baseball season featured record-breaking home run performances by both Mark McGwire and Sammy Sosa. The home-run race may not have been the sole attraction that saved baseball from doldrums attributed by many to the baseball strike and shortened season several years earlier. Nevertheless, the two sluggers are credited with bringing baseball "all the way back" as America's sport.

Because sports in America is big business, with $150 billion in gross annual revenue, an unseemly side frequently crops up in sports coverage. The impasse between players and owners in the National Basketball Association (NBA) was only the latest instance that caused fans to lose patience with both the wealthy owners and the highly paid players. A satirical chain letter swept across the Internet calling for donors to adopt an NBA player. This grassroots spoof of genuine giving programs for needy children included appeals for a mere $10,000 per month to defray the athlete's car payments or cover his "walking around" money for incidental spending.

Public relations plays a critical role in sports far beyond promotion of celebrities. Two important areas are sports crisis management and sponsorship management. According to John Eckel of Hill and Knowlton Sports, professional communicators must deal with the media focus on issues ranging from player strikes to high ticket and concession costs and

Athletic event sponsorship: Muhammad Ali uses the Olympic torch to ignite the Olympic flame, opening the 1996 games in Atlanta. Janet Evans, right, watches. The torch had been paraded across the United States by a series of runners to promote the games, under sponsorship of Coca-Cola.

boorish athletes who deny that they are role models while they benefit from their visibility as . . . role models.

Management of sports sponsorships has become systematic and deliberate. For example, Edelman Event and Sponsorship Marketing uses its "M.U.S.T.S. system" to evaluate sponsorships. The acronym means:

Media Appeal

User Friendliness

Sales Appeal

Thematic Applications

Special Event Potential

The advertising agency DDB Needham studied the effectiveness of a very high-profile sponsorship, the Summer Olympics. The agency found that the Olympic Games require a huge commitment of $40 million per sponsor plus extensive costs of marketing that sponsorship to the company's benefit in sales and goodwill. Only about half of sponsors successfully linked their names to the games. The agency recommends an integrated plan that uses the sponsorship as the focal point, but includes many opportunities for coverage.

The Olympic Games are subject to inevitable crises associated with what C. Richard Yarbrough, director of communication for the 1996 Atlanta Games, called "the world's largest special event." Salt Lake City was still enjoying the glow of its public relations coup associated with becoming host of the 2002 Winter Olympics when a major crisis broke in national news coverage. Scandalous charges of blackmail and bribery were leveled against the Salt Lake Committee, especially for providing International Olympic Committee (IOC) members and their families with scholarships meant as humanitarian aid to needy athletes. Salt Lake City officials rapidly investigated and then admitted that six relatives of IOC members had benefited from scholarship aid. Resignations of committee directors followed shortly.

TRAVEL PROMOTION

With money in their pockets, people want to go places and see things. Stimulating that desire and then turning it into the purchase of tickets and reservations is the goal of the travel industry. Public relations has an essential role in the process, not only in attracting visitors to destinations but in keeping them happy after they arrive.

Like entertainment and sports, travel draws from the public's recreation dollars. Often its promoters intertwine their projects with those of entertainment and sports entrepreneurs.

Phases of Travel Promotion

Traditionally the practice of travel public relations has involved three steps:

- Stimulating the public's desire to visit a place

- Arranging for the travelers to reach it

- Making certain that visitors are comfortable, well treated, and entertained when they get there

Recently, terrorist bombings have forced emphasis on a crucial new element:

- Protecting the travelers' safety

Stimulation is accomplished by travel articles in magazines and newspapers, alluring brochures distributed by travel agents and by direct mail, travel films and videos, and presentations on the World Wide Web. Solicitation of associations and companies to hold conventions in a given place encourages travel by groups.

Some publications have their own travel writers; others purchase freelance articles and pictures. Well-done articles by public relations practitioners about travel destinations often are published too, if written in an informational manner without resorting to blatant salesmanship and purple prose. Aware of public resistance to such exaggeration, *Condé Nast Traveler* magazine carries the slogan "Truth in Travel" on its cover. In fact, *O'Dwyer's PR Services Report* warns that "PR overkill" results from indiscriminate distribution of news releases, nagging follow-up calls to editors about releases, ignorance about the publication being pitched with a story, and excessive manipulation of the writer's itinerary on arranged trips so that the writer finds it difficult to get a complete picture of the travel destination.

Arrangements for travel are made through travel agencies or by direct booking at airlines, airports, and railroad and bus stations. Complicated tours and cruises are arranged most frequently by travel agencies, which charge customers retail prices for accommodations and receive a 10-percent commission from the travel supplier. Wholesalers create package tours that are sold by travel agencies.

To promote sales, the 38,000 U.S. travel agencies distribute literature, sponsor travel fairs, and encourage group travel by showing destination films at invitational meetings. Cities and states operate convention and travel departments to encourage tourism. A widely used method of promoting travel is the *familiarization trip,* commonly called a "fam trip," in which travel writers and/or travel salespeople are invited to a resort, theme park, or other destination for an inspection visit. Fam trips in the past often were loosely structured mass junkets. Today they are smaller and more focused.

Good treatment of travelers is a critical phase of travel promotion. If a couple spends a large sum on a trip, then encounters poor accommodations, rude hotel clerks, misplaced luggage, and inferior sightseeing arrangements, they come home angry. And they will tell their friends vehemently how bad the trip was.

Even the best arrangements go awry at times. Planes are late, tour members miss the bus, and bad weather riles tempers. This is where the personal touch means so much. An attentive, cheerful tour director or hotel manager can soothe guests, and a "make-good" gesture such as a free drink or meal does wonders. *Careful training of travel personnel is essential.* Many travelers, especially in foreign countries, are uneasy in strange surroundings and depend more on others than they would at home.

Fear of Terrorism

Two explosion tragedies in the United States within days in 1996 created an upsurge of fear and uncertainty about traveling. The midair explosion of TWA Flight 800 off Long Island killed 230 persons en route to Paris from New York, and a terrorist bomb that exploded in

How Many "Freebies" to Accept?

Creation of newspaper and magazine stories about travel destinations, so essential in tourism promotion, poses a problem for writers and public relations people. Who should pay the writer's expenses in researching them?

Some large newspapers forbid their travel writers to accept free or discounted hotel rooms, meals, and travel tickets. They believe that such subsidies may cause writers to slant their articles too favorably, perhaps subconsciously.

Many smaller publications and most freelance writers cannot afford such an expensive rule, however, and by following it would be unable to prepare travel articles. One freelance travel writer, Jeff Miller, took the publishing industry to task in *Editor & Publisher* magazine for paying $150 per newspaper story and $500 to $1000 per magazine story while banning writers from taking subsidized trips. Travel writers claim the hypocritical policy makes the publication look good, but has to be regularly ignored by travel writers who simply cannot make a living without subsidized trips. The writers contend that pride in their professional objectivity keeps them from being influenced by their hosts' "freebies." Some point to critical articles they have written on subsidized trips.

For the public relations director of a resort, cruise, or other travel attraction, the situation presents two problems: (1) How much hospitality can be given to the press before the "freebies" become a form of bribery? and (2) How does the director screen requests from self-described travel writers who request free housing or travel?

The Society of American Travel Writers (SATW) sets this guideline:

Free or reduced-rate transportation and other travel expenses must be offered and accepted only with the mutual understanding that reportorial research is involved and any resultant story will be reported with the same standards of journalistic accuracy as that of comparable coverage and criticism in theater, business and finance, music, sports, and other news sections that provide the public with objective and helpful information.

What do you think of the SATW guidelines? Are they specific enough to guide you in your public relations position for a gorgeous Caribbean resort? What of the "no sponsored trips" policy at some newspapers and magazines? Do you believe that heavily discounted trips tend to buy writer loyalty in the same way that free trips do?

the midst of an international crowd at the Olympic Games in Atlanta startled the world. Americans were shocked to realize how vulnerable their country was to terrorism. After the U.S. Embassy bombings in Kenya and Tanzania, they recognized, too, that they were especially vulnerable while traveling abroad.

Travel Business on the Internet Takes Off

Airline tickets, hotel accommodations, and travel packages can readily be shopped and then booked on the World Wide Web. Consumers have found the convenience and the discounted Internet specials to be highly attractive, resulting in an increase in online travel transactions from $275 million in 1996 to $2.1 billion in 1998. Websites such as *Travelocity.com* not only offer complete airline booking services but also provide e-mail notification to members of fare changes for itineraries selected by the online user. Airlines and hotels find that

An important tool in travel promotion is the familiarization trip, in which tour operators and travel writers are taken as guests to inspect a travel destination. Here, a group organized by the Daniel Edelman public relations firm samples a host resort's food.

last-minute inventory of seats or rooms can be sold effectively online. Because of such online commerce, hotels, resorts, and cruise lines can afford to mount extensive websites that provide outstanding information to consumers and journalists alike.

Appeals to Target Audiences

Travel promoters identify target audiences, creating special appeals and trips for them.

Britain's skillfully designed publicity in the United States is a successful example. Its basic appeal is an invitation to visit the country's historic places and pageants. It also offers London theatrical tours, golf expeditions to famous courses in Scotland, genealogical research parties seeking family roots, and tours of the cathedrals. Special groups can be arranged for other purposes as well.

"Packaging" is a key word in travel public relations. Cruises for family reunions or school groups, family skiing vacations, university alumni study groups, archeological expeditions, even trips to remote Tibet—these and other so-called niche travel packages are offered. A package usually consists of a prepaid arrangement for transportation, housing, most meals, and entertainment, with a professional escort to handle the details. Often supplementary side trips are offered for extra fees.

Appeal to Seniors   The biggest special travel audience of all is older citizens. Retired persons have time to travel, and many have ample money to do so. Hotels, motels, and airlines frequently offer discounts to attract them. As a means of keeping old-school loyalties alive, many colleges conduct alumni tours, heavily attended by senior citizens.

A large percentage of cruise passengers, especially on longer voyages, are retirees. Alert travel promoters design trips with them in mind, including such niceties as pairing compatible widows to share cabins and arranging trips ashore that require little walking. Shipboard entertainment and recreational activities with appeal to older persons—nostalgic music for dancing to rather than rock 'n' roll, for example—are important, too.

TIMES OF CRISIS

Public relations in travel requires crisis management, just as in corporate work. Crises come in many forms, from those of dangerous magnitude to the small but embarrassing varieties.

Ocean cruising, a major aspect of the travel industry, is highly competitive and requires intensive public relations effort. The arrival of the new *Grand Princess*, the world's largest cruise ship, in New York was greeted by a dockside party and heavy national television coverage. Porter Novelli, the public relations firm handling the event, reported that 42 TV crews and 15 radio reporters came aboard to describe the ship's features.

The spate of attacks against Florida tourists in the early 1990s led to one of the highest-stake crisis management efforts of all time. A multibillion-dollar source of revenue, Florida tourism suffered a deluge of damaging international publicity when nine foreign tourists were killed in separate incidents, mostly during robberies. Some victims were exchange students, while others were tourists gunned down only a few days after their arrival from abroad. Attempting to limit the damage, the Florida Division of Tourism sent faxes to 28,000 travel agents in North America, England, and Europe describing steps taken to help travelers and providing an 800 number for inquiries. Travel to Florida from Europe that winter decreased almost 50 percent from normal.

Florida's strenuous public relations efforts to repair the damage to its tourism have paid off. The U.S. Department of Commerce reported that in 1995 Florida played host to 5,346,000 overseas visitors, the most of any state. This total represented a 9-percent increase in one year.

Sometimes a crisis results from a fluke. The supersonic Concorde flew to Tucson, Arizona, to pick up about 100 tourists who had paid up to $12,000 each for a flight to England, five days in London, and a return cruise. As the Concorde was pulling out from the gate, a tow bar broke and a flying piece punctured two tires on the plane. Since the Concorde carried only one spare, a second tire had to be flown out from New York. During the anticipated wait of several hours, passengers were entertained by an impromptu champagne breakfast on the taxi strip. Then airline officials realized that because of the Tucson delay the Concorde could not make its necessary refueling stop in New York without violating that city's noise curfew law. The flight had to be postponed until the next day. Passengers who had expected to fly across the Atlantic at twice the speed of sound spent the night instead in a Tucson hotel and lost a day of their London visit.

CASE PROBLEM

Zimbabwe in southern Africa wants to attract more overseas visitors. Its tourism industry is well developed and the country has a number of attractions. Some of these include Victoria Falls, Hwange National Park, the ruins of Great Zimbabwe, the Eastern Highlands, and outstanding arts and crafts.

Your public relations firm is hired to create awareness of Zimbabwe as a desirable tourist destination in the American market. What key publics will you try to reach and how will you segment them? What communication strategies and messages will you utilize? What media will be most appropriate for your purposes?

QUESTIONS FOR REVIEW AND DISCUSSION

1. Why do public relations students need to understand how the personal publicity trade functions, even if they do not plan to handle theatrical or sports clients?

2. Which of the five motivating factors in the cult of personality (fame, notoriety, self-glorification, repair of bad image, desire for money) make most sense to you, and why?

3. Name two psychological factors underlying the American obsession with celebrities.

4. When politicians say something they wish they hadn't and it is published, they often claim that they were misquoted. Why is this poor policy?

5. What is the first step in preparing a campaign to increase the public's awareness of an individual client?

6. What is a "bio"? What should it contain?

7. "Cheesecake" photographs once were commonplace in American newspapers, but few are published now. Why is this so?

8. What do "planters" and "bookers" do?

9. Why do practitioners put emphasis on certain players on sports teams?

10. What are the basic phases of travel promotion?

The Internet and Other New Technologies

18

Preview

The objective of this chapter is to give students an understanding of the global communications explosion caused by development of new technologies and to describe how these can be used in public relations.

Topics covered in the chapter include:
- The interactive "information superhighway"
- The Internet
- Uses of the computer
- Facsimile transmission
- Satellite transmission
- Teleconferencing
- Software and other electronic tools

THE COMMUNICATIONS EXPLOSION

The explosive growth of the Internet during the 1990s has created a form of mass communications unlike all others. In 1990 the Internet merely exchanged scientific information. Today a household word, the Internet has become a global communications tool for millions of people. According to a study commissioned by *PR Reporter* in 1998, use of the new technology is the leading trend in public relations.

Internet users exchange messages around the world electronically. They "surf" the Internet, tapping the masses of information and entertainment that the interlocking system of computer networks offers, virtually unconstrained by time and space. Through the Internet's World Wide Web, thousands of companies, organizations, other media, and individuals tell the world about themselves, sell their wares, and promote their ideas. By posting *pages* of printed words, graphics, photographs, and sounds, these cyberspace hosts communicate with millions of "netizens" worldwide. According to Angus Reid Group, a Canadian market research firm, "Global usage of the internet is well on its way to reaching 1 billion users by 2005."

The Internet is the most intriguing of the new electronic methods that are changing mass communications in general and providing public relations practice with innovative tools.

Familiar Systems Merging

Three familiar methods of communication—telephone, television, and the computer—are blended together in new forms of transmission such as the much-publicized *information superhighway.* A fundamental fact is that a large portion of the emerging services is interactive—that is, two-way. Instead of depending on the programs television networks and cable systems provide, for example, viewers can order pay-per-view movies onto their screens, or move seamlessly between TV programming and high-speed Internet access on their television sets. Among the goals of engineers and scientists, on which huge corporations are risking billions of dollars, are 500 or more TV channels, delivery of cable TV programs to homes by telephone companies, and videophones.

Much of the world's communication today flashes upward through satellite dishes like these, bounces from transponders on satellites, and is caught by dishes at receiving points on earth.

Two key factors in this electronic outburst are:

- Use of fiber-optic cable—multiple strands of glass thinner than hairs—in place of the traditional copper cable. This tremendously increases transmission volume and speed. The GTE Corporation reports that one of its fiberglass cables could transmit a 500-page novel in slightly more than two seconds.

- Digital transmission of sounds and pictures; that is, transmission of messages in code numbers that are reconstructed at the receiving end into words and pictures. Digitalization will vastly improve TV reception through development of high-definition television (HDTV), now emerging from the experimental stage.

The enormous cost of development and construction has delayed general use of some electronic applications, but each year additional ones reach consumers.

In this chapter we shall explain how the principal new technologies can be applied to accomplish public relations objectives.

THE COMPUTER

For public relations practitioners, the computer serves many purposes. It handles office procedures faster and more extensively than the old do-it-by-hand methods. As a research tool, it makes an immense amount of information easily accessible. Through electronic mail and "chat" forums, it provides a stimulating exchange of ideas.

Even more intriguing, the personal computer is the vehicle that can carry the practitioner into the maze of the Internet.

Each commercial online service contains masses of stored information: news reports, complete texts of major newspapers and magazines for years back, encyclopedias, government records, texts of books, and more. They provide rich sources for public relations researchers. (See Chapter 6, "Research.")

The step beyond these services is the Internet itself.

THE INTERNET

Created in the late 1960s by researchers who found how to link computers in separate cities, the Internet first functioned as an academic-government tool. It came into public use in the early 1990s; tie-ins developed between the American system and those in more than 150 other countries. Communication occurred by typing words on the computer screen through e-mail, newsgroups, and special-interest discussion forums.

An upsurge in Internet use developed with the creation of graphics and sound on the World Wide Web portion of the Internet. Aware of the Web's commercial possibilities but not quite sure how to exploit them, hundreds of companies established *sites* on the Web. A site consists of one or more pages, the first of which is the home page. A searcher enters the home page by using its code name of letters, figures, and punctuation marks. An effective home page is a colorful mixture of text and graphics on which the sponsoring organization introduces itself. The Internet has no official central control headquarters, so obtaining valid statistics on use of the global system is difficult.

The number of "hits" for each page can be determined; that is, the number of times users enter the page. Since many hits are by "surfers" hunting around to see what they can find, this figure is of limited commercial value. Figures for hits can be wildly inflated because complex pages may generate hits for each major component of the page rather than one hit per page. Furthermore, each time a user returns to a page during a visit, another hit is recorded. Several organizations, including the Audit Bureau of Circulation (ABC), are working on more sophisticated tracking methods that count the number of visitors to a site.

The worldwide total of computer owners having access to the Internet, and using it, can only be estimated. A Nielsen Media Research 1999 study estimated that there were approximately 101 million Internet users, but the number grows every month.

The Internet and Public Relations

The Internet gives public relations practitioners a many-faceted form of worldwide communication, primarily involving message exchange by e-mail; information delivery and persuasion by its World Wide Web, and research.

These are the primary *Internet* uses:

- **E-mail distribution.** This electronic mail includes messages to individuals, newsletters to staff members, transmission of news releases and "pitch" letters to media offices, and

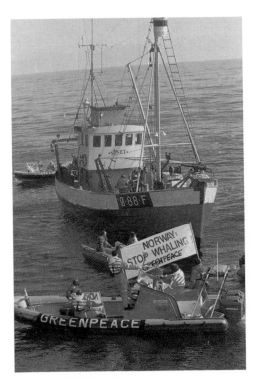

Greenpeace, the activist environmentalist organization, uses its website to publicize its confrontations at sea with vessels whose work it opposes. Here, a Greenpeace ship tries to block passage of a Norwegian whaling vessel. The website carries news reports and background information from the Greenpeace point of view.

dispatch and receipt of copy between public relations firms and clients. Many e-mail systems now accept hypertext e-mail that presents images in full color when the e-mail is opened. Professional Training Associates, a newsletter publisher, was able to send its direct mail postcard on the Internet to selected editors and reporters. The postcard announced a new website titled *Hard@Work* with a whimsical shot of the publisher and editor perched on a rock in the middle of a stream.

- **World Wide Web sites.** These sites provide a way for organizations to tell Internet users what they do, publicize projects, and advocate policies. Edelman Public Relations Worldwide, for example, provides information about its clients. Ketchum Public Relations offers recipes from its food product clients.

- **Brochureware.** Although this term is used ironically by those who envision websites as a unique new channel, much of the content on websites is little more than an online version of the brochures and collateral materials that organizations provide to stakeholders. Over time, interactivity and video clips will distinguish brochureware from its print predecessor. Public relations professionals should capitalize on such characteristics.

- **Usenet discussion groups.** Individuals concerned with a certain issue discuss it by making comments and reading the responses of other participants. Sometimes this exchange is called an *electronic bulletin board*. Usenet groups also are used for audience research, in which a participant requests opinions and facts. An estimated 10,000 such groups operate.

- **Listservs;** such as PRFORUM, offer a similar interactive and dynamic opportunity for public relations professionals to query members on the discussion list. A participant must enroll with the list manager, thereby gaining access to the discussions.

An example of how public relations firms use the Internet is this home page of Edelman Public Relations Worldwide, offering a variety of information.

Here are specific examples of how the Internet is used in public relations practice:

- Firms not only pitch stories to journalists via e-mail, but also respond rapidly to stories.

- Organizations increasingly set up websites to serve informational needs of reporters, especially during a crisis or a breaking news situation. The Starr Report of the investigation of President Clinton's affair with Monica Lewinsky was released to the Web for wide and immediate dissemination. News organizations then made it available on their own websites, where an estimated 24.7 million people read parts of it in a matter of days.

- Xerox's Web PR website offers answers to any question—any question at all. In response to an online question, the offbeat site reported its calculation that it would require 33,661 years to vacuum the state of Ohio! Publicity in People magazine and various TV news features resulted.

- LifeSavers, like many websites, offers free online games that attract users to the website, where they are exposed to the LifeSaver brand. Sweepstakes serve a similar role of attracting traffic to websites.

- Companies such as Boeing and Compaq have used webcasting to increase coverage of important news conferences by broadcasting video footage over the Web via Medialink's website, *NewStream.com.*

- At least 400 health care organizations and companies use their websites to distribute medical information. Two examples are: (1) the American Medical Association, which provides information for physicians and patients about treatments, medical developments, and other health care news and (2) the National Alliance of Breast Cancer Organizations (NABCO), which provides current information about breast cancer research and treatment, events, and links to Internet sites.

- The United Nations High Commissioner for Refugees conducts a website to increase public awareness of the global refugee problem. It provides maps, photographs, and news about people who have left their homes to escape war and persecution.

Key Aspects of the Internet

Public relations professionals should keep in mind these important facts about the Internet:

1. Its reach is worldwide. A message intended for local or regional use may draw reactions, good or bad, from unexpected places.

2. The content of the Internet is virtually uncontrolled. Anyone can say or show anything without passing it through "gatekeepers," the editors and producers who approve the material that reaches the public through commercial channels. Lack of editorial control permits unfettered freedom of speech but also permits distribution of unconfirmed, slanted, or erroneous information.

The potential for damage resulting from unconfirmed information on the Internet was demonstrated by Pierre Salinger, press secretary for President John F. Kennedy and retired ABC television correspondent. He received worldwide attention with an announcement in France that he had obtained a security document confirming that TWA Flight 800, which exploded off Long Island with 230 deaths in 1996, had been shot down accidentally by a

U.S. Navy missile. In fact, his source was a bogus story, previously discredited, that someone had circulated on the Internet.

Public Relations Tactics, published by the Public Relations Society of America, welcomes this freedom from editorial control. In its March 1996 issue about the World Wide Web, it asserts: "PR pros can now get messages out without passing them through the filter of editors and journalists. Traditional media gatekeepers have lost their power in today's point-and-click world."

3. Issue-tracking can be more thorough using the Internet, and far more immediate. Services such as NewsEdge monitor Web-based news and wire services and alert users when relevant topics appear in Internet news sources. By monitoring the Internet, practitioners can keep track of what competitors, opponents, and the public are saying. Thus informed, they can better shape their own tactics and messages as well as respond in *real time* to forestall erroneous or unbalanced stories from gaining momentum without correction A PRNewswire executive recalled how a story released by his service at 7:30 a.m. prompted an e-mail response by a public relations person. The result was a factually corrected release on PRNewswire by 7:35.

Internet Problems

The global spiderweb of interlocking computer networks has problems, along with its manifest benefits. The following should be kept in mind as users plan Internet communication programs:

- The difficulty in finding the information they desire through the complexities of the system frustrates some users.

- Controversial problems of security and legal questions of copyright infringement, libel, invasion of privacy, and pornography remain unsolved.

In sum, the Internet is a still-developing form of mass communication that fascinates participants but must pass through a trial-and-error period before its effectiveness as a public relations tool can be fully determined.

OTHER COMPUTER USES

Among the most valuable uses of the computer:

Word Processing

In the computer's function as a word processor, its two principal values are: (1) the capacity to store created material in its memory system for instant recall, and (2) the ability to make corrections, insert fresh material, and move material from one portion of a document to another. Ingenious software programs used in the computer greatly enhance the range of services it provides writers.

Dictation and Voice Generation Most computers being sold today have the memory and processing speed needed to recognize human speech. Software called Via Voice not only recognizes the user's speech, but improves its accuracy by taking into account corrections the user makes in the dictated text on the computer screen. The program becomes more accurate in converting speech to word processing, presentation, Web, database or spreadsheet content. Computer commands may also be spoken, including the command "Read Text," which prompts the computer to generate speech by reading the written text to the user.

Processing of News Releases   Word processing is valuable in preparation of news releases. Like letters, releases can be reworded by computer for different types of publications, such as trade magazines, daily newspapers, and the business press. The draft of a news release can be placed in computer storage while the client makes revisions on a printout copy. Also, the draft of a news release can be entered in storage by its writer and later called up on another screen by the supervisor for review.

Correction of Spelling and Grammar   Special software programs—sets of instructions telling the computer what to do—can improve the public relations writer's work by correcting spelling and grammatical mistakes. Some programs contain a dictionary of more than 100,000 words and a thesaurus of more than 10,000 words. They detect errors and suggest more appropriate words.

Electronic Mail   When a writer creates copy for a brochure, the edited text can be recorded on a disk for delivery to the printing company. Or, if the printing company has suitable computer connections, the brochure copy can be transmitted electronically from the writer's computer into the printing company's computer. No paper is used. That computer in turn can feed the copy into a phototypesetting system, from which it will emerge as type on paper ready to be reproduced, with headlines included. The frequent collaboration of public relations professionals with clients and colleagues has been greatly enhanced through the sharing of draft documents via e-mail. When compatible word processing, graphics, or desktop publishing software is used by both parties, documents attached to e-mail can be opened, edited, and returned, even when one person uses Mac and the other is on a Windows machine.

Desktop Publishing

Recent advances in computer techniques make possible the creation of professional-looking newsletters and graphically illustrated material on a personal computer right in the office. This is known as desktop publishing.

Desktop publishing allows the public relations writer and editor to design and lay out reports, newsletters, brochures, and presentations by manipulating copy and graphics directly onto a computer screen instead of on a drawing board. It produces camera-ready pages for offset printing.

Desktop publishing saves cost and time. Less than $5000 will buy all the components necessary for producing high-quality newsletters and graphics: a personal computer, a word-processing program, a graphics program, page-making software, and a laser printer. Producing camera-ready materials in-house reduces the fuss and expense of involving a commercial printer.

Mailing Lists

Up-to-date mailing lists are vital in public relations work. Lists of names are typed into a computer and stored in its memory. Changes of address or other alterations can be made by calling up a name and using a few keystrokes. When a mailing is to be made, the desired names on the master list can be activated and printed on adhesive labels or on the individual envelopes.

The capability to select groups of names from the master list assists the practitioner in reaching target audiences. For example, when introducing its new models, Ford sought to generate ample publicity for more than 2000 of its dealers located in primarily rural areas. As reported in *Public Relations Journal,* the automaker created a computer file on each dealer, including address, phone number, and name of local spokesperson. By combining this file with its standard news release, Ford created 9600 customized releases. Every release mentioned a local dealer by name. These were sent to carefully culled mailing lists within the dealer's territory.

Public relations departments and firms may compile their own computer lists of media contacts or purchase standard diskettes from press-directory companies such as *Bacon's Media Source Software,* which lists mail, e-mail, and phone data for nearly 30,000 editors.

Lists of Contacts   In a related application, public relations offices use the storage and call-up facilities of computers to maintain ready-reference lists of individuals with their telephone numbers and addresses, job titles, and other personal data, which can be listed by category.

Online Conferences

When two or more persons tie their computers together by telephone line, they can hold discussions by exchanging a series of typed messages. In order to do so, their computers must be equipped with a *modem* (short for *modulator/demodulator*) or a connection to a local network such as a university computer network; this converts the computer's electronic signals into signals that can move along the phone line. While two computers can communicate in this fashion, any number of participants may join the conversation in private chat rooms.

Online conferences are increasingly valuable in public relations work. Practitioners "converse" with clients and suppliers or participate in forums on professional matters with groups of their peers. The text of what has been said can be retained for the record in computer storage or typed out by a hard-copy printer.

Because of their mobility—some are even palm-sized—properly equipped personal computers can be used in out-of-office situations, such as while traveling.

Graphics

Use of computers to design for publications eye-catching colored graphics—drawings, graphs and charts, and text—has emerged as a new technology in public relations practice. Recent developments in computer software make such graphics possible.

Attractive graphics give visual impact to annual reports and employee publications, as well as to video programs and slide presentations. Imaginative visual effects may be obtained

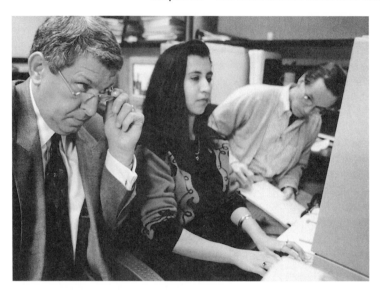

Jerry Colangelo, president of the Phoenix Suns, explains to questioners nationwide on an American Online computer interview why he fired the coach of that National Basketball Association team. He is assisted by online operator Suzanne Lopez while Phoenix *Republic* reporter Chris Cobbs takes notes. Such online interviews are becoming a frequently used public relations method.

with only a modest investment of time and money. Slide presentations in particular can be enhanced dramatically with computer-generated graphics.

Facsimile Transmission

An invaluable tool in public relations practice is facsimile transmission, commonly called *fax.* Such frequently heard remarks as "I'll fax it to you" have added a new verb to the language.

Facsimile transmission moves an exact copy of printed matter and graphics by telephone circuit from a machine or computer in one office to one in another office, across town, or the other side of the world. A news release, a draft of a client's newsletter, instructions from headquarters to a branch office—these are merely three among scores of ways in which practitioners use fax. Office workers even fax their lunch orders to nearby restaurants.

By using *broadcast fax,* a sender can transmit a single document to hundreds of recipients simultaneously. A corporation, for example, can distribute a news release swiftly and equally to competing news media. In another application, a customer can call a major vendor such as PR Newswire and Business Wire by a toll-free 800 number, request information, and receive it by fax within minutes.

A word of caution: Discretion should be used in sending news releases to editors by facsimile. Send only those you consider to be truly important and urgent. Editors complain, often quite sharply, about the amount of "junk fax" they receive. They say that the inpouring of materials useless to them, including advertisements and irrelevant announcements, ties up their machines and may delay delivery of important news material. Some states have enacted laws restricting distribution of unsolicited fax items.

Increasingly, the lines between fax and e-mail have blurred. It is now possible to use services that will convert an e-mail message into a broadcast fax delivered to the physical fax machines of the target public.

SATELLITE TRANSMISSION

Text messages and pictures can be flashed around the world in seconds by using satellite transmission, a fact of enormous significance to public relations communicators.

Satellite transmission on a reliable 24-hour basis became possible when a satellite was shot aloft to the altitude of 22,300 miles above the equator. There a satellite has an orbital period of 24 hours. It thus remains stationary above a fixed point on the earth's surface, available for relaying back to receiving dishes on the earth the transmissions beamed up to it from originating points on the ground. A constantly growing number of satellites are being parked above the equator in what scientists call the *geostationary belt.*

When information is dispatched by computer through a ground "uplink" station to a transponder pad on a satellite, then bounced back to a receiving dish on the ground and into a receiving computer, enormous amounts of material can be transmitted. One computer can "talk" to another via satellite about 160 times faster than can be done over land lines, and at much lower cost.

The *Wall Street Journal,* New York *Times,* and *USA Today* use satellites to transmit entire page layouts to regional printing plants. The Associated Press, United Press International, and other news services transmit their stories and pictures by satellite. The television and radio networks deliver programs in the same manner.

News Release Delivery

More than a dozen American companies deliver news releases electronically to large newspapers and other major news media offices. In the receiving newsrooms these releases are fed into computers, to be examined by editors on video display terminals.

The difference between news release delivery firms and the traditional news services such as the Associated Press is this: newspapers, radio, and television stations pay large fees to receive the reports of the news services, which maintain staffs of editors and reporters to gather, analyze, select, and write the news in a neutral style. On the other hand, the news release delivery companies are paid by creators of news releases to distribute those releases to the media, which pay nothing to receive them. These delivery services are prepaid transmission belts, not selectors of material. They do enforce editing standards and occasionally reject releases as unsuitable.

One of the largest news release companies is Business Wire. Using electronic circuits and satellite communications, the company can simultaneously reach more than 1600 media points in the United States and Canada and more than 500 in Europe, Latin America, East Asia, and Australia. In addition, Business Wire provides rapid dissemination of financial news releases to more than 600 securities and investment community firms worldwide.

Electronically delivered news releases have an advantage over the conventional variety—releases transmitted by satellite tend to receive closer, faster attention from media editors than those arriving by mail.

Another large news release delivery company, PR Newswire, was the first to distribute its releases by satellite. PR Newswire's computers distribute releases and official statements from more than 7500 organizations directly into the newsroom computers of the media.

Video and Audio News Release Distribution

Transmission by satellite also makes possible fast distribution of video news releases (VNRs). The picture-and-voice releases are sent primarily to cable television networks, local cable systems, and local television stations. Nearly 30 companies produce and distribute hundreds of video news releases for clients. Only relatively few of the most newsworthy, technically superior VNRs succeed in obtaining airtime. (See Chapter 23 for a discussion of video news releases.) Successful VNRs usually feature video footage that would be difficult for a station to obtain, as in these examples:

- A VNR sponsored by OshKosh B'Gosh bib overalls quotes the winner of its Search for the Oldest Bib Overall contest, 89-year-old Claude Mehder, who owns a pair of circa-1901 bibs: "We'll keep having kids, as long as the bib overalls hold up."

- Ringling Brothers & Barnum & Bailey Circus clowns helped *PC Computing* magazine conduct the Notebook Torture Test of laptop computers.

- "The Car of the Future", a VNR distributed by D.S. Simon Productions, included DVD video screens, on-board message systems, global positioning, and a home security monitor.

Global Transmission of Messages

Still another use of satellite communication is found in *global electronic mail.* For example, Apple Computer of California regularly communicates with its foreign offices through a dedicated, private e-mail system. A public relations manager using an Apple computer in California can send a message anywhere in the world within seconds.

Some American corporations send facsimile pages of annual reports by satellite to printing firms in Japan and Korea. These corporations find that the cost of overseas transmission, printing, and air shipment back to the United States is lower than if the printing were done by American companies.

Teleconferencing

The most spectacular use of satellite transmission for public relations purposes is *teleconferencing,* also called *videoconferencing.* Through it, groups of conferees separated by thousands of miles can interact instantaneously with strong visual impact.

Use of this technique is growing rapidly. Around the United States some 20,000 sites have been equipped to handle such events. A traditional conference consists of a group of men and women assembled at a central location for discussion, exchange of information, and inspiration. Participants frequently come from distant points. Their travel costs and hotel bills are often high, they may be plagued by the nuisances of flight reservations and connections, and they may be away from their offices for days.

Satellite-relayed television has changed this concept radically. Now the conferees can remain at their home offices, or gather in groups in nearby cities, and hold their conferences by television. Travel time and cost are reduced or eliminated. In one five-year period, the

Boeing Company used teleconferencing for 5699 meetings and eliminated the need for more than 1.5 million miles of travel.

Long-distance discussions among widely separated groups began in the 1930s when the telephone company created conference calls that enabled three or more parties to talk among themselves. Satellites and fiber optics have dropped transmission costs to several hundred dollars per hour, and a company can easily arrange a teleconference by employing a firm that specializes in this form of communication.

The most widely used form of teleconferencing blends one-way video and two-way audio. This one-way video technology, a form of direct broadcast satellite (DBS), broadcasts a live presentation to many locations simultaneously. DBS is the least expensive method because cameras, transmitters, and other expensive equipment are needed only at one end. The video signal can be received by small, relatively inexpensive antennas at locations around the world via satellite. Figure 20.1 shows, in schematic form, how the satellite transmission works.

Guests at receiving locations view the presentation on large screens. Regular telephone circuits back to the point of origin enable the guests to ask follow-up questions. Teleconferencing also has great potential for employee relations. Ford Motor Company, for example, has installed a $10 million system connecting more than 200 Ford locations in North America. Other companies have similar systems.

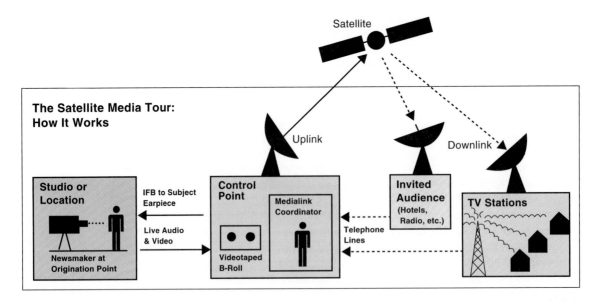

Figure 20.1

This graph explains how a satellite media tour is conducted, enabling the person being interviewed to remain in one place while appearing on screens in other cities.

Source: Media Link, Inc. *

Here are examples of teleconferencing in operation:

* The Whirlpool Corporation in the United States and an N.V. Philips division in the Netherlands needed to explain their new $2-billion joint-venture agreement. So they held an international teleconference for their respective stockholders and employees, the media, and financial analysts.

* Hill and Knowlton, on behalf of several government agencies, arranged a two-hour conference between Cairo, Egypt, and five U.S. cities that permitted several hundred U.S. investors to talk directly with high-ranking Egyptian officials about private investment in that nation.

A more economical system is the "slow scan" conference. This provides for transmission of still pictures or slides over a telephone circuit between conference points, with voice transmission over a separate line.

Those who use teleconferencing emphasize that it is most effective for reaching large audiences for such purposes as introduction of a product, sales meetings, and announcement of new corporate policies. It lacks the personal warmth that comes from a handshake and a face-to-face conversation.

Webconferencing   Although in its infancy, the Web has become a less expensive alternative for videoconferencing. Called "see-you-see-me" or CUCME technology, cameras and microphones mounted on the computer monitors of two users enable them to engage in an Internet version of videophone. One of the authors of this text participated in a student's defense of his master's thesis using Microsoft Netshow. Audio was carried by telephone with video displayed on the computer screen via the Web. A 15-second delay in video feed and the student's preference for the comfort and support of a human presence suggest that such conferencing requires further development.

Satellite Media Tours   Instead of having a personality—an actor or author, for example—criss-cross the country on an expensive, time-consuming promotional tour, public relations sponsors increasingly use the so-called satellite tour.

The personality is stationed in a television studio, and TV reporters interview him or her by satellite from their home studios. Two-way television is used, permitting a visual dialogue. Each station's reporter is put through to the personality at a specified time; thus a series of interviews, five to 10 minutes each, can be done in sequence. Corporations also employ satellite media tours to promote their products or services, using a well-known performer or other "name" figure as spokesperson.

Before his paralyzing spinal injury, actor Christopher Reeve set an endurance record by doing 45 consecutive interviews at one sitting. Tiresome mentally and physically, no doubt, but much faster and cheaper than visiting all those cities!

OTHER TOOLS

Numerous other tools created through electronic technology also are used regularly in public relations practice. New instruments based on digital transmission appear frequently.

Hewlett-Packard Leads in Video Communication

Hewlett-Packard, headquartered in Palo Alto, California, spends more than $20 million annually on video communications and produces some of the nation's most sophisticated business television.

The company began live, interactive broadcasts in 1981, using a transmitter to reach more than 80 plant and sales sites nationwide. This enabled an executive to address many audiences simultaneously. By 1996, HP had 127 sites linked to its video communications network, including several in Canada, South America, and Europe.

HP also has 48 teleconference rooms at 44 locations in the United States, Europe, and Asia. These facilities allow participants to hold meetings with people in as many as eight locations. Two-way audio and video allows a truly interactive meeting format; participants can also share information, including files and graphics, on personal computers.

HP is developing a desktop interactive multimedia network so that employees will eventually be able to view live videos on their personal computers, including the company president's semi-annual address. "Until the majority of employees can view video on their PCs or workstations, I don't think business television is going to advance much," said Mary Anne Easley, manager of HP's employee communications.

To communicate with employees, HP also produces a high-quality video magazine. Released four times a year at a cost of $50,000 an issue, it is formatted after television's "evening magazine." According to Easley, "Television is an effective medium for reaching the baby boomers—the production and clerical workers."

The CD-ROM

The CD-ROM (Compact Disc-Read Only Memory) is the multimedia version of the familiar compact disc that plays music, but it can contain video, audio, and text on the same surface. With an enormous capacity, the CD-ROM can display up to 300,000 pages of text, color pictures, and graphics.

As an example of the CD-ROM's potential, Yale University Press issued a disk called Perseus for use in teaching Greek language and history. The disc has 25 volumes of Greek text with English translation, a 35,000-word Greek dictionary, and 6000 photos and drawings of architectural sites and artifacts. In Norway, a public health effort to enhance appropriate interaction and respect between boys and girls was modeled in a computer game distributed on CD-ROM.

Computer Disks

One digital form of the informational brochure is the computer disk, which a person "reads" on a personal computer. Buick, for example, mailed 20,000 disks to users of Apple personal computers to tell them about its new models.

Breakthroughs in software design made it possible for recipients of the Buick disk to "interact" with the information presented. By pushing a few buttons, computer users could load the trunk with luggage and ask questions about mileage, standard equipment, and how the Buick compared with other auto makes.

A "press disk," the computer disk or CD version of a press kit, is increasingly used by reporters. A more efficient use of the disk technique is distribution to targeted audiences that seek information, such as stockholders in corporations that distribute their annual reports on diskettes. As these reports grow in graphic splendor, memory demands outstrip ordinary disk capacity. Superdisks enable multimedia presentation of extensive content. The Zip disk has become common "coinage" in public relations firms for the transfer of Web pages, graphics, and entire publications among account or project team members.

Electronic Blackboards

Blackboards with chalk now belong to the past as companies begin to use "whiteboards," which serve the same function as facsimile machines. A person can write on a whiteboard with a liquid marker during a presentation, and the image is electronically scanned to allow a printer rapidly to produce multiple copies of the image for future reference.

CASE PROBLEM

Ashland Community Hospital is deeply involved in health education as part of its approach to preventive care. In the past, the hospital has distributed leaflets about various diseases and conducted community seminars on such topics as how to stop smoking, the importance of physical fitness, and how to detect early signs of cancer.

The new technologies, however, now enable the hospital to expand its potential in health education. Write a proposal on how the hospital would use the Internet, the World Wide Web, e-mail, CD-ROM, fax, and diskettes to disseminate health care information to the community.

QUESTIONS FOR REVIEW AND DISCUSSION

1. What part of the Internet has "home pages," and what does that term mean?

2. What is the "information superhighway," and what are some of its uses?

3. Define such terms as *electronic mail, direct broadcast system (DBS), interactive video, desktop publishing, modem, database, teleconference, slow scan,* and *CD-ROM.*

4. Satellites are placed in geostationary orbit. What does that mean?

5. What is the difference between a news release delivery system such as Business Wire and a news service such as the Associated Press?

6. Teleconferencing is growing in popularity. Explain how it operates.

7. Authors frequently make satellite media tours. How do they work and why do authors prefer them to traditional book promotion tours?

8. What are some of the ways Hewlett-Packard uses its video communication system?

9. As a public relations practitioner, how might you use online computer conference calls?

10. Why is transmitting signals by fiber optics superior to sending them over an ordinary telephone line?

Written Tactics

19

Preview

The objective of this chapter is to show students how to write news releases and to understand the preparation and purpose of other written tools of public relations, including the annual report.

Topics covered in the chapter include:
- News releases: their content and distribution
- Newsletters
- Company periodicals
- Brochures and handbooks
- Annual reports
- Corporate advertising

THE NEWS RELEASE

Basically, a *news release* is a simple document whose purpose is the dissemination of information in ready-to-publish form. Editors of print and broadcast media to whom news releases are sent judge them on the basis of news interest for their audience, timeliness, and in some instances their adaptability to the medium's form. No payment is made to the publication or station if the material appears in print or on the air. If an organization or individual purchases space in a publication to present its material, this is a paid advertisement and the purchaser controls the content.

Releases should be prepared so that the media can relay their news content to audiences easily with confidence in their accuracy. Editors want the main facts stated succinctly in the opening paragraph of a release, for quick recognition. A news release is a purveyor of information, not an exercise in writing style, except in those cases of longer releases that are clearly intended to be feature stories. The writer of a basic news release should leave the clever writing to staff members of the media.

A news release faces intense competition when it arrives on an editor's desk, against scores or even hundreds of other releases. As they scan the releases, editors make almost instant decisions, assigning each release to one of three categories:

1. *Obvious news.* Copy that is certain to be used.

2. *Maybe.* Stories possibly worth developing if a reporter has the time. A sharp news angle in a release may put it in the "obvious news" category instead of the risky "maybe" pile. Potentially good stories placed in the "maybe" pile face the danger of being thrown away after a second reading if the key information is poorly developed.

3. *Discard.* Releases of insufficient interest to the receiving editor's audience and those of marginal value that would require too much effort to develop. These go into the recycling box or the wastebasket.

News releases that are prepared according to the criteria described in the following sections have the best chance of being accepted for publication, assuming that their content is newsworthy.

Physical Appearance

There is a standard format for news releases:

- Use plain white 8 ½-by-11-inch paper.

- Identify the sender in the upper-left-hand corner of the page, listing name, address, and telephone number. Many releases also include a fax number and an e-mail address. Especially if the sender is a large organization, also give the name of an individual within the organization as a point of contact. It is important that the listed phone be answered by an informed person, usually a public relations specialist, not by a recording.

- Below the identification state *For Immediate Release* if the material is intended for immediate publication, as most news releases are. If a time restriction is necessary, as with an advance copy of a speech to be delivered at a specified hour, indicate the desired publication time; for example, *For Release at 6 p.m. EST Feb. 12.* This is called an *embargo*. Media recipients of embargoed material have no legal obligation to obey its restrictions, but they normally do so out of courtesy and mutual convenience unless they believe that the embargo is an obvious effort to manipulate the news. Embargoes should be used only when genuinely necessary.

- Leave 2 inches of space for editing convenience before starting the text.

- Start the text with a clearly stated summary lead containing timely, relevant, important information.

- Leave at least a 1.5-inch margin. Double-space the copy to give editors room in which to edit the material.

- Never split a paragraph from one page to the next. Put (*more*) at the bottom of each unfinished page.

- Place an identifying slugline and page number at the top of each page after the first.

Some public relations practitioners place a summary headline above the text to tell an editor quickly what the release contains.

Content

There are a few essential rules for content:

- Begin the news release with a tightly written summary lead and state the fundamentals—who, what, when, where, and why—early in the copy. The first sentence should state the most important point in the story. *Do not bury the lead.* The opening paragraph should be three to five lines maximum.

- Be concise. Edit the copy to remove excess words and "puff" terminology. A competent editor would cut them out, anyway. Few news releases need to be more than two pages long; most can be written in a single page. A reporter may obtain additional details by telephoning numbers listed or by sending an e-mail. Reporters also routinely access the organization's website for additional background information.

- Caution: avoid clichés and fancy phrases. When editors receive a news release using such terms as "unique," "revolutionary," and "state-of-the-art," they are likely to throw it away.

- Never use excessively technical language in a release for a general audience. The objective is communication, not confusion.

- Be absolutely certain that every fact and title in the release is correct and that every name is spelled properly. Check the copy closely for grammatical errors. Errors can be embarrassing and costly. In a news release announcing a Mexican cruise, distributed nationally, Cunard Lines mistakenly listed the 800 telephone number of a San Francisco optical company instead of its own. The optical company received more than two thousand calls in the first week; its phone lines were tied up and it had to assign personnel to redirect the calls. Cunard compensated for its blunder by giving the optical proprietor and his wife a free cruise to Europe.

For protection against errors and misunderstandings, a public relations counselor is wise to have the client initial a file copy of each news release before its distribution. In company public relations departments, similar initialing by a superior is desirable and in some cases mandatory. Corporate review can become excessive, however. Writing in *Editor & Publisher,* Ron Cantera, a former public relations executive who became a journalism professor, reported: "In one corporate job I held, my news releases were reviewed by at least six different insiders—my boss, his boss, a product manager, the marketing vice president, an agency copyreader and, believe it or not, a word-processing supervisor . . . that led to communication by committee."

Those who issue news releases should welcome follow-up inquiries from reporters and be able to provide additional information. Often reporters complain that the public relations personnel aren't available or don't promptly return phone calls.

To counter this complaint, many public relations people make it a point on news releases to list contact numbers that are direct lines to a real person instead of voicemail or an answering machine. In addition, many practitioners provide cellular and home phone numbers so that they can be reached after regular business hours.

When a story is controversial, and the organization or individual issuing the news release is in a defensive position, this openness sometimes diminishes or even vanishes. The attitude of some upper-management executives toward the media in controversial situations is, "Tell them only what we want the public to know. Let them find out the rest for themselves, if they can." This attitude on the part of management may persist to the point of having the public relations department omit relatively simple information.

Citing "company policy," Quadrex Corporation refused to answer press inquiries about how many people were being laid off. An editorial in the local newspaper called the company to task. It said, in part: "A public company should be relatively open. There is no reason or excuse—except short-term stonewalling to harbor the company's stock from truth—to withhold such information as the number of persons in a layoff. . . . In the long run, Quadrex would generate a better public image by disclosing rather than withholding information."

This management attitude of playing it close to the vest is a source of mistrust among the media toward companies that follow the practice. A survey by a unit of the J. Walter Thompson advertising agency showed that 55 percent of the business editors who responded criticized corporate press releases for burying important information.

Gradually, many firms are adopting a more forthright approach. A company has no reason to wash its dirty linen in public in a voluntary outburst of confession. Yet greater frankness in news releases and willingness to volunteer answers to reasonable questions that good reporters will ask anyway help to build a company's credibility. Professors Glen T. Cameron of Missouri, Lynne Sallot of Georgia, and Patricia A. Curtin of North Carolina reviewed several decades of studies of the relationship between reporters and public relations persons. The researchers noted in *Communication Yearbook 20* the increasing respect among reporters for the professionalism of their news sources. Positive experiences with ethical and forthright practitioners has improved the standing of public relations in the eyes of the media.

Delivery of News Releases

News releases should be conveyed to the media in a timely and effective manner. As pointed out previously, releases should be addressed to recipients by name whenever possible. Releases may be sent in a broadside manner to large numbers of recipients, in an approach called *macrodistribution,* or to carefully selected target media sources, in the *microdistribution* technique. The high cost of postage and of specialized delivery services causes most public relations practitioners to select recipients of their news releases with care, omitting those unlikely to use the material. Therefore, practitioners should determine the appropriate media sources for their firm or their clients.

Locally, releases can be delivered by first-class mail, fax, messenger, or e-mail if they contain urgent material. Use of bulk mail to save postage is unwise. Delivery is subject to delay, and recipients of bulk mail tend to dismiss it as unimportant.

Delivery of releases regionally or nationally is more complicated because of timing problems and the need to reach the proper outlets and individuals in areas where the sender lacks knowledge of local situations. Accurate, current mailing lists substantially influence the amount of exposure a news release obtains. For this reason, many organizations employ distribution firms to handle their mailings. One of these firms, Media Distribution Services, states that it maintains current lists of more than 150,000 editors and reporters at more than 40,000 print and broadcast media in the United States and Canada, and lists the media in 2,500 categories of editorial interest.

Distribution of releases by mail still is the cheapest, most common, and least attention-getting method. It is also the first preference of reporters and editors. Overnight delivery by Federal Express, Express Mail, United Parcel Service, or DHL is more expensive but gives the news release an aura of importance. Faxed messages are a popular way of delivering invitations to meetings and events.

Electronic Delivery   Newswire companies offer various types of news release delivery, usually aimed at carefully targeted lists of recipients. The public relations practitioner writes a news release and turns over the copy to one of these distribution companies. Depending on the type of distribution the practitioner chooses, the commercial firm prints and mails it to a selected mailing list, distributes it by high-speed private wire to outlets chosen by the author, or distributes it on the Internet and Web. The release arrives in newsrooms on special public relations printers in the same ready-to-publish form as if it had been mailed. Recognizing the growing dependence on computers in newsrooms, distribution companies also will dispatch news releases from their computers directly into the computers of newsrooms, just as news services send copy to most newspapers.

Business Wire and PR Newswire, the principal distribution firms, handle heavy volume at moderate cost. A 400-word news release distributed nationally costs about $500. They claim better usage of a release sent electronically.

Camera-Ready Feature Services   Still another way of distributing news about products, services, and events nationally is through a distribution service that provides newspapers with "camera-ready" copy. A company or firm sends a featurized news release about its project or product to the promotion service. If the service's editors deem the content to be newsworthy and written in competent news story style, they lay out the story in newspaper format and distribute it by mail or in digital form on a CD-ROM or a website. Photographs and appropriate drawings may be included to illustrate the release. Brand names are permitted, although they usually are placed inconspicuously well down in the stories. Smaller newspapers in particular use editorial promotion service copy as textual matter in special advertising sections on such themes as gardening, home repair, Mother's Day, auto repair, and fashions. To win acceptance by an editorial promotion service, copy must be free of hard-sell "puffery."

Localizing a News Release

National corporations realize that when the releases they send out are localized, media use will be substantially higher. The local angle should be placed in the lead if possible. Inclusion of local names or statistics attracts editors; they know it interests readers. For example, a corporation with offices and plants in 20 cities sends out a release reporting that it currently has 30,000 employees systemwide, who last year received total wages and health benefits of stated amounts. The release may be published rather inconspicuously in the newspapers of some company cities but will receive little or no broadcast attention because it is too general. Even company employees will have difficulty relating to it. However, if the releases sent to the media in each company city tell how many employees the company has in that locality, and how much these workers receive in payroll and health benefits each year, likelihood of widespread use will be high.

In a period of large layoffs such as the 1990s, and the closing and reorganizing of plants, localized information by corporations is especially important because the futures of workers and their families are at stake.

Lack of localization in the news releases they receive is a major cause of complaint by editors. In a comprehensive study of news releases and their usage, Professor Linda P. Morton of the University of Oklahoma found that fewer than 10 percent of the releases that she reviewed were localized. When they were localized, usage jumped. Of one group she studied, Morton reported, "For instance, of 174 localized releases, 78 were published. Comparably, 1174 general releases resulted in only 87 being used."

Using computer techniques, a corporation can prepare a standard national news release giving general information for use by all recipients. It also can prepare paragraphs containing the local information for each company city. These paragraphs are inserted by computer appropriately into the releases intended for each specific city.

FACTSHEETS AND MEDIA ADVISORIES

Although factsheets are distributed by public relations personnel to the same media as news releases are, and somewhat resemble releases physically, they are in outline form instead of in news story format.

A *factsheet* is essentially a quick-reference tool for reporters: it summarizes the key points about an event, a product, or a company to help reporters get a quick grasp or overview. Susan Antilla, New York bureau chief of *USA Today*'s Money section, said in *Jack O'Dwyer's Newsletter,* "PR people can really help a lot by providing background on companies . . . good factsheets are considered gold and are kept on file."

A *media advisory,* also called a media alert, differs from a factsheet. It gives basic facts about an event, in the hope of attracting media coverage, and it also describes interview prospects as well as photo and video possibilities.

The Pitch Letter

The purpose of the *pitch letter,* an important tool in a public relations campaign, is to obtain coverage of an event in the print and electronic media.

A pitch letter to an editor or producer should be so brisk and bright that it will catch the recipient's attention in the daily stack of mail. These letters offer the writer an opportunity to be clever, even offbeat, but they also must include the basic facts about an event or new product and offer reasons why the editor should assign someone to cover it.

The letter should be addressed personally to an individual, not merely to "Editor." Several directories are available to identify the current editor of a publication as well as its editorial calendar—the planned topics and special issues for the coming year. *Bacon's Publicity Checker* is a large set of annual directories that also include an update service for a fee to the purchaser of the volumes. Frequent updates of the annual directory are provided so that news releases and pitch letters are targeted to the current editor or reporter at a publication. Although reporters and editors move and change positions frequently, they are nonetheless sensitive about receiving mail directed to their predecessor.

The Press Kit

A *press kit* is often prepared when a company announces a new product or sponsors a major event; frequently elaborate, it gives media representatives a thorough background and provides information in various formats. Press kits may be sent to the media or distributed at a news conference (discussed in the next chapter).

The basic format consists of a large folder cover with pockets inside that contain news releases, factsheets, backgrounders (background articles), collateral company materials, black-and-white publicity photos, color slides, and even article reprints. The folder usually is visually attractive, incorporating graphic design and color.

Typical of such press kits is one prepared by LMS International, a new company formed as a joint venture of Control Data and Philips corporations. The public relations objective was to announce the new organization and develop a stronger understanding among the electronic trade media of its products; consequently, the press kit contained the following materials:

- Backgrounders on (1) the company/management team, (2) product areas/markets, and (3) major new products

- Separate news releases on each new product

- A six-page, four-color brochure on glossy paper about the new company and its products

- Black-and-white product publicity photos of major products

- Color slides of major products

The budget for the press kit was $10,000. One thousand press kits were distributed to (1) senior editors and reporters of the computer press around the world, (2) business and financial editors covering computer technology, and (3) market researchers and analysts. As a result, articles and photographs about the company appeared in more than 200 publications worldwide. Secondary articles appeared in more than 400 publications; also, the company received more than 100 requests for special features, industry trend/position articles, and technical articles.

Levi Strauss & Co. also prepared a fairly elaborate kit to publicize the results of a national survey about the fashion and lifestyle tastes of today's college students. The survey, conducted on 25 campuses among 7700 undergraduates, was called the Levi's 501 Report.

This kit contained (1) four news releases, (2) a factsheet on Levi's 501 jeans, (3) a backgrounder on the statistical findings of the survey, and (4) a sampling of fashion publicity photos of college-age models wearing, of course, jeans. A special press kit cover and letterhead also were designed.

The cost to write, produce, and distribute the press kit was $20,000. The cost of the survey was $25,000. The package was distributed to fashion editors at the top 500 newspapers around the United States, the news services, college media news services, and radio syndicates. Within three months, 345 articles appeared.

THE NEWSLETTER

Designed as an informal publication to deliver information to a target audience at regular intervals, the newsletter is precisely what the two portions of its name indicate: *news* transmitted in the chatty, brisk style of a *letter.* Newsletters are used frequently by corporations to communicate with employees and stockholders, by nonprofit agencies and associations to reach members and friends, and by sales organizations to deliver information and personnel chitchat to representatives in the field. Expert opinion and inside advice in specialized fields also are sold to subscribers in newsletter form by commercial publishing firms.

The typical newsletter is a four-page folder of 8 ½-by-11-inch pages, often set in computer type rather than regular printer's fonts. This style projects an air of informality and urgency. Ample use of white space increases readability.

The newsletter can be double-folded into a No. 10 business envelope, or it can be a self-mailer—that is, when folded, it has space on an outside surface for the address and stamp. Envelope mailing has greater impact, but the self-mailer is more economical. The choice is a question of budget.

Newsletters for internal audiences typically report to employees on trends in their field of work, forthcoming events, personnel changes and policy announcements within the organization, news from field offices, introduction of new products, unusual achievements by employees, results of surveys, and new publications. The goal is to make employees feel that they are informed about company affairs.

A newsletter aimed at an outside audience, members of an organization, or both, may contain items about political trends that could affect the organization or field of interest, announcements of new programs and policies, brief human interest stories about personnel or recipients of organization services, promotions and retirements—whatever news the editor believes is of interest to readers that can be told succinctly. On complicated stories, the newsletter should give the basic facts and indicate where readers can write or telephone for additional details. A newsletter is a brisk compilation of highlights and tidbits, not a place for contemplative essays or discussion.

Punchiness in writing style is essential for a successful newsletter. Sentences are short and direct. The writing is authoritative and no-nonsense in tone, from a busy writer to a busy reader. Another secret of the successful newsletter is to cover several topics that will appeal to a variety of readers. The single-topic edition should be avoided.

For internal use among departments and branches of large corporations with extensive word-processing facilities, the electronic newsletter is popular. The editor composes the letter in the usual way. The copy then is coded into the computer system, dispatched, and delivered to everyone on the receiving list on hard copy from the recipients' printout machines.

COMPANY MAGAZINES

Hundreds of well-written, well-edited, and attractive periodicals published in the United States never are seen by the general public. They are produced by public relations departments of companies or their counseling firms and distributed free to carefully selected audiences. Whether designed to be read by employees, stockholders, customers, or combinations of these audiences, periodicals are among the most effective channels of continuing communication that a company can use. Like any publication issued at regular intervals, the company magazine or newspaper creates a sense of anticipation of its arrival. This helps to strengthen the ties between management and the groups it seeks to inform and influence.

Although it is commonly assumed that employees with long-term service in a company are the most avid readers of company newsletters and magazines, research has disputed this. Professor John Pavlik, of Columbia University, studied employees of Honeywell, Inc., in Minneapolis, and found that an employee's career aspirations are a much better predictor of readership. Quite simply, Pavlik says, "An employee with higher career aspirations tends to place greater importance on reading to keep track of changes in management and to find out what is going on in the company generally."

Women seem to show strong interest in reading to keep track of their friends, while men primarily want to follow the company's business activities. Of course, this finding may be skewed in that traditionally women have been assigned more to lower-level clerical functions, and many have had no real career path in the company.

Experts emphasize the importance of four elements in maintaining a good relationship between management and employees—employee recognition, communication, a sense of belonging, and emotional security. When all of these elements function well, productivity tends to rise. Workers who believe that their jobs are secure and their personal worth recognized will contribute more than disgruntled ones.

Along with other forms of internal communication, company periodicals help substantially in the development of all four elements. The periodicals communicate information and decisions from management to employees. They increase the workers' feeling that they know what is going on in the company, and why. Management can use the periodicals to influence the attitudes of employees. However, this purpose must be accomplished with caution and finesse. If employees sense that management is talking down to them and using the periodical merely as a propaganda vehicle, the publication may become an object of derision. Periodicals also can serve as channels for communication from employees to management through letters to the editor, question-and-answer features, and similar devices.

Major corporations sometimes produce sleek, sophisticated-appearing magazines and colorful newspaper-style publications that are in the forefront of contemporary design. Four-color covers and splashy graphics help attract readers in this age of visual emphasis. Examples of this lavish approach are AT&T's management-oriented *AT&T Magazine* and Transamerica Corporation's *Transamerica*. Some of these, such as the American Express *Dateline International*, circulate worldwide. Kvaerner, a multinational company founded in Norway centuries ago, distributes tens of thousands of copies of its corporate magazine across the globe in English, Finnish, and Norwegian.

Company publications vary in size, use of color, graphics, photos, and frequency of publication, depending on the size of the budget and the target audience management seeks to reach. Some companies have found that their blue-collar employees get more satisfaction from a periodical that is simple in design and presentation than from an elaborate, multicolored, sophisticated-looking magazine that might be intended for stockholders or investment advisers.

Large corporations frequently publish several periodicals, each designed for a different audience. Usually the objective of a publication is stated in small type in its masthead. Typically, *Chevron World,* published quarterly by Standard Oil Company of California, states, "The *Chevron World* is published and distributed by the company's Public Affairs organization for the information of shareholders, employees, and other interested parties." Knowledge of this stated purpose helps a person to scrutinize the content of a periodical and analyze why various elements were included. (*Chevron World* is described in detail later in the chapter.)

Nonprofit organizations publish periodicals for much the same purposes that corporations publish theirs. Instead of trying to please stockholders and customers, nonprofit organizations must seek the support of contributors. Their product is service. Therefore, periodicals aimed at contributors and possible donors emphasize the quality and social value of the service the organization delivers.

Company magazines fall into four major categories, grouped by the audience they serve. To illustrate how the various types function, the following sections analyze the contents of typical magazines in each category: those for employees and retirees, for stockholders and employees, for marketing staff and wholesaler customers, and for customers and association members.

Magazines for Employees and Retirees

The employee magazine is a means by which management can inject a personal touch into company affairs. As a humanizing tool, it helps offset the feelings of some employees, especially in large corporations, that they have little significance as individuals to management.

Employee publications, like most periodicals, usually have stated objectives. The Clorox Company publishes a quarterly magazine, *The Diamond,* for its 4,800 employees. *The Diamond* has the following objectives:

- To assist management in securing employee understanding and support for the company's operations, activities, objectives, and plans

- To recognize employee accomplishments on and off the job to maintain high morale and develop a sense of participation in the company's affairs and its relationship with local communities

- To educate employees about subjects such as the U.S. economic system, safety, and the obligations of responsible citizenship to make employees more valuable members of the Clorox family and their communities

The editor of *The Diamond* follows a story mix intended to recognize people in different divisions, departments, and various locations while covering issues important to the company. The magazine exemplifies effective employee communication with a limited staff and budget. In a primarily one-person operation, the editor plans content, interviews people, writes all copy, handles all approvals, takes most photographs, and supervises design, production, and printing. The editor also handles all phases of a monthly two- to four-page newsletter.

Magazines for Stockholders and Employees

Because a magazine of this type is aimed at two audiences, its approach must be broader. Although stockholders and employees share concern about the success of their company, their interests are not identical. News about the activities and milestones of individual employees does not interest stockholders. The magazine's focus needs to be more on technical and economic developments in the corporation's field and on the company's strategy to take advantage of them. It must be kept in mind that many employees also are stockholders, often as participants in company-sponsored stock purchase programs.

An example of the company periodical distributed to both stockholders and employees is *Chevron World,* published quarterly by Standard Oil of California as a colorfully printed, 30-page, slick-paper magazine.

A typical issue of *Chevron World* contains a policy statement by the chairman of the board about oil exploration, articles about natural gas reserves and oil taxation, a feature about Chevron's TV school in which the company instructs its executives on how to appear on television programs, and a story about bird life on the company's North Sea oil platforms.

In this publication, employees are given a carefully crafted picture of their company's ambitious search for new energy sources. Their pride in the company's size and ingenuity is stimulated. They receive strong exposure to management's views. Corporate image-building is the dominant theme.

Magazines for Marketing Staff Members and Wholesalers of Company Products

These periodicals are unabashedly promotional, edited to encourage sales through inspirational essays and how-to-do-it articles.

An excellent example of these direct sales-booster periodicals is *Team Talk,* published by Anheuser-Busch of St. Louis to promote its group of beers. Articles contain cheerleader sentences of a type the reader would be unlikely to find in the magazines previously analyzed. Quotations like this from wholesalers are included in articles about their activities:

> Everybody loves a winner and wants to be associated with a class organization . . . our retailers and the general public know we are proud of our products. Anheuser-Busch is a winner, and we want to be one, too.

In general, the content of *Team Talk* urges marketing people to exploit established events by pushing exposure of their products and to create special events for the same purpose. The publication's goal is motivation of its readers.

Magazines for Customers and Association Members

As a psychological link to their customers to remind them of company products and services, some firms publish magazines addressed exclusively to this group. Magazines published by national organizations for their members are similar in purpose and character. The cost of a membership magazine normally is included in the annual dues.

The customer magazine is not a catalogue, although it may contain pages offering services or products, often packaged in special offers. Primarily its objective is to present a favorable image of the company, rather than direct selling.

A colorful example of the customer magazine is *Silver Circle,* a 48-page quarterly published by Home Savings of America and distributed free to members of its Silver Circle. The circle is a device designed to increase deposits. Home Savings depositors who have at least $10,000 in accounts become Silver Circle members. They receive the magazine and a membership card entitling them to discounts on numerous travel and entertainment items.

The editors of *Silver Circle* can make several important assumptions about their audience: (1) those who receive the magazine have at least a moderate amount of spare money; (2) members may be expected to have substantial interest in travel; (3) all probably have at least a fundamental understanding of financial matters. Those attributes of the *Silver Circle* readership are the framework on which the magazine is built.

The tie-ins between the magazine and the hotels, restaurants, and amusement parks offering discounts in it illuminate the techniques of entertainment sales promotion. Those who give discounts know they are reaching an audience with money to spend. Home Savings, in turn, earns goodwill from magazine recipients by offering such bargains.

BROCHURES AND HANDBOOKS

Writing informational publications to fill innumerable needs is among the most common duties of public relations practitioners. Some printed pieces are issued at stated intervals, such as quarterly reports to stockholders and college catalogues. The majority, however, are designed to last for indefinite periods, subject to updating as required. Most of this material is distributed free.

Whatever their purpose, these publications share clearly defined writing requirements. Clarity is essential. Frequently the writer must explain technical material or simplify complex issues for a reader who knows little about the topic. This calls for explanations that are straightforward, shorn of jargon, and stated in terms of reference that a casual reader can comprehend quickly. Paired with clarity is conciseness. Informational writing should be tightly done.

Every brochure, handbook, or other form of printed information should be organized on a firm outline that moves the reader forward comfortably through unfamiliar territory. Frequent subheads and typographical breaks are desirable. The writer often operates under budget restrictions that dictate the size of the publication-perhaps a four-page folder, perhaps a large-format brochure of 30 pages consisting primarily of illustrations with short blocks of type. Space limitations should be regarded as a challenge to the writer's skill at condensation.

The following are the types of publications in this category that a public relations writer is most frequently called upon to create.

Informational Brochures

These describe the purposes, policies, and functions of an organization. Tour-guide folders given out at museums are an example of this form.

Handbooks

More elaborate than basic brochures, these usually include policy statements, statistical information, and listings of significant facts about the issuing organization and its field of operation. Handbooks often are designed for distribution primarily to news media sources as handy references for a writer or broadcaster in a hurry.

Typical examples of the handbook are the following:

- *"Sharing the Risk," published by the Insurance Information Institute.* Nearly 200 pages describe property and casualty insurance concepts, regulations, and policies, ranging from homeowners' losses to nuclear risks.

- *"Oil & Gas Pocket Reference," published by Phillips Petroleum Company.* This is a 60-page small-format booklet of statistics about the oil industry. Included are such lists as the top 10 U.S. oil-producing states; the top 15 oil-producing nations, with amounts; oil and gas imports by year; and significant reference dates.

Corporate Brochures for External Use

Frequently aimed at specific audiences rather than at the general public, these may be such items as the inserts utility companies include with their bills, financial documents such as quarterly reports to stockholders and proxy statements for potential stock purchasers, owners' manuals, and teaching materials.

Duffey Communications, Inc.
Public Relations • Marketing

INTRODUCING THE *NEW* SAN FRANCISCO TREAT FACT SHEET	

When:	October 15, 1998
What:	Duffey Communications expands its nationally recognized brand of public relations, business marketing and public affairs with the opening of its new West Coast office in San Francisco.
Where:	Duffey Communications, Inc. 357 Tehama Street Third Floor San Francisco, California 94103
Contact Information:	Phone 415/597-4597 Fax 415/597-4554 E-mail info@duffey.com Web site www.duffey.com
Why:	The continued growth of Duffey's technology, telecommunications and interactive marketing practice areas, combined with the increasing need for public affairs counsel in the technology industry, make San Francisco and the Silicon Valley an important geographical area for the firm.
Who:	Founded in 1984, Duffey Communications has grown into one of the largest independent firms in the nation, specializing in public relations, business marketing and public affairs for clients in the public and private sector. Duffey Communications is ranked among the **top 100 U.S. public relations and marketing firms** and has been named one of America's *12 Hot Creative Firms, Top 10 New Media Pioneers* and *Best Strategic Counseling Firms* by *Inside PR* magazine. Overall, the firm has earned more than 300 national and international awards.
Staff:	Mike Neumeier, group director of technology, will oversee San Francisco operations.

For More Information:	*Contact*	*Telephone*	*E-mail*
	Mike Neumeier	404/266-2600	miken@duffey.com
	Denise Kitchel	404/266-2600	denisek@duffey.com

Additional Offices:	Duffey Communications, Inc. (Headquarters) Eleven Piedmont Center Suite 600 Atlanta, Georgia 30305 404/266-2600	Duffey Communications, Inc. 700 13th Street, NW Suite 800 Washington, D.C. 20005 202/347-5444

Eleven Piedmont Center • Suite 600 • Atlanta, Georgia 30305 • 404/266-2600

Affiliated offices in Baltimore • Boston • Boulder • Chicago • Cleveland • Columbia, SC • Dallas • Denver • Framingham, MA • Ft. Lauderdale • Honolulu • Houston • Indianapolis • Kansas City • Los Angeles
Miami • Minneapolis • Nashville • New Orleans • New York • Philadelphia • Phoenix • Pittsburgh • Sacramento • Salt Lake City • San Antonio • San Diego • San Francisco • Seattle • St. Louis
Washington, D.C. and other major cities in Canada, Europe and Asia

This fact sheet and the first page of a news release (see next page) illustrate the difference between the two types of material distributed by a public relations organization. One is a factual summary, the other a news story in publishable form.

Corporate Brochures for Internal Use

To inform and train their employees, companies issue a broad range of brochures and handbooks. These may be distributed at in-plant meetings or to individuals at work, or mailed to the employees' homes. In simplest form, information sheets may be posted on company bulletin boards.

Duffey Communications, Inc.
Public Relations • Marketing

FOR IMMEDIATE RELEASE

CONTACT: Denise Kitchel
Duffey Communications
404/266-2600
email: denisek@duffey.com

MOVE OVER RICE-A-RONI
THERE'S A NEW ICON IN SAN FRANCISCO

--Duffey Communications Goes West--

ATLANTA (October 15, 1998) -- Duffey Communications energized its
continued expansion efforts with the announcement of its new office in downtown San
Francisco. The Atlanta-based public relations, business marketing and public affairs firm
also has an office in Washington, D.C. Billings for the award-winning firm are expected
to approach six million in 1998.

"The explosive growth of our technology, telecommunications and interactive
marketing practice areas, combined with our expertise in public affairs issues for the
technology industry, make San Francisco and the Silicon Valley an important
geographical area for our company," explains Lee Duffey, president and founder of
Duffey Communications. "Our approach to business marketing has earned our firm more
than 300 domestic and international honors for results. We are very excited to expand
our operations to the West Coast and look forward to continuing our seamless client
service operations nationally and abroad."

(more)

Eleven Piedmont Center • Suite 600 • Atlanta, Georgia 30305 • 404/266-2600

DUFFEY GOES WEST.../2

Inside PR magazine ranks Duffey as one of the nation's *12 Hot Creative Firms,*
Top 10 New Media Pioneers and *Best Strategic Counseling Firms*. With offices in
Atlanta, San Francisco and Washington, D.C., Duffey Communications is noted as one of
the **top 100 public relations firms in the United States.**

Lee Duffey is the current chairman of the board of Pinnacle Worldwide, the
nation's oldest consortium of independently owned public relations firms. Through
Pinnacle, Duffey offers clients global service via 27 domestic and 36 international
affiliate offices. Visit Duffey on the World Wide Web at http://www.duffey.com.

# # #

Examples of in-company brochures and manuals include the following:

- *Atlantic Richfield Company's 12-page booklet to assist older employees in making the transition from work to retirement.* It answers questions that concern every employee approaching retirement, such as financial planning, use of leisure time, and health benefits.

- *A manual describing proper telephone techniques, given to employees of Washington Federal Savings and Loan Association in Seattle.* Employees discuss the manual in seminars during which they see a 25-minute film depicting "telephone traps" in which they might find themselves.

THE ANNUAL REPORT

"The principal purpose of the annual report is to tell the company's story to a multiplicity of audiences," says David F. Hawkins, a professor at the Harvard Business School. "It's a public relations document with a regulatory requirement."

Indeed, preparation of a corporation's annual report is a major function of a company's public relations department or counseling firm and is probably the company's most expensive written contact with its stockholders and the financial community. According to a study by the National Investor Relations Institute, investor relations executives devote about 13 percent of their time to preparing annual reports.

Technically, the corporate annual report is an informational document required of all publicly traded companies by the Securities and Exchange Commission. But there is no legal requirement that annual reports be extravaganzas. Under Rule 14a-3 of the Securities Exchange Act, publicly traded companies are required to include only basic financial information and other material such as a list of directors and the auditor's opinion letter. Once these requirements are met, the rule states, "the report may be in any form deemed suitable by management."

Companies publish expensive and attractive annual reports for public relations purposes. These include (1) impressing current and potential stockholders that the company is well managed and successful, (2) encouraging potential investors to purchase stock, and (3) using the annual report as a vehicle for recruiting new employees.

Increasingly, large corporations use striking new graphic techniques in their reports to stimulate reader interest and project an image of power.

A corporate annual report is divided into two general sections:

1. *Detailed financial information about the company's condition and performance during the past year.* A consolidated balance sheet and management's discussion of the financial condition are essential elements. A letter from the corporation's auditing firm is included, along with breakdowns of certain aspects. The material in this section, prepared by the financial department and approved by top management, is coldly objective and must be completely accurate. Other relevant information about the corporation is published in this section for reference.

2. *Management's presentation of accomplishments during the past year, its goals, and outstanding problems.* This material, appearing in the first portion of the report just after a one-page summary of financial highlights, is designed to give a good impres-

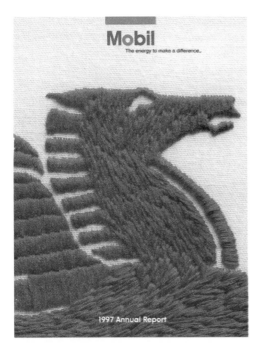

Corporations issue annual financial reports required by the federal government. Many of them expand their reports with promotional material presented in strong graphic form. This cover of a Mobil Corporation report, including the company symbol, is especially eye-catching.

sion of management's work. While the prose is restrained, use of striking color photographs and other graphics helps suggest corporate vigor.

The centerpiece of this front section is a report to stockholders by the board chairperson or the chief executive officer. This is the "message,".

When companies have had a bad year financially or have been involved in an embarrassing episode, they frequently bury that fact in their annual reports. In general, trends in annual reports during the 1990s moved toward more informality in writing, more focus on employees, and, when a company's operations justify it, emphasis on its roles in the international market and the environmental movement.

On occasion, a company breaks out of the usual mold with a creative approach. Bell-South, for example, used an annual report to focus on the year 2000 by including essays from nationally known authors, commentators, and experts about our lives now and in the future. And First Hawaiian, Inc., a bank-holding group, used color photos of its executives in Hawaiian shirts instead of three-piece suits.

As supplements to printed annual reports, but never as replacements for the financial section, some companies issue videotaped annual reports for showing to employees, stockholders, and financial groups. Teleconferencing an annual meeting is an increasingly common practice.

CORPORATE ADVERTISING

Traditionally, *advertising* is defined as purchased space or time used to sell goods or services, while public relations space in the media is obtained free. The line of demarcation becomes fuzzy when a company engages in *corporate advertising,* also called *institutional advertising.* Such advertising is processed and purchased in the regular manner. Its purpose, however, is not to sell the company's products or services directly but to enhance public conception of the company or to advocate a company policy.

A corporate advertisement, as defined by Leading National Advertisers, a checking service, must deal with a company's policies, functions, facilities, objectives, ideas, and standards; build favorable opinions of the company's management, skill, technology, or social contributions; enhance the investment qualities or financial structure of the company; or promote it as a good place to work.

Recently, a type of corporate advertising called advertorial advertising has been used to push products, sometimes rather subtly, to the extent that the distinction between product and corporate advertising becomes blurred. Professor Glen T. Cameron of the Missouri School of Journalism believes this blurring results in information pollution. He and colleagues have found evidence that readers are confused by such practices. He calls for prominent labels to indicate advertising and a statement early in the ad copy declaring the commercial nature of the message.

The largest amounts of corporate advertising appear on television and in magazines.

Corporate advertising may be divided into three basic types: (1) *general corporate image-building,* (2) *investor and financial relations programs,* and (3) *advocacy.*

Image-Building

Image-building advertising is intended primarily to strengthen a company's identity in the eyes of the public and/or the financial community. Conglomerates whose divisions market unrelated products seek through such advertising to project a unified, readily recognized image. Others use it to correct an unfavorable public impression. Increasingly, corporations use institutional advertising to show their concern for the environment, and by doing so seek to demonstrate what good corporate citizens they are.

Phillips Petroleum, for example, published a full-page magazine advertisement dominated by a photograph of a bird's head and beak, with the headline, "You'd sing too if someone created a sanctuary for you." The text read:

> Thousands of songbirds had no voice. So we gave them one. We helped expand the High Island Sanctuary, a crucial resting place on the Texas coast for migrating songbirds. Originally it was just five acres. But now it spans 170 acres. To make it happen, Phillips Petroleum brought together government agencies, conservation groups, and another oil company. Did it make a difference? Just ask the next gray catbird you happen to meet. Respect for wildlife. At Phillips, that's what it means to be The Performance Company.

A warning: any corporation that strikes a proenvironmental posture, then is caught polluting or otherwise damaging the environment, immediately becomes the object of derision for hypocrisy.

Financial Relations Programs

The second form of corporate advertising is aimed straight at the financial community. The advertiser tries to depict its financial strength and prospects so favorably that securities analysts will advise their clients to purchase its stock. When a corporation has millions of shares outstanding, even a fractional improvement in its price is beneficial. Such advertising is used extensively during proxy fights for control of companies, or when a company is undertaking a major reorganization and needs to keep the financial community informed.

Advocacy

The third, sometimes controversial, form of corporate advertising is advocacy. In such advertisements, a corporation or association tries to influence public opinion on a political or social issue. Only a small portion of corporate advertising expenditure goes into advocacy advertising, but because these advertisements sometimes touch public sensibilities, they receive considerable attention.

Parents…Grandparents…Families…This is for YOU

TV Is Leading Children Down A Moral Sewer
How You And I Can Stop It

Are you as disgusted as I am at the filth, vulgarity, sex and violence TV is sending into our homes?

Are you fed up with steamy unmarried sex situations, filthy jokes, perversion, vulgarity, foul language, violence, killings, etc.?

Are you as outraged as I am at how TV is undermining the morals of children…encouraging them to have pre-marital sex…encouraging lack of respect for authority and crime…and shaping our country down to the lowest standards of decency?

Well now you and I can end it. Yes we can, actually and literally. We can do it by reaching the TV sponsors whose ad dollars make it possible. And here's how:

Steve Allen

A Parents' Appeal To
TV Sponsors
Look At The Evidence
These Are Some Of The Tragic Consequences Of The TV Filth, Sex And Violence You Send Into Our Homes

- Since television started around 1000 studies, reports, etc. concerning the impact of TV violence have been published.
- The National Institute of Mental Health and 7 more national organizations say there is overwhelming evidence that violent entertainment causes violent behavior.
- An ABC network study found 22 to 34 percent of young felons imprisoned for violent crimes said they had consciously imitated crime techniques learned from watching television programs.
- Homicide rates doubled in 10 to 15 years after TV was first introduced into specific areas of the U.S. and Canada.
- In a survey of 10 to 16-year olds, 62 percent said sex on TV influences their peers to have sex when they're too young.

TV sponsors: This is just a small sampling of the massive evidence showing the terrible damage you are causing by paying to send TV filth, sex and violence into American homes. We beg you to stop sponsoring it.

Please don't tell us to take our complaint to the TV networks. For years network officials went to Washington and promised to reduce violence on TV. Janet Reno, U.S. Attorney General, called their promises "worthless". We know, and YOU know, that without your advertising dollars the TV programs that are desensitizing an entire nation to killing, violence, promiscuous sex and vulgarity WOULDN'T BE BROADCAST.

We Want It Stopped!

A Message From Steve Allen
Together We Can Make It Happen

I'm asking every person who agrees with this ad (virtually EVERYONE we speak to DOES) to send in the Appeal To TV Sponsors on the right. Every month we at Parents Television Council will total the number received and notify the sponsors.

They're going to KNOW that we, their customers, are angry and we want them to stop sponsoring sex, filth, violence and sleaze… and instead put their ad dollars in *the kinds of decent, family-safe programs that are getting huge ratings.*

The heads of the companies are fine people. Many are parents and grandparents. The trouble is they have been letting their ad agencies and others decide which programs to sponsor and they are unaware of the harm they are doing.

We can really get them to stop sponsoring the TV that is so harmful to our children and our country. All it takes is for enough of us to make our voices heard. Here's *proof:*

Recently viewers critical of just one TV program let the sponsors know of their anger, and over 35 sponsors cancelled their ads! This project is going to succeed!

So please, mail YOUR Appeal To TV Sponsors to me *today.* We'll do the rest.

Please don't put it off. Our children and our country are being hurt too badly for any one of us to remain silent. Mail your Appeal to me NOW!

Parents Television Council
600 Wilshire Boulevard, Los Angeles, CA 90017
Steve Allen, Honorary Chairman

An Appeal To The Heads Of Every Company Supporting TV Programs That Undermine America

Mail to:
Steve Allen
Parents Television Council, Dept. 6SAC68
600 Wilshire Blvd., Suite 700, Los Angeles, CA 90017

Yes Steve, I want to be counted as one who agrees that TV is leading us down a moral sewer. I think it is unconscionable for fine companies to use their ad dollars to send filth, vulgarity, coarse humor, pre-marital sex situations, violence, killings and all the rest into American living rooms and children's bedrooms. Let's bring back Family-Safe TV.

Name _____

Address _____

City _____ State _____ Zip _____

☐ I'd also like to help you run more ads like this so you can overwhelm the sponsors with the number of these Appeals you receive. Enclosed is my tax-deductible contribution to help buy another full-page ad in another city. (Please make checks payable to: Parents Television Council.)

☐ $100 ☐ $50 ☐ $25 ☐ $10 ☐ Other

IMPORTANT: You don't need to send any money to have this Appeal added to the total we report. But we do need all the help we can get. This is a grassroots campaign. These ads cost up to $36,000.00 each. Every penny you send will go for the ads and notifying the sponsors. We will not give your name to the sponsors. Thanks.

The Parents Television Council is the Hollywood project of the Media Research Center, which is recognized by the IRS as a tax-exempt non-profit organization under Sec. 501(c)(3). Contributions can be accepted for unlimited amounts and are tax-deductible.

8401B

Advocacy advertisements by organizations or individuals are intended to sell an idea rather than a product. This one, placed by longtime television personality Steve Allen, deals in ardent tones with a social issue in an industry with which he is closely connected.

Evaluating Corporate Advertising

Ogilvy & Mather, a major advertising agency, studied corporate advertising. It announced these conclusions:

> We have learned that good corporate advertising can:
>
> - Build awareness of a company
>
> - Make a favorable impression on investors and securities analysts
> - Motivate employees and attract recruits
> - Influence public opinion
> - Strengthen relations with dealers
> - Influence legislation
>
> We have learned that corporate advertising cannot:
>
> - Gloss over a poor record or a weak competitive position
>
> - Boost the price of your stock next month
> - Swiftly turn the tide of public opinion
>
> There are no quick fixes. Advertising can spread the truth about your company but cannot *conceal* it.

Thomas F. Garbett, a recognized authority on the subject, offered this justification for corporate advertising, in an article published in the *Harvard Business Review:*

> Although many companies assume that the safest course is to keep a low profile, this may in fact be a dangerous tack. If some inadvertent disclosure brings high visibility or even incidental exposure, an unknown company maintains little credibility as it moves to counter public criticism. . . . When people first get acquainted with a company through an unfortunate disclosure, they often distort what little they know and make generalizations about missing information. The less filled out a company's image is, the more subject that image is to wild distortions.

CASE PROBLEM

The Cleveland Repertory Theater will move into a new home next month. The $25 million building is part of the city's downtown redevelopment plan. The facility has state-of-the-art lighting and sound, seating for 750, and rooms for drama workshops. The architect is Skinner & Associates, and the contractor is BK Industries. Julie Andrews, star of stage and screen, will be the guest of honor at the official opening.

Write a general news release about the Repertory Theater and its planned grand opening. Second, write a pitch letter to the local media encouraging them to do feature stories about the new facility in advance of the opening. Third, write a media alert or advisory letting the press know that Julie Andrews will be available for interviews on a particular day. Fill in the appropriate quotations and information that you deem necessary.

QUESTIONS FOR REVIEW AND DISCUSSION

1. What is an *embargo* on a news release? Does it have any legal standing?

2. What are the physical requirements for an attractive news release?

3. A public relations counselor should have a client initial a file copy of each news release before distribution. Why?

4. Describe the difference between a news release and a factsheet.

5. To what audiences might a corporate public relations department send a newsletter?

6. As editor of a company magazine intended for employees and retirees, what would be your objectives?

7. Handbooks are issued frequently by corporations and trade associations. What types of material do they usually contain?

8. To what federal agency must corporate annual reports be submitted?

9. Corporate or institutional advertising differs in purpose from ordinary advertising. Explain this difference.

10. What risk does a corporation take when it uses aggressive advocacy advertising?

20

Spoken Tactics

Preview

The objective of this chapter is to explain spoken tactics in public relations and how such assignments as writing speeches and conducting news conferences are handled. The problem of rumors also is examined.

Topics covered in the chapter include:
* Face-to-face discussion
* Speech-writing techniques
* Staging a speech
* Conducting a news conference
* Press parties and tours
* Interviews
* Conducting meetings
* Word-of-mouth

FACE-TO-FACE DISCUSSION

A recent inductee into the hall of fame sponsored by the Atlanta Chapter of the Public Relations Society of America shared his keys to career success. He stated that the crucial component was personal communication. Speaking to students at his induction, he offered a tip learned decades before from his own mentor: your highest daily priority should be to return all phone calls in person before any other work is done.

A conversation *face to face* between two persons is widely regarded as the most effective form of interpersonal communication. This is certainly true in the world of work. The chemistry of personality that can develop by calling on a client or colleague is not easily defined but can be tremendously valuable.

Telephone or face-to-face conversation also offers immediate clarification and feedback so that misunderstandings are minimized. Although e-mail also offers this immediacy and can emulate some characteristics of conversation, it is no substitute. Because the written word does not convey nuance or emotional tone, it can be easily misconstrued. E-mail messages often appear harsh and curt, leading to communication problems.

Visualize these typical situations: a public relations representative at an editor's desk explaining the reasons for her hospital client's fund drive; a corporate vice president for public affairs calling on a city council member to urge the opening of a new street to reduce traffic congestion outside the company's manufacturing plant. In each case, the logic of the persuader's arguments is reinforced (or undermined) by the impact of the individual's personality. Sincerity impresses the listener. An aggressive, demanding approach arouses irritation. A smile, perhaps a casual quip, and a friendly but respectful manner help immeasurably in getting one's message across.

The personal call is among the most potent methods a public relations practitioner can use. It may fail, however, no matter how good the cause, if the caller arrives ill prepared and handles the presentation clumsily. Here, from a veteran newspaper editor who has listened to hundreds of across-the-desk public relations presentations, is advice on how to present a case effectively:

1. *Telephone in advance for an appointment.* Then be on time. Don't walk in "cold" and expect a hearing.

2. *Identify yourself and your purpose immediately.* Present a business card if possible, so the recipient has your name and affiliation at hand during the discussion and for filing later.

3. *Be concise.* Editors, program directors, and other opinion makers on whom you call are busy. Even those who appear relaxed and casual have other work waiting to be done. Make your presentation succinctly. Describe what your client plans to do, explain the purpose of the program, tell how it will help the public, and state specifically what support you hope to receive from the person you are addressing. Respond to your host's questions without meandering up side conversational paths, politely seek a commitment if that seems appropriate, then leave.

4. *Don't oversell.* Don't plead. Persons who receive presentations dislike being pressured and instinctively build defense mechanisms against excessively emotional "pitches" Never say, "You must help us!" Persons whose aid you seek resent being told that they "must" do anything.

5. *Express appreciation for your host's time and for anything he or she can do to assist your cause.*

6. *Leave behind written material—a brochure, a news release, a factsheet—for your host to study later.* Be certain that the material includes a telephone number at which you can be reached for further information. Asking your host to read the material while you

sit there is a poor tactic, unless it is very short; the result may be a hasty, reluctant scanning rather than the thoughtful reading you desire.

If the presentation can be made at lunch, over coffee or perhaps over a drink, outside the office setting, its impact may be stronger.

7. *Follow up with a note of appreciation for the reception, expressing hope that the recipient can use the information you left.* It subtly reminds the person to read the material, if that hasn't happened, and to do something about it.

If you are working with an editor or program director in a small community, or with a person you know well, the approach can be more informal.

Face-to-face discussion also is an essential tool for open communication within business organizations. Such conversations between management representatives and supervisors, supervisors and foremen, and management and union officers spread understanding of a company policy or a new product among the employees. Slightly less intimate, but almost as effective if well done, is the small-group discussion directed toward the same goal. Internal communication through staff study meetings, employee training sessions, and department meetings creates a more competent, motivated work force and identifies areas of employee dissatisfaction. (A discussion on how to conduct an effective meeting appears later in this chapter.)

A blind spot in company management, in small firms as well as large ones, is the too-frequent assumption that employees down the line know the reasons for company policies. The cynical wisecrack "There's no reason for it, it's just company policy" shows a weakness of management. Explaining *why* something is done is just as important as explaining *how* it should be done.

Each of these spoken methods will be discussed in detail. The text will first examine the speech: how to plan it, how to write it, and how to assist the speaker who delivers it.

ASSIGNMENT: SPEECH-WRITING

Public relations practitioners frequently are called on to write speeches for their employers or clients. As speech-writers, their role is a hidden one. In the White House, the wraps of anonymity usually are drawn around the writers who churn out speeches and statements for the president of the United States. A president who utters a memorable phrase gets the credit, but some unknown writer in a back office probably created it. There is nothing discreditable about this. Presidents have more urgent tasks than to think up catchy quotations.

Most of the largest corporations employ speech-writers, some of whom receive annual salaries from $70,000 to $120,000. Freelance writers often command from $1,000 to $10,000 for a speech. The writer's copy must be approved by numerous executives, and it sometimes becomes badly mangled in editing battles.

Turning loose a speaker, especially an inexperienced one, before an audience without a text, or at least a careful outline, may be an invitation to boredom. The "and . . . uhs" and "as I was sayings" will proliferate like rabbits. The audience will squirm, inwardly at first and then conspicuously in their chairs, as the speaker stumbles along. The opportunity to deliver a message that informs, persuades, and entertains listeners has been thrown out the window. That is why speakers who lack the time or the skill to do their own preparation need able speech-writers.

Some speakers prefer to work from notes rather than read a text. In that event, the writer should prepare a full speech for the speaker to study, then reduce the main elements of it to note cards arranged in proper sequence.

The Basic Points of Speech-Writing

Whatever the assignment, here are basic points for the speech-writer to keep in mind:

1. *A speech should say something of lasting value.* Even a talk intended to entertain, full of fluffy humor, should be built around a significant point.

2. *A speech should concentrate on one, or at most two, main themes.*

3. *A speech needs facts.* The information must be accurate. The writer's skill as a researcher is put to the test, to dig up information that will illustrate and emphasize the speaker's theme.

4. *The type of audience should influence the style and content of the speech.* When a company celebrates its fiftieth anniversary with a reception and dinner dance for its employees, they don't want to hear the president drone on for 30 minutes about the corporate financial structure. The setting calls for some joking, a few nostalgic stories, references to some individuals by name, words of appreciation for what the employees have contributed, and a few upbeat words about the future.

5. *Clarity in speech-writing is essential.* If the listeners don't understand what the speaker is saying, everyone's time is wasted. This happens when the speech contains complicated sentences, technical information that the speaker fails to explain in terms the audience can comprehend, and excessive jargon or "inside" talk. The speech-writer's challenge is to simplify the message, while keeping its significance.

An Example of Speech-Writing

To determine how the speech-writing process works, consider how a specific assignment could be handled. The assistant public relations director of a large regional restaurant chain is assigned to prepare a speech for the general manager to deliver at a chamber of commerce banquet in a middle-sized city where the company has recently opened a luxury restaurant. What does the practitioner do?

First, she must know what the speaker desires to emphasize. The management has heard extensive word-of-mouth criticism about the high dinner prices the new restaurant charges. Some business has been lost because of this. The general manager sees the speech invitation as an opportunity to explain why the restaurant must charge these prices and to stress what good values the dinners really are. To do so, he must give the audience a frank look at the restaurant business—an opening for the speech-writer to spice up the necessary financial information with whimsical backstage anecdotes.

Twenty minutes of such material, brightly presented, will entertain and inform this business-oriented audience. It will demonstrate that the restaurant organization is efficiently run and does its best to provide residents with a distinctive place to dine at the lowest feasible cost. Indeed, here is an excellent public relations moment.

The speech-writer must use her speech-planning appointment with the general manager to learn what he wants to say and to study his style. Does he speak intensely or in a casual, wry manner? Is his speech staccato or a bit fulsome? Probably he can provide her with one or two of his favorite restaurant anecdotes.

A speech is built in blocks, joined by transitions. The following pattern for assembling the blocks provides an all-purpose outline on which most speeches can be built:

1. *Introduction (establishment of contact with audience)*

2. *Statement of main purpose of speech*

3. *Development of theme—with examples, facts, and anecdotes.* Enumeration of points in 1, 2, 3 order is valuable here. It gives a sense of structure and controlled use of time.

4. *Statement of secondary theme, if there is one*

5. *Enunciation of principal point to which speaker has been building—the heart of the speech*

6. *A pause at this plateau, with an anecdote or two.* This is a soft place while audience absorbs principal point just made.

7. *Restatement of theme in summary form*

8. *Brief, brisk conclusion*

This plan of speech organization is *deductive;* that is, the central theme is stated almost at the beginning, and the points that follow support and illustrate the theme. A less common type of organization is *inductive.* In it the speaker presents points of information and arguments leading up to a statement of the principal theme near the end.

Introduction Following the preceding deductive outline, the speech-writer uses the first two minutes of the allotted 20 to build rapport between the general manager and the audience. The manager explains that when his company first considered coming to this city, he doubted that the area would support the luxury type of restaurant it operates. But the chamber of commerce convinced him that it would, and he is delighted that he had the good sense to listen (a light, slightly self-disparaging touch). He congratulates the chamber on the excellent statistical material it provided.

Then come the building blocks leading up to the conclusion.

Statement of Main Purpose The speaker says he wants to tell the audience about how a luxury restaurant operates, what its problems are, and why the customer sees things done a certain way. A summary of purpose in a single theme sentence at this point gives the speech a solid foundation. Almost as an aside he remarks, "Perhaps this will help you understand why our dinners cost as much as they do."

Development The manager states his company's total investment in opening this restaurant and reveals the number of people needed to run it . . . mentions kitchen jobs the diner never knows about . . . lists how many potatoes, steaks, heads of lettuce, and pounds of coffee are consumed in a week . . . relates a story about the night when the *maitre d'* had a full book of reservations and the salad chef walked out in a huff after a quarrel with his waitress girlfriend . . . describes how the chain's bill for pork and beef has soared.

Statement of Secondary Theme   The speaker explains how the restaurant chooses its menus. He describes research into which entrees sell well or poorly.

Enunciation of Principal Point   Operation of a top-flight restaurant in a time of high labor costs and rising food prices is a risky business, subject to the vagaries of weather, the economy, and the largely unpredictable turns of public fancy. By its steady growth, his organization has proved that a significant percentage of the public, "including here in this city," will patronize a restaurant that serves fine food with attentive service in a distinctive setting. "Our challenge is to do this at the lowest prices we can."

Pause on Plateau   The manager relates an anecdote about a diner who tried to steal some silverware, only to have it drop out of his pocket near the front door.

Restatement of Theme   The speaker's summary emphasizes his pride in the way local diners have patronized the new restaurant, proving his belief that the establishment provides the city with a type of high-quality dining that its citizens want and appreciate.

Brief Conclusion   The audience hears a bit of news: the speaker announces that the restaurant has arranged to receive ample supplies of a popular but relatively rare fish. Next week the restaurant will add the fish, prepared in an unusual manner, to the menu at a special low introductory price. He invites everyone to come and try it.

One more step remains to make this a thoroughly successful public relations appearance. The speaker knows that the audience will be invited to ask questions; he has had the speech-writer give him a list of antagonistic queries he may receive. His ability to answer the tough ones will improve the good impression his speech has made.

SPEECH-WRITING TECHNIQUES

The first principle in writing words to be spoken is to make them flow in the way a person usually talks. Writing intended for the ear must be simpler in construction and more casual in form than writing meant for the eye.

Short, straightforward sentences are best. To provide variety, an occasional long sentence is acceptable if its structure is simple. A spoken sentence is heard only once. Thus a speaker should repeat key points of the speech, couching them if possible in slightly different form.

Studies indicate that the average person listens four times as rapidly as the average person speaks. Thus the listener may be thinking about other matters while hearing the speaker. Holding the listener's undivided attention is difficult; recapitulation of main points helps the listener retain at least the main thrust of the speech.

Here, for example, is a sentence from a published news story that would be unacceptable in a speech text because of its intricate structure:

> Wright, who has agreed to pay the fine, said she believes the commission's action, which comes three weeks before the Nov. 2 election, will have no effect on her reelection campaign against Democrat C. D. (Dick) Stine.

If the material were written as follows, listeners could comprehend it far more easily:

Wright has agreed to pay the fine. The commission's action comes only three weeks before the November 2nd election. But Wright believes that it will not affect her campaign for reelection against Democrat Dick Stine.

An excellent way to grasp the concept of writing for speech is to close your eyes and listen to people around you talk. Do the same thing while hearing a radio newscast, which has been written especially for the ear. Visualize how the words you are hearing would appear on paper. Notice how often people use fragments of sentences.

The incomplete sentence is used quite effectively in this excerpt from a speech by John C. Bedrosian, president of the American Federation of Hospitals. His topic, the high cost of medical care, was complex, and he dealt with the problem in depth. A brief text, however, kept the speech from bogging down. Brief sentences, sentence fragments, and short words are used to offset such necessary long ones as *catastrophic* and *ambulatory:*

Hospital care is expensive. There is no denying that. It is essentially designed to provide care to the critically ill. Catastrophic illnesses. Major surgeries. Serious injuries. Any institution that is equipped and staffed to provide the highest level of care is by its very nature not economically appropriate for low-level care.

That's why we are witnessing the growth of alternative care and treatment sources. Satellite clinics, for example, surgi-centers, and other ambulatory care facilities. Skilled nursing homes for recuperation from illness or surgery. Home health care, a concept that has really only gotten started.

All of these are approaches that match the level of care to the need, and at a significant reduction in cost.

A speaker normally delivers a text at the rate of about 150 words a minute. So when preparing a 20-minute speech, the writer must produce about 3000 words.

Tips from Professional Speechwriters

Here are tips on writing from professional speech-writers:

- Read aloud the words you have written, to be certain that they sound natural to the ear.

- Avoid clauses that complicate sentences.

- Use smooth transitions to move from one section of the speech to the next.

- Use rhetorical questions.

- Draw verbal pictures.

- Be wary of jokes.

- Quote statistics sparingly.

VISUAL AIDS FOR A SPEECH

A speech often can be strengthened by use of visual devices. Graphs and charts, a common kind of visual aid, are only as good as their visibility to the audience. A chart too complicated for easy comprehension or too small to be read from the rear of the room is almost useless. Slides projected onto a screen are frequently used. They must be simple in content; holding a slide on the screen long enough for the audience to study involved information creates restlessness. (Audiovisual aids are discussed in Chapter 21.)

STAGING A SPEECH

Effective speeches don't just happen. They have to be rehearsed and prepared—or, in the language of the theater, "staged." Organizations frequently rely upon a practitioner's understanding of potential audiences to ensure that a speaking engagement helps the organization get a positive message across. And to create a pool of talented speakers, some organizations establish training programs.

In some instances, visual effects of staging can be inadvertent and humorous. During a gubernatorial campaign stop in Pennsylvania, a speech meant especially for television coverage was staged in a library where the candidate listed programs he would fund if elected. Unfortunately, he was standing just under the sign for the "Fiction" section.

The Practitioner's Role

Public relations practitioners who write speeches are frequently called on by management to give their opinion about whether the company should accept an invitation to speak and, if so, how the firm should use such a forum to present its views and policies in the most favorable light.

Management also is likely to seek out the practitioner's opinion when a speaker must appear before a hostile audience—a real test of public relations skill. While not always pleasant, the experience can pay dividends. A land developer who proposes construction of a shopping center close to a school cannot expect a cordial welcome when addressing an audience of parents. If the speaker can command respect by a pleasant, frank manner, however, some members of the audience may realize that he is not the ogre they had imagined. Having achieved this, the speaker can lay out his arguments and at least make the audience aware of his reasoning. People usually respect frankness.

Speech Training Programs

Even a brilliantly written speech can fail if it is delivered poorly. Upper-echelon executives for whom speeches are a required part of the job should be offered training by professionals in the techniques of public speaking. Progressive organizations also search among their employees for men and women who can be trained to speak effectively.

Employees selected may be assigned to attend on-the-job training sessions in speechmaking. They are instructed in such basics as diction, stage presence, voice projection, reading audience reaction, and handling questions. Videocassette tapes and other teaching aids enhance the instruction.

When a company needs to explain its policy to employees and seek their cooperation, top-echelon officials aren't always the best ones to do it. A well-trained fellow worker in a department may succeed better in convincing his or her colleagues to authorize automatic payroll deduction for United Way contributions than a speaker sent out from the executive offices. When management trains speakers from various work levels, provides them with well-written speeches appropriate for their needs, and gives them a suitable setting, they can fill a valuable role in the internal communication chain. What's more, they can give management enlightening feedback from their colleagues.

HELPING THE SPEAKER POLISH AND PRESENT THE SPEECH

After writing a draft of a speech, the writer should go over it with the speaker, who may request changes. By listening to the speaker read the material aloud, the writer can detect clumsy portions and smooth them out. The more frequently a speaker reads the text aloud in practice, the better the on-stage performance will be. A videotape made of a practice session will show the speaker where improvement is needed.

The finished version of a speech should be typed on $8^{1/2}$-by–11-inch pages in easily read type, without excessive crowding.

Writing an introduction and sending it to the person who will present the speaker is a good tactic. This assures that the information about the speaker will be correct. Although the introducer may alter the material, the content will probably be approximately what the public relations representative desires.

At the scene of the speech, the public relations representative should take several actions:

- *The microphone and other apparatus should be tested.* The audiovisual equipment should be set up and checked and the slide projector focused. Charts or flipcards should be numbered and arranged in correct order on an easel.

- *Extra copies of the speech should be brought along.* Additional copies are for distribution to the news media and to listeners who request a copy.

- *The speech should be recorded on tape.* The tape can be used to settle any disputes over what the speaker said, to provide "actuality" excerpts for local radio stations, and to assemble material for a postmortem session between speaker and writer analyzing the performance.

Two other steps can be taken to obtain additional exposure for an important speech: (1) copies can be mailed to a selected list of opinion leaders, and (2) the speech can be rewritten as an article for a company publication or submitted to a suitable trade magazine. Robert Dilenschneider, principal of the Dilenschneider Group, delivered an address about "spin" and public relations at the *Bulldog Reporter*/PR Newswire Media Relations '98 Conference in New York City. Dilenschneider then converted the speech into an op-ed piece for the *Wall Street Journal* (June 1, 1998). The speech achieved far wider exposure for Dilenschneider as a leader in the public relations industry than if it had been used only as an address to industry insiders.

SPEAKERS' BUREAUS AND HOTLINES

Speakers' bureaus operated by trade associations, social agencies, and corporations constitute an important instrument for bringing speakers and audiences together. They function something like a company's pool of internal speakers, but on a more elaborate scale.

Speakers developed within an organization are made available by the bureaus upon request. The bureaus also seek to place speakers before influential audiences. Typically, a telephone company in Illinois has a bureau with 42 trained speakers who talk before all types of clubs and civic organizations. Before being sent out to represent the company, the speakers receive professional training and must pass auditions.

Talent-booking agencies that place professional speakers for a fee sometimes also call themselves speakers' bureaus. The roles of these two types of speakers' bureaus are quite dissimilar: one provides speakers without charge, to promote the sponsor, while the other does so on a direct profit-making basis. It is important to distinguish between the two types of speakers' bureaus.

Somewhat related to the organizational speakers' bureau is the telephone hotline service operated by some trade associations and companies to provide quick answers, especially to the news media. This facility generally offers toll-free telephone service using the 800 prefix.

SPECIAL TYPES OF SPEAKING OPPORTUNITIES

A speaker addressing an audience represents one-way communication. Listeners receive the message, either accepting or rejecting it, but do not engage in a dialogue during which they can challenge the speaker's statements. The speaker commands the situation. The only exception occurs when a speaker agrees to accept questions from the floor—a practice that some speakers relish but others avoid, either because they realize that they do not perform well spontaneously or because they desire to avoid embarrassing questions.

The News Conference

At a news conference, communication is two-way. The person speaking for a company or a cause submits to questioning by reporters, usually after a brief opening statement. A news conference makes possible quick, widespread dissemination of the sponsor's information and opinions through the news media. It avoids the time-consuming task of presenting the information to the news outlets individually and assures that the intensely competitive newspapers and electronic media hear the news simultaneously. From a public relations point of view, these are the principal advantages of the news conference. Against these important pluses must be weighed the fact that the person holding the conference is open to severe and potentially antagonistic questioning.

In public relations strategy, the news conference can be either an offensive or a defensive device, depending on the client's need.

Most news conferences—or press conferences, as they frequently are called—are *positive* in intent; they are affirmative actions to project the host's plans or point of view. A corporation may hold a news conference to unveil a new product whose manufacture will create many new jobs, or a civic leader may do so to reveal the goals and plans for a countywide charity fund drive she will head. Such news conferences should be carefully planned and scheduled well in advance under the most favorable circumstances.

Public relations specialists also must deal frequently with unanticipated, controversial situations. A business firm, an association, or a politician becomes embroiled in

*E*DISON *EXPRESSions is Southern California Edison's employee-volunteer speaker organization. Since 1971, our speakers have given thousands of free, multilingual presentations to service clubs, schools, senior and consumer groups, business organizations, and community groups throughout the region on a broad range of electric industry topics. Whether it is a classroom presentation, a luncheon or a community event, we are your one-stop speakers' bureau for all occasions.*

SOUTHERN CALIFORNIA
EDISON

An *EDISON INTERNATIONAL*SM Company

www.sce.com

THE POWER BEHIND PEACE OF MINDSM

Recognizing the immense ethnic diversity in its service area, Southern California Edison operates a speakers' bureau, EDISON EXPRESSions. Consisting of company employees, speakers are available in several Asian languages and in Spanish. More than 26 percent of Southern California Edison customers speak Spanish with limited English capability, and 16 percent speak an Asian language.

News conference: Reporters and photographers crowd around independent counsel Kenneth Starr at one of his infrequent new conferences during his investigation of the relationship between President Clinton and Monica Lewinsky, a White House intern, that led to the impeachment trial of the President.

difficulty that is at best embarrassing, possibly incriminating. Press and public demand an explanation. A bare-bones printed statement is not enough to satisfy the clamor and may draw greater press scrutiny of the "stonewalling" organization. A well-prepared spokesperson may be able to achieve a measure of understanding and sympathy by issuing a carefully composed printed statement when the news conference opens. According to experimental research funded by Ketchum PR's SMART Grant program, when the company has a good reputation, audiences will accept a sincere apology. Researcher Lisa Lyon found, however, that organizations with a bad reputation may actually be better off taking a defensive stance.

No matter how trying the circumstances, the person holding the news conference should create an atmosphere of cooperation and project a sincere intent to be helpful. The worst thing he or she can do is to appear resentful of the questioning. The person should never succumb to a display of bad temper. A good posture is to admit that the situation is bad and that the organization is doing everything in its power to correct it, the approach described by Professor Timothy Coombs at Illinois State University as the "mortification" strategy. (Further discussion of crisis public relations appears in Chapter 8.)

Rarely, an organization or public person caught in an embarrassing situation foolishly attempts to quiet public concern by holding a news conference that really isn't a news conference. The host reads a brief, inadequate statement, then refuses to answer questions from reporters. This practice alienates the press.

Two more types of news conferences are held. One is spontaneous, arising out of a news event: the winner of a Nobel Prize meets the press to explain the award-winning work, or a runner who has just set a world's record breathlessly describes his feelings. The other type is the regularly scheduled conference held by a public official at stated times, even when there is nothing special to announce. Usually this is called a briefing—the daily State Department briefing, for example.

Planning and Conducting a News Conference   First comes the question: "Should we hold a news conference or not?" Frequently the answer should be "No!" The essential element of a news conference is *news.* If reporters and camera crews summoned to a conference hear propaganda instead of facts, or information of minor interest to a limited group, they go away disgusted. Their valuable time has been wasted—and it *is* valuable. If editors send reporters to a conference that has been called merely to satisfy the host's sense of self-importance, they resent the fact. If the material involved fails to meet the criteria of significant news, a wise public relations representative will distribute it through a press release.

Every news outlet that might be interested in the material should be invited to a news conference. An ignored media outlet may become an enemy, like a person who isn't asked to a party. The invitation should describe the general nature of the material to be discussed, so an editor will know what type of reporter to assign.

What hour is best? This depends upon the local media situation. If the city has only an afternoon newspaper, 9:30 or 10 A.M. is good, because this gives a reporter time to write a story before a midday deadline. If the city's newspaper publishes in the morning, 2 P.M. is a suitable hour.

Another prime goal of news conference sponsors is the early evening newscasts on local television stations, or even network TV newscasts if the information is important enough. A conference at 2 P.M. is about the latest that a television crew can cover and still get the material processed at a comfortable pace for inclusion in a dinner-hour show. This time period can be shortened a little in an emergency.

A warning: a public relations representative in a city with only an afternoon newspaper who schedules a news conference after that paper's deadline yet in time for the news to appear on the early evening television newscasts, makes a grave blunder. Newspaper editors resent such favoritism to television and have long memories. Knowledge of, and sensitivity to, local news media deadlines are necessary.

Deadlines for radio news reporters are less confining.

Here are two pieces of advice from longtime public relations specialists to persons who hold news conferences:

1. *The speaker should never attempt to talk off the record at a news conference.* If the information is so secret that it should not be published, then the speaker shouldn't tell

Focus on Ethics

"No Tough Questions, Please"

Shortly after the Arizona Diamondbacks major league baseball team signed a $52 million contract with Randy Johnson to pitch for them for four years, he held an introductory news conference. More than 100 media people attended, consuming soft drinks and popcorn provided by the management.

Johnson walked in, embraced his mother conveniently placed in front of the cameras, and said that it wasn't really the money that had brought him to Phoenix. It was the pleasant family environment.

A public relations man spoiled the euphoric mood, however, by telling reporters what questions to ask. He said, "Hold off asking your tough questions for another day." The reporters, of course, did just the opposite.

The *Arizona Republic* reported, "His plea went unheeded, and he visibly showed displeasure as unpleasant questions were asked."

Was the publicist's request unethical? It is a borderline call. He neither put out false information nor directly covered up anything. He did try to manipulate the coverage, however, by luring the reporters into one-dimensional stories through omission.

At the very least, his request was a foolish violation of good public relations practice.

it to reporters. Many editors forbid their reporters to honor off-the-record statements, because too often the person making them is merely attempting to prevent publication of material that is legitimate news but might be embarrassing. Any statement made before a group will not stay secret long, anyway.

2. *The speaker should never lie!* If he or she is pushed into a corner and believes that answering a specific question would be unwise, it is far better to say, "No comment" in some form than to answer falsely. A person caught in a lie to the media suffers a critical loss of credibility.

Bulldog Reporter, a West Coast public relations newsletter, suggests the following checklist for a practitioner asked to organize a news conference. The time factors given are normal for such events as new product introductions, but conferences concerning spot news developments for the daily press and electronic media often are called on notice of a few days or even a few hours.

- Select a convenient location, one that is fairly easy for news representatives to reach with minimal travel time.

- Set the date and time. Times between midmorning and midafternoon are good. Friday afternoons are deadly, as are days before holidays.

- When possible, issue an invitation to a news conference about six to eight weeks ahead of time, but one month is acceptable. The invitation should include the purpose of the conference, names of spokespersons, and why the event has significant news value. Of course, the date, time, and location must be provided.

- Distribute a media release about the upcoming news conference when appropriate. This depends on the importance of the event.

- Write a statement for the spokesperson to give at the conference and make sure that he or she understands and rehearses it. In addition, rehearse the entire conference.

- Try to anticipate questions so the spokesperson can readily answer difficult queries. Problem/solution rehearsals prepare the spokesperson.

- Prepare printed materials for distribution at the conference. These should include a brief factsheet with names and titles of participants, a basic news release, and basic support materials. This is sometimes called a press kit.

- Prepare visual materials as necessary. These may include slides, transparencies, posters, or even a short videotape.

- Make advance arrangements for the room. Be sure that there are enough chairs and leave a center aisle for photographers. If a lectern is used, make certain that it is large enough to accommodate multiple microphones.

- Arrive 30 to 60 minutes early to double-check arrangements. Test the microphones, arrange name tags for invited guests, and distribute literature.

Some organizations provide coffee and possibly sweet rolls for their media guests as a courtesy. Others find this gesture unnecessary because most of the newspeople are in a hurry.

Liquor should not be served at a regular news conference. Such socializing should be reserved for the press party, discussed in the next section.

At some news conferences, still photographers are given two or three minutes to take their pictures before questioning begins. Some photographers complain that, thus restricted, they cannot obtain candid shots. If free shooting is permitted, as usually is the best practice, the physical arrangements should give the photographers operating space without allowing them to obstruct the view of reporters.

A practitioner should take particular care to arrange the room in such a way that the electronic equipment does not impede the print reporters. Some find it good policy for the speaker to remain after the news conference ends and make brief on-camera statements for individual TV stations, if their reporters request this attention. Such statements should not go beyond anything the speaker has said to the entire body of reporters.

A final problem in managing a news conference is knowing when to end it. The public relations representative serving as backstage watchdog should avoid cutting off the questioning prematurely. To do so creates antagonism from the reporters. Letting a conference run down like a tired clock is almost as bad. A moment comes when reporters run out of fresh questions. A speaker may not recognize this. If not, the practitioner may step forward and say something like, "I'm sorry, but I know some of you have deadlines to make. So we have time for just two more questions."

Presidential press conferences do not have this problem. Long-standing custom limits these conferences to 30 minutes. At that point, the senior news service reporter present calls out, "Thank you, Mr. President!" and the conference ends. Everyone concerned with public relations should study a presidential press conference on television. The kinds of questions asked, the manner in which the president answers them, the nature of any opening announcements, and the physical facilities—all of these provide clues for organizing news conferences of a more mundane nature.

Global PR

News Conference Styles Vary

News conferences are a universal public relations tool, but there are local differences. Carole M. Howard, former vice president of public relations and communications policy for the Reader's Digest Association, has organized press events in a number of nations. She writes:

> News conferences in Moscow, for example, often last more than an hour rather than our [U.S.] normal 20–30 minutes because Russian journalists like historical perspective in the presentations. In Poland the skeptical press likes numerical research from a reputable outside firm to support product claims. In Central and Eastern Europe food is a major enticement to attend a news conference. As soon as the speeches and questions are over, everyone rushes to the food—traditionally a full meal consumed at record speed. In Asia they expect lots of local dignitaries to be on stage with your company's presenters—the more VIPs there, the more important your company must be.

Source: Carole M. Howard, "Going Global: How to Expand Your Horizons While Avoiding the "Ugly American' Syndrome." *Public Relations Quarterly,* Fall 1997, p. 22.

The Press Party and the Press Tour

In the straightforward news conference, the purpose is to transmit information and opinion from the organization to the news media in a businesslike, time-efficient manner. Often, however, a corporation, an association, or a political figure wishes to deliver a message or build rapport with the media on a more personal basis; then a social setting is desirable. Thus is born the press party or the press trip.

The Press Party   This gathering may be a luncheon, a dinner, or a reception. Whatever form the party takes, standard practice is for the host to arise at the end of the socializing period and make the "pitch." This may be a hard-news announcement, a brief policy statement followed by a question-and-answer period, or merely a soft-sell thank-you to the guests for coming. Guests usually are given press packets of information, either when they arrive or as they leave.

The press party is a softening-up process, and both sides know it. The party opens the channels of communication.

Also, if the host has an important policy position to present, the assumption—not necessarily correct—is that editors and reporters will be more receptive after a social hour. The host who expects that food and drink will buy favorable press coverage may receive an unpleasant surprise. Conscientious reporters and editors will not be swayed by a free drink and food.

Until a few years ago, though, *freeloading* by news people at parties was widespread and accepted as normal practice. Often press guests were given expensive gifts. In large cities, the expectations of certain reporters, especially those covering business and entertainment, became absurdly high. One coauthor of this book recalls attending a new-model announcement dinner for the press given some years ago by the Chevrolet division of General Motors. During dinner, the public relations director announced that there would be gifts for the guests when they went home. Each guest was asked to fill out a color preference card—blue, green, or tan.

One guest at the author's table asked another, quite seriously, "Do you think they are going to give us cars?" The other responded, with equal gravity, that perhaps they might. The actual gift proved to be an expensive blanket of the preferred color, packed in an individualized cedar chest. This type of payoff for attending the presentation became known as "loot." None of the media guests refused to accept the gift. (Present practice concerning gifts will be described shortly.)

Here is an actual example of a press party:

> A land developer invited local media guests and civic leaders to a luncheon at which he disclosed plans for a major shopping center at the edge of the city. Arriving guests received paste-on tags imprinted with their names, large folders containing news releases, photographs of the developer and of an artist's rendering of the project's exterior and interior, and a factsheet giving the developer's biography and a list of projects he had built. The artist's renderings stood on easels around the room; a scale model of the project was displayed on a table. Drinks and luncheon were served. Then the developer spoke about the project and answered questions.

The normal adjournment hour for luncheon sessions is 1:30 P.M. This one ran a few minutes past that hour because of the number of questions. No press luncheon ever should run past 2 P.M.

The Press Tour   There are three kinds of press tours. The most common is a trip, often disparagingly called a "junket," during which editors and reporters are invited to inspect a company's manufacturing facilities in several cities, ride an inaugural flight of a new air route, or watch previews of the television network programs for the fall season in Hollywood or New York. The host usually picks up the tab for transporting, feeding, and housing the reporters.

A variation of the press tour is the familiarization trip. "Fam trips," as they are called, are offered to travel writers and editors by the tourism industry. Convention and visitor bureaus, as well as major resorts, pay all expenses in the hope that the writers will report favorably on their experiences. Travel articles in magazines and newspapers usually result from a reporter's fam trip.

In the third kind of press tour, widely used in high-technology industries, the organization's executives travel to key cities to talk with selected editors; for example, top Apple Computer executives toured the East Coast to talk with key magazine editors and demonstrate the capabilities of the new Apple iMac computer.

The Ethics of Who Pays for What   In recent years, severe self-searching by media members as well as by professional public relations personnel who feel it is unethical to offer lavish travel and gifts, has led to increased self-regulation by both groups as to when a press tour or "junket" is appropriate and how much should be spent.

The policies of major dailies forbid employees to accept any gifts, housing, or transportation; the newspapers pay all costs associated with a press tour on which a staff member is sent. In contrast, some smaller dailies, weeklies, and trade magazines accept offers for an expense-paid trip. Their managers maintain that they don't have the resources of large dailies to reimburse an organization for expenses and that such trips are legitimate for covering a newsworthy activity.

Some newspapers with policies forbidding acceptance of travel and gifts don't extend the restrictions to all departments. Reporters in the "hard news" area, for example, cannot accept gifts or travel, but such policy may not be enforced for reporters who write "soft news" for sports, travel, and lifestyle sections. Few newspapers, for example, pay for the press box seats provided for reporters covering a professional football game, nor does the travel editor usually pay the full rate for rooms at beach resorts that are the focus of travel articles.

Given the mixed and often confusing policies of various media, the public relations professional must use common sense and discretion. He or she, first of all, should not violate the PRSA code of ethics that specifically forbids lavish gifts and free trips that have nothing to do with covering a legitimate news event. Second, the public relations person should be sensitive to the policies of news outlets and should design events to stay within them. A wise alternative is to offer a reporter the option of reimbursing the company for travel and hotel expenses associated with a press tour.

In terms of gift-giving, the sensible approach is a token of remembrance such as a pen, notepad, or a company paperweight. Some large newspapers will not permit even these token gifts. (Ethics are discussed extensively in Chapter 3.)

Organizing a Press Party or Press Tour   The key to a successful event is detailed organization. Every step of the process should be checked out meticulously.

In planning the press event, the practitioner has to consider a variety of details. Menus for a luncheon or dinner should be chosen carefully. Do any of the guests have dietary restrictions?

Has the exact hour of serving been arranged with the restaurant or caterer to allow sufficient time for the program? The usual check on microphone and physical facilities is essential. Even such a seemingly trivial item as a name tag requires the practitioner's careful attention.

Fouled-up transportation is perhaps the worst grief for a person conducting a press tour. Maintaining a firm tour schedule is essential. At stops, the host should begin to round up the strays a few minutes before the announced departure time.

As much as possible, the tour host should "walk through" the entire route to confirm arrangements and look for possibly embarrassing hidden troubles. When North American Aviation introduced a new jet fighter to the national press at the Palmdale, California, airport in the Mojave Desert, it asked the pilot to impress the guests by diving and creating a sonic boom. He did so—and pieces of glass went flying through the reception area from windows broken by the impact of the boom. The pilot climbed to do it again, but the hosts stopped him in time by yelling into the radio, "Call it off!"

The Interview

Another widely used spoken method of publicizing an individual or a cause is the interview, which may appear in print form in newspapers and magazines or on a television and radio. Online computer interviews are a popular new method. The ability of the person being interviewed to communicate easily is essential to success. Although required to stay in the background with fingers crossed that all goes well, a public relations specialist can do much to prepare the interviewee.

Andrew D. Gilman, president of CommCore in New York City, emphasizes the need for preparation. Said he: "I would no more think of putting a client on a witness stand or through a deposition without thorough and adequate presentation than I would ask a client to be interviewed by a skillful and well-prepared journalist without a similar thorough and adequate preparation."

Techniques for arranging interview appearances by clients are discussed in Chapter 11. This section will examine the steps the public relations representative can take to increase the odds for an effective performance.

Clear Purpose   In all interviews, the person being questioned should say something that will inform or entertain the audience. The practitioner should prepare the interviewee to meet this need. An adroit interviewer attempts to develop a theme in the conversation—to draw out comments that make a discernible point or illuminate the character of the person being interviewed. The latter can help the interviewer—and his or her own cause as well—by being ready to volunteer specific information, personal data, or opinions about the cause under discussion as soon as the conversational opportunity arises.

In setting up an interview, the public relations person should obtain from the interviewer an understanding as to its purpose. Armed with this information, the practitioner can assemble facts and data for the client to use in the discussion. The practitioner can also aid the client by providing tips about the interviewer's style.

Some interviewers on the radio talk shows that have proliferated in recent years ask "cream puff" questions, while others bore in, trying to upset the guest into unplanned admissions. Short, direct answers delivered without hesitation help a guest project an image of strength and credibility.

Print Differs from Broadcast   A significant difference exists between interviews in print and those on radio and television. In a print interview, the information and character impressions the public receives about the interviewee have been filtered through the mind of the writer. The man or woman interviewed is interpreted by the reporter, not projected directly to the audience. On radio and television, however, listeners hear the interviewee's voice without intervention by a third party. During a television interview, where personality has the strongest impact of all, the speaker is both seen and heard. Because of the intimacy of television, a person with a weak message who projects charm or authority may influence an audience more than one with a strong message who does not project well. A charismatic speaker with a strong message can have enormous impact.

The Print Interview   An interview with a newspaper reporter may last about an hour, perhaps at lunch or over coffee in an informal setting. The result of this person-to-person talk may be a published story of perhaps 400 to 600 words. The interviewer weaves bits from the conversation together in direct and indirect quotation form, works in background material, and perhaps injects personal observations about the interviewee. The latter has no control over what is published, beyond the self-control he or she exercises in answering the questions. Neither the person being interviewed nor a public relations representative should ask to approve an interview story before it is published. Such requests are rebuffed automatically as a form of censorship.

A talk with an entertainment personality is among the most common forms of newspaper interview. Many personality interview stories carrying Hollywood or New York datelines are proposed by practitioners endeavoring to build up a performer's image or publicize a new motion picture or television series.

Excellent promotional results can be achieved in far less popular fields of endeavor than entertainment when the person interviewed has something unusual to offer.

Magazine interviews usually explore a subject in greater depth than those in newspapers, because the writer may have more space available. Most magazine interviews have the same format as those in newspapers. Others, such as those published in *Penthouse* and *U.S. News & World Report,* appear in question-and-answer form. These require prolonged taped questioning of the interviewee by one or more writers and editors. During in-depth interviews, the person interviewed must guard against saying something that has unfortunate repercussions.

A famous instance of this occurred when Jimmy Carter was running for president against President Gerald Ford. Carter is a deeply religious man, a fact his public relations advisers emphasized by publicizing his work as a Sunday School teacher and lay preacher in a Southern Baptist church. When they sensed that these pursuits made Carter appear too sanctimonious to voters less religiously inclined, his advisers sought to have him offset this image by being interviewed in *Playboy.*

In the published interview Carter, although happily married, admitted that he had "looked upon a lot of women with lust" and "committed adultery in my heart many times." Angry reactions from his conservative followers were swift. He had besmirched their perceived image of him. Although this frank admission of a common-enough human trait made Carter seem more "human" to some voters, overall the interview statements damaged his campaign. He was, of course, elected anyway.

A third, even more elaborate, form of magazine interview story is the long profile, such as those published in *The New Yorker.* Reporters doing profiles usually travel with the interviewee, observing the subject at close range over extended periods. Before trying to interest a magazine in doing such a profile on a client or employer, the public relations adviser should be satisfied that the intended subject of the profile is willing to accept the interviewer on an intimate basis for long periods and will wear well under close scrutiny. Outbursts of anger, a dictatorial manner toward assistants, excessive drinking, and similar private habits produce a bad effect when revealed in print.

Radio and Television Interviews   The possibilities for public relations people to have their clients interviewed on the air are immense. The current popularity of talk shows, both on local stations and syndicated satellite networks, provides many opportunities for on-air appearances in which the guest expresses opinions and answers call-in questions. (See Chapter 11.) A successful radio or television broadcast interview appearance has three principal requirements:

1. *Preparation.* Guests should know what they want to say.

2. *Concise speech.* Guests should answer questions and make statements precisely and briefly. Responses should be kept to 30 seconds or less, because seconds count on the air.

3. *Relaxation.* "Mike fright" is a common ailment for which no automatic cure exists. It will diminish, however, if the guest concentrates on talking to the interviewer in a casual person-to-person manner, forgetting the audience as much as possible.

A public relations adviser can help an interview guest on all of these points. Answers to anticipated questions may be worked out and polished during a mock interview in which the practitioner plays the role of broadcaster. A tape recording or videotape of a practice session will help the prospective guest to correct weaknesses.

All too often, the hosts on talk shows know little about their guests for the day's broadcast. The public relations adviser can overcome this difficulty by sending the host in advance a factsheet summarizing the important information.

Conducting a Meeting

Meetings are a major public relations tool in contemporary American life. They can be an extremely effective form of communication, or they can be incredible bores. Speakers who drone on too long and discussions that degenerate into petty quibbling act as soporifics on the audience. Far from accomplishing a worthwhile purpose, such meetings alienate their audiences. Everyone's time is wasted.

Meetings held for public relations purposes take many forms and vary greatly in size. Sessions may be informational and friendly, they may be heated and controversial, or they may be largely formalized gatherings such as banquets and dedications. Whatever the size and form of a meeting, good planning and an alert presiding officer can assure that the meeting accomplishes its purpose without leaving participants glassy-eyed with fatigue.

Guidelines for Meetings   Preparation and firmness discreetly applied can control the dynamics of a meeting. The program should move briskly toward a goal. Few people have ever been heard to complain that a meeting was too short. Participants should have a feeling of movement without the appearance of hurry. By following these 13 guidelines, the organizers and presiding officer can create an effective session:

1. If the meeting is open to the public, an audience should be built through distribution of news releases and through other forms of publicity such as posters and announcements at clubs.

2. An agenda should be made and followed.

3. The meeting should start promptly at the announced hour.

4. Speakers should be allotted specified amounts of time and urged to cooperate.

5. Physical arrangements of the hall should be checked in advance—acoustics, seating of the audience so that it is centered in front of the speakers, adequate lighting and fresh air, advance placement of visual aids, and the like.

6. If possible, the reading of minutes and reports should be avoided. Distribution of these documents in printed form is one way to solve this time-consuming problem.

7. Printed material should be distributed to an audience at the start or the close of a meeting, not while the session is in progress. The latter is distracting.

8. Discussion should be controlled evenhandedly so that the audience has adequate opportunity to express itself but isn't allowed to wander from the theme.

9. In a controversial situation, public involvement techniques become especially valuable. Establish a time limit on each speaker from the floor—five minutes, perhaps—and enforce it. Sometimes, one or two verbose individuals will dominate a discussion or a string of speakers will repeat similar harangues. Public involvement specialists employ nominal group techniques to defuse anger, to generate meaningful discussion, and to turn the event into a problem-solving session. Groups of four to six persons work on the issue at hand and then report to the plenary session, where their ideas are duly recorded.

10. In a panel discussion, the presiding officer should give all panel members equal opportunity to be heard. The moderator should try to distribute questions from the floor equitably among the panelists.

11. In long meetings such as a seminar or a training session, periodic recesses should be called; the meeting should resume promptly after the allotted time. A recess should be at least 10 minutes, 15 or 20 if the crowd is large. Provide comfortable chairs.

12. The meeting should be brought to a constructive conclusion. If there are several speakers, the best one should be scheduled last, if possible. At the end of a discussion, the presiding officer should summarize for the audience what was said. If a motion for action will be needed, arrangements may be made in advance for someone to offer it.

13. A closing time should be set and enforced.

AUDIO NEWS RELEASES

Another form of spoken public relations is the audio news release, sent to radio stations in ready-to-broadcast form. This is commonly called a public service announcement (PSA).

The amount of air time required to read a PSA, normally 30 or 60 seconds, is stated in the top of the release—vital information in tightly timed radio programming. PSAs are written in conversational radio style, often employing partial sentences.

Audio news releases often are written in interview form, in which an announcer asks questions and another voice gives responses.

The following 30-second example, distributed by the American Red Cross, illustrates the brisk, short-sentence style commonly used in these releases.

The American Red Cross

"R-Well Received"
Radio:30
ZDMA-0378
As Produced Script
10/2/95

Announcer: Ever give a gift that didn't go over real big?

One that ended up in the closet the second you left the room?

There *is* a gift that's guaranteed to be well received.

Because it will save someone's life.

The gift is blood, and the need for it is desperate.

Over 20,000 people must choose to give this gift every day.

We need your help.

Please give blood. There's a life to be saved right now.

Call the American Red Cross at 1–800–GIVE LIFE.

Tag: This public service message brought to you by The Advertising

Council and The American Red Cross.

WORD-OF-MOUTH

Often called "interpersonal communication" by academics, "word-of-mouth" is an ephemeral form of spoken communication difficult to isolate or measure but which has a major impact on the formation of public opinion. (See Chapters 8 and 10.)

Research shows that people seldom accept new ideas or products unless friends and relatives also endorse them. Studies also show that informal conversations among peers and friends influence our thinking and behavior more than television commercials or newspaper editorials do.

The American automobile industry provides an example. The message traveled by word-of-mouth that imported cars were more reliable and better-crafted than American cars. Despite massive advertising campaigns to change public perception, American automakers lost millions of buyers. Then, subtly, the mood changed, and talk among buyers became far more favorable to American cars.

One study shows that a person dissatisfied with a product tells a minimum of 10 to 15 people about the experience; in turn, these people tell others in an ever-widening ripple effect that condemns the product. On the other hand, if word-of-mouth designates a product as "hip," sales soar.

The Insidious Problem of Rumors

Every professional communicator should understand how rumors start and, more important, how to combat them.

Simply stated, rumors are pieces of "information" that cannot be confirmed or verified by personal experience or a highly credible secondary source. They thrive when a combination of uncertainty and anxiety exists and authentic, official information is lacking or incomplete.

Results of a study commissioned by the Institute for Public Relations suggest that rumors are a common problem faced by public relations professionals. The study authors, Nicholas DiFonzo and Prashant Bordia, suggest that taking a proactive approach and providing formal communication to address the rumor are effective strategies to reduce uncertainty that leads to belief in the rumor.

James Esposito and Ralph Rosnow, writing in *Management Review,* give four strategies for defusing rumors in a company:

1. *Keep employees informed.* Employees are especially sensitive about situations that may affect them directly, such as management-union relations, job advancement, opportu-

---

PR Insights

Tips on Combating Rumors

Here are general guidelines for combating rumors:

1. Analyze the nature and impact of the rumor before taking corrective action. Many rumors are relatively harmless and dissipate within a short time.

2. Attempt to track the cause of the rumor and the geographical locations where it is prominent. This will help determine whether the rumor should be dealt with on a local, state, or national level.

3. Compile complete, authentic information that will either refute or confirm the rumor.

4. When denying a rumor, avoid repeating it more than necessary.

5. Use outside experts and credible public agencies to refute the rumor. The public views the U.S. Food and Drug Administration as more trustworthy than the president of a company defending the firm's product. If the rumor is only among certain highly identifiable groups, enlist the support of the groups' leaders.

nities for relocation, and potential layoffs. Be fully honest, because half-truths encourage additional rumors and destroy the credibility of official spokespersons.

2. *Pay attention to rumors.* If the source of employee anxiety can be determined, the underlying cause of the rumors is obvious. Then, by giving feedback to employees—letting them know how the situation is being dealt with—their fears should be allayed.

3. *Act promptly.* Rumors become more difficult to control as they harden with time. Get the facts out rapidly but don't repeat a false rumor, because repetition may foster belief. If the rumor is true, it must be confirmed.

4. *Educate personnel.* Conducting a workshop on rumors and their destructive potential can help to stop rumors before they get started.

External rumors are more difficult to c6ontrol, and they can have a devastating effect on a company or its products. Many rumors of this type circulate on the Internet.

Plagued by rumors that their company was connected with the Ku Klux Klan, the makers of Snapple ready-made teas decided to attack the problem head-on with an advertising campaign in San Francisco denouncing the tales as "outrageous."

One version of the rumor claimed that the illustration of a sailing ship on a label represented a slave ship. Actually, it depicted the Boston Tea Party. Another rumor charged that the encircled letter K on some labels symbolized the Klan. In fact, it indicated that the product was Kosher. The company was unable to discover the source of the rumors.

Rumors that cannot be tracked to any particular cause are more difficult to deal with. McDonald's had to cope with a rumor that its ground beef contained earthworms as a protein supplement, and General Mills had to contend with the rumor that its Pop Rocks candy was explosive.

With a few exceptions, little evidence exists to support the suspicion by many people that rumors are started by commercial competitors. Instead, social psychologist Frederick Koening says, "Rumors validate the world view of those who believe them. If you believe in Satan—and many people do—you're likely to welcome a rumor that he's alive and well in Akron, Ohio."

People spread rumors by word-of-mouth for a number of reasons: (1) they are advocates of conspiracy theories and distrust all institutions of society; (2) they feel victimized by a complex, uncaring society and have high anxiety; (3) they seek recognition from peers by claiming to have "inside" information; and (4) they find the rumor somewhat plausible.

Measuring the Effects of Word-of-Mouth Communication

Although efforts to measure the specific effects of word-of-mouth communication have been relatively few and of minor value, the Coca-Cola Company did obtain enlightening information from a study it sponsored concerning public reaction to its handling of consumer complaints.

Questionnaires were sent to hundreds of persons who had filed complaints with Coca-Cola's consumer affairs department. Responses showed that individuals who felt that their complaints had not been resolved satisfactorily told a median of nine to ten persons about their negative experience. Those who were completely satisfied told a median of four to five persons about their good results—a word-of-mouth distribution of bad news over good by a ratio of approximately two to one. Nearly 30 percent of those who felt that their complaints had not been resolved satisfactorily said they no longer bought Coca-Cola products. On the other hand, nearly 10 percent of the satisfied complainers reported that they now bought more Coca-Cola products as a result of the good treatment. Two lessons for companies trying to preserve a favorable image emerge from this survey:

1. The best service possible should be given, so that complaints are held to a minimum.

2. Complaints should be handled promptly and thoroughly, so that customers feel the company really cares about them. As an example, an eight-year-old girl sued the makers of Crackerjack because she didn't find a prize in a box she purchased. She had written to the company about the mistake, but it failed to answer the letter. The lawsuit she brought gave the company bad nationwide publicity.

CASE PROBLEM

Pace Industries, a manufacturer of cordless phones, has a morale problem among its 1200 employees. There is a widespread rumor that the company will lay off from one third to one half of its employees. The rumor apparently started because of two environmental factors: (1) many news stories in recent years have reported the "downsizing" of corporate America, and (2) the company recently lost the bid on a major contract.

The rumor is false, and Pace executives are worried that it will affect productivity and cause an exodus of valued employees. What steps should the company take to dissipate the rumor and reassure employees that their jobs are secure? What kinds of messages and communication channels should be used?

QUESTIONS FOR REVIEW AND DISCUSSION

1. List three tasks a public relations representative should perform when preparing for and making a face-to-face presentation to an editor.

2. How many themes should a speech have?

3. What are some key building blocks a writer uses in constructing a speech?

4. Which type of sentence structure should a speech-writer use? Explain your answer.

5. Why do companies sometimes use fellow workers rather than high executives to address audiences of employees?

6. How should a company executive prepare to hold a news conference?

7. Should a spokesperson speak off the record at a news conference? Why or why not?

8. What might a corporate host hope to accomplish by holding a press luncheon instead of a morning news conference?

9. How can a public relations representative help a client prepare for a television interview?

10. A company may be harassed by malicious rumors about its policies. If it decided to strike back, how might it do so?

Visual Tactics

Preview

The objective of this chapter is to help students understand the advantages and disadvantages of numerous visual and audiovisual techniques, and to explain the visual needs of the various mass media outlets.

Topics covered in the chapter include:
- News delivery to television
- Video news releases (VNRs)
- News on cable television
- Personal appearances on television
- Other uses of videotape
- Motion pictures
- Still images for projection
- Still photography
- Comic books and cartoons
- Outdoor displays
- Corporate design

TELEVISION

The human eye is a magnificent channel for communication, carrying messages to the brain at astounding speeds, often so subtly that the recipient is not consciously aware of absorbing them. These images are stored in the brain, combining with the intake of audible and tactile impressions to help form opinions, trigger decisions, and generate actions. Since these are the goals of public relations, the role of visual communication in public relations practice obviously is vital.

Television is the dominant form of visual communication in contemporary life. The Nielsen survey reports that the average American family has its TV set turned on about seven hours a day. During the late 1990s, however, the World Wide Web of the Internet emerged as a visual communicator in competition with television. (See Chapter 18 for a discussion of the World Wide Web.) The Web has increased the average hours that people devote to media use and has caused a definite shift of hours from television viewing to Web browsing.

Chapter 11 examined how the television industry is organized and listed ways in which public relations practitioners can use television to advance their causes. This chapter will look more closely at techniques employed for this purpose.

News Releases

Practitioners can provide news releases to television stations in several ways, ranging from a simple sheet of paper to an expensively produced videotaped story ready to go on the air. The type of news material, the time factor, and the originator's budget will determine which method is best for each story.

The Printed News Release   Identical to that sent to newspapers, the so-called handout frequently is sufficient. If the news director or assignment editor at a station judges the material to be newsworthy, a staff member is assigned to handle the story, rewriting it briefly in television style or, if the material justifies, going to the scene with a camera crew to obtain visual support for the facts. Information about coming events also is sent to TV stations in the form of a *media advisory* (see Chapter 19). When a television reporter and crew come on assignment in response to a news release, the public relations practitioner who sent out the release should do everything possible to assist them.

A fundamental difference between a news story on television and one in a newspaper is *motion*. Stories that can be illustrated easily and effectively often will receive more air time than ones that cannot. The rule for a practitioner trying to place a news story on television is: *think pictures!* The representative never should tell a reporter and photographer what pictures to shoot or what questions to ask, but may discreetly suggest possible picture and story angles.

The other primary factor in television news coverage is *brevity*. A story that runs 400 words in a newspaper may be reported in only two or three sentences in a newscast. If a television crew spends an hour shooting a story with a practitioner's help, and the story then receives 30 seconds or less of air time, the inexperienced public relations representative may feel let down. All that work, with such a brief result! As any veteran will advise, however, there is no reason for disappointment. The impact of even a very brief item on a popular newscast can be heavy.

The Prepared Script   This second, more elaborate, form of television news release is accompanied by one to four slides to illustrate the text. In this method, the public relations representative does most of the television news department's work on the story. Smaller stations with limited news staffs may be especially willing to air such ready-to-use material if it is deemed newsworthy. In preparing scripted news releases, the writer should avoid

Use of graphic humanlike figures to illustrate the results of an employee opinion survey gives the reader a quick grasp of the statistics. The survey was taken by the American States Insurance Company of Indianapolis.

terminology that sounds like advertising or "puff" publicity. Graphics created by computers can be used effectively in news releases.

For a fee, specialist commercial firms will prepare a news release script with slides from a practitioner's material, send the script to stations, and report on its use.

Videotaped excerpts from local speeches made by the practitioner's client, delivered to a television station along with a written news release explaining the circumstances in which the speech was made, may be used in the station's newscasts.

The Videotaped News Release   The most elaborate and expensive form of news delivery to television stations is the videotaped news release (VNR). This report, prepared by a public relations organization, presents information about a product, a service, or an idea, usually in featurized style.

Delivered to selected stations by satellite feed or by package, the VNR may be a ready-to-use tape of visual and voice material that a TV station may put on the air exactly as received—the use most desired by the supplier. Or, to give the station more editorial control, the release may consist of separate elements an editor can use in preparing the station's own presentation. These may include unedited video pictures, called B-roll footage, any of which the editor may select; brief "sound bites"; a separate voice-over narration by the producer's announcer, which may be aired as-is or instead read by a station announcer; and a script to be used or rewritten.

In the motion picture, *Titanic*, passengers chat on deck a few hours before the ship struck an iceberg and sank with heavy casualties. Home video versions of motion pictures like *Titanic* have huge sales and are an important form of visual communication.

B-roll footage is especially popular with newscast producers because the journalist maintains greater control over the tone and nature of the story that is broadcast. One study of air checks (news stories derived from a VNR) found that television producers used B-roll almost exclusively. Material used from the VNR tended to be stock footage of the façade of the organization and sound bites from news conferences and interviews. The authors of the study, David Blount and Glen T. Cameron, concluded that VNRs provide news producers with access to basic visuals for their craft.

Obviously, preparation and distribution of such VNR packages is expensive—from $5000 to $50,000 for most releases and even higher for elaborate ones. Yet TV stations receive hundreds of VNRs each year, many of inferior technical quality. Several factors should be considered before an organization commits that much money to a news release. Is the story sufficiently newsworthy, so that many stations probably will put it on the air? Can the story be told well visually? Does the producer have sufficient time to prepare the release—perhaps as much as six weeks? If the VNR concerns a legitimate health issue or scientific breakthrough, its chances of being widely used are better than those for introductions of commercial products.

VNRs featuring a celebrity also stand a better chance of garnering airtime. Prince Naseem Hamed was a European professional boxer with several major titles and an undefeated record. Although not well known in the United States, his European fame justified

Video news release: When some customers claimed they had found syringes in Pepsi cans, the company distributed a video news release (VNR) showing that intrusion into its high-speed bottling process was virtually impossible. The claim proved to be a hoax.

an outlay of $16,000 by sponsor Addidas International for a VNR produced by Medialink. The total audience for news stories based on the VNR exceeded 20 million.

In producing successful video news releases, sponsoring organizations must create a feeling of news or offer an interesting feature idea. A VNR that is clearly an attempt to obtain free advertising goes automatically into a station's wastebasket.

This restriction creates the need for ingenuity. Writing in the *Wall Street Journal,* Michael Klepper described how a company seeking mass exposure for a new talking doll produced a successful VNR about the history of artificial voice synthesis, using the doll as an example of the technology. Not only do such stories downplay commercial messages, they serve the station's need for "evergreen" stories of human interest that do not become immediately dated.

To introduce a new picture book *America Then & Now,* DWJ Television shot part of a video news release from the top of the Brooklyn Bridge, interviewing a still photographer who took a picture from the spot that duplicated one taken from the same place 116 years earlier. The book, published by HarperCollins, compared recent photos of events and locations with pictures taken at the same places many years earlier. Thus the VNR stimulated the viewers' historical interest while promoting the book.

A tie-in satellite media interview was conducted by the author with TV reporters in more than 30 states in which pictures for the book had been taken. (See Chapter 18.) A B-roll containing those pictures was sent in advance to each station, so it could select home-state shots for use in its interview.

Ethical Problems in the Use of VNRs   Video news releases are intended to present the sponsoring organization's story in a favorable light, subtly or more obviously. Knowing this, news editors of some television stations refuse to use them, and many stations that use some VNR material refuse to broadcast the ready-to-air versions they receive. That is why the makers of VNRs increasingly supply B-roll footage with their submissions.

Ethical responsibility for the airing of video news releases lies equally with those who produce the VNRs and the television stations that run them. Producers should make clear who is paying for the releases. Stations in turn should tell their viewers the sources of the releases they use.

Infomercials   An expanded form of VNR, called an *infomercial or program length commercial,* is a lengthy presentation made to look like an editorial examination of a topic when in reality it is a slightly disguised sales pitch for everything from mops and muscle-strengtheners to children's action figures. Such programs turn up on the screen in the late-evening hours and Saturday mornings, especially on cable systems. Some channels and stations announce that the shows are paid programs; others fail to do so or make announcements so inconspicuous that viewers easily miss them.

Presentation of infomercials in prime-time viewing hours has been undertaken by two small cable networks, Consumer Resources Network and Cable Time Direct. A few mainstream companies, such as Ford and State Farm Insurance, have shown 30-minute infomercials in prime time. Their approach is less hard-pitch salesmanship, more an extended explanation of their products. Infomercials have become so clever at looking like regular TV programs that Disney ran a commercial for its Duckman cartoon in an infomercial for a music anthology—a commercial within a commercial. Infomercials are sent to the station's advertising department, and airtime must be purchased.

News on Cable Television

An emerging battle in distribution of news by cable television provides new opportunities for public relations exposure. Innovative practitioners will find additional placement possibilities for the cable-viewing audience.

Disturbed by the way Ted Turner's Cable News Network (CNN) has flourished around the world, four over-the-air broadcasting networks struck back in 1996 by forming their own cable news networks. NBC joined with Microsoft to create MSNBC, a 24-hour cable network combined with a World Wide Web news service; the new Fox news service arranged to have its news distributed on the cable systems of the huge Tele-Communications, Inc.; and Westinghouse/CBS entered the global cable market by purchasing the Spanish-language cable channel TeleNoticias.

Numerous newspapers have obtained local cable channels on which they produce newscasts, using their own staff-gathered material as resources. Using satellite distribution, nationwide superstations such as WTBS-TV in Atlanta and WGN-TV in Chicago reach large numbers of cable viewers from coast to coast.

PR Casebook

Book Promotions Reach High-Tech Audiences

Recording artist Jewell read poetry from her recent book, *A Night Without Armor,* to more than 1000 fans who gathered in the New York Virgin Megastore. The singer-songwriter drew quite a significant crowd for a poetry reading, especially when you consider that the live audience was supplemented by crowds gathered at Virgin Megastore's retail outlets in Orlando, Los Angeles, and San Francisco. Fans in all locations were able to listen and ask questions of the rock star and poet. The event was good for store traffic, book sales, and positioning of Jewell as an artist.

Personal Appearances on Television

Anyone invited to appear on television in a talk show or for an interview should prepare for the occasion. The beaming red light of a television camera aimed at a guest, indicating that he or she is on the air, can have a terrifying effect on an inexperienced performer. The throat goes dry. The words won't come out. The guest projects discomfort.

Public relations practitioners can help their clients avoid this unpleasantness by coaching them in what to say and how to behave. Playing the role of interviewer in practice sessions, the coach can rehearse the guest by asking anticipated questions. If the subject matter is controversial, the practitioner should fire antagonistic questions to test the guest's mettle. As much as possible, the guest's prepared responses should be honed down to 30 seconds or less. (Preparation for appearances on television is discussed in Chapter 20).

Professional coaches who prepare guests for television appearances make these suggestions for their personal conduct:

- *Use of gestures.* The guest should create movement for the camera, even though seated, by changing facial expressions and by moving the hands, arms, head, and shoulders to emphasize points. Potential guests can observe these tricks by watching professional actors on talk shows.

- *Use of eye contact.* The guest should look at the interviewer, as in a private conversation. If the camera is focused directly at the guest, he or she should talk to it. The trick is to think of the camera eye not as an electronic device but as another person whom the speaker is trying to inform or convince.

- *Proper placement of the body.* Persons being interviewed should not cross their legs; the position is awkward. It is better to sit with one foot in front of the other. Leaning forward in the chair makes a person appear more aggressive. Keeping the hands apart allows the guest to use them for gesturing.

OTHER USES OF VIDEOTAPE

Videotape is so flexible and cheap that it is used by public relations people in many ways in addition to video news releases. Commercial firms and nonprofit organizations use it to reach external audiences and to communicate information and instruction to their staffs. Here are two examples:

- The state of Nevada aimed a 16-minute video, "What's the Deal with Yucca Mountain?" at school children in its fight against creation of a federal nuclear waste dump there.

- American Express sponsored a video, "It Could Never Happen to Me: Preventing Campus Crime," to be loaned free to colleges nationwide.

Videotaped Financial Reports

Corporations increasingly are putting their financial information onto videotape for showing to shareholders and securities analysts. Videotaping of annual meetings is one aspect of this trend. Specially prepared reports with graphs and other visual aids are also taped.

Internal Corporate TV News Programs

Large corporations with thousands of employees scattered in many locations keep hunting for ways to give their employees a sense of company pride and common purpose. Among the print media, company newspapers and magazines have that goal. The audiovisual equivalent is the corporate television news program.

Such programs need a strong professional touch in production; hence, they are expensive to create. They should have a well-defined formula for content. Management-oriented material should be presented discreetly in news style. The techniques of brevity, visual storytelling, human interest, and touches of humor that mark a successful commercial television newscast need to be applied to a corporate news program.

Showing of these programs to employees on a voluntary basis is done at lunch hours or other convenient times. Videotape cassettes of the shows can be distributed to sales and other employees working in the field. Playing the programs on cable television in cities where corporate plants are located is another possibility.

TV News, a corporate TV magazine for employees of SmithKline Beecham, is an excellent example. A pioneer in the field, it has appeared weekly since 1972. Although some corporations use a TV newscast format with an anchor person, *TV News* has employees do voice-over narrations of stories involving them, such as veterans of the Persian Gulf War and Hurricane Andrew survivors.

Videotaped Training and Marketing Programs

An estimated $3 billion is being spent annually on employee video programs, according to the American Society for Training and Development. The flexibility and economy of videotape makes it ideal for training employees and updating their skills.

Videotaped Sales Messages

A recent development, as the electronic revolution changes publicity methods, is distribution of sales messages on tape to selected potential customers. *Videocassettes* are mailed upon request to prospective buyers who can play these illustrated sales messages on home recorders. A stamped, self-addressed envelope for return of the cassettes to the firm may be included. Because of the costs involved, this method is used primarily for higher-priced items by companies selling direct to the consumer.

Looking into the future, some electronics enthusiasts predict that a prospective purchaser, after seeing an item advertised, will be able to dial a toll-free number on a home telecomputer, watch the sales demonstration on the home television screen, and order the item by pushing the proper button on the computer terminal. Payment for the item will be drawn by computer from the customer's bank account. Whether or not future sales methods follow this precise line, the use of electronic selling inevitably will grow. Meanwhile, home-shopping channels on cable TV offer a similar service.

Home Video

Three fourths of American families now have videocassette recorders (VCRs) with which they record television shows or view rented or purchased movies. A Newspaper Advertising

Bureau study showed that VCR owners rented an average of 108 movies a year, while the average American visited a movie theater only five times annually.

Taking advantage of this viewing potential, a growing number of organizations and companies now use videotape to reach key audiences.

In politics, candidates and groups use videotapes as today's "high-tech leaflet." A Massachusetts congressional candidate distributed a 15-minute videotape of himself for campaign workers to show in voters' homes. In Orinda, a community across the bay from San Francisco, proincorporation forces produced a videotape on the advantages of being a city, for showing at neighborhood meetings and in homes. The measure passed, and the city's first mayor credited the videotape as a major factor in the victory.

Increasingly, employees can check out videotapes of company-produced materials ranging from the corporate video news magazine to informational videos such as an explanation of the new health benefits. According to *PR Reporter,* as audiences relinquish time devoted to reading in favor of visual stimulation through television, video games, and the Web, visually oriented strategies must be adopted to convey information. Video production gives organizations an opportunity to communicate with audiences that are increasingly inclined to visual literacy.

MOTION PICTURES

Hollywood commercial feature films viewed by millions of customers in theaters constitute only a fraction of the films produced in the United States and Canada every year. Hundreds of motion pictures, often equal in quality to theatrical films, are made annually by sponsors for showing to selected audiences. Only a handful of these ever will appear on commercial theater screens, and then only as supporting films on programs of mass-market entertainment.

Sponsored films have a major role in public relations work, as noted in Chapter 11. Designed to inform, instruct, and persuade, often subtly, they play to a huge cumulative audience. Unlike commercial films, most of them are shown to viewers without charge. The makers of these films, and in some instances the organizations showing them, bear the cost in order to further their purposes directly or indirectly.

Hollywood Entertainment Films

Moviegoers are frequently exposed to publicity projects in the films they watch, although they rarely are aware of it. Public relations specialists who arrange mentions of their clients' products or causes in movies obtain high visibility because Hollywood motion pictures often are seen by millions of viewers.

Such mentions dropped into the middle of the story line are not accidental. They are arranged by negotiations between public relations specialists and the film's producer, in which the filmmaker receives payment in money or services. The show business weekly *Variety* calls the practice "product *pluggola.*"

Two examples:

• Oldsmobile arranged for its Silhouette minivan to appear in *Get Shorty,* the MGM film in which John Travolta goes to Hollywood to collect on a debt. He expects to pick up a Cadillac but instead gets "the Cadillac of minivans"—a line repeated several times in the film.

• Internal memos disclosed that Brown & Williamson Tobacco Corporation paid $950,000 in four years to have its cigarette brands shown in more than 20 movies. At least $300,000 of this went to action-film star Sylvester Stallone. The company said that it stopped this activity several years ago.

Sponsored Films and Videos

The range of films and videos made to be shown free of charge or to be rented or purchased for showing to external audiences is immense. A well-produced film or video with minimal commercial emphasis is an excellent way for companies and organizations to reach members of school, church, social, cultural, professional, and business groups.

Sponsored films and videos, despite their expense, serve several public relations purposes. They can (1) inform audiences about a topic of educational interest, (2) create understanding of a company or organization's activities, and (3) generate goodwill and name recognition among important audiences. Charms Candy, for example, reached an important audience—schoolchildren—by producing a film on school-bus safety that school administrators often show in school assemblies.

Cable television is another important outlet for sponsored films. Consumer education films and videos in which the company's commercial message is reduced to perhaps just the opening and closing credit lines find widespread acceptance by cable operators.

A limiting factor on use of videotape is the projection method. Unless a large group meeting place is equipped with a large television screen or multiple television monitors, viewing is difficult. School-assembly or service-club rooms rarely have large television monitors. And even if the group is small enough for a standard television monitor, there is the problem of standardization in tape size and equipment. Some players take $\frac{1}{2}$-inch tape, others take $\frac{3}{4}$-inch; the Beta and VHS cassettes are incompatible, with VHS the dominant form. Although the availability of playback equipment is improving, the standard movie projector is still a workhorse in classrooms and small membership organizations. Recently TV monitors have been installed in many classrooms by some cable TV systems so students can watch their programs.

The length of sponsored films and videos varies greatly. A survey by Modern Talking Picture Service, however, shows a strong audience preference for films 21 to 30 minutes in length. But there are exceptions. "Where's the Cap'n?" is a four-minute music video sponsored by the Quaker Oats Company to develop awareness among children six to 12 years old about a cereal promotion. The video was used on nationally and locally produced video music programs, reaching an estimated audience of 7.9 million viewers.

At the other end of the spectrum, Pepsi-Cola sponsored a 40-minute film titled *Amber Lights* that received widespread acclaim as a high school assembly program. It combined popular film clips and music in an MTV format to address the No. 1 killer of teenagers in the United States—drunk drivers.

STILL IMAGES FOR PROJECTION

Slides, filmstrips, and transparencies—all of them methods for projecting still images onto a screen—often are referred to as *audiovisual aids*. Properly, the word *audiovisual* encompasses all forms of sound-and-picture projection, including motion pictures, but in practice it frequently is applied only to these simpler forms. Inclusion of such visual aids in programs stimulates audiences.

Audiovisual aids are much cheaper than motion pictures and videotapes, and have simple projection requirements. All that is needed are a relatively inexpensive slide projector, an electrical outlet, and a small screen. A presentation of still images accompanied by live or recorded narration often is the most efficient method for bringing a message to a small audience. Audiovisual aids are now frequently designed in public relations departments and firms using popular software such as Powerpoint, Harvard Graphics, or Presentations. Several advantages are afforded by the use of presentation software. A uniform, stylish look is afforded through the software. Selected portions of the scripts written for the speaker can be turned into bulleted items on the digital slides—with subsequent changes in the script automatically updated on the appropriate slide. Presentations made for printing onto transparencies can also be "mounted" on a website. Finally, public relations presentations such as pitches to prospective clients can be projected using machines called LCD Projectors that convert the computer file into images. Quality of image, fluidity of presentation and the addition of animation, short video clips, and audio are all facilitated. Most top firms now make presentations with this technology.

Slide Shows

Slide presentations now range upward from Uncle Chester showing the dinner guests slides he made during his trip to Europe—usually too many and occasionally upside-down—to the projection of intricate triple-screen, three-dimensional productions issued by some corporations. For his performance before the captive audience in the living room, Uncle Chester selects the slides he likes best and delivers a rambling ad-lib narration about them as they flash on the screen. This is the exact opposite of the way a professional slide show should be constructed.

A slide show should be built on a well-defined theme to tell a story and deliver a message. The script should be written and approved first, then the visual elements should be developed to illustrate and emphasize points in the script. The standard technique is for a visually oriented person to study the script, marking places in it that lend themselves to illustration by photograph or drawing. An artist then creates rough storyboards, indicating the illustration perceived for each point. Photographer and artist go to work, producing 35-millimeter slides that meet the requirements of the storyboards. Slides and motion picture film can be coordinated.

Depending on its purpose, a slide show might consist of photographs, as in a program made by a state tourist board to publicize the scenic attractions of the state. Or, if intended to explain retirement benefits to an internal audience of employees, it might be made entirely with drawings and explanatory text slides. A combination of photographs, drawings, and text also can be effective. Stock shots of scenery, people, and events from commercial firms can be leased.

Text-only slides often help to give a presentation cohesion and to emphasize key points. The content of each text slide should be brief, making a single clear statement in a maximum of 25 words, preferably fewer. A slide containing 10 words or fewer can be powerfully effective. Color slides containing text and/or drawings need strong contrast, usually a dark background of blue, black, or brown with letters and pictures in white or yellow. An occasional black-and-white slide may be mixed into a color sequence.

A narrator may deliver the script of a slide show live, or it may be accompanied by a taped voice synchronized with the progression of slides. Slides can be shown on an automatic projector controlled by a button the speaker presses to change them.

Overhead Transparencies

A simple, economical form of audiovisual aid is a sheet of transparent acetate or similar material on which illustrations and/or lettering have been placed. When this sheet is laid on a flat glass surface in the projector, the images are reproduced on a screen behind the speaker by light transmitted by mirrors and lenses. Overhead transparencies are especially good in classrooms and small discussion groups because of their flexibility. They can be made by running a master on regular paper through a photocopier onto the acetate plastic. Large type (at least 24 point) should be used on overheads, and only about 10-12 words of copy.

Masking a transparency permits a speaker to show several steps in a process with only one transparency. If the same series of steps were shown by slides, a separate slide would be necessary for each step.

When a speaker wishes to show the operation of a piece of machinery, for example, masking can be done in the following way: the transparency contains a diagram of the entire machine. A piece of onionskin or white opalescent plastic is laid over each portion of the diagram and taped lightly into place. As the blanked-out transparency appears on the screen, the speaker removes each sectional overlay progressively and explains the revealed portion of the diagram, until the entire diagram is visible. The speaker can draw or write on a transparency while it is being displayed on the screen.

STILL PHOTOGRAPHY

A story in the print media, especially newspapers and magazines, may, and frequently should, be told in pictures as well as words. Still photography is an essential tool for every practitioner who works with publications.

Newspaper Requirements

Newspaper editors like to receive photographs of persons mentioned in news releases. The presence of a photograph with a release sometimes increases the likelihood that the story will be published. Or, as frequently happens, a photograph of a newsworthy individual or group will be published without an accompanying story, the necessary information having been condensed into the photo caption.

The type of photograph most easily placed in a newspaper by a practitioner is the head-and-shoulders portrait of a client. These portraits, known in the trade as *mug shots,* frequently are published in one-column or half-column size to illustrate textual material. Group shots are published less often than individual pictures because they require multiple-column space. Practitioners submitting group photographs should keep the number of persons in a picture small and have them tightly grouped—a maximum of three or four persons unless the picture is a highly unusual one.

Photographs on the main news pages of a newspaper usually are taken by staff photographers or are provided by the news picture services. They stress action or personality

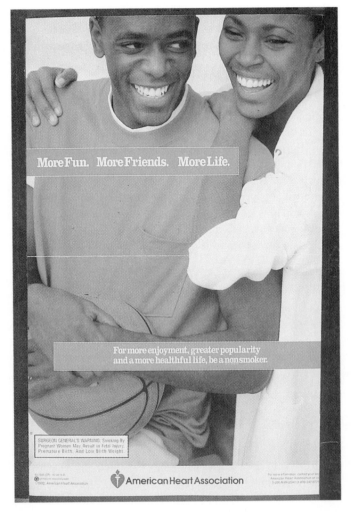

An effective poster delivers a simple message in a few words and includes a striking illustration. This poster by the American Heart Association, urging youths not to smoke, is a good example.

to capture attention. The chances for a public relations practitioner to have a submitted photograph published in these up-front pages are relatively small, except for one-column portraits. When spot news is involved, the practitioner is better advised to telephone the photo editor of a newspaper and call attention to a picture possibility that a staff photographer can cover. Staff photographers know their editors' space limitations and deadlines.

Other sections of a newspaper provide abundant opportunities for publication of photographs submitted by practitioners.

The business pages regularly include photographs of meetings, new products, and individuals appointed to new positions. Sports editors welcome photographs of athletes and coaches in various poses. Entertainment editors need pictures of performers, individually and in groups, and publish still photos taken from scenes in locally playing motion pictures and television shows. Travel editors desire photographs of interesting scenes and modes of transportation.

An especially broad target for the practitioner is the section of a newspaper called "Family Living," "Life Styles," "Today's Scene," or something similar.

While retaining the traditional elements of social life and homemaking, these sections have added material about family life and problems, personal finances, careers, and contemporary lifestyles. This broadened appeal has multiplied the photographic possibilities for the public relations practitioner, both to submit photographs and to query editors with ideas for illustrated feature stories by staff members about activities of their clients.

"Family Living" sections often publish pictures of groups planning charity events, civic affairs, and social organization parties. These pictures generate interest in the event, help to sell tickets, and incidentally serve as an ego payoff to workers who appear in them. Unfortunately, far too many such pictures belong to the waxworks school of photography—stilted, self-conscious poses in which the participants appear ramrod-stiff and painfully artificial. A photographer's ingenuity is challenged to invent an interesting piece of business for the participants to do, and to coax them to relax.

When shooting a publicity shot, a clever photographer will include, if possible, a prop that helps to carry the message. A picture promoting a Red Cross blood drive, for example, would be strengthened by inclusion of a Red Cross poster or similar symbol.

This photograph of Marilyn Monroe is a classic example of the staged photo arranged for publicity purposes. To promote her film, *The Seven Year Itch*, she stood over a grating while wind blowers hidden beneath it swirled her skirt upward. Publicists claimed the resulting photo was "accidental."

Publicity shots may be submitted by the practitioner, or arrangements may be made with an editor for a staff photographer to handle the assignment. If a staff photographer is assigned, the practitioner must make certain that all participants in the picture assemble at the appointed place on time, appropriately dressed. The photographer is busy and, in a sense, the editor is doing the organization a favor.

Photographs submitted to newspapers normally are eight by 10 inches in black and white, with caption material attached either to the back or bottom of the picture. *The practitioner should be absolutely certain that the names in the caption are spelled correctly and match up in left-to-right sequence with the photograph itself.* An added precaution is to count the number of persons in the picture and the number of names in the caption, to be sure that they correspond. Smaller prints usually are acceptable for head-and-shoulders portraits.

Use of Color   Most newspapers publish some pictures in color daily, and the practice is growing. Excellent public relations opportunities exist to place color pictures in feature sections. Living sections often run color photos of prepared foods; travel sections show enticing color shots of destinations.

The practitioner should submit color slides, not color prints. To increase the chances that a picture will be used, it is a wise precaution to determine in advance from the picture editor or chief photographer what special technical requirements for color work the newspaper may have. Newspapers now regularly use photographs downloaded from wire services and the Web, so it is also a good idea to ask whether the photo should be submitted in digital form on diskette or as an attachment to an e-mail message.

Keep File Pictures Current   Since newspapers maintain large files of published and unpublished photographs, it is not unusual for a mug shot of a newsworthy personality to be published more than once—a bonus for the practitioner who submitted it. Individuals change in appearance as they age, and occasionally an editor will reach into the files in a hurry and publish an obviously outdated picture of a news figure. The public relations person handling a prominent individual can avoid this embarrassment by submitting an up-to-date photograph from time to time. Since journalists also increasingly look to the Web for graphic material, including photographs, it is important to maintain up-to-date photos on the website. Doing so serves the interests of the reporter and the public relations person.

The importance of including a selection of photographs in a press kit introducing such projects as a new shopping center, a sales program, a political campaign, or a fund drive is obvious. The kit should contain pictures of the key persons involved and of physical aspects of the projects.

On a national or regional basis, the alert practitioner may obtain space by appealing to newspaper editors' interest in hometown angles. At trade conventions or sales conferences, the public relations staff can run a "production line" in which individual delegates are photographed in company with a celebrity. As with media use of VNRs, the celebrity does enhance chances that a photo will appear in print. At least rudimentary knowledge of photographic techniques is an important asset for everyone working in public relations.

Magazine Requirements

Magazine requirements resemble those of newspapers, although emphasis is primarily on feature photographs. Some magazines use only color photographs, some only black-and-white, some both. The practitioner should study each magazine before submitting pictures to it.

Trade and professional magazines frequently use submitted photographs of individuals, new products, and industrial installations. When sending in a proposal for a feature story about a client, the practitioner should offer to provide photographs to accompany the text, regardless of whether the story is written by the practitioner, by a freelance writer, or by a magazine staff member. Many magazines do not have photographic staffs or budgets and facilities for acquiring pictures and so depend upon submitted pictures. Attractive photographs accompanying a manuscript enhance the possibility that it will be accepted for publication.

Public relations departments and counseling firms should include in their annual budgets a substantial amount for photographic service. In addition to submitting pictures to the media, representatives often find it effective to send souvenir prints of these pictures to persons appearing in them and to important persons such as dealers and customers. Such small gestures have a flattering effect.

COMIC BOOKS AND CARTOONS

Another eye-catching way to deliver visual messages in print is to use comic books and cartoons. The artwork must be of professional quality, however, or the effect is diminished. Drawings are especially good for illustrating steps in a process, as in an owner's instruction manual. If an artist can create a whimsical cartoon character that symbolizes the service or objective, entire campaigns can be built around it.

A note of warning: published cartoons and comic strips are covered by copyright and may be reproduced only by permission of the owner.

OUTDOOR DISPLAYS

Although billboards, building signs, and other forms of outdoor announcements are erected primarily for advertising and identification, they have potential uses as public relations tools. Billboards may remind motorists and pedestrians of a citywide charity fund drive in progress. A changing electric sign outside a bank showing time and temperature performs a public service and creates goodwill for the bank; so does a signboard on which announcements of forthcoming civic events are placed. An ingenious practitioner working for a nonprofit organization may be able to find numerous outlets of this type to deliver a message, at little or no cost.

A public relations specialist should know the fundamentals of billboard design and economics, in case a situation arises in which outdoor displays will fit into a publicity program. Billboard companies quite fairly maintain that their medium may be the only mass medium remaining in an era of multiple broadcast channels and publications that reach only portions of the total populace. The standard billboard of the type seen along streets and on buildings is 12 by 25 feet. The colorful paper posters pasted onto it are slightly smaller, leaving a white frame around them. The standard poster is called a 24-sheet, because at one time 24 sheets of paper were needed to cover the space on a full-sized billboard. Modern printing processes do it with 10 sheets. Small posters called 3-sheets are designed to attract pedestrian readers at sidewalk level. Recent development of computer-controlled painting on vinyl billboards permits use of larger boards.

Outdoor advertising companies rent display space on their billboards on the basis of what they call a *100-showing*—that is, the number of boards in a market area calculated to expose the advertiser's message to approximately 100 percent of the people at some time during the 30 days it is posted. The number of boards that constitute a 100-showing fluctuates from market to market, based on traffic studies.

Successful billboard copy must be short and illustrations simple, because the duration of viewing time as motorists pass is brief. Eye-catching impact is the goal. That requires powerful design and strong colors. Two lively examples: "Heaven Can Wait . . . Wellness Works" and "We Don't Do That in Clarke County," an antilittering billboard in Georgia. One message was five words long, the other seven, quickly absorbed. Billboards have reinforcement value in support of a program using other methods as well. Design and preparation of billboard posters are handled by advertising agencies, while physical placement is done by the billboard companies.

CORPORATE DESIGN

The need to present a unified visual image to the world is becoming increasingly evident to corporations and nonprofit organizations. Especially among corporations that have grown rapidly by acquiring many subsidiaries, the uncoordinated proliferation of letterheads, signs, publication symbols, news release sheets, packages, and other visual public representations of the organization gives a jumbled, unfocused appearance.

Creation of a simple, powerful logotype for use on all printed matter and signs projects an image of the company as a tightly knit contemporary operation. An impressive logo suggests quality and strength.

In the acquisition-minded climate of corporate life today, companies often add so many subsidiaries that the original names of the parent firms become inadequate. So these corporations adopt generalized names, usually of one or two words. United States Steel Corporation changed its name to USX Corporation.

Because it no longer makes cans but has moved into such varied fields as life insurance, direct mail, recorded music, and stock brokerage, the American Can Company decided to change its name. It paid Lippincott & Margulies consultants $200,000 to help it choose a new one. The choice was Primerica, a synthetic word intended to reflect the company's "prime" growth prospects and ability to finance them.

Corporate redesign usually involves coordinated effort by the public relations and marketing departments. First, management must define the objectives to be sought in the new design. Should the graphic style be ultramodern, formal and conservative, or perhaps old-fashioned to suggest historical continuity? A counseling firm and graphics specialist are usually brought into the discussion. A detailed audit of existing printed materials and signs is necessary to establish the areas where the new design will be used. In a corporation with numerous divisions, the logotype may be color-coded—a different color for each division, with identification of the division in type below.

As companies enter the international market, they often find that their traditional identifying logotypes are unsuitable in foreign countries because of language complications and cultural differences. So they seek logos that are easily identified around the world. The Fuji

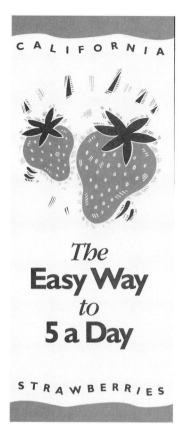

A catchy slogan illustrated by a bright drawing or cartoon draws attention to a product. Readers attracted to the slogan, "The Easy Way to 5 a Day" turn the page to find recipes for serving strawberries.

Bank of Japan, for example, replaced its symbol using Japanese letters with a simple design consisting of a drawing of Mount Fujiyama and the words Fuji Bank.

Creation of a symbolic person to represent a corporate product is another effective graphic method—the Pillsbury Doughboy, for example.

Goodwill Industries formerly had as its symbol a cartoon character, a smiling young man, feather in his hat and a lunch box in his hand, pictured rolling along in a wheelchair. The national help-the-handicapped organization found that the symbol, while clever, did not print well and lacked sales appeal on signs outside its retail outlets. The design consultant Goodwill employed replaced the symbol with a rectangular logo in which a large lowercase *g* in the upper-left corner looks like half of a smiling face.

Creation of a graphics standards manual helps a large organization to enforce its unified designs throughout all its operations. A consistent use of paper color and texture, print style and size, and standard specifications for ink colors offers a subtle but constant identity for an organization. For example, most consumers of soft drinks can readily recognize the Coca-Cola red.

CASE PROBLEM

The local chapter of the American Lung Association needs to update its ten-minute slide presentation about the activities and services of the organization. Do some research on the American Lung Associa- tion and what it does. Then write the script on the right side of the paper. On the left, briefly describe the slides that would be keyed to the basic points of the script.

QUESTIONS FOR REVIEW AND DISCUSSION

1. What is the fundamental difference between a news story in a newspaper and one on television?

2. Under what conditions might a public relations adviser recommend distribution of a videotaped news release?

3. In what ways can a corporation make use of videotaped presentations?

4. If you were handling public relations for an airline, what types of publicity tie-ins might you develop with a Hollywood motion picture producer?

5. A food manufacturer plans to produce a sponsored film about a new oat-bran cereal. What elements might it include in the film? To what target audiences might it show the film?

6. Why is it desirable to write the script of a slide show before the pictures are taken?

7. What is a storyboard?

8. Why is a mug shot a useful photographic tool in public relations practice?

9. Billboard companies rent display space on the basis of a *100-showing*. What does this mean?

10. How can graphics design help to strengthen a corporation's public image?

Photo Credits

Page 4 : © Paul McErlane/AP/Wide World Photos; 12: GTE Communications Corporation; 18: © J. Scott Applewhite/AP/Wide World Photos; 19: © Reuters/Gary Carmen/Archive Photos; 26: Culver Pictures; 33: AP/Wide World Photos; 36: © Marie Hansen/LIFE Magazine © Time Inc.; 37: AP/Wide World Photos; 38: Courtesy Edward L. Bernays; 40: Courtesy Edward L. Bernays; 74: Courtesy of the American Cancer Society, Inc.; 81TL: Courtesy Marsha Appel, Musiclan; 81TR: Courtesy Margo L. Barnes, Bayer Corp.; 81TCL: Courtesy Barie S. Carmichael, Dow Corning; 81TCR: Courtesy Jean L. Farinelli; 81BCL: Courtesy Kathy Lane, Lucent Technologies; 81BCR: Courtesy Mary Carroll Linder, Estee Lauder Companies; 81BL: Courtesy Katherine B. Rohrbach, Charles Schwab & Company; 81BR: Courtesy Anita K. Russell, Coors Brewing Company; 124: AP/Wide World Photos; 130: © Loren Santow/Tony Stone Images; 161: Courtesy Pepsi-Cola Company 1993; 189: Save the Children, Westport, CT; 200: Courtesy The Ad Council and The American Red Cross; 214: © Alan Singer/AP/Wide World Photos; 215: © Edward Keating/NYT Pictures; 233: Courtesy Federal Express Corporation/BBDO; 258: Firestone Tire and Service Centers; 259: Hausback Pickle Company, Saginaw, MI; 261: Courtesy of Aetna, Inc.; 271: © Robert Trippett/Sipa Press; 281: © Joe Marquette/AP/Wide World Photos; 286: © Bob Edme/AP/Wide World Photos; 298: © Xinhua, Hu Haixing/AP/Wide World Photos; 300: Amann & Associates Public Relations; 301: © David Brauchli/AP/Wide World Photos; 306: Phi Kappa Phi; 307: © Paul Warner/AP/Wide World Photos; 308: Religious Communication Congress 2000; 309: Reprinted with permission of the Chesapeake Bay Foundation; 311: Mothers Against Drunk Driving (MADD); 314: Phoenix Newspapers, Inc.; 318: Courtesy Retired and Senior Volunteer Program, Senior Service Corps.; 321: Courtesy of UC Museum of Paleontology, Berkeley, CA.; 333: Bettmann/Corbis; 336: UC Berkeley Foundation; 347: Copyright 1999, USA TODAY. Reprinted with permission; 354: © Bob Child/AP/Wide World Photos; 356: AP/Wide World Photos; 360: © Edeleman; 361: Courtesy Princess Cruises and Porter Novelli; 365: © Bob Child/AP/Wide World Photos; 367: © Morgan/Greenpeace; 368: Courtesy Edelman; 373: Phoenix Newspapers, Inc.; 394: Duffey Communications; 395: Duffey Communications; 397: Courtesy Mobil Corporation; 399: Parents Television Council; 412: Southern California Edison, An Edison International Company; 413: © Tyler Mallory/AP/Wide World Photos; 431: © Merie W. Wallace/Kobal Collection; 432: Courtesy Pepsi-Cola Company; 440: Reproduced with permission © More Fun. More Friends. More Life. Copyright American Heart Association.; 441: Bettmann/Corbis; 445: California Strawberry Commission.

INDEX